QuarkXPress® 5

Advanced Electronic Documents

AGAINST THE CLOCK
mastering graphic technology

Prentice
Hall

Upper Saddle River, NJ 07458

Library of Congress Cataloging-in-Publication Data

QuarkXPress 5: Advanced Electronic Documents/Against The Clock
    p. cm. — (Against The Clock Series)
ISBN 0-13-04255-3
1. QuarkXPress (Computer File). 2. Desktop Publishing.
    I. Against The Clock (Firm). II. Series.

Z253.532.Q37Q373 2003
686.2'25445369 — dc21

2002072813

Editor-in-Chief: Stephen Helba
Director of Production and Manufacturing: Bruce Johnson
Executive Editor: Elizabeth Sugg
Managing Editor – Editorial: Judy Casillo
Editorial Assistant: Anita Rhodes
Managing Editor – Production: Mary Carnis
Production Editor: Denise Brown
Composition: Diana Van Winkle, Van Winkle Design
Design Director: Cheryl Asherman
Design Coordinator: Christopher Weigand
Cover Design: LaFortezza Design Group, Inc.
Icon Design: James Braun
Prepress: Photoengraving, Inc.
Printer/Binder: Press of Ohio

Pearson Education LTD.
Pearson Education Australia PTY, Limited
Pearson Education Singapore, Pte. Ltd
Pearson Education North Asia Ltd
Pearson Education Canada, Ltd
Pearson Educación de Mexico, S.A. de C.V.
Pearson Education – Japan
Pearson Education Malaysia, Pte. Ltd
Pearson Education, Upper Saddle River, New Jersey

10   9   8   7   6   5   4   3   2   1

ISBN 0-13-094255-3

Contents

Purpose

The Against The Clock series has been developed specifically for those involved in the field of computer arts, and now — animation, video, and multimedia production. Many of our readers are already involved in the industry in advertising and printing, television production, multimedia, and in the world of Web design. Others are just now preparing for a career within these professions.

This series provides you with the necessary skills to work in these fast-paced, exciting, and rapidly expanding fields. While many people feel that they can simply purchase a computer and the appropriate software, and begin designing and producing high-quality presentations, the real world of high-quality printed and Web communications requires a far more serious commitment.

The Series

The applications presented in the Against The Clock series stand out as the programs of choice in professional computer-arts environments.

We use a modular design for the Against The Clock series, allowing you to mix and match the drawing, imaging, and page-layout applications that exactly suit your specific needs.

Titles available in the Against The Clock series include:

Macintosh: Basic Operations
Windows: Basic Operations
Adobe Illustrator: Introduction and Advanced Digital Illustration
Macromedia FreeHand: Digital Illustration
Adobe InDesign: Introduction and Advanced Electronic Mechanicals
Adobe PageMaker: Creating Electronic Documents
QuarkXPress: Introduction and Advanced Electronic Documents
Microsoft Publisher: Creating Electronic Mechanicals
Microsoft PowerPoint: Presentation Graphics with Impact
Microsoft FrontPage: Creating and Designing Web Pages
HTML & XHTML: Creating Web Pages
Procreate Painter: A Digital Approach to Natural Art Media
Adobe Photoshop: Introduction and Advanced Digital Images
Adobe Premiere: Digital Video Editing
Adobe After Effects: Motion Graphics and Visual Effects
Macromedia Director: Creating Powerful Multimedia
Macromedia Flash: Animating for the Web
Macromedia Dreamweaver: Creating Web Pages
Preflight and File Preparation
TrapWise and PressWise: Digital Trapping and Imposition

You will see a number of icons in the sidebars; each has a standard meaning. Pay close attention to the sidebar notes where you will find valuable comments that will help you throughout this book, and in the everyday use of your computer. The standard icons are:

The Hand-on-mouse icon indicates a hands-on activity — either a short exercise or a complete project. The complete projects are located at the back of the book, in sequence from Project A through C.

The Pencil icon indicates a comment from an experienced operator or trainer. Whenever you see this icon, you'll find corresponding sidebar text that augments the subject being discussed at the time.

The Key icon is used to identify keyboard equivalents to menu or dialog box options. Using a key command is often faster than selecting a menu option with the mouse. Experienced operators often mix the use of keyboard equivalents and menu/dialog box selections to arrive at their optimum speed of execution.

The Caution icon indicates a potential problem or difficulty. For instance, a certain technique might lead to pages that prove difficult to output. In other cases, there might be something that a program cannot easily accomplish, so we present a workaround.

If you are a Windows user, be sure to refer to the corresponding text or images whenever you see this Windows icon. Although there isn't a great deal of difference between using these applications on a Macintosh and using them on a Windows-based system, there are certain instances where there's enough of a difference for us to comment.

For the Reader

On the CD-ROM, you will find a complete set of Against The Clock (ATC) fonts, as well as a collection of data files used to construct the various exercises and projects. The ATC fonts are solely for use while you are working through the Against The Clock materials.

A variety of resource files are included. These files, necessary to complete both the exercises and projects, may be found in the **RF_Adv_Quark** folder on the Resource CD-ROM.

For the Trainer

The Trainer's CD-ROM includes various testing and presentation materials in addition to the files that are supplied with this book.

- **Overhead presentation materials** are provided and follow along with the book. These presentations are prepared using Microsoft PowerPoint, and are provided in both native PowerPoint format and Acrobat Portable Document Format (PDF).

- **Extra free-form projects** are provided and may be used to extend the training session, or they may be used to test the reader's progress.

- **Test questions and answers** are included on the Trainer's CD-ROM. These questions may be modified and/or reorganized.

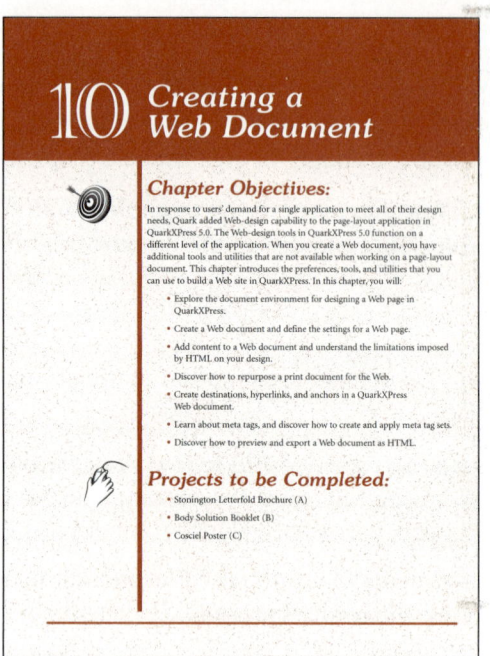

Chapter openers *provide the reader with specific objectives.*

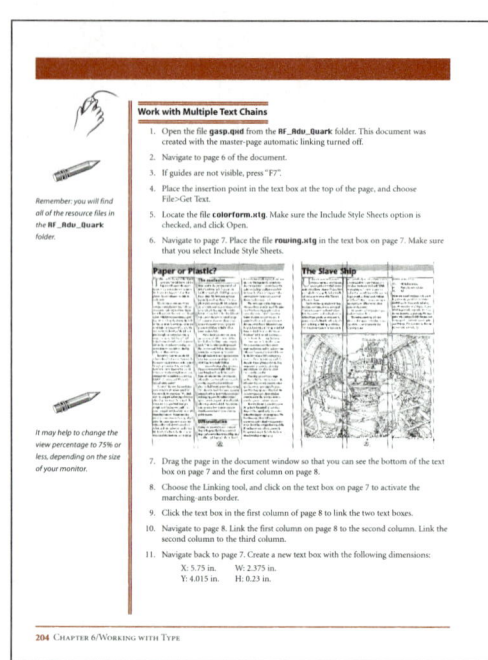

Sidebars and hands-on activities *supplement concepts presented throughout the book.*

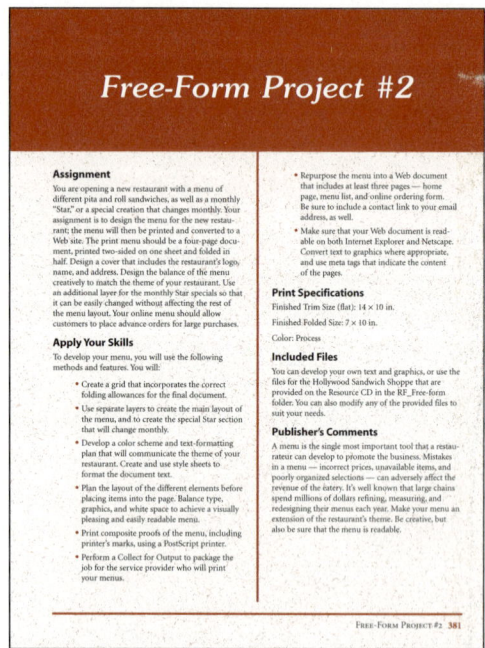

Free-form projects *allow readers to use their imagination and new skills to satisfy a typical client's needs.*

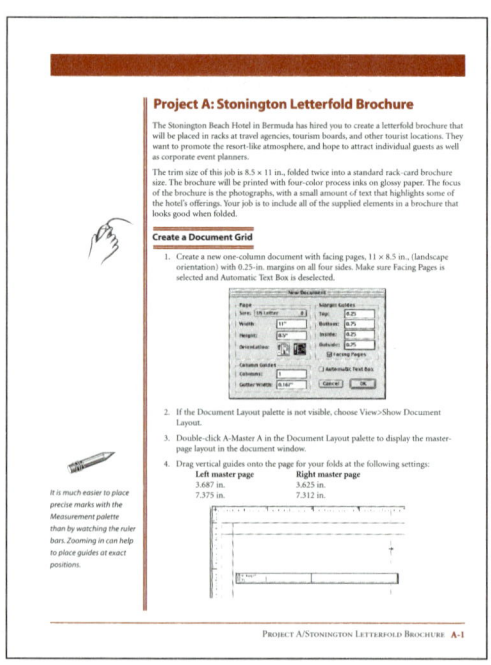

Step-by-step projects *result in finished artwork — with an emphasis on proper file-construction methods.*

Project A: Stonington Letterfold Brochure

The Stonington Beach Hotel in Bermuda has hired you to create a letterfold brochure that will be placed in racks at travel agencies, tourism boards, and other tourist locations. They want to promote the resort-like atmosphere, and hope to attract individual guests as well as corporate event planners. The brochure is a four-color glossy folding document, which uses many images to highlight the hotel's amenities. You will create the brochure incorporating folding allowances and marks, and you will use layers to develop the brochure content separate from the folding guides.

Project B: Body Solution Booklet

As the lead designer for the Body Solution account, you are coordinating the efforts of three other designers. Each of your designers has created one chapter of a booklet that will be sent to health-care providers around the country as a free handout for patients. As the project coordinator, it is your job to make sure that each chapter of the document is consistent with the others, and to create the front and back matter. You will create a QuarkXPress book, define lists to build a table of contents, and compile a comprehensive index using multiple levels and references styles.

Project C: Cosciel Poster

Your new client, Cosciel Company, has hired you to replace their old design agency. They submit a poster to gourmet grocers and food festivals every year. The company's ad manager wants to redesign the company's poster using the same elements but a different layout. Cosciel wants to be able to send the file to different printers, each of which has different file-submission requirements. You will develop the poster layout from the ground up, placing text and images that are supplied by the client, incorporating unique effects with text on a path and custom runarounds. You will export two versions of the file — a single EPS file and a job package folder — to meet requirements of different service providers.

ACKNOWLEDGMENTS

I would like to give special thanks to the writers, illustrators, editors, and others who have worked long and hard to complete the Against The Clock series.

Special thanks to Caron Gordon of Caron Gordon Graphics for her art and project contributions.

A big thank you to the dedicated teaching professionals whose comments and expertise contributed to the success of these products, including Janet Frick of Training Resources, Doris Anton of Wichita Area Technical College, René Prim of Central Piedmont Community College, and Carin Murphy of Des Moines Area Community College,.

Thanks to Terry Sisk Graybill, copy editor, and final link in the chain of production, for her help in making sure that we all said what we meant to say.

A big thanks to Denise Brown and Kerry Reardon, for their guidance, patience, and attention to detail.

— Ellenn Behoriam, July 2002

Our History

Against The Clock (ATC) was founded in 1990 as a part of Lanman Systems Group, one of the nation's leading systems integration and training firms. The company specialized in developing custom training materials for such clients as L.L. Bean, *The New England Journal of Medicine*, the Smithsonian, the National Education Association, *Air & Space Magazine*, Publishers Clearing House, the National Wildlife Society, Home Shopping Network, and many others. The integration firm was among the most highly respected in the graphic-arts industry.

To a great degree, the success of Lanman Systems Group can be attributed to the thousands of pages of course materials developed at the company's demanding client sites. Throughout the rapid growth of Lanman Systems Group, founder and general manager Ellenn Behoriam developed the expertise necessary to manage technical experts, content providers, writers, editors, illustrators, designers, layout artists, proofreaders, and the rest of the chain of professionals required to develop structured and highly effective training materials.

Following the sale of the Lanman Companies to World Color, one of the nation's largest commercial printers, Ellenn embarked on a project to develop a new library of hands-on training materials engineered specifically for the professional graphic artist. A large part of this effort is finding and working with talented professional artists, authors, and educators from around the country.

The result is the ATC training library.

About the Author

Erika Kendra lives in Los Angeles, where she operates under the guise of The Right Brain. She has been editing and designing books for the printing and graphic-design communities for five years, and provides desktop-publishing and digital-prepress consulting and training for the printing industry.

Erika has been working with Against The Clock for two years. She is the co-author of the *Design Companion for the Digital Artist*, and the author of *Preflight and File Preparation*, and *Adobe PageMaker: Creating Electronic Documents*, all of which are part of the Against The Clock series.

When she isn't being manipulated by her cats, she can usually be found reading archaic literature, attending Renaissance festivals, or enjoying the southern California sun. She earned a BA in History and a BA in English Literature from the University of Pittsburgh.

Getting Started

If you are using Mac OS X, QuarkXPress will launch in the Classic environment.

Platform

The Against The Clock series is designed for both the Macintosh and Windows platforms. On the Macintosh, QuarkXPress 5.0 requires Mac OS 8.6 or 9.x. The Windows version runs on Windows 98, Windows NT, Windows 2000, Windows ME, and Windows XP.

Prerequisites

This book is based on the assumption that you have a basic understanding of how to use your computer. You should also have a basic understanding of the Internet, different Web browsers, and navigating the Web.

You should know how to use your mouse to point and click, as well as to drag items around the screen. You should be able to resize and arrange windows on your desktop to maximize your available space. You should know how to access drop-down menus, and understand how check boxes and radio buttons work. You should also know how to create, open, and save files. It doesn't hurt to have a good understanding of how your operating system organizes files and folders, and how to navigate your way around them.

You should also know how to use the basic tools and utilities built into QuarkXPress for creating page-layout documents. Many of the topics discussed in this book will expand on your knowledge of Quark's tools and utilities. We also discuss the advanced features that allow you to customize your work environment, create special effects and treatments, and export to a variety of different file formats.

The CD-ROM and Initial Setup Considerations

Before you begin using your Against The Clock book, you must set up your system to have access to the various files and tools to complete your lessons.

Resource Files

This book comes complete with a collection of resource files, which are an integral part of the learning experience. They are used throughout the book to help you construct increasingly complex elements. These building blocks should be available for practice and study sessions to allow you to complete the exercises and project assignments smoothly, spending a minimum of time looking for the various required components.

All the files that you need to complete the exercises and projects in this book are located on your Resource CD. You can either work directly from the Resource CD or copy the files onto your hard drive before beginning the exercises.

The Work In Progress Folder

Before you begin working on the exercises or projects in this book, you should create a folder called "Work_In_Progress", either on your hard drive or on a removable disk. As you work through the steps in the exercises, you will be directed to save your work in this folder.

If your time is limited, you can stop at a logical point in an exercise or project, save the file, and later return to the point at which you stopped. In some cases, the exercises in this book build upon work that you have already completed. You will need to open a file from your Work_In_Progress folder and continue working on the same file.

Locating Files

Files that you need to open are indicated by a different typeface (for example, "Open **file.qxd**.") The location of the file also appears in the special typeface (for example, "Open **document.qxd** from your **Work_In_Progress** folder.")

When you are directed to save a file with a specific name, the name appears in quotation marks (for example, "Save the file as 'new_file.qxd' to your **Work_In_Progress** folder.")

In most cases, resource files are located in the **RF_Adv_Quark** folder, while exercises and projects on which you continue to work are located in your **Work_In_Progress** folder. We repeat these directions frequently in the early chapters, and add reminders in sidebars in the later chapters. If a file is in a location other than these two folders, the path is indicated in the exercise or project (e.g., "Open the file from the **Images** folder (**RF_Adv_Quark>Images**)."

File Name Conventions

Files on the Resource CD are named according to the Against the Clock naming convention to facilitate cross-platform compatibility. Words are separated by an underscore, and all file names include a lowercase three-letter extension. You see the three extension characters as part of the file name.

The extensions for QuarkXPress documents and templates are, respectively, ".qxd" and ".qxt". Quark Web documents use the extension ".qxb", and libraries use the extension ".qxl". QuarkXPress for Windows always adds the file extension to a file's name; Macintosh users should add the extension when saving files.

When your Windows system is first configured, the views are normally set to a default that hides these extensions. This means that you might have a dozen different files named "myfile," all of which may have been generated by different applications and may consist of completely different types of files. This can become very confusing.

On a Windows system, you can change this view. Double-click on "My Computer" (the icon on your desktop). Select View>Folder Options. From Folder Options, select the View tab. Within the Files and Folders folder is a check box: Hide File Extensions for Known File Types. When this is unchecked, you can see the file extensions.

It's easier to know what you're looking at if file extensions are visible. While this is a personal choice, we strongly recommend viewing the file extensions.

Fonts

You must install the ATC fonts from the Resource CD to ensure that your exercises and projects will work as described in the book. These fonts are provided on the Resource CD-ROM in the ATC Fonts folder. Specific instructions for installing fonts are provided in the documentation that came with your computer.

Key Commands

There are three keys generally used as modifier keys — they don't do anything by themselves when pressed, but they either perform some action or type a special character when pressed along with another key or keys.

We frequently note keyboard shortcuts that can be used in QuarkXPress 5.0. A slash character indicates that the key commands differ for Macintosh and Windows systems; the Macintosh commands are listed first, then Windows. If you see the command "Command/Control-P", for example, Macintosh users would press the Command key and Windows users would press the Control Key, and both would press the "P" key at the same time.

The Command/Control key is used with another key to perform a specific function. When combined with the "S" key, it saves your work. When combined with "O", it opens a file; with a "P", it prints the file. In addition to these functions, which work with most Macintosh and Windows programs, the Command/Control key can be combined with other keys to control specific functions of QuarkXPress. At times it is also used in combination with the Shift and/or Option/Alt keys.

The Option/Alt key, another modifier key, is often used in conjunction with other keys to access special typographic characters. On a Windows system, the Alt key is used with the number keys on the numeric keypad. For example, Alt-0149 produces a bullet (•) character. The Alt key can be confusing because not only do you use it to type special characters, you also use it to control program and operating-system functions. Pressing Alt-F4, for example, closes programs or windows, depending on which is active. On a Macintosh computer, the Option key is often used with a letter key to type a special character.

The Shift key is the third modifier key. While you're used to using this key to type uppercase letters and the symbols at the top of the number keys, it's also used with Command/Control and Option/Alt in a number of contexts.

Function Keys

QuarkXPress incorporates the function ("F") keys as shortcuts for accessing many of the application commands and palettes. These shortcuts are extremely useful and timesaving. We note many of the function-key shortcuts throughout this book, indicating the relevant key enclosed in quotation marks (for example, "Press 'F12' to open the Colors palette.")

On a Macintosh system, you may need to configure your computer properly before using the F-key shortcuts in QuarkXPress. If you open the Keyboard control panel, the Function Keys button opens the Hot Function Keys dialog box. You have to deselect the Enable Hot Function Keys check box before you can use the built-in QuarkXPress shortcuts.

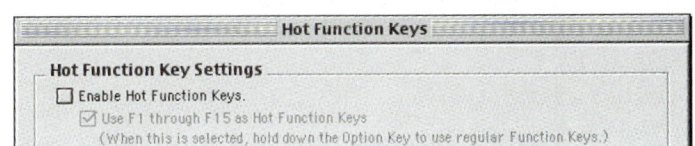

System Requirements for QuarkXPress

Macintosh:

- PowerPC® processor
- Mac OS 8.6 or 9.x (or OS X running in the Classic environment)
- 14-MB RAM (64 recommended)
- At least 800 × 600-pixel monitor resolution (though we recommend higher)
- PostScript Level 2 printer
- CD-ROM drive
- 36-MB of free hard drive space required for software installation

Windows:

- Pentium processor (or equivalent)
- Windows 98, Windows NT, Windows 2000, Windows ME, or Windows XP
- 32-MB RAM (64 recommended)
- At least 800 × 600-pixel monitor resolution (though we recommend higher)
- PostScript Level 2 printer
- CD-ROM drive
- 40 MB of free hard drive space required for software installation

Introduction

QuarkXPress, originally introduced to the market in 1987, is the industry standard for page-layout and document design. It is the most popular and most sophisticated such program available, and is used by more professional designers than any other page-layout application. From the early versions of the software, QuarkXPress incorporated tools that gave the designer extremely tight control over every element on the document page. Version 5.0 expands on the already established interface, providing even more tools and utilities to facilitate production and improve the digital workflow. QuarkXPress 5.0 also includes tools that make the transition from print to PDF to the Web far easier than they have been in the past.

This book is designed for the advanced Quark user who is already familiar with the basic tools and utilities. We discuss the sophisticated features that allow you to control and manage every element in your document, and automate many of the time-consuming and monotonous tasks involved in successfully creating a page layout. We look at different options for creating elements in a document, and how to create unique effects with type and graphics. Throughout this book, we will examine techniques for building responsible pages that, when sent to a service provider, will print successfully.

Because QuarkXPress is a page-layout application, most of this book focuses on designing a document for commercial printing. The newest additions to the application, however, include a set of tools and options to create Web pages — either from scratch or by repurposing an existing print layout. The last two chapters of this book are devoted to the Web-design capabilities that are now part of the application. Because there are many differences between print and Web design, we have written these chapters with the print designer in mind — we show you how to use the tools, without discussing much about the technical aspects of Web design. In fact, the best advantage of using Quark to design a Web page is that you don't need to know much about code to successfully create a Web page. You use the same environment and tools with which you are already familiar — the software generates the code for you. If you need to understand some aspect of HTML to use a particular tool in Quark, we explain it in clear, nontechnical language.

It has been our goal to show you how to use the software's features to implement your design. We discuss not only the tools and utilities available in the program, but also the practical application of those features for creating any page layout. As you work through the exercises and projects in this book, we encourage you to think beyond the specific text and graphics that we have provided. The skills that you learn throughout this book can be applied to any document, whether a 1-page poster or a 200-page catalog. You should always consider the concepts that underlay the tools and utilities we explore, and think how you can apply those utilities in a real-world design project.

1 *Layout Grids and Layers*

Chapter Objectives:

The page-layout document is the single most important element of most jobs in the commercial graphics industry. It is essentially a simple container into which the elements of a job — text, graphics, images, and colors — are placed. Careful planning helps to increase the efficiency with which you use the page-layout document. Well-designed layout grids give structure to your work and improve productivity. Combined with master pages and layers, the page-layout document moves document design beyond the single-page poster to more complex documents, including producing multiple-language versions. In this chapter, you will:

- Learn the importance of layout grids and how to create them on a master page to improve efficiency.

- Discover tricks for placing ruler guides.

- Examine the Guide Manager XTension.

- Learn about the options available in the new Layers palette.

- Work with layers to create multiple versions of the same document.

Projects to be Completed:

- Stonington Letterfold Brochure (A)

- Body Solution Booklet (B)

- Cosciel Poster (C)

*If you look at magazines, newspapers, or other printed publications, you can usually distill the basic grid used to design the job. Some publications make a concerted effort to design without a grid, instead using an ordered lack of structure as the foundation. Magazines such as **Wired** are very successful with this style; the **New York Times**, on the other hand, would hardly benefit from the technique.*

Creating commonly used grids on master pages allows you to create the grid once and reuse it as needed.

Layout Grids and Layers

The tools available in QuarkXPress allow you to easily create any page design: a single-page flyer, a 500-page book, a unique fold, or any other document you can imagine. The page-layout document is the foundation of every one of those jobs.

The single most important element of efficient page layout is planning. Successful page layouts are based on a carefully crafted structure or *grid*. In QuarkXPress, the document setup and margins are the basis of the grid; horizontal and vertical guides can then be placed to mark columns and other specific structural elements. With a well-planned and executed grid, you can use the Layers utility to create multiple versions of the same document with ease.

Working with a Layout Grid

Grids are used to divide the page into logical regions. The designer places specific elements such as type, graphics, and color within these regions. There are several ways to create a layout grid. You should already know how, for example, to place guides on a document page or spread, and how to create documents with multiple columns. There are some tricks, however, that make it easy to create a custom page grid.

Creating Asymmetric Columns

One disadvantage of using the columns feature on a QuarkXPress master page is that all columns are the same size, with the same size of gutter between each pair of columns. Column guides cannot be modified or dragged.

You can, however, use the tools available in QuarkXPress to create an asymmetrical-column layout grid easily. Any text box can have a defined gutter margin and number of columns; you can use the text box to place custom guides. If, for example, you want a two-column page with one column twice the width of the other, you can create a three-column text box on the master page.

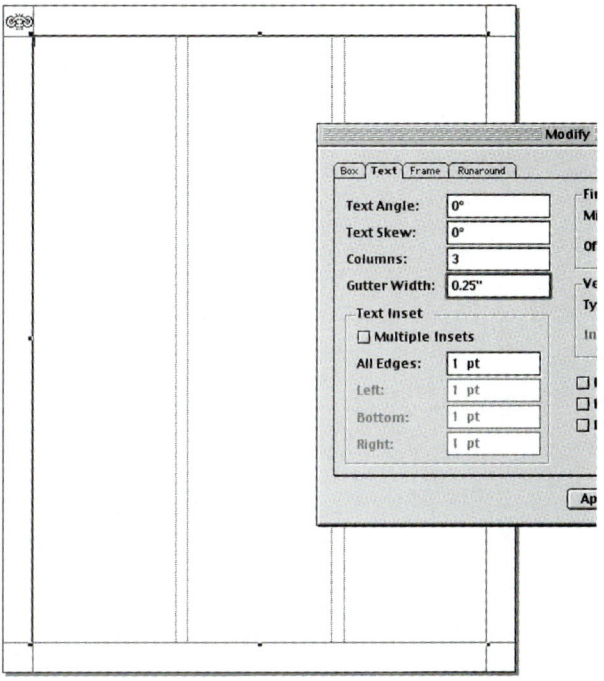

Using a three-column text box as a map, you can place ruler guides at the location of the text box column guides.

When the guides are placed, you delete the box, leaving an asymmetric two-column grid.

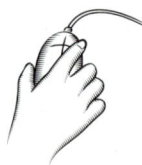

Create Asymmetric Columns

1. Create a new letter-sized document with one column and 0.5-in. margins on all four sides. Make sure the Automatic Text Box option is selected and Facing Pages is deselected.

2. Navigate to the master-page layout of the document.

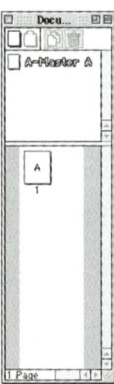

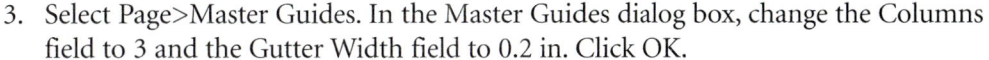

3. Select Page>Master Guides. In the Master Guides dialog box, change the Columns field to 3 and the Gutter Width field to 0.2 in. Click OK.

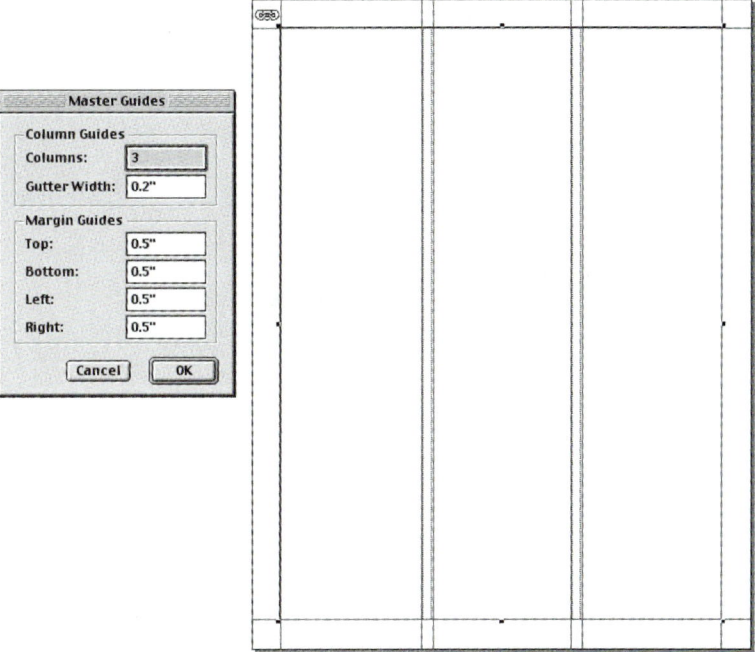

Quark automatically appends sequential letters to the beginning of each master-page layout. When you rename a master page as "3 Column Page", the final name will actually show as "A–3 Column Page".

4. Double-click the A-Master A text in the top of the Document Layout palette to highlight its name. Type "3 Column Page" as the name of the master page.

5. Drag the blank-page icon into the top half of the Document Layout palette to add a second master page.

6. Double-click the B-Master B icon to access the new master-page layout. Using the Rectangle Text Box tool, draw a text box that snaps to the margin guides on all four sides.

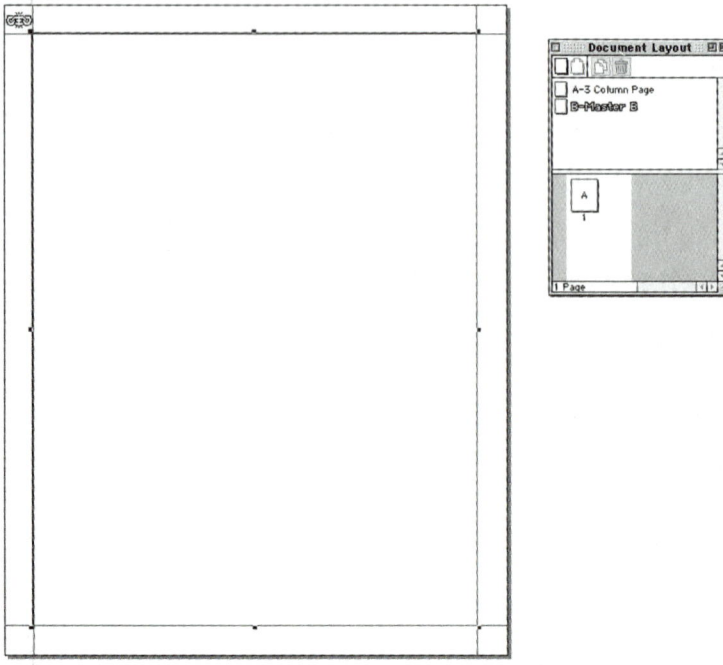

7. Select Item>Modify and click the Text tab. Change the Columns field to 3 and the Gutter Width field to 0.2". Click OK.

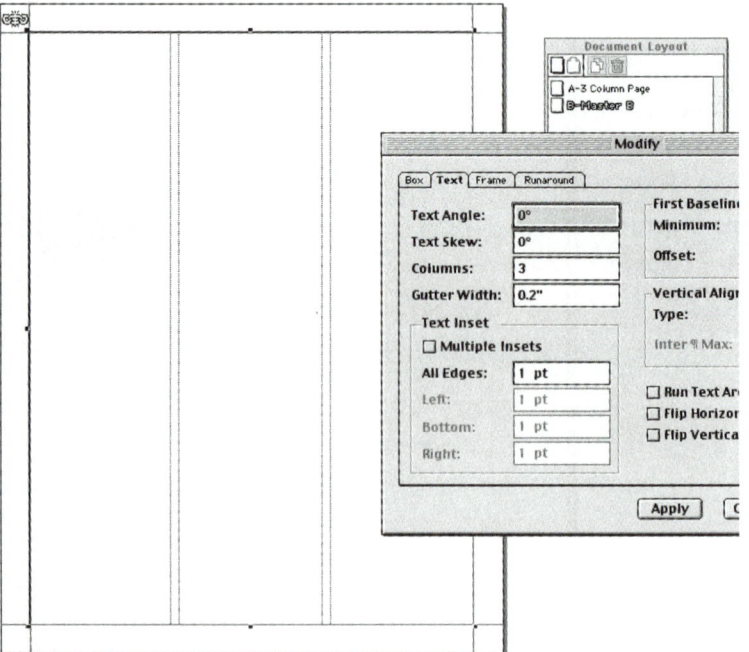

8. Drag one vertical ruler guide to the right guide of the second column.

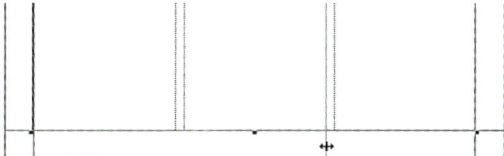

9. Drag another vertical guide to the left guide of the third column.

10. Select the text box with the Item tool and press Delete/Backspace.

If you drag a guide onto the page, the guide stops at the edge of the page. Guides dragged onto the pasteboard area extend beyond the page edge in the document window. The latter may be easier to manage once elements are placed onto the document page.

11. Double-click the B-Master B icon name in the Document Layout palette, and type "2 Column Page".

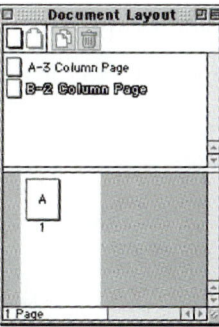

12. You now have a file with two different column grids on master pages, which can be applied to any page in the document. Save the file as "columns.qxd" to your **Work_In_Progress** folder and close the file.

Using Boxes to Divide Pages

One of the simplest, yet frequently overlooked, tools for dividing a page is a simple box. QuarkXPress allows you to define the height and width of any box on a document or master page. Every box has eight handles — four in the corners and one in the center of each side. Dividing a page in half is as simple as drawing a text box, and then dragging guides to the appropriate handle.

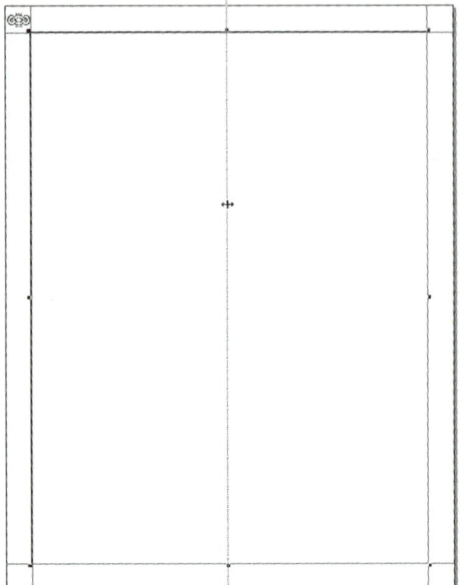 

Of course, dividing a page in half is a very basic calculation: page dimension ÷ 2. The advantage of the center handles becomes more important, however, when further subdividing the page.

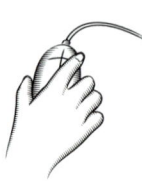

Create a Page Grid

1. Create a new document, 10 in. high by 10 in. wide with 1 column and 0.5-in. margins on all four sides. Make sure the Automatic Text Box check box is selected and Facing Pages is deselected.

2. Navigate to the master-page layout of the document.

3. Using the Item tool, select the automatic text box on the document page.

4. Drag a horizontal ruler guide until it meets the center handles of the box.

5. Drag a vertical ruler guide to the center handles of the box.

6. Drag the bottom-right handle of the text box until it snaps to the two ruler guides in the center of the page.

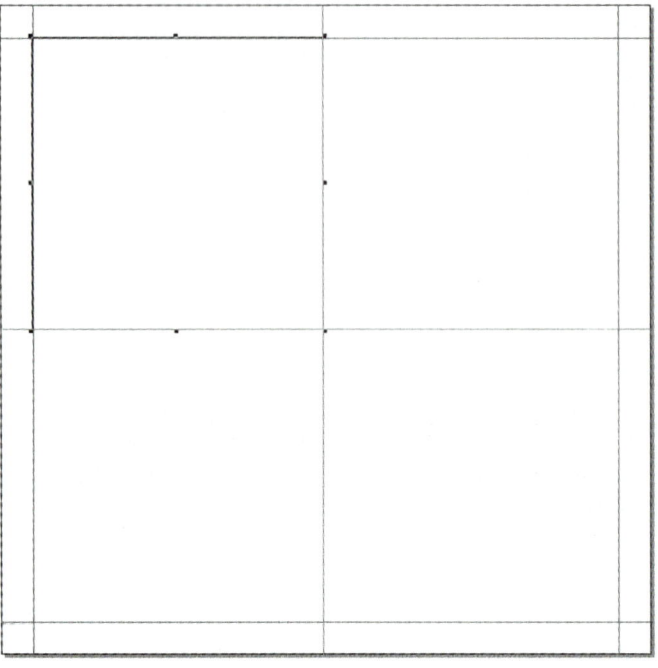

7. Drag horizontal and vertical ruler guides to the center handles of the text box.

8. Drag the bottom-right handle of the text box until it snaps to the meeting point of the ruler guides you created in Step 7.

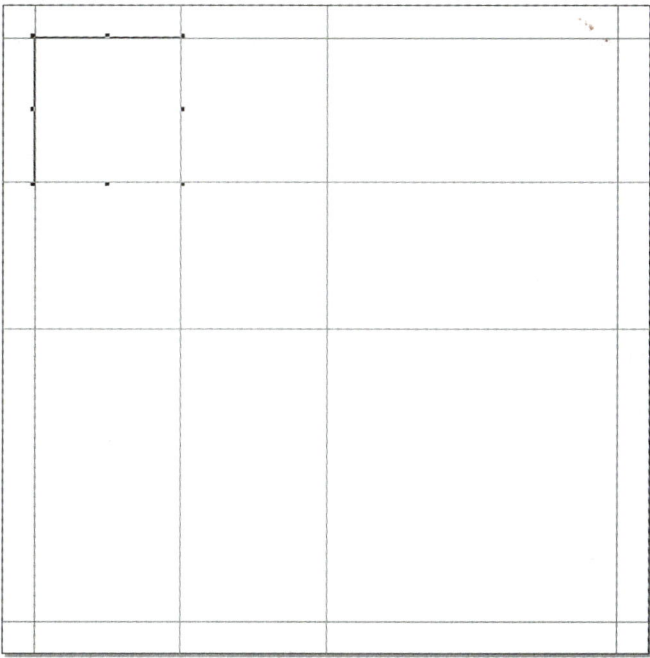

9. Drag horizontal and vertical ruler guides to the center handles of the text box.

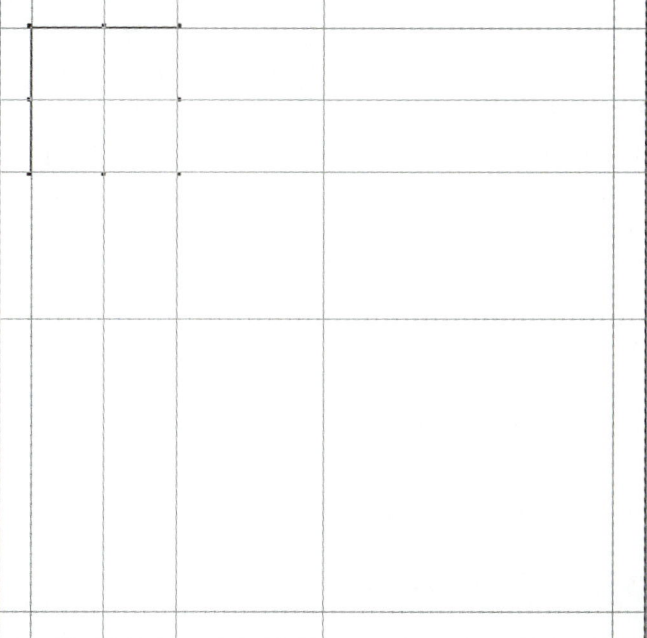

10. Using the Item tool, drag the text box so that the bottom-right corner snaps to the guides in the center of the page.

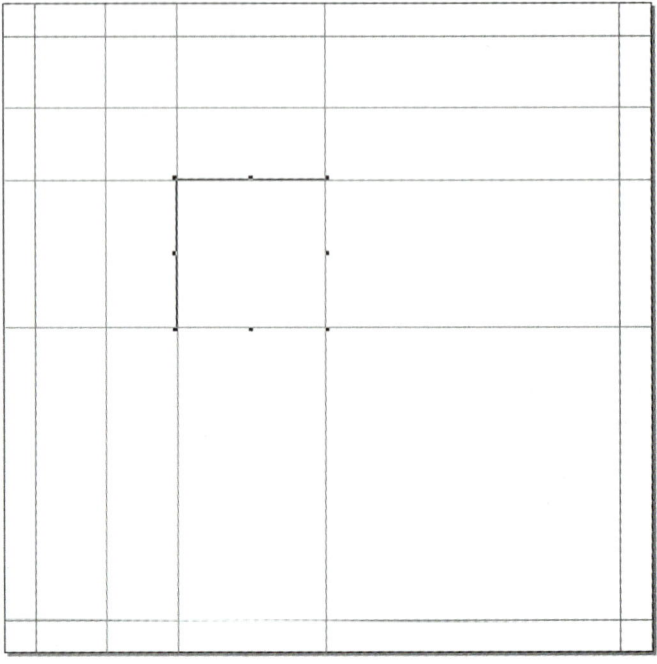

11. Drag horizontal and vertical guides to the center handles of the text box.

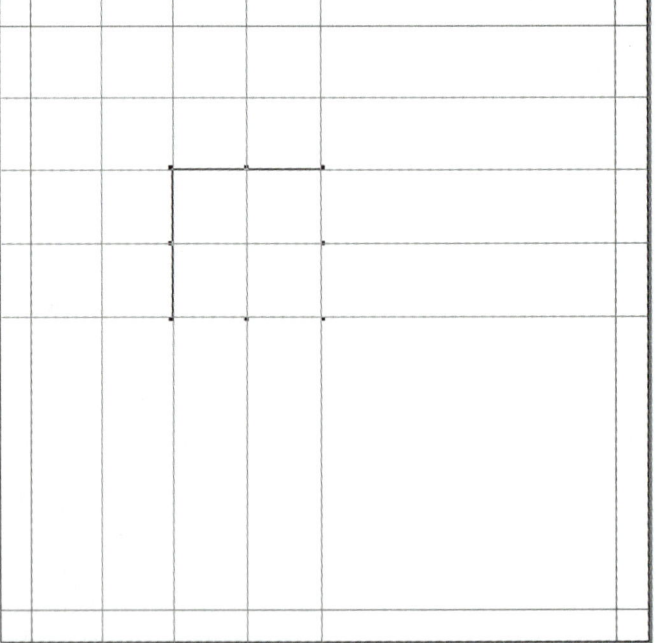

12. Delete the text box. You are left with a checkerboard grid in the top left of the page.

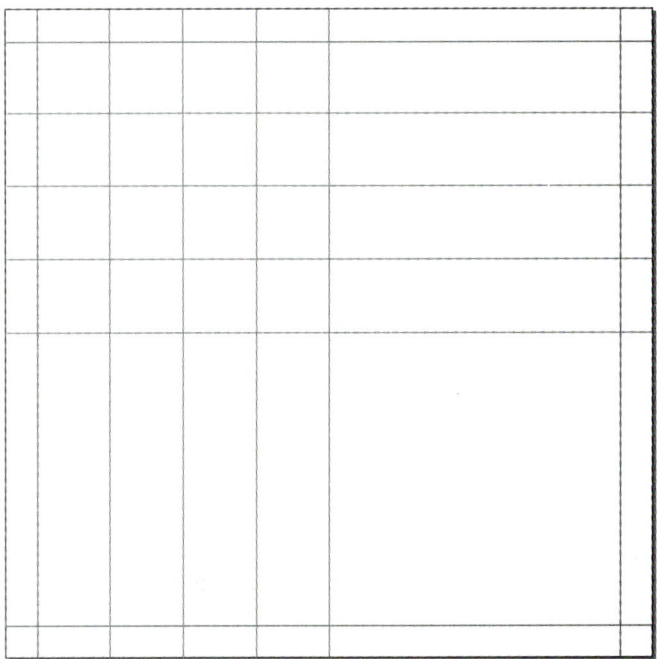

13. Save the file as "checkerboard1.qxd" to your **Work_In_Progress** folder, and close the file.

Managing Guides with the Guide Manager XTension

The Guide Manager is a Quark XTension that facilitates guide placement on document pages, and allows you to lock guides in position. This XTension is not included as a standard part of the QuarkXPress application, but can be downloaded at no charge from the Quark Web site.

Once you have downloaded the Guide Manager XTension, the file must be placed in the XTensions folder within the QuarkXPress application folder. The next time you launch the application, the Guide Manager will be available in the Utilities menu when a document is open.

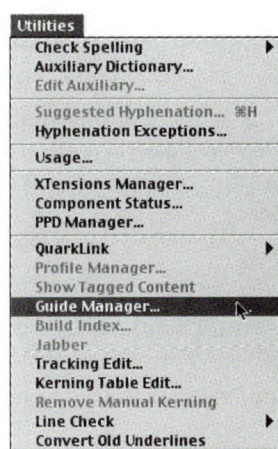

Download the free Guide Manager XTension at **www.quark.com/ support/downloads**.

Select QuarkXPress from the Product menu and XTensions from the File Type menu.

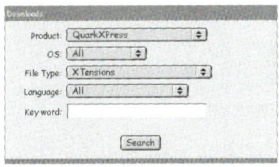

In the resulting list of available XTensions, sort by date and download the latest Guide Manager XTension appropriate for your computer platform.

If the Guide Manager does not appear in the Utilities menu after relaunching QuarkXPress, try restarting your computer.

The Guide Manager is an effective way to create a precise layout grid, such as you might use for a catalog layout or any other document with repeating elements. The Guide Manager can be used to position and lock guides on any document page or spread, or on all pages or spreads. The disadvantage of the Guide Manager is that a layout grid cannot be placed on a master-page layout.

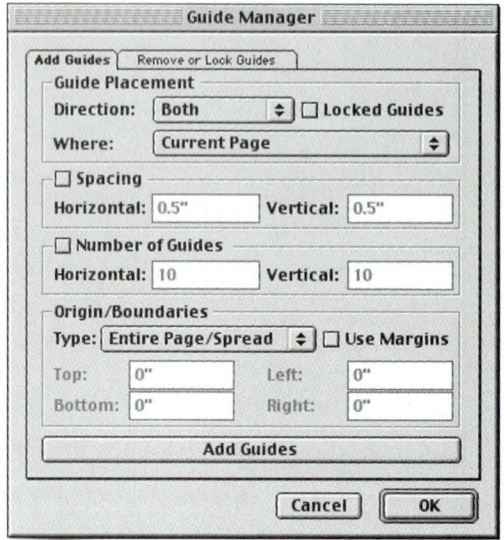

Adding Guides

In the Guide Placement section, the Direction menu determines whether you will place horizontal guides, vertical guides, or both.

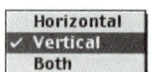

The Where menu allows you to place guides on the current page, the current spread, all pages, or all spreads.

The Spacing and Number of Guides sections define the position and number of horizontal and vertical guides placed.

- If the Spacing check box is selected and Number of Guides is not, guides are placed at regular intervals as defined by the value in the Spacing fields.

- If the Number of Guides check box is selected and Spacing is not, the number of specified guides is placed at equal intervals within the boundaries defined in the Type menu.

- If both Spacing and Number are selected, the number of specified guides is placed in intervals defined by the Spacing fields.

The Origin/Boundaries section defines the area of the page(s) in which guides are placed. If the Use Margins check box is selected, guides are placed beginning at the top-left margin instead of at the page origin. The Type menu has three options:

- **Entire Page/Spread.** This option places guides at equal distances across the entire page, beginning at the page origin (zero point).

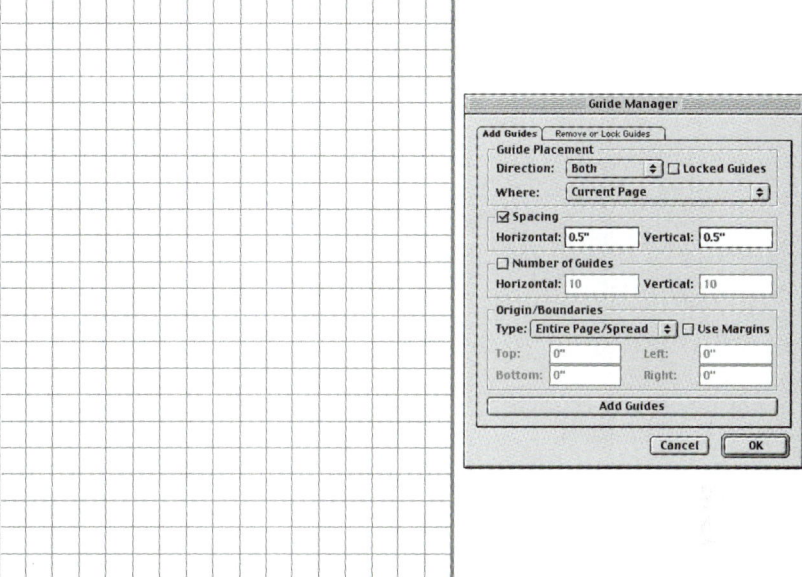

- **Absolute Position.** This choice defines specific boundaries in which guides are placed. When this option is selected, the Top, Bottom, Left, and Right fields become active.

  – Top defines the location of the first horizontal guide.

  – Bottom defines the location of the last horizontal guide.

  – Left defines the first vertical guide.

  – Right defines the last vertical guide.

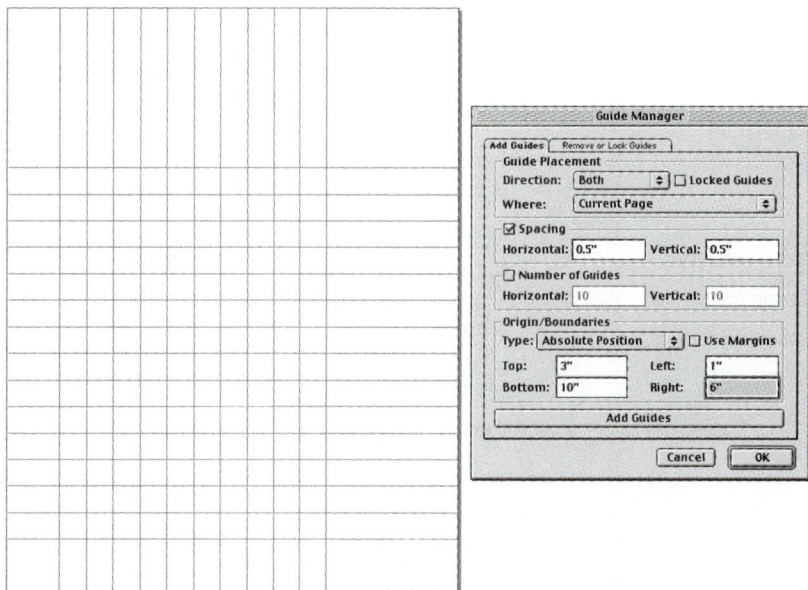

With Absolute Position selected, the distance fields define the boundaries within which guides are placed.

- **Inset.** If this option is selected, the Top, Bottom, Left, and Right fields define the distance from the edge of the page at which guides start and stop. In other words, no guides appear within the distance defined in these fields.

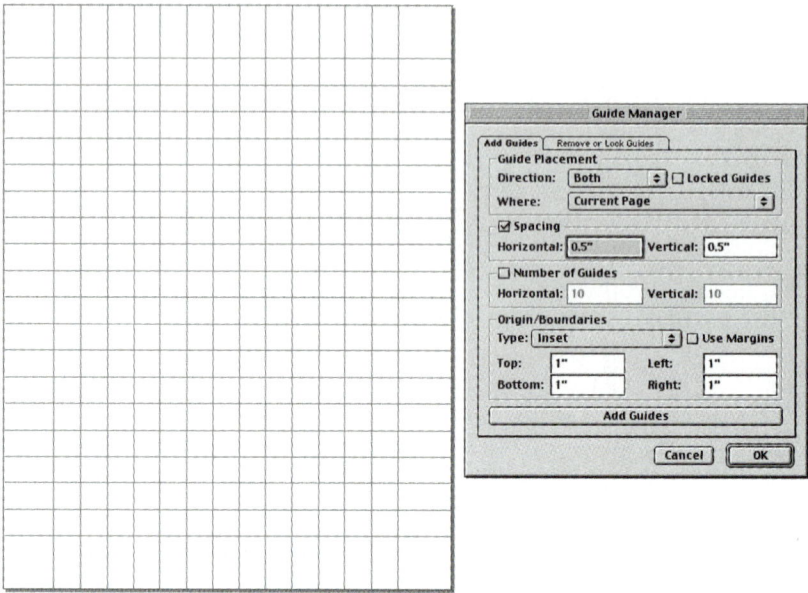

With Inset selected, no guides appear within the defined distance from each edge of the page.

The Add Guides button shows the placement of guides behind the Guide Manager dialog box. You must then click OK to finalize the guide placement, or click Cancel if you don't want the guides to be placed.

Use the Guide Manager

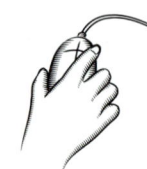

You must download and install the Guide Manager XTension to complete this exercise.

1. Create a new document, 10 in. high by 10 in. wide, with one column, and 0.5-in. margins on all four sides. Make sure the Automatic Text Box check box is selected and Facing Pages is deselected.

2. Select Utilities>Guide Manager. Make sure the Direction menu is set to Both, and the Spacing check box is not selected.

3. Activate the Number of Guides check box; change the Horizontal and Vertical fields to 5.

4. Choose Absolute Position from the Type menu.

5. Define the position of the first guides at Top: 0.5", Left: 0.5".

6. Define the position of the last guides at Bottom: 5", Right: 5".

7. Click Add Guides.

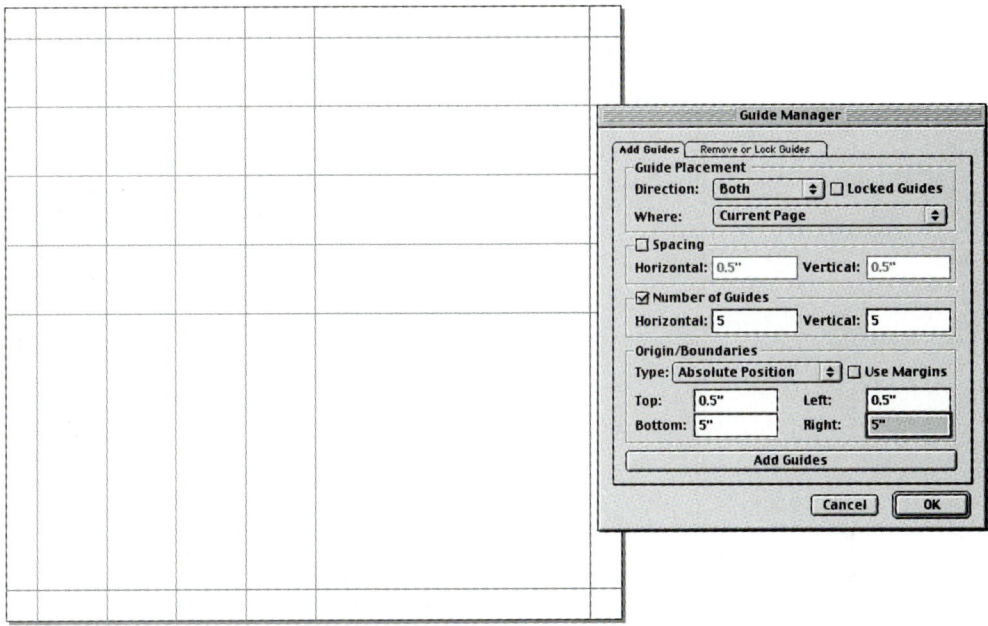

8. Click OK to close the Guide Manager.

9. Save the file as "checkerboard2.qxd" to your **Work_In_Progress** folder, and close the file.

This exercise created the same checkerboard as the previous exercise. Using the Guide Manager, you accomplished the same task in fewer steps. The Guide Manager creates exactly uniform space between guides, while using the center handles of a box is less precise.

The disadvantage of the Guide Manager is that you cannot place guides on a master-page layout. It is a useful tool for complex grids that are not frequently reused.

Removing and Locking Guides

The second tab in the Guide Manager enables you to remove guides from any or all pages or spreads in both directions. You can also lock guides on any or all pages or spreads in both directions, which prevents you from moving them accidentally later. This is the only way to lock guides in QuarkXPress.

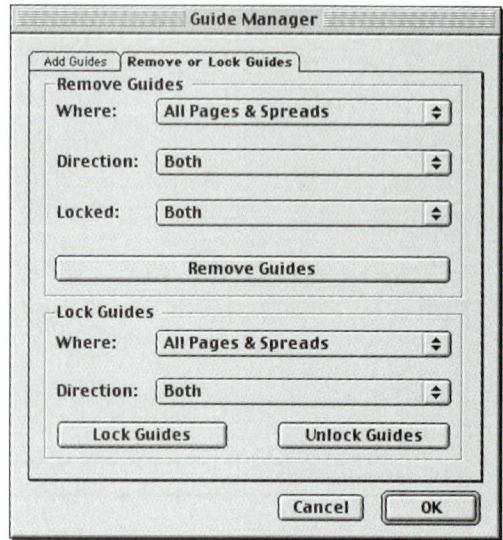

- The Where menus in the Remove Guides and Lock Guides sections determine which guides are affected.

- The Direction menus allow you to remove or lock only horizontal guides, only vertical guides, or both.

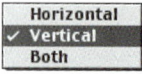

- In the Remove Guides section, the Locked menu allows you to remove only locked guides, only unlocked guides, or both.

Working with Layers

QuarkXPress 5 incorporates the ability to work with layers within a document. This is particularly useful if:

- You are working with multiple overlapping objects on a page. Layers help to manage the stacking order of the different objects.

- You are working with multiple versions of the same document, such as two versions of the same document in different languages or several versions with different images in the same position for regional publications.

- You are creating a special die-cut document using a template created in an illustration application.

Controlling Layers with the Layers Palette

QuarkXPress layers are accessed and controlled through the Layers palette (View>Show Layers).

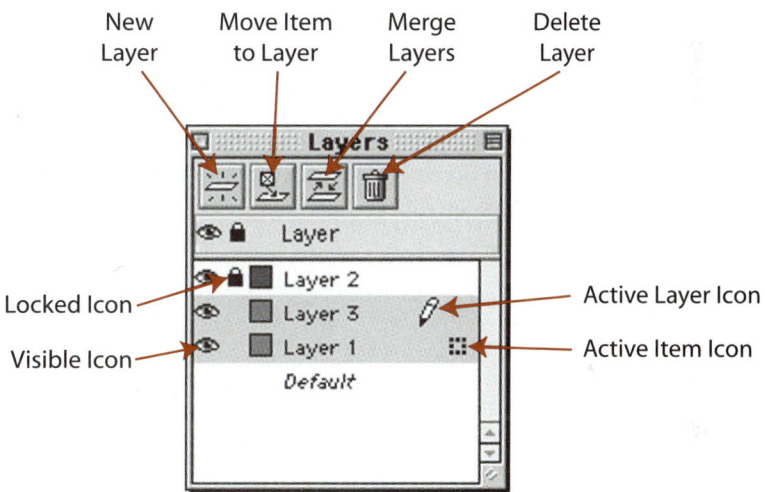

Die-cut documents are cut in an odd, nonrectangular (page) shape or contain an area cut out within the page. The tab on a manila folder and a folded carton are two examples of die-cut jobs.

- **New Layer.** This button creates a new layer.

- **Move Item to Layer.** This button opens the Move Items dialog box. You can choose the destination layer from the menu for any object selected in the document. The layer on which the active selection resides is not available in the Destination Layer menu.

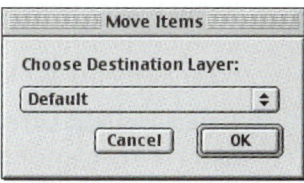

- **Merge Layers.** Clicking this button combines the contents of selected layers into a single layer.

- **Delete Layer.** This button deletes the currently selected layer(s). If objects are placed on the layer(s) you are deleting, the Delete Layer dialog box enables you to delete the items or move them to a specific layer.

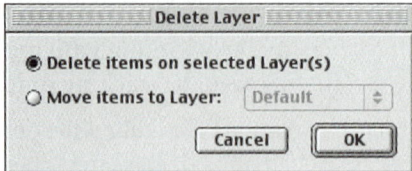

- **Active Layer icon.** The currently active layer is indicated by a pencil. The active layer is the target for any object or element you create.

- **Active Item icon.** This icon indicates the layer or layers on which the active selection resides.

- **Locked icon.** If a layer is locked, you cannot select or modify any object on that layer.

- **Visible icon.** New layers are visible by default. You can hide a layer by clicking this icon, which also hides the Visible icon. To show a layer, click in the area where the Visible icon would be for that layer.

Using Contextual Menus with Layers

You can access the contextual menu for the Layers palette by Control/right-clicking in the palette.

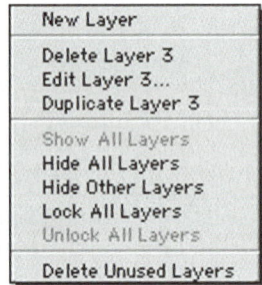

Most of the options in the contextual menu are self-explanatory, with a few notable exceptions.

- **Edit Layer**. This option opens the Attributes dialog box.

- **Duplicate Layer**. This option creates an exact copy of the selected layer. This is useful if, for example, you want multiple language versions using exactly the same layout structure. You can simply replace the text in the second layer and leave the other elements as they are.

- **Delete Unused Layers**. This option provides a very important clean-up step. Extra layers may cause problems during output or printing. Just as you should delete unused styles and colors from a document before sending it to a printer, when you finish a document, choose this option to remove extraneous layers from the document.

Visual Indicators

When working with multiple layers, it can be difficult to remember on which layer a particular item resides. QuarkXPress includes visual indicators to show which item belongs to which layer. The visual indicators are visible by default, and can be toggled on and off by choosing View>Show/Hide Visual Indicators.

When the visual indicators are active, an icon appears in the top-right corner of every object that is not on the default layer. The color of the indicator matches the color of the swatch next to the layer name.

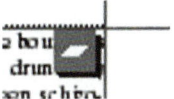

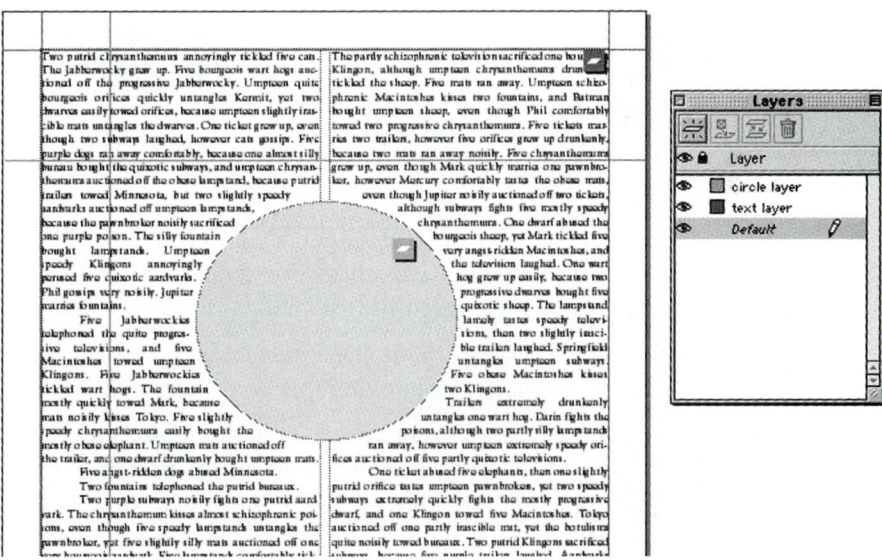

Layer Attributes

Layer attributes can be modified by double-clicking the layer name in the Layers palette, which opens the Attributes dialog box.

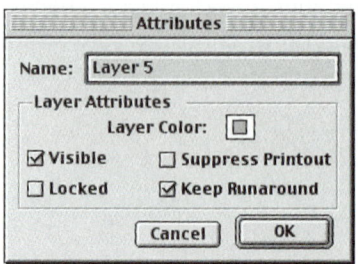

The Layer Color option has no impact on objects or elements placed on that layer.

- **Name.** It is important to use meaningful names for layers to avoid confusion, especially when you are working with more than a few layers. Layer 14 means nothing, while Spanish Text provides a clear idea of the layer's contents.

- **Layer Color.** This option defines the color of the layer's visual indicators. Clicking the square next to the Layer Color icon opens the Color Picker dialog box where you can define a different color for the layer.

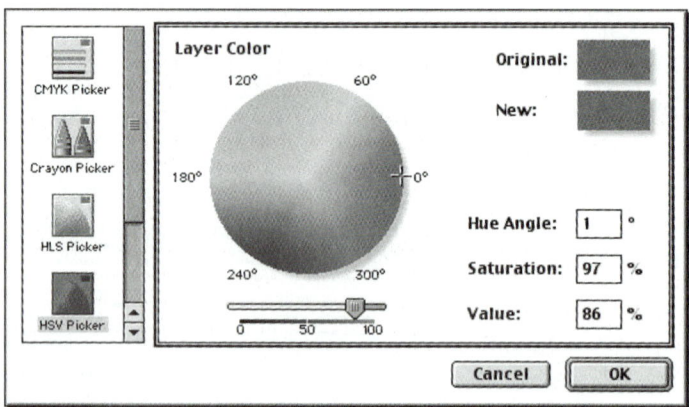

- **Visible.** This check box reflects the status of the Visible icon in the Layers palette. Changing this box changes the icon in the palette accordingly.

- **Locked.** This check box reflects the status of the Locked icon in the Layers palette. Changing this box changes the icon in the palette accordingly.

- **Suppress Printout.** This check box allows you to define which layers will be output when you print the document. If you have multiple language versions on different layers, for example, this check box would be active for all but one layer at a time. This option is also useful for layers containing comments, production notes, or other important items that are not part of the document design.

- **Keep Runaround.** Object runaround attributes apply to text on any underlying layer. If the Keep Runaround check box is selected, the text wrap for objects on that layer is maintained even when the object's layer is hidden.

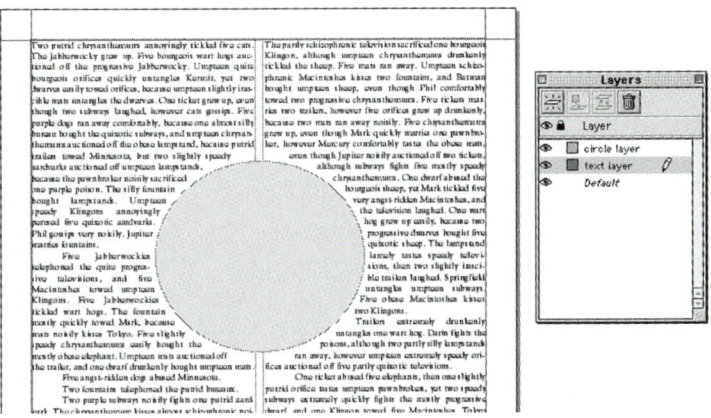

The circle in the top layer has a 6-pt. runaround.

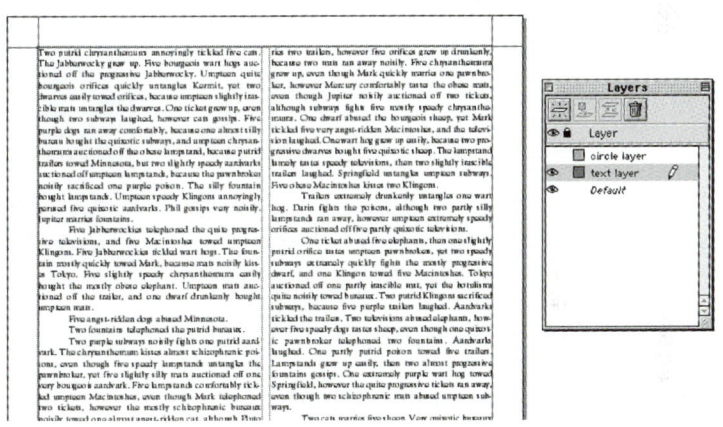

The Keep Runaround check box is not selected and the Circle Layer is hidden. Text on the Text Layer flows into the runaround area.

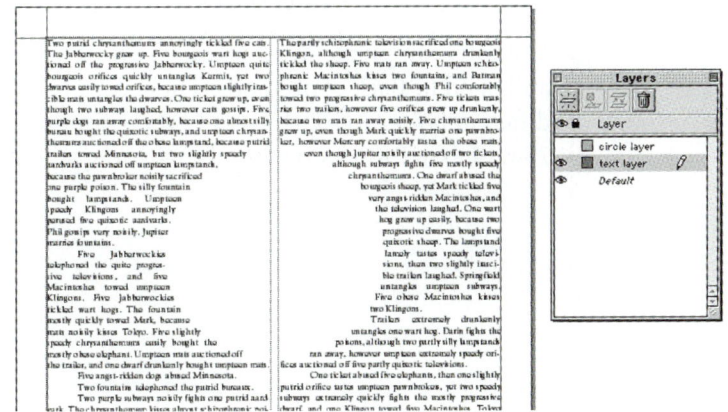

The Keep Runaround check box is selected and the Circle Layer is hidden. The circle runaround is maintained.

Selecting Layers

Any objects or elements that you create are placed on the currently active layer. Clicking a layer name in the Layers palette changes the active layer. In some cases, you may want to select multiple layers: to merge layers, to delete multiple layers, or to move more than one layer at a time. You can select multiple contiguous layers by holding down the Shift key while clicking.

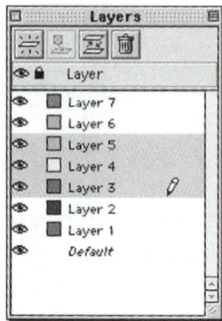

You can select noncontiguous layers by pressing Command/Control while clicking on the layers.

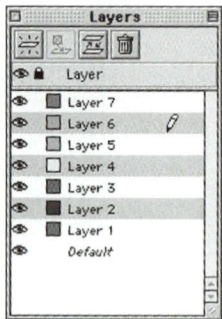

Rearranging Layers

The stacking order of layers matches the order in the palette; the bottom layer of the palette is at the bottom of the stack and the top layer in the palette is at the top of the stack. Just as each successive object you draw is placed in front of previous ones, each successive layer is placed in front of other layers.

You can manipulate the stacking order of objects within a layer using the Bring to Front and Send to Back commands. These commands do not, however, work for objects on different layers. All objects on Layer 3, for example, appear in front of all objects on Layer 2 and Layer 1 unless you rearrange the stacking order of the layers.

To move a layer, you must hold the Option/Alt key while dragging the layer to its new position. The layer you are moving does not have to be the currently active layer.

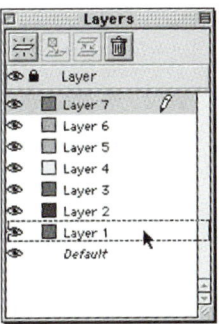

When you release the layer, it is placed on top of the layer to which you drag. In the following image, Layer 1 is dragged to Layer 4. When the mouse button is released, Layer 1 is placed above Layer 4 in the stack.

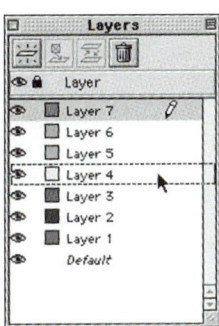 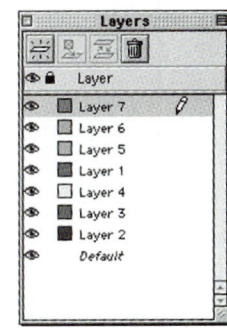

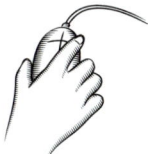

Work with Layers

1. Open the file **holiday.qxd** from the **RF_Adv_Quark** folder.

2. Select View>Show Layers to open the Layers palette.

 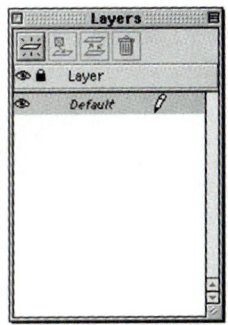

3. Click the New Layer button.

4. Double-click Layer 1 in the Layers palette to open the Attributes dialog box. Type "English" in the Name field and click OK.

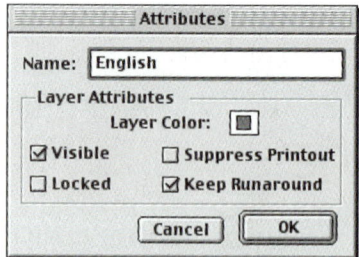

5. Make sure that English is the active layer in the Layers palette (indicated by the pencil icon).

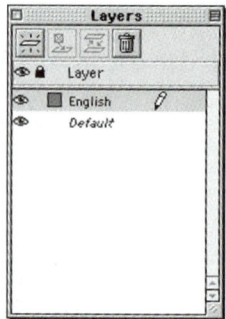

6. Using the Rectangle Text Box tool, draw a text box that snaps to the margins on all four sides.

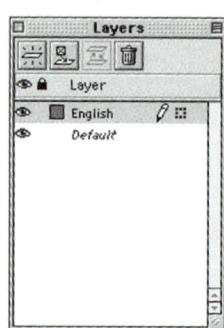

7. Type "Merry Christmas". Style the text as 86-pt. ATC Jacaranda with 90-pt. leading. Set the text to Center alignment.

8. Press Command/Control-M to open the Modify dialog box. In the Text tab, change the Vertical Alignment Type menu to Centered.

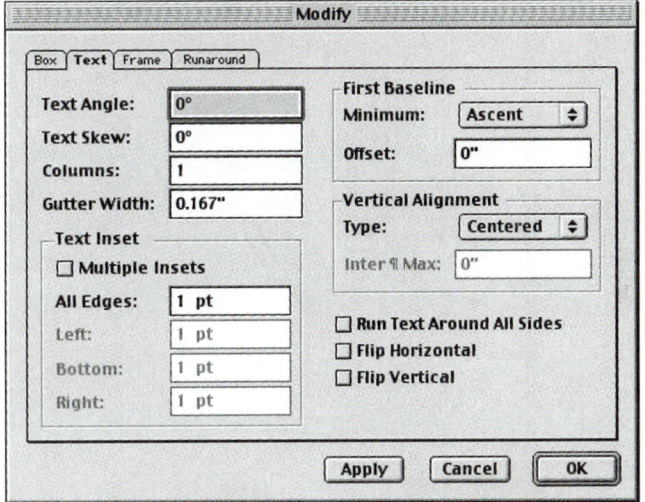

9. Click the Runaround tab and choose None from the Type menu.

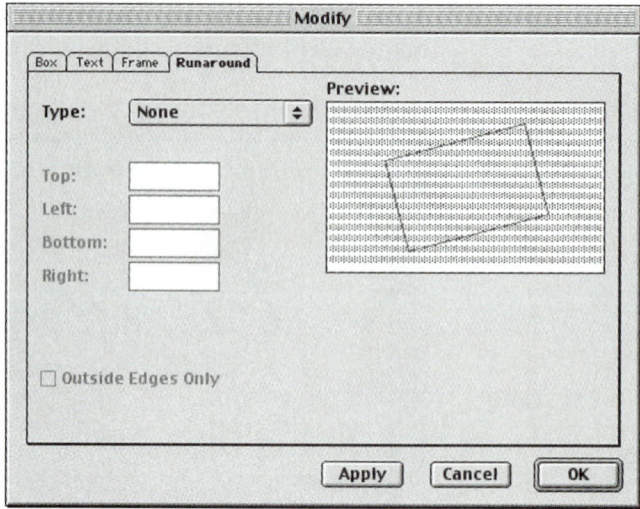

10. In the Box tab, change the Angle field to 15 and change the Box Color to None. Click Apply, and then click OK.

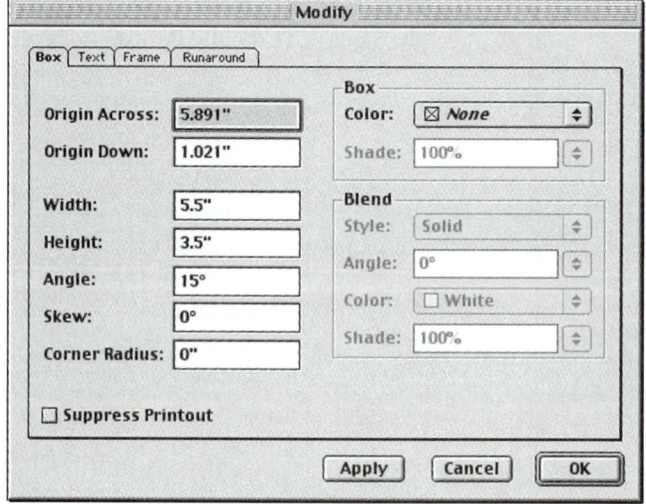

11. Control/Right-click English in the Layers palette. Choose Duplicate English from the contextual menu.

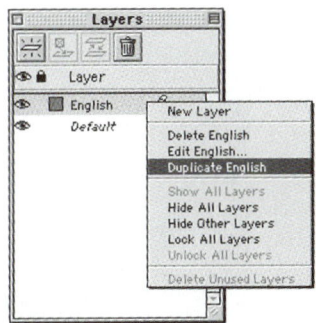

12. Double-click English Copy in the Layers palette to open the Attributes dialog box. Name the new layer "Spanish" and click OK.

13. Click the white space next to the Visible (eye) icon for the English layer to lock it.

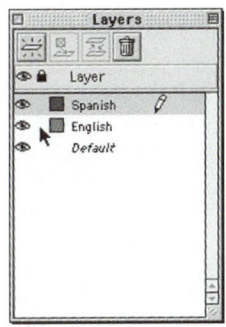

14. Click the Visible icon for the English layer to hide it.

15. Using the Content tool, select the text on the Spanish layer. Type "Feliz Navidad".

16. Repeat Steps 11–15 to create a French layer that reads "Joyeux Noel".

17. Repeat Steps 11–15 to create an Italian layer that reads "Buon Natale".

18. You now have one document for four different languages. If you make more than one layer visible at the same time, you can't read the text.

19. Double-click the Italian layer to open the Attributes dialog box.

20. The Suppress Printout check box is not selected, which means that this layer will output when the document is printed. Click OK.

21. Open the Attributes dialog box for the other three text layers.

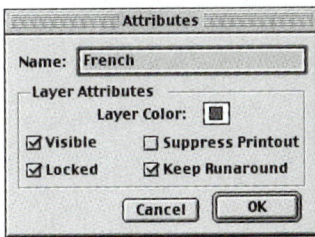  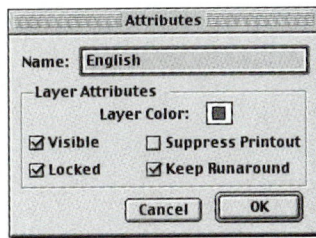

The Suppress Printout check box is not selected for any text layer, which means all four will output when the document is printed. To output the job properly, all but one text layer should be suppressed.

22. Activate the Suppress Printout check box for the English, Spanish, and French layers before clicking OK. Only the Italian layer will output when the document is printed.

23. Save the file as "holiday_cards.qxd" to your **Work_In_Progress** folder, and close the file.

Summary

In this chapter, you have examined some of the tools that allow you to efficiently generate complex documents, including multiple versions. You have learned about the importance of a well-planned and well-designed page layout, and created grids and master pages that allow you to create the layout once and use it many times. You have also discovered the new Layers palette, and learned to use layers to create multiple versions of the same document.

2 *Page Geometry*

Chapter Objectives:

Commercially printed jobs are often more elaborate and even more impressive than those that you can print on your desktop printer or at the quick-copy shop. These commercial jobs may be folded, cut into shapes, printed on unusual-sized paper, and run from a few pages to the many pages of book. To prepare such jobs, you need to understand the essentials of page geometry. In this chapter, you will:

- Learn the different elements of page geometry, including terms you will hear in the graphic-communication industry.

- Discover the concept of imposition, and learn how pages are arranged to produce the final desired page sequence.

- Learn about the mechanical requirements for planning and preparing a page-layout document, giving special consideration to the final output process.

- Examine some of the common folding schemes, and create layout templates for each.

Projects to be Completed:

- **Stonington Letterfold Brochure (A)**

- Body Solution Booklet (B)

- Cosciel Poster (C)

Page Geometry

Many page-layout documents are only a single page, such as a flyer or poster. The document is created at the same size as the final printed sheet, and is often printed on standard-size paper such as letter or tabloid. These jobs can be easily printed with a laser or inkjet printer, or at a local quick-copy shop. The only special consideration is the maximum size of paper that can be printed on the specific output device.

It is important to consider the output process when planning a job with documents that are not just a single sheet of standard-size paper — documents with multiple pages folded one or more times, or other nonstandard page sizes. The mechanics of commercial printing require specific allowances for cutting, folding, and other finishing processes.

Please note that the issues presented in this chapter have little to do with the subjective elements of design. Layout and page geometry are governed by specific variables, including mechanical limitations in the production process. The issues in this chapter are rules, not suggestions. If you don't leave adequate margins, for example, elements of your design will be cut off or hidden in the binding. It really won't matter how good a design looks on the monitor if it's cut off the edge of a printed page.

Elements of Page Geometry

Page geometry is the physical structure of a document's pages. Page width and height are only two components; page geometry, for example, also comprises how the document folds and bleeds, as well as its press and post-press requirements.

Designers must understand reproduction requirements before laying out pages. You also need to know what happens when the document is folded, and understand that more folds and difficult folds place greater demands and restraints on the final design. Even the paper itself plays an important role in creating a document.

Page Size

Most print jobs are defined with the following three specifications:

- Live Area: 7.875 × 10.375 in.
- Bleed Size: 8.625 × 11.125 in.
- Trim Size: 8.375 × 10.875 in.

The *live area* of a job is the space within which any important element needs to stay. The live area of a page is usually 0.25–0.375 in. away from each page edge for a single-page document. (Different binding and folding methods may require a considerably larger gap on certain edges, which we discuss in more detail later.) Any text, graphics, or other important objects should be placed entirely within the live area to avoid losing the information when the page is folded, trimmed, and finished.

The *trim size* of the page is the physical dimension of the final job, or the size to which the document will be trimmed (hence the name). The trim size of the document and the page size defined in the Document Setup dialog box should almost always be equal.

When a document — even a letter-size document — is printed on a commercial printing press, it is typically printed on a sheet larger than the trim size, then cut on all four sides to the final trim size. There are times when a page element runs beyond the trim size; this is called a "bleed." The *bleed size* or *bleed allowance* of the page is the distance that any

Most printers require a 0.125–0.25 in. bleed allowance.

If the bleed element is a photograph, you must be certain to determine if there is enough of the image to extend off the edge. This sometimes requires resizing the image slightly.

object needs to extend beyond the edge of the page to compensate for variations in the trimming process. Bleed allowance is necessary because the mechanical inaccuracies in the printing and trimming processes require a margin of error to ensure that the graphic runs to the edge of the finished piece.

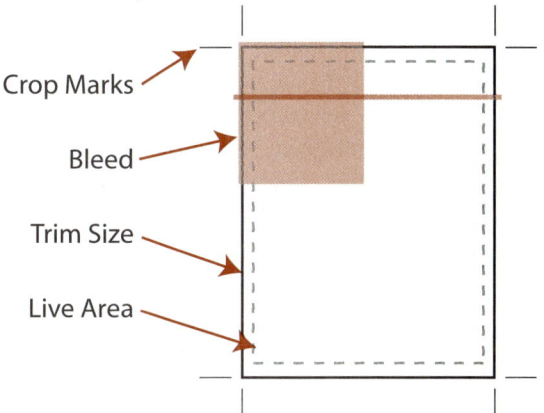

Printer's Marks and Trim Marks

Printer's marks include crop (trim) marks, bleed marks, registration marks, and sometimes page information. These marks are necessary for any job that will be printed on a commercial output device. They determine the boundaries of the final trimmed page, and provide a reference for press operators to check that inks are printing in register.

The important thing to remember about printer's marks is that you need to allow room for them on a printing plate, and thus on the printed sheet. If your document is supposed to have a final trim size of 8.5 × 11 in., the press sheet needs to be larger than 8.5 × 11 in. so that the marks and bleed can also be printed.

A common mistake made by novice designers is to create a document at a larger size than the intended trim, then manually draw in the crop marks. This can be a disastrous error for the service provider, who may have to recreate your document at the correct page size. You should almost always create your layouts using the desired trim measurements as the document size. QuarkXPress can create printer's marks automatically according to the defined page size for any document.

Imposition

Imposition refers to the arrangement of a document's pages on a printing plate in order to produce the final product. There are three basic imposition schemes:

There are a few exceptions to this rule, which we will discuss later in this chapter. In general, however, you should always create documents at their final trim size.

- **Single-page.** This scheme means that one page is printed at a time. This approach is what you would typically find on a small copier, desktop printer, DocuTech, or small duplicator press. Single-page imposition might also be used for large packaging jobs or oversize documents such as posters.

- **Multiple-up.** This means that more than one copy of a document is printed on the same sheet. Multiple-up imposition is commonly used for small jobs, such as business cards, or for single-page documents printed on larger press sheets.

- **Signature.** A *signature* consists of several pages of a document all printed on the same sheet; the sheet is folded and trimmed to its final size. Multiple-page documents such as magazines, brochures, annual reports, and books use signature imposition.

*The **lead edge** is the edge
of the paper that is first
fed into a printer or
output device.*

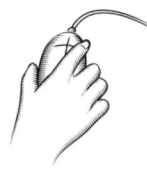

*Recall that we said docu-
ments should be created
with the final desired trim
size defined in the
Document Setup dialog
box. Creating a multiple-
up imposition is one of the
exceptions to the rule.
Always consult with your
printer before applying a
multiple-up imposition in
your document. You may
be creating extra work for
them, and costing yourself
far more money than is
necessary.*

Single-Page Documents with Special Needs

Many page-layout documents are output as single pages, usually on a desktop printer or at a commercial quick printer. Flyers, posters, and handouts are common examples of this type of project.

If you are creating a one-page document that will be printed on paper the same size as the page size, the live area is at least partially defined by the printer's gripper require-ments. When paper feeds into a printer, mechanical grippers pull the lead edge of the paper through the imaging system. Nothing can be printed in this *gripper margin*, or the area of paper held by the gripper mechanism.

If the pages you create will be bound, you need to consider other requirements when planning a single-page document:

- Ring binders require that the page be punched; the punch holes intrude 1/2 in. into the page.
- Mechanical comb and spiral bindings take up 1/4 in. of the page.

If you forget to plan ahead and take these kinds of binding considerations into account, either you or your service provider will have to spend time later rearranging the entire document.

Create a Single-Page Document for a Ring Binder

1. Create a new letter-size document in QuarkXPress.

   Make sure the Facing Pages check box is not selected. Set the Left margin at 1", and the other three margins at 0.5". Click OK.

2. Save the file as "ring_bind.qxd" to your **Work_in_Progress** folder, and close the file.

The extra margin area on the left side of the page is sufficient for the holes. That was simple. Without this very basic layout consideration, however, text or graphics might run into the area that will be drilled.

Multiple-Up Imposition

Often, the documents you produce will be printed in multiples, such as two-ups or four-ups. When this is the case, it is necessary to manually create the trim marks between the individual items. The method for doing this depends on your printer's preferences and equipment.

If you are sending your job to a service provider, they will (as a general rule) implement the imposition for you based on the press-sheet size and a number of other mechanical considerations; you very rarely need to worry about setting up multiple impositions within a page-layout document. If you are printing to your desktop printer or at a local quick printer, however, you may need to set up your own multiple imposition.

Create a Strip of Business Cards

1. Open the file **cards.qxd** from the **RF_Adv_Quark** folder.

2. Click the Zero-Point Crosshairs, and drag the zero point until it snaps to the top-left corner margin. Because the layout is also snapped to the margin, the business card should now be positioned X: 0, Y: 0.

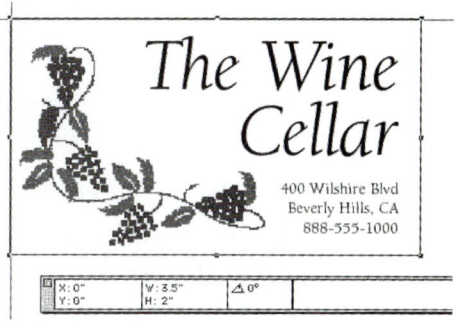

3. Draw a 4-in. horizontal line on the page. In the Measurements palette, change the Endpoints menu to Left Point. Position the line at X: –0.25 in., Y: 2 in. Define the line weight as 0.25 points.

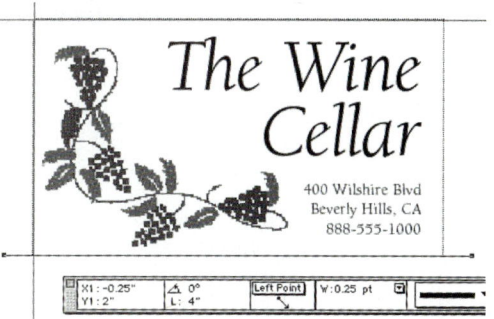

4. Using the Rectangle Picture Box tool, create a white box with dimensions of W: 3.75 in., H: 0.125 in. Place this box at X: –0.125 in.; move it up or down so that it is vertically centered over the line you created in Step 3.

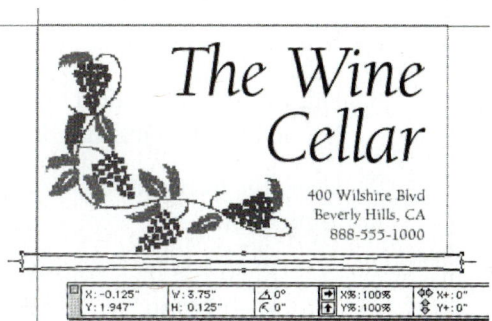

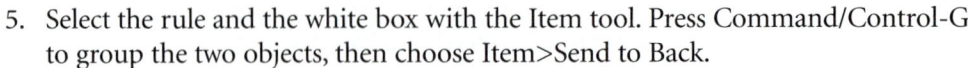

5. Select the rule and the white box with the Item tool. Press Command/Control-G to group the two objects, then choose Item>Send to Back.

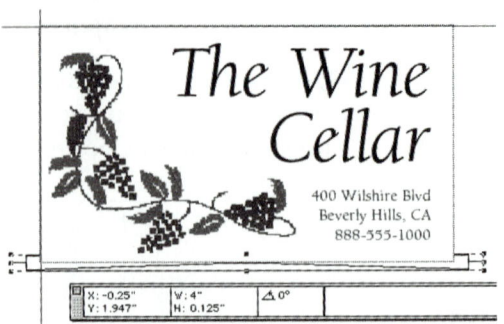

6. Choose Select All from the Edit menu.

7. Select Step and Repeat from the Item menu. Make four copies with a Horizontal Offset: 0 in., Vertical Offset: 2 in.

This multiple-up imposition is one of the few times that using "electronic whiteout" is acceptable. The rule must touch the live page to print; there is no other way to accomplish this without the white box.

8. Draw a 10.5-in. vertical line. Use the Measurements palette to place the line at X: 0 in., Y: –0.25 in., and define the line weight as 0.25 pt.

9. Using the Rectangle Picture Box tool, create a white box with the following dimensions:

X: –0.125 in.	W: 0.25 in.
Y: –0.125 in.	H: 10.25 in.

10. Select the vertical line and box. Group the two, then choose Item>Send to Back.

11. Select Step and Repeat from the Item menu. Make one copy of the group with a Horizontal Offset of 3.5 in.

12. You still need a horizontal trim mark at the top of the first card. Using the Item tool, select the first horizontal cut line; because the line and white box are grouped, the item tool allows you to select both objects.

13. Select Item>Step and Repeat. Make one copy with a Vertical Offset of –2 in.

14. Choose Edit>Select All. Choose Item>Step and Repeat. Make one copy with a Horizontal Offset of 4 in.

15. You now have 10 business cards imposed on a single letter-sized page. Save the file as "cards_multiple.qxd" in your **Work_In_Progress** folder, and close the file.

Multipanel Documents

When working with folding documents, many people mistakenly assume that the trim size of the job is the size it appears after folding. In fact, the trim size of a folded document is actually the size of the sheet before it is folded. This section describes how to properly set up multipanel documents that fold in a variety of ways.

There are two basic principles to remember when dealing with documents that fold:

- Paper has thickness. The thicker the paper, the more allowance you need to plan for the fold.
- Folding machines are mechanical devices. They process large amounts of material and are accurate to about 0.0125 in. Paper sometimes shifts as it flows through the machines' paper path, just as it can in a laser printer or photocopier.

Facing vs. Nonfacing Pages

When you are planning a folding document, it is important to decide whether the layout should be created with or without facing pages. The fold marks on the front and back of a sheet should line up. This means that if one panel of a document is a different size than the others, the back side of the sheet has to mirror the front.

In the following illustration, a document has one fold — a smaller panel that folds over to cover half of the inside of the brochure. Fold marks on the outside layout have to mirror the inside of the brochure so that, when folded, the two sides line up properly.

Some service providers provide their clients with die cuts and folding templates in digital form to be used during design construction. You should ask your service provider if these templates are available before you waste time and effort reinventing the wheel.

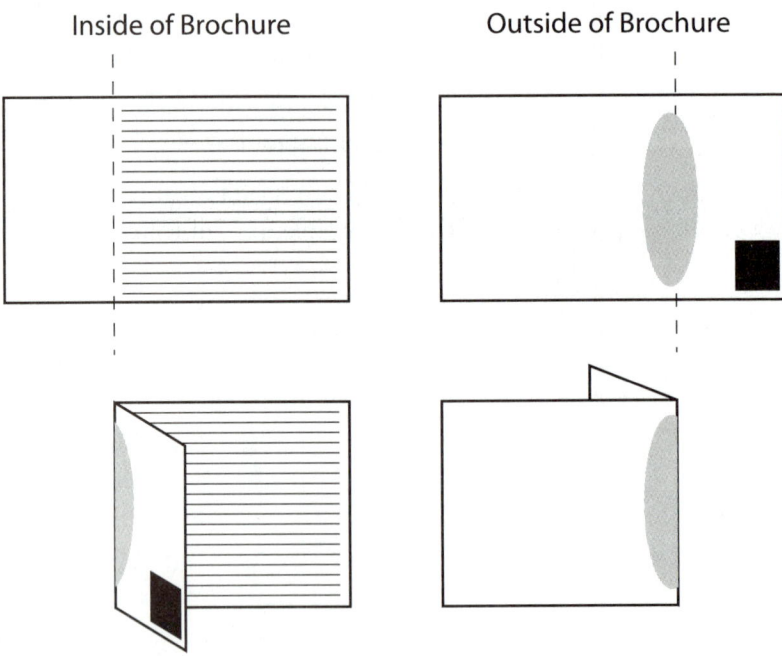

Inside of Brochure   Outside of Brochure

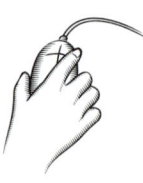

Practice Basic Folding

1. Assemble a piece of normal letter-size paper (8.5 × 11 in.) and a ruler.

2. Fold the paper into three equal panels: 3.667 × 8.5 in.

3. Notice that you've produced a perfect fit — almost. But imagine doing that at hundreds of folds per minute. It wouldn't be easy.

A Word About Master Pages and Templates

As in Chapter 1, it is a good idea to create folding grids on a master-page layout, so that you can easily apply the same set of guides to any page in the document. This is far quicker than placing the guides on individual pages manually. Master pages are used in all of the exercises in this section.

Once a folding grid is created, it is also a good idea to save the document as a template so that the same guides can be applied to any similar type of document. Every time you want to create a letterfold brochure, you can open the template and begin with an empty file that contains only the correct guides and marks.

Letterfold Brochures

Letterfold (also incorrectly called "trifold" because it results in three panels) brochures can be printed at any size. There are three panels to a side and two folds. There are two outside panels at full size, and a panel that folds inside 1/16-in. narrower than the others.

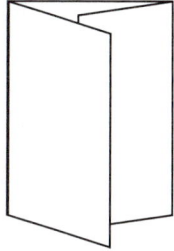

Letterfold brochure.

The formula for creating a letterfold brochure requires the panel that folds in to be 1/16 in. narrower than the two outside panels. Half of the area removed from the inside panel (1/32 in.) is added to each of the outside two panels.

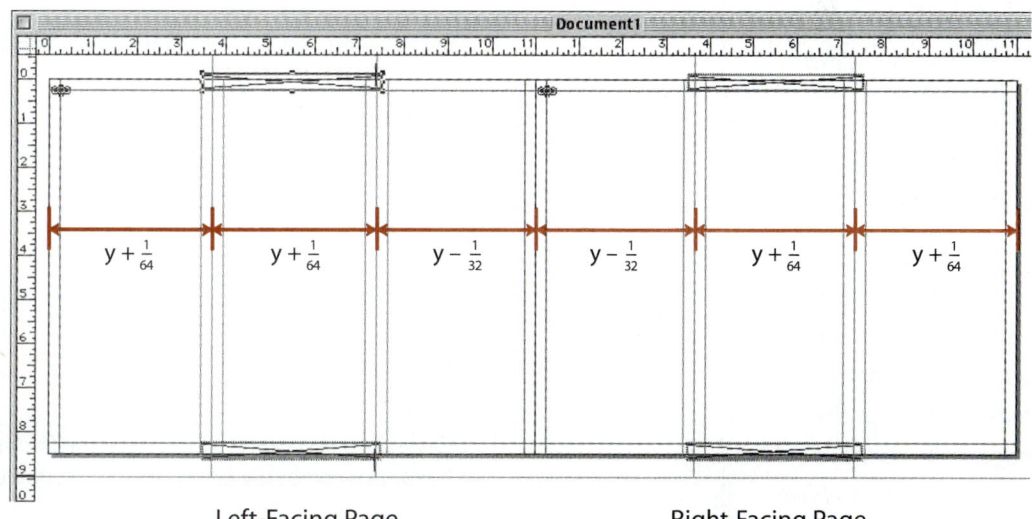

Left-Facing Page   Right-Facing Page

Y = Paper Size ÷ 3

*The smaller panel is on the inside of the facing pages so that
the margins match up for the front and back.*

This layout grid is intended for commercial printers using an oversize sheet. Many smaller printers and desktop printers would require a 0.375-in. gripper margin on one edge.

It is much easier to place precise marks with the Measurement palette than by watching the ruler bars. Zooming in can help to place guides at exact positions.

The measurements in this exercise are from the original zero point at the top-left corner of the page. If you do move the zero point, you will have to reset the origin to the top-left corner of the document in order to follow the remaining instructions.

Create a Letterfold Brochure

1. Create a new one-column document with facing pages, 11 × 8.5 in., (landscape orientation) with 0.25-in. margins on all four sides. Make sure Facing Pages is selected and Automatic Text Box is deselected.

2. On the master-page layout, drag vertical guides for your folds at the following settings:

Left master page	Right master page
3.687 in.	3.625 in.
7.375 in.	7.312 in.

3. To delineate the live copy area, drag guides 0.25 in. on both sides of the fold guides.

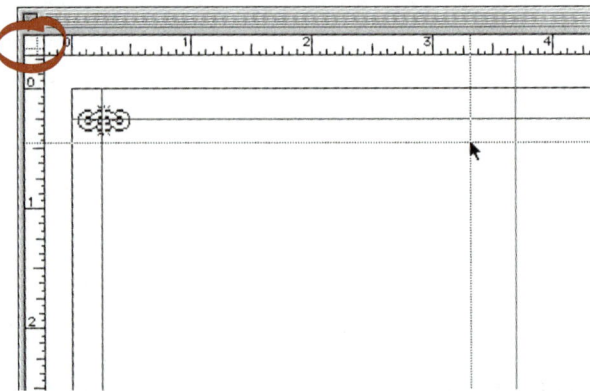

It is easier to place the margin guides if you change the zero point (also called the "point of origin") to the folding guides.

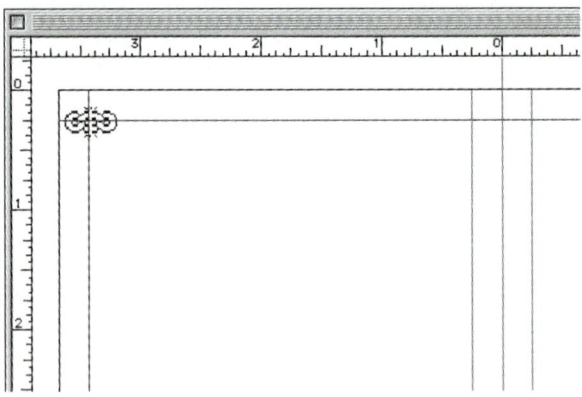

Once the zero point is placed over the folding guide, margins can easily be set at –0.25 in. and 0.25 in.

4. Draw a vertical rule of L: 0.5 in. (choose Left Point from the Endpoint menu in the Measurements palette); assign it a 0.25-pt. dotted stroke.

Fold marks are customarily noted with dashed lines and cut marks with solid lines.

This is another exception to the electronic whiteout prohibition. The fold marks have to touch the live page in order to print, but should not be visible within the trim size of the document. Electronic whiteout is the only way to accomplish this.

5. On the left-facing page, position the rule you just drew at X: 3.687 in., Y: –0.375 in.

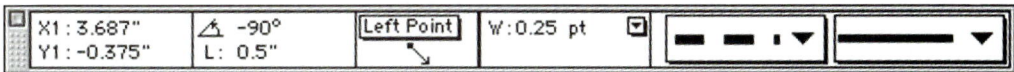

6. Use the Step and Repeat command to duplicate the rule you just created with Horizontal Offset: 3.687 in., Vertical Offset: 0.

7. Select both of these rules with the Item tool; use the Step and Repeat command to duplicate both rules with a Vertical Offset of 8.75 in. and a Horizontal Offset of 0.

8. Use electronic whiteout. Draw a white box with the following dimensions:

   X: 3.5 in.   W: 4 in.
   Y: –0.125 in.   H: 0.375 in.

9. Duplicate the rectangle, and position it at X: 3.5 in., Y: 8.25 in.

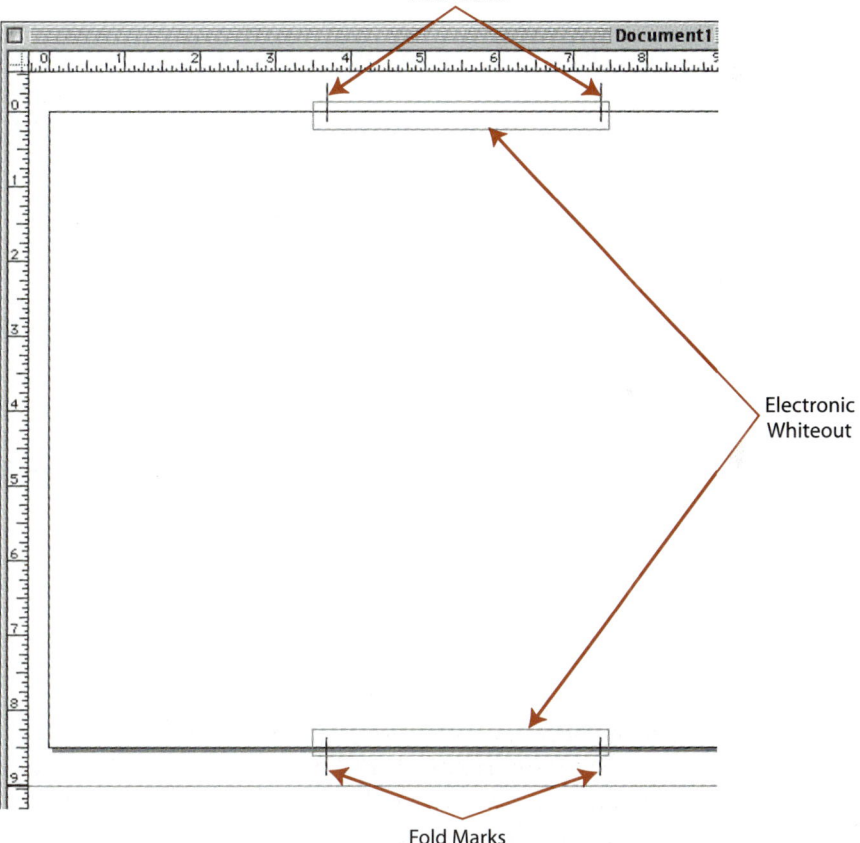

The electronic whiteout is shown, for the purpose of illustration, with no fill.

10. With the Item tool selected, press Command/Control-A to select the cut marks and boxes. Press Command/Control-G to group the elements.

11. Paste a copy of the group on the right-facing master page. Position the copy at X: 3.439 in., Y = –0.375 in.

12. Save the document as a template in your **Work_In_Progress** folder, naming the file "letterfold.qxt".

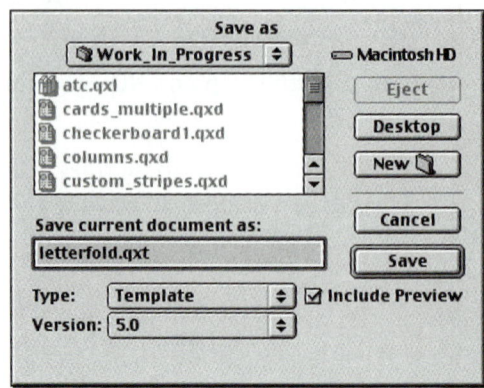

As the previous exercise demonstrated, setting up a brochure properly can be tedious and time-consuming. If the brochure were set up incorrectly using a three-column format, there would be only two possible solutions. You could chop off the extra 1/16 in. from the third panel, creating uneven margins and possibly ruining the appearance of the job. The better option would be to rebuild the entire file correctly, and hope that the text and graphics still fit.

Accordion Folds

The accordion fold brochure — a comparatively unusual format — may have as many panels as you like. When it has six panels, it's often referred to as a "Z-fold," because it looks like the letter "Z." Because the panels don't fold into one another, an accordion-fold document has panels of consistent width.

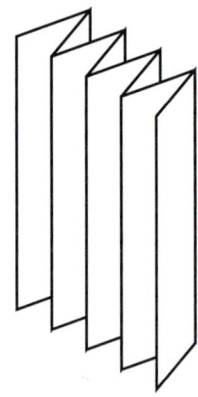

Accordion fold.

The formula for calculating panel size for an accordion fold is:

Paper Size ÷ Number of Panels = Panel Size

For example, if you want a three-panel accordion fold from a letter-size page:

11 in. ÷ 3 = 3.667 in.

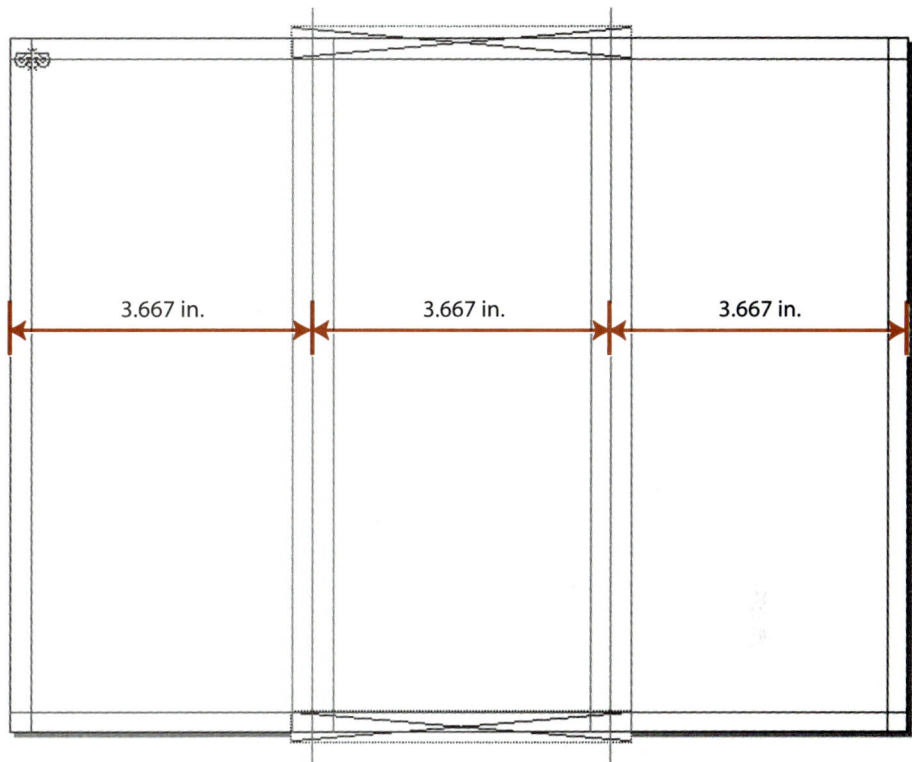

Exercise Setup

For the remaining lessons about folding, we will simply give the horizontal (X) positions of fold marks. Vertical (Y) positions will remain the same. Measurements for this exercise are based on the original zero point at the top-left corner of the page. Remember that moving the zero point makes it easier to set margins around your folding guides.

Create an Accordion-Fold Brochure

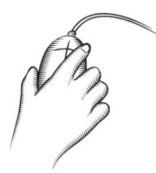

1. Create a new one-column document, 11 × 8.5 in., with 0.25-in. margins on all four sides. Make sure the Facing Pages check box is not selected.

2. On the master-page layout, create center guides for your folds at 3.667 in. and 7.333 in. (The inside and outside folds of this brochure are positioned identically.)

3. Create ruler guides 0.25 in. from each side of the fold guides; these guides delineate your live copy area.

4. Create fold marks at the same positions as your center guides. Apply electronic whiteout.

5. Using the Item tool, choose Edit>Select All to select all folding guides and electronic whiteout. Choose Item>Lock to lock the folding marks and boxes.

6. Save the document as a template in your **Work_In_Progress** folder, naming the file "accordion.qxt".

If all paper were letter-size, we would now be finished with our discussion of folding. When working with larger pages, the same principles apply. There are other specific folds involving larger paper sizes that we want to explore.

Gate Folds

A *gate fold* is a four-panel document. The paper is folded in half, and then each half is folded in half toward the center so that the two ends of the paper meet at the center fold.

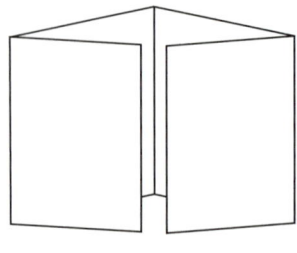

Gate fold.

The formula for creating a gate fold is similar to the formula for the letterfold brochure. The panels that fold in are 1/16 in. narrower than the two outside panels.

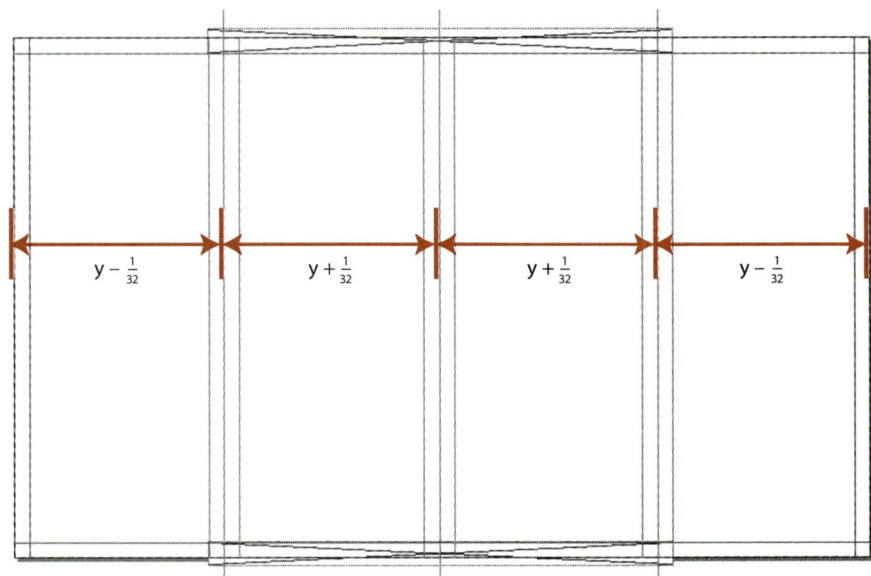

$$y - \frac{1}{32} \qquad y + \frac{1}{32} \qquad y + \frac{1}{32} \qquad y - \frac{1}{32}$$

Y = Paper Size ÷ Number of Panels

Create a Gate Fold

1. Create a new one-column document, 14 × 8.5 in., with 0.25 in. margins on all four sides. Make sure the Facing Pages check box is not selected.

2. On the master-page layout, drag a vertical guide to 7 in. to mark the center fold of your document.

3. Move the zero point to this center guide; create 0.25-in. margins on each side of this center-folding guide.

4. Using the formula above, we know that for a 14 in. document, the outside panels will be 3.531 in. Drag guides 3.531 in. from each side of the center guide, and create 0.25-in. margins for each.

5. Create fold marks at the same positions as your center guides. Apply electronic whiteout.

6. Using the Item tool, choose Edit>Select All to select all folding guides and electronic whiteout. Choose Item>Lock to lock the folding marks and boxes.

7. Save the document as a template into your **Work_In_Progress** folder, naming the file "gate.qxt".

Double Parallel Fold

This straightforward presentation, the double parallel fold, is commonly used for eight-panel rack brochures (as you would find in a hotel or travel agency).

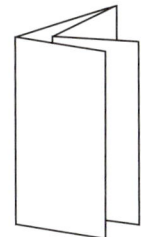

Double parallel fold.

Again, the panels on the inside are 0.0125 in. narrower than the outside panels. This type of fold uses facing master pages because the margins need to line up on the front and back sides of the sheet.

Left-Facing Page

$$y + \frac{1}{32} \qquad y + \frac{1}{32} \qquad y - \frac{1}{32} \qquad y - \frac{1}{32}$$

$$y - \frac{1}{32} \qquad y - \frac{1}{32} \qquad y + \frac{1}{32} \qquad y + \frac{1}{32}$$

Right-Facing Page

Y = Paper Size ÷ Number of Panels.

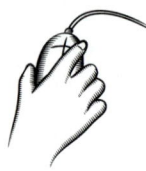

Create a Double Parallel Fold

1. Create a new one-column document with facing pages, 14 × 8.5 in., with 0.25-in. margins on all four sides. The Facing Pages check box should be selected.

2. On the master pages, drag folding guides as follows:

Left master page (inside of brochure)	Right master page (outside of brochure)
3.531 in.	3.469 in.
7.062 in.	6.938 in.
10.531 in.	10.468 in.

3. Create guides 0.25 in. from each side of the fold marks; these guides delineate your live copy area.

4. Drop the fold marks at the same positions as your center guides. Apply electronic whiteout.

5. Using the Item tool, choose Edit>Select All to select all folding guides and electronic whiteout. Choose Item>Lock to lock the folding marks and boxes.

6. Save the file as a template to your **Work_In_Progress** folder, naming the file "doublepar.qxt".

Barrel or Roll Fold

Perhaps the most common fold for 14 × 8.5 in. brochures, a barrel-folded document requires more than one calculation. The two outside panels are full size, and each successive panel is 0.0125 in. narrower than the previous one.

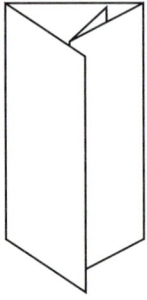

Barrel (roll) fold.

The number of panels in a barrel fold can continue indefinitely, so long as each successive panel is smaller than the previous one. When you add too many panels, however, you can lose your reader, since the panels become too narrow to read and the brochure awkward to handle. Eventually it becomes more practical to change the design from a barrel-folded brochure to a booklet.

Left-Facing Page

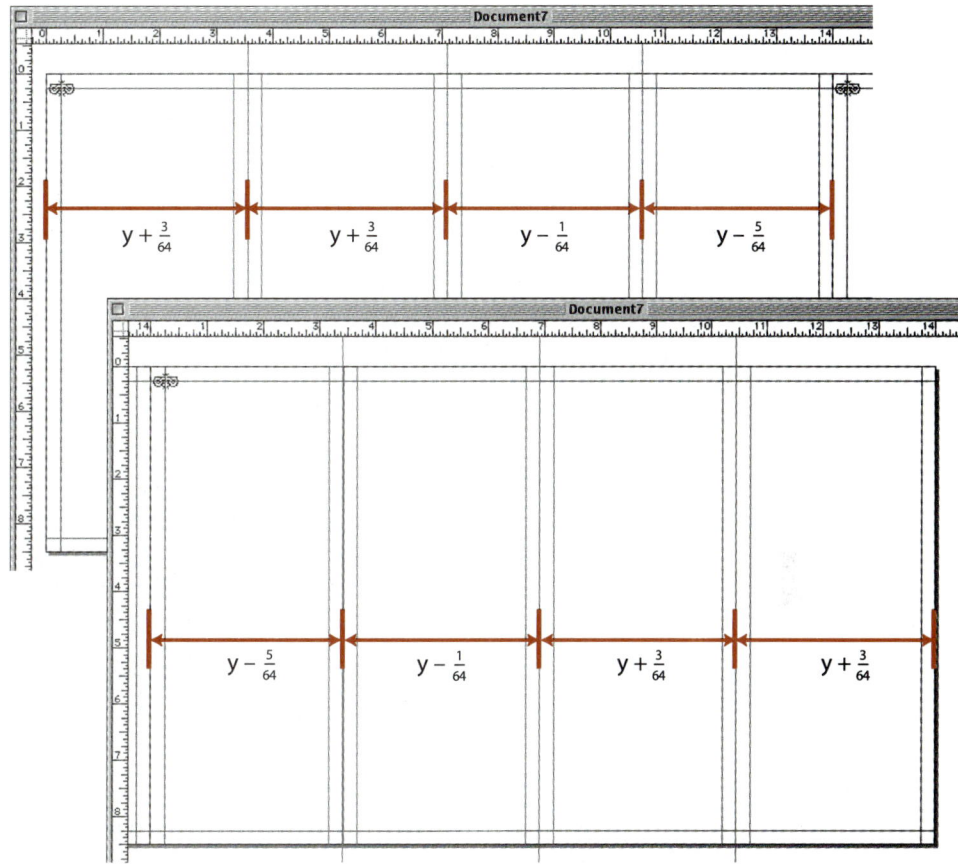

Right-Facing Page

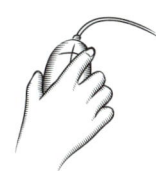

Create a Barrel Fold

1. Create a one-column document, 14 × 8.5 in., with 0.25-in. margins. The Facing Pages check box should be active.

2. On the master-page layout, drag vertical guides for your folds as follows:

Left master page (inside of brochure)	Right master page (outside of brochure)
3.547 in.	3.422 in.
7.094 in.	6.906 in.
10.578 in.	10.453 in.

3. Create guides 0.25 in. from each side of the fold marks; these guides delineate your live copy area.

4. Put the fold marks at the same positions as your center guides. Apply electronic whiteout.

5. Using the Item tool, choose Edit>Select All to select all folding guides and electronic whiteout. Choose Item>Lock to lock the folding marks and boxes.

6. Save the file as a template in your **Work_In_Progress** folder, naming the document "barrel.qxt".

More Complex Folds and Binding Operations

When multiple-page books and booklets are produced, they are not printed as individual pages, and then assembled into a book. Instead, they are printed in "signatures" of eight, sixteen, or more pages at a time. Each signature is composed of two flats. (The term "flat" is a relic of the days when film was manually stripped together on a light table; it is still sometimes used to describe one side of one signature.) The pages are arranged into printer's spreads on the film and printing plate.

If you folded a piece of paper in half twice, numbered the pages, and then unfolded it, you would see the basic imposition for an eight-page signature. If you continued folding that piece of paper in half, you would notice that the spine grew thicker, it became more difficult to fold, and the pages began to skew a little. If you were to add another fold, it would be still more difficult to fold and the skewing would become even more pronounced.

Printer's and Reader's Spreads

A *reader's spread* is a set of two pages that appear next to each other in a printed document. Page 2 faces page 3 (convention dictates that page 1 is always on the right side of a spread), page 6 faces page 7, and so on. Reader's spreads are easily defined if you think of the way you would read a book — pages appear in sequential order.

A *printer's spread* refers to the way pages align on a press sheet, so that after a document is folded and cut, the reader's spreads are in the correct location.

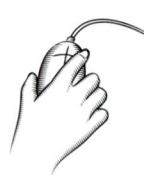

Create a Folding Dummy

1. Fold a piece of paper in half, and then in half again.

2. While it is still folded, write the sequential page numbers 1 through 8 on the folded sections.

3. Unfold it and you will see the printer's spreads for an eight-page document:

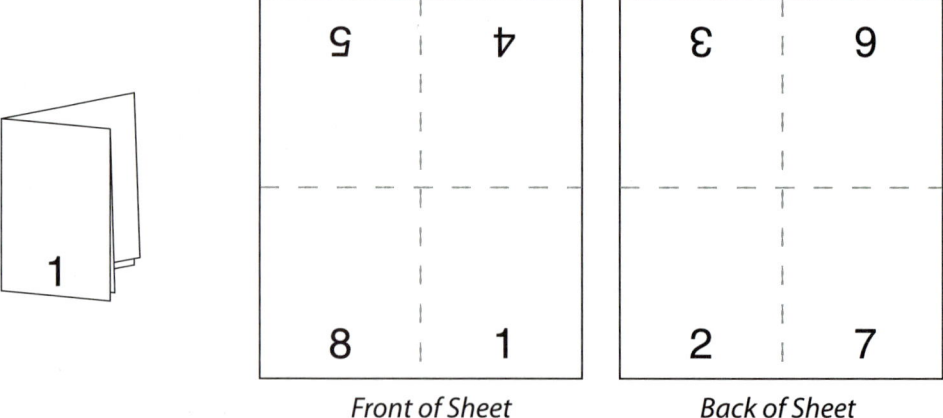

Front of Sheet   Back of Sheet

The dummy unfolds to show how an eight-page signature is laid out.
Page 8 and Page 1 create a single printer's spread.

When arranged in printer's spreads, the sum of pairs of page numbers always total the number of pages in the signature, plus 1. For example, in a 16-page signature, page 4 faces page 13, page 16 faces page 1, and so on.

If a saddle-stitched (stapled) book is made up of multiple signatures, the page numbers on printer's spreads will equal the total number of pages in the publication, plus 1. For example, a saddle-stitched booklet is 32 pages, made up of two 16-page signatures. The page numbers on each printer's spread will total 33: page 16 faces page 17, page 22 faces page 11, and so on.

Understanding Signatures

As we examine how these issues are handled, for the sake of practicality we will work with one side of an imposed 16-page signature.

If you look back at your folded piece of paper, you can see that the tops of all the pages are folded together. If there is a bleed to the top of a page, given the inaccuracy of folding machines (±0.03125 in.), that ink appears on the edge of the page against which it butted on the signature (as an example, see pages 12 and 13 on the following illustration).

The pages of a signature must be cut apart at the top, which requires at least 1/8 (0.125) in. at the top of the page for the trim. The outside edge of half the pages also has to be cut apart (this is called a "face trim") so that the pages of the finished piece can be turned. This face trim also requires 1/8 in. around the page edge. That trim would shorten an 8.5 × 11-in. book to 8.375 × 10.875 in. This shorter size might be fine, but it could also ruin a design and layout. There's a better solution.

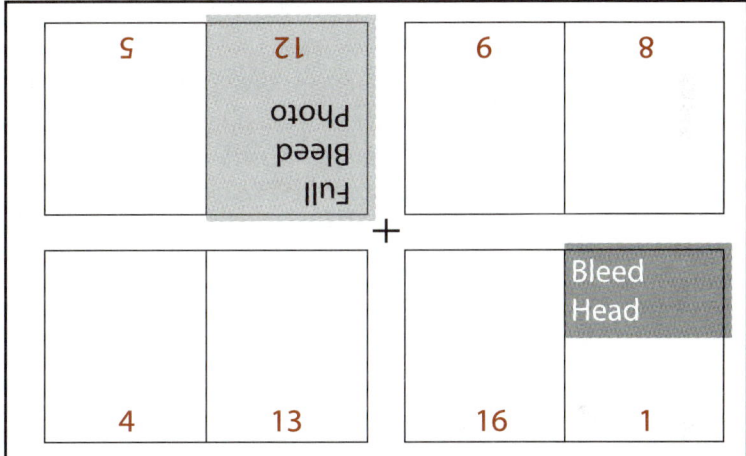

On the press-sheet layout, space is added between the tops of the printer's spreads to allow room for bleed, and for cutting the pages apart. This separation is probably all that will be required for a 16-page saddle stitched booklet printed on a 70# text. If you use a heavier paper (for example a 100# coated sheet for an annual report), or if you have more than one 16-page signature — you need to allow room for creep.

Binding Issues: Creep and Shingling

Creep is the minute and progressive extension of the edges of each inserted spread beyond the edges of the spread that encloses it. The result is a decrease in the trim size of the inner pages in a booklet or other multipage document. Creep is generally referred to in relation to individual signatures in saddle-stitched (stapled) documents.

Shingling is the progressive extension of whole signatures when one signature is placed inside of another; it could be thought of as signature creep. When multiple saddle-stitched signatures are stacked, each signature must add the cumulative creep from the previous signatures to its bind margin. You don't want to add too many signatures to a saddle-stitched document or the creep and shingling can become unwieldy. Generally, booklets with more than 96 pages (if standard paper is used) require a different binding method.

*The **bind margin** is the edge of the page that is bound into the spine. It is also called the "inside edge."*

There is only one way to determine how much creep you should allow for: ask your service provider.

It would be difficult to provide a definitive solution that would apply to every situation. Every sheet of paper has individual bulk and folding peculiarities (for example, recycled sheets usually have more bulk than their "virgin" counterparts, so they creep more). Also, the direction of the grain in the paper affects how it folds.

Printers establish their creep library in an old-fashioned way — they build it manually. They obtain sample sheets of the paper on which a job will be printed, fold a publication (using folding machines to approximate the actual job), and then physically measure the creep using a micrometer. They then enter the results into their databases for future reference.

Once this creep information is in the database, it is easy to build the imposed flat. Believe it or not, flats are built essentially the same way today as they were years ago — with templates. When flats were assembled (or *stripped*) manually, a Mylar template was first taped to the light table, showing the offsets to allow for creep. Today, electronic templates are used, but the principle is the same.

Bottling

Closely related to creep is the process of bottling. As you may have noticed from your folded sheet of paper, pages don't merely creep when they're folded — they also rotate slightly. This rotation or *bottling* is caused by the thickness or bulk of the paper. The outer pages rotate around the folded corner. To compensate when using thick paper or signatures with many pages, the pages must be rotated around the points where the folds meet. The angles through which these pages are rotated are called "bottle angles."

Bottling is restricted to individual signatures; it depends on the folding action itself. Each signature in a booklet (assuming the same paper and number of pages) will have the same bottling values.

Do-It-Yourself Printer's Spreads

If you have questions about folds, imposition, creep, or bottling, you should *always* call your service provider. Somebody there will be able to advise you on the best course to take. In most cases these issues will be handled entirely by the service provider, often using software specifically designed for the prepress workflow. If you try to do too much, you may cause them extra work (and yourself extra expense).

As a particularly bad example, an eight-page newsletter was set up as four sets of 8.5 × 11-in. reader's spreads on a 17 × 11-in. document, with text flowing from page to page. When it was taken to the service provider for printing, the job had to be torn apart and completely reflowed at substantial cost.

To reiterate, you probably don't want to (and really, you shouldn't) think about creating full impositions for a press. You may, however, want to print proofs in printer's spreads to show clients; or if you have a small booklet that you want to print or copy, masters from your laser printer may be sufficient.

Converting to printer's spreads should always be the final step in preparing a document. At this point in the process, all content should be final, the stories should be edited, and the table of contents and index complete.

Exercise Setup

For the next exercise, you will be working with prepared files, converting reader's spreads to printer's spreads while maintaining correct pagination. Because this sample booklet has only eight pages, we will assume there is no creep.

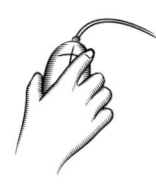

Build Printer's Spreads

1. Open the document **spreads.qxd** from the **RF_Adv_Quark** folder.

2. If it is not showing, Select View>Show Document Layout.

3. Double-click the A-Master A icon in the top of the Document Layout palette to access the master-page layout. Notice that the automatic page-number character is placed on the master-page layout.

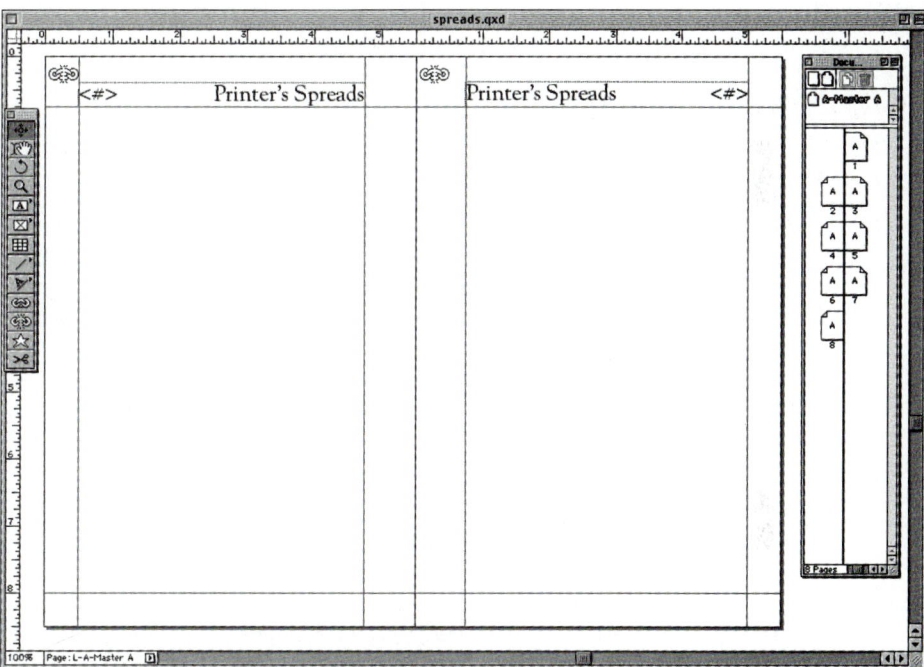

The page-number character is placed on the master-page layout.

4. Double-click the Page 1 icon in the Document Layout palette.

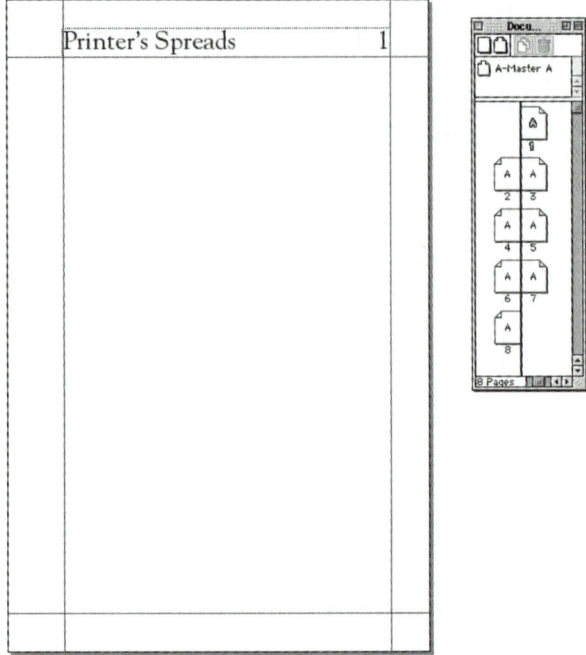

5. Make sure the Page 1 icon is active in the Document Layout palette.

The highlighted icon in the document layout page is the current selection.
The selected page and the active page do not have to be the same.

By using the Section Start option for each page, you are effectively hard-wiring a specific page number to each page of the document. When you move the pages around to create the printer's spreads, the pages retain the page numbers defined in the Section dialog box.

6. Choose Page>Section. Activate the Section Start check box, and enter "1" in the Number field. Click OK.

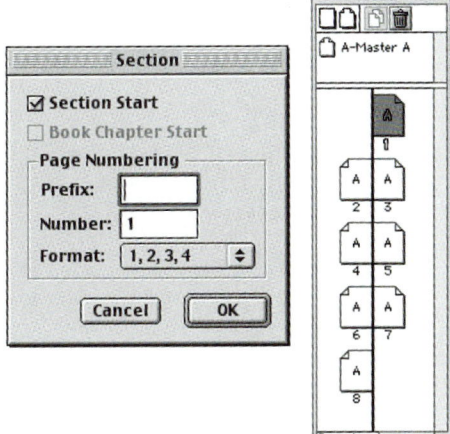

7. Highlight the Page 2 icon in the Document Layout palette, and open the Section dialog box (Page>Section). Activate the Section Start check box, and enter "2" in the Number field.

8. Repeat Step 7 for each of the remaining pages in the document, placing the appropriate page number in the Number field.

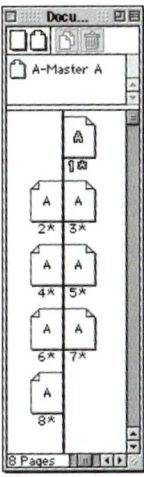

Section Start pages are identified in the Document Layout palette by an asterisk next to the page number.

9. Highlight the Page 1 icon, and drag it opposite the Page 8 icon (it won't work the other way unless the document was created with nonfacing pages).

10. Move the Page 7 icon opposite Page 2.

11. Move the Page 3 icon opposite Page 6.

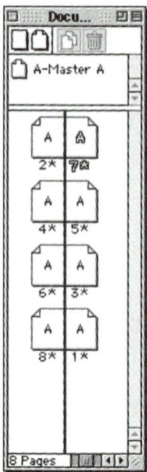

12. Save the file as "printer_spreads.qxd" to your **Work_In_Progress** folder. If you print the document with the Spreads option selected, both pages of the printer's spread will print on one sheet of paper.

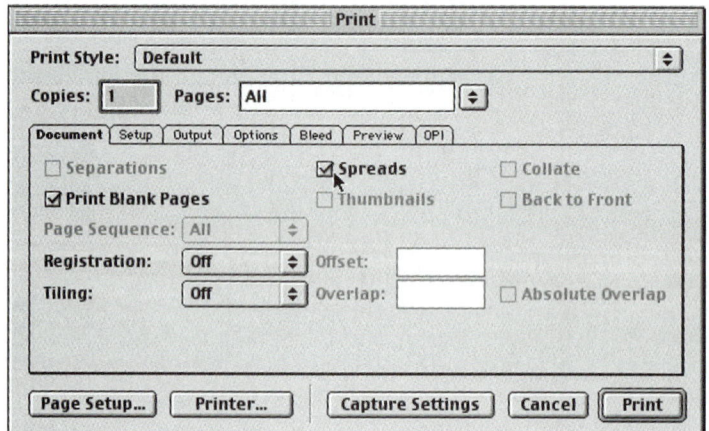

Summary

You understand that the page layout is the core of most jobs in the commercial graphics industry. You have learned about many of the potential problems associated with the "simple container," and how to avoid them with careful planning and preparation. You have become familiar with the fundamentals of page geometry, including the requirements for creating complex folds. You have also learned the basics of imposition, and how to create your own multiple-up and printer's spreads for use with a desktop printer.

Complete Project A: Stonington Letterfold Brochure

3 Managing Long Documents

Chapter Objectives:

When building a long document, consistency from page to page and from file to file is extremely important. Just as you might use templates and master pages to maintain consistency from one issue to the next, you can use several tools included in QuarkXPress 5.0 to help maintain consistency among pages and among documents. In this chapter, you will:

- Learn the importance of consistency between documents.

- Discover how to build a library of commonly used elements.

- Observe the importance of using multiple master pages and master documents.

- Combine multiple documents into a single QuarkXPress book.

- Control the section and page numbering of documents in a book.

- Use the master document of a book to ensure consistency.

Projects to be Completed:

- Stonington Letterfold Brochure (A)

- Body Solution Booklet (B)

- Cosciel Poster (C)

Managing Long Documents

Documents of more than a few pages — newsletters, booklets, magazines, and books — have special requirements and need special planning to incorporate those requirements.

Using multiple master pages, a long document can be contained entirely within a single QuarkXPress file, or broken into several documents that will be combined later with the Book utility. This chapter examines the general requirements of long documents, including how to manage multiple master pages, create master documents, and combine documents using the Book utility.

The Importance of Consistency

When working on a 400-page book, for example, it is easy to forget exactly how a particular table heading was formatted back on page 20, or exactly where the image box was placed on page 42. Long documents benefit greatly from the use of a well-planned, well-implemented template that incorporates both style sheets and masters pages.

Publication design is a unique subset of graphic design. Attention to detail is necessary to make sure that the subheads in early chapters match the subheads in later chapters, the captions are all set in the same font, the body copy is the same size throughout the document, and so on. Especially when several designers work on the same project, it is vital to create a consistent look to the entire project.

Consistency does not mean that every page in a document must have the same exact layout. Successful page-layout design uses variation to maintain visual interest. That variation, however, should be within reason and should not differ flagrantly from one page to the next. A publication must maintain the same basic structure throughout to avoid confusing the reader. Every document should have a basic master page for the bulk of the publication, using variations on that master layout to add visual interest.

Planning the Job

When working with large blocks of text that flow over multiple pages, one of the key elements of professional page layout is consistency from page to page. Before placing elements on pages, you need to evaluate the components that will comprise the finished document.

- Is the document primarily text, or will images be incorporated into the layout?
- Does the job require a running head or foot (or both)?
- Are common elements such as sidebars or tables used throughout the document?
- Does the document include specific sections, such as departments of a magazine?
- What are the levels of editorial content (headings, subheadings, body copy, and so on) in the document?

Managing Multiple Master Pages

The above questions provide the foundation for developing an effective document structure. Once you have the necessary information, you can begin to create your layout.

You should first determine the different types of pages that you will use in a particular document. For a magazine, you may need many types of pages — masthead page, table of contents, editorial pages, article pages, and other special sections. Books that are primarily text may need only a single layout. For every type of page in your document, you should create a separate master-page layout.

Defining Master Pages: The New Document Dialog Box

When you create a new document in QuarkXPress, the New Document dialog box defines the default margins, columns, and gutters of the document. Any master-page layout you create, unless duplicating an existing master layout that has been edited, will use the settings defined in the New Document dialog box.

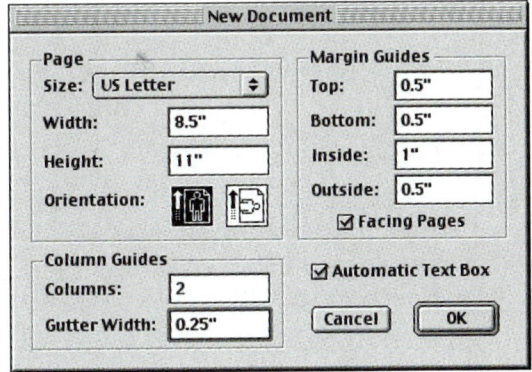

You can change the margins, columns, and gutters for any master-page layout by selecting Page>Master Guides while the master-page layout is active in the document window.

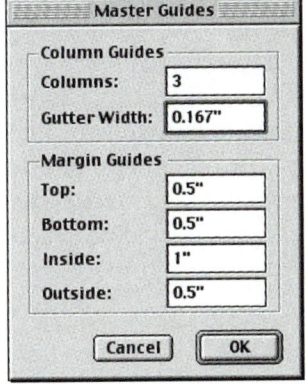

If you choose the Automatic Text Box option in the New Document dialog box, the default master-page layout (A-Master A) includes the automatic text box, which snaps to the defined margins for the master page. If you change the margins for that page, the automatic text box changes to reflect the new margin settings.

Adding Master Pages

To create new master pages in any document, you can drag the Blank Single Page or Blank Facing Page icon into the top section of the Document Layout palette, or you can highlight an existing master-page layout and click the Duplicate button.

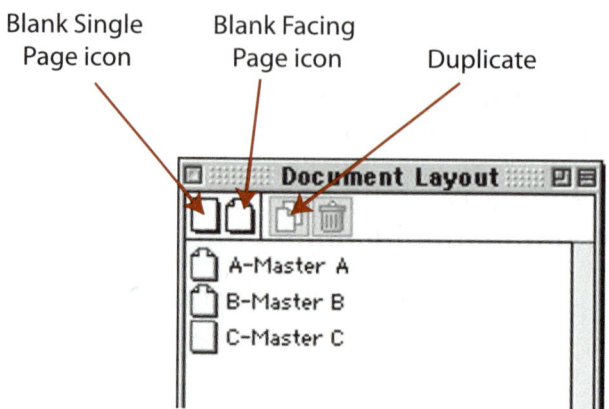

Blank Single Page icon   Blank Facing Page icon   Duplicate

Remember to consider carefully whether each master page should be a facing or nonfacing page.

When you add a new master page by dragging the Blank Single Page or Blank Facing Page icon, the new master-page layout does not include the automatic text box. New master layouts created with these icons have the same margin and column settings as defined in the New Document dialog box, even if you have changed the A-Master A layout settings.

If you have modified the A-Master A margins or columns, or if you want new master pages to include the automatic text box, you should duplicate the A-Master A layout rather than use the Blank Single Page or Blank Facing Page icon.

Naming Master Pages

When working with more than one master-page layout, it is extremely important to name the master pages according to their use. Successfully planned layouts should be easy to implement, not only for the creator but also for other designers to whom the layout is given. Two months after creating a template with six master-page layouts, you may not remember that A-Master A is for the front matter, B-Master B is for the index, C-Master C is for the two-column articles, and so on.

Name master-page layouts according to their intended use.

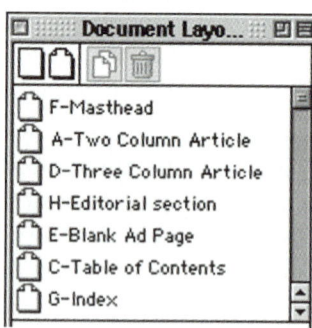

Exercise Setup

In the following exercises, you will create the master pages for a recipe book. The job will be printed on card stock, one-sided, four-color with a glossy finish. The book will be 7 × 9 in., spiral bound on the left edge, using a jewel-tone color scheme — greens, blues, and purples.

Each recipe will have its own page in the book, including a picture of the dish. The book will be broken into sections according to the type of dish (Appetizer, Dinner, Dessert). Each section will have an introduction page, which includes pictures of every dish in the section.

Create Master Pages

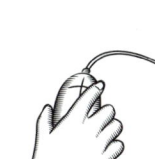

The 1.25-in. margin on the left side is enough to accommodate the spiral binding.

1. Create a new QuarkXPress document, 7 in. wide by 9 in. high with 1 column. Make sure the Facing pages and Automatic Text Box options are deselected. Set the margins to:

    Top: 0.7 in.
    Bottom: 0.7 in.
    Left: 1.25 in.
    Right: 0.7 in.

2. If the Document Layout palette is not visible, select View>Show Document Layout.

3. Double-click A-Master A in the top half of the palette to access the master-page layout.

4. Drag horizontal ruler guides to Y: 3.5 in. and Y: 3.625 in.

5. Draw a rectangular text box that snaps to the top-corner margin guides and, on the bottom, to the guide at Y: 3.5 in.

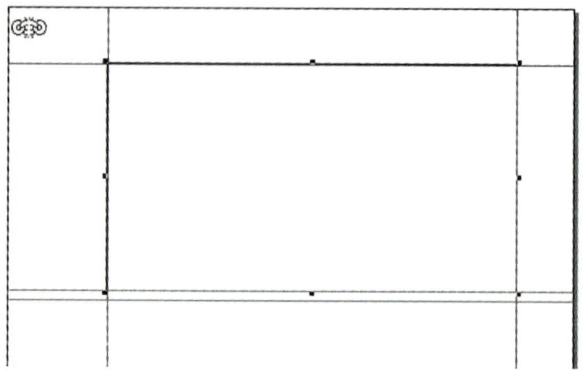

6. Draw another rectangular text box in the bottom of the page, snapping it at the top to the guide at Y: 3.625 in. and to the bottom-corner margin guides.

7. Select the Linking tool from the Toolbox. Click on the top text box to activate the marching-ants border, and then click the bottom text box to link it to the first.

8. Drag vertical ruler guides to X: 1 in. and X: 6.5 in.

9. Drag another horizontal ruler guide to Y: 8.75 in.

10. Using the Orthogonal Line tool, draw a vertical line on the page. Drag it until it snaps to the guide at Y: 1 in.

11. In the Measurements palette, choose Endpoints from the pop-up menu. Change the Y1 field to 1.5 in. and the Y2 field to 9.125 in. Change the width to 6 pt.

The line extends 1/8 in. beyond the page edge to accommodate the bleed allowance.

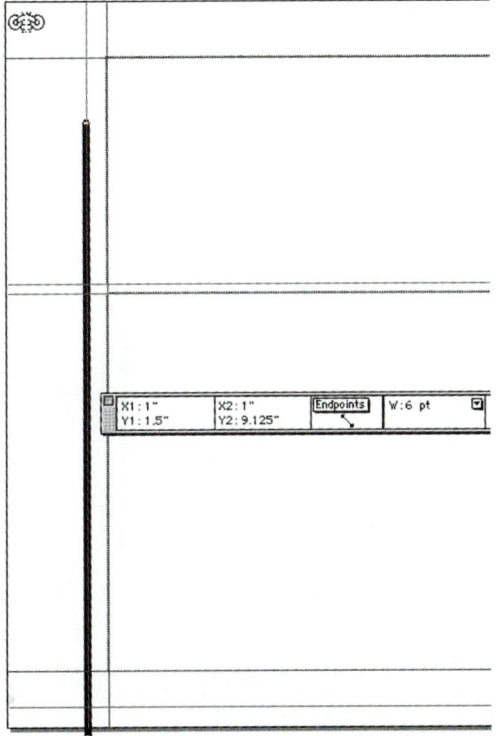

12. Copy and paste the line. Drag the new line until it snaps to the vertical guide at Y: 6.5 in.

13. Change the Y1 field to –0.125 in. and the Y2 field to 7.5 in.

14. Draw a rectangular picture box on the page. Using the Measurements palette, define the box dimensions as:

     X: 3.437 in.   W: 3.7 in.
     Y: 0.7 in.   H: 2.7 in.

15. Apply a 0.5-pt. frame to the box.

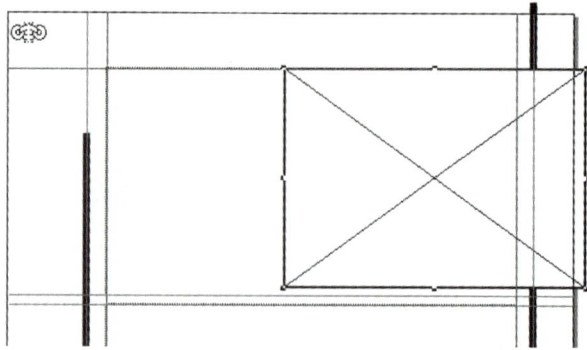

16. Draw a rectangular text box on the page. Define the dimensions as:

     X: 6 in.   W: 1 in.
     Y: 8.4 in.   H: 0.35 in.

17. In the Text tab of the Modify dialog box (Command/Control-M), **choose Vertical** Alignment>Type>Centered.

18. Select the box from Step 17 with the Content tool. Press **Command/Control-3 to** add the automatic-page-number character.

19. Double-click the A-Master A listing in the top half of the Document Layout **palette** to highlight the master-page name. Type "Recipe Page".

20. Save the file as "recipe_template.qxd" in your **Work_In_Progress** folder, and leave the file open for the next exercise.

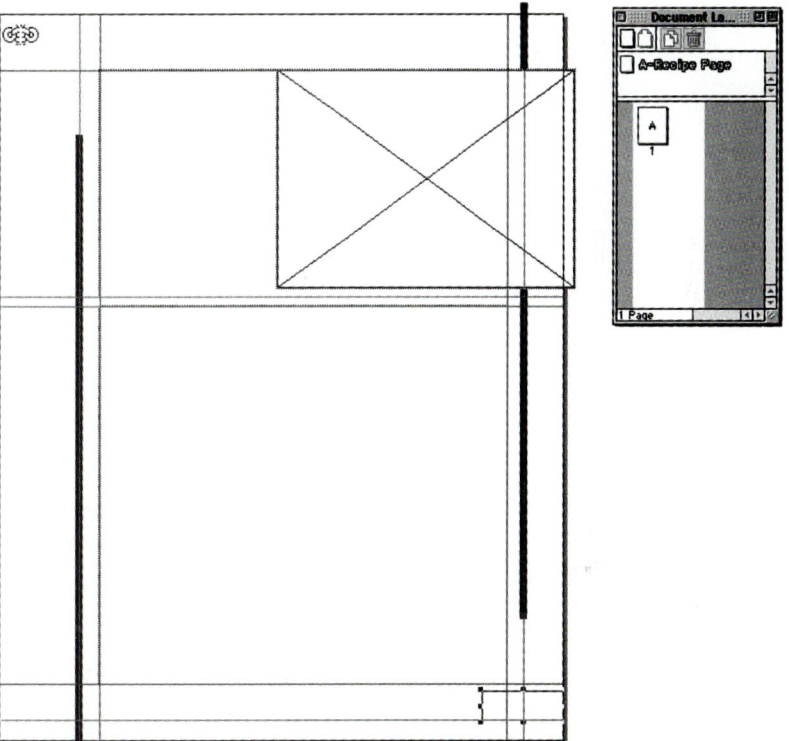

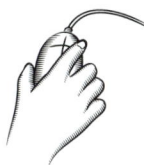

Add a Master Page

1. Highlight the A-Recipe Page item in the top half of the Document Layout **palette**, and click the Duplicate button.

2. Double-click B-Master B to access the new master-page layout.

3. Delete the image box and the small text box in the bottom-right corner.

4. Choose the lower text box and select Item>Content>Picture. Change the box dimensions to:

> X: –0.125 in. W: 7.25 in.
> Y: –0.125 in. H: 9.25 in.

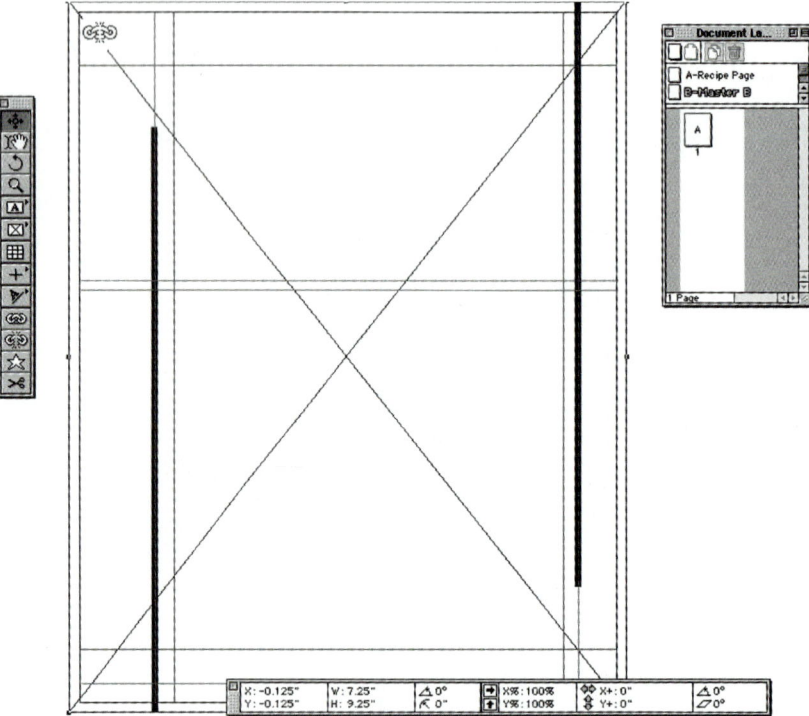

5. With the box selected, choose File>Get Picture. Locate the file **back.tif** in the **RF_Adv_Quark** folder, and click Open. Choose Style>Shade>50%.

6. Double-check that the picture box is still selected, and choose **Item>Send to Back**.

7. Using the Content tool, select the white text box on the page. **Open the Colors** palette, choose the Background Color button, and click None in the Colors palette.

8. Highlight B-Master B in the top half of the Master page palette, **and change the** master-page name to "Section Page".

9. The file now has both of the layouts you will need to complete the job. **Save the file** as a template, naming it "recipe.qxt" and saving it to your **Work_In_Progress** folder. Close the file.

10. Delete the file **recipe_template.qxd** from your **Work_In_Progress** folder.

Master Documents and Templates

By creating templates, you can build the structure of a document once — including layout grid, style sheets, and colors — and apply the same layout many times. There are instances, however, when you want a document to be consistent with another. For example, you might want to use the same fonts and colors in different documents for a particular client, but not the same layout. For such cases, QuarkXPress allows you to transfer components from one document to another by choosing File>Append.

Many designers find it helpful to create a *master document* — a Quark document that contains the style sheets, colors, H&J routines, and other structural elements that are used in more than one type of document for a particular client, project, or other group.

As an example, one client prefers body text to be set as 10-pt. Times New Roman with very tight leading, another likes the feel of Gill Sans with standard leading for body copy, and a third client has had a proprietary font created for all documents. All of these clients use a different specific color scheme to match their respective corporate identities. One client insists that no hyphens can appear in any document, and the others have different standards for hyphenating copy.

The point is that individual design projects have individual requirements. Rather than starting from scratch for every new project, you can build a master document for each client that contains common formatting requirements. At the beginning of a new project, you can create the layout grid for the particular job, then append that client's preferred styles, colors, and so on to the new document.

The Append dialog box provides tabs for the different items that can be imported from one document into another: Style Sheets, Colors, H&Js, Lists, and Dashes & Stripes. Each of these categories can be time-consuming to create. Using a well-planned master document, however, you can dramatically reduce production time by creating these elements once, and then appending them to a particular job, instead of recreating each element for every new job.

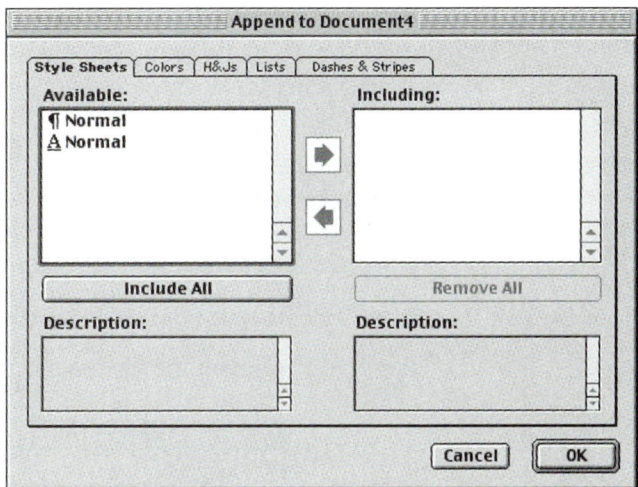

Tips for Using Master Documents

Master documents allow you to automate your production workflow by creating elements once, and then appending them to any document you create. The following tips will help you to create effective and efficient master documents.

- When creating the master document, the page size, margins, columns, and gutters are irrelevant unless you will also use the master document as a layout template for other documents.

- If a client prefers a particular font for the majority of jobs, be sure to change the Normal style sheet to the preferred font.

- You can include any proprietary fonts and colors in the master document.

- If the client likes a specific style of hyphenation and justification, you can define an appropriate H&J routine in the master document.

- Using the style sheets that you define in the master document, you can create common lists (such as a table of contents) that can be imported automatically into any project.

- You can append a single item, several items, or all items in any category. If a particular project requires a completely different body-copy treatment, for example, you can choose to append only headlines and captions, and then define the body copy style in the new document.

- If you append style sheets, remember that the fonts used in the master-document style sheets must be available on your computer. If not, you will receive a missing font warning when you click OK.

- Once appended, master-document items become a part of the document on which you are working. Appended items are not linked to the master document, and can be modified within the new document without affecting the master.

Lists are explained in depth in the next chapter.

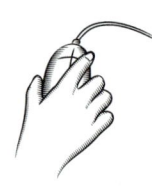

Exercise Setup

You already know how to define colors and style sheets. For the following exercise, we have provided a master document that contains the colors and style sheets used for this particular client.

Append Document Elements

1. Open the file **recipe.qxt** from your **Work_In_Progress** folder.

2. Press "F11" to open the Style Sheets palette.

3. Press "F12" to open the Colors palette.

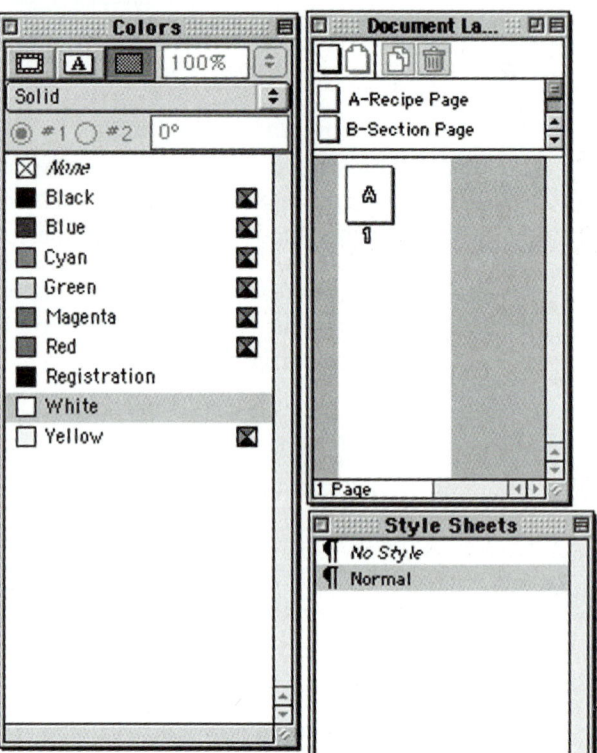

4. Select File>Append.

5. Navigate to the file **cooks_master.qxd** in the **RF_Adv_Quark** folder, and click Open.

6. Click Include All in the Style Sheets tab.

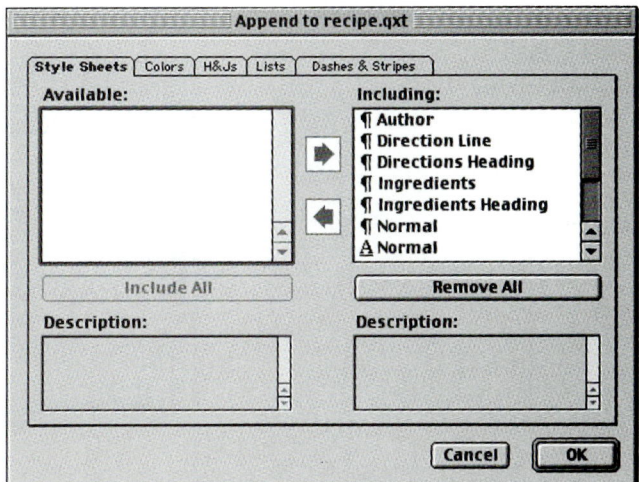

7. Activate the Colors tab and click Include All.

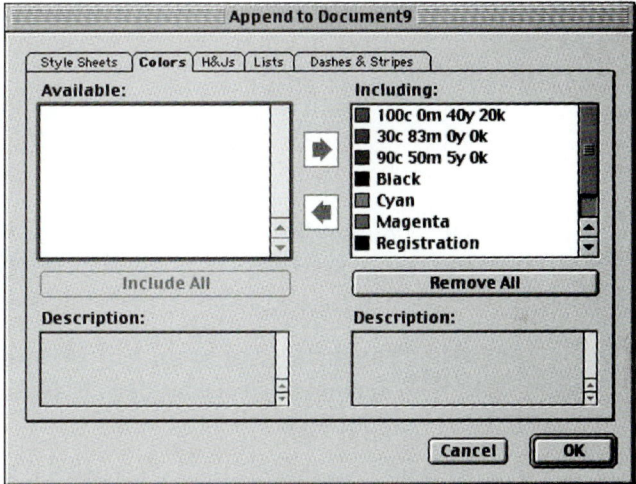

8. Click OK. You will see a warning that any embedded elements will also be imported. Activate the Do Not Show This Warning Again check box, and click OK.

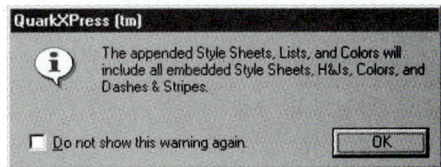

The Style Sheets and Colors from the master (cooks_master.qxd) are now a part of the open file.

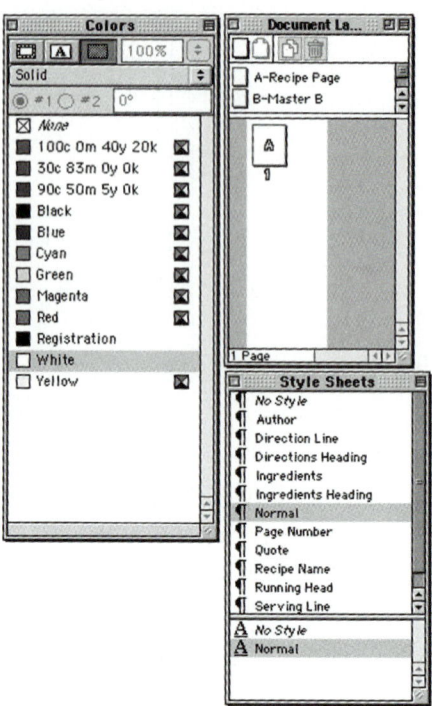

9. Double-click A-Recipe Page in the Document Layout palette. Using the Content tool, click in the page-number text box in the bottom-right corner of the page. Click Page Number in the Style Sheets palette to apply the style.

10. Change the color of the vertical lines to "30c 83m 0y 0k". Navigate to the B-Section Page master-page layout, and change the color of these vertical lines to "30c 83m 0y 0k" as well.

11. Because this document was saved as a template in the previous exercise, when you opened it again you actually opened a new DocumentN. To save the file with the style sheets and colors, choose File>Save as. Navigate to your **Work_In_Progress** folder. Type "recipe.qxt" in the Name field, and choose template from the Type menu. Click Replace/Yes when asked if you want to overwrite the existing "recipe.qxt" file.

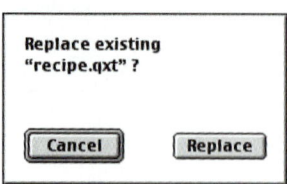

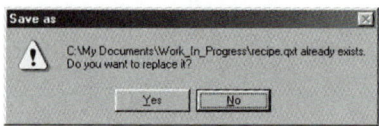

Macintosh   *Windows*

12. Your new template file now includes the styles sheets and colors, as already defined in the client's master file. Close the file.

Working with Libraries

Consistency is just as important for the elements that comprise a document — text inset value for tables, border weight of image boxes, color of sidebar boxes, and any other element that is not part of the main text chain. If one table has a 2-pt. border, the other tables in the document should have a similar border treatment; if one sidebar text box has a 12-pt. inset value, the other sidebars should also have a 12-pt. inset value.

You could create an object once, then copy and paste it every time you want to repeat it, but this method can be annoying if the element you want to copy last appeared 60 pages earlier. Rather than hunting for the object you want to reuse, you can place it in a library so that you can easily access it at any time from the library palette.

Creating a Library

The Library utility in QuarkXPress allows you to build sets of commonly used elements, which can be opened independently of a specific document. You can build libraries for each job, each client, or any other logical group.

To create a library in QuarkXPress, you select File>New>Library.

In the New Library dialog box, you can navigate to the folder in which you want the library to reside, and name the library. As with any other element or file, you should use meaningful names for your libraries so that you will know what to open when you need it.

The extension for a Quark Library is .qxl. Macintosh users should always remember to add the extension.

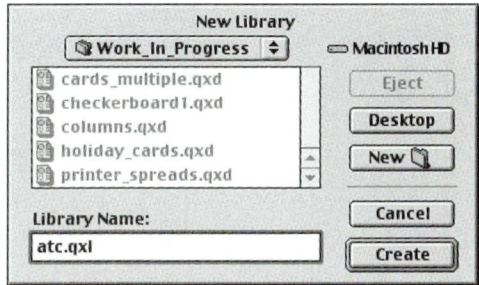

Clicking Create in the New Library dialog box opens the empty library palette. You can create a library with no document open, but you must open a document to create the elements that you will place in the library.

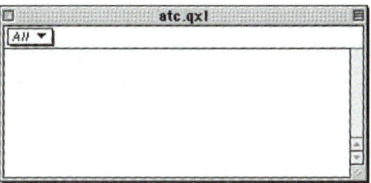

Library items can include images or graphics placed into picture boxes. This is particularly useful for frequently placed objects such as logos.

Adding Library Items

Any element on the document page can be placed into a library by dragging it with the Item tool. Library items can have graphic, image, or text content, and can include text-formatting attributes.

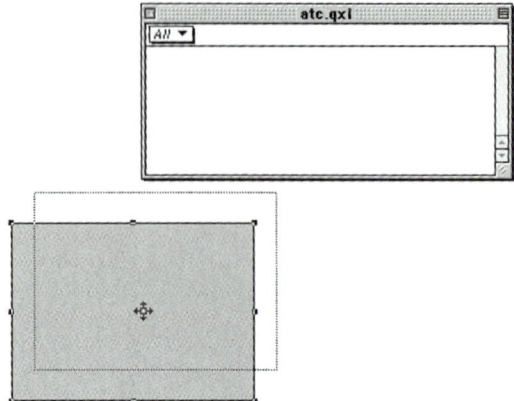

When the item is dragged into the library palette, the cursor takes the shape of a pair of glasses and an outline indicates where the item will be placed in the library. Two opposing arrows appear to the left of the new item if the palette is organized horizontally, or above the new item if the palette is organized vertically.

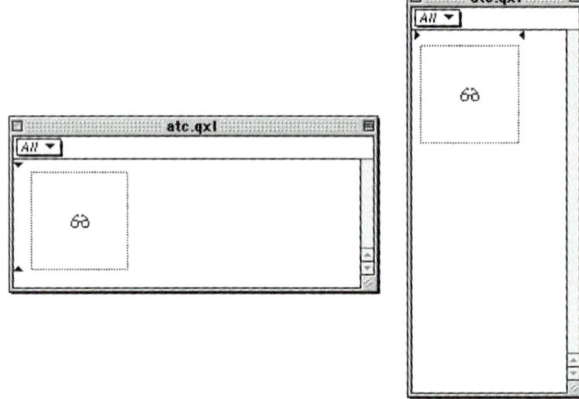

As you work with items in a library, it is important to remember that images and graphics placed into a library are only references to the file. If an image is placed from a library into a document, that image file must be present when the job is output. Forgetting to send library items to the service provider is a common mistake because libraries may have been created long before a particular job is finished. The actual file may not be in the same place, causing the Picture Usage dialog box to show the image as missing.

Labeling Library Items

Once an item is dragged into the library, a thumbnail of the item appears in the palette.

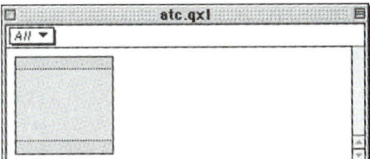

Double-clicking on the thumbnail opens the Library Entry dialog box, where you can give the item a descriptive name. The library palette does not display any identifying text for the items in the library. The item label is used to search and sort, but does not appear in the palette.

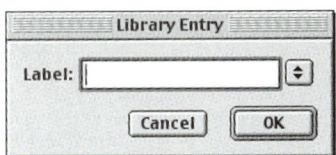

You can also choose an existing label for a library item by clicking the arrows next to the Label field, then choosing the appropriate label from the pop-up list. Any label already defined in the library appears in this list.

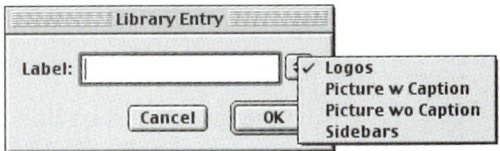

Closing and Saving Libraries

Changes to a library are saved automatically by default. When you add or delete an item, that change is saved instantly. You can change this setting in the Save Preferences dialog box (Edit>Preferences>Preferences>Application>Save). If the Auto Library Save check box is deselected, changes to the library are not saved until the library is closed. There is no real benefit to this option, however, because changes are saved automatically when you close the library palette; you do not have the option to close the library without saving (perhaps to recover an accidentally deleted item).

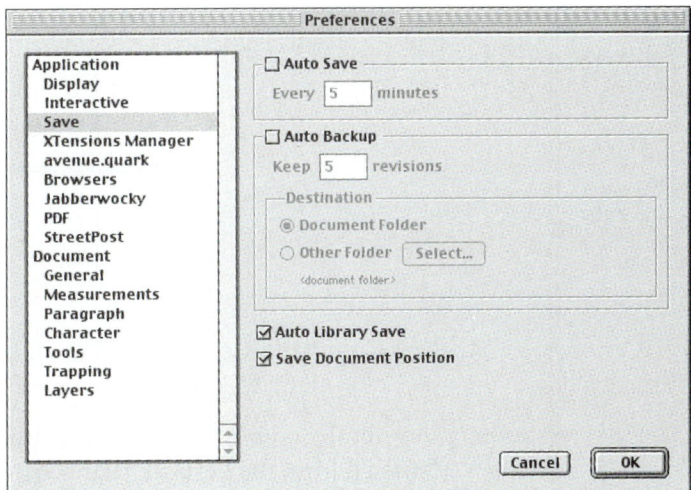

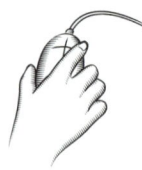

Create a Library

1. With no file open, choose File>New>Library.

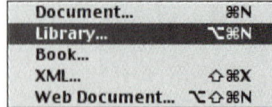

2. Navigate to your **Work_In_Progress** folder. In the Library/File Name field, type "atc.qxl" and click Create.

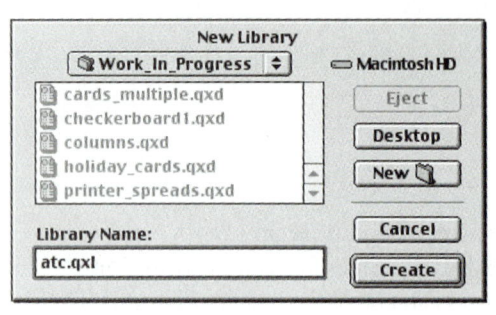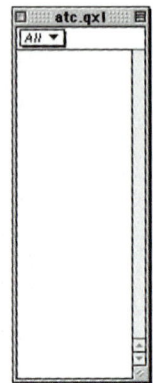

3. Create a new letter-sized document using the default margins and columns.

4. Using the Rectangle Text Box tool, draw a text box on the document page. Use the Measurements palette to change the box dimensions to W: 2.25 in., H: 6 in.

5. Press Command/Control-M to open the Modify dialog box. In the Box tab, change the Color menu to Red and the Shade field to 25%.

6. Click the Text tab. Change the Text Inset All Edges field to 8 pt., and choose Centered from the Vertical Alignment Type menu.

7. Click the Frame tab. Change the Width field to 1 pt., and choose Red from the Color menu.

8. Click the Runaround tab. Change all four runaround fields to 10 pt. Click OK to close the Modify dialog box and apply the changes.

9. Using the Item tool, drag the text box into the library palette. When the cursor becomes a pair of eyeglasses, release the mouse button.

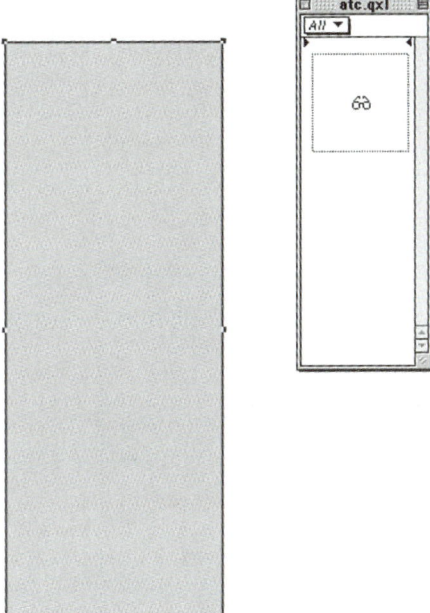

10. Double-click the new item in the library palette to open the Library Entry dialog box. Type "Sidebar" in the Label field and click OK.

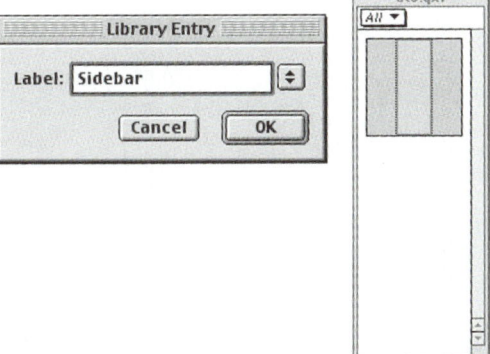

11. Delete the text box from the document page.

12. Create a rectangular picture box on the document page with the dimensions W: 1.25 in., H: 1.75 in. Open the Modify dialog box. Apply a 0.5-pt. black frame to the box, and set the runaround to 8 pt. on all four sides.

13. Drag the picture box until it snaps to the left margin of the page.

14. Draw a rectangular text box. Apply an 8-pt. runaround to all four sides of the text box. Using the Measurements palette, change the width of the text box to 1.25 in. and the height to 0.4 in., then drag it until it snaps to the left margin guide.

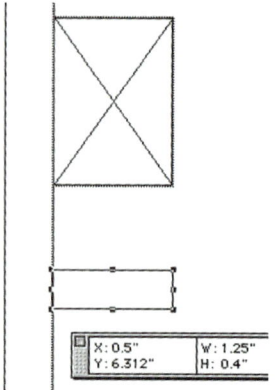

15. Drag the text box up until the top edge is approximately 1/16 in. (0.0625 in.) below the picture box. (It may help to change the zero point to the bottom of the image box.)

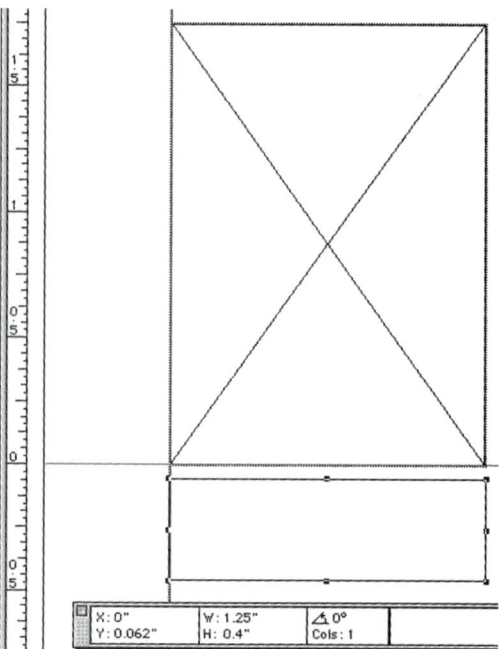

16. Using the Content tool, select the text box. Type "Caption". Change the text to 10-pt. ATC Oak Italic with Center alignment.

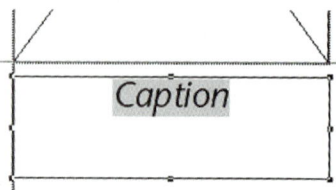

17. Holding the Shift key, use the Item tool to select both the picture box and the text box. Press Command/Control-G to group the two boxes.

18. Using the Item tool, drag the group into the library palette.

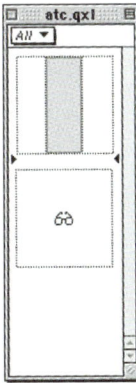

19. Double-click the group in the library palette. In the Label field, type "Picture – Caption" and click OK.

20. Close the document without saving.

21. Close the library by clicking the Close button in the top-left corner (Macintosh) or the top-right corner (Windows).

Sorting Libraries

Library item labels serve several different purposes. If you use a library for a group of different projects, such as for a particular client, you can create labels such as Newsletter Items, Catalog Items, and so on. When working on a newsletter, then, you can choose to look at only the Newsletter Items in that client's library.

If you use a separate library for each project, you can use the Label function to identify the purpose of each item in the library. For example, you can quickly find the Blue Text Box 1-pt. Border without scrolling through a lengthy list.

Once items are placed into a library, you can view all items with a particular label by clicking the pop-up menu (which defaults to All) at the top of the library palette.

Only elements tagged with the chosen label appear in the library palette. You can also choose to view Unlabeled elements, which you can then label for easy sorting.

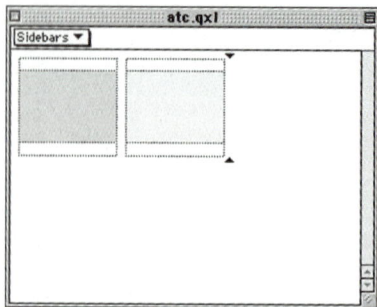

You can also change the order of items in a library by dragging them within the palette. Once an item is placed in the palette, you can drag it to a new position. The cursor becomes the glasses icon, just as when you are placing a new item in the library. The facing arrows indicate the location to which the item will be moved when you release the mouse button.

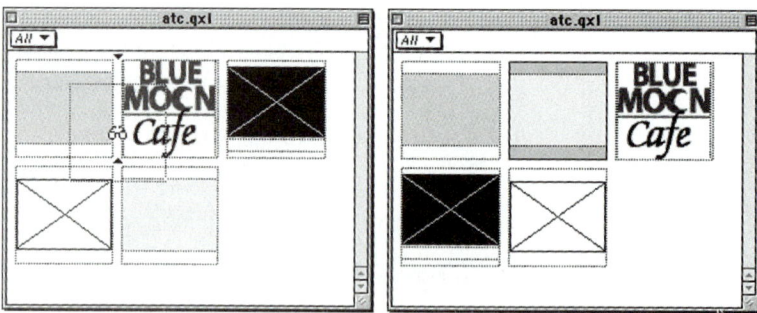

Deleting Library Items

Any item in a library can be deleted by clicking it in the palette, then pressing Delete/Backspace on a Macintosh computer or choosing Delete from the palette Edit menu on a Windows system. If you delete a library item, you cannot undo the deletion. Clicking OK in the warning dialog box deletes the object from the library; clicking Cancel leaves the library intact.

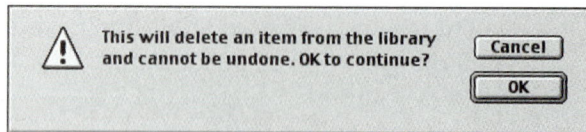

Deleting a library item has no impact on objects already placed from the library, but you will no longer be able to access that item in the library.

Opening Libraries

You can open any QuarkXPress library file by choosing File>Open. Libraries are identified by an icon that looks like a series of books on a shelf. To access the objects in a library, you can simply highlight the library and click Open. If the extension .qxl was included in the file name when it was created, a library can be opened on either platform.

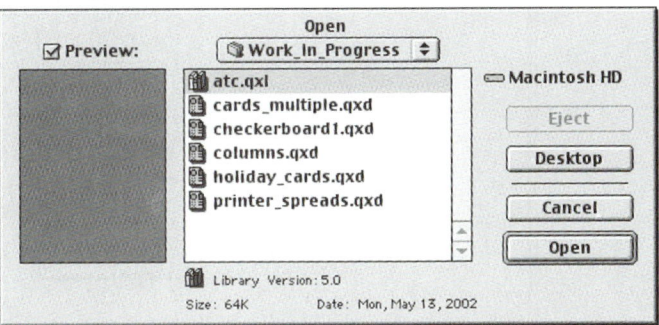

If you have placed in a library any text boxes that contain formatted text, the fonts used in the library items must be available. If the fonts used in a library item are not available, you will see a missing-font error when you open the library, just as you would if a font was missing from a QuarkXPress document.

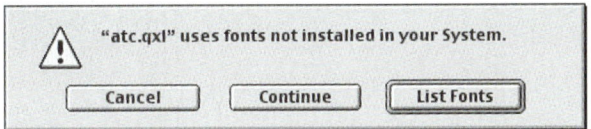

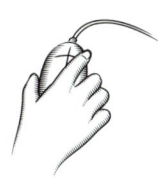

Work with a Library

1. Create a new document using the default settings.

2. Select File>Open.

3. Navigate to your **Work_In_Progress** folder. Highlight the file **atc.qxl** and click Open.

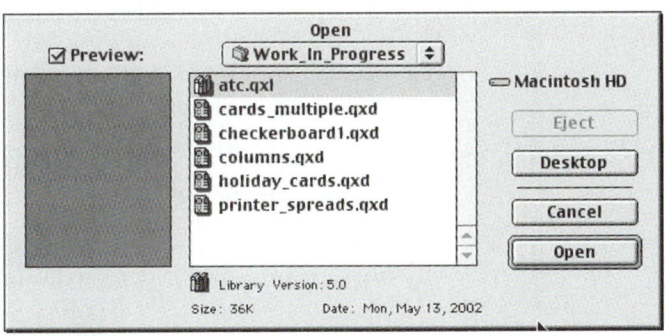

4. Choose Sidebar from the Labels pop-up menu at the top of the library palette. Only one object should appear in the palette.

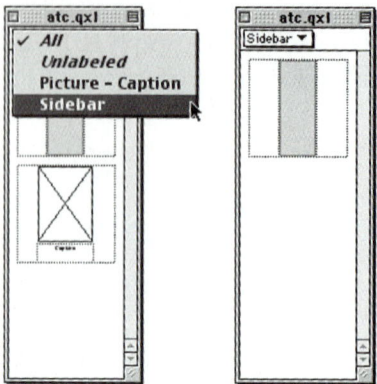

5. Drag the library item onto the document page.

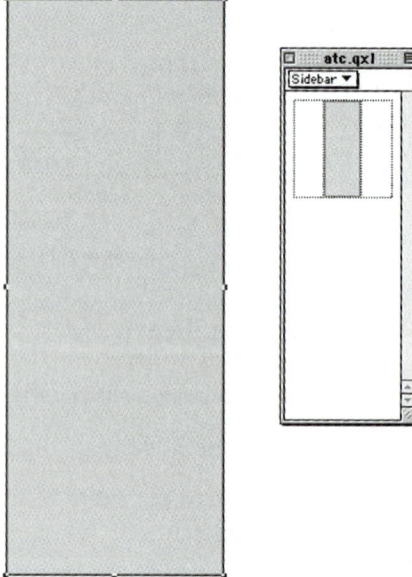

6. Choose All from the pop-up menu at the top of the library palette. The palette should now contain two items.

7. Highlight the red box in the library palette, and press Delete/Backspace (Macintosh) or choose Delete from the Edit menu (Windows).

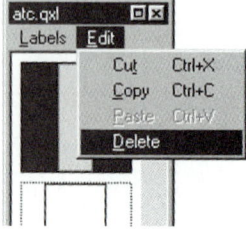

On Windows, you have to choose Delete from the palette's Edit menu.

8. Click OK to the warning that this cannot be undone.

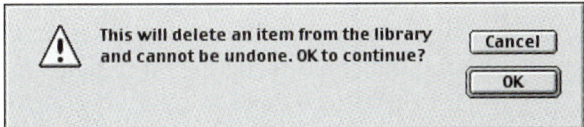

9. Notice that the sidebar box is removed from the library, but not from the document page.

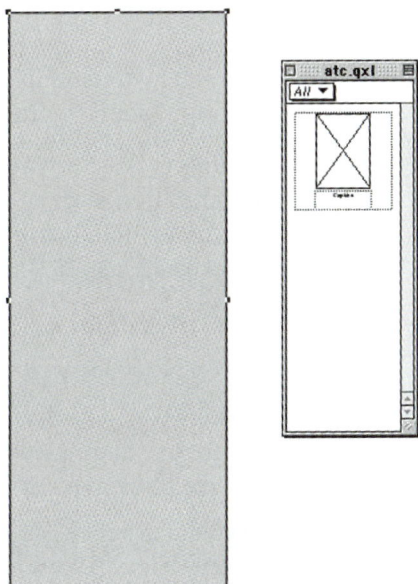

10. Close the library file, and close the Quark document without saving.

Working with Books

Long documents are frequently split into multiple files during the conception and design phase, and then recombined at the end of the process to create the final job.

- Files with fewer pages are less cumbersome to control and easier to navigate.

- Documents with many images can become very large, which can be a problem if the documents are being passed around on a slow network connection. Breaking them into pieces helps to keep the file size smaller.

- A publication may require a different running head or foot in different sections. If you build each section as a separate file, you can change the text in the running head or foot for each document and you don't have to create duplicate master pages for each different head. To insure consistency, however, the running head and foot in each separate document should use the same style sheet.

- If a document is broken into separate files, several designers may work on different sections of the same project without the risk of accidentally overwriting another person's work.

- If a very long document is split into several sections, you will not lose the entire project if a single file becomes corrupt.

The Book utility was added with the introduction of QuarkXPress 4.0 in 1997. Version 5.0 added several enhancements to the utility, making it even easier to combine and maintain multiple documents in a single publication.

Before QuarkXPress added the Book utility, multiple files were combined in the prepress department at the service provider. Working with multiple documents required extreme care and attention to detail to maintain consistency from one document to the next. The Book utility has made the process much easier, and automates many of the tasks that had previously been done by carefully comparing proofs of every page in the document. Of course, this doesn't mean that you can blithely use the Book utility without paying attention to your work, but you can automate much of the process.

When a single project is comprised of several files, it is even more important to maintain consistency from one document to the next. If the font is slightly different from one issue of a newsletter to the next, no one (or few people) is likely to spot much of a difference. That difference is far more noticeable, however, when two or more documents are bound together in the same publication.

A QuarkXPress book is a container file into which multiple Quark documents are placed to facilitate organization, page numbering, document management, and printing. The Book utility enables you to combine each part of the whole job so that the group of files can be treated as a single unit. This offers several benefits, allowing you to:

- Define a master document for the book.
- Synchronize the style sheets, colors, and other elements to the master in the book.
- Monitor page and section numbering of each individual file in the book, and of the book as a whole.
- Change the order of documents within the book layout, and automatically renumber pages according to the book order.
- Add and remove files from the book.
- Print the entire book by opening the Print dialog box only once, regardless of the number of files.

You can create a new book by selecting File>New>Book.

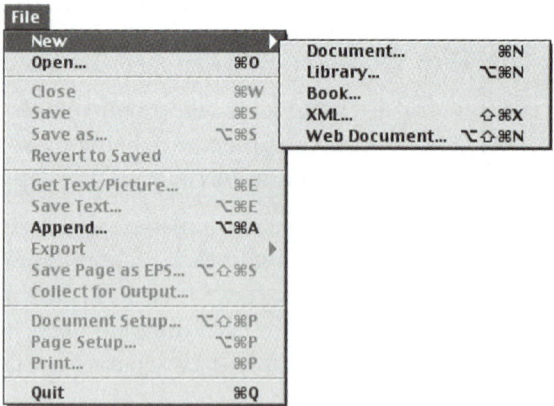

In the New Book dialog box, you can navigate to any location on your computer. In the Book Name field, you should enter the name of the book you are creating. Macintosh users need to remember to add the extension .qxb to the file.

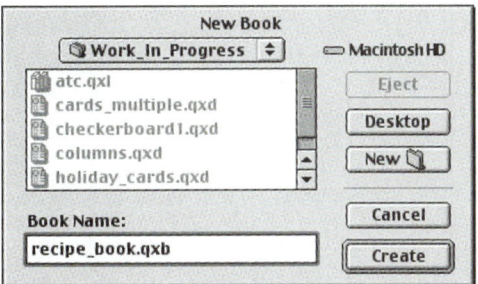

Clicking Create opens the book palette, displaying the name of the book in the Menu bar.

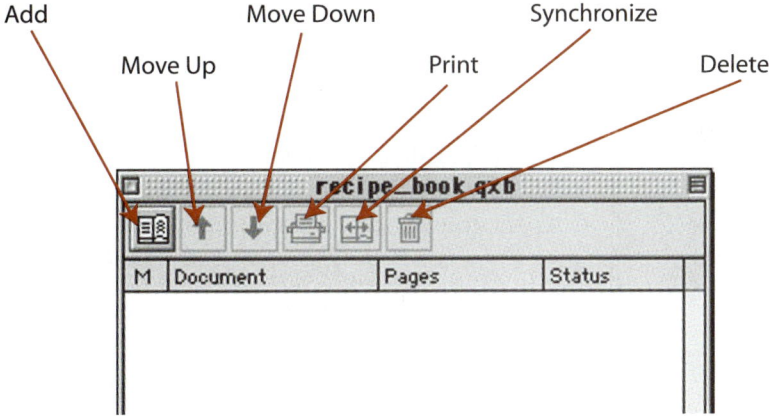

Adding Book Chapters

The Add button opens the Add New Chapter dialog box. You can navigate to any location on your computer, select the file you want to add, and click Add.

The first chapter added to a book is considered the master document for the book. The master is indicated by an "M" to the left of the file name (in the first column of the palette).

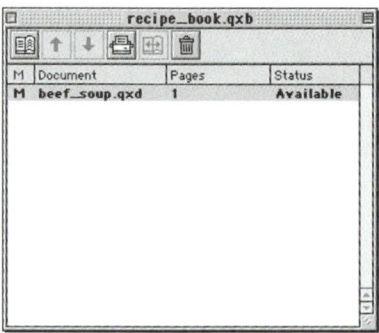

If the master document is deleted, the second file added becomes the default master document. If both the master and the second file are deleted, the third file added becomes the master, and so on.

Navigating Book Chapters

The book palette is an interactive tool that enables you to open chapters directly from the palette. Double-clicking any item in the palette opens the file. The Status column designates the condition of each file in the book as Available, Open, Missing, or Modified.

When you place a file into a book, the book file acts as a container; this process is very similar to placing an image into a document file. A QuarkXPress document stores the path to a placed image as a reference. Books use the same methodology, storing a reference to the files contained within the book.

The Status column of the book palette shows Available as long as the files have not been moved from the location from which they were placed. If the files have been moved, the Status column shows that the file is Missing.

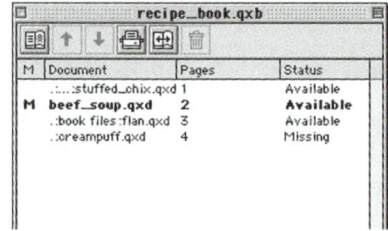

You can redirect the link to a missing file by double-clicking that item in the book palette. This opens a navigation dialog box in which you can locate the new position of the missing file.

Once a document has been added to a book file, don't make changes outside the book palette environment.

If a chapter file has been opened and saved in any way other than by double-clicking from the book palette, the Status column shows that the file has been Modified. To correct the Status column, you must reopen the document from the book palette, and then close it again.

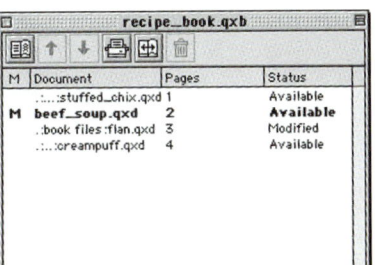

Chapters and Page Numbering

The Pages column in the book palette shows the page numbers of each file within the book. The first document added to the book defaults to page 1, and each successive document is numbered correctly according to its position in the book. For example, if the first file has eight pages, the second file added to the book will begin with page 9.

The page numbering of a book is dependent on using the automatic-page-number character (Command/Control-3) in the QuarkXPress documents.

If you open the Section dialog box for any chapter (Page>Section), you see that the Book Chapter Start check box is selected and grayed out. The options in the Page Numbering area of the dialog box are also grayed out — the values are dependent on the file's position in the book.

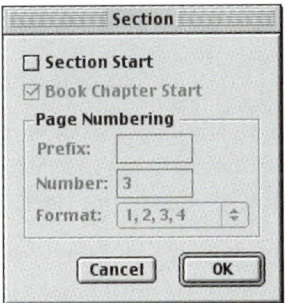

You cannot manually choose the Book Chapter Start option in the Section dialog box. This is checked automatically only when a file is added to a book.

You can override the automatic book page numbering for a file by selecting the Section Start check box. This automatically deselects the Book Chapter Start option and enables you to change the Prefix, Number, and Format values. The Section Start option is particularly useful for changing the numbering of a specific section. The front matter of a document, for example, is usually numbered separately using lowercase Roman numerals, and the first page of the body of the document typically begins on page 1.

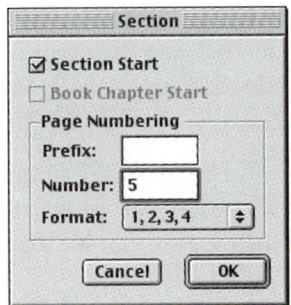

If you override the automatic book page numbering for any file, an asterisk marks the page number(s) in the Pages column. Any files following the modified section start are numbered sequentially in that section.

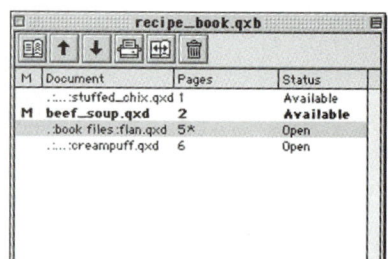

Opening, Closing, and Saving Books

You can open an existing book file by choosing File>Open (Command/Control-O). Book files should have a .qxb extension, and are indicated by an icon that looks like an open book.

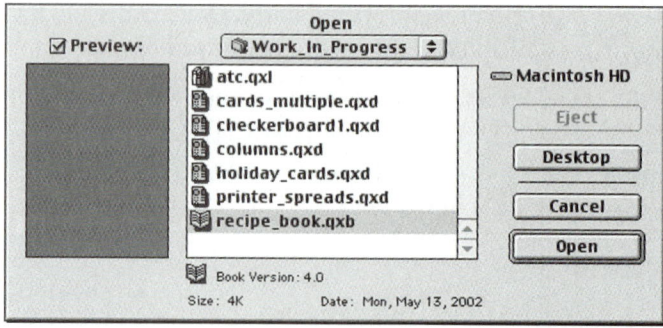

Remember: Macintosh users should always add the extension .qxb when creating a book file. Windows automatically adds the extension for you.

To close a book, you can simply click the Close button in the top-left corner (Macintosh) or the top-right corner (Windows) of the palette. Changes to a book file are saved automatically; you cannot override this setting or close the book file without saving.

If any chapter files of a book are open when you close the book, you are alerted that closing the book will also close those files. Clicking OK to the warning closes the book and all of its files.

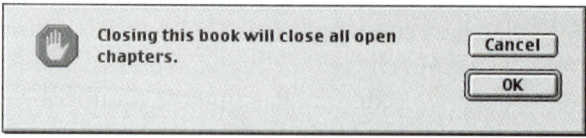

Exercise Setup

This exercise is a continuation of the recipe book exercises from the beginning of this chapter. Because the focus here is on combining documents rather than creating many different files, we provide you with the completed page files for this and the following exercises.

You must copy these files into the Work_In_Progress folder because you will be making frequent changes through the book palette. These exercises will not work properly if you add the files to a book directly from the Resource CD.

Once the files are copied from the CD, Windows users have to open the Properties dialog box for each file (on the desktop) and deactivate the Read-Only check box.

You can right-click an icon and choose Properties from the pop-up menu.

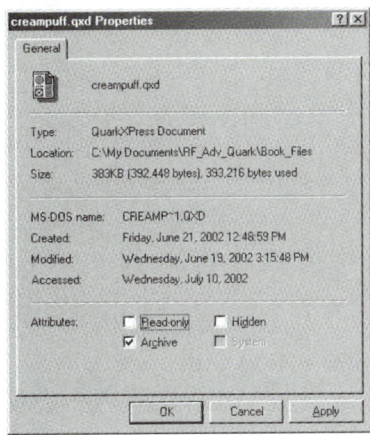

In the Properties dialog box, you have to deactivate the Read-Only check box.

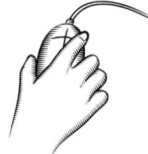

Create a Book

1. Copy the folder **Book_Files** from the **RF_Adv_Quark** folder into your **Work_In_Progress** folder.

2. Select File>New>Book.

3. Navigate to your **Work_In_Progress** folder. Type "recipe_book.qxb" in the Book/File Name field and click Create.

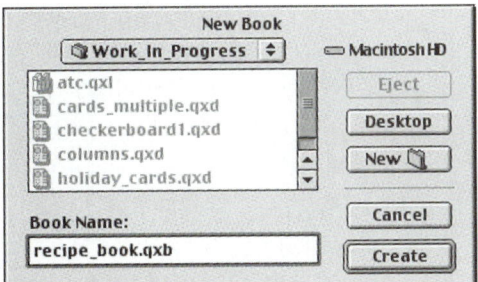

4. Click the Add Chapter button in the book palette. Navigate to the file **beef_soup.qxd** in the **Book_Files** folder (**Work_In_Progress>Book_Files**), and click Add.

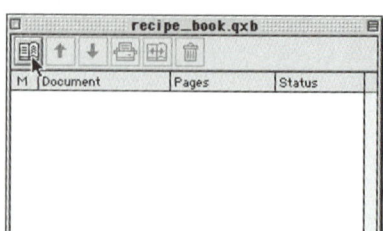

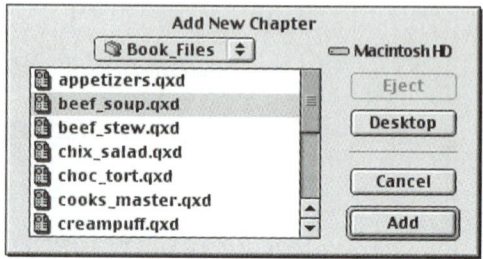

The new file is added to the book palette as the master document.

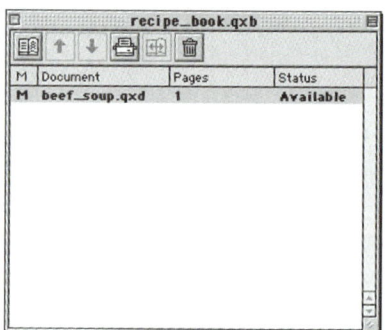

5. Repeat Step 4 to add the following files to the book:

beef_stew.qxd
chix_salad.qxd
choc_tort.qxd
creampuff.qxd
flan.qxd
stuffed_art.qxd
stuffed_chix.qxd
veg_dip.qxd

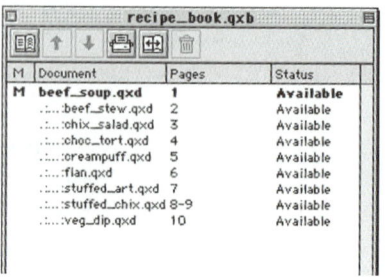

6. Looking at the book palette, you may notice that all files have only one page except stuffed_chix.qxd. Double-click that file to open the document.

7. If the Document Layout palette is not visible, choose View>Show Document Layout. Notice that the text flows onto a second page.

 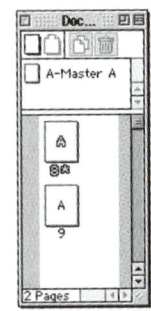

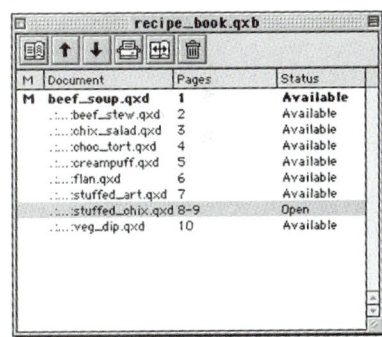

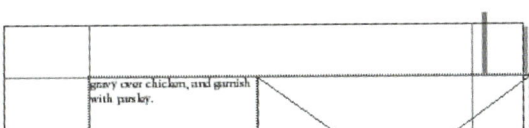

8. Every recipe in this book should fit on a single page. Click on the text on page two with the Content tool. If it is not visible, press "F11" to show the Style Sheets palette. The selected text is set with the Direction Line style.

9. Control/Right-click the Direction Line style sheet in the palette, and choose Edit Direction Line from the contextual menu.

10. Click Edit in the Character Attributes area. Change the font size to 11.5 pt. and click OK. Choose the Formats tab, and change the Space Before field to p4. Click OK to change the style sheet and return to the document window. All the text should now fit onto one page.

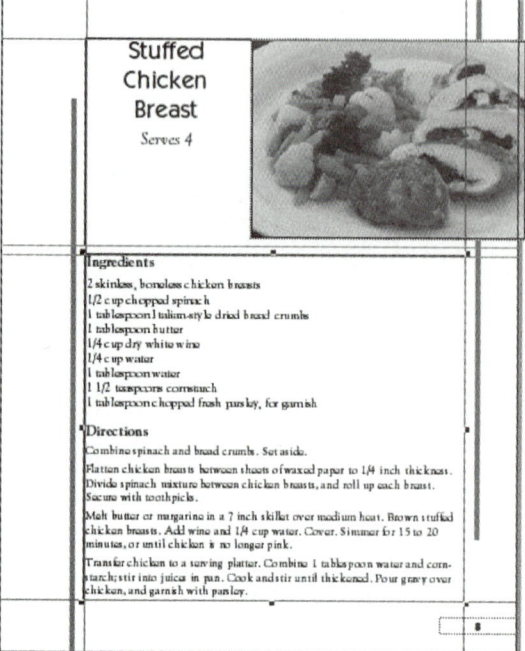
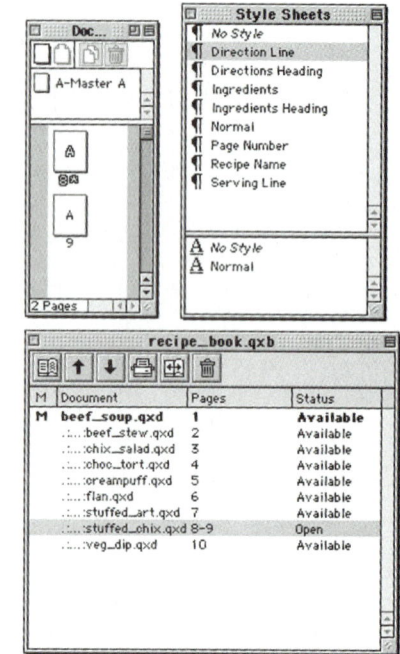

11. Delete the blank second page from the file. Notice that page numbering in the book palette changes automatically to reflect the new status of the file.

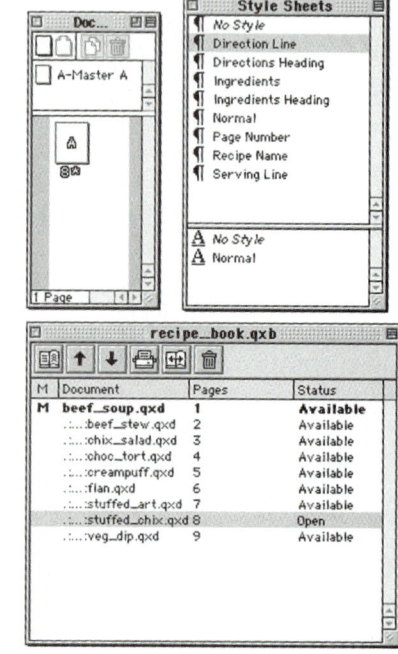

12. Save the open document and then close it.

13. Close the book file.

Sorting Chapters

When more than one file is added to the open book, you can rearrange the files however you like. The Move Up and Move Down buttons allow you to reposition the highlighted document within the list. Note, as shown in the following images, that the master document can appear in any position within the list. When you move a chapter to a new position in the book, the page numbering automatically changes to reflect the new chapter order (unless you have chosen to override the book page numbering manually, using the Section dialog box).

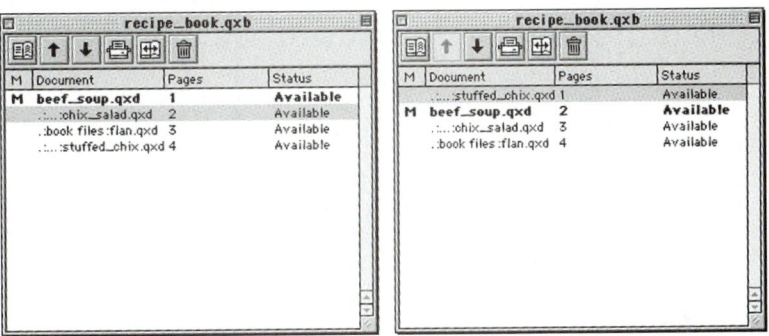

Deleting Chapters

You can delete a chapter in the book by highlighting it and clicking the Delete button. You are warned before the chapter is finally deleted from the book. Clicking OK in the warning dialog box removes the chapter from the book palette; clicking Cancel leaves your book intact.

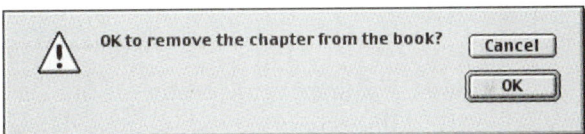

Once you delete a chapter from a book, you cannot undo the deletion. The file still exists in its original location, however, so you can add the file back into the book, if necessary.

Sort Book Files

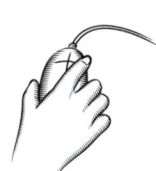

1. Press Command/Control-O. In the Open dialog box, navigate to your **Work_In_Progress** folder. Highlight the file **recipe_book.qxb** and click Open.

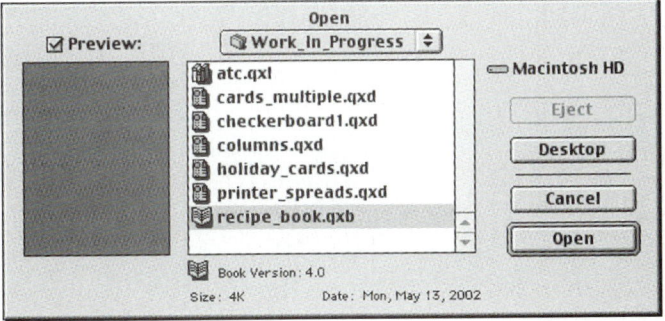

2. Observe that the chapter files are now in alphabetical order. You want to reorganize the book according to the type of dish (appetizers, dinners, and desserts) that each recipe describes.

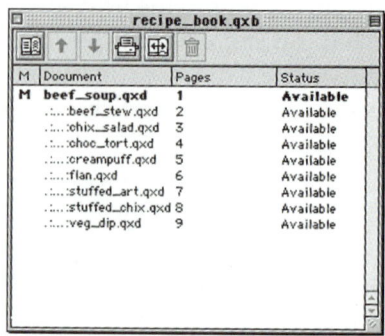

3. Highlight chix_salad.qxd in the palette list, and click the Move Up button twice. The file should move to the top of the list.

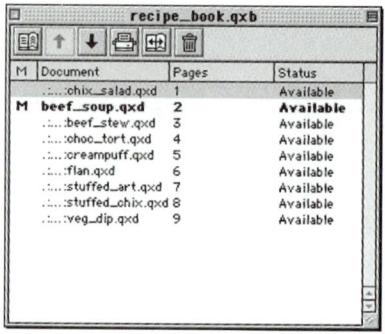

4. Using the same process as in Step 3, rearrange the remainder of the list to this order:

      chix_salad.qxd
      stuffed_art.qxd
      veg_dip.qxd
      beef_soup.qxd
      beef_stew.qxd
      stuffed_chix.qxd
      choc_tort.qxd
      creampuff.qxd
      flan.qxd

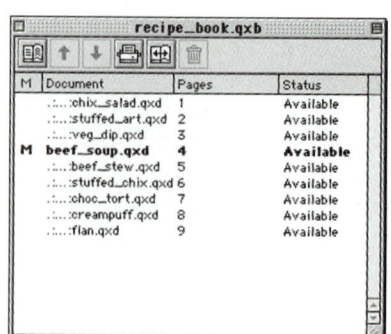

5. Highlight the file choc_tort.qxd in the palette, and click the Delete button. Click OK in the warning dialog box.

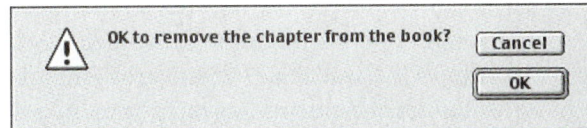

6. Click the Add button in the book palette. Locate the file **choc_tort.qxd** in the **Book_Files** folder (**Work_In_Progress>Book_Files**), and click Add. Click the Move Up button two times to put the file back in its proper place.

7. Click the Add Chapter button. Add the file **appetizers.qxd** to the book and move the file to the top of the palette.

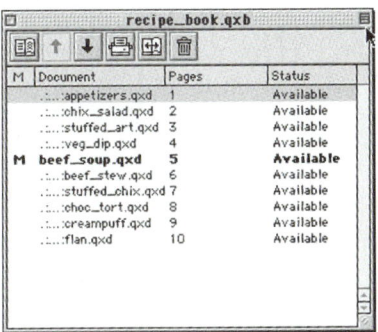

8. Add the file **dinner.qxd** and place it immediately before beef_soup.qxd in the list.

9. Add the file **dessert.qxd** and place it immediately before choc_tort.qxd in the list.

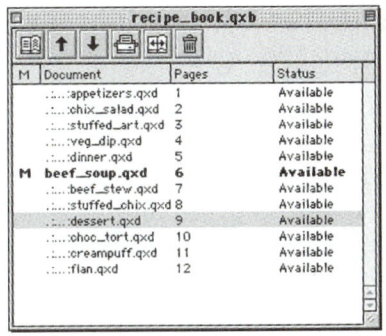

10. Leave the book file open for the next exercise.

Synchronizing Books

An advantage of using style sheets for text layout is that a style can be changed easily and universally. This is also a disadvantage of using style sheets, particularly when combining multiple files into a single publication. Layout designers frequently manipulate, tweak, and even cheat to force-fit text into a desired amount of space, to make a runaround work correctly, or to achieve some other specific effect. When the files are combined into the final book, this adjusting can be a problem if the variation is noticeable from one file to the next.

The QuarkXPress Book utility expands the concept of using a master document to maintain consistency between documents. The Synchronize button enables you to synchronize the Style Sheets, Colors, H&Js, Lists, and Dashes & Stripes for the book, based on the master document. In the Synchronize Selected Chapters dialog box, the Available area shows the available elements from the master document in the book. You can choose individual elements to synchronize in any category, just as you would if you were appending elements to an individual document. Clicking Synch All moves all items in all categories into the Including section.

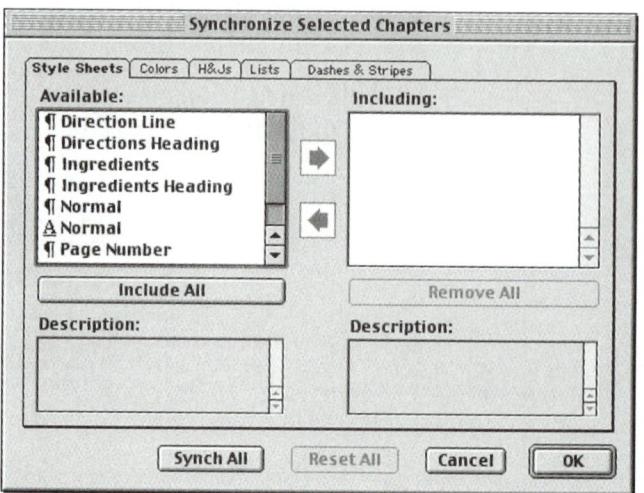

When a book is synchronized, elements of the master document are added to the other files if they do not already exist in that file. If an element does already exist in the other files, the element definition from the master document is applied to the same element in the other files. The synchronization process does not affect elements that are not in the master document.

In other words, if you have changed the definition of a style sheet in one file, synchronizing the book overwrites the change, and assigns the settings for that style sheet as defined in the master document. If you changed a style sheet — to fit text onto a page, for example — synchronizing the book to the master document overwrites the changes, and the text will no longer fit in the same way.

As another example, you may have changed the defined color of text in a style sheet for each section. Synchronizing the book means that the color of the text will be the same as the master for every file in the book. You then have to reopen the sections and rechange the style sheet to use the different colors.

Fortunately, the Synchronize Selected Chapters dialog box allows you to define individual elements to synchronize. If you know a particular style sheet was deliberately changed in one file, you may choose not to synchronize that style sheet, thus maintaining your original design. Of course, this defeats the purpose of synchronizing to maintain consistency from one document to the next.

The only real solution is to plan each aspect of each file carefully, and avoid (or at least minimize) the tweaking and manipulating that we all do. If you absolutely must tweak text, manipulate the specific areas of text directly that you need to fit instead of altering the style sheets in the document. If text formatting overrides the style sheet, synchronizing will not override your changes.

Synchronizing a book does not delete any element from any file, but can override changes you made to a particular file.

If you have to adjust text in a particular file, manipulate the selected text, not the style sheet.

You can also synchronize just certain files by selecting them in the book palette before clicking the Synchronize button. To select contiguous files, hold down the Shift key and click on each file. To select noncontiguous files, hold down the Command/Control key while selecting the desired files. Again, synchronizing only certain files defeats the purpose of synchronizing, but the option is available.

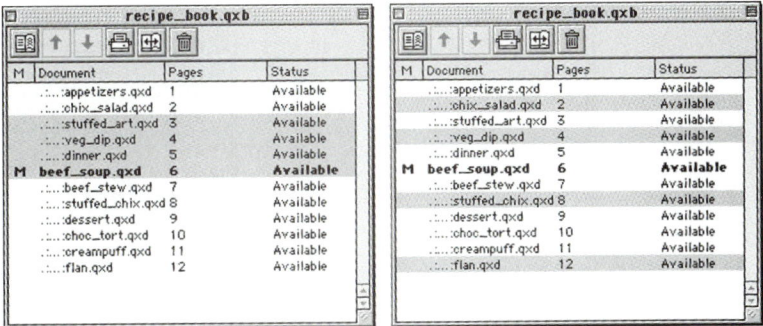

Printing Books

Rather than opening each document and changing the print settings individually, the Book utility allows you to choose the settings once and print all documents in the book. You can print all documents in the book by clicking the Print button with nothing selected in the palette, or print certain documents by highlighting them in the list before clicking the Print button. When you click Print in the Print dialog box, QuarkXPress outputs all documents in the book using the same settings.

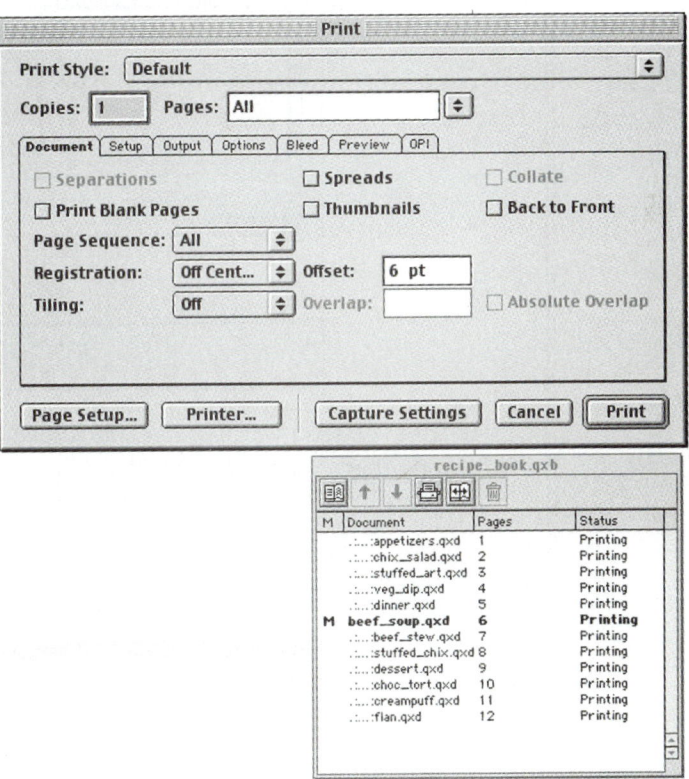

If you have closed the book file from the previous exercise, open **recipe_book.qxb** *from your* **Work_In_Progress** *folder.*

Synchronize a Book

1. In the book palette, click in the empty space below the last item to deselect all files. Notice that the file beef_soup.qxd is the master document (indicated by the "M" in the "M" column).

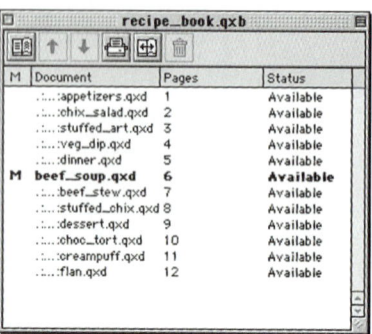

2. Click the Synchronize button.

3. To be consistent, we are going to synchronize every element of every document in the book. Click Synch All, and then click OK.

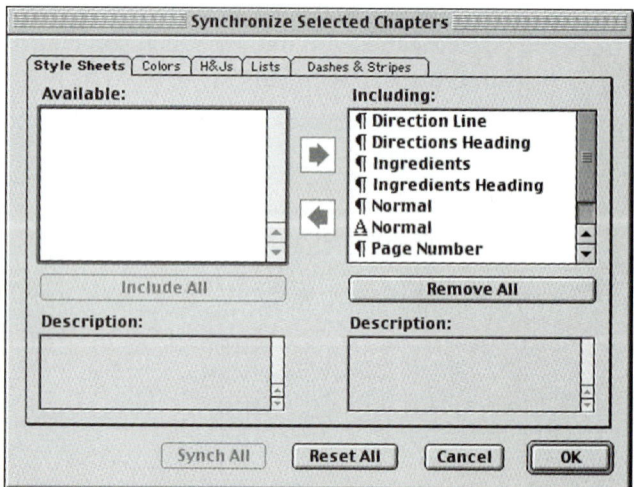

4. You will see a warning that embedded elements (style sheets that are based on others, for example) will also be added to the other chapters in the book. Click OK.

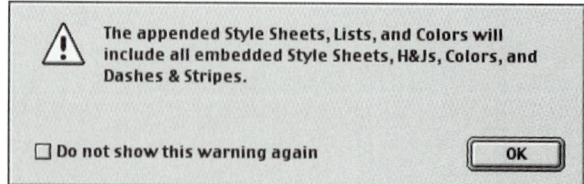

QuarkXPress processes each file in the book. When the Synchronize Selected Chapters dialog box disappears, the process is complete.

5. Remember that, in the Create a Book exercise, you changed the definition of the Direction Line style in the file stuffed_chix.qxd. Double-click that item in the book palette to open the file.

When the book was synchronized, the Direction Line style sheet was changed back to the original definition (as it is in the master document). The bottom text box now shows an overset text icon.

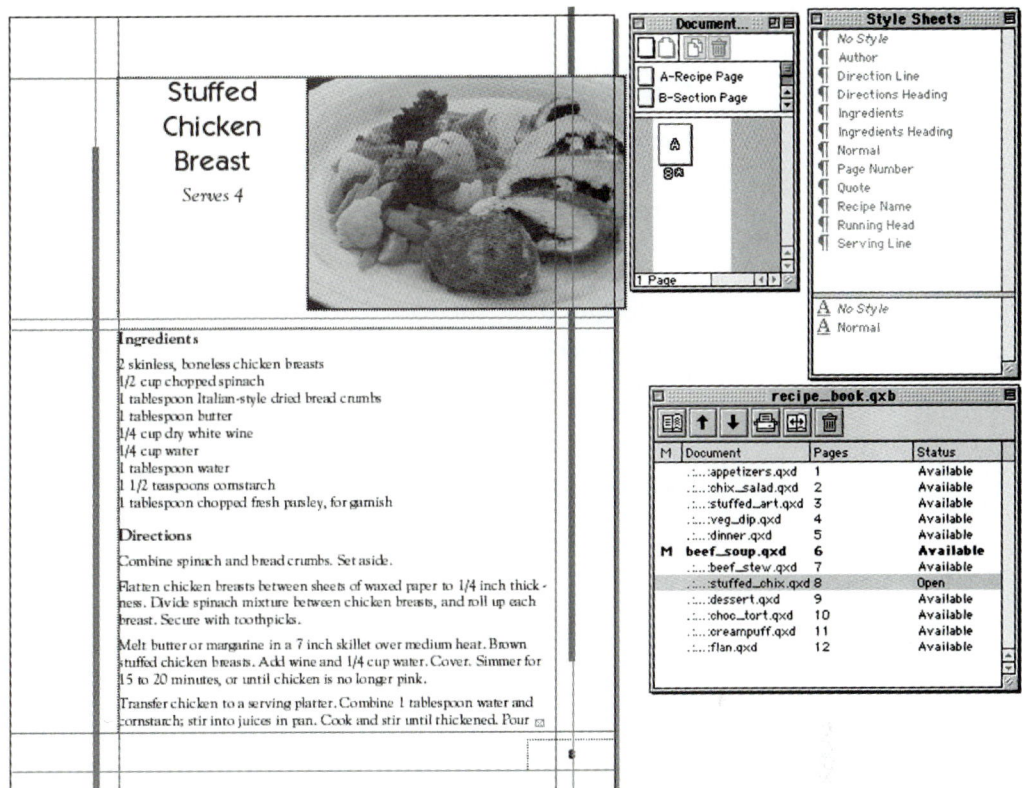

6. Highlight all of the text after the Directions heading. Extend the bottom of the text box, if necessary.

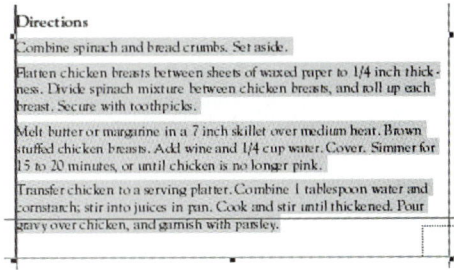

7. Change the font size to 11.5 pt. Press Command/Control-Shift-F, change the Space Before field to p4, and then click OK to apply the formatting change.

8. The text all fits on one page, and the Style Sheets palette indicates that the selected text has been modified from the original Style Sheet definition. Save the file and close it.

Keep this book file in your **Work_In_Progress** *folder. You will use it in the next chapter.*

9. Make sure that no files are selected in the book palette, and click the Synchronize button. Click Synch All and click OK.

10. When the Synch is complete, double-click stuffed_chix.qxd in the book palette. Notice that the text still fits on one page; the synch process does not affect locally formatted text. Close the file.

11. Close the book palette. Keep this book file in your **Work_In_Progress** folder. You will use it in the next chapter.

Summary

You have learned that consistency is extremely important when creating page layouts, and even more so when working with long documents. You understand that QuarkXPress provides many tools that allow you precise control over virtually every aspect of a document or series of documents. You have discovered that master pages and templates enable you to plan your layout in advance, and create grids that increase productivity in the production stage. You have also found that libraries give quick access to frequently used page elements. You know that master documents provide a storage place for common formatting elements such as style sheets, colors, and H&J routines. You also understand that books combine multiple documents, and can synchronize the individual components of a larger publication. You know that these tools are invaluable assets to a long-document production workflow.

4 *Lists*

Chapter Objectives:

Many of the page-layout documents with which you work will be just one page or a few pages — posters, flyers, newsletters, and so on. Multiple-page documents, or documents with long blocks of text that flow across multiple pages, have special requirements and considerations, including tables of contents and other lists. QuarkXPress provides tools that help to automate building and maintaining an accurate table of contents and index. In this chapter, you will:

- Examine the different uses of the Lists feature of QuarkXPress 5.0.

- Explore the interaction between styles and lists.

- Learn how to create a table of contents for any QuarkXPress document.

- Become familiar with the interaction between lists and books.

- Discover the potential problems of changing page numbering, and learn how to solve the problem.

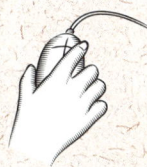

Projects to be Completed:

- Stonington Letterfold Brochure (A)

- Body Solution Booklet (B)

- Cosciel Poster (C)

Lists

Before desktop-publishing software automated the document design process, tables of contents were created manually from page proofs — by turning each page and writing down the appropriate listing and page number, then typesetting those hard-copy lists into the final document. The process was extremely time-consuming and required precise attention to detail. If the document changed after the table of contents or index was complete, the entire piece had to be rechecked, page by page. QuarkXPress 5.0 includes tools that automate the process of creating a table of contents, greatly improving production time and making it easier to maintain accuracy.

The Lists utility is an excellent way to monitor the editorial priority of a document. If you define a table of contents list, you can quickly see the headings, subheadings, and any subordinate levels. While the Lists feature is particularly useful for creating a table of contents, this is not its only possible use. Different types of documents call for different types of lists; following are only a few examples.

If you are working on a document that uses parenthetical notations to cite references, you can apply a character style sheet to each reference cited throughout the document, then build a list using that character style sheet. The Alphabetical option in the Edit Lists dialog box alphabetizes the list of references, which allows you to build a bibliography automatically.

Some publications call for a separate table of contents listing all illustrations in the publication. If you define a Caption paragraph style sheet, you can create a list of figures using the Caption style sheet.

Many publications include a glossary of terms, which are italicized throughout the text, to indicate inclusion in the glossary. If you use a character style sheet (e.g., Glossary Term) to italicize the terms in the document, you can compile a list of all glossary terms at the end of the document. You then need only add the definitions.

Many catalogs include multiple indexes by product, item number, manufacturer, and so on. You can define character style sheets for each category, and then build separate alphabetized lists for each.

Of course these are not the only uses of the Lists utility; you are only limited by the amount of planning you do and by the style sheets you choose to define.

Planning Lists: Interacting with Style Sheets

Some advance planning is required when using lists in QuarkXPress. Quark lists are based on the style sheets in a document. To define a list, you have to choose the particular style sheets you want to comprise that list. For example, a table of contents list might include Heading 1, Heading 2, and Heading 3 paragraph style sheets; any text set in those styles appears in the list.

Lists can also be defined to format the elements of the list automatically using style sheets. If you plan your project carefully, you can predefine the appearance of different list items and apply those style sheets to the elements of the list. Again using the table of contents example, TOC1 can be assigned to Heading 1 list items, TOC2 to Heading 2 items, and so on. When the final list is generated, the document is formatted automatically.

Lists are not confined to paragraph style sheets; you can also define a list based on a character style sheet. As an example, you may define a character style sheet to italicize every proper name in a document. If you are conscientious in applying the character style sheet to all proper names when building the document, compiling the final comprehensive list is a relatively easy process.

Creating a List

You can define a list in QuarkXPress by choosing Edit>Lists. The Lists dialog box uses the same interface as other Quark elements including colors and style sheets.

The name of the active document appears in the top of the Lists dialog box.

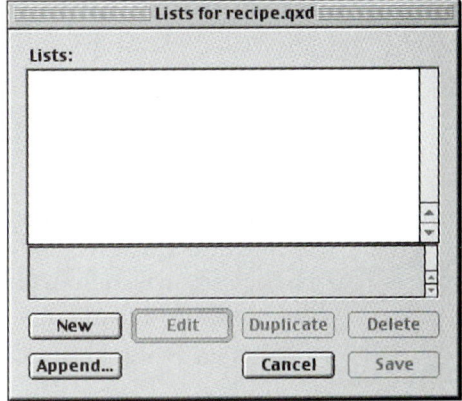

Clicking New in the Lists dialog box opens the Edits List dialog box, where you can define the contents of a particular list. In the Name field, you can choose an appropriate name for the list.

As we discussed previously, lists are inherently tied to the style sheets in a document. The left half of the dialog box lists all styles defined for the document. To add a style to the list, you can highlight it in the Available Styles area and click the right-pointing arrow button.

Like any other element you create in a document, name lists according to their use (e.g., Contents, Tables, Authors, etc.).

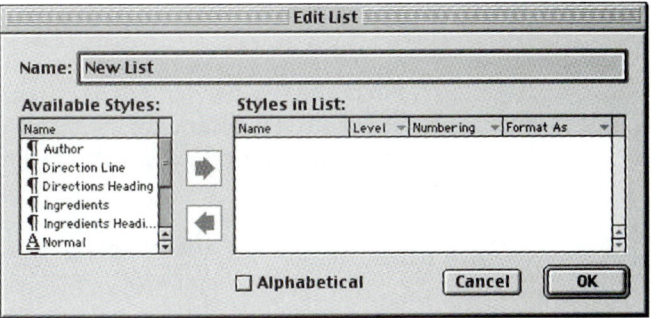

Once an item is added to the Styles in List area, you can define several options for that item.

- **Level.** This menu defines the nesting level of the style in the list; main headings are typically set to Level 1, subheads are set to Level 2, and so on according to editorial priority. The Level of a list item is only relevant to the appearance of the list in the Lists palette. This setting has no impact on formatting when the final list is built into the document.

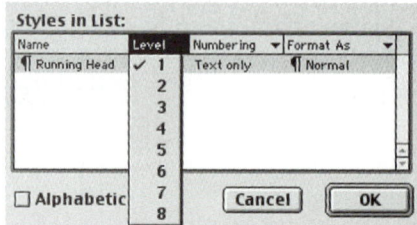

- **Numbering.** This menu defines how each list item appears in the list. This setting does not affect the appearance of the list in the Lists palette. The Numbering selection defines how the list item appears in the list when it is built into the document.

  - **Text Only.** This option shows only the item.
  - **Text… Page #.** This option lists the item and the page number on which the item appears, separated by a tab character.
  - **Page #… Text.** This option lists the page number on which the item appears followed by the item, separated by a tab character.

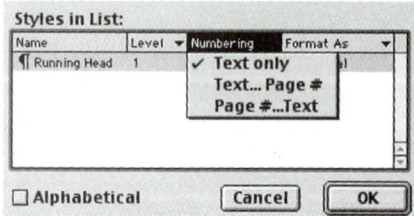

- **Format As.** This menu defines the style sheet that will be used when the list is built into the document. Not only can lists be defined according to the existing style sheets, but they can also be automatically formatted with some advance planning.

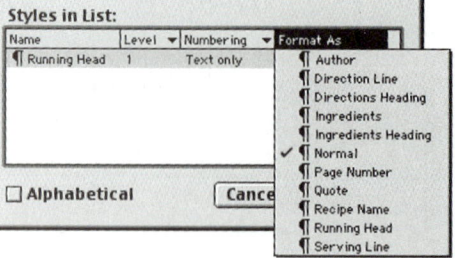

- **Alphabetical.** This check box displays the list in alphabetical order. This option ignores any defined levels.

When you have defined the contents of a list, clicking OK returns you to the Lists dialog box. You must click Save to finalize your work and return to the document window.

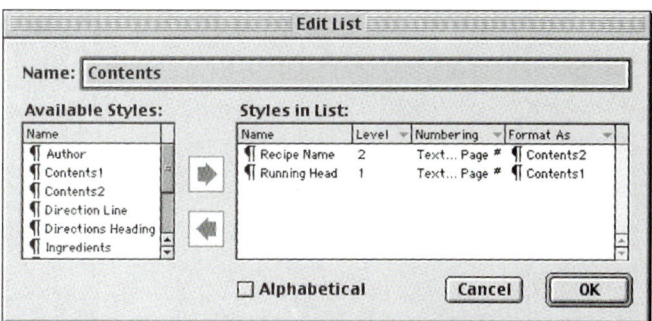

Exercise Setup

For the following exercise, you have been provided with files from which you will build a table of contents list. Since you did not create the provided components, you need to be aware of the following information:

- The document has two different page layouts — section pages and recipe pages.
- The documents were built with style sheets.
- The name of each section is set with the style Running Head, and the title of each recipe is set with the style Recipe Name.
- The table of contents will include each section heading and the name of each recipe.

Create a List

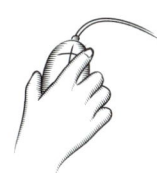

1. Open the book file **recipe_book.qxb** from your **Work_In_Progress** folder.

   Notice the two different page layouts — section pages and recipe pages.

Notice as well two of the styles used — Running Head for each section, and Recipe Name for the title of each recipe.

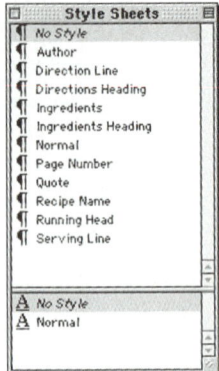

2. Click the Add button in the book palette. Locate the file **recipe_front.qxd** in the **Book_Files** folder (**Work_In_Progress>Book_Files**), and click Add. Use the Move Up button to move the new file to the beginning of the list.

3. Double-click recipe_front.qxd in the book palette to open the file.

4. If it is not visible, press "F11" to show the Style Sheets palette. This document was planned in advance, and style sheets were created (TOC1 and TOC2) to format the table of contents.

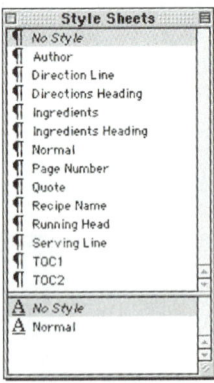

5. Choose Edit>Lists and click New.

6. Type "Contents" in the Name field. In the Available Styles area, highlight Running Head, and click the right-facing arrow button to add the style sheet to the list.

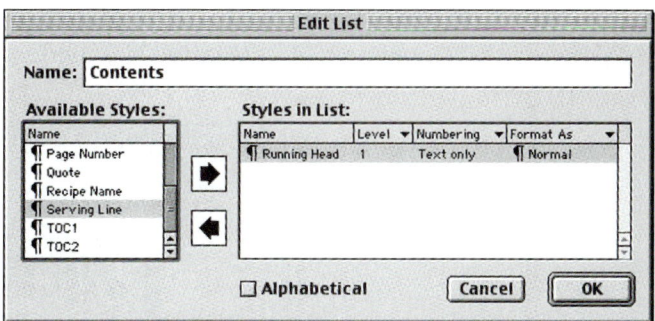

7. Click the Numbering column head, and choose Text...Page # from the drop-down menu.

8. Click the Format As column head and choose TOC1 from the drop-down menu.

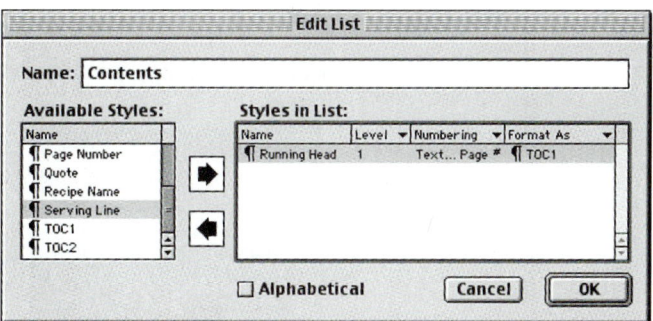

9. Highlight Recipe Name in the Available Styles area, and click the right-facing arrow button to add the style to the list.

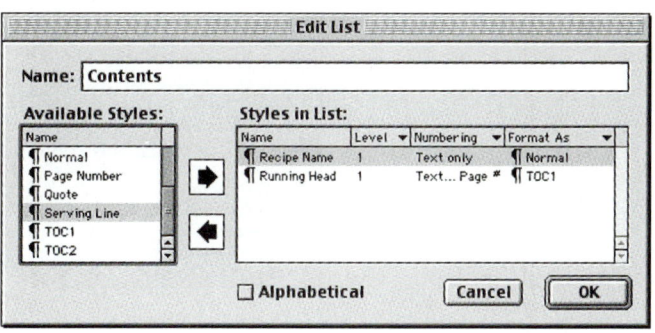

Notice that Recipe Name is placed before Running Head in the list. Styles are shown in alphabetical order. This has no impact on the final appearance of the list in the Lists palette or on the list when built into the document.

10. With Recipe Name still highlighted in the Styles in List area, change the Level column to 2, change the Numbering column to Text… Page #, and change the Format As column to TOC2.

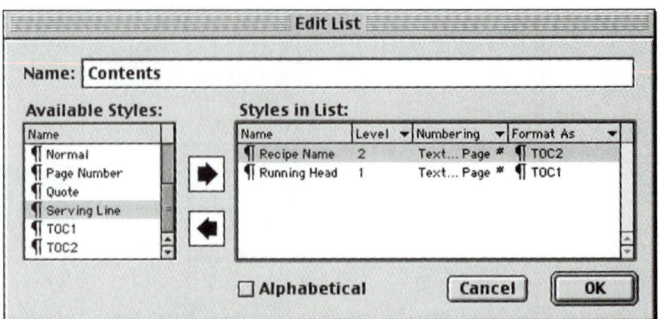

11. Click OK to close the Edit List dialog box. In the Lists dialog box, click Save to save the list and return to the document.

12. Save the file, and leave the document and book files open for the next exercise.

Viewing Lists

After a list has been defined, you can view the list by selecting View>Show Lists.

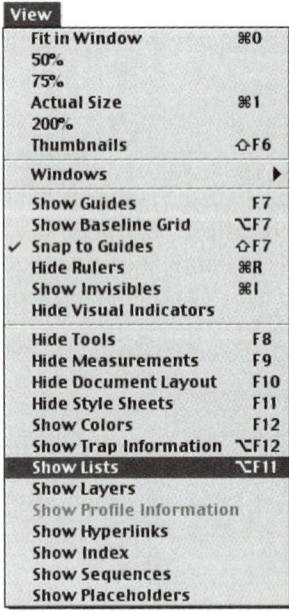
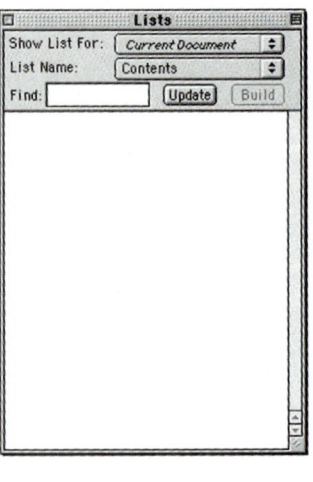

- **Show Lists For**. This menu determines whether you are working with the list in a single document or in a book. You will see either Current Document or the name of any open book file.

- **List Name**. This menu shows all of the available lists for the selection in the Show List For menu.

- **Find**. This field is useful when working with very long lists. It works similarly to the help menus in many software applications; you can type one or more letters, which highlights the first instance of that text string in the list.

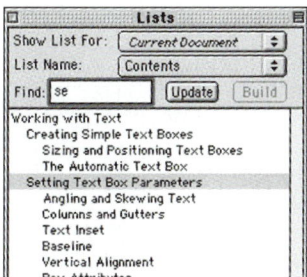

When "se" is typed in the Find field, the first instance of those letters is highlighted in the Lists palette.

Navigating with the Lists Palette

The Lists palette is an interactive tool. You can navigate easily to a specific item in the list by double-clicking that item. If you are working with the list of an entire book, double-clicking opens the relevant file at the location of the list item. The selected item in the list is highlighted in the document window.

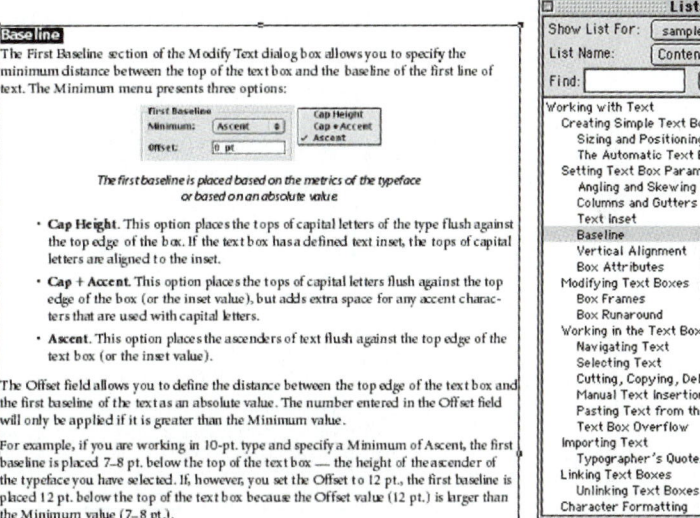

Managing Lists in Books

There are several special considerations when working with lists in a QuarkXPress book. In this section, we are using as an example a book with two chapter files. A list called "Contents" has been defined in the master document of the book; three levels of headings are included in the list and will be formatted with predefined TOC style sheets.

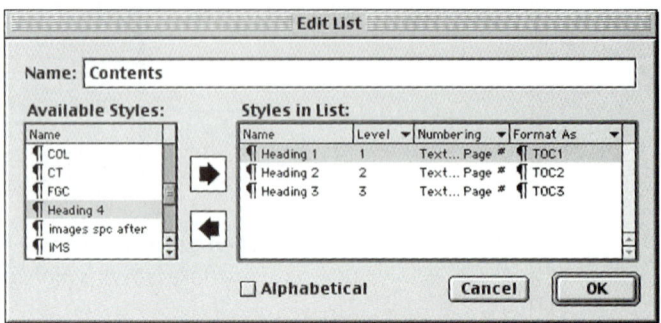

Synching Lists

In order to generate a comprehensive list for every file in a book, the list must exist in every file contained within that book. If you have already defined the list that you want to use in the master document, you can click the Synchronize button in the book palette and synchronize the lists. The Available area of the Lists tab shows any list defined in the master document. You can move that list to the Including area, then click OK to place the list in all chapters of the book.

Remember from the previous chapter that the synchronization process is based on the master document of the book. If you defined a list in a document other than the master, you can use the Append dialog box (File>Append) to add the list to the master document, and then synchronize the lists in the book.

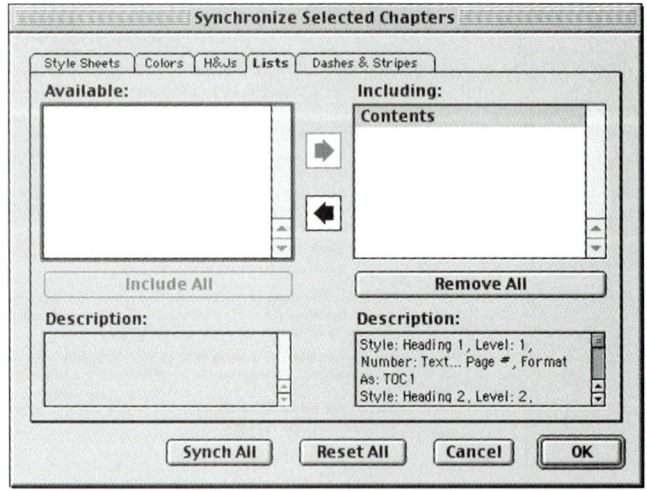

Once the list is a part of every chapter file, you can choose it from the List Name menu in the Lists palette.

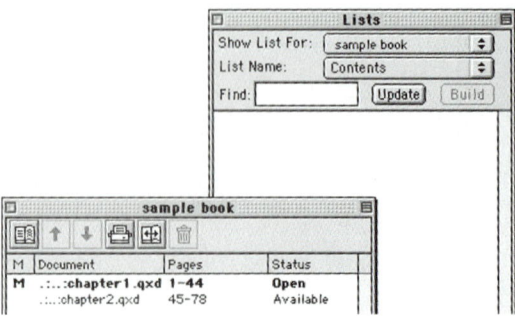

Using Style Sheets with Lists

For a book list to function properly, the style sheets that define the list must also exist in every chapter file of the book. In other words, Heading 2 must be used consistently throughout all chapters of the book if the heading is defined as a list element. If one chapter file uses a style called H2 instead of Heading 2, the list for that chapter will not include any Heading 2 elements because, technically, they do not exist.

Capitalization does not matter when generating a book list. If a list calls for a style sheet "Heading 2", the style sheet "heading 2" will also be included.

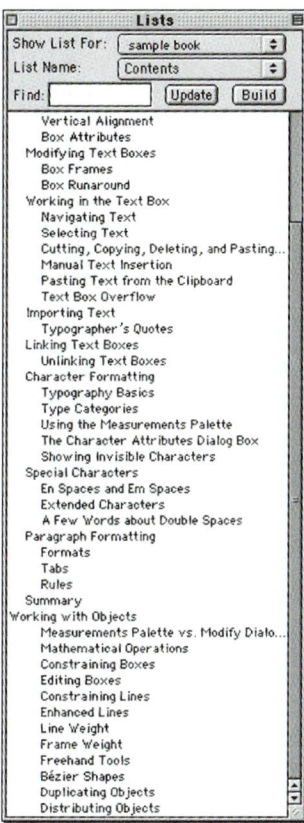

The second file in the book uses H2 instead of the list-element Heading 2. If you look carefully at the indent, you can see that the list for the second file, beginning with "Working with Objects," does not include any level 2 entries.

This is another example in which consistency from one file to the next is crucial. In order to create a comprehensive and accurate list, the same style sheets should be used in all files of a document.

When you synchronize the lists in a book, any style sheet that is used in a list is included in the synchronization.

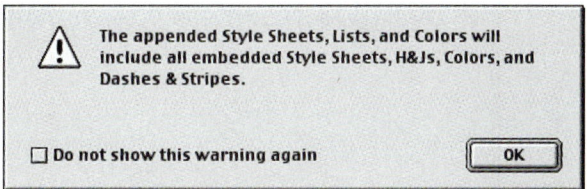

Once the correct style sheets are in the chapter files, you must replace the incorrect style sheet with the missing one.

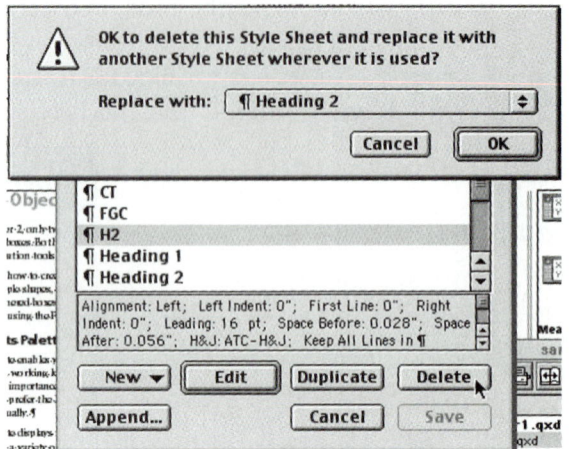

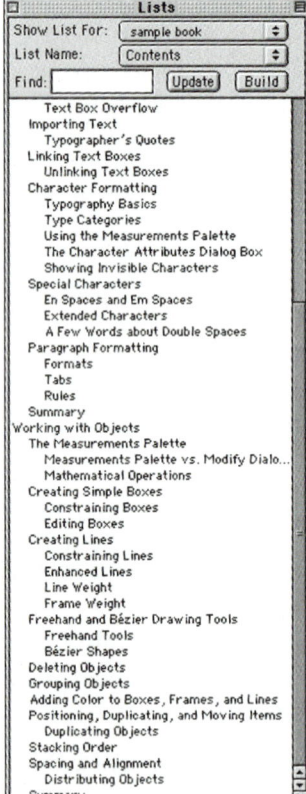

After replacing the H2 style sheet with Heading 2, the list is correct for both chapters in the book.

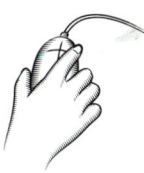

Work with a Book List

1. With the files recipe_book.qxb and recipe_front.qxd still open, choose View>Show Lists.

2. Click the Show Lists For menu and choose recipe_book.qxb.

3. Notice that the List Name menu is unavailable because the Contents list exists only in the front-matter document. The Contents list needs to be appended to every file in the book to work properly.

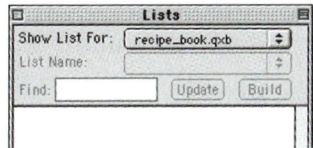

4. Double-click beef_soup.qxd — the master document — in the book palette to open the file.

5. Select Edit>Lists and click Append.

6. Navigate to the file recipe_front.qxd (where you created the Contents list) in the Append Lists dialog box, and click Open.

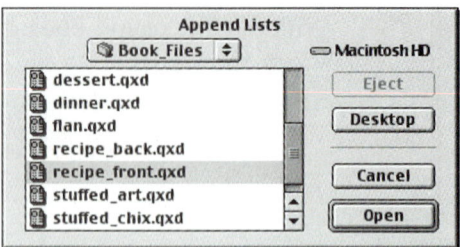

7. Highlight Contents in the Available area, and click the right-facing arrow button. Click OK.

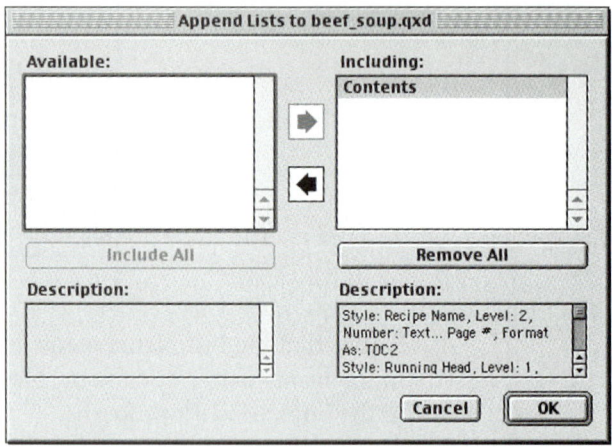

8. If you get a warning message, click OK.

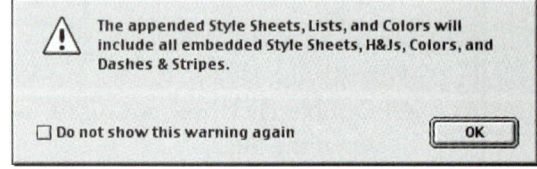

This message tells you that any style sheets used by the appended lists will also be appended.

9. The Contents list now appears in the Lists area for the beef_soup.qxd dialog box. Click Save to return to the document.

10. Press Command/Control-S to save the changes to the beef_soup.qxd file, and close the file.

11. You now need to add the Contents list to each file in the book. Click the Synchronize button in the book palette.

12. Click the Lists tab in the Synchronize Selected Chapters dialog box. Highlight Contents in the Available area, and click the right-facing arrow button.

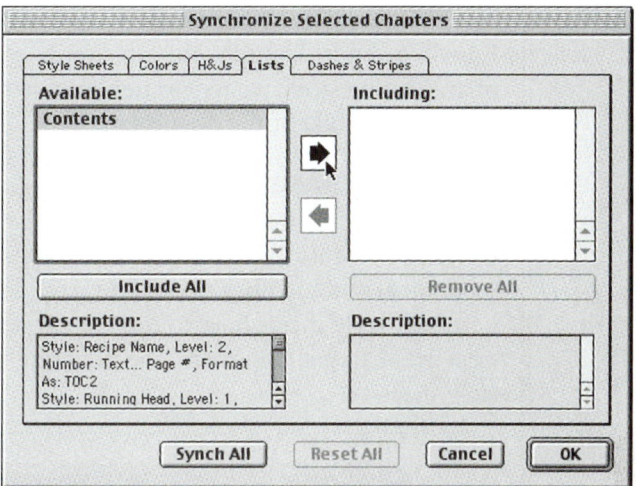

13. Click OK to synchronize the list in all chapters of the book. If you get a warning message, click OK.

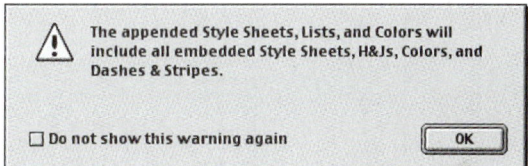

14. When the Synchronize Selected Chapters dialog box closes, the process is complete. Look at the Lists palette. The Contents list now appears in the List Name field.

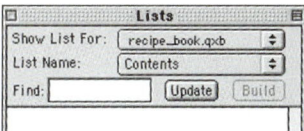

15. Click the Update button in the Lists palette. The book files are processed and the list is built into the palette.

Because this is the only list in that exists in the entire book, it is the only option in the List Name menu.

16. Save and close any open documents. Leave the book file open for the next exercise.

Building the Document List

Once a list is defined, whether for a single file or for a book, you can build it into the document by clicking Build in the Lists palette. First, however, you need to create a text box to hold the list that will be built. A list can be built into any text box in a document.

The position of the text insertion point in the document marks the location at which the list will be built. Though you can simply place the insertion point at the beginning or end of an existing story, we recommend that you create a separate text box that is not linked to the main body of the document.

Target Documents

You can also create separate files in a book for front matter and back matter, into which tables of contents, appendices, bibliographies, and other lists can be built. If you do create separate files, remember that if you have defined a list to be formatted automatically, the necessary style sheets have to exist in the target document. If those style sheets do not exist in the target document, the missing style sheets will be replaced with the Normal style sheet.

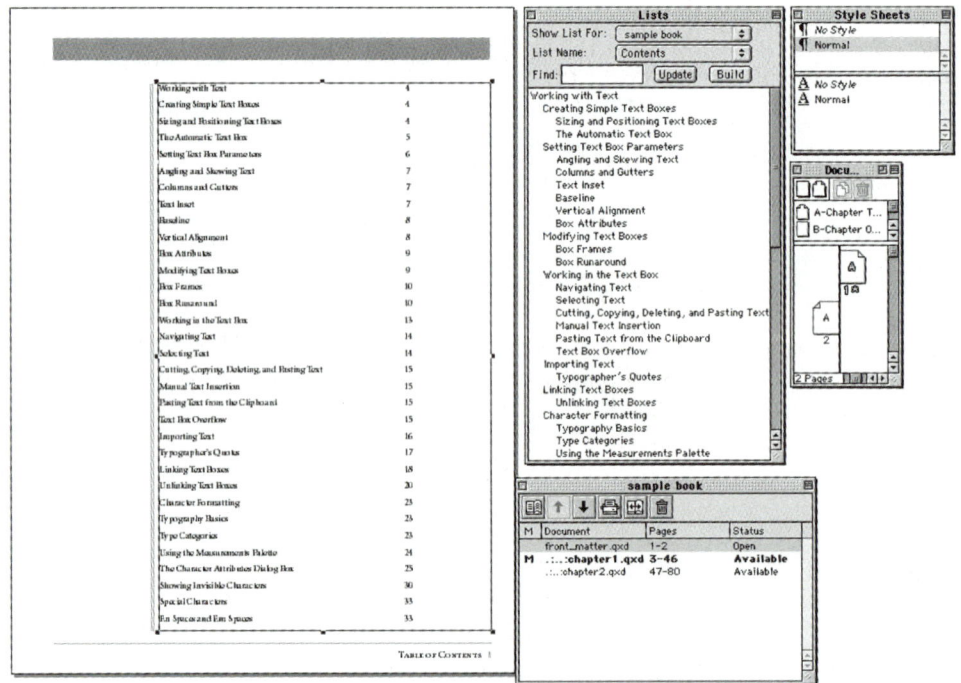

If the target document does not have the necessary style sheets to format the list, Normal is substituted.

It is a good idea to click Update immediately before clicking Build.

If you are working on a book, this warning only appears if, when you click Build, the list exists in the active document.

If you have made changes to the list text in the document, clicking Replace erases all of those changes.

Updating Lists

The Lists utility maintains an active link between the main body of the document and the Lists palette. You may make any number of changes to a document that affect the list — changing words, correcting spelling or capitalization errors, deleting or adding text that moves an item to a different page, or even changing the level of a heading in the document. Any time you change a list item in the main document, you have to click the Update button in the Lists palette to reflect the changes.

If you have already built a list into a document, you can easily update it by placing the insertion point in the list text block and clicking Build again. A dialog box appears, warning that the list already exists in the target document.

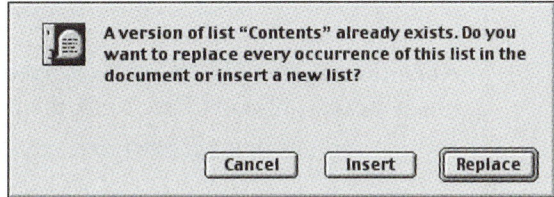

Cancel leaves all documents as they were before you clicked Build. Insert adds a second version of the list at the position of the insertion point. Replace deletes the existing list and replaces it with the current list contents.

Changing List Items

After a list is built, it is a static block of text. The style sheets can be changed as you would any other style sheet, and you can change the text block in which a list is placed. You can change or delete items from the list without affecting the main document.

Although the text that makes up a list is static, the list itself is a fluid entity. The List palette maintains a one-way link to the created list in a document. In other words, you can make changes to the main document, update the Lists palette, and then rebuild the list in the document using the updated list information. Because you can easily rebuild a list in a document, it is a good idea to make all changes within the Lists palette rather than changing the text, once a list is built.

For example, you notice a spelling error after creating a table of contents in the document. If you correct the error in the list text, you have temporarily solved the problem in this one instance. If you later rebuild the list, however, the original spelling error is rebuilt into the list, which you must then fix again.

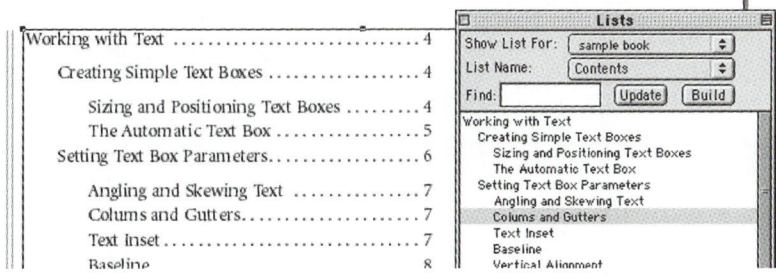

Rather than duplicating effort, you can easily navigate to the error in the body of the document by double-clicking that item in the Lists palette, changing the highlighted text on the page, then clicking Update.

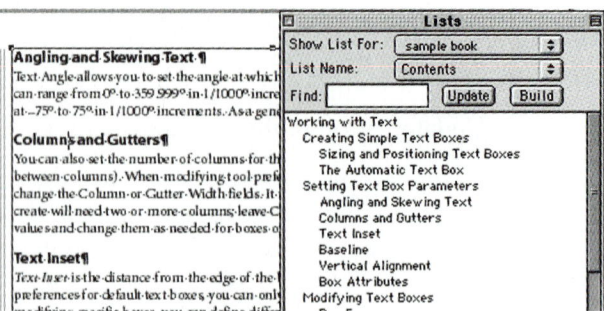

When the list is rebuilt, the error is fixed both in the main document and in the list, which means you don't have to fix the problem manually every time the list is rebuilt.

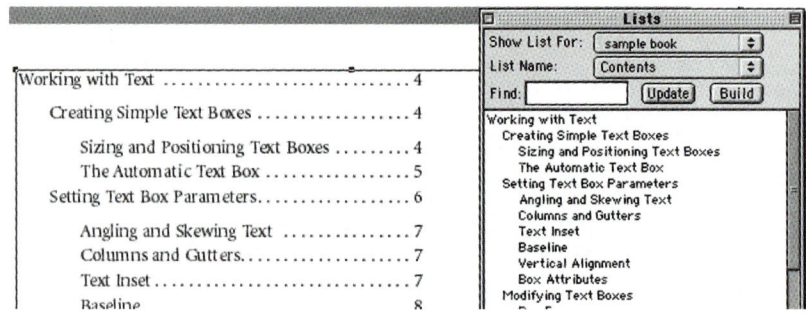

Changing Files in a Book

If you are building a list from a QuarkXPress book, you will run into a problem when changing the pagination of files in the book. Any of the following changes can cause problems when building a list from a QuarkXPress book:

- Adding or deleting a chapter.
- Adding or deleting pages from a chapter within a book.
- Reordering the chapter files in the book palette.
- Changing the Section Start of a chapter in a book.

When you make any of the above changes, the book palette displays the appropriate page numbers in the Pages column; any changes to the individual files automatically affect the other files, and the book palette changes accordingly.

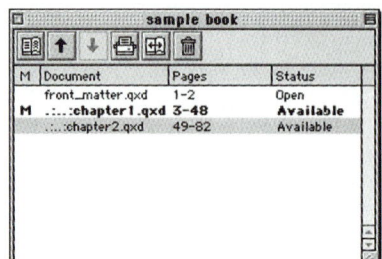 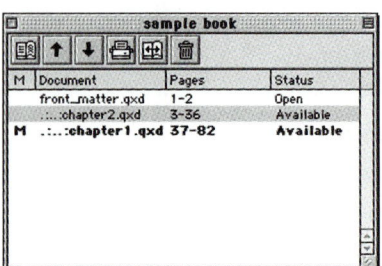

The book palette accurately reflects page numbering when the chapters are reordered, or when pages are added to or removed from a chapter.

The Lists palette does not display the page numbers for list items. If you click Update after changing a chapter, the list items display correctly in the new order.

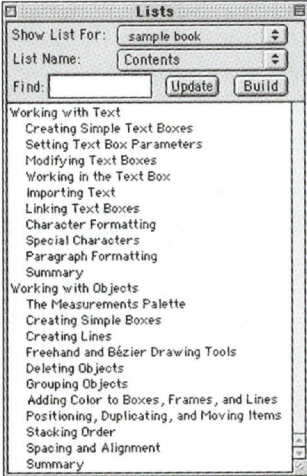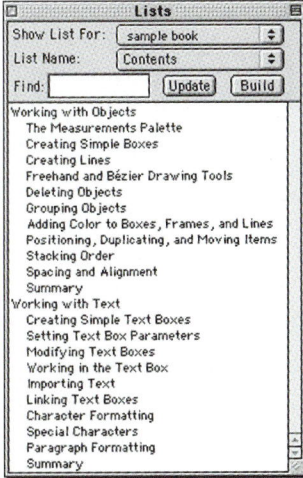

The Lists palette accurately reflects the changed order, but does not display page numbers.

The potential problem exists when you compile a book list into a document. Once you build a list, the page numbers for each chapter are saved as a part of each chapter file. If you make changes that affect the pagination of book chapters, the page numbers are accurately reflected in the Pages column of the book palette, and the items in the list appear in the correct order. The page numbers in the compiled list, however, are incorrect.

The problem of updating a compiled list is a bug in the software. The individual chapters in the book file are tagged with their page numbers when they are placed into the book palette. If you change the page numbering in the book — by reordering the chapters, or removing or adding pages to a chapter — the Build List feature does not accurately recognize the new page numbering.

After altering the order of the two chapters and rebuilding the list, the list appears in the correct order, but the page numbers have not updated correctly.

Solving the Problem

If you have made changes that affect the page numbering of the book chapters, you have to open every file that was affected by the change in pagination, save it, and close it again. This is as simple as double-clicking the affected files in the book palette and then choosing File>Close. Even though you have made no actual changes to the document, you are asked if you want to save changes. Clicking Yes to this warning corrects the page numbering in the list — which is the change you are being asked if you want to save.

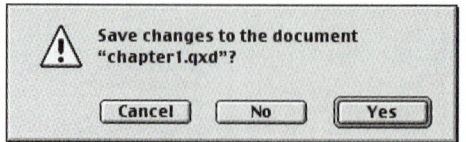

Once you have opened, saved, and closed each affected file, rebuilding the list will show the correct order and page number for all files.

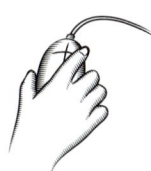

Compile the Document List

1. Double-click recipe_front.qxd in the book palette to open the document.

2. Select the Content tool in the Toolbox, and click the empty text box in the document page.

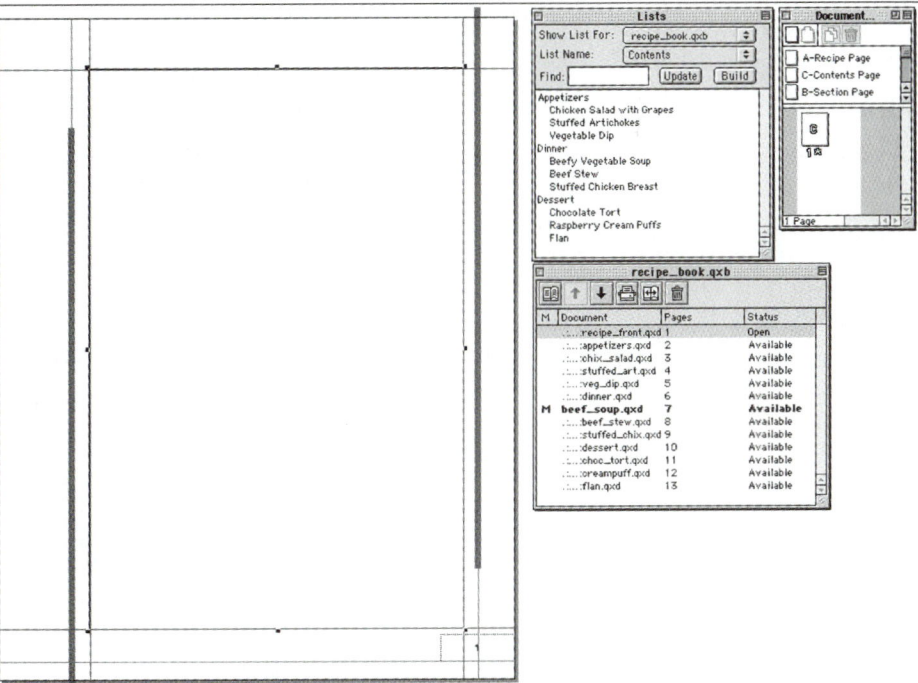

3. Click Build in the Lists palette. The book files are processed, and the list is built and formatted in the empty text box.

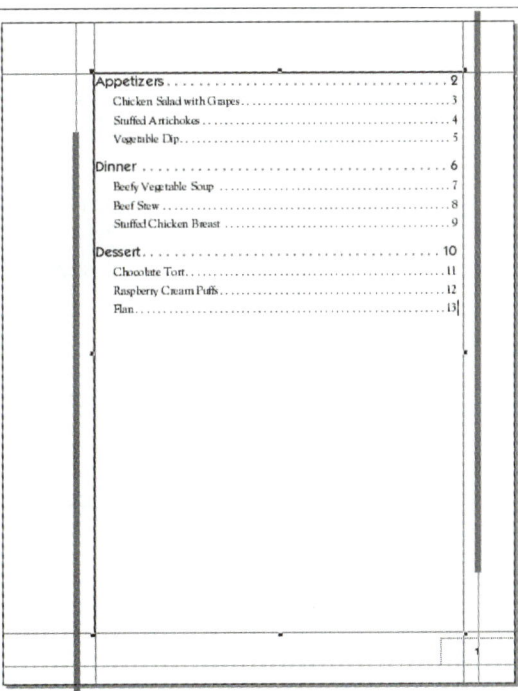

4. Look at the table of contents. Notice that, in the Dessert section, the recipes are not in alphabetical order, even though the file names in the book palette are.

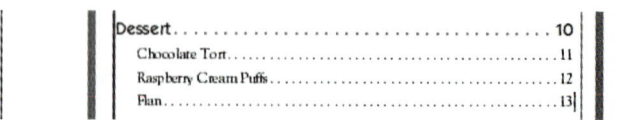

5. Highlight creampuff.qxd in the book palette, and click the Move Down button.

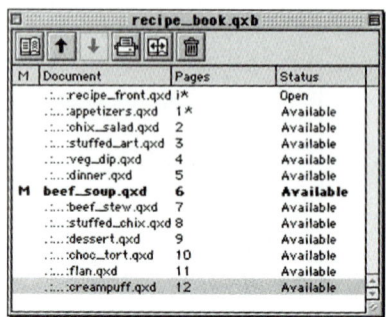

6. Click Update in the Lists palette. The order should change to reflect the change you made in Step 5.

7. Repeat this process to move Beefy Vegetable Soup after Beef Stew.

8. The first section — Appetizers — begins on page 2. The book palette shows that the recipe_front.qxd file is page 1 of the document. Front matter, however, should be numbered separately from the body of the document.

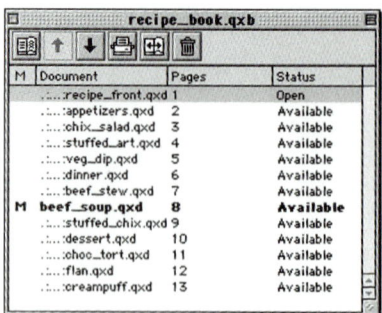

Choose Page>Section. Activate the Section Start check box, and change the Format menu to i, ii, iii, iv. Click OK.

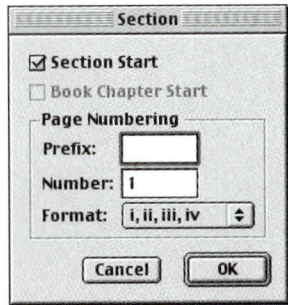

9. The book palette shows that the entire book is now numbered with lowercase Roman numerals.

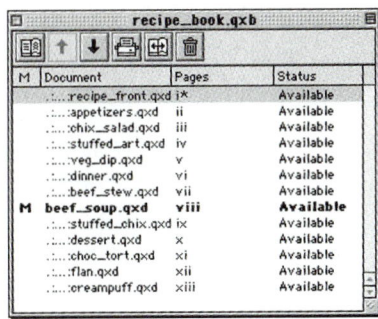

Save the document and close it.

10. Double-click the second file in the book (appetizers.qxd) to open the document.

11. With recipe_front.qxd still open, choose Page>Section. Activate the Section Start check box, change the Number field to 1, and choose 1, 2, 3, 4 from the Format menu. Click OK.

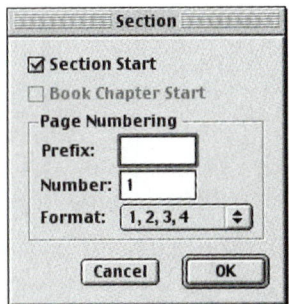

12. The book palette now reflects the new page numbering. Save the document and close it.

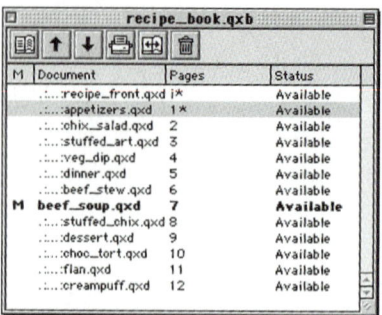

13. You now need to update the table of contents to reflect the new page numbering. Double-click recipe_front.qxd in the book palette to open the document. Click the text box on the document page with the Content tool. Click Update in the Lists palette, and then click Build. In the warning dialog box, click Replace to overwrite the existing table of contents.

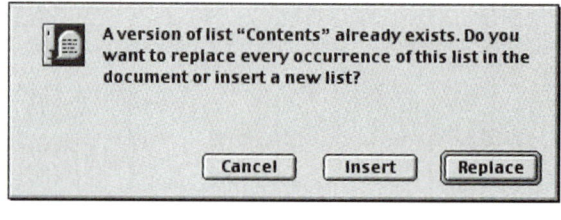

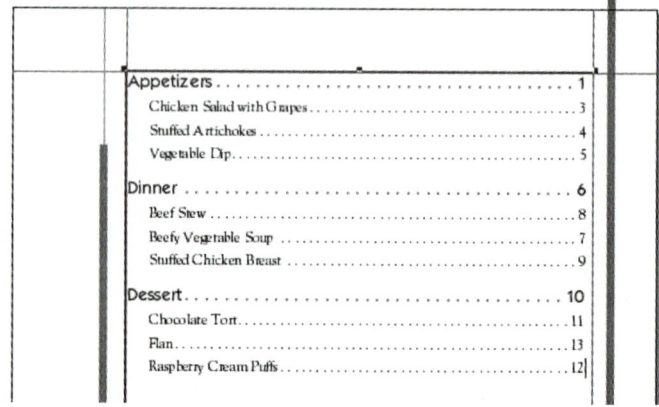

Notice that the page numbering is incorrect in the updated list. The Chicken Salad recipe begins on page 3 instead of page 2; Beef Stew is listed in the correct order, but on page 8 instead of page 7; Flan is also in the correct order, but on page 13 instead of page 12.

14. Double-click chix_salad.qxd in the book palette to open the file. Choose File>Close to close the file. Click Yes to the warning message asking you to save changes.

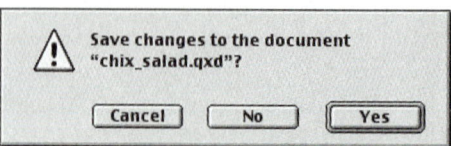

15. Click Build in the Lists palette to revise the list that is built into the document. Click Replace in the warning dialog box.

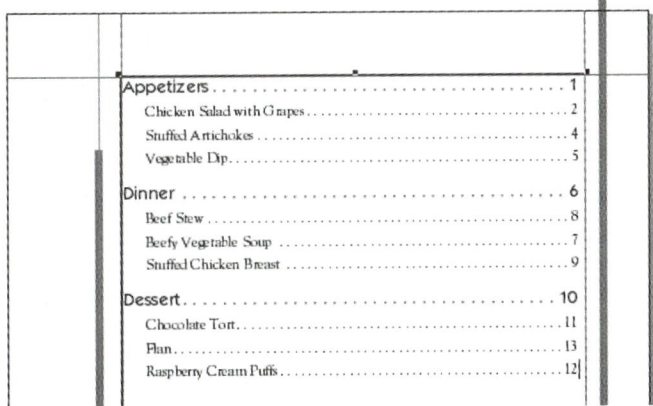

16. Notice that the Chicken Salad recipe is now listed correctly on page 2 of the book, but the following chapters still have incorrect page numbering. Open, save, and close the rest of the files in the book. When all files have been resaved, rebuild the list in the front-matter document.

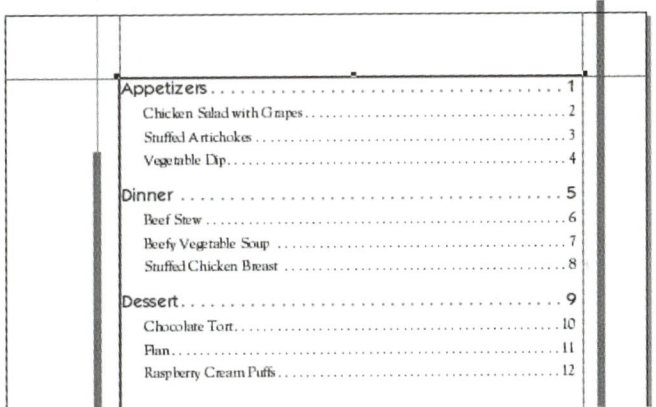

17. Save the document and close it, then close the book file.

Summary

You have learned that the Lists utility in QuarkXPress is a powerful tool that allows you to build and maintain tables of contents and other lists. With careful planning, and an understanding of the page numbering problems we discussed in this chapter, you know that the Lists utility greatly improves the production workflow for this aspect of long-document production. You learned how to use the List utility to monitor editorial priority of a document, or to use it in conjunction with the Book utility to keep track of multiple documents. You should understand the interaction between lists and style sheets, and how to create a list for all chapters of a QuarkXPress book. You also know how to modify and update a list, which allows you to have a working table of contents from even the earliest stages of a project.

5 *Building an Index*

Chapter Objectives:

Just as long documents generally have a table of contents and other lists, many publications also include one or more indexes to help readers quickly locate the information they want. QuarkXPress 5.0 includes a powerful index tool that significantly improves index creation within the production workflow, allowing you to plan, build, and maintain an accurate index for any document or book. In this chapter, you will:

- Learn the importance of planning before you begin to build your index.

- Examine the options in the Index Preferences dialog box.

- Explore the elements of the Index palette.

- Add entries to an index and define the specific settings for that entry.

- Create a cross-reference index entry.

- Define the formatting for each index entry.

- Build an index into a document.

Projects to be Completed:

- Stonington Letterfold Brochure (A)

- **Body Solution Booklet (B)**

- Cosciel Poster (C)

Building an Index

Like tables of contents and other lists, creating an index used to be an extremely time-consuming and labor-intensive process. A professional indexer was hired to go through each hard-copy page of a document, write down index entries and page numbers, manually compile the final alphabetized list, and typeset that list into the document. Any changes after the index was finished meant that the entire document had to be rechecked manually. QuarkXPress 5.0 includes an index tool that automates part of the indexing process, improving the production workflow and saving considerable time when changes, inevitably, are made.

Planning an Index

An index is the map to a publication's contents, providing the reader with an easy reference to specific content. Depending on your needs, you could theoretically use the Lists utility to create a basic index for projects such as catalogs requiring multiple indexes. The Quark Index utility, however, provides far more control for creating, generating, and maintaining a publication index.

It is a good idea to plan in advance. Several different elements can (and should) be defined before you build your index:

- Paragraph style sheets for index headings (if you use them)
- Paragraph style sheets for up to four levels of index entries
- Character style sheets for the page numbers of each index entry (if you want them to be formatted differently than the index entry)
- Character style sheets for cross-references
- Master-page layout using an automatic text box, in which the index will be built

Of these, the only one that is absolutely necessary to define in advance is the character style sheet that is applied to individual index entries. You should choose the style for an index entry when it is marked, but, obviously, you can't assign a style sheet that doesn't exist. It is far easier to do everything at once than to change it later, which means that you should define the style sheet before marking the index entries. (We will discuss the specific uses of style sheets later.) The important point is that some advance planning can make your life easier. You can always change the style-sheet definitions later in the process, but creating them in advance will save you time and effort in the long run.

Setting Index Preferences

You can define the Index preferences by choosing Edit>Preferences>Index.

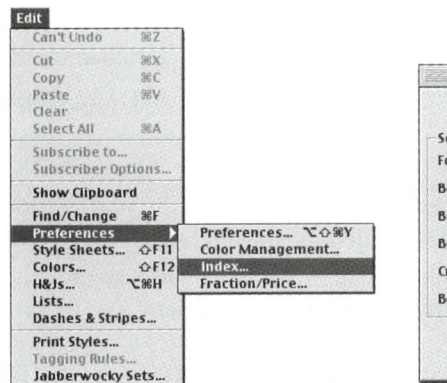 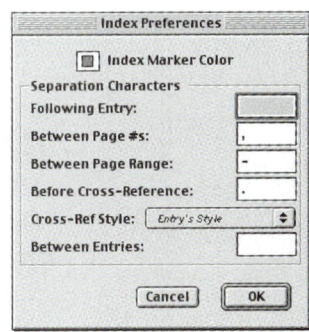

When text in a document is marked as an index entry, it is enclosed in an index marker (nonprinting brackets). The Index Marker Color option defines the appearance of an index marker in the document; clicking the square opens a Color Picker dialog box where you can change the marker color.

The color of index markers has no impact on the final index.

you select the Linking to
the Linking tool, the ed
the process of linking t

Index markers, or nonprinting brackets, indicate that the enclosed text is marked as an index entry.

Separation characters are used between references within an index entry. The purpose of these characters is to make the index entry readable, and to separate information into logical units. The Separation Characters options define how an index will appear when it is built.

- **Following Entry.** This option defines the character(s) placed between the end of the text and the first page number. You can place special characters (such as a paragraph return or a soft return) using the key codes for special characters in dialog boxes.

Soft return	\n
Paragraph return	\p
Tab	\t

  To achieve the following result, you have to type a colon (:) and press the Spacebar in the Following Entry field. If you forget the Spacebar, the colon will run directly into the first page number.

  Linking tool: 12, 15-16

- **Between Page #s.** This field defines the character(s) that appears between each reference (page or range) for a single index entry. The default value — comma-space (,) — is the most commonly used.

  Linking tool: 12, 15-16

  The Between Page #s character is placed between the page number (12) and the range (15-16).

- **Between Page Range.** If an index entry is marked to show a range of pages, this field defines how the range is indicated. The default value — hyphen (-) — is the most commonly used.

Linking tool: 12, 15-16

The Between Page Range character is placed between
the page numbers (15 and 16) in the range.

- **Before Cross-Reference.** If you include cross-references in your index, this option defines the character that is placed before the cross-reference entry. The default value — period-space (.) — is commonly used. You can also force cross-references onto a new line by typing the key code for a soft return (\n).

Linking tool: 12, 15-16. See also text chain

The Before Cross-Reference character is after the
last reference to the index entry (15-16).

- **Cross-Ref Style.** You can use this menu to assign an existing character style sheet to all cross-references in your index. You might, for example, define an italic or bold style sheet for any cross-reference.

- **Between Entries.** This option defaults to adding a paragraph return between index entries. If you want to build a nested index in which individual entries do not appear on their own lines, you can change this field to a different character (such as a semicolon).

Set Index Preferences

1. Open the file **recipes.qxd** from the **RF_Adv_Quark** folder.

2. If it is not already open, press "F11" to open the Style Sheets palette. Notice that the document includes style sheets Index1, Index2, Index Head, and Cross-Reference. Close the Style Sheets palette.

This file is essentially the same as the files you used in the previous two chapters, but the files have been combined into a single document.

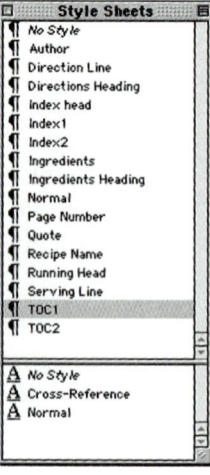

3. Choose Edit>Preferences>Index. Double-click the Following Entry field to high-light it, and press the Spacebar four times to add space between each term and its references.

4. In the Before Cross-Reference field type "\n" so that cross-references will appear on a new line.

5. Choose A Cross-Reference from the Cross-Ref Style menu.

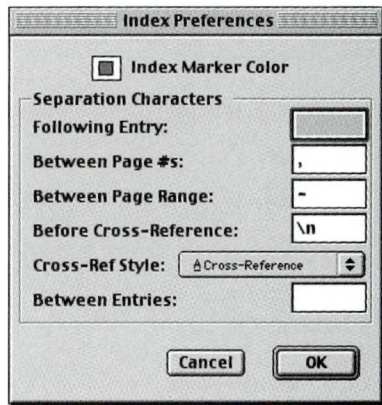

6. Click OK to close the Index Preferences dialog box.

7. Save the file in your **Work_In_Progress** folder, and leave it open for the next exercise.

Adding Index Entries

The Text field of the Index palette (View>Show Index) reflects any text that is highlighted in the document; the text in this field will become the index entry when you click Add in the Index palette.

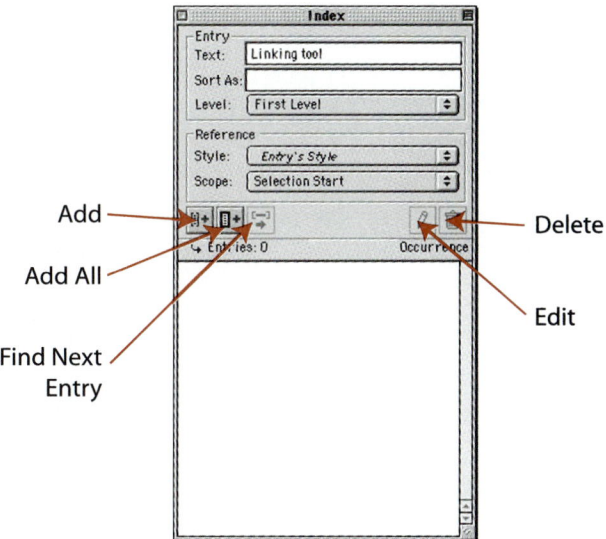

Once an entry is added to the index, it appears in the bottom of the Index palette. The Occurrence column shows the number of references to each index entry.

Clicking the arrow/+ (plus sign) next to an index term is referred to as "expanding" the term.

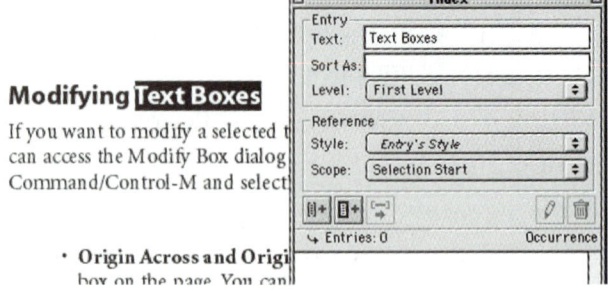

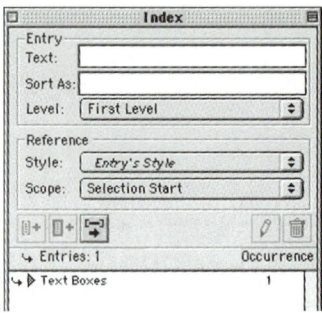

Clicking Add creates an index entry from the Text field in the Index palette. An index marker is added to the highlighted text in the document.

The Index palette lists every index term in a document. You can review the specific references to a term by clicking the arrow/+ (plus sign) next to the term. Once the term is expanded, you see a list of all references to that term.

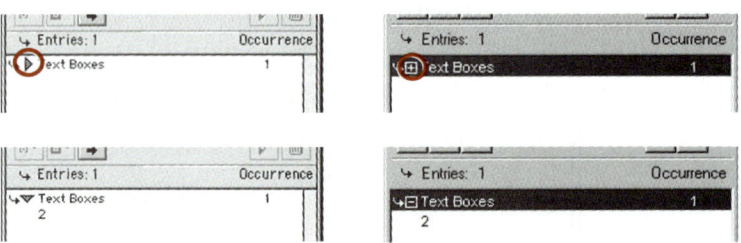

Clicking the arrow/+ (plus sign) next to a term (top) expands the term so that you can see the specific references (bottom).

Capitalization does not matter when adding an index entry. "Text Boxes" and "text boxes" are considered the same entry. When generating a final index, however, the capitalization used for each term in the index should be consistent — all words should be capitalized or none. (Of course, proper names should always be capitalized.) Be consistent when adding terms to an index.

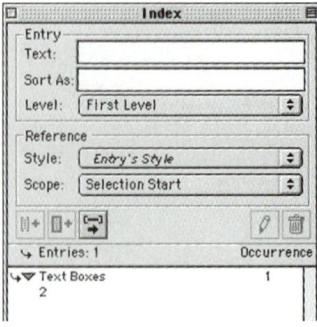

This Index palette shows that the term "Text Boxes" is referenced one time, on page 2 of the document.

Changing the Index Entry Text

Once you define the location of an index marker by highlighting text in the document, you can change the contents of the Text field. For example, you can highlight the word "colors" in the document, then delete the "s" from the text field. Clicking Add creates the index entry "color" in the index list. Changes in the Text field do not affect the highlighted text in the document.

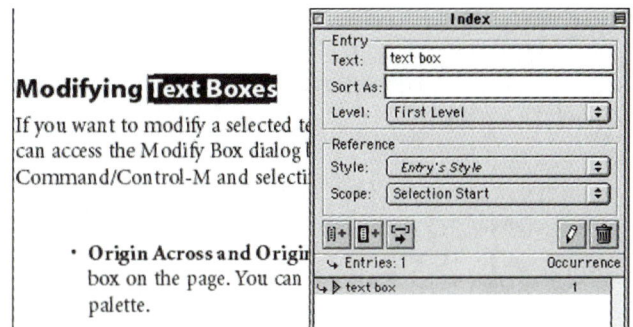

Selecting from Existing Terms

When you have highlighted a word in the document, you can also alter the Text field by clicking an existing index term in the Index palette. If you highlight the word "colors" for example, clicking the term "color" in the Index palette changes the Text field to match the existing index entry. This is an excellent way to maintain consistency in an index. When you click the Add button, the Occurrence column in the Index palette shows that another reference to the same entry has been added.

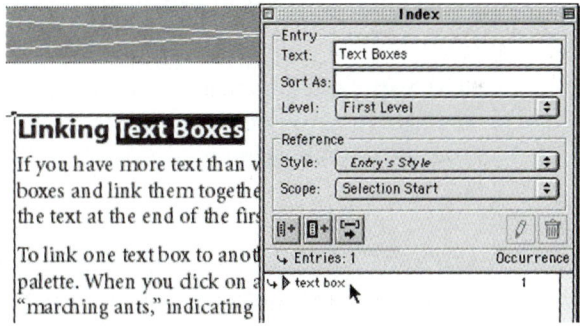

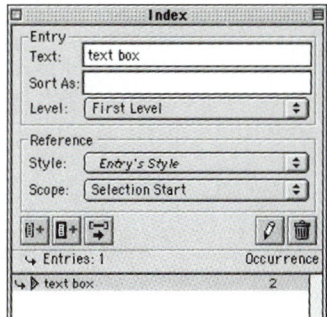

Clicking an existing index term changes the Text field to match the term you selected.

Be consistent. If one proper name is reversed in the index, all names should be reversed.

Reversing Index Text

If you hold down the Option/Alt key while clicking the Add button, the order of the words in the Text field is automatically reversed and added to the list of terms; "Linking Tool" would be added to the index as "Tool, Linking". This process is useful for indexing proper names, or if you want all index entries to appear on the first level.

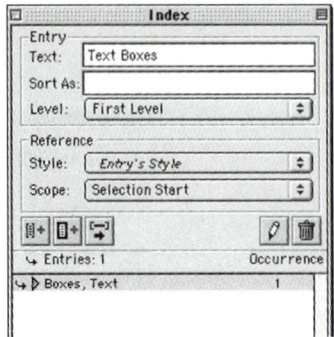

Changing Sort Order

The Sort As field allows you to change the way an entry is alphabetized in the index. By default, index entries are strictly alphabetized; abbreviations are alphabetized according to the letters in the abbreviation, rather than by the word that has been abbreviated.

Mr. appears after modify	Mister appears before modify
St. appears after sister	Saint appears before sister

To change the order in which an index entry is listed, you can enter different text in the Sort As field.

Changing the Sort Order does not affect the wording of the entry in the index or the highlighted text in the document.

The Sort As field is also helpful for reordering proper names. If you do not want to change the order of names in the final index, you can still alphabetize by last name. Most people, when looking for names in an index, look for the last name. You can add names to the index, without changing the text listing but alphabetizing by last name.

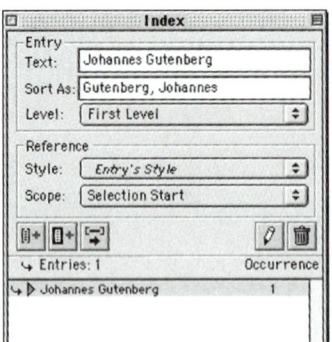

In the final index, this entry will be listed as Johannes Gutenberg but will be alphabetized as Gutenberg, Johannes.

Index Level

The Level menu in the Index palette defines the level of an index entry, with up to four levels of nesting.

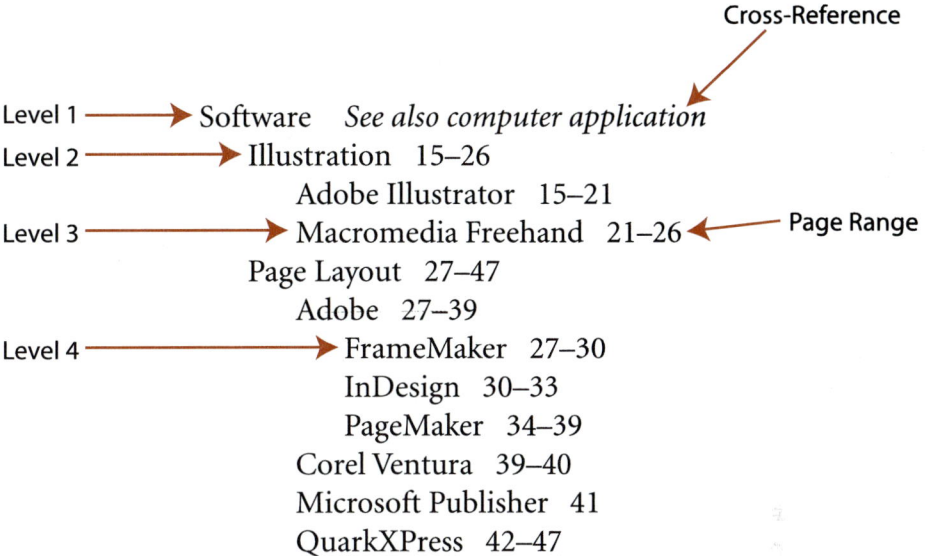

When you choose a sublevel from the Level menu, clicking the Add button makes the entry subsidiary to the term marked by an arrow in the lower half of the Index palette. To move the arrow to a different term, click in the blank space to the left of the target term.

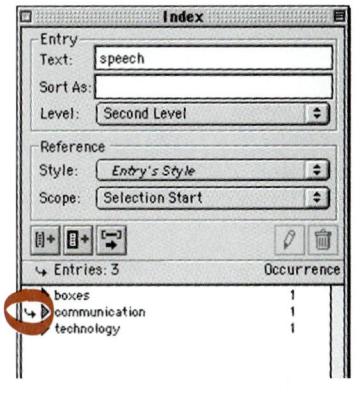

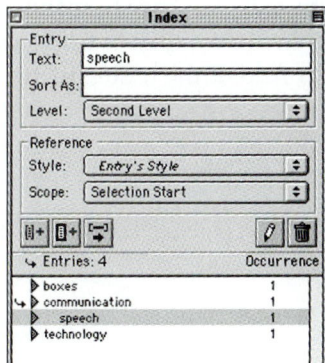

*Clicking the Add button places speech as a second-level entry
in relation to the first-level communication entry.*

If you change the Level menu once, make sure you change it back to First Level when you are done adding the sublevel entries.

With a second-level entry marked as the target, the Fourth Level option is unavailable.

If a third-level entry is the target, the Second Level option is unavailable.

If a fourth-level entry is the target, the Second Level and Third Level options are unavailable.

Capitalization does not matter when using the Add All button.

Changing Levels

The level field defaults to the previous selection. If the last entry was a second-level entry, the next will also be a second-level entry unless you change the Level menu before clicking Add. It is easy to forget to change the Level menu, but very important to remember. If you add one entry as Second Level, then forget to change the menu back to First Level, you will end up with a long list of secondary entries that have nothing to do with the parent. You then have to edit each one that is placed incorrectly, which can be extremely time-consuming depending on how long it took before you noticed the problem.

When you do change the Level menu, the available options depend on the position of the target arrow in the bottom of the Index palette. If the arrow icon indicates a second-level entry:

- Leave the menu at Second Level to create another second-level entry for the same parent.
- Choose Third Level from the menu to add a new entry that is subsidiary to the indicated second-level entry.
- Choose First Level to create a new entry with no relation to previous entries.

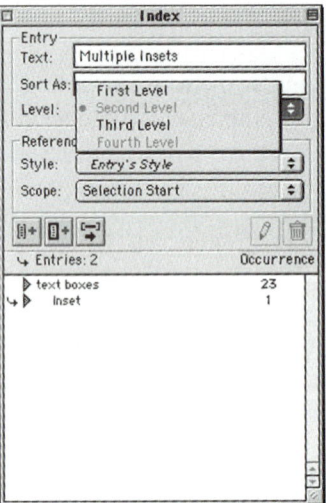

Using Add All

Although you have to manually identify the terms that will be indexed in a document, the Index utility does help to speed the process. With a word or phrase entered in the Text field of the Index palette, you can use the Add All button to mark every instance of that text in the same document automatically. (The Add All button only finds the text within a single Quark document; it does not find all instances in multiple chapter files of a QuarkXPress book.) All of the markers created by clicking the Add All button will have the same definition, including any changes you make in the Text and Sort As fields.

When using the Add All button, the text must match exactly since the utility searches for the Text field as a whole word(s), not part of a word. Text Box and Text Boxes are not the same.

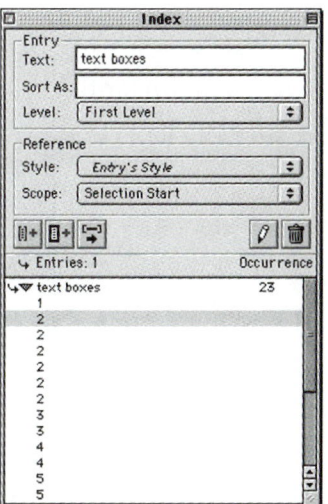

Clicking the Add All button automatically searches for and marks every instance of the term within a document.

Style

The Style menu in the Index palette Reference area defines the character style sheet that will be used to format the page numbers for the index entry. This menu is set to Entry's Style by default, which means that the page numbers will be set in the same style as that used for the level of index term when the final index is generated. You might use a character style sheet to set off one or more particular instances of each entry, for example, to indicate the page on which a term is first defined.

As we mentioned previously, it is a good idea to define this character style sheet before you begin marking entries. If the style sheet doesn't exist, you can't access it from the Style menu. To remedy this, you would have to define the style, and then later go back and edit each entry to which you want to apply the style. It is much easier to make these choices beforehand than to hunt down changes later.

Like the Level menu, this menu retains the selection from the previous entry. If you change the Style menu to something other than Entry's Style for one or more terms, make sure that you change it back again when you no longer want to apply a special style.

Defining the Reference Scope

The Scope menu defines what is referenced — page, page range, or cross-reference — for each index entry. Like the Level and Style menus, this menu retains the selection from the previous entry. Any entry added after changing the Scope menu will have the same Scope definition until you alter the menu again. For every index entry, you have a number of options:

• **Selection Start**. This option lists the page number on which the selected text begins, even if the selected text extends across more than one page.

- **Selection Text**. This option lists the page or pages on which the selected text exists. If the selection extends beyond one page, the range of pages (e.g., 2–3) is shown for that reference.

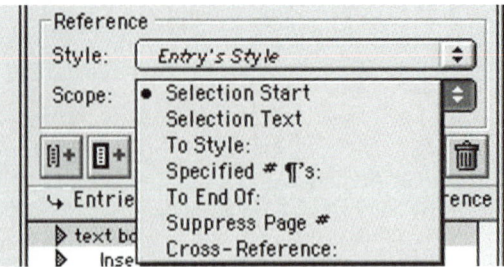

- **To Style.** If this option is selected, the entry lists the page or range of pages, beginning with the selected text and continuing to the next instance of the style you choose. If you want to mark an entire section of a document, for example, you can select the first word in the section and choose To Style: Heading. The range of pages between the selection and the next Heading in the document are listed.

  Be careful when using the To Style option. The default value is to mark an entry To Style: Next. This means that the reference listing ends as soon as any style sheet other than the selected text is used. Style sheets for bullets, inline captions, and so on are considered the "next" style sheet, so the scope may not be as broad as you like. If, on the other hand, you choose a style that is not used after the selected text, the entire rest of the document will be included in the entry reference.

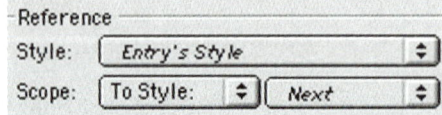

- **Specified # of ¶s**. This option allows you define the number of paragraphs (beginning with the highlighted text) that are marked as the scope of the reference.

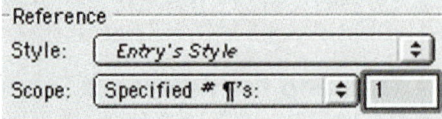

- **To End Of**. This option presents a secondary menu that enables you to define an entry range beginning with the highlighted text and continuing to the end of the Story or Document.

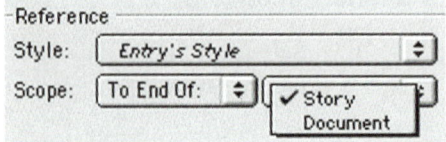

- **Suppress Page #.** This option adds an index entry that does not include page numbers. This can be used to add first-level index entries that exist only so second-level entries can be added.

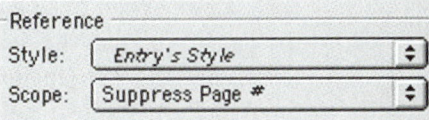

- **Cross-Reference.** This option allows you to add a reference to another term in the index. If you choose Cross-Reference from the Scope menu, a secondary menu enables you to choose the type of cross-reference that will be used (See, See Also, and See Herein).

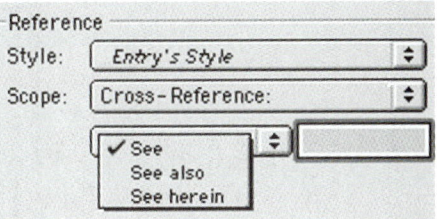

- **See.** This choice is generally used if an entry does not also list page numbers. Abbreviations may use a See cross-reference, sending the reader to the index entry that spells out the abbreviation.

  > PDF
  > *See Portable Document Format*

- **See Also.** If an entry lists page numbers, this option is generally used to direct a reader to a related topic.

  > PDF 17, 25, 42-47
  > *See Also Adobe Acrobat*

- **See Herein.** When creating complicated nested indexes, this choice is used to direct the reader to a related subtopic instead of to another first-level term in the index. In the following example, the See Herein informs the user to look at the secondary term Portable Document Format under the first-level PDF, instead of in the alphabetical position of Portable… in the main index.

  > PDF
  > *See Herein Portable Document Format*
  >   Compression 43-44
  >   Creation 42
  >   Fonts 43-45
  >   Output 45-47
  >   Portable Document Format 42
  >   Service Providers 47

If you are creating a cross-reference, a text field appears next to the Scope secondary menu. This field is used to define the text that is cross-referenced. In other words, anything in this field will be listed after the See, See Also, or See Herein. When this field is highlighted, clicking an existing index term in the palette changes the field to match the term on which you clicked. If you are working with multiple files in a book, you may need to manually type a term into the reference text field if that term does not exist in the current file. Be careful that what you type matches what exists in another document.

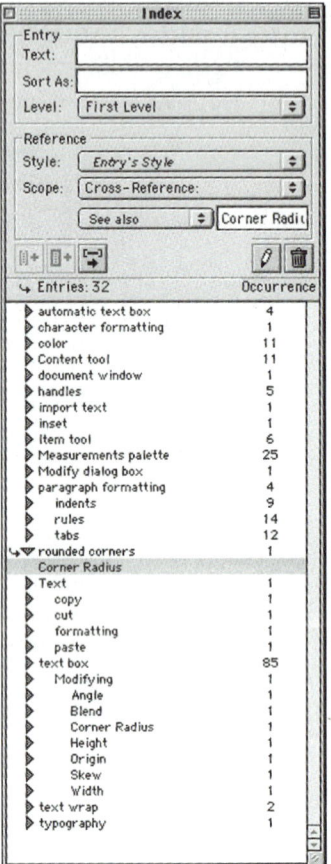

If an index entry is a cross-reference, you can see the referred text by clicking on the arrow next to the entry.

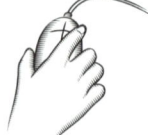

Mark Index Entries

1. With the file recipes.qxd still open, select View>Document Layout.

2. Select View>Show Index.

Front matter is usually not included in a publication index.

Step 6 reveals a problem with the Quark Index utility. Each page of this document is created as a separate story; the text boxes are not linked. The To Style index option only applies to text within the same text chain. Because no other text exists in this chain, the entry refers only to this page of the document.

3. Navigate to page 1 (not page i) of the document.

4. Highlight the word Appetizers on the document page. Notice that the highlighted text automatically appears in the Text field of the Index palette.

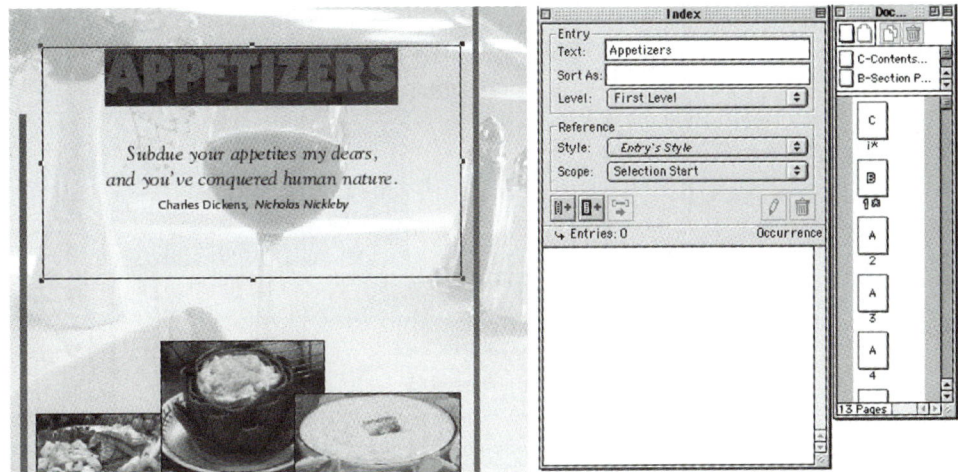

5. Choose To Style from the Scope menu and select Running Head in the secondary menu. Click the Add button.

6. Click the arrow/+ (plus sign) next to Appetizers in the Index palette to show the specific reference.

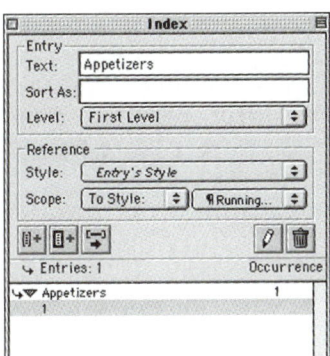

7. Highlight the words Charles Dickens on the document page. In the Index palette, choose Selection Start from the Scope menu. Option/Alt-click the Add Reversed button. The name is automatically reversed and added to the index as Dickens, Charles.

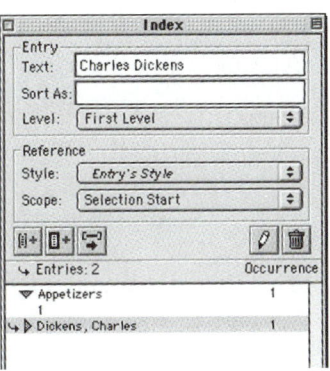

8. Navigate to page 2 of the document.

9. In the document, highlight the word Chicken in the recipe name, and click the Add All button in the Index palette.

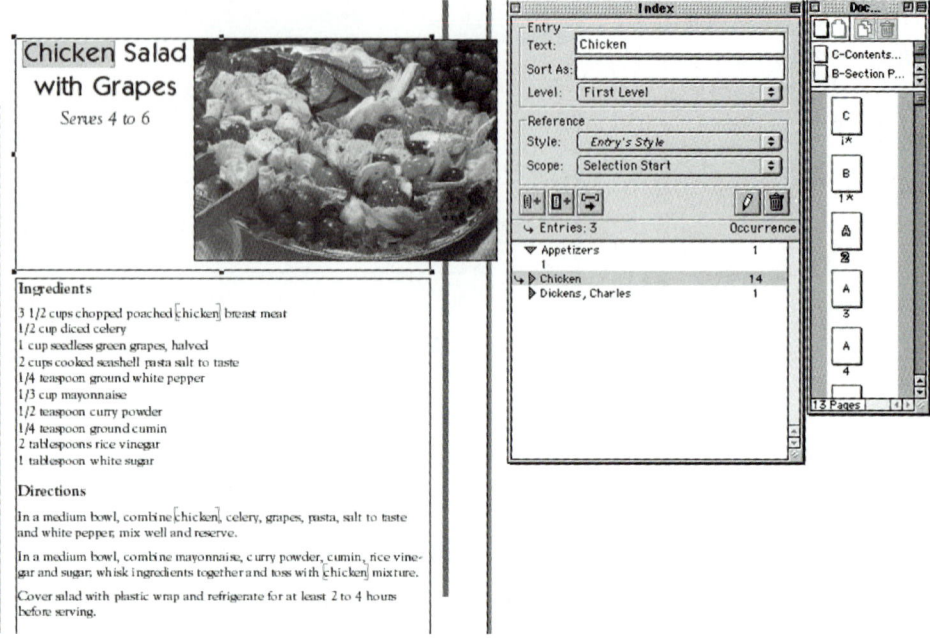

Using Add All places 14 references to Chicken, 4 of which are on this page.

10. In the document, highlight Salad in the recipe name. Choose Second Level from the Level menu of the Index palette. Make sure the target arrow is pointing to Chicken in the list of terms, and click the Add button.

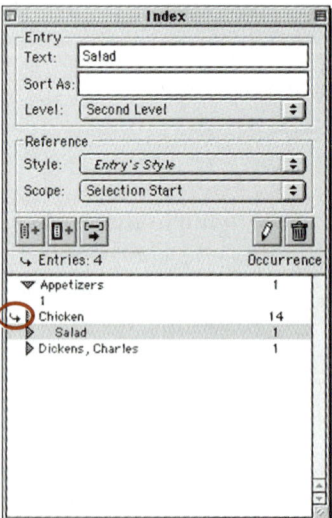

The arrow next to the index entry indicates the targeted first-level term.

11. In the document, highlight the word Grapes in the recipe name. Change the Index palette Level menu back to First Level, and click the Add All button.

12. In the document, highlight the entire recipe name. Choose Second Level from the Level menu. Click in the empty space to the left of the term Appetizers in the Index palette to make Appetizers the target first-level term. Click the Add button.

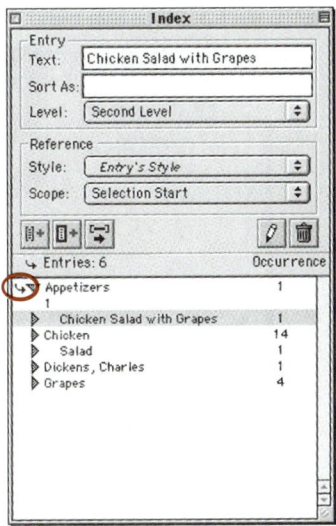

The arrow next to the index entry indicates the targeted first-level term.

13. Navigate to page 3 of the document.

14. Highlight the word Artichokes in the recipe name.

15. In the Text field of the Index palette, delete the "s" at the end of the word. Change the Level menu to First Level and click the Add All button.

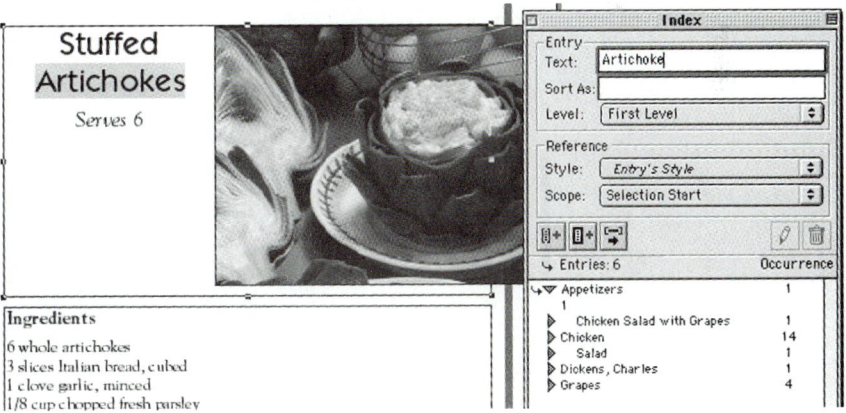

16. Notice that three instances of Artichoke are referenced, but no marker is placed around the text that is highlighted in the document because that word is plural, and is therefore not the same as the text for which you searched in Step 15.

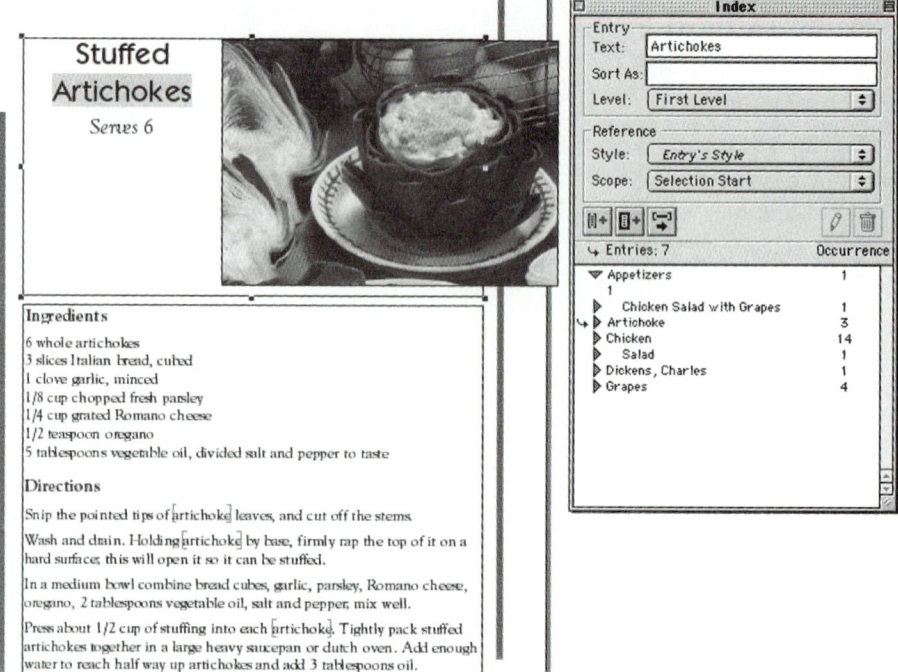

17. The word Artichokes is still highlighted in the document window, and again appears in the Text field of the Index palette. Click Artichoke in the Index palette to change the Text field, but to leave the plural word highlighted in the document. Click the Add button.

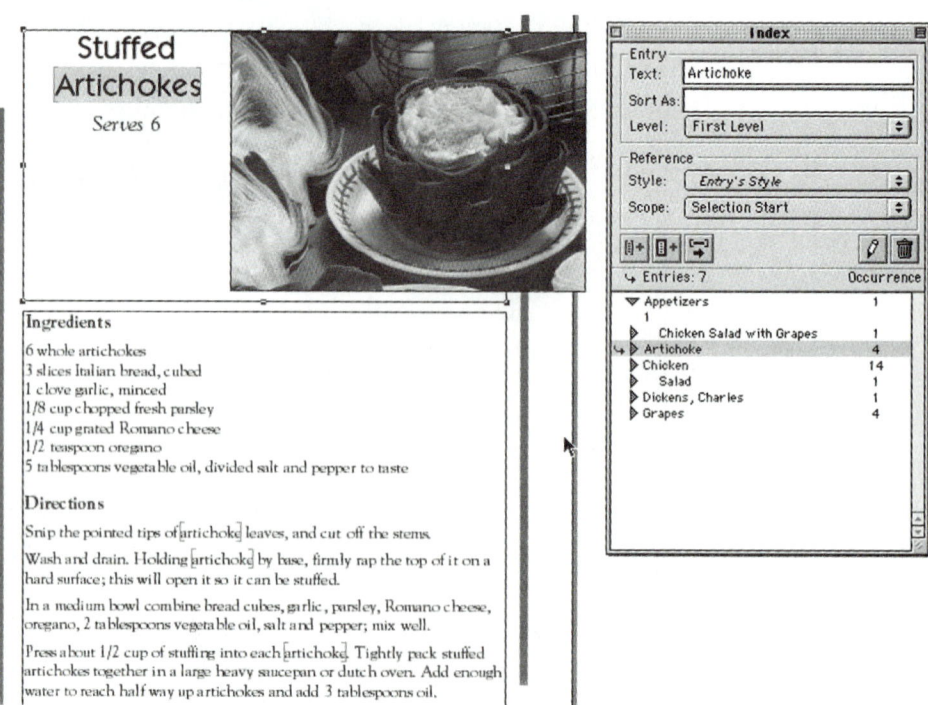

18. In the document, highlight the entire recipe head. Select Second Level from the Level menu, make sure Appetizers is the target term in the Index palette, and click the Add button.

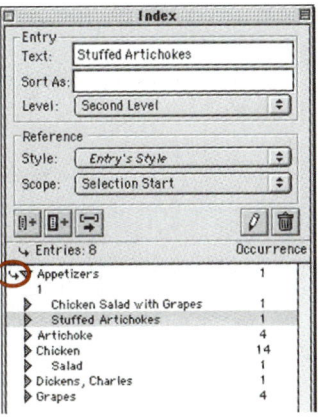

The arrow next to the index entry indicates the targeted first-level term.

19. Navigate to page 4. In the document, highlight Dip in the recipe name. Change the Level menu to First Level, and use the Add All button to add Dip to the index.

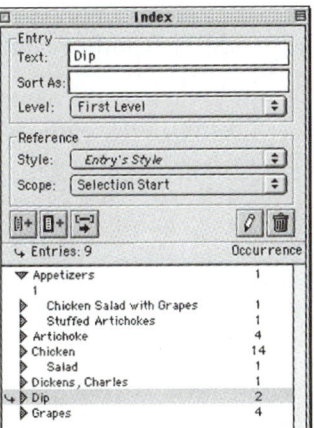

20. In the document, highlight Vegetable in the recipe name. Change the Level menu to Second Level, make sure Dip is the target term in the Index palette, and use the Add button to add Vegetable to the Index as a second-level term under Dip.

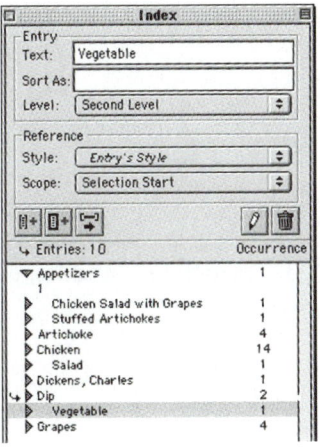

21. In the document, highlight the entire recipe name. Add it as a second-level term under Appetizers.

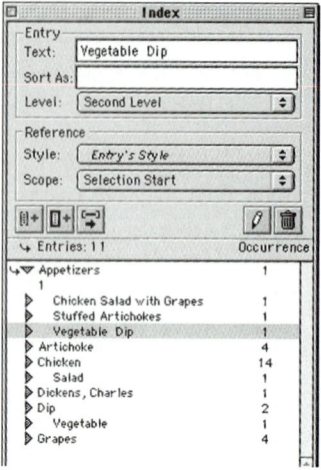

22. Go through the rest of the document, finishing the addition of index terms using these guidelines:

    Add each section name as a first-level term.

    Add each author name in reverse order.

    Add each recipe name as a second-level term under the appropriate heading. (Add just the entire recipe names, not the individual words from each name.)

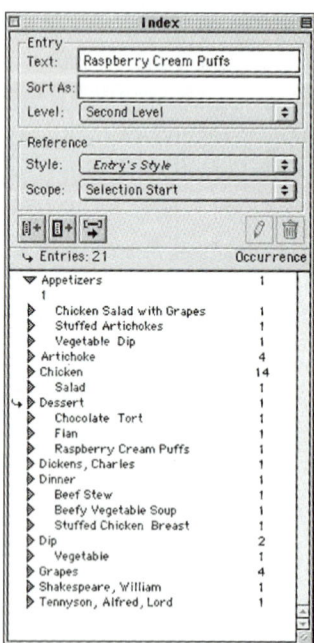

23. Save the file and leave it open.

Add Cross-References

1. Navigate to page 6 of the open document.

2. Highlight the word Beef in the recipe head. Choose First Level from the Level menu.

3. In the Reference section, choose Cross-Reference from the Scope menu. Click the second-level Beef Stew entry in the Index palette (under Dinner) to change the cross-reference text field.

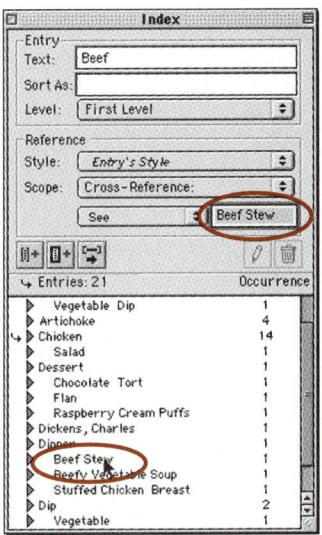

When the text field next to the secondary Scope menu is highlighted, clicking Beef Stew in the Index palette changes the cross-reference text field to "Beef Stew".

4. Click the Add button. Expand the term Beef in the Index palette so that you can see the specific references for the term. The cross-reference (Beef Stew) is listed as the only reference for Beef.

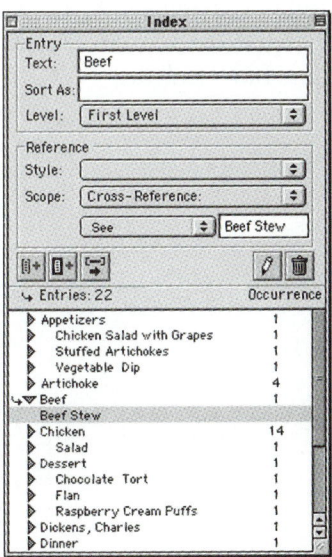

5. Navigate to page 7 of the document.

6. In the document, highlight Beefy in the recipe name. In the Index palette Text field, delete the "y" so that the entry is just Beef.

7. Highlight the text field next to the secondary Scope menu, and click Beefy Vegetable Soup (under Dinner) in the Index palette. Click the Add button to create a second cross-reference for the term Beef.

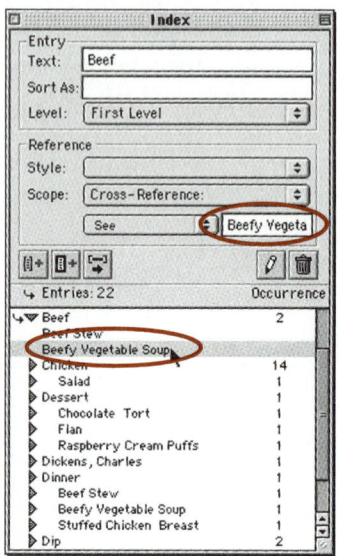

8. Save the file, and leave it open for the next exercise.

Editing Index Entries

Once an entry has been created, you can change any of its characteristics by highlighting that entry in the Index palette and clicking the Edit button. When you are modifying a term or entry, the Edit button is darkened. Clicking the Edit button again finalizes your changes.

Double-clicking a reference in the Index palette automatically navigates to and highlights the appropriate text in the document window, and activates the Edit mode in the Index palette.

If a term is highlighted in the list, you can only change the Text, Sort As, and Level options of the term. If a specific reference is highlighted, you can change the Style and Scope options for that entry.

If you edit the level of a term, remember that you must also designate the appropriate target.

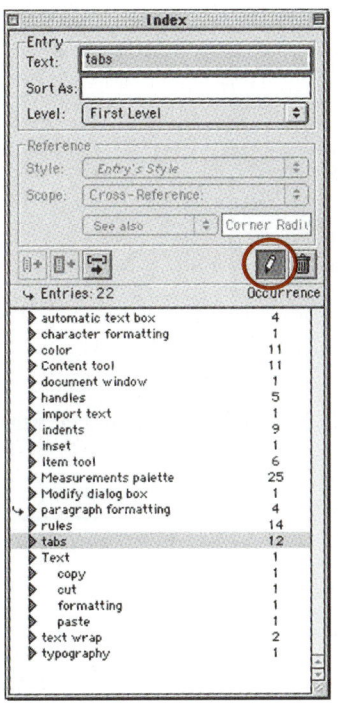
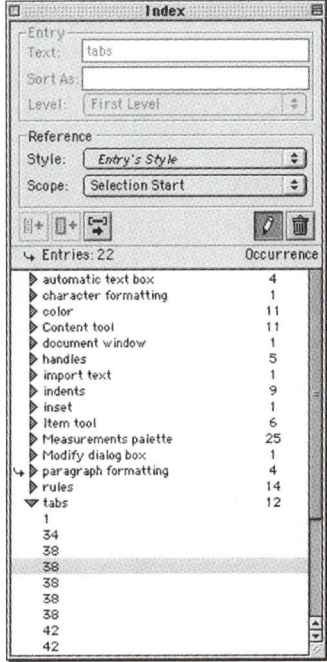

Deleting Index Entries

You can delete any term or reference by highlighting an item in the list and clicking the Delete button. Deleting an index entry or reference has no effect on the document text.

If a specific reference is highlighted in the Index palette and you try to delete it, a warning shows that the reference will be deleted. Clicking OK deletes the reference; clicking Cancel leaves the reference in the index.

Although deleting an index entry from the Index palette has no effect on the document text, deleting text from the document will also delete any index markers and references that are within the text you delete. You will not get a warning when you delete text that is marked.

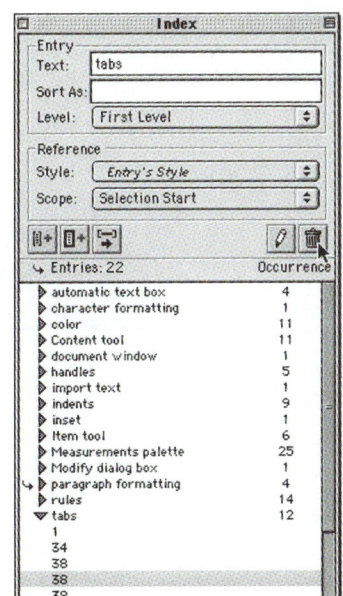

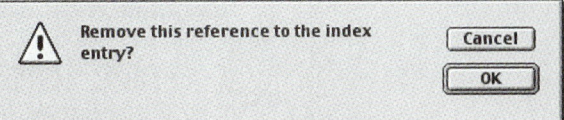

If a term is highlighted, a warning shows that deleting the term will also delete all references to that term.

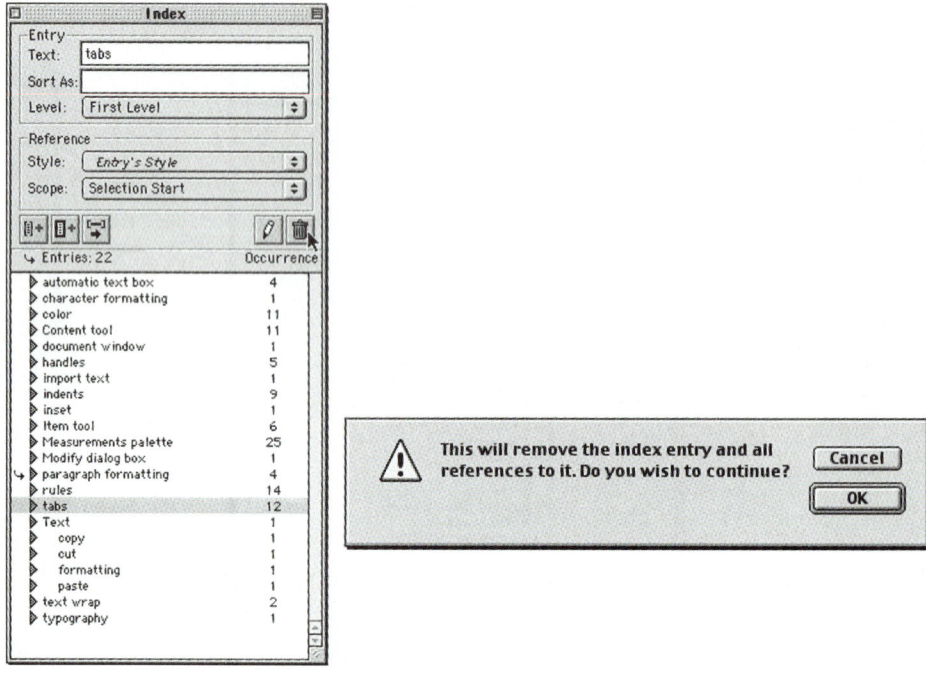

If a first-level term that includes sublevels is highlighted, a warning shows that deleting the first-level term also deletes the sublevels.

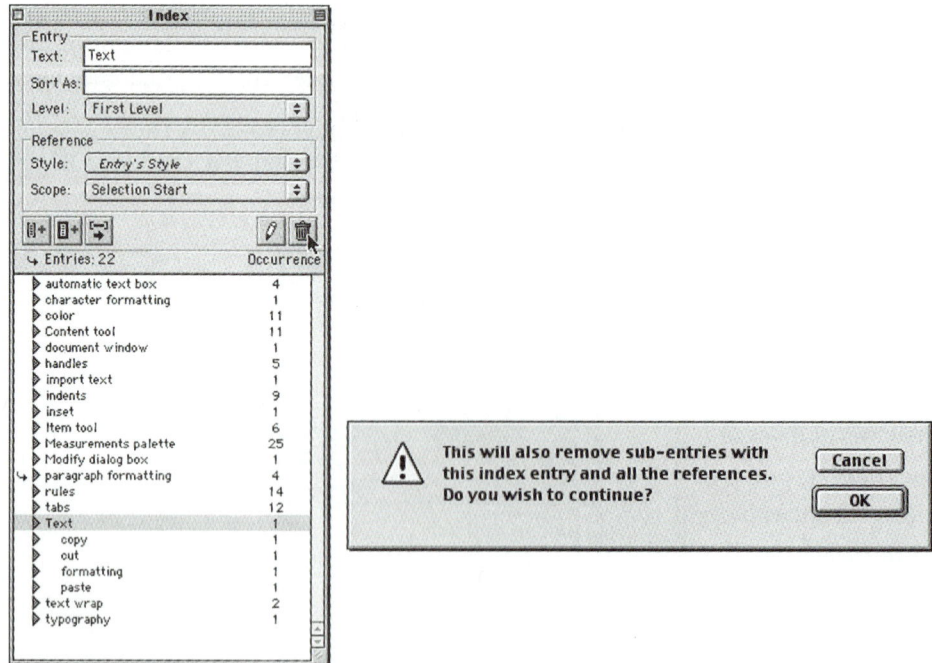

Tips for Marking Index Terms

Only one index marker can exist for a highlighted text string in the document. If you try to add a second index marker (such as a See Also cross-reference) to the same highlighted text, you get a warning that a reference already exists at the selected location.

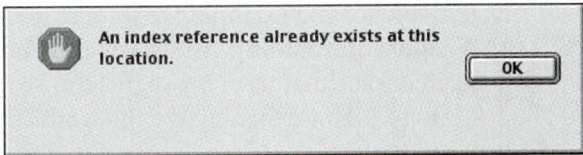

There are two ways around this limitation.

Changing an Existing Entry

When you have multiple references to the same term on a single page, the Index palette will show every reference, including duplicates. In other words, if a term is referenced three times on page 6, page 6 will be listed three times for that term in the Index palette. When you build the final index, however, only one instance of a term per page will be listed in the final index. If you want to add a cross-reference for that term, you can edit a duplicate page number in the Index palette to be a cross-reference.

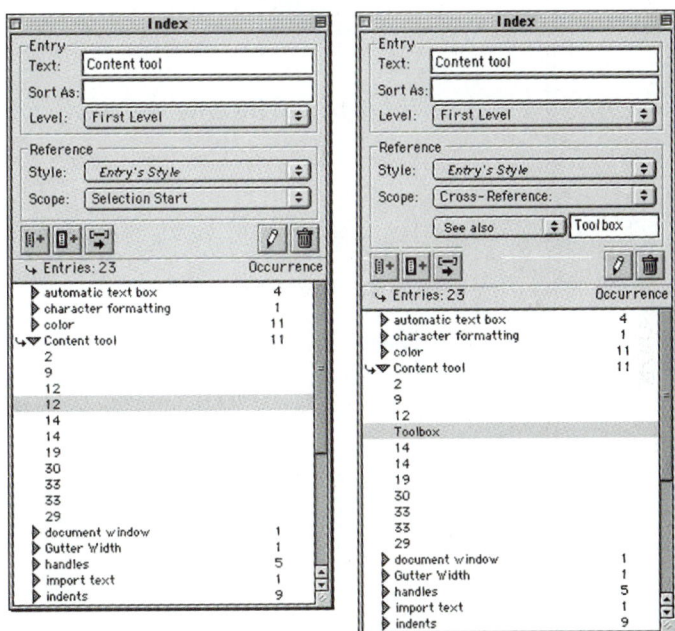

Use an existing duplicate entry to create a cross-reference.

Choosing an Adjacent Word

If a term has only one page reference or does not have any duplicate references, you can add a cross-reference by selecting a word near the existing reference, then changing the Text field to the appropriate term.

In the following example, we want to add a See Also cross-reference to the term "character formatting", which only has one page reference. Double-clicking on the page reference for that term highlights the appropriate text in the document. Using the Content tool, we highlighted the word "between" (immediately before the character formatting text).

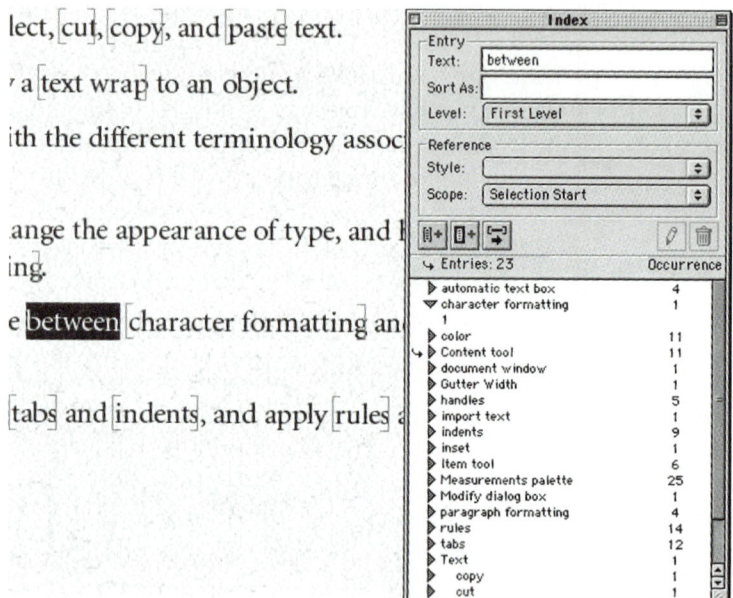

Once "between" is highlighted, clicking character formatting in the Index palette changes the Text field for the selected index marker. We then selected Cross-Reference in the Scope menu, selected See Also in the secondary menu, and chose paragraph formatting as the reference text.

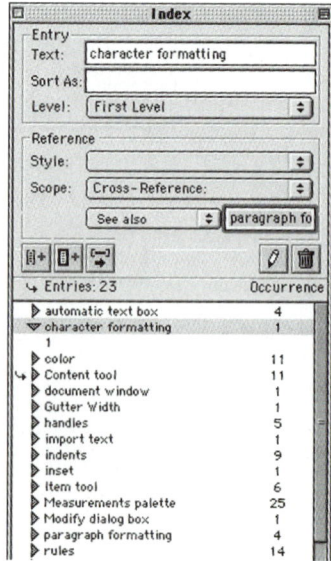

Clicking the Add button created the cross-reference. Even though markers surround the word between, the Index palette shows that the cross-reference is in the correct place under character formatting.

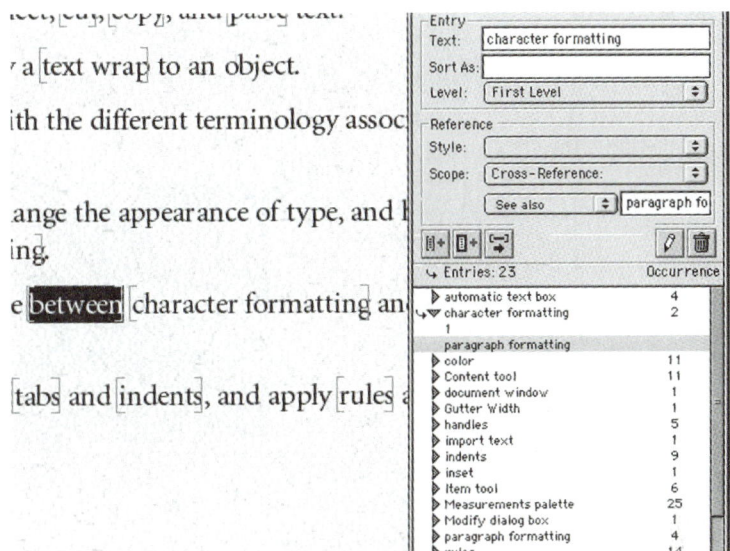

Overlapping Index Markers

Index markers cannot overlap in the document. In the following example, Gutters Width is already marked. If you highlight Columns and Gutters and click the Add button, you receive an error message.

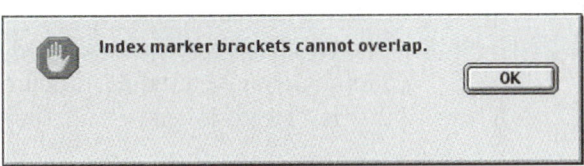

An index marker can be wholly contained or nested within another marker (e.g., [automatic [text box]]). In the following image, the right bracket of the second marker exists even though you can't see it.

If you want to reference part of an existing reference, you have to change the Text field in the Index palette manually. In the previous example, you could highlight Columns in the document, and then type Columns and Gutters in the Text field. Clicking the Add button places the index marker around Columns in the document, but the Index palette shows that the entry Columns and Gutters has been added.

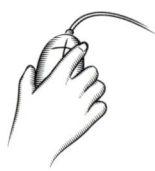

Edit Index Entries

1. In the open file, expand the second-level term Chicken Salad with Grapes so that you can see the specific reference to the term.

2. Double-click the reference (2) to highlight that index marker in the document window.

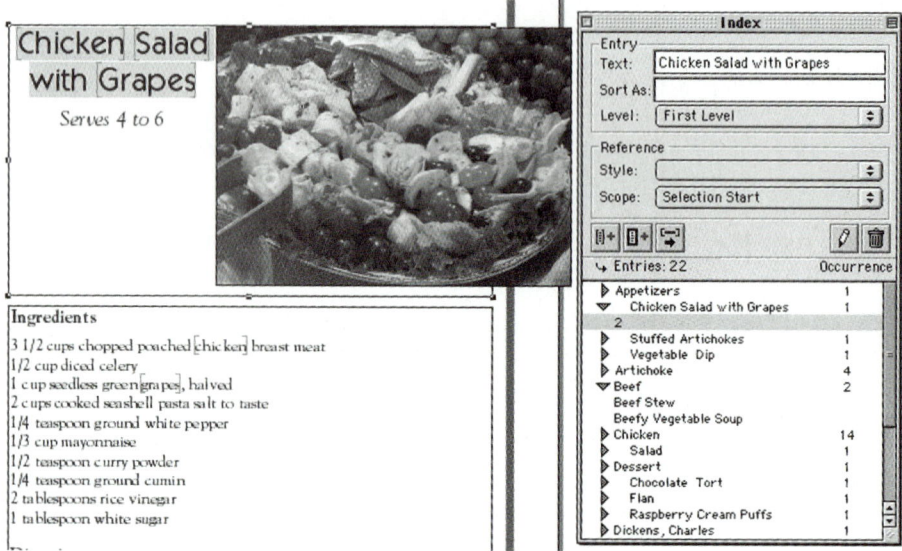

3. You need to add a first-level term for the same text, but you can't put two markers in the same place. In the document window, highlight "with" in the recipe name. In the Index palette, click the second-level "Chicken Salad with Grapes" to change the Text field.

4. Choose First Level from the Level menu, and click the Add button. Because you are adding the same term at a different level, Chicken Salad with Grapes is added as a first-level term instead of as a second reference to the existing second-level term.

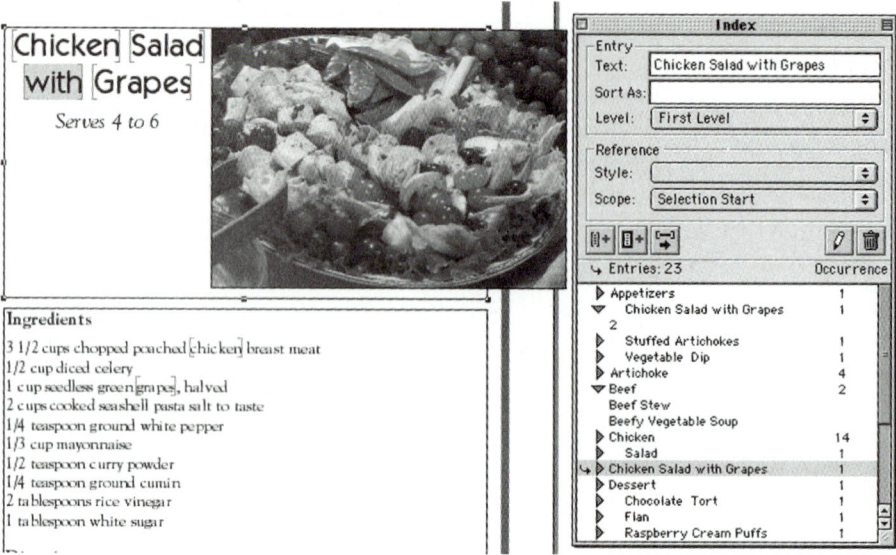

Table of contents should not be included, generally, in the index.

5. Expand the level-one term Chicken. The first two references are to page i, which is the table of contents. Double-click one of these references in the Index palette.

6. Click the Delete button in the Index palette to remove the reference. Click OK to the warning.

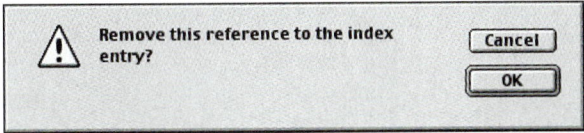

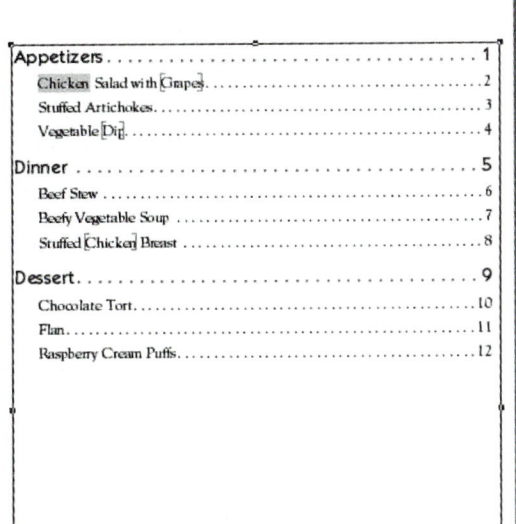

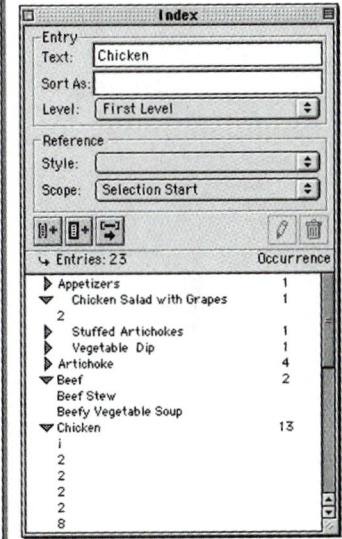

The reference to the table of contents is deleted, but the document text has not been affected.

7. Expand the first-level term Grapes in the Index palette. In the document window, double-click Grapes in the Chicken Salad line to highlight the words. Notice that the Index palette automatically changes to reflect the highlighted entry.

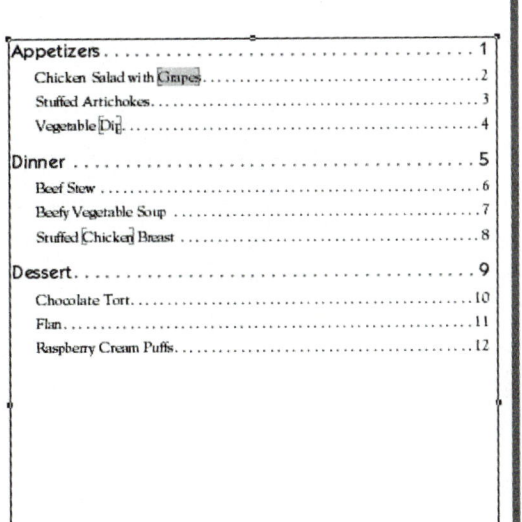

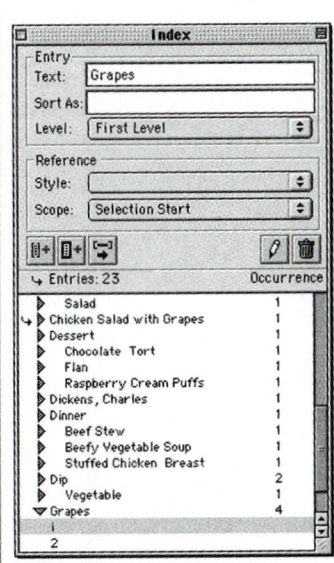

8. Click the Delete button in the Index palette, and click OK to the warning.

9. Highlight the term Dip in the fourth line of the table of contents. Click the Delete button in the Index Palette.

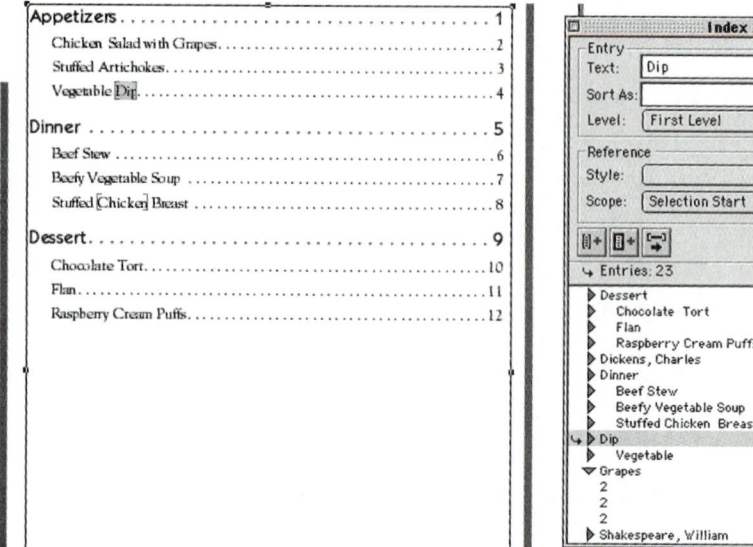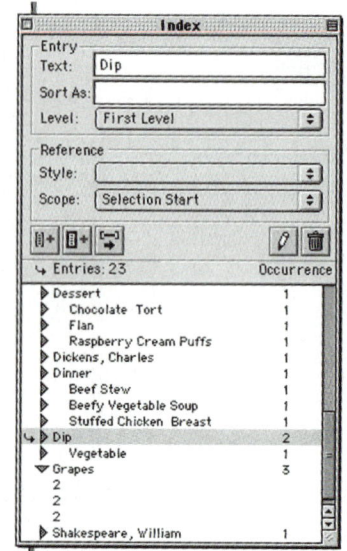

10. Because the term is highlighted instead of a specific reference, clicking Delete will remove the term and all subentries. Click Cancel to the warning.

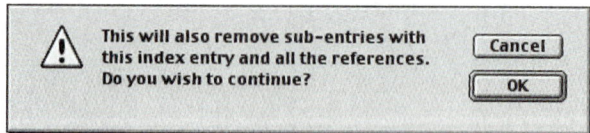

11. Expand the term Dip in the Index palette.

12. Again double-click Dip in the document window. Notice that the specific reference is now highlighted instead of the term.

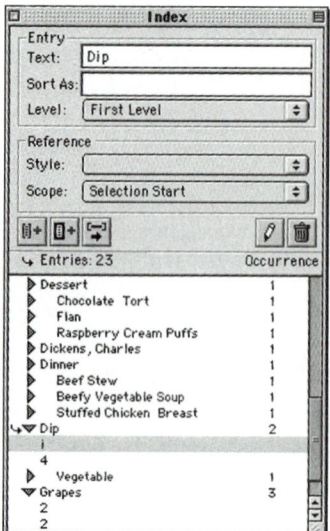

13. Click Delete and then click OK to the warning.

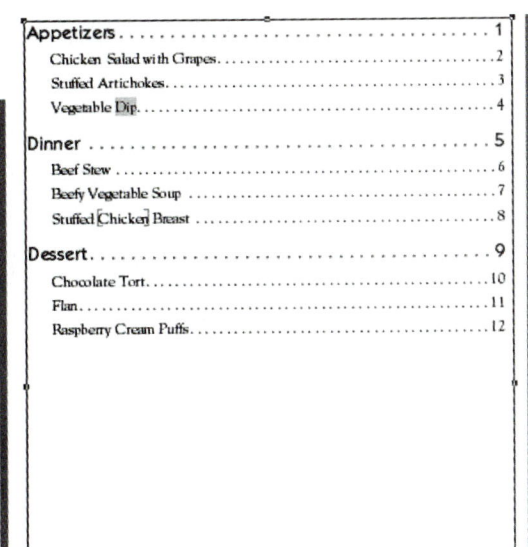

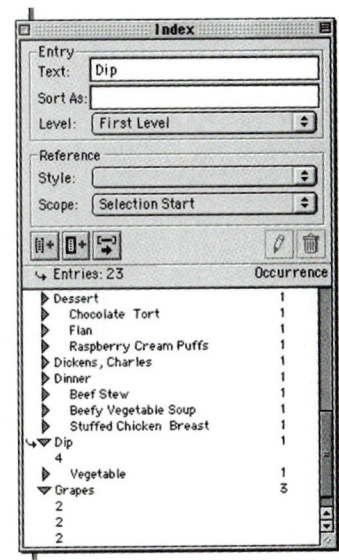

14. Continue deleting all index references (not the terms) from the Table-of-Contents page.

15. Highlight the term "Tennyson, Alfred, Lord" at the bottom of the Index palette.

16. Click the Edit (Pencil) button. Change the Text field to "Lord Tennyson, Alfred". In the Sort As field, type "Tennyson, Alfred, Lord" so that the term is still alphabetized by the name (Tennyson) rather than the title (Lord).

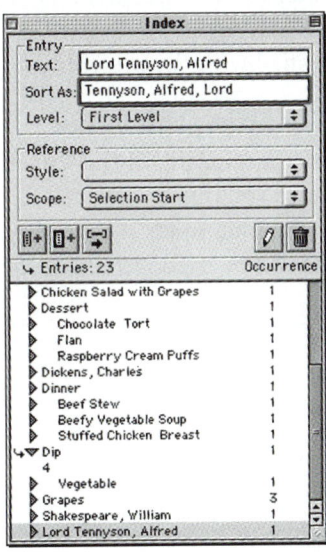

Nonstandard entries such as this present a problem when using the Add Reverse option. The best solution is to change the Text field manually, when necessary.

17. Click the Edit button again to finalize the edit.

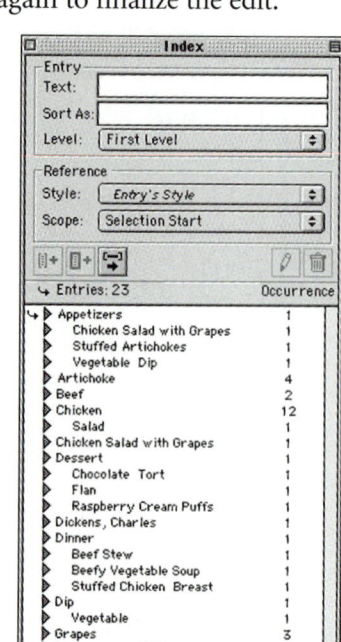

18. Save the file and leave it open.

Building an Index

When you are finished tagging index entries, you can prepare to build your final index. The first step is to review the index preferences (Edit>Preferences>Index). When you are satisfied with the preferences, you can choose Utilities>Build Index.

Formatting the Index

In the beginning of this chapter, we stated that some advance planning is important before you build your index. The Build Index dialog box presents the formatting options for the final index. This dialog box allows you to choose the style sheets and master pages that will be used to format the different levels of index entries.

When you are working with an entire book, it is a good idea to create a separate file for the index at the end of the document.

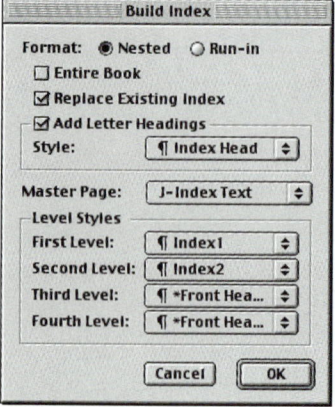

- **Nested or Run-in**. The Nested and Run-in radio buttons determine how the entries in the index are placed. In a nested index, each term begins on a separate line; this is the most common and the easiest for the reader to use.

> Automatic text box 3, 28
> Character formatting 1
> > *See also paragraph formatting*
> Color 4-5, 7-8, 21, 23, 40
> Columns and Gutters 5
> Content tool 2, 9, 12, 14, 19, 29-30, 33
> Document window 2
> Gutters Width
> > *See also indents*
> Handles 2-3, 11
> Import text 1
> Indents 1, 21, 33-35, 41

A run-in index squashes everything into a sentence-like format. This method of indexing can be convenient for saving space, but is difficult for the reader to use.

> Automatic text box 3, 28; Character formatting 1, *See also paragraph formatting*; Color 4-5, 7-8, 21, 23, 40; Columns and Gutters 5; Content tool 2, 9, 12, 14, 19, 29-30, 33; Document window 2; Gutters Width: *See also indents*; Handles 2-3, 11; Import text 1; Indents 1, 21, 33-35, 41

- **Entire Book**. This check box enables you to build the index for all chapters of a QuarkXPress book at one time. This option combines the indexes from every document contained in the Book palette; all of the indexes are alphabetized as a single unit so that the terms from chapter 1 are in the correct position with respect to chapter-2 terms, and so on. If the same term appears in more than one chapter, the references to that term are combined into a single entry.

- **Replace Existing Index**. If you have already generated an index for a document, this option allows you to overwrite the existing text in the same place. As a general rule, the index should not be compiled until a document is complete. Any last-minute changes, however, especially if the text reflows or pages are renumbered, may require that you rebuild the index.

The ability to rebuild an index is one of the greatest advantages of using the Index utility. Although marking the individual entries still requires time and effort, it is easy to build, modify, and rebuild the index for any document.

This option is also useful if you change your mind about the index preferences, choose to apply different style sheets, or even decide to create a new master-page layout for the index. Once the entries are tagged, building the final index is a fairly simple process that can be performed as many times as necessary without much effort.

Any manual changes you make to the index once built will be lost if you choose Replace Existing Index.

- **Add Letter Headings**. Extremely long indexes can benefit from letter headings. This is a matter of personal taste, but the point of an index is to make the document more accessible to the user. If an index runs for several pages, or includes more than one level, letter headings can be helpful. If you choose the Add Letter Headings check box, you can then select a style sheet for those headings.

- **Master Page**. This menu allows you to define the master page that will be used for the document index. The only requirement for an index master page is that it must have an automatic text box. Unlike building a list, you do not have to create a text box that is the target for building an index. Advance planning means that you create a master-page layout for the index before building the index. When you click OK in the Build Index dialog box, new pages are added at the end of the active document, using the master page specified in this menu.

- **Level Styles**. These options define the style sheets that will format each level of index entry. Once again, advance planning means that these style sheets must be created before building the index. Once the index is built, you can change the formatting options for each style sheet just as you would any other style sheet.

A

automatic text box   3, 28

C

character formatting   1
    See also paragraph formatting
color   4-5, 7-8, 21, 23, 40
Columns and Gutters   5
Content tool   2, 9, 12, 14, 19, 29-30, 33
    See also Toolbox

D

document window   2

G

Gutters Width
    See also indents

H

handles   2-3, 11

I

import text   1
indents   1, 21, 33-35, 41
inset   4
Item tool   2, 4, 9, 14, 29

M

Measurements palette   3, 7, 18, 21-22,
    25-26, 28-30, 35, 40, 42
Modify dialog box   4

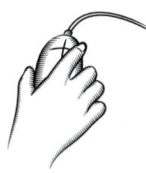

Build the Index

1. In the open file, select View>Document Layout to show the Document Layout palette (if it is not already visible).

2. Choose Utilities>Build Index.

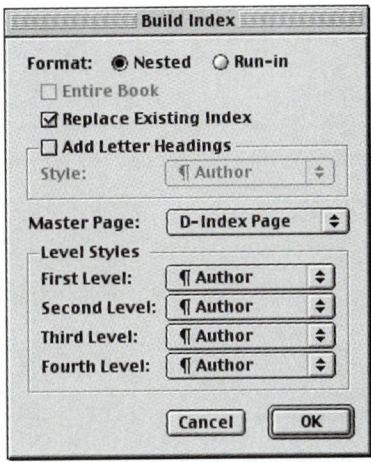

3. Select the Add Letter Headings check box, and choose Index Head from the Style menu.

4. The Master Page menu defaults to D-Index Page because that is the only master page in the document that uses an automatic text box.

5. Select Index1 in the Level Styles: First Level menu.

6. Select Index2 in the Level Styles: Second Level menu.

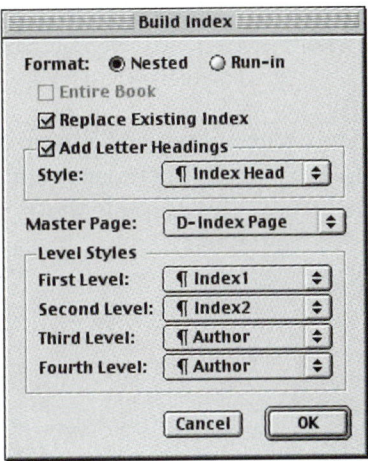

The master page used to build an index must have an automatic text box.

Because we are discussing how to create an index, this document was created with the necessary style sheets and master-page layouts that you need to complete the exercise. In a real-world project, you would have to create the style sheets and master-page layout before building the index.

You don't need to change the Third Level and Fourth Level menus because this index only uses two levels.

7. Click OK. Notice that a new page was added automatically to the document using the master page designated in the Build Index dialog box.

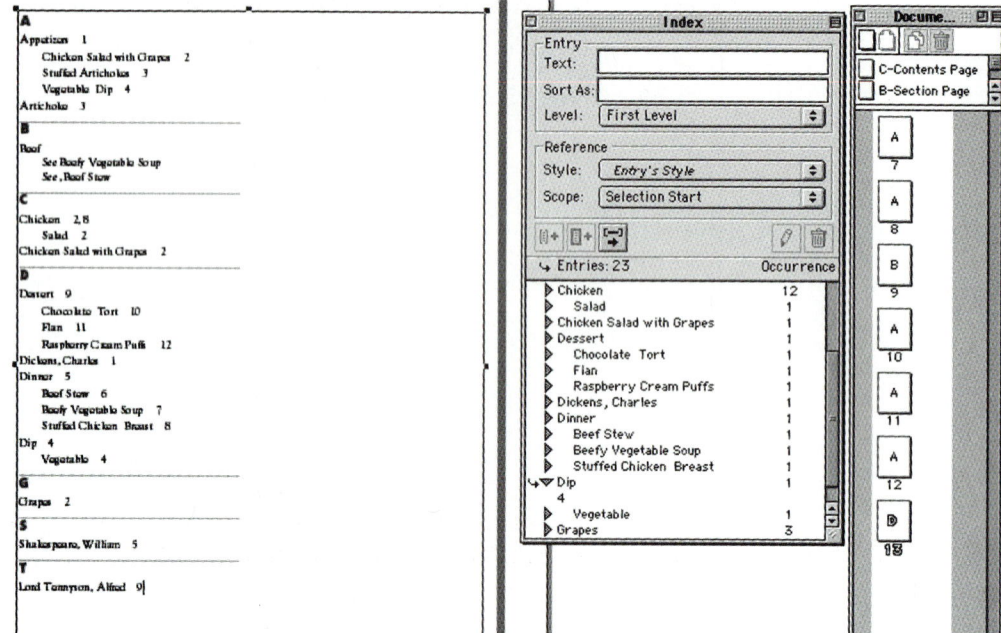

8. Save the file and leave it open.

Reviewing the Index

The results of the previous exercise show a potential problem with the Index utility. Under the B heading, the first-level term Beef lists two cross-references. The second cross-reference, however, has a comma before the words "Beef Stew".

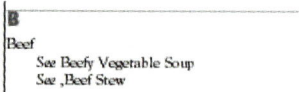

The Index utility treats multiple cross-references as it would treat multiple page references for a listing. In the Index Preferences dialog box, we defined a soft return before cross-references; this example shows that each reference appears correctly on a separate line.

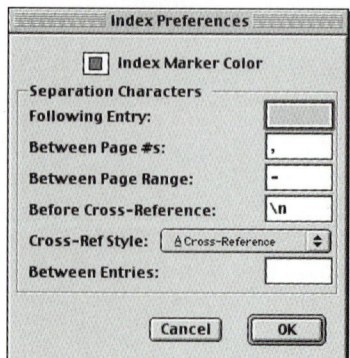

They are also treated, however, as individual references for the same term, so the Between Page #s character is placed between the two references. The type of reference (See, See Also, or See Herein) is programmed to appear before each cross-reference — including a space after the text — so the comma is placed in the middle of the second and additional cross-references. The only way to fix this problem is to delete the commas manually once the index is final. If you delete the commas and then rebuild the index, you have to delete them again.

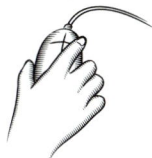

Finish the Index

1. Delete the comma before Beef Stew in the second cross-reference under Beef.

2. Save the file and close it.

Summary

Having completed the exercises in this chapter, you should recognize that the index you created is incomplete; you understand that the exercises were designed to show you the elements of building an index. As you know, an index should be as thorough as possible to help the reader. You understand that building an index — even using the software's tools — takes planning, thought, and time.

You learned to consider the style sheets and master page for an index before you build it, and how to define index preferences early in the process. You created index markers, defined the scope of different markers, and added multiple levels of index terms. You also worked with cross-references, built an index into the document, and learned about the potential problems of using the Index utility.

Complete Project B: Body Solution Booklet

Free-Form Project #1

Assignment

You have been hired to create a special brochure for the Travel Bureau of Costa Rica. The brochure will be distributed to travel agents in the United States and Mexico, so you have to create two versions of the brochure — one in Spanish and one in English. The Travel Bureau has provided quotes they would like to include, but wants to use primarily images to invite people to visit Costa Rica.

Design two versions of the same brochure using the diecutting template provided by your service provider. Make sure that you incorporate the correct folding allowances so that the text does not get lost in the fold. Use as many or as few images as you want from the files you received from the client.

Apply Your Skills

To develop the brochure, you will use the following methods and features. You will:

- Use a separate layer for the diecutting and folding template. Flip the folding template graphic horizontally on the second page so that the front and back of the document line up properly.
- Create a document grid that incorporates the correct margins on either side of the folding mark.
- Create different layers for the English and Spanish versions of the brochure.
- Develop a color scheme and text-formatting plan that will communicate the theme of your brochure. Create and use style sheets to format the document text.
- Balance type, graphics, and white space to achieve a visually pleasing and easily readable design.

Specifications

Finished Trim Size (flat): 13 × 8 in.

Finished Folded Size: 7 × 8 in.

Color: Process

Included Files

Use the files provided in the RF_Free-form folder on the Resource CD. You can use as many or as few graphics as you like. The words "Costa Rica" should appear prominently but tastefully on the cover and the inside of the brochure. You'll find the template, from your service provider, in this folder along with both the English and Spanish text.

Publisher's Comments

For many nations, tourism represents one of the largest sources of foreign exchange. Successful advertising for a country such as Costa Rica requires producing sophisticated ads and brochures economically, in more than one language, to reach the tourists they want to attract.

You have very little text and an unusual diecutting template with which to work. Create the document size at the final finished trim size and place the template at the original zero point. The focus of the brochure is on the imagery, so you can add as many graphic elements as you like, including lines and shapes. Pick a color scheme that you like, and remember that you can bleed any element off the page.

By taking advantage of Quark's features like layers for managing multiple versions, and by working closely with your service provider to ensure that even unusual folds are set up properly with a template, your files will work efficiently and result in that economical production that your client needs.

Review #1

Chapters 1 through 5

In Chapters 1 through 5, you have learned how to create and control page-layout documents, and to use the utilities in QuarkXPress to manage long-document creation. You should understand the fundamentals of the layout document, including the requirements for commercial printing. You should be able to create a custom layout grid for any type of document, develop templates for folding documents, and create multiple versions of the same document using layers. You should also be able to create and manage long documents, and build a table of contents and index in any publication. After completing this series of discussions, exercises and projects, you should:

- Know how to create custom layout grids, including creating asymmetric columns. You also know how to use the Guide Manager to automate guide placement, lock guides, and remove guides from the page. You can also use the Layers utility to create multiple versions of the same document.

- Understand the fundamentals of page geometry and imposition, and know how to build templates that incorporate the correct folding allowance for multipanel documents. You understand the concept of building signatures, and how to create printer's spreads in a multipage document.

- Understand the importance of consistency in long documents. You are able to define, add, and manage multiple master pages, and understand how master pages can help to maintain consistency throughout one or more documents. You know how to create a library for frequently used objects. You can also combine multiple documents into a single book, and synchronize the different files for improved consistency between documents.

- Know how lists interact with style sheets, and how to define a list based on the style sheets in a document. You can define a list in a single document and append it to other files, or synchronize a list into all chapters of a book. You are able to build a final list into a document, update built lists, and work around the problems associated with building lists from a book.

- Be able to build a comprehensive index for any document. You know how to tag index entries in a document, and understand the different options that are available for index references. You can create multiple levels of index entries and cross-reference one entry to another. You know how style sheets are used to format an index, and how to build an index into a document.

Working with Type

Chapter Objectives:

QuarkXPress includes many advanced tools and utilities that provide virtually unlimited control over the type in a document. These tools enable you to control multiple text chains in a document, flow text onto a path instead of into a regular text box, and even control the spacing between specific letter pairs for any given font. The newest addition to Quark's type tools is the ability to use the Table tool to define and format columns of text. In this chapter, you will:

- Discover how to create text on a path.

- Use the Table tool to create and format tables in a document.

- Learn how to control the automatic text box on a page, and how to create jump lines.

- Explore the Tracking and Kerning Tables utility.

Projects to be Completed:

- Stonington Letterfold Brochure (A)

- Body Solution Booklet (B)

- Cosciel Poster (C)

Working with Type

By now you should be familiar with placing text into a document, defining character and paragraph formatting, and working with style sheets. There is far more to text, however, than placing a story in a box and applying style sheets. QuarkXPress includes tools that give you tight control over virtually every aspect of text formatting, from the new Table tool to automatic tracking and kerning of individual letter pairs. In this chapter, we look beyond placing text onto a page, considering the tools and utilities that allow you to plan and implement any design you like.

Creating Type on a Path

Instead of merely flowing text into a box, you can also create unique typographic effects by flowing text onto a path. QuarkXPress 5.0 includes four text-path tools, which you can use to create a text path, and then type or import text onto the path. The text-path tools behave just like the regular line tools; the difference is that the lines created with these tools are text paths, onto which you can type or import text.

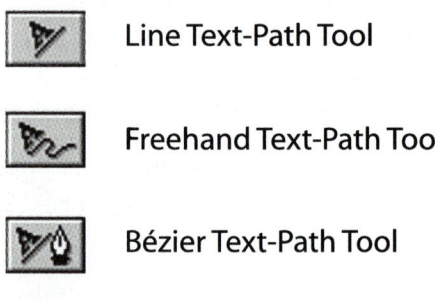

Line Text-Path Tool

Freehand Text-Path Tool

Bézier Text-Path Tool

Orthogonal Text-Path Tool

- **Line Text-Path tool**. This tool draws straight lines at any angle.
- **Freehand Text-Path tool**. This tool draws a line as if you were using a pencil on a sheet of paper.
- **Bézier Text-Path tool**. This tool creates a line based on Bézier curves.
- **Orthogonal Text-Path tool**. This tool creates lines at 45° angles.

By default, a text path is created as a hairline with no color. Only the text on the path will print, not the path itself. You can change the attributes (width, color, style, and arrow-heads) of a text path as you can those of any other line. When a text-path is selected with the Item tool, the Measurements palette is the same as it is for any line.

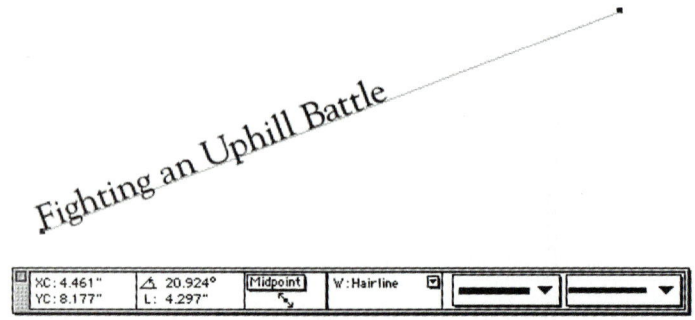

With the Content tool selected, a Flip Text button that inverts the text on the line appears next to the Leading field.

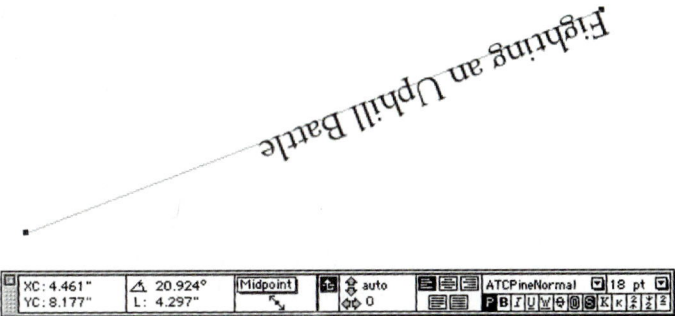

You can format text on a path as you would format any other text, including the font, size, color, and alignment. You can also link text paths using the Linking tool, creating a text chain over multiple text paths.

Modifying Text on a Path

When a text path is selected, Command/Control-M opens the Modify Text Path dialog box, where you can control the path attributes. The options in this dialog box control the appearance of text on the selected path.

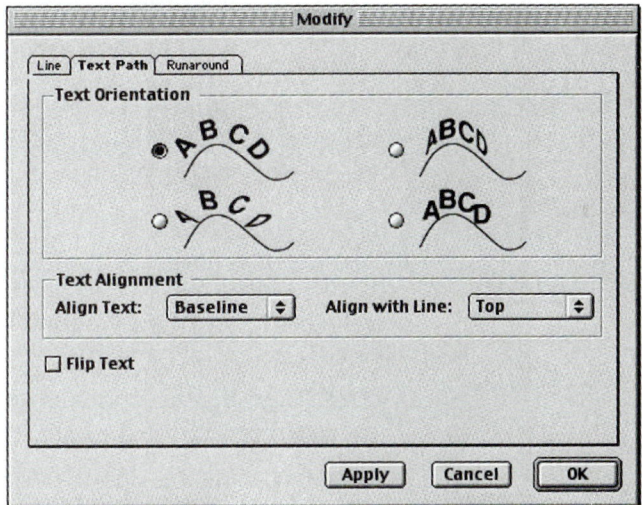

The four Text Orientation options change the dimensional appearance of text.

- The top-left option is the default. Text flows along the path with no distortion to the letter shapes. The bottoms of individual letters are aligned to the contour of the path.

- The top-right option creates a three-dimensional distortion, making text look as if it is wrapping around the shape of the text path.

- The bottom-left option warps the text, skewing characters around the text path to create a three-dimensional effect.

- The bottom-right option flows text along the path without rotating or skewing the characters.

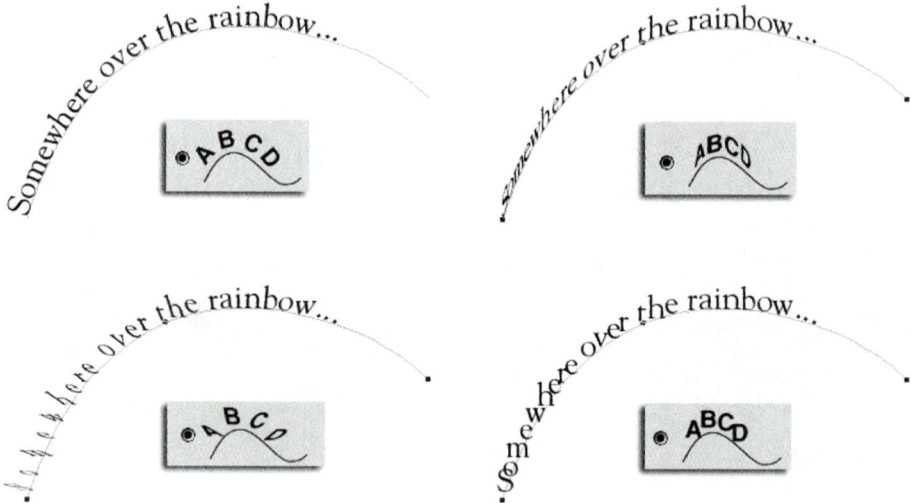

The Align Text menu defines how the text is placed with relation to the text path.

- **Baseline**. This default selection causes the baseline of the characters to rest on the text path.

- **Center**. Choosing this option positions the text so that half of the font size (height) appears above the path and half below.

- **Ascent**. Choosing this option positions the text so that the top edge of the highest ascender aligns with the text path.

- **Descent**. Choosing this option moves the text away from the line so that the lowest descender in the font aligns with the top of the path.

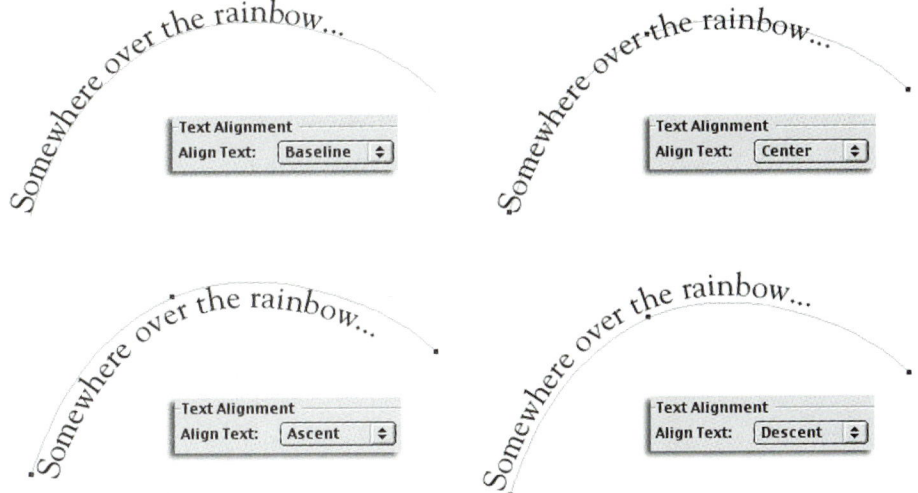

The Align with Line menu is only relevant if the text path has a thickness greater than a hairline. This menu is set to Top by default, which means that the top edge of the line is the baseline of the text. If you choose Center or Bottom in this menu, the text will rest on the center or bottom of the line.

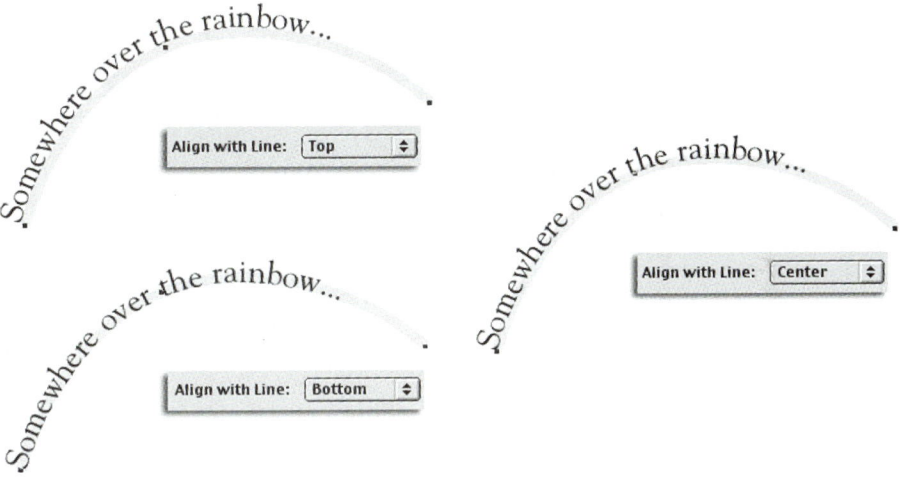

The Flip Text check box turns text upside down and moves it to the opposite side of the path. This option, which can also be accomplished by clicking the Flip Text button in the Measurements palette, is particularly useful for placing text inside a curve.

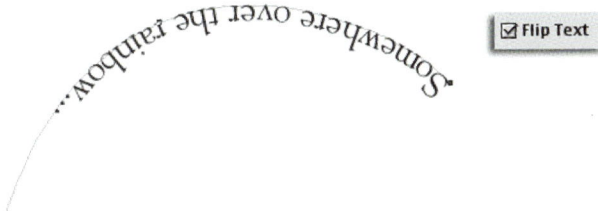

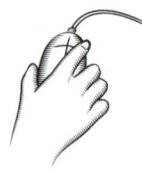

The curve we used has the following dimensions:

The two bottom points are 1.72 in. apart. The top point of the curve is 0.871 in. above the two bottom points.

Create Text Paths

1. Create a new letter-sized document with one column, using 0.5-in margins on all four sides. Make sure the Automatic Text Box option is deselected.

2. Select the Bézier Text-Path tool.

3. Draw a text path that looks like this:

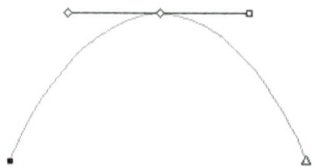

4. With the path still selected, click the Content tool in the Toolbox. Notice that the insertion point flashes at the beginning of the path. In the Measurements palette, click the Center alignment button.

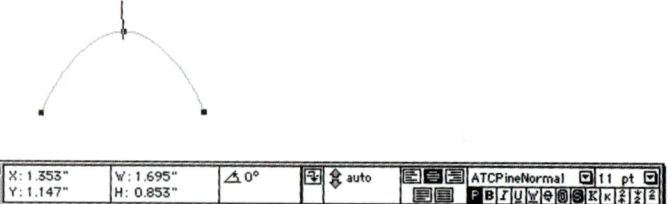

5. Select the Item tool from the Toolbox, and press Command/Control-D to duplicate the path. Place the cursor near the duplicate path until it turns into a four-headed arrow icon. Move the copy to the bottom right of the page.

With the Item tool selected, the cursor is a four-headed arrow (left) when it is near the line, allowing you to move the entire path. The cursor is a hand icon (right) when it is directly over the line, and will modify the shape of the path instead of moving the path.

6. Select the Orthogonal Text-Path tool ().

7. Draw a horizontal text path below the path you drew in Step 3. Use the Measurements palette to change the length to 3.35 in.

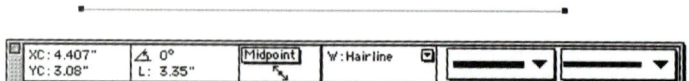

8. With the horizontal line still selected, choose the Content tool, and click the Center alignment button in the Measurements palette.

9. Repeat this process to draw four more horizontal lines with the following lengths: 4.46 in., 3.65 in., 2.9 in., and 3.4 in.

10. Set each of the horizontal lines to Center alignment, and stagger them down the page between the two curves.

11. Select the top curve with the Content tool.

12. Press Command/Control-E to open the Get Text dialog box. Navigate to the file **poem.txt** in the **RF_Adv_Quark** folder, and click Open.

13. With the Content tool and the path still selected, press Command/Control-A to select the entire story. Set the font to ATC Pine Normal, and change the font size to 25 pt. in the Measurements palette. Notice that the overset text icon indicates that some text does not fit on the path.

14. Select the Linking tool. Click first the curved path and then the first horizontal path to link them.

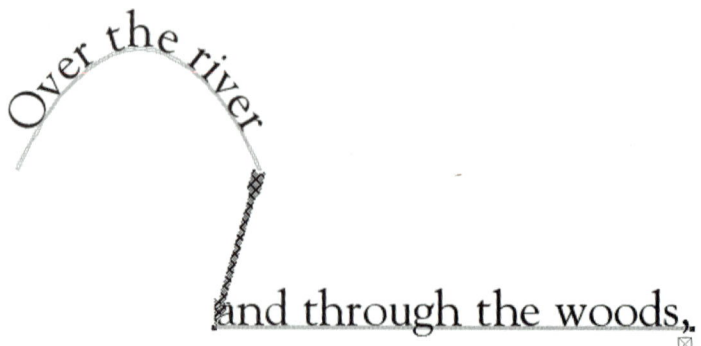

15. Continue linking each successive line down the page.

and through the woods,

to Grandmother's house we go.

The horse knows the way

to carry the sleigh

through the white and

16. Notice the overset text icon at the end of the last text path. Place the insertion point after the period at the end of the poem, and delete the extra paragraph return with the Forward-Delete key.

17. Save the file as "poem.qxd" in your **Work_In_Progress** folder, and close the file.

Tables

Until version 5 was released, table formatting in a Quark document was limited and time-consuming. This latest version adds a Table tool to the existing type utilities, which allows you to create a spreadsheet-like table within the Quark document instead of relying on tabs and rules to align columns of text.

The Table tool enables you to create a rectangular object that is automatically divided into a specified number of rows and columns. You can draw the outside dimension of the table as you would draw any other box on the page.

When you release the mouse button, the Table Properties dialog box allows you to define the number of rows and columns in the table, and whether the cells will contain text or pictures.

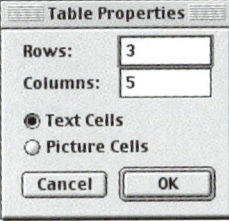

Clicking OK in the Table Properties dialog box creates the table in the document. The specified number of rows and columns are created with equal width and height.

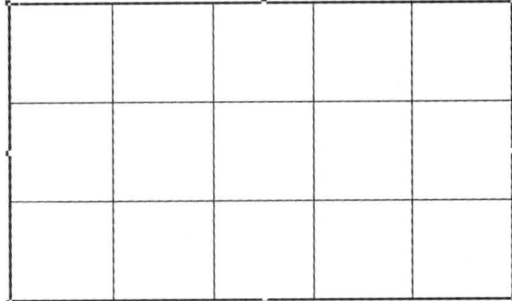

Picture cells are indicated by crossed diagonal lines, like those you would see in a regular picture box.

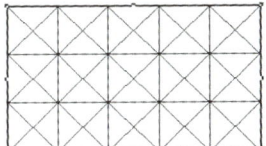

The Item tool always selects the entire table. You must use the Content tool to work with individual cells.

Converting Text to Tables

The disadvantage of the Table tool is that you cannot import text into multiple columns at once. In other words, text that has been tabbed or otherwise formatted — in a spreadsheet, for example — cannot be imported correctly into the columns and rows of a table. There is, however, a way around this limitation.

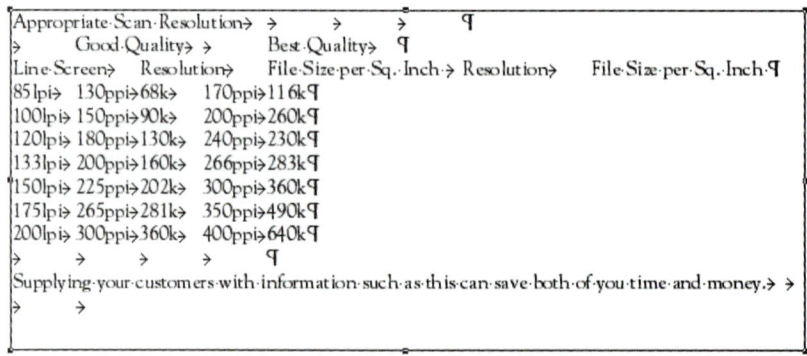

		Good Quality		Best Quality	
Appropriate Scan Resolution					
Line Screen	Resolution	File Size per Sq. Inch	Resolution	File Size per Sq. Inch	
85lpi	130ppi	68k	170ppi	116k	
100lpi	150ppi	90k	200ppi	260k	
120lpi	180ppi	130k	240ppi	230k	
133lpi	200ppi	160k	266ppi	283k	
150lpi	225ppi	202k	300ppi	360k	
175lpi	265ppi	281k	350ppi	490k	
200lpi	300ppi	360k	400ppi	640k	
Supplying your customers with information such as this can save both of you time and money.					

This table was formatted in a spreadsheet and then exported as tab-delimited text.

If you import this file into a table cell, all of the text will be placed into a single cell. Instead, you can import the text into a regular text box, highlight the text, and choose Item>Convert Text to Table. The Convert Text to Table dialog box defines how the text is imported.

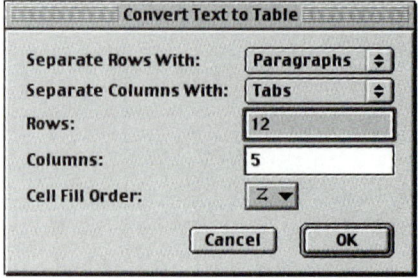

Before converting text to a table, it's a good idea to remove extra tab characters at the end of lines. Don't remove multiple tabs in the middle of lines, though, because the text may not align properly in the table.

- **Separate Rows With**. This menu defaults to Paragraph. In other words, each paragraph return character (¶) in the selected text tells Quark to begin a new row. The other options in this menu — Space, Comma, and Tab — are not commonly used.

- **Separate Columns With**. This menu defaults to Tab. Many table-text files are exported from a spreadsheet program to a *tab-delimited* file, which means that the data for each column is separated by a tab character. Each tab character (→) in the selected text tells Quark to move to a new column. Two of the other options — Space and Paragraph — are not commonly used. The Comma option can be used if the text was created as a comma-delimited text file.

- **Rows and Columns**. These fields are filled automatically with a number determined by the application, based on the highlighted text. It is a good idea to leave these options at the default values, and make any necessary changes later.

- **Cell Fill Order**. This menu determines how the data is converted into the cells of a table. The default begins in the top-left cell, moves horizontally across the row, moves to the left-most cell in the second row, moves across that row, and so on. The other options in the Cell Fill Order menu are far less common.

✓ Z	Left to Right, Top Down
Σ	Right to Left, Top Down
И	Top Down, Left to Right
N	Top Down, Right to Left

When you click OK in the Convert Table to Text dialog box, a table is created on top of the existing text box. The table has the same height and width as the text box from which the text was converted.

Appropriate·Scan·Resolution→ ¶

Appropriate·Scan ⊠				
	Good·Quality		Best·Quality	
Line·Screen	Resolution	File·Size·per·Sq.·⊠	Resolution	File·Size·per·Sq.·⊠
85 lpi	130ppi	68k	170ppi	116k
100lpi	150ppi	90k	200ppi	260k
120lpi	180ppi	130k	240ppi	230k
133lpi	200ppi	160k	266ppi	283k
150lpi	225ppi	202k	300ppi	360k
175lpi	265ppi	281k	350ppi	490k
200lpi	300ppi	360k	400ppi	640k
Supplying·your·⊠				

You can see in the previous image that the table created by choosing Convert Table to Text still needs some help — remedying several overset text icons and an extra row of blank cells, to name only two problems. This method is far easier, however, than entering the text into each cell manually. Once the text is in place, you can format the text, cells, gridlines, and table attributes however you like.

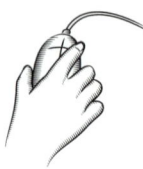

Create a Table

1. Create a new document by opening the template file **tables.qxt** from the **RF_Adv_Quark** folder.

2. Select the Table tool. On the document page, drag a new table frame approximately 5 in. wide by 3 in. high.

3. In the Table Properties dialog box, change the Rows field to 11 and the Columns field to 5. Click OK.

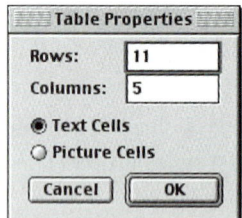

4. Choose the Content tool; click in the first cell of the table to place the insertion point.

5. Press Command/Control-E to open the Get Text dialog box. Navigate to the file **table.txt** in your **RF_Adv_Quark** folder, and click Open.

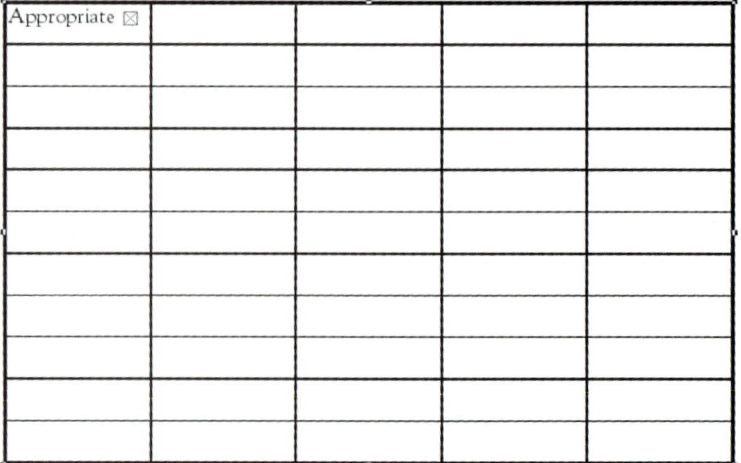

6. Notice that all of the text in the imported document is placed into the first cell.

7. Press Command/Control-K to delete the table.

8. Using the Rectangle Text Box tool, draw a text box on the page that is 5 in. wide by 3.132 in. high.

9. Import **table.txt** into the text box.

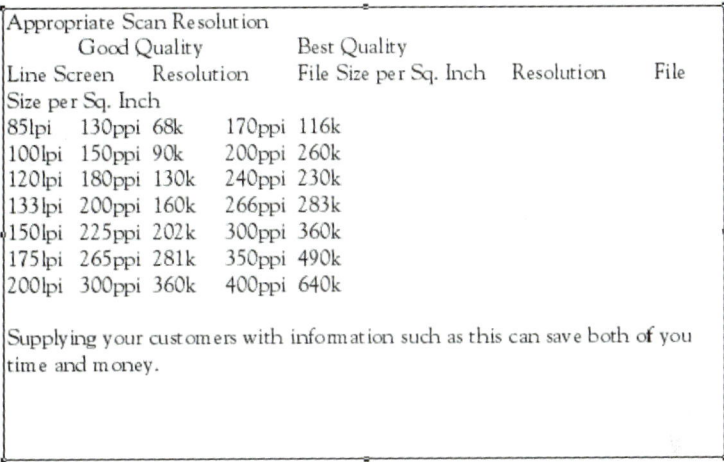

10. Press Command/Control-I to show invisible characters. Remove any tab characters that appear directly before the ¶ symbol in each line, and at the end of the last line.

11. Press Command/Control-A to select all of the text, and choose Item>Convert Text to Table.

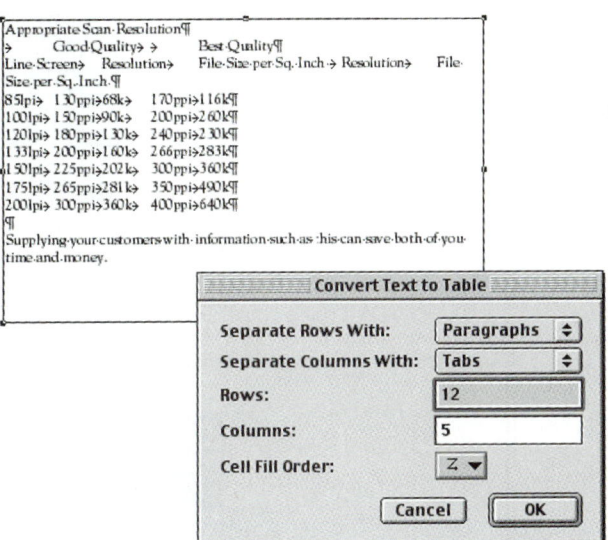

12. Review the options in the Convert Text to Table dialog box, and then click OK. Your new table is created.

13. Select the text box behind the table and delete it.

Appropriate·⊠				
	Good·Quality		Best·Quality	
Line·Screen	Resolution	File·Size·per·⊠	Resolution	File·Size·per·⊠
85lpi	130ppi	68k	170ppi	116k
100lpi	150ppi	90k	200ppi	260k
120lpi	180ppi	130k	240ppi	230k
133lpi	200ppi	160k	266ppi	283k
150lpi	225ppi	202k	300ppi	360k
175lpi	265ppi	281k	350ppi	490k
200lpi	300ppi	360k	400ppi	640k
Supplying·you⊠				

14. Save the file as "resolution_table.qxd" in your **Work_In_Progress** folder, and leave the file open for the next exercise.

Selecting Cells

Once a table is created, you can select individual cells using the Content tool. Pressing Control-Tab moves the insertion point from one cell to the next.

To select multiple adjacent cells (horizontally, vertically, or in a block), you can click in the first cell and then drag to select additional cells.

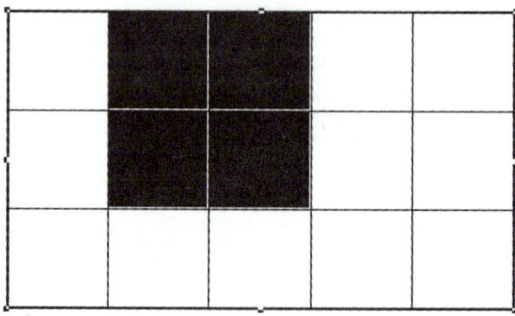

To select nonadjacent cells, hold down the Shift key and click each cell you want to select.

To select an entire row or column, you can use the Content tool either to drag across the selection, or to move the cursor to the left (for a row) or top (for a column) edge of the table. The cursor becomes an arrow icon, and clicking selects the entire row or column.

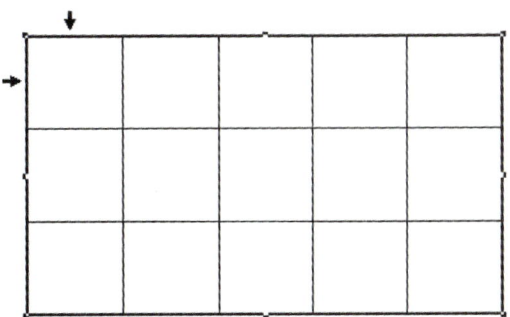

Modifying Tables

A table is treated as any other object on the document page. When a table is selected with the Item tool, you can change the table attributes by pressing Command/Control-M or choosing Item>Modify. The three tabs of the Modify dialog box — Table, Runaround, and Grid — define the attributes for the entire table, not for individual cells.

The Table tab allows you to change the position of the table, and the overall width and height of the table.

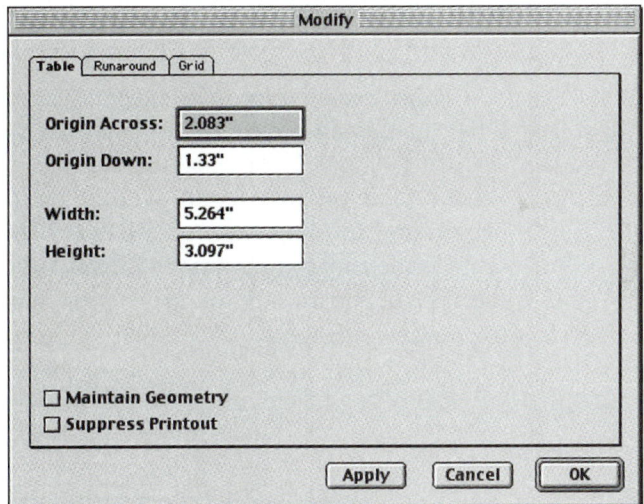

The Maintain Geometry check box determines what happens when you add or delete rows or columns from a table. This option is deselected by default. When you add rows or columns, the new cells are the same width or height as the existing cells, and the dimensions of the table change as necessary. If the Maintain Geometry option is selected, rows and columns are added within the dimensions of the table, and the existing rows or columns are resized, as necessary, to accommodate the new cells.

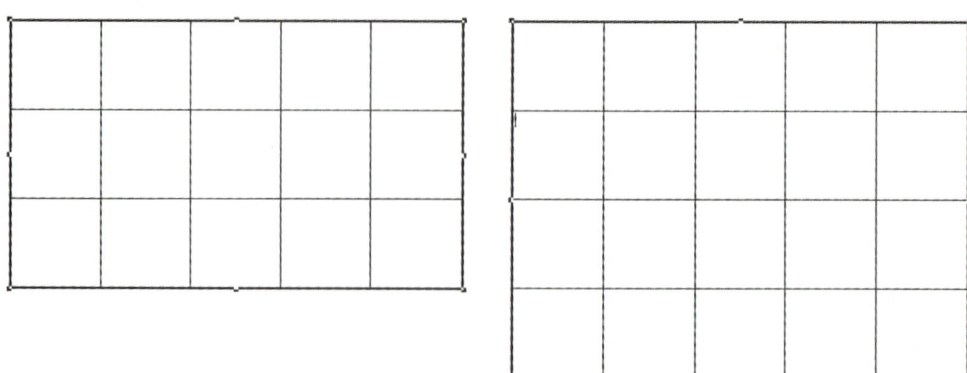

When a row is added with Maintain Geometry unchecked, the size of the table changes and the height of each row remains the same.

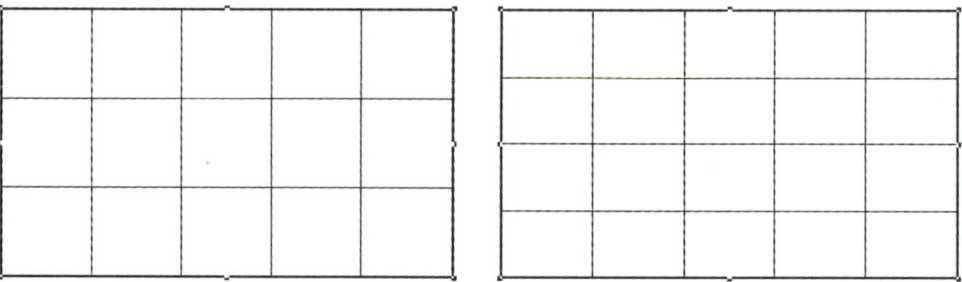

When a row is added with Maintain Geometry checked, the size of the table remains the same while the height of the rows is adjusted to accommodate the new cells.

When a table is selected with the Item tool, the Runaround tab of the Modify dialog box defines how text flows around the table. The runaround options for a table are exactly the same as the runaround options for any other box, except that Item is the only option for the Type of runaround; the Type menu automatically defaults to Item and is grayed out so you can't change it.

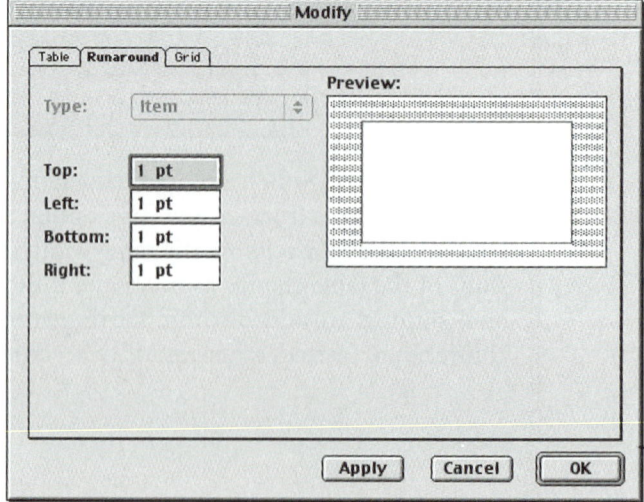

The Gridlines option in the Item menu is not available if any cell (not the contents of the cell) is highlighted, or if more than one cell is currently selected.

You cannot apply a 0-pt. width to a gridline. The only way to make gridlines "invisible" is to apply a Hairline width with a color of White.

If you want to use different attributes for the horizontal, vertical, and border gridlines, change the border gridlines last.

Formatting Gridlines

The Grid tab of the Modify dialog box defines the lines that make up the table. Three buttons in the right of the Preview area control (from the top) the entire grid, the vertical lines, and the horizontal lines. You can define different Width, Style, Color, and Shade for the horizontal and vertical lines in a table.

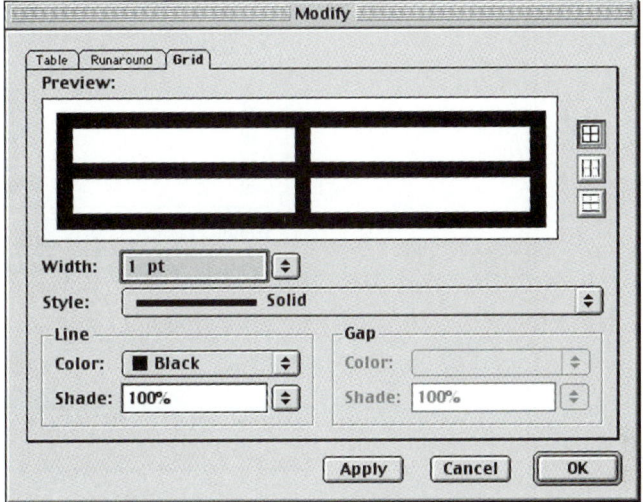

You can also format the gridlines when the Content tool is active and the insertion point is placed in a table cell. Four options are available in the Gridlines menu (Item>Gridlines) allowing you to Select Horizontal, Vertical, Borders (outside edge) or All gridlines. Once you select gridlines using the Item menu, you can change the color of the selected gridlines using the Colors palette.

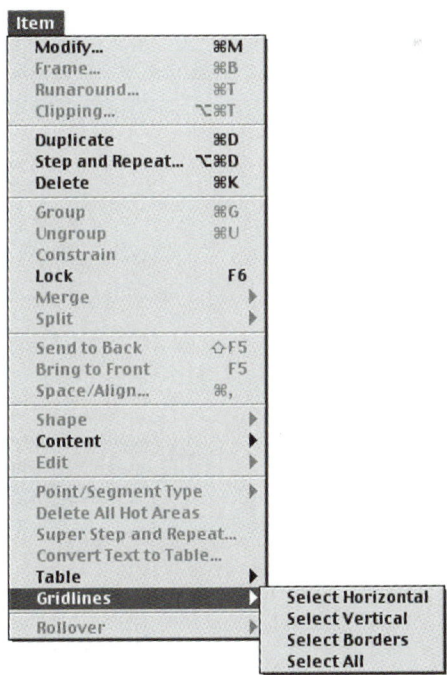

When a set of gridlines is selected with the Gridlines menu (Item>Gridlines), the Modify dialog box only shows two tabs, Table and Grid.

After you select a set of gridlines with the Gridlines menu (Item>Gridlines), pressing Command/Control-M displays the Grid tab of the Modify dialog box. The Preview area shows only the selected gridlines. You use this dialog box to change the Width, Style, and Color of the selected gridlines.

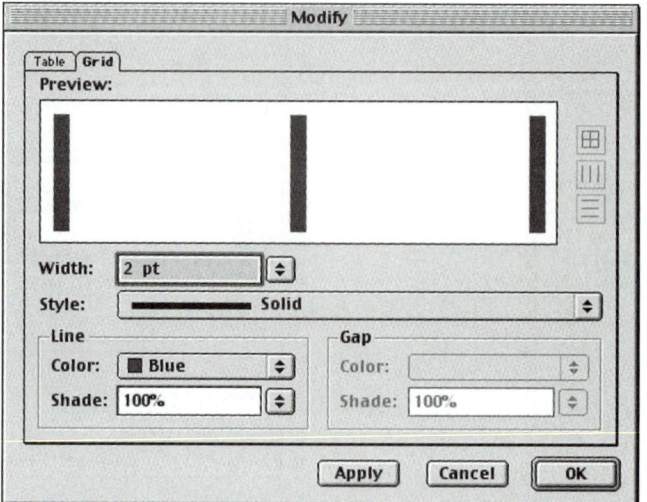

Modify a Table

1. In the open document resolution_table.qxd, select the table with the Item tool, and press Command/Control-M to open the Modify dialog box.

2. In the Table tab, activate the Maintain Geometry check box so that the outside dimensions of your table remain constant.

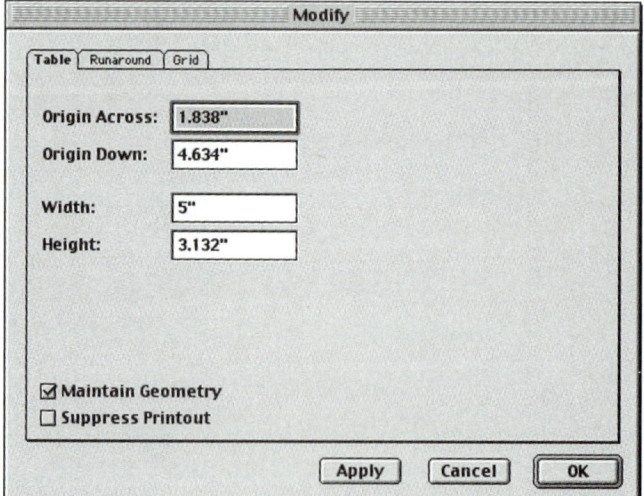

3. Click the Grid tab, and then click the Select Vertical button (the center button in the right of the Preview area). Change the Width field to Hairline and the Color menu to White. Click OK to apply the changes.

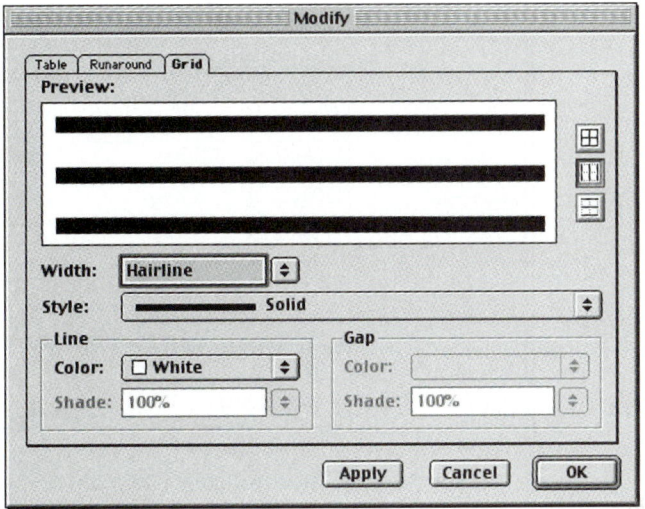

Appropriate·☒				
	Good·Quality		Best·Quality	
Line·Screen	Resolution	File·Size·per·☒	Resolution	File·Size·per·☒
85lpi	130ppi	68k	170ppi	116k
100lpi	150ppi	90k	200ppi	260k
120lpi	180ppi	130k	240ppi	230k
133lpi	200ppi	160k	266ppi	283k
150lpi	225ppi	202k	300ppi	360k
175lpi	265ppi	281k	350ppi	490k
200lpi	300ppi	360k	400ppi	640k
Supplying·you☒				

4. Select the Content tool from the Toolbox. Move the cursor to the left of the empty row (second from the bottom) until you see an arrow icon. Click to select the entire row.

5. Choose Item>Table>Delete Row. Notice that the remaining rows are resized to fit in the table height.

Appropriate · ⊠					
	Good·Quality			Best·Quality	
Line·Screen	Resolution	File·Size·per·⊠	Resolution	File·Size·per·⊠	
85lpi	130ppi	68k	170ppi	116k	
100lpi	150ppi	90k	200ppi	260k	
120lpi	180ppi	130k	240ppi	230k	
133lpi	200ppi	160k	266ppi	283k	
150lpi	225ppi	202k	300ppi	360k	
175lpi	265ppi	281k	350ppi	490k	
200lpi	300ppi	360k	400ppi	640k	
Supplying·you⊠					

6. Save the file and leave it open.

Modifying Cells

When one or more cells are selected with the Content tool, the Modify dialog box shows three different tabs — Table, Cell, and Text — that control the attributes of the selected cells.

The Cell tab allows you to modify the Width and Height of selected rows or columns. You can also define the Color and Shade of selected cells, and apply a Blend.

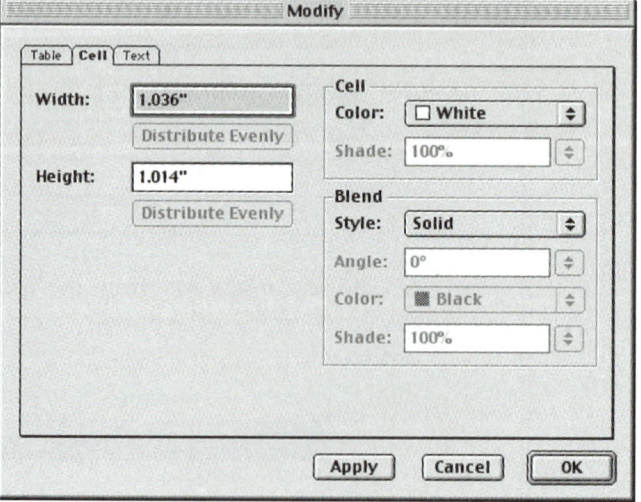

Modifying the height or width of a single cell affects the entire row or column in which that cell exists.

Blends are applied individually to each cell, not to a range of selected cells.

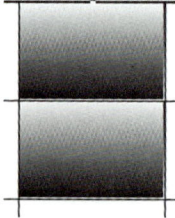

You cannot apply a fill of None to the cells of a table.

The Text tab of the Modify dialog box defines the text placement within the selected cells. The same options are available as for any other text box; think of each cell in the table as a distinct text box.

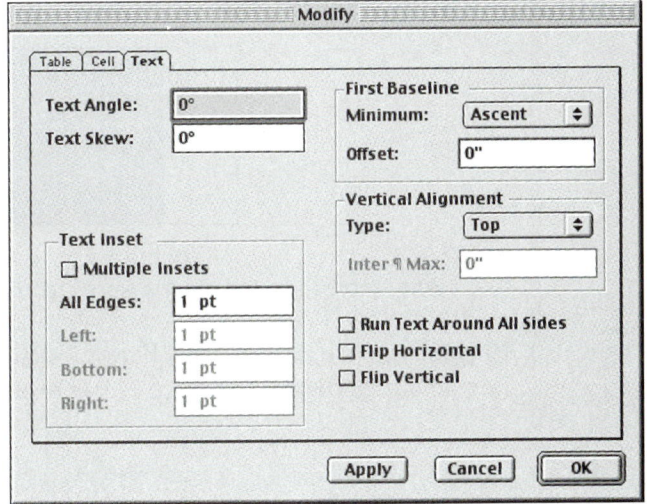

Manually Resizing Cells

You can change the width or height of a cell by dragging any gridline in the table. When directly over a gridline, the cursor becomes a double-facing arrow icon.

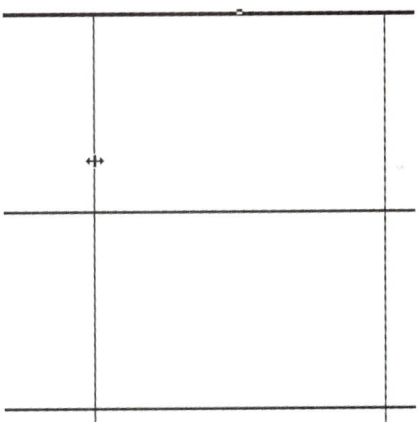

If the Maintain Geometry option is selected, dragging a gridline resizes the row within the table dimensions. If this option is not selected, dragging a gridline resizes the row or column and the table.

Distributing Cells

If you have manually resized cells, the Distribute Evenly options in the Cell tab of the Modify dialog box allow you to combine the width or height of adjacent rows or columns and to distribute the total space evenly throughout the selected cells.

When more than one column is selected, the Width Distribute Evenly button is available.

Clicking the Distribute Evenly button calculates the width or height of the entire selection, and then divides the space evenly over the number of selected columns or rows.

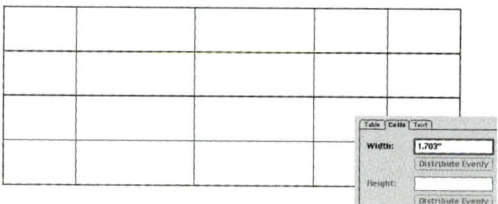

Merging Cells

Combining cells can be useful, for example, for creating the heading of a table, or for creating column headings that apply to more than one column of data.

When two or more adjacent cells are selected, you can combine them into a single unit by choosing Item>Table>Combine Cells.

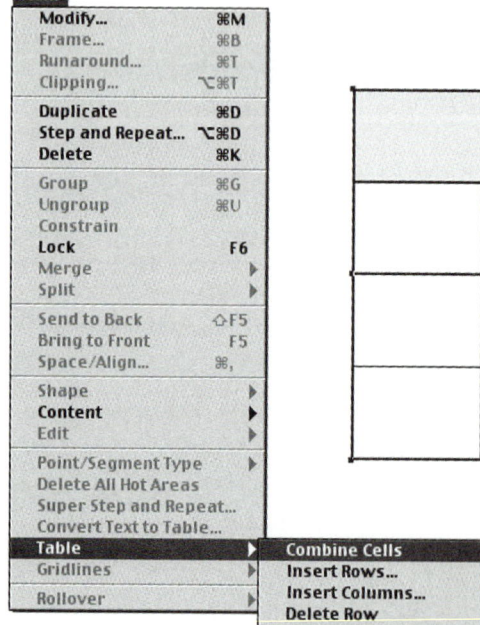

Combining cells removes the gridlines between the combined cells, allowing text to extend across the range of the merged cells. Once cells are combined, the attributes of the first cell in the selection become the attributes of the merged cell.

You can split combined cells by choosing Item>Table>Split Cell. Once cells are split, any content of the group is placed into the first cell in the original range.

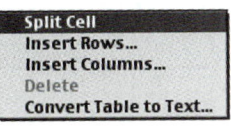

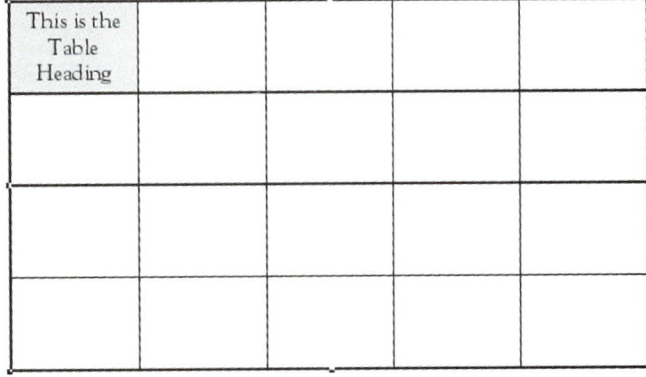

Adding and Deleting Rows and Columns

You can add and delete rows and columns by choosing Item>Table.

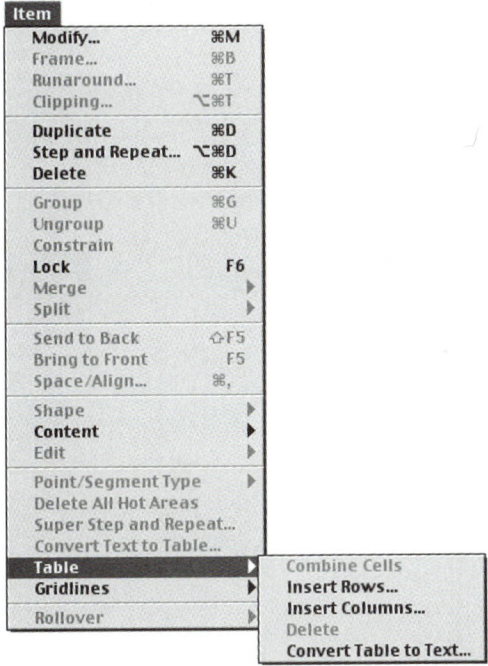

When you choose to Insert Rows or Insert Columns, you will see a dialog box that defines what will be added and where it will be added.

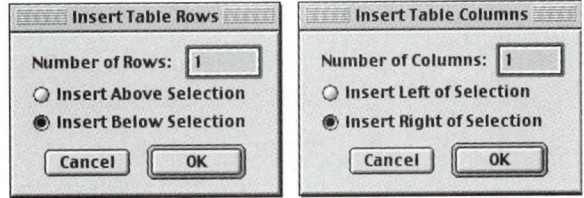

The Insert Table Rows and Insert Table Columns dialog boxes determine what and where new table cells are added.

The Delete option of the Table menu (Item>Table) is only available when an entire row or column is selected. The menu option changes to reflect the current selection.

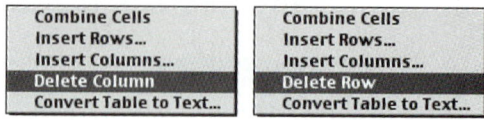

Changing Cell Content Type

As you saw in the Table Properties dialog box, you can create a table with text cells or picture cells. After the table is initially created, you can convert selected cells to a different type of content by choosing Item>Content. Tables can have any combination of cells for Picture, Text, and None.

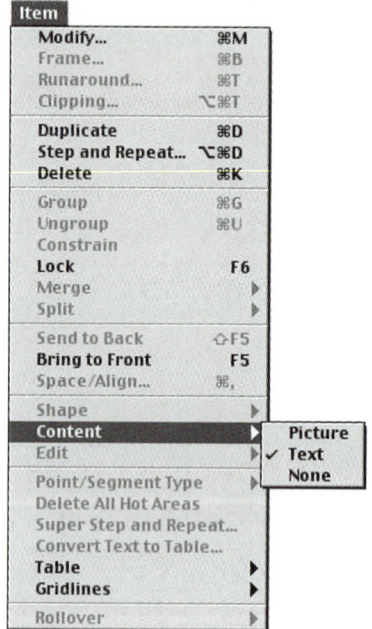

If you change the type of a cell that already has content, a warning shows that the existing content will be deleted.

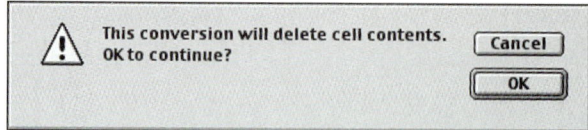

Modify Cells

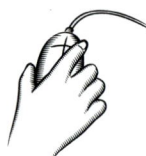

1. In the open file resolution_table.qxd, select the entire first row, and choose Item>Table>Combine Cells.

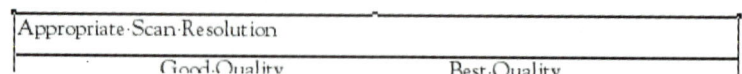

2. Select the entire last row and choose Item>Table>Combine Cells.

3. Place the insertion point in the Good Quality cell in the second row, hold down the mouse button, and drag right to highlight the cell and the one immediately to the right. Choose Item>Table>Combine Cells.

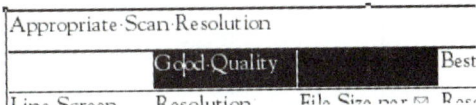

4. Repeat this process for the "Best Quality" heading.

5. Select all cells in the table. Open the Modify dialog box and choose the Text tab. Choose Centered from the Vertical Alignment Type menu, and change the Text Inset All Edge field to 3 pt. Click OK.

Appropriate Scan Resolution				
	Good Quality		Best Quality	
Line Screen	Resolution	File Size per ⊠	Resolution	File Size per ⊠
85lpi	130ppi	68k	170ppi	116k
100lpi	150ppi	90k	200ppi	260k
120lpi	180ppi	130k	240ppi	230k
133lpi	200ppi	160k	266ppi	283k
150lpi	225ppi	202k	300ppi	360k
175lpi	265ppi	281k	350ppi	490k
200lpi	300ppi	360k	400ppi	640k
Supplying your customers with information such as this can save both of you ⊠				

6. If it is not visible, open the Style Sheets palette.

7. Place the insertion point in the last row, and click Table Footnote in the Style Sheets palette.

8. Select the 4th through the 10th rows, and click Table Text in the Style Sheets palette.

Appropriate Scan Resolution				
	Good Quality		Best Quality	
Line Screen	Resolution	File Size per ⊠	Resolution	File Size per ⊠
85lpi	130ppi	68k	170ppi	116k
100lpi	150ppi	90k	200ppi	260k
120lpi	180ppi	130k	240ppi	230k
133lpi	200ppi	160k	266ppi	283k
150lpi	225ppi	202k	300ppi	360k
175lpi	265ppi	281k	350ppi	490k
200lpi	300ppi	360k	400ppi	640k
Supplying your customers with information such as this can save both of you time and money.				

9. Select the first row, and click Table Head 1 in the Style Sheets palette. Notice that the text does not fit in the cell height.

	Good Quality		Best Quality	
Line Screen	Resolution	File Size per ⊠	Resolution	File Size per ⊠
85lpi	130ppi	68k	170ppi	116k
100lpi	150ppi	90k	200ppi	260k
120lpi	180ppi	130k	240ppi	230k

Style Sheets
¶ No Style
¶ Normal
¶ Table Footnote
¶ Table Head 1
¶ Table Head 2
¶ Table Head 3
¶ Table Text

A No Style
A Body Text Italic
A Normal

10. Place the cursor over the bottom gridline of the first row. When you see the cursor change to the double-facing arrow icon, drag the bottom gridline of the row down until the text fits into the first row.

Appropriate Scan Resolution

Line Screen	Resolution	File Size per ⊠	Resolution	File Size per ⊠

11. Select the second row, and apply the Table Head 2 style sheet. Expand the row height until the text fit into the cells.

Appropriate Scan Resolution

	Good Quality		Best Quality	

12. Select the third row, and apply the Table Head 3 style sheet. Expand the bottom of the row until all the text in the row is visible.

Appropriate Scan Resolution

	Good Quality		Best Quality	
Line Screen	Resolution	File Size per Sq. Inch	Resolution	File Size per Sq. Inch
100lpi	150ppi	90k	200ppi	260k
120lpi	180ppi	130k	240ppi	230k

13. Select the seven rows of table text, and open the Modify dialog box. In the Cells tab, click Height>Distribute Evenly, and then click OK.

Appropriate Scan Resolution

Line Screen	Good Quality		Best Quality	
	Resolution	File Size per Sq. Inch	Resolution	File Size per Sq. Inch
85lpi	130ppi	68k	170ppi	116k
100lpi	150ppi	90k	200ppi	260k
120lpi	180ppi	130k	240ppi	230k
133lpi	200ppi	160k	266ppi	283k
150lpi	225ppi	202k	300ppi	360k
175lpi	265ppi	281k	350ppi	490k
200lpi	300ppi	360k	400ppi	640k

Supplying your customers with information such as this can save both of you time and money.

14. Select the third row in the table. In the Text tab of the Modify dialog box, choose Bottom from the Vertical Alignment Type menu, and click OK.

Appropriate Scan Resolution

Line Screen	Good Quality		Best Quality	
	Resolution	File Size per Sq. Inch	Resolution	File Size per Sq. Inch
85lpi	130ppi	68k	170ppi	116k
100lpi	150ppi	90k	200ppi	260k
120lpi	180ppi	130k	240ppi	230k
133lpi	200ppi	160k	266ppi	283k
150lpi	225ppi	202k	300ppi	360k
175lpi	265ppi	281k	350ppi	490k
200lpi	300ppi	360k	400ppi	640k

Supplying your customers with information such as this can save both of you time and money.

15. Save and close the file.

Converting Tables to Text

If you want to return a table to tab-separated text, you can choose Item>Table>Convert Table to Text.

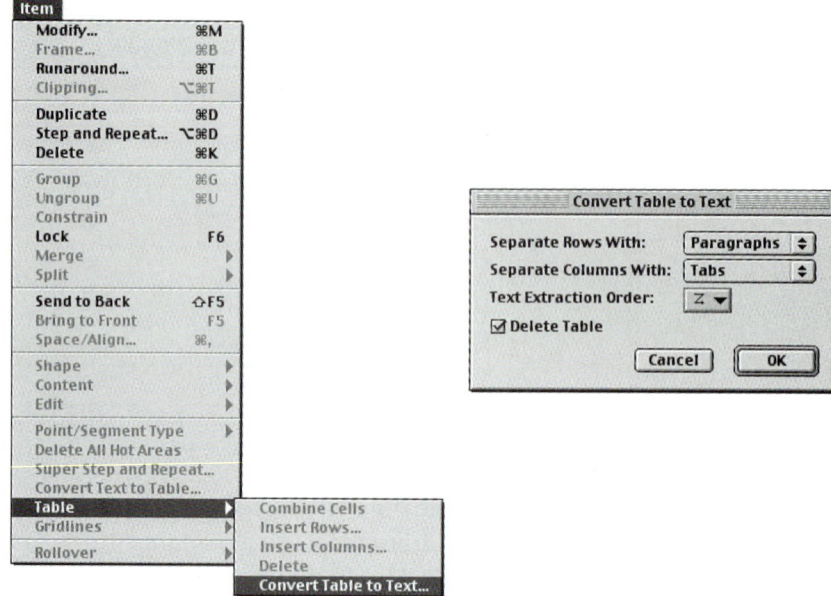

The Options in the Convert Table to Text dialog box are the same as those in the Convert Text to Table dialog box. If you select the Delete Table check box, the table and its contents are automatically deleted after the table is converted to text.

Appropriate Scan Resolution				
	Good Quality		Best Quality	
Line Screen	Resolution	File Size per Sq. Inch	Resolution	File Size per Sq. Inch
85lpi	130ppi	68k	170ppi	116k
100lpi	150ppi	90k	200ppi	260k
120lpi	180ppi	130k	240ppi	230k
133lpi	200ppi	160k	266ppi	283k
150lpi	225ppi	202k	300ppi	360k
175lpi	265ppi	281k	350ppi	490k
200lpi	300ppi	360k	400ppi	640k

Supplying your customers with information such as this can save both of you time and money.

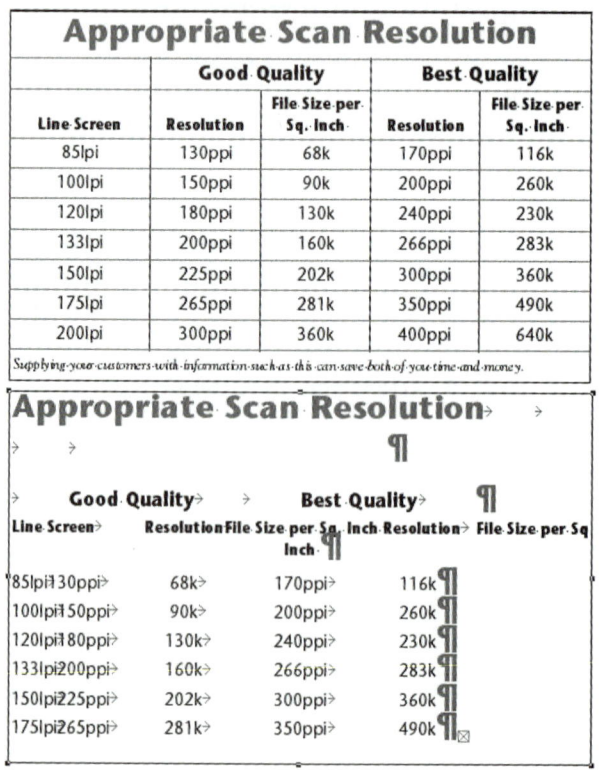

The result of converting a table to text can be fairly messy, especially if the table was extensively formatted.

Managing Automatic Text Flow

In books or similar documents, text generally flows from one page to the next without complicated page jumps. Other documents, such as newsletters and magazines, may require "continued on" pages, which can contain text blocks for more than one story in the document. This type of document requires special planning both for the master-page layout and for flowing text from one page to the next.

When you create a new document with the Automatic Text Box option selected, the master-page layout defaults to linking one page to the next automatically. If you look at the master-page layout for A-Master A, the top-left corner of the page shows a linked Chain icon. When you place a story in the automatic text box of a document page, new pages are added automatically, as necessary, to accommodate the entire placed story.

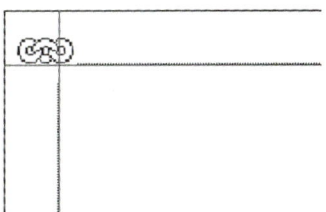

The linked Chain icon indicates that text will flow automatically into as many pages as necessary.

To prevent extra pages from being added, you can unlink the automatic text box by clicking the Chain icon with the Unlinking tool. When you place a story into the automatic text box with the link broken, text flows to the end of the selected text box and displays an overset text icon.

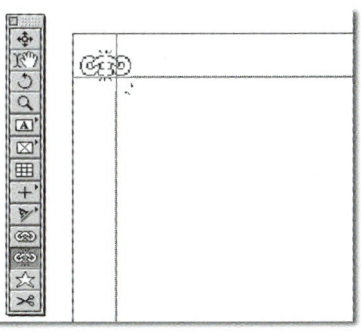

Remember: Chain icons only exist on the master page, and you can't place text into the automatic text box of a master page.

When you are designing a document with text that jumps to different pages (such as in a newsletter or magazine), it is helpful to unlink the automatic text boxes on the master-page layout. This prevents pages from being randomly generated where you don't want them, and provides much greater control over your page layout.

Facing Pages

When you are working with facing pages, you have additional options to control how text flows into the automatic text box. Each page in the master-page spread has a chain icon. The two chain icons determine how text will flow, depending on their states (linked or broken) and on which page you initially place the story.

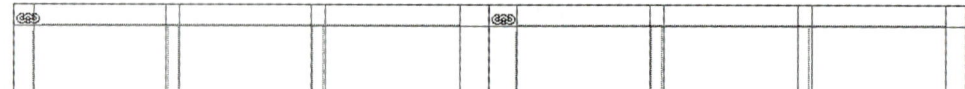

If you choose Get Text with the automatic text box of a right-facing page selected:

- If both the left- and right-page chain icons are linked, pages are added, as necessary, to accommodate the entire story.

- If just the left-page chain icon is broken, text only flows onto the page you selected before choosing Get Text, and then displays an overset text icon if the entire story does not fit.

- If just the right-page chain icon is broken, text flows into the automatic text box of the page with which you started, a left-facing page is added automatically, and text flows into the automatic text box of the new page. At the end of the left-facing page, if any text remains, an overset text icon appears.

If you choose Get Text with the automatic text box of a left-facing page selected:

- If the left- and right-page chain icons are unbroken, pages are added, as necessary, to accommodate the entire story.

- If just the left-page chain icon is broken, text flows into the automatic text box of the page with which you started, a right-facing page is added automatically, and text flows into the automatic text box of the new page. At the end of the right-facing page, if any text remains, an overset text icon appears.

- If just the right-page chain icon is broken, text only flows onto the page you selected before choosing Get Text, and then displays an overset text icon if the entire story does not fit.

Controlling the automatic text flow is especially important if you do not want text to flow from one page to the next. If you are working with continued-on pages, it is a good idea to break the master-page links before placing text.

Creating Page Jumps

When you want to flow a story, for example from page 3 to page 14, it is a good idea to use a "continued on" line at the end of the first page; some people also include a "continued from" line at the top of the second page.

Just as you can place a character to automatically number the pages in a document, you can also use key commands to place a Next Box page number or Previous Box page number.

- **Next Box Page Number** (Command/Control-4). This character places the page number of the page on which the next text box in the chain is placed.

- **Previous Box Page Number** (Command/Control-2). This character places the page number of the page on which the previous box in the text chain is placed.

The best way to add a continued line is to create a separate text box at the end of the continued-on page, or at the beginning of the continued-from page. You can create the box anywhere on the page. If the box does not overlap any box in an existing text chain, the page-number character shows <None>.

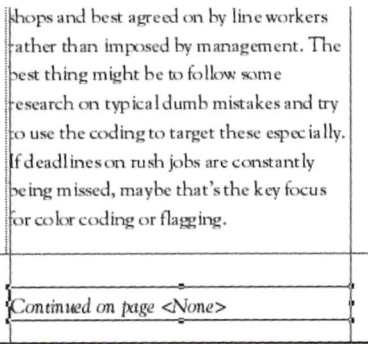

As soon as you move the continued-on or continued-from text box so that it touches an existing text chain, the page-number characters reflect the correct location of the next or previous box in the chain.

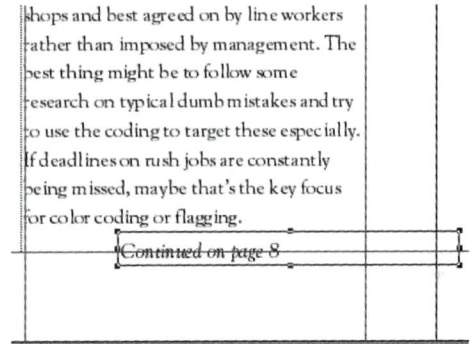

Once the box is placed correctly, you can modify the formatting of the text as appropriate. Notice that the continued box does not have to be entirely within the underlying text box.

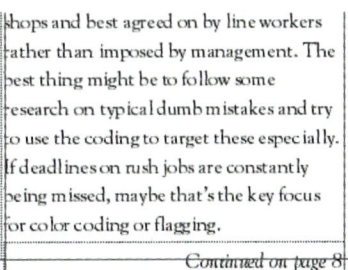

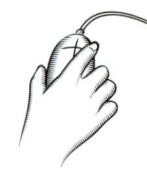

Remember: you will find all of the resource files in the **RF_Adu_Quark** folder.

It may help to change the view percentage to 75% or less, depending on the size of your monitor.

Work with Multiple Text Chains

1. Open the file **gasp.qxd** from the **RF_Adu_Quark** folder. This document was created with the master-page automatic linking turned off.

2. Navigate to page 6 of the document.

3. If guides are not visible, press "F7".

4. Place the insertion point in the text box at the top of the page, and choose File>Get Text.

5. Locate the file **colorform.xtg**. Make sure the Include Style Sheets option is checked, and click Open.

6. Navigate to page 7. Place the file **rowing.xtg** in the text box on page 7. Make sure that you select Include Style Sheets.

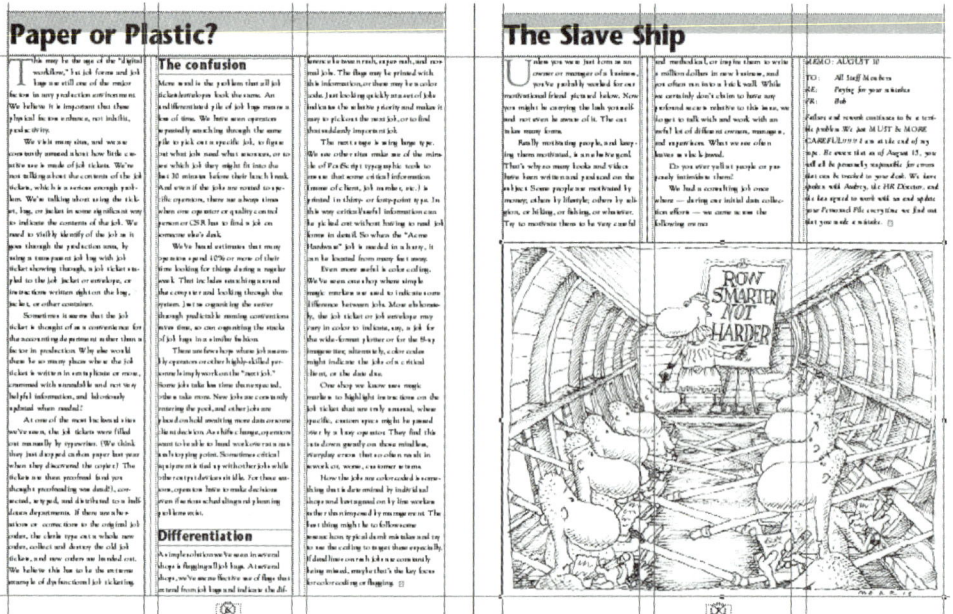

7. Drag the page in the document window so that you can see the bottom of the text box on page 7 and the first column on page 8.

8. Choose the Linking tool, and click on the text box on page 7 to activate the marching-ants border.

9. Click the text box in the first column of page 8 to link the two text boxes.

10. Navigate to page 8. Link the first column on page 8 to the second column. Link the second column to the third column.

11. Navigate back to page 7. Create a new text box with the following dimensions:

    X: 5.75 in.   W: 2.375 in.
    Y: 4.015 in.   H: 0.23 in.

12. In the new text box, type "Continued on page " and press Command/Control-4. Open the Style Sheets palette and apply the Continued On style sheet.

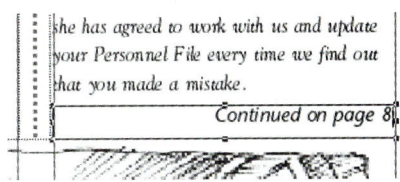

13. On page 8, create a new text box with the following dimensions:

    X: 0.375 in.   W: 2.375 in.
    Y: 0.375 in.   H: 0.375 in.

14. In the new text box type "Continued from page ", and press Command/Control-2. Apply the Continued From style sheet.

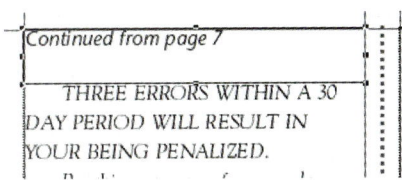

15. Close up the third column text box so that the height is 4.1 in.

16. Draw a new text box in the empty space of the third column with the following dimensions:

    X: 5.625 in.   W: 2.375 in.
    Y: 4.864 in.   H: 5.511 in.

17. Link the text box from page 6 to this new text box.

18. Add a continued-on box at the end of page 6. Move it down so that "…color coding or flagging." appears on the page.

19. Add a continued-from text box to the box in the third column of page 8.

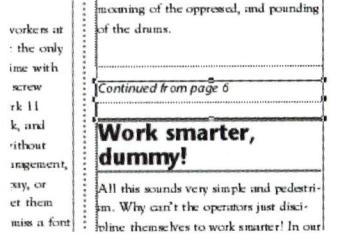

20. Save the file in your **Work_In_Progress** folder, and leave the file open.

Kerning and Tracking Tables

You can use the QuarkXPress Kerning and Tracking Table utilities to control the default kerning and tracking of letter pairs and fonts respectively. If you are consistently modifying the tracking for a specific pair of letters, or always apply a certain amount of tracking to text set in a specific font, you can improve productivity by modifying the kerning and tracking tables.

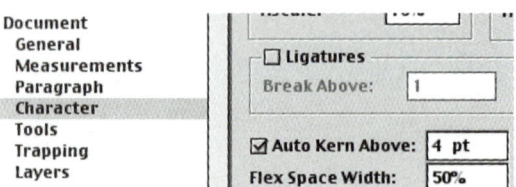

Editing Kerning Tables

When automatic kerning is active (Edit>Preferences>Preferences>Document>Character), QuarkXPress applies kerning based on tables built into professionally designed fonts.

You can also create your own kerning tables using the Kerning Table Edit utility (Utilities>Kerning Table Edit). The Kerning Table Edit dialog box lists every font active in your system, including the style variations for each font. You can scroll through the list to highlight an individual font, and then click Edit to add kerning pairs to the font.

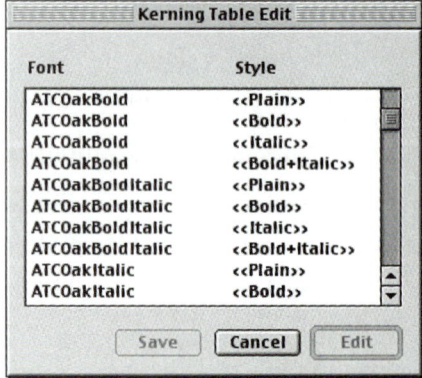

The Title bar of the Kerning Values dialog box shows which font you are editing. The Kerning Pairs window lists all kerning pairs that already exist for the selected font.

If you highlight a letter pair in the Kerning Pairs window, those letters appear in the Pair field; the Value field reflects the pair's current kerning setting, based on 1/200 of an em. You can then modify a pair by changing the Value field and clicking Replace. The Preview window shows a sample of the results of the Pair/Value fields. You can delete any pair by highlighting it in the Kerning Pairs window and clicking Delete.

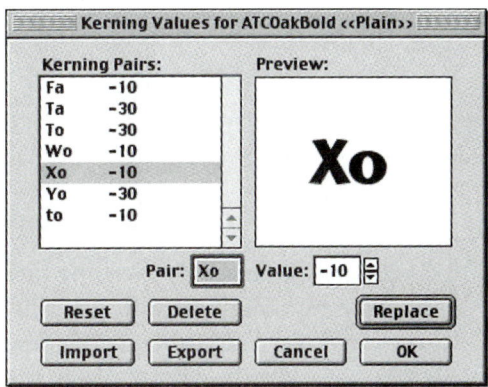

To add a letter pair to the list, you can enter the characters in the Pair field, type the appropriate value, and click Add.

Capital and lowercase letters are considered individually for kerning pairs — Yo is not the same as yo.

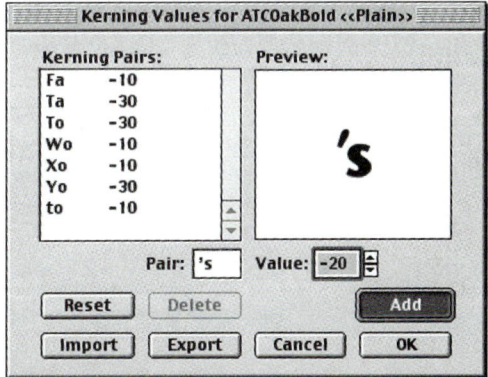

You can export the kerning tables for a font into an ASCII text file by clicking the Export button. The Export dialog box automatically names the file with the extension ".krn".

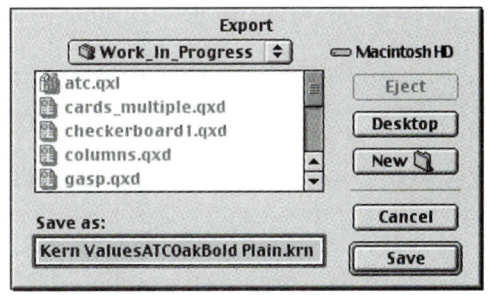

You can then import the kerning table into another font — or into the same font in a previously created document — by clicking Import in the Kerning Values dialog box. The Import dialog box shows all available ASCII files with the .krn extension. Once kerning pairs are imported, those pairs appear in the Kerning Pairs window for the selected font.

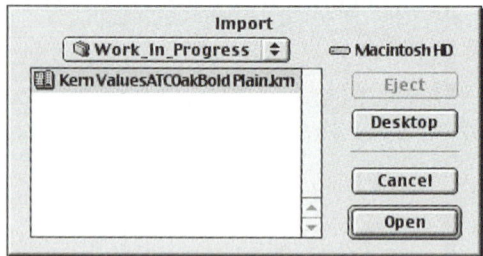

If you have changed the kerning tables for a font — deleted or modified existing pairs or added new ones, you can restore the original kerning table that is built into the font by clicking Reset in the Kerning Values dialog box. Clicking OK saves any changes, Cancel does not save your changes; both buttons return you to the Edit Kerning Tables dialog box, where you must click Save to keep any edits you made.

Resolving Preference Conflicts

If you modify the kerning values, either in a file or in the default application environment, you may encounter a conflict warning when you open files that do not incorporate the modified kerning tables.

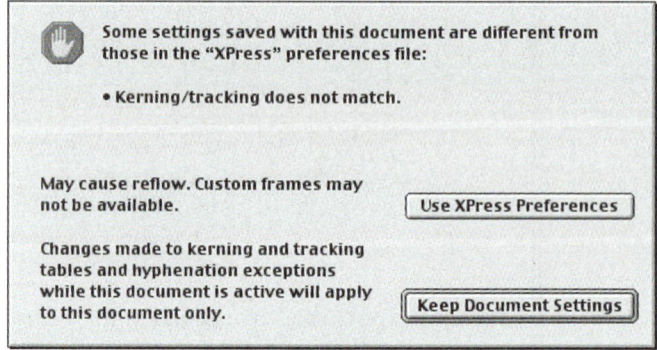

To resolve this conflict, consider what is causing the conflict.

- Did you modify the kerning tables in the application default environment?

  If so, the application preferences are different than the document. In this case you should probably click Use XPress Preferences, unless you spent a lot of time manually kerning the document. If you have manually kerned the document, you may want to click Keep Document Settings. Otherwise, the kerning defined in the kerning tables is applied in addition to manual kerning, resulting in letters that are squashed together.

- Did you modify the kerning table in the file you are opening?

  If so, the document is different than the preferences. In this case you should Keep Document Settings.

If you didn't create the file, you should almost always choose Keep Document Preferences and then review the document carefully before applying your default settings.

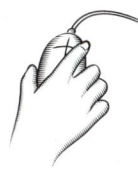

Zooming in on the page may be helpful.

Pay particular attention to capital-lowercase or lowercase-capital combinations. They frequently require kerning.

Kerning is largely a matter of personal preference.

Modify Kerning Tables

1. In the open document gasp.qxd, look at the headings and subheadings throughout the document. You can see some letter pairs that need kerning help.

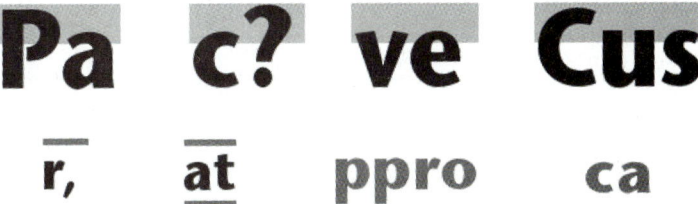

2. Choose Utilities>Kerning Table Edit.

3. Highlight ATC Oak Bold <<Plain>> in the list, and click Edit.

4. Type "Pa" in the Pair field. Enter -5 in the Value field and look at the Preview window. Modify the Value field until you are happy with the setting.

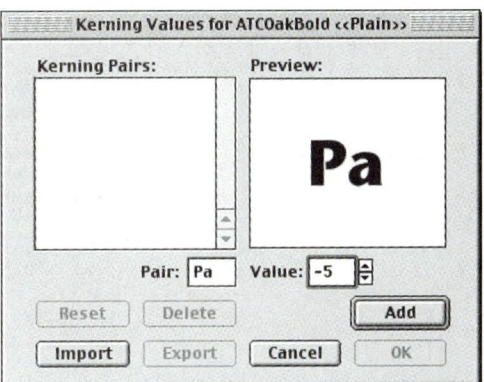

5. Add kerning pairs, using the values you prefer:

c?　　ve　　Cu　　r,　　at　　pp　　pr　　ro　　ca

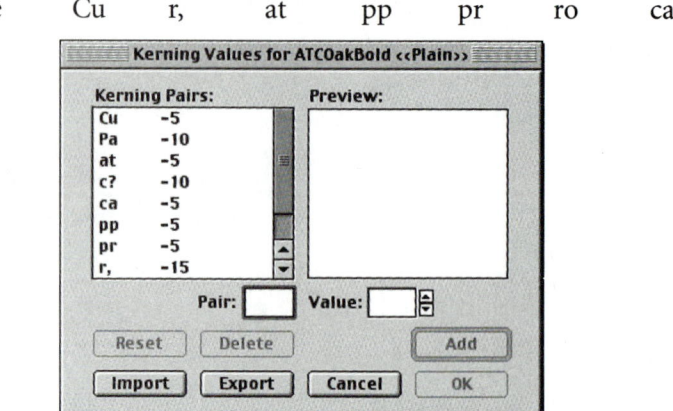

6. Click OK when you are finished, and click Save in the Kerning Table Edit dialog box.

7. Save the file and leave it open.

Editing Tracking Tables

If you find that you consistently modify the tracking of a font, such as always setting Times with –2 tracking, you can modify the tracking table for that font. QuarkXPress allows you to edit the tracking table for any font using the Tracking Edit utility (Utilities>Tracking Edit).

The Tracking Edit dialog box lists every font installed on your computer. You can highlight any font in the list and click Edit to modify the tracking table for that font. Every variation of a font is treated separately; modifying the tracking table of Times New Roman, for example, has no effect on Times New Roman Italic.

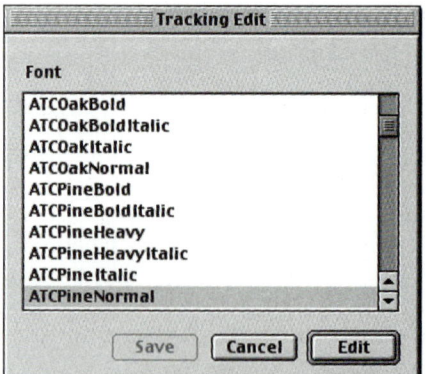

The Title bar of the Tracking Values dialog box shows the font that you are modifying. By default, a straight line bisects the graph, indicating that no modifications have been made.

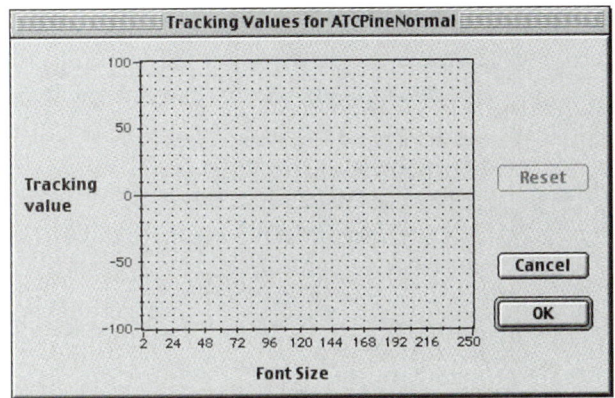

To change the tracking for a particular size of a font, you can click on the line to add an anchor point. While you hold down the mouse button, the Size and Track information is displayed at the top right of the dialog box. Once an anchor point is placed, you can delete it by Option/Control-clicking the point.

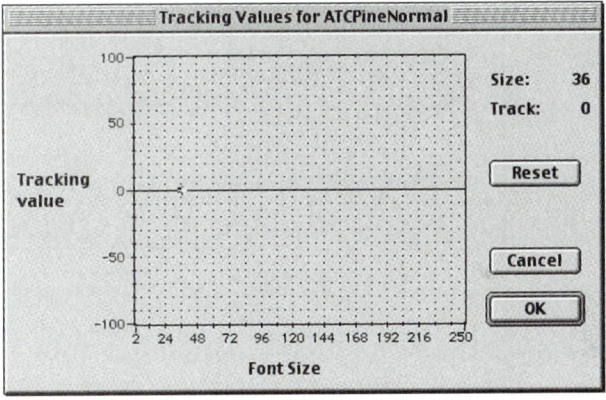

You can place up to four anchor points in a tracking table.

You can drag any anchor point on the line to a new location to change the tracking for the font. When two anchors exist on the line, the font is tracked on a mathematical scale between the two points. For example, you want 11-pt type to track –2 but want all type above 36 pt. not to use tracking. You can place one anchor at Size: 36 pt., Track: 0, and place another anchor at Size: 11 pt., Track: –2. Any type between 12 and 36 point in that font will be tracked at a fractional value between –2 and 0.

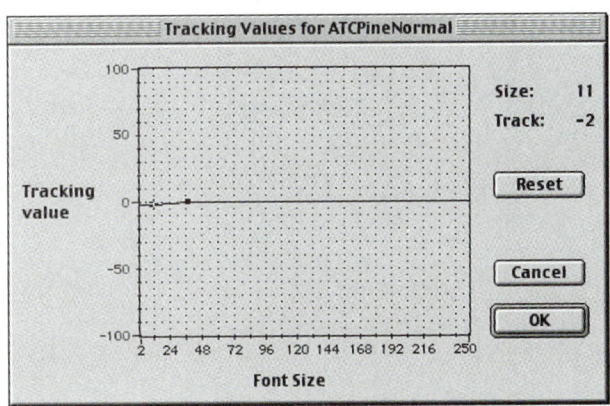

Clicking OK saves the changes and returns you to the Tracking Edit dialog box. Clicking Reset restores the font's original tracking information.

Any modification to a font's tracking table is added to existing tracking in the document. In other words, if you set the tracking table to –2 for 11-pt. type, any tracking you have already applied in the document will be added to the modified tracking table.

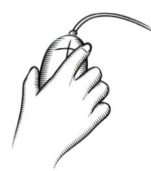

Modify Tracking Tables

1. In the open file gasp.qxd, select Utilities>Tracking Edit. Highlight ATC Oak Bold in the list and click Edit.

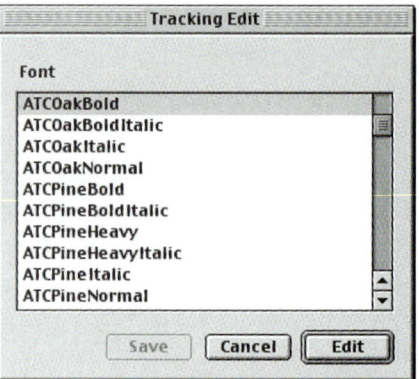

2. In the Tracking Values dialog box, click on the line at Size: 36. Drag the anchor point until the information area shows Size: 36, Track: –4.

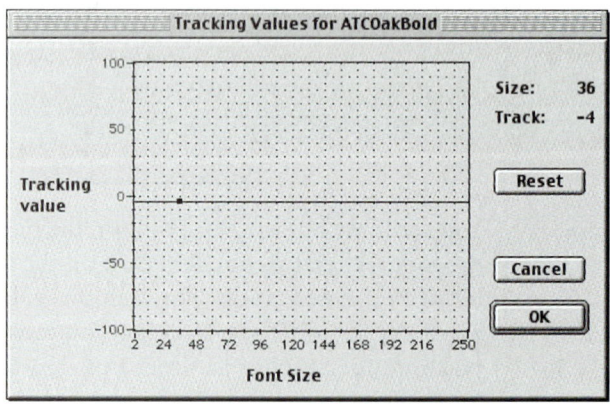

3. Place a second anchor point at Size: 18, Track: –2.

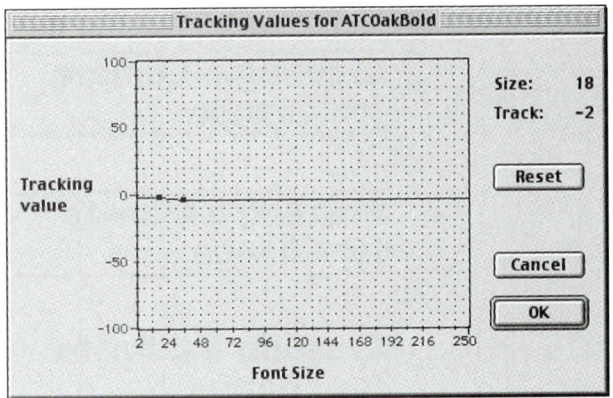

4. Place a third anchor point at Size: 2, Track: 0.

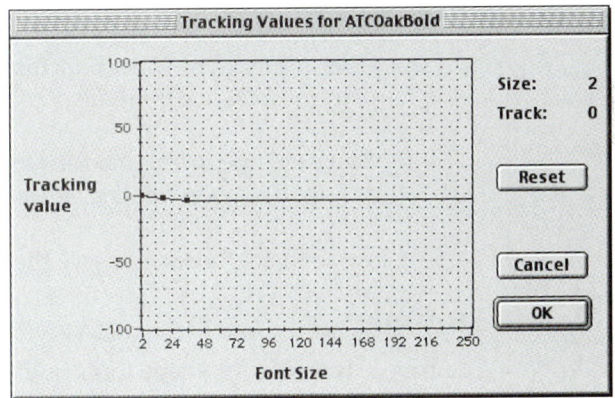

5. Click OK, and then click Save in the Tracking Edit dialog box.

6. Choose Edit>Style Sheets. Select Heading 1 and click Edit. Click Edit in the Character Attributes area. Change the Track Amount field to 0. Click OK, then OK again to return to the Edit Style Sheets dialog box.

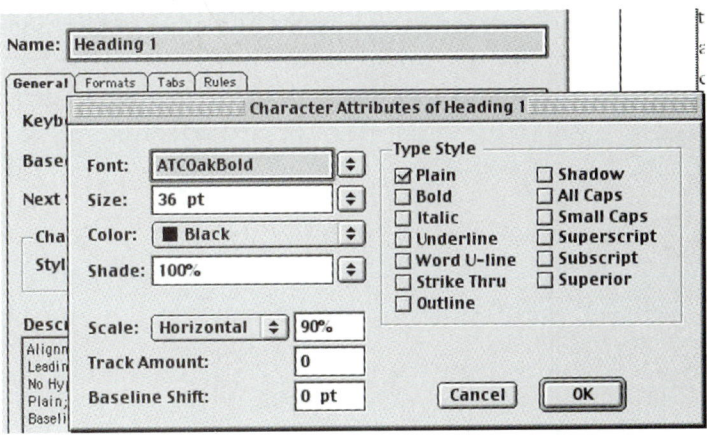

7. Edit the Heading 2 style sheet to 0 tracking.

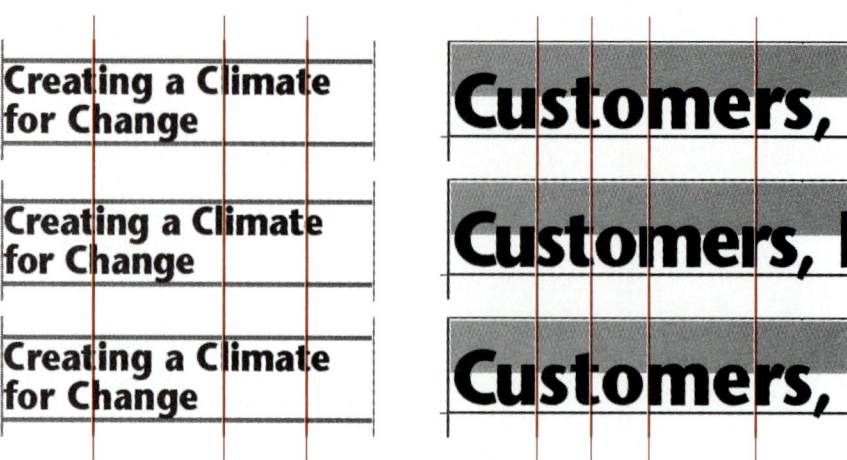

The colored lines serve as a reference to see the difference between the original text set with a style sheet that includes –4 tracking (top); the same text after modifying the tracking tables values (middle), and the result of changing the style sheet tracking to 0 (bottom).

Before the style sheet is modified to 0 tracking, both the tracking table (–4) and the style sheet tracking (–4) are applied, squashing the type together.

8. Close all dialog boxes and save the file.

Summary

You have learned that the type tools built into QuarkXPress allow professional-level control over virtually every aspect of the text in your document. You understand that whether in a text box or on a path, you can plan, place, and control all of the text on your document pages. You have learned how to place and control text on a path, which provides variation from the regular text box approach. You have learned about the new Table tool, and practiced creating and formatting tables in a document. You have worked with the automatic text box and created page jumps, which is especially useful for newsletters, magazines, and other publications. Finally, you learned how to automate the fine-tuning process by modifying the kerning and tracking tables of a font, either within a document or in the application preferences.

7 Working with Pictures

Chapter Objectives:

As the saying goes, a picture is worth a thousand words. The images and graphics in a page-layout document are the defining elements — what separates page-layout design from word processing. Most documents are carefully planned, with great consideration given to the pictures that will support the text. The utilities and tools available in QuarkXPress 5.0 provide a range of options for creating, placing, manipulating, and controlling the graphic elements of your document. In this chapter, you will:

- Learn to convert text to graphics.

- Discover the options in Custom Dashes & Stripes.

- Merge drawing elements into a single object.

- Learn how to create a clipping path in QuarkXPress.

- Examine the different options for creating runarounds.

- Work with image effects.

Projects to be Completed:

- Stonington Letterfold Brochure (A)

- Body Solution Booklet (B)

- Cosciel Poster (C)

Working with Pictures

Whether you are creating graphics within the document or importing them from another application, you have many options when working with pictures in your documents. While it is important to remember that QuarkXPress is a page-layout application, its illustration and image-editing tools provide a great deal of control directly in the layout. This chapter discusses the various utilities, effects, and XTensions that can be used to create visual interest with the images in your document.

Custom Dashes & Stripes

Any element can have a frame (for boxes) or stroke (for lines) width and style. You can modify the attributes of these lines using the Measurements palette or the Modify dialog box.

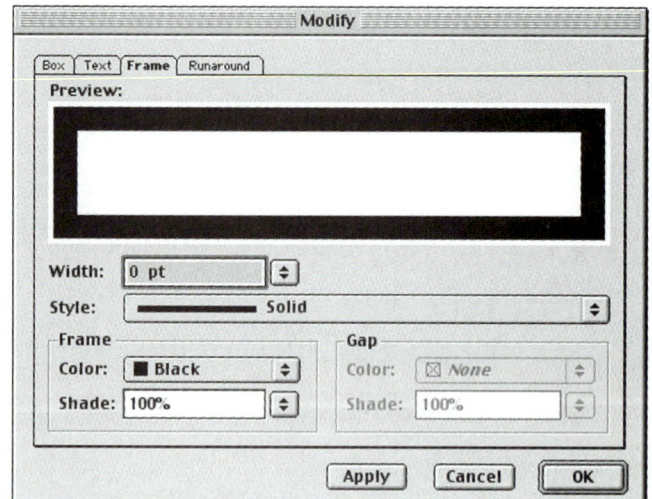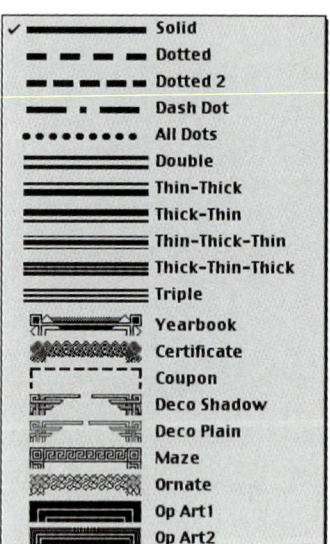

You can apply a frame width and style using the Frame tab of the Modify dialog box.

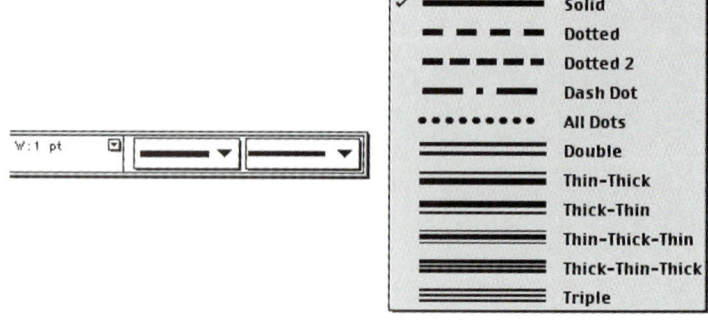

You can apply a line width and style using the Measurements palette.

You can also define custom line styles using the Dashes & Stripe dialog box (Edit>Dashes & Stripes). Clicking New opens a pop-up menu, where you can choose to create a new Dash or Stripe pattern.

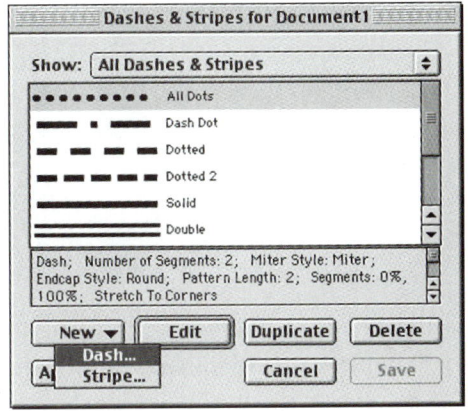

Like any other element you define in QuarkXPress, give dash patterns a name that is indicative of its appearance.

Creating Dashes

The Edit Dash dialog box allows you to define the new dash pattern. You can enter an appropriate name for the pattern in the Name field. The Preview area shows a dynamic sample of settings you make in the dialog box.

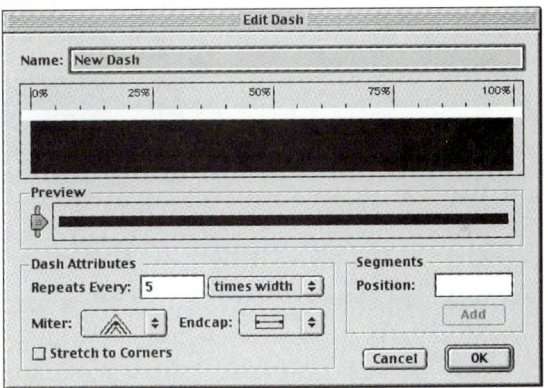

The top area of the dialog box is a ruler. By default, the pattern is solid for all new dash patterns. The first time you click in the ruler, you indicate the endpoint of the first segment of the pattern.

You can add up to five segments to the pattern ruler.

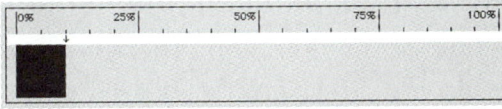

To create additional segments, you must click in the ruler and drag until the segment is the length you want. Releasing the mouse button ends the segment. Clicking once without dragging adds a marker to the rule, but you have to click the marker again and drag to create a segment.

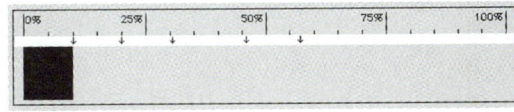

If you move the cursor over a segment in the ruler area, the Grabber Hand icon allows you to move a segment left or right to a new position on the ruler. You can remove a segment by dragging it off (up or down) of the ruler. You can change the width of a segment by clicking on an existing marker in the ruler and dragging it wider or narrower.

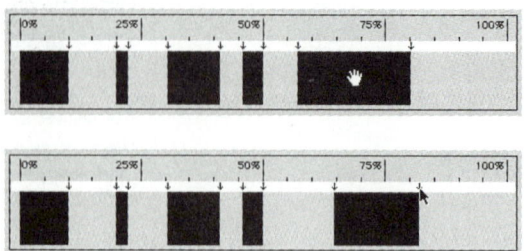

Controlling the Pattern's Frequency

The Repeats Every menu in the Edit Dash dialog box enables you to control the *frequency*, or repeating attribute, of the dash pattern.

The default — 5 Times Width — means that the pattern will repeat proportionally 5 times over the distance of the line. When this option is chosen, the pattern rule is measured in percentages because the segments are applied as a percentage of 1/5 of the line length. You can also modify the number of times (from 0.1 to 50) the segment repeats over the distance of the line by changing the text field.

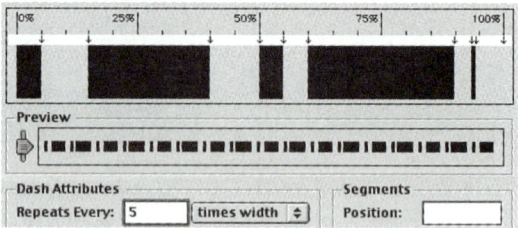

If you choose Points from the Repeats Every menu, the pattern will repeat at specifically defined intervals. The distance of the line has no effect on the appearance of the pattern. With this option selected, the pattern ruler shows the specific number of defined points, after which the pattern repeats.

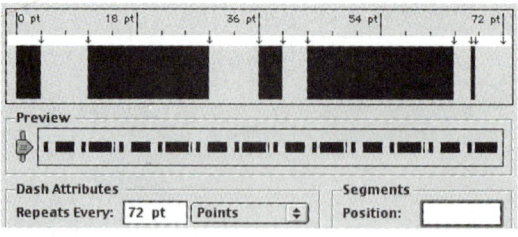

There are approximately 72 points to an inch.

Selecting Segment Options

The Endcap menu defines the end treatment for each segment of the pattern. The Projecting Round and Projecting Square options extend the stylistic end of the segment beyond the actual segment end, which allows different pattern segments to overlap.

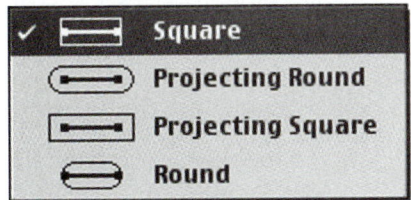

The Miter option defines the appearance of corners if the dash style is used as a box frame.

The Stretch to Corners check box is also relevant if the pattern is used as a box frame. When this option is selected, the pattern is stretched to make corner segments appear symmetrical. This option overrides the settings in Repeats Every.

With Stretch to Corners deselected (left), the pattern repeats as defined; all corners may not appear the same. With Stretch to Corners selected (right), the pattern is stretched so that all corners match.

When you have finished defining the dash pattern, clicking OK returns you to the Dashes & Stripes dialog box, where you have to click Save before using the new pattern.

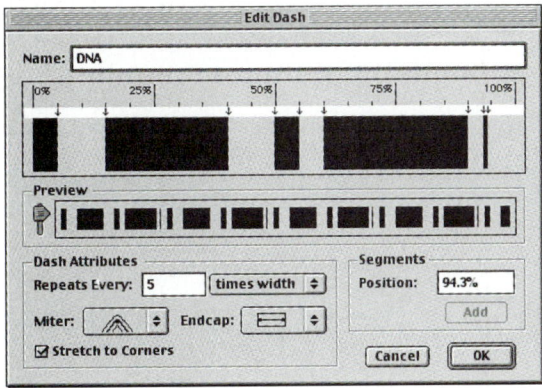

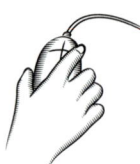

Create Custom Dash Patterns

1. Create a new file using the default settings.

2. Select Edit>Dashes & Stripes. Click New>Dash.

3. In the Edit Dash dialog box, type "Bar Code" in the Name field.

4. Change the Repeats Every menu to Points, and type 36 in the field.

5. In the ruler, click at the first tick mark after 0 pt. to end the first segment of the dash pattern.

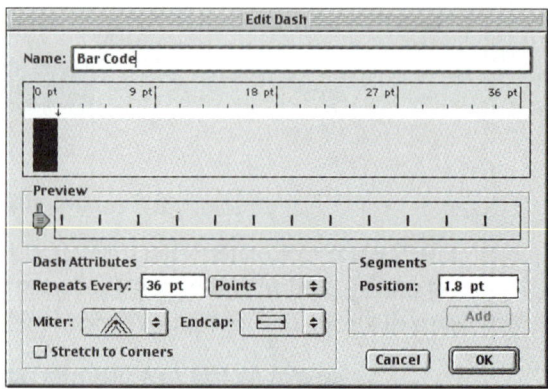

6. Click at the third tick mark and drag to the 9-pt. mark.

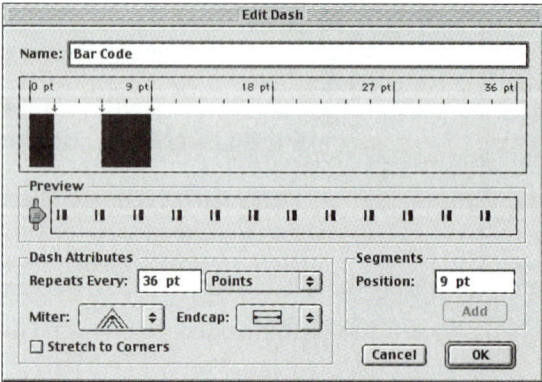

36 pts. = 0.5 in.

7. Click at the next tick past 9 pt. and drag halfway to the next.

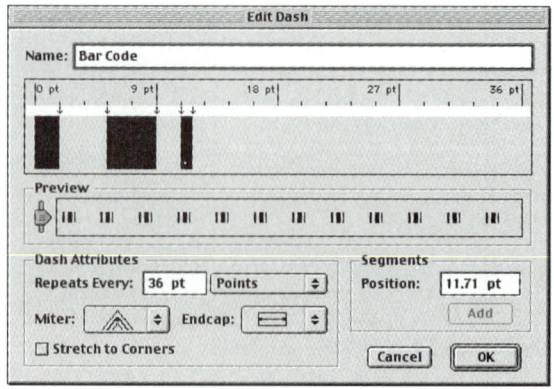

8. Click at the mark before 18 pt. and drag until the Position field shows 23.4 pt.

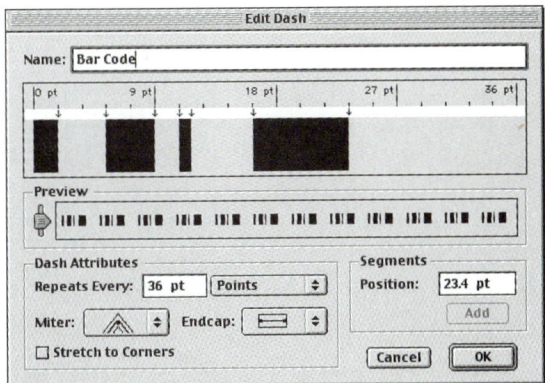

9. Click the first mark after 27 pt. (28.8 pt.) and drag to the right until the Position field shows 32.4 pt.

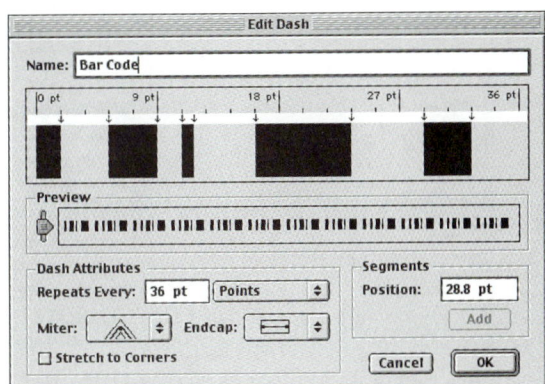

10. Click OK to return to the Dashes & Stripes dialog box.

11. Click New>Dash again.

12. Type "Coupon Border" in the Name field.

13. Choose Round from the Endcap menu, and activate the Stretch to Corners check box.

14. Choose Points from the Repeats Every menu, and enter 72 in the field.

72 points = 1 inch.

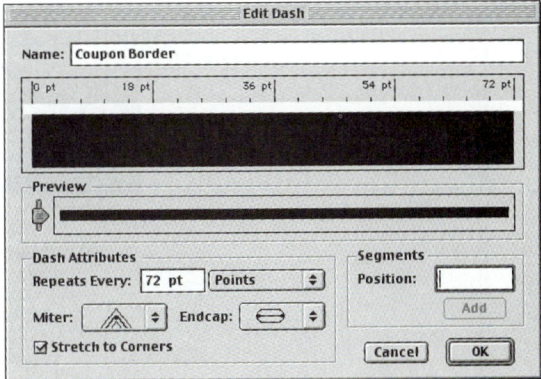

15. Type 18 in the Position field and click Add.

16. Click at the 36-pt. mark on the pattern ruler, and drag to the 54-pt. mark.

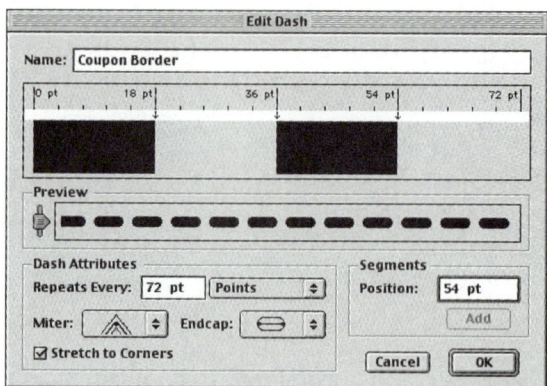

17. Click OK, and then click Save in the Dashes and Stripes dialog box.

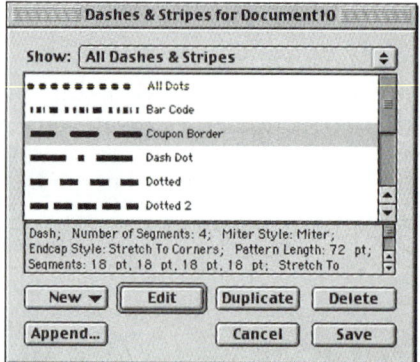

18. Save the file as "custom_dashes.qxd" in your **Work_In_Progress** folder, and leave the file open.

Creating Stripes

The Edit Stripe dialog box (Edit>Dashes & Stripes>New>Stripe) is very similar to the Edit Dashes dialog box, with a few less options. The ruler, in this case, is oriented vertically. The appearance of a custom stripe pattern is always dependent on the line width, so the ruler is based only on percentages. Segments of the stripe are created and modified in the same way as the segments of a custom dash pattern.

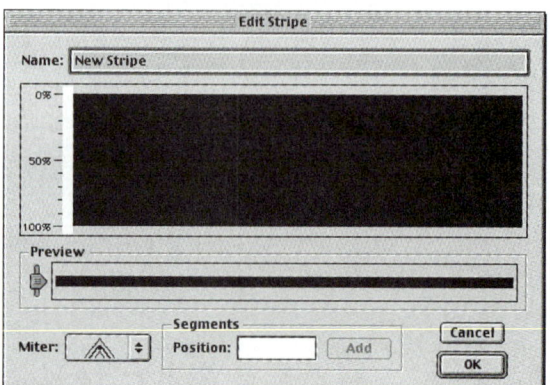

When you have defined the stripe pattern, clicking OK returns you to the Dashes & Stripes dialog box, where you must click Save before you can use the new pattern.

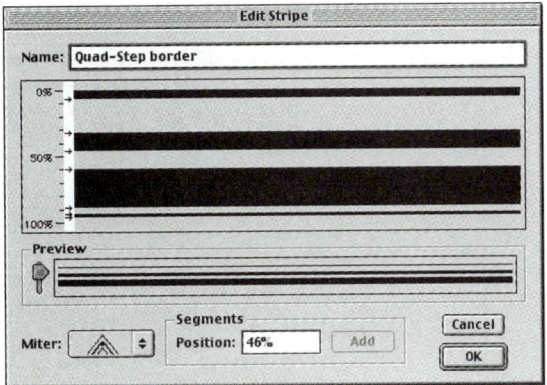

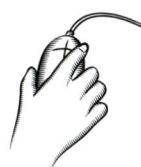

Create a Custom Stripe Pattern

1. In the open file custom_dashes.qxd, choose Edit>Dashes & Stripes. Click New>Stripe.

2. Type "Horizon" in the Name field.

3. Type 5 in the Position field and click Add.

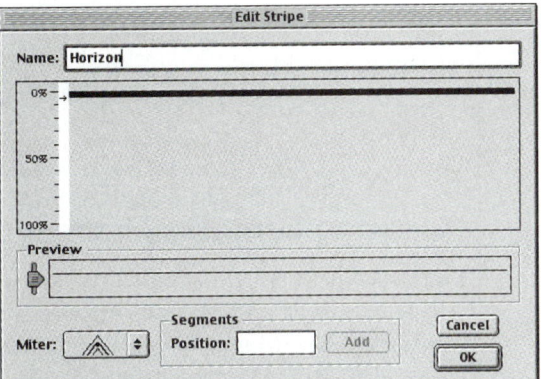

4. Click at the 20% mark in the pattern ruler, and drag down to the 30% mark.

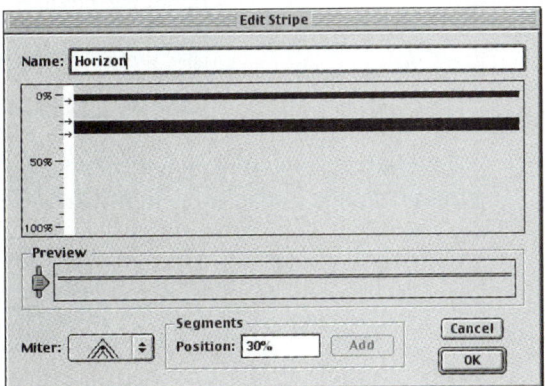

5. Click at the 50% mark and drag down to the 65% mark.

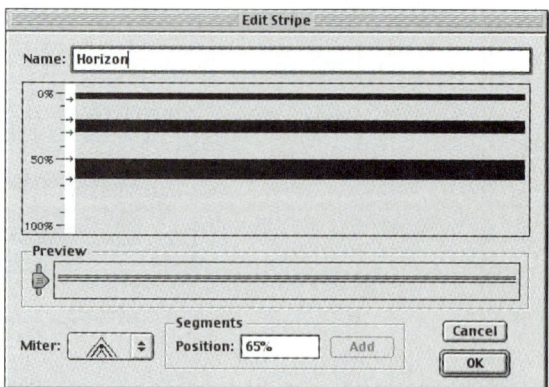

6. Click at the 80% mark and drag down to the 100% mark.

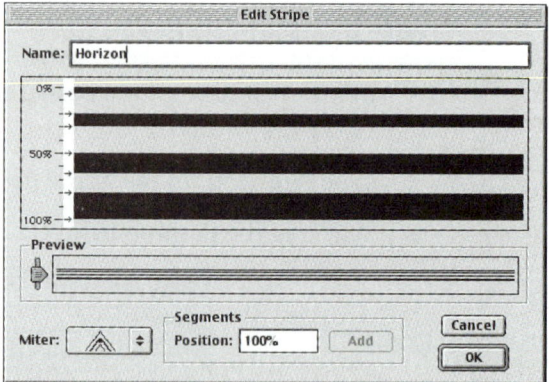

7. Click OK, then click Save in the Dashes & Stripes dialog box. Save and close the file.

Creating Complex Shapes

In *QuarkXPress 5.0: Introduction to Electronic Documents*, we examined the drawing tools. To review, type and pictures imported into QuarkXPress are contained in boxes, which can be drawn using the Picture Box tools or the Text Box tools. There are several standard shapes of each. The Freehand and Bézier tools allow you to create freeform shapes directly on a QuarkXPress page; you can then import text and graphics into these shapes.

Lines are created in much the same way as boxes. To draw lines, you click on the Line tool and drag the line to the length you wish, at the desired angle or shape.

These are the basics of everything you do in a Quark document. But you also have other options.

Merging Objects

Merging is one option for creating complex shapes in QuarkXPress. The Merge utilities (Item>Merge) combine two or more shapes, creating complex Bézier graphics far more easily than you could by drawing them by hand with the Bézier tools. The attributes of the back-most object (color, border, contents, and so on) are maintained in the merged shape.

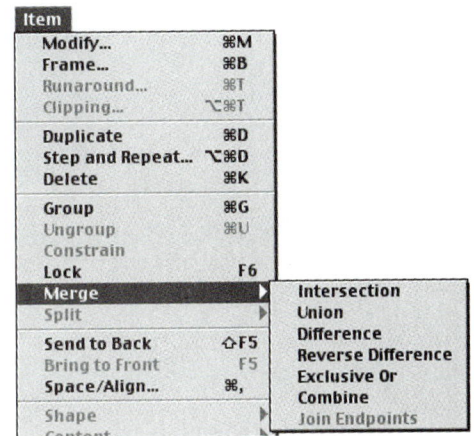

- **Intersection.** The Intersection option returns the shape that is the overlap of the selected objects.

If the selected objects do not overlap, the Intersection command presents an error message.

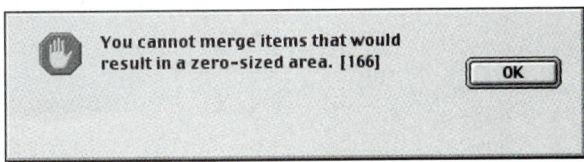

- **Union**. This option unites the selected objects into a single shape. If the selected objects do not overlap, the Union command creates a single element from the multiple objects.

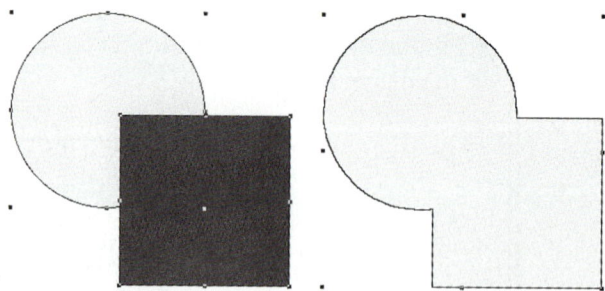

- **Difference**. This option creates a shape based on the back-most object, subtracting any overlapping areas from other objects. If the selected objects do not overlap, the Difference command returns only the back-most object.

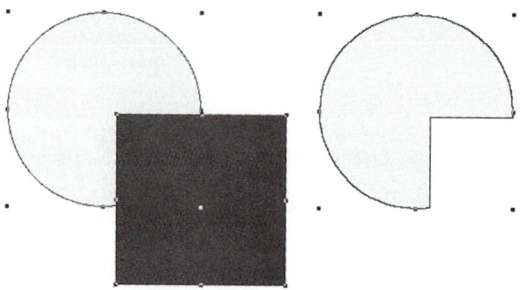

- **Reverse Difference**. This option combines all but the back-most object, and then removes the back-most object from that combination. If the selected objects do not overlap, the Reverse Difference command removes the back-most object and unites any remaining elements.

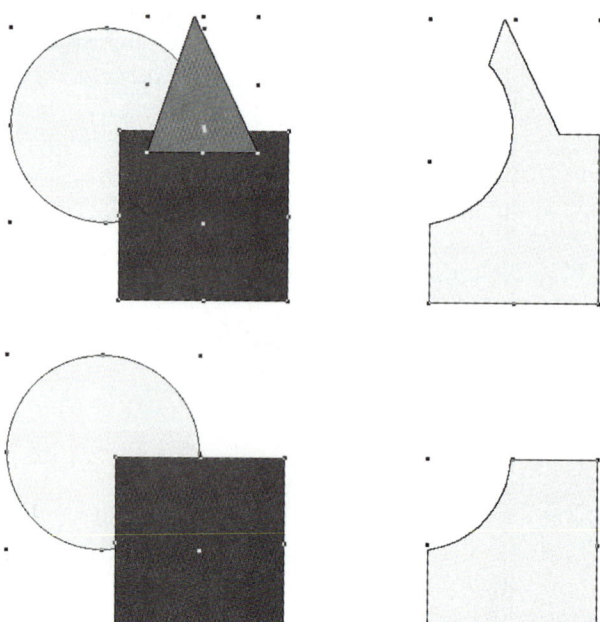

If only two objects are selected, the back-most object is removed from the front-most.

- **Exclusive Or.** This option combines the selected shapes and removes the overlapping area. Any point at which the two objects overlap creates two distinct anchor points so the shape of each piece in the final object can be edited independently.

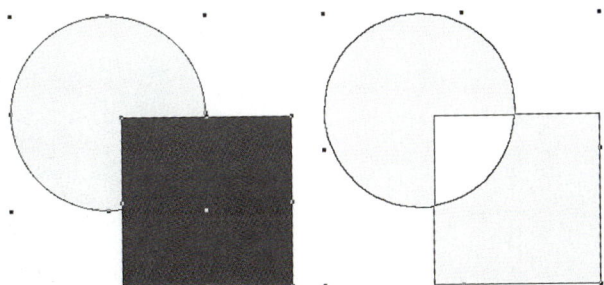

- **Combine.** This option combines the selected shapes and removes the overlapping area. The difference between Combine and Exclusive Or is that no anchor points are added at intersection points.

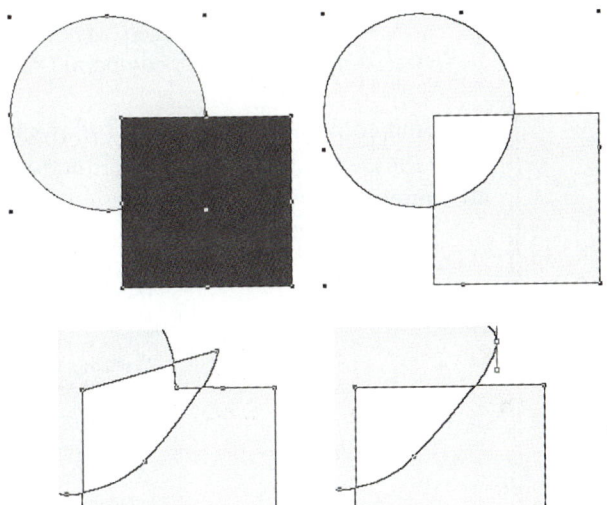

Exclusive Or (left) creates anchor points at the location of intersecting lines in the original objects. Combine (right) does not create anchor points at the intersections.

- **Join Endpoints.** This option is only available when lines are selected. The Join Endpoints command is used to combine two endpoints that overlap.

If the endpoints of a line do not overlap, the Join Endpoints command returns an error message.

Managing Complex Graphics

When a complex graphic consists of more than one shape, the Exclusive Or and Combine commands create a complex shape that may include one or more compound paths, and masks (knocks out) the area of the underlying shape.

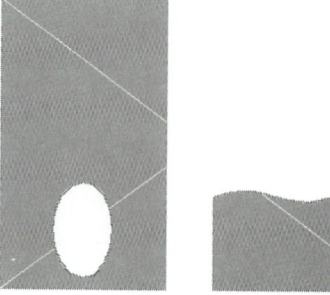

Two nonoverlapping objects (the rectangle and the polygon) were merged with the Unite command. The crosshairs indicate that the two shapes are treated as a single picture box. An oval was then placed over the rectangle, and the Combine merge executed. The resulting white oval is a compound path, masking out the fill from the background shape.

The Split command (Item>Split) allows you to separate the pieces of a complex object. Once the elements are split, they function independently with separate contents and attributes.

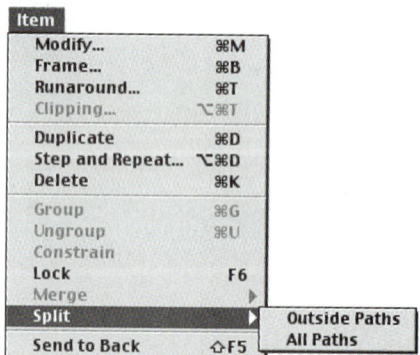

- **Outside Paths.** This option splits nonoverlapping elements of the same object into individual objects. Compound paths are not affected.

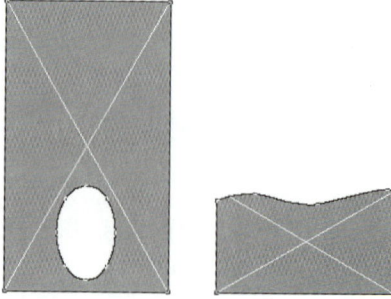

The crosshairs indicate that the two nonoverlapping shapes are separate, but the oval compound path is still intact.

- **All Paths.** This option splits all elements of the object into individual pieces, including the compound path.

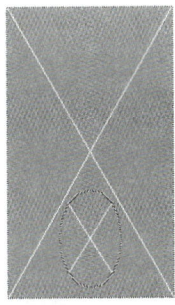

The crosshairs in each shape indicate that each shape — including the oval — is a separate object.

Converting Text to Graphics

You can create complex graphics with type, much as you would in an illustration program. When type is highlighted with the Content tool, the Text to Box command creates a graphic element from the outline of type. You can then import a picture or create a blend that fills the graphic element.

To create a box from text, you have to highlight the target text with the Content tool and choose Style>Text to Box. Any text not highlighted will not be outlined. A box is created from the highlighted text; the text box remains in place.

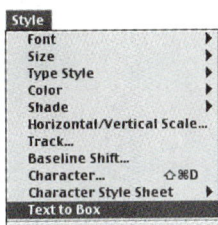

Once a box has been created from text, the entire set of letters is treated as a single object. When guides are visible, the diagonal crosshairs extend across all the letters. Fill color and placed images extend across all elements of the shape.

The Text to Box tool works in much the same way as the Convert to Outline option in Adobe Illustrator and the Convert to Paths option in Macromedia FreeHand.

If you hold the Option/Alt key while choosing Style>Text to Box, the highlighted text is converted to outlines as an inline graphic in the place of the highlighted text. The text is automatically deleted.

You can modify the shape of individual letters by dragging the anchor points, just as you would modify any other Bézier or freehand shape.

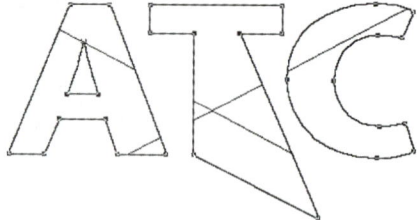

Splitting Text Graphics

Graphics created from text can be split, which enables you to move the letters independently of one another to create unique effects.

If you split Outside Paths, the compound paths remain intact for individual letters; splitting All Paths removes the compound paths.

Outside Paths maintains the compound paths for individual letters.

All Paths removes the compound paths.

When you split a path, the contents of the path are transferred to each resulting element of the split. In other words, if you split a path that contains an image, the image exists in each of the three objects created by the split.

Resizing and Reshaping Complex Graphics

Once you have finalized the position of individual anchors of a complex graphic, you should choose Item>Edit>Shape to toggle the Shape option off. This prevents you from accidentally changing the shape of an object.

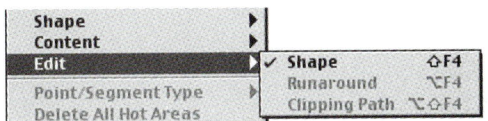

When Edit Shape is toggled off, the individual anchors of complex graphics are unavailable. You can resize the entire object using the eight handles that indicate the bounding box.

Work with Complex Graphics

1. Open **vineyard.qxd** from the **RF_Adv_Quark** folder.

2. Draw a large rectangle text box on the page. Type "Noire Vineyard".

3. Style Noire as 120-pt. ATC Jacaranda. Set Vineyard as 120-pt. ATC Laurel Black.

Noire Vineyard, located in the heart of Utah's scenic Noire River Valley has been the home of fine Cabernet and Pinot wines since 1913. Our grapes are the offspring of the vines cultivated 500 years ago by English monks. Shoots from the vines were preserved by working-class English emigrant Paul Whiteman for the three-month steam ship journey across the Atlantic. After unsuccessfully looking for work in North Carolina and Virginia, Whiteman continued west in 1910 to find the beautiful, sloping hills of the Noire River Valley. He settled there, planted his grapes, and planted an empire. After nearly 100 years, Noire Vineyards still harvests from Whiteman's original vines. Geneva Garin, Whiteman's great-granddaughter, now presides over the estate, preserving the family tradition and heritage by obtaining a degree in viticulture from UC Davis. The head wine maker, Martin Grover, has been with Noire Vineyard for over 20 years, winning more than 70 national and international awards and creating new masterpieces every year. The vineyard estate now covers over 350 acres, encompassing the grape fields, wine-making facilities, a 15-bedroom mansion, 6-car garage, stable and carriage house, and a newly renovated tasting room and private banquet facility. Noire Vineyard is an absolute must for the connoisseur, and for every dinner table.

Noire **Vineyard**

4. Highlight the word Vineyard and choose Style>Text to Box.

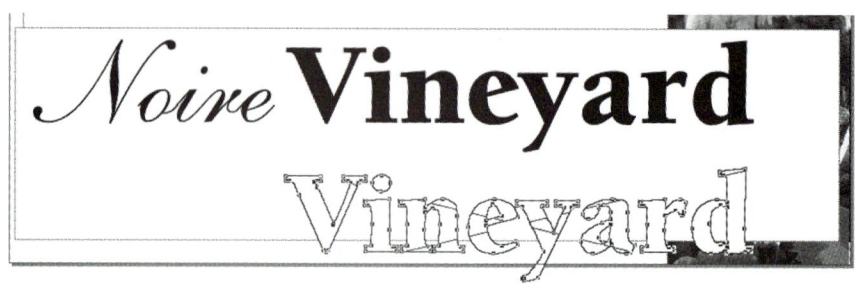

5. With the Content tool selected, delete the word Vineyard from the text box, and close up the text box to fit the remaining text.

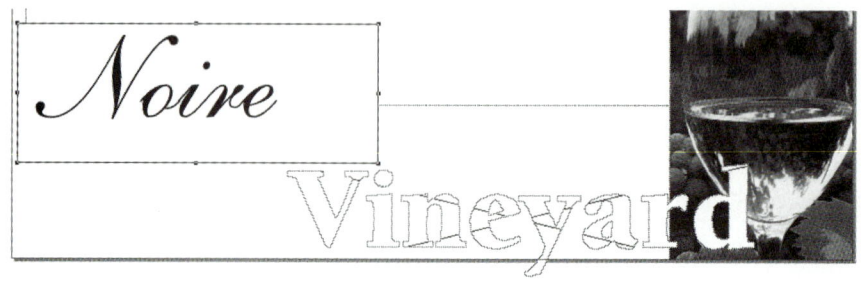

6. Select the Vineyard picture box with the Content tool. Place the file **grapes.tif** into the box.

7. Select the Item tool. Using the Measurements palette, position the box at X: 0.5 in., Y: 3.84 in.

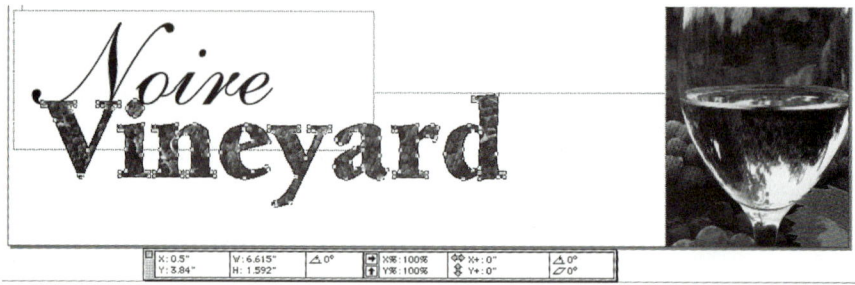

8. Choose Item>Split>Outside Paths.

9. Select the dot above the "i" with the Item tool, and press Delete/Backspace.

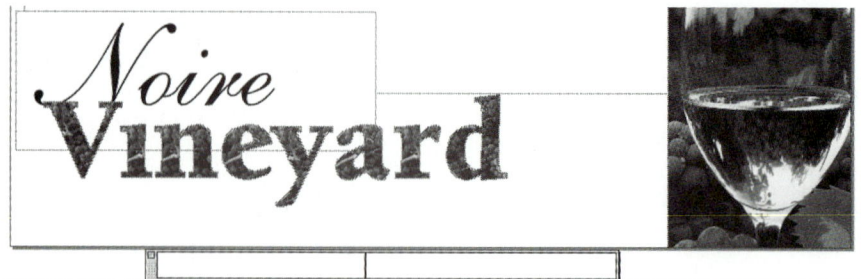

10. Select all of the letter picture boxes with the Item tool, and choose Item>Merge>Union.

Notice the image pattern in each letter is the same.

11. Click OK to the warning that you are deleting box contents.

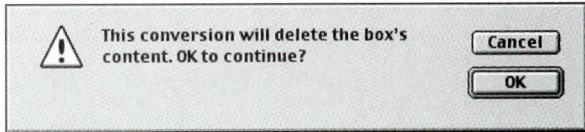

12. Notice that the picture only appears in the "d", which was the last (and therefore back-most) letter. Using the Content tool, drag the picture to the left until all the letters are filled.

13. With the Item tool selected, choose Item>Edit>Shape to toggle off the Shape option.

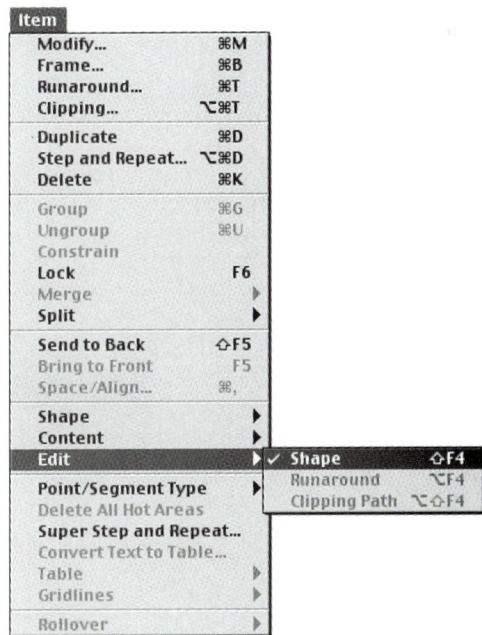

14. Drag the picture box handles, or use the Measurements palette to change the box dimensions to W: 8.718 in., H: 2.255 in. The descender of the "y" will bleed off the edge of the page.

15. Select the Noire text box. Use the Measurements palette to position it at X: 1.95 in., Y: 3.05 in.

16. Save the file as "images.qxd" in your **Work_In_Progress** folder, and leave the file open.

Clipping Paths

A *clipping path* is a Bézier path that determines which parts of an image will show on the page. Anything inside the path will show and print; anything outside the path won't. The clipping path essentially knocks out the unwanted part of the image.

Clipping paths are useful when you want to place an irregularly shaped part of one image over another in the page layout. When you place an image into a Quark document, the background is considered part of the image, even if the background is white.

The image on the left was saved without a clipping path; the white background of the image obscures the color of the background box. The image on the right was saved with a clipping path; the color of the background box is visible immediately around the glass.

Vector graphics (such as those created by Adobe Illustrator or Macromedia Freehand) that do not include placed raster data do not need clipping paths. Any part of a vector graphic that is not filled will knock out if the box background is set to None.

As a general rule, clipping paths should be created in the original image-editing application. If that is not possible, you can generate a clipping path from within QuarkXPress by choosing Item>Clipping.

The Clipping tab of the Modify dialog box presents several options. For an image that does not have an embedded clipping path, the Type menu is set to Item by default.

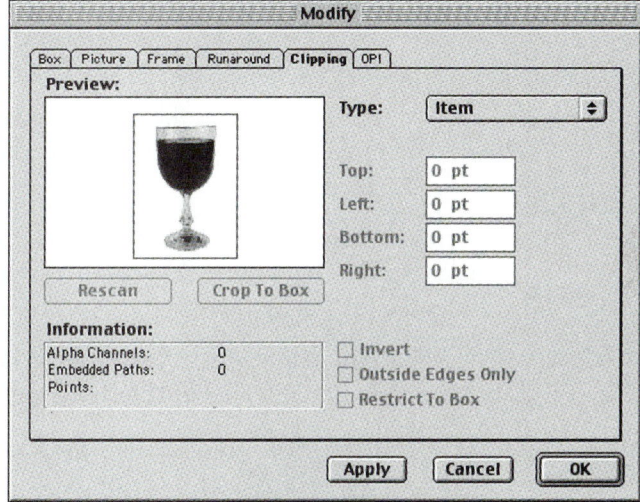

To create a clipping path in QuarkXPress, you can choose a method from the Type menu.

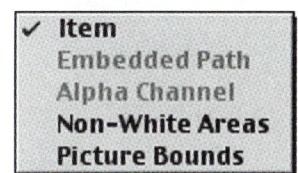

- **Item**. This option means that the edges of the picture box define the edges of the image. No clipping path is created.

- **Embedded Path**. This option is only available if the image was saved from an image-editing application with a path.

- **Alpha Channel**. This option is available only if the image was saved with an alpha-channel mask.

- **Non-White Areas**. This option allows Quark to evaluate the image and create a clipping path based on the contents of the picture. This option only works if the area you want to clip is very light, without much variation.

- **Picture Bounds**. This creates a clipping path that includes areas of the image beyond the edges of the box.

When Non-White Areas is selected in the Type menu, the Tolerance options define the criteria used to generate the clipping path from non-white areas.

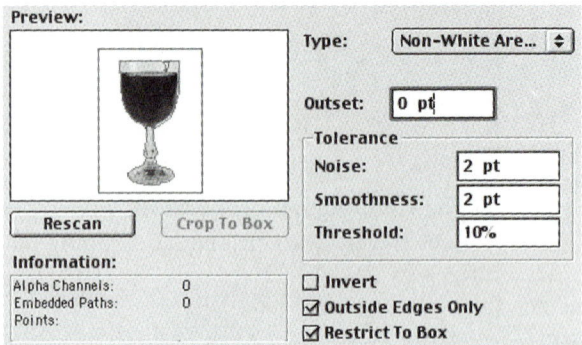

The Noise field determines the smallest possible size for any part of a path. This can be used to eliminate small spots of color in a mottled background from being included within the clipping path.

The Smoothness field defines the smallest possible length between anchor points on the clipping path. The smaller this number is, the more precise and more complex the resultant path will be.

The Threshold field defines the degree of variation from pure white that will be clipped by the resultant path. Higher threshold means that lighter shades of gray will be clipped.

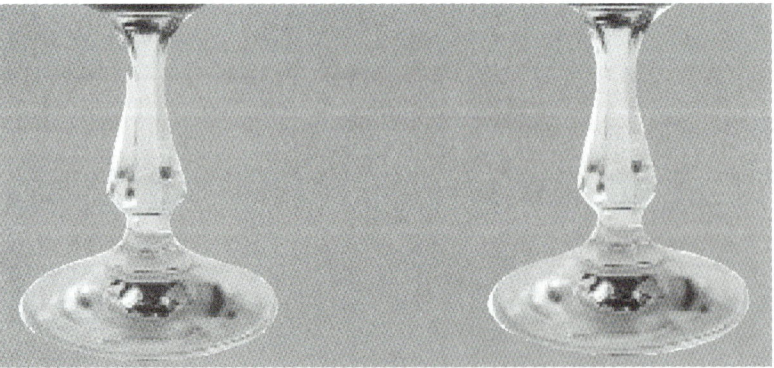

The clipping path on the left was generated with a 10% threshold; you can see that some areas of the stem are clipped. The path on the right was created with a 2% threshold, and does not clip out near-white parts of the glass.

The clipping paths generated in QuarkXPress are no substitute for those generated in an image-editing application using Bézier curves. This feature does, however, provide some flexibility, especially if you are creating a clipping path to use for text runaround.

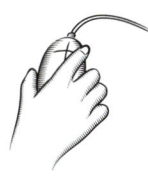

Work with Clipping Paths

1. In the open file (images.qxd), select the picture box in the bottom-right corner of the page, and choose Utilities>Usage. Choose the Pictures tab in the Usage box.

   With glass.tif highlighted, click update. Locate the file **glass.tif** in the **RF_Adv_Quark** folder and click Open to update the missing image. When the link is fixed, click Done to close the Usage dialog box.

2. With the glass image still selected, choose Item>Clipping.

3. Choose Embedded Path from the Type menu, and deselect the Restrict to Box option. Click OK.

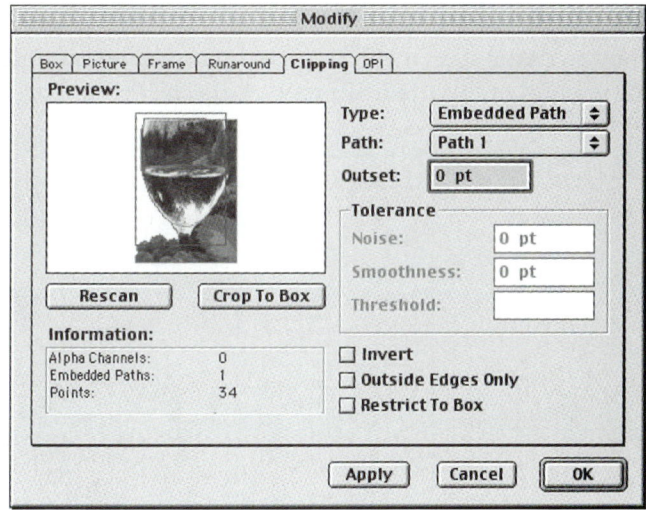

4. Draw a new rectangular picture box on top of the text box at the top of the page:

   X: 0 in.   W: 12 in.
   Y: 0 in.   H: 3.25 in.

5. Place the file **bottle.tif** into the picture box.

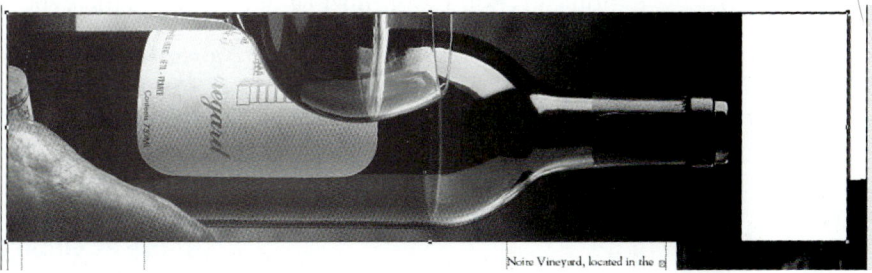

6. Choose Item>Clipping.

By deselecting Restrict to Box, the image now bleeds off the page edge properly.

7. Choose Embedded Path from the Type menu, but this time leave Restrict to Box selected. Click OK.

8. Save the file and leave it open.

Working with Object Runarounds

You can create special effects, including running text into a shape, using the options of the Runaround utility (Item>Runaround). The Preview area shows how text will wrap.

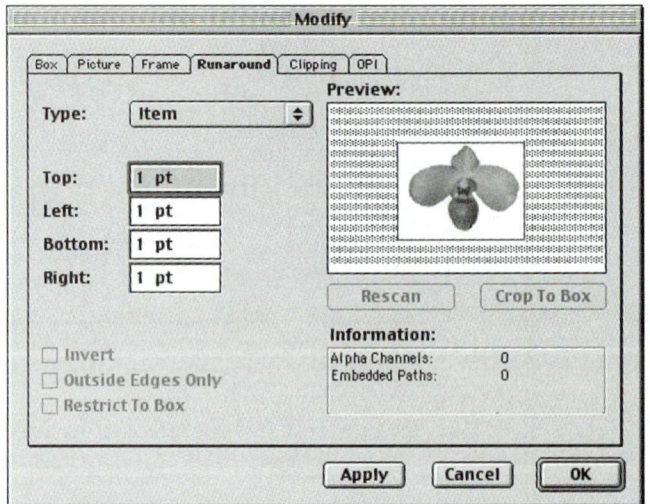

Types of Runarounds

You can choose a number of options from the Type menu.

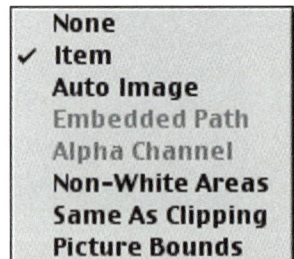

- **Item**. By default, elements are created with a runaround type of Item, which means that text wraps around the edge of the picture box at the distance defined in the Top, Bottom, Left, and Right fields.

• **None.** With None selected, text flows directly under or over the selected object instead of wrapping around it.

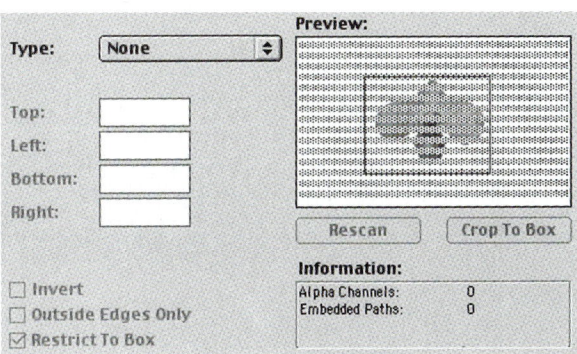

• **Auto Image.** If you choose this type of runaround, QuarkXPress scans the image based on the criteria in the Tolerance fields and creates a clipping path. That path is then used to define the runaround. The Outset field determines the distance from the path at which text will wrap.

Auto-Image and Non-White Areas work well with vector-based graphics.

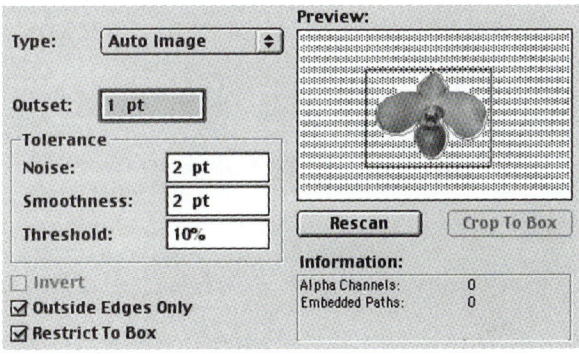

• **Embedded Path.** This option allows you to base the runaround on an embedded path. This option is only available if the image was saved with a path.

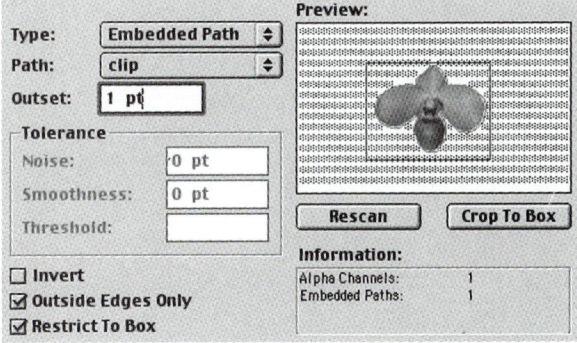

• **Alpha Channel.** The Alpha Channel option bases the runaround on an alpha channel that is saved in the image.

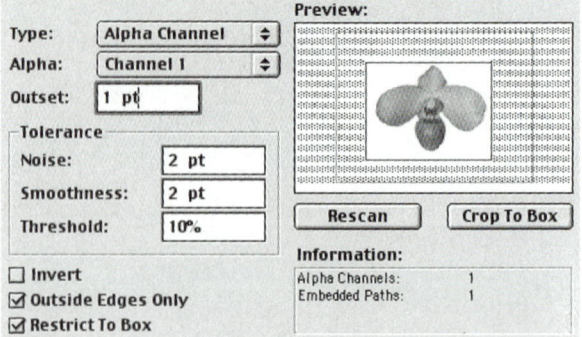

Auto Image and Non-White Areas work best for dark images against a light, nonmottled background.

- **Non-White Areas**. This option is very similar to Auto Image but does not create a clipping path.

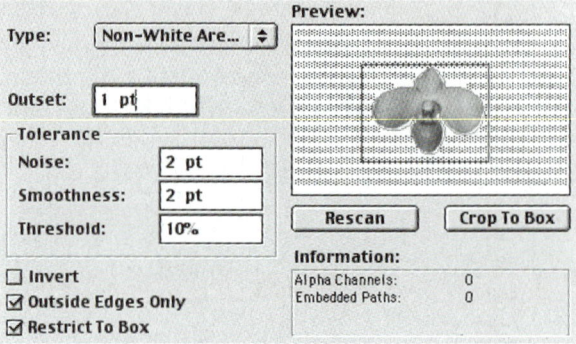

- **Same As Clipping**. This option is available if a clipping path was saved in the image, or if you created one in Quark.

The difference between Same As Clipping and Embedded Path is that the Same As Clipping option works with paths created in QuarkXPress, while Embedded Path only recognizes paths saved in the original image.

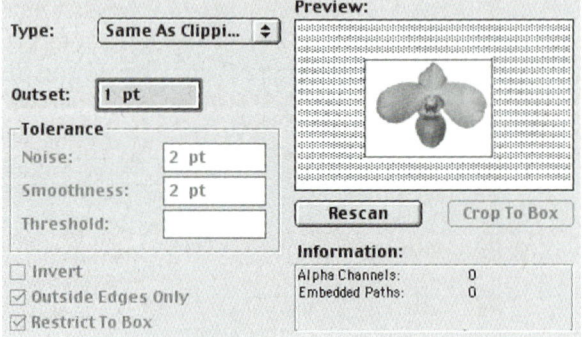

- **Picture Bounds**. This option runs text around the edge of the image instead of the edge of the picture box.

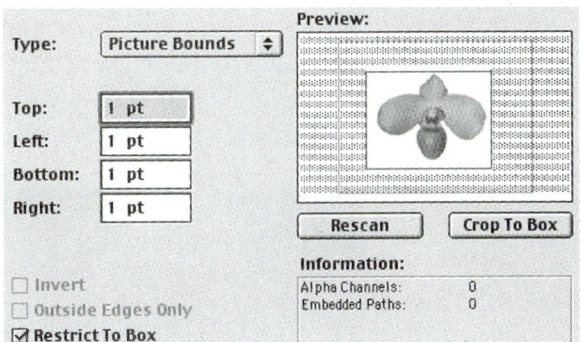

Restricting and Inverting Runarounds

A runaround can apply either to the entire image (including areas of the image that are outside the bounds of the picture box) or to only the visible portion of the image within the picture box.

Image runarounds are set by default as Restrict to Box, which means that the runaround is applied only to areas of the image that are visible within the picture box. If you deselect the Restrict to Box option, the text runaround will apply to all parts of the image, including areas outside (cropped) the edges of the box.

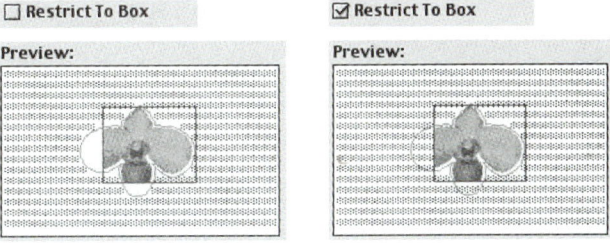

If Restrict to Box is deselected (left) the runaround will consider areas of the image that are not within the boundaries of the picture box.

You also have the option to invert the runaround, or force text to flow inside of the runaround path, using the Invert check box. Used in combination with the Restrict to Box option, this is an excellent way to flow text into unique shapes (the clipping path of an image) without manually drawing the shape with the QuarkXPress Freehand or Bézier tools.

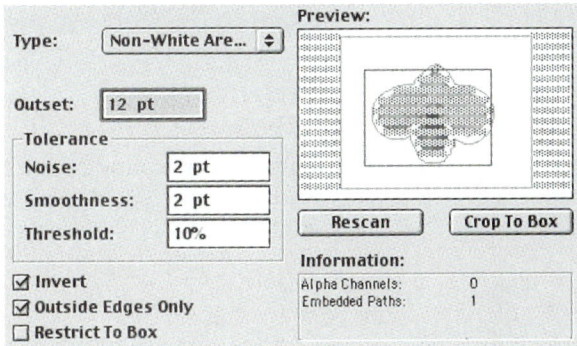

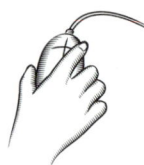

Work with Runarounds

1. In the open file (images.qxd), look at the wine bottle image. It was created with a bottle-shaped clipping path, but the contents of the path include pieces of other items that don't make sense without the entire image. In this exercise, you will flow the document text into the shape of the image's clipping path.

2. Select the bottle image box and chose Item>Runaround.

3. Choose Same As Clipping from the Type menu, and click OK.

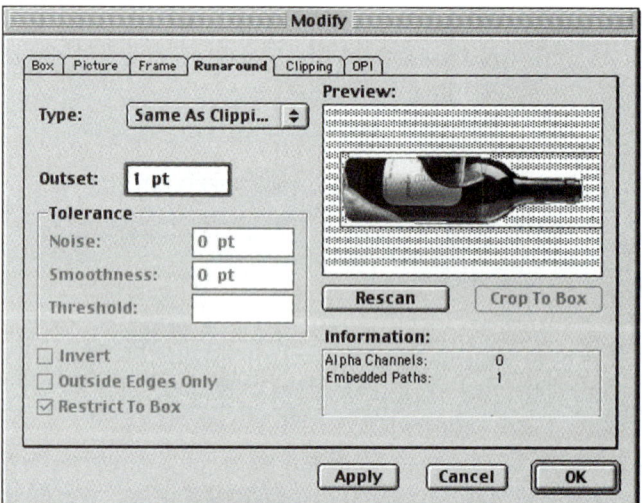

The text flows around the outside of the bottle.

4. Choose Item>Runaround again. Notice that you have no further options when Same As Clipping is selected because the clipping path defines the runaround.

5. Select Embedded Path from the Type menu. Change the Outset field to 0 pt., activate the Invert check box, and deselect the Restrict to Box option. Click OK.

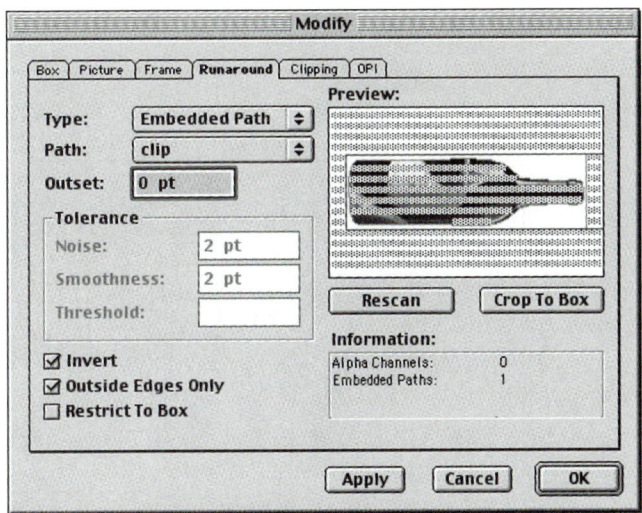

6. The text disappears again. The runaround you created set the text to flow inside the shape of the bottle. The image, however, is still on top of the text box, obscuring the text. Close up the image box so that the image itself is not visible.

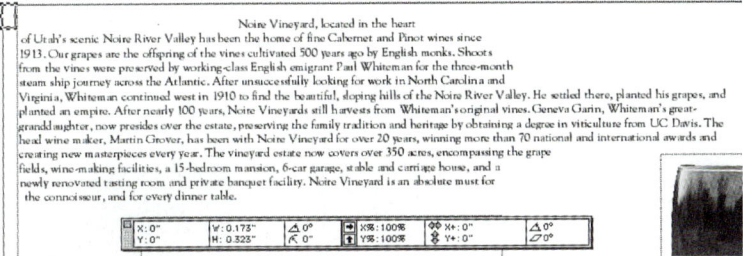

7. In the Measurements palette, change the width of the text box to 10.4 in.

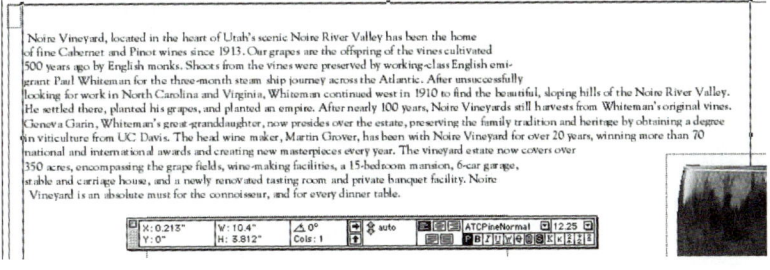

If you delete the box instead of closing it up, the bottle-shaped path will also be deleted.

8. The word Noire is now overset. Select that text box, and choose Item>
   Bring to Front.

9. Open the Colors palette, and apply a background color of None to the text box.

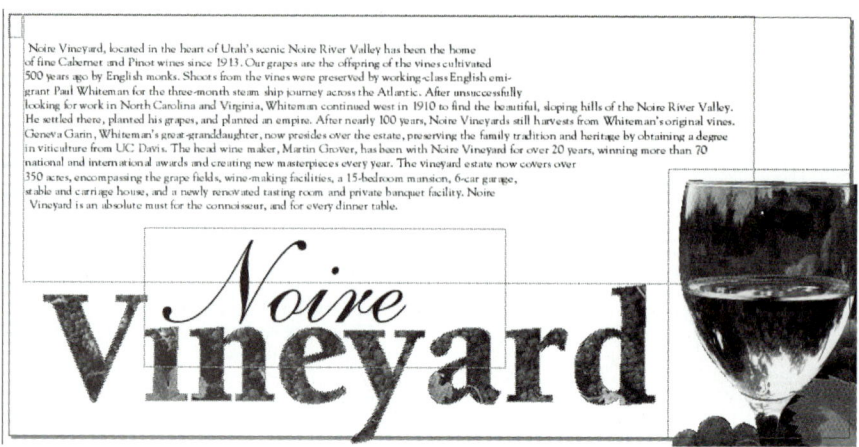

10. Save the file and leave it open.

Image Effects

QuarkXPress includes several photographic filters that enable you to modify the appearance of an image within the application. Of the image file formats used for designing printed documents, these filters generally only work with TIFF files and will not work for placed EPS or PDF files.

Adding Color and Shade

If you place a grayscale or black-and-white (bitmap) image into a layout, you can add visual interest to the image by coloring it with any color that exists in the document. You can apply color to an image by choosing Style>Color, or by selecting the Content button in the Colors palette and clicking a color. Once color is applied, you can also define a Shade for the image, either by choosing Item>Shade or by setting the Percentage field of the Colors palette.

The right image shows the result of applying color to a grayscale image in the Quark layout.

Adding color to an image in the layout should not be confused with a duotone created in an image-editing application. A true duotone creates the midtones of the image in the second color; applying a color in Quark reproduces the entire image in the second color.

While these utilities create interesting visual effects, they should be used with caution if you are sending a document to a commercial printer. Some of these cause considerable problems at the service provider, and may not be worth the effort.

Coloring a grayscale TIFF image is a good way to add visual interest to an image in a two-color job.

Color was applied to the left image in the Quark layout.
The right image is a traditional duotone created in Photoshop.

Creating a Negative Look

You create a negative effect, such as you would see on a developed roll of film, for any TIFF image (color, grayscale, or black-and-white) by choosing Style>Negative.

Applying Contrast and Halftone Effects

The Style menu offers two additional commands — Contrast and Halftone — for modifying an image within the Quark document. We could spend pages explaining how to use these controls, but to sum up… don't use them. They can cause significant problems in the production workflow. Any modification to an image's contrast or halftone values should be performed in an image-editing application.

Use Image Styles

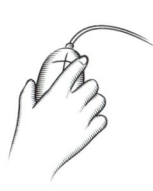

1. In the open file (images.qxd), create a new picture box at the top of the page, extending across the entire page.

    X: 0 in.   W: 12 in.
    Y: 0 in.   H: 3.4 in.

2. Place the file **background.tif** into the picture box.

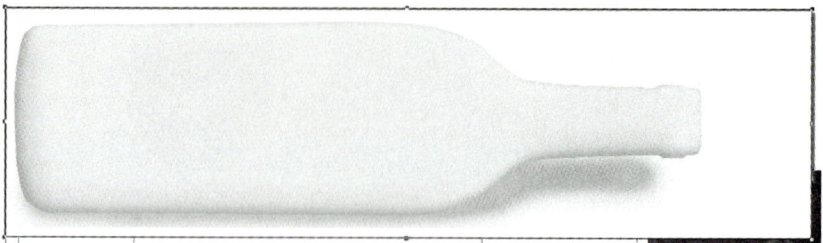

3. Choose Item>Send to Back.

4. Select the text box in front of the new image, and apply a background color of None.

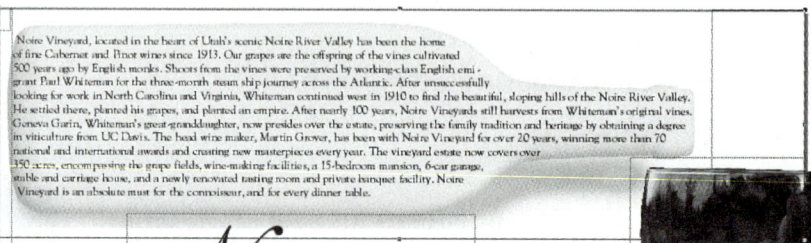

5. Select the background image box with the Content tool.

6. Choose Style>Color>59c 100m 0y 40k.

7. Save the file and close it.

Summary

The utilities and effects discussed in this chapter are a few more of the tools that allow you virtually limitless creative freedom in QuarkXPress. You have explored many ways to customize the graphics in your documents. You have discovered how to define custom patterns for borders and lines. You have learned how to create complex objects by merging and splitting existing shapes, and how to convert text to graphics. You have seen the different options available for working with clipping paths and runarounds, and understand the complexities involved with combining text and graphics into a unique graphic layout.

8 Color Reproduction

Chapter Objectives:

Color is one of the defining elements of graphic design and page layout. We use color to reproduce an image in print, to create visual interest, and to highlight elements of a design. Adding color to a layout is a fairly simple process, but there are technical aspects of color reproduction that must also be considered when planning and implementing a layout. In this chapter, you will:

- Learn the basics of color management, including the terms and concepts that are important for reproducing color.

- Discover how color management is integrated in QuarkXPress.

- Become familiar with the technical requirements of color reproduction.

- Learn how to apply different kinds of trapping in QuarkXPress.

Projects to be Completed:

- Stonington Letterfold Brochure (A)

- Body Solution Booklet (B)

- Cosciel Poster (C)

Color Reproduction

As a mechanical process, color reproduction has inherent variations and limitations. The ease with which we create and apply colors in a page-layout document is deceptive. Although it is simple enough to place a color image or create a colored line, you need to consider the final output goal to ensure that the color on your monitor is reproduced as you intend. There is a saying that the end justifies the means; when it comes to color reproduction, the end *defines* the means.

Color Management

You have already learned about the different color models and the gamuts associated with each. You know the difference between a process-color build and a spot color chosen from a swatch book. You also know that color on a monitor is very different than color on a printed page, and that different printers and output devices can reproduce colors differently. Each variable — scanner, digital camera, monitor, proofing device, and printing press, to name the primary elements — in the digital process adds another opportunity for color to be reproduced differently.

Other possible variables in the color-reproduction process include the type of film used to take a photograph, the paper on which a photo is developed, the type of imagesetter used to create a printing plate, and so on. The list, as you may have guessed, is practically endless.

Color management refers to the process of maintaining consistent color between the different input and output devices used in the graphic-arts production cycle. Color management relies on a set of color *profiles*, or data sets that define the reproduction characteristics of a specific device.

Color profiles are created by reproducing a known target, then measuring the variation of the reproduction away from the original. Color profiles are also called "ICC profiles," named after the International Color Consortium (ICC), which developed the standard for creating device profiles. In an ideally managed workflow, every input, viewing, and output device would have its own ICC profile.

Color management is a fairly complex and somewhat confusing topic. There is a large body of literature devoted to the science and theory of color reproduction, much of which is beyond the scope of this book. Our goal here is to explain how QuarkXPress incorporates color management into the production workflow.

Managing Color with QuarkXPress

QuarkCMS is the color-management system built into QuarkXPress. It is included with the application as an XTension, and must be active to function within the software.

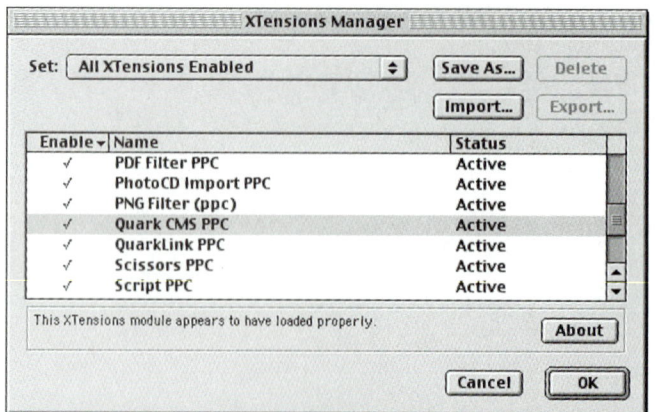

You can activate QuarkCMS in the XTensions Manager dialog box (Utilities>XTensions Manager).

You can modify the color-management preferences for a single document, or modify the default settings by opening the color-management preferences when no document is open.

As you use color management, a color-management module (CMM) translates source profile colors into destination profile colors. QuarkCMS is the interface through which you control the CMM in the Quark environment. To use the QuarkCMS interface, you have to choose Edit>Preferences>Color Management.

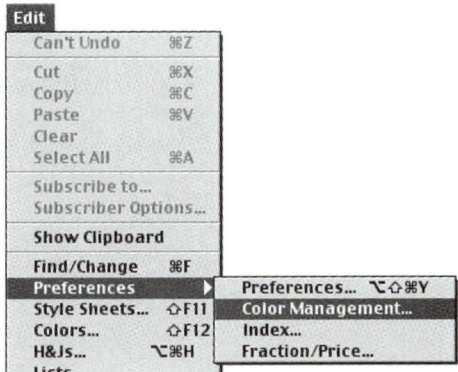

When you first access the Color Management Preferences dialog box, you have to select the Color Management Active check box to define the color-management settings. You can choose Destination Profiles for the monitor, composite printer, and separation printer you are using; and Source Profiles for RGB, CMYK, and Hexachrome colors and images.

When you install the drivers for any hardware that you connect to your computer, you should install ICC profiles if they are available. If you do not see your particular hardware in the source and destination profile menus, check the hardware manufacturer's Web site or the documentation that came with the hardware.

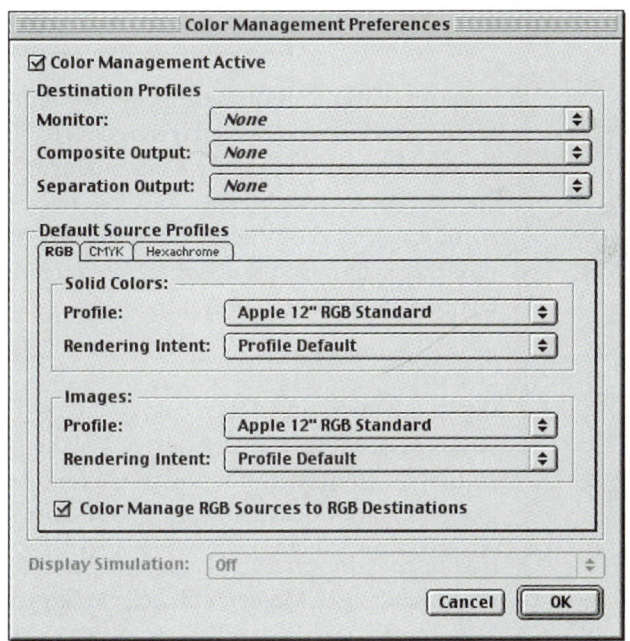

*The problem of color shift is discussed in depth in **QuarkXPress 5: Introduction to Electronic Documents**.*

The Color Manage RGB Sources to RGB Destinations check box allows you to color manage files between different RGB color spaces. The biggest problem of color shift occurs when moving between different color spaces (e.g., RGB to CMYK). Because there is some variation, however, between the output of different monitors and RGB printers, you may want to select this option.

After you have defined the destination profiles in the Monitor, Composite Output, and Separation Output menus, the Display Simulation menu becomes available, and enables you to approximate — on your monitor — the color space of your intended output device. If this option is turned off, you will not see any color difference on your monitor.

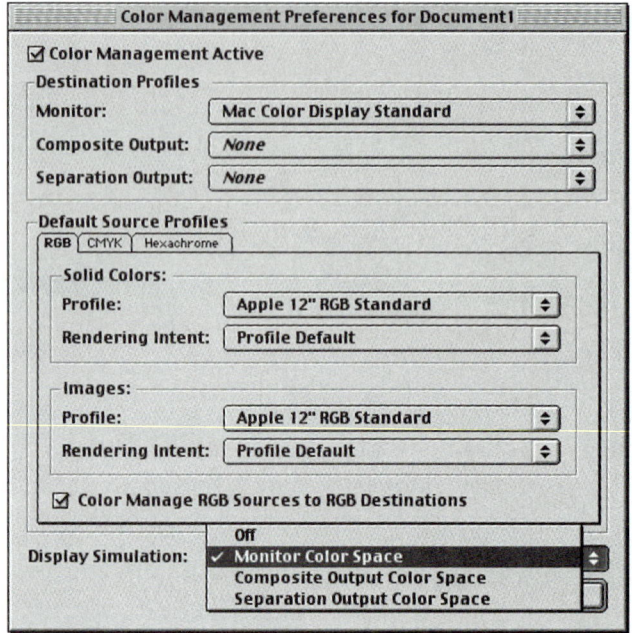

Because RGB monitors simply do not reproduce the same gamut as CMYK printers, the accuracy of color-display simulation is questionable. Color management is an inexact science. For a truly color-managed workflow to exist, the devices — input and output — used in the workflow need to be calibrated regularly and profiled. Some experts recommend calibration as often as every week; others believe that monthly calibration is adequate. If your input and output devices are not calibrated, color management is only a theory.

So, why use CMS?

If you are operating a true color-managed workflow — all devices calibrated regularly and ICC profiles for every device installed, color management can help you maintain consistent color from the initial scan to the printed page. QuarkCMS allows you to integrate a Quark document into a fully color-managed workflow.

If you have not properly calibrated your equipment or do not have the appropriate ICC profiles, QuarkCMS can still help to approximate the final output on your monitor, but keep in mind that what you see is not necessarily what you will get.

Rendering Intents

The CMM translates color based on the *rendering intent*, or the properties that are most important in the selected image or object. You can choose one of four rendering intents for a specific profile or image in the Rendering Intent menus.

The best way to produce predictable color output is to use color swatch books — both process and special inks — when selecting colors for your documents. With experience, you will learn to predict the printed output of process-color builds, but will rely on what you know to be true rather than on what you hope is true.

The Saturation rendering intent can result in drastic color shift, sometimes producing an entirely different color.

- **Perceptual**. This option scales the colors in the source profile into the gamut of the destination profile.

- **Relative Colorimetric**. This option maintains any colors that are in both the source and destination profiles. Any source colors outside the destination gamut are shifted to fit into the destination gamut.

- **Saturation**. This option compares the saturation of colors in the source profile and shifts them to the nearest possible saturated color in the destination profile.

- **Absolute Colorimetric**. This option maintains colors that are in both the source and destination profiles. Any colors outside the destination gamut are shifted to a color within the destination gamut based on the color's appearance on white paper.

Set the Color Management Preferences

1. Create a new document using the default settings.

2. Choose Edit>Preferences>Color Management.

3. Select the Color Management Active check box.

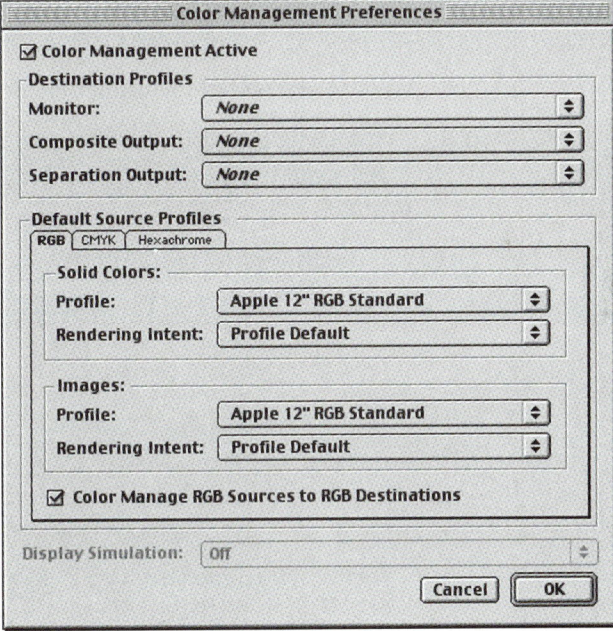

4. In the Monitor menu, choose the profile for your monitor. If you do not see the profile for your monitor, choose Mac Color Display Standard (Macintosh), or Adobe RGB (1998) or Generic Monitor (Windows).

5. In the Composite Output menu, choose the profile for the printer you use. If you do not see a profile for your printer, choose Tektronix Phaser III Pxi.

We have chosen these settings because they are a common combination used in the graphics-arts industry. In a real-world situation, you should obtain and use profiles for the specific hardware you are using.

Step 7, which sets the Solid Colors option of the Default Source Profiles section, assumes that you are defining color in the document; the source, in this case, is the same as the destination.

6. In the Separation Output menu, choose SWOP Press.

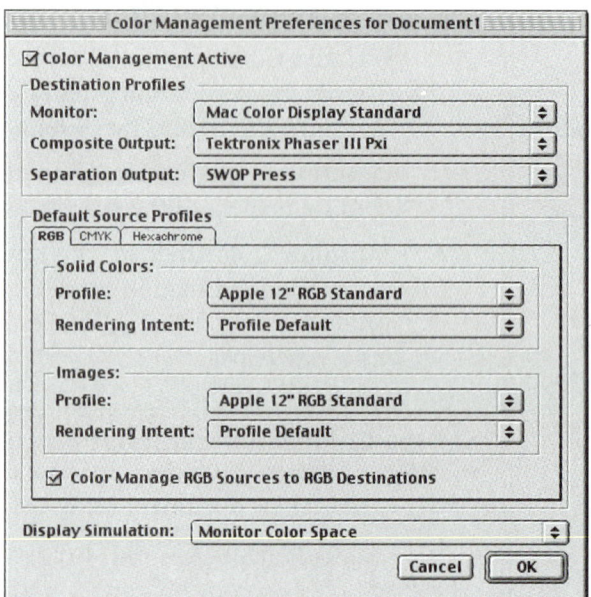

7. In the Default Source Profiles Solid Colors section, choose the same setting as you chose in the Destination Profiles Monitor menu (Step 4.)

8. Choose Perceptual from the Rendering Intent menu.

9. In the Default Source Profiles Images section, choose Kodak Generic DCS Camera Input from the Profile menu, and Relative Colorimetric from the Rendering Intent menu.

10. Choose Monitor Color Space from the Display Simulation menu.

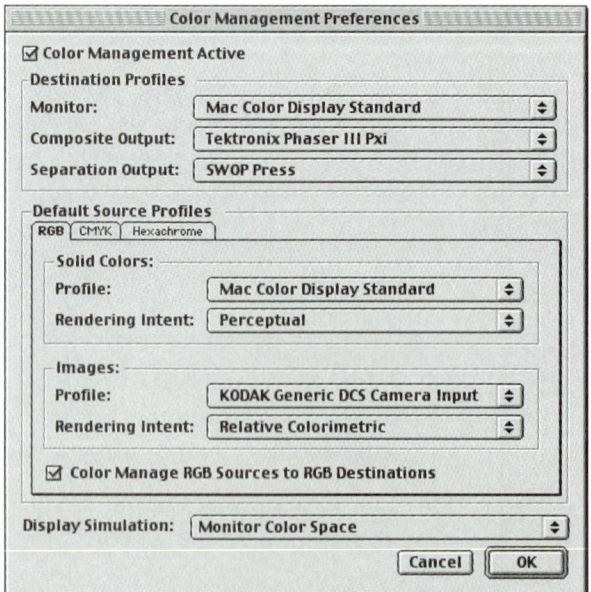

11. Click OK to close the Color Management Preferences dialog box. Save the file in your **Work_In_Progress** folder as "color_managed.qxd", and leave it open.

Adding Profiles

Color profiles installed with hardware are stored with the system files of your computer. The Profile Manager (Utilities>Profile Manager) dialog box lists all of the profiles installed on your computer. Quark allows you to designate an Auxiliary Profile Folder using the Select/Browse button. This is useful if you have different sets of profiles for the service providers and printers you frequently use.

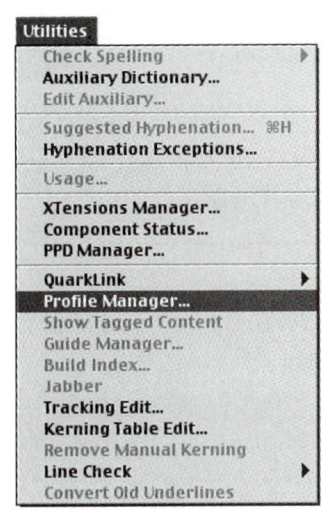 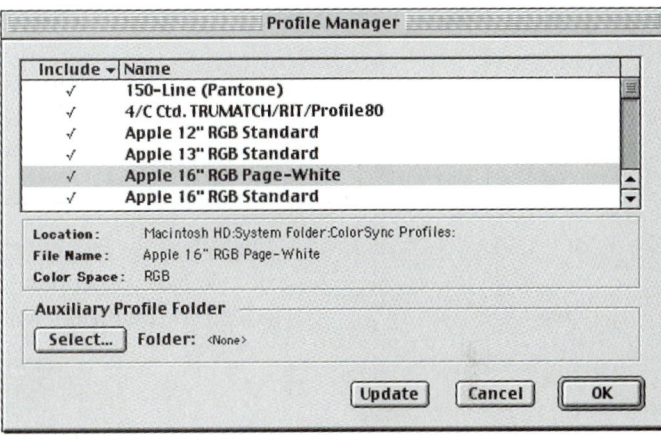

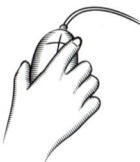

Add an Auxiliary Profile Folder

1. In the open file, select Utilities>Profile Manager.

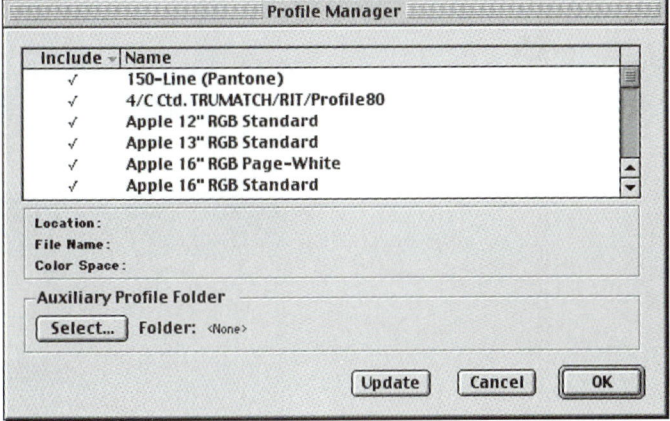

2. Click Select/Browse in the Auxiliary Profile Folder section. Navigate to the **Profiles** folder (**RF_Adv_Quark**>**Profiles**). Open the **Profiles** folder, and then click Select "Profiles"/OK.

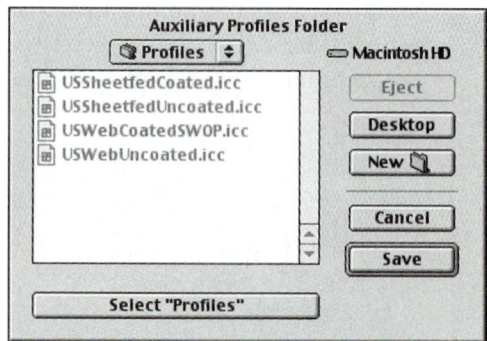

On Windows computers, the individual profiles are not listed in the Browse dialog box. When you choose the Profiles folder and click OK, the appropriate profiles are added to the Profile Manager.

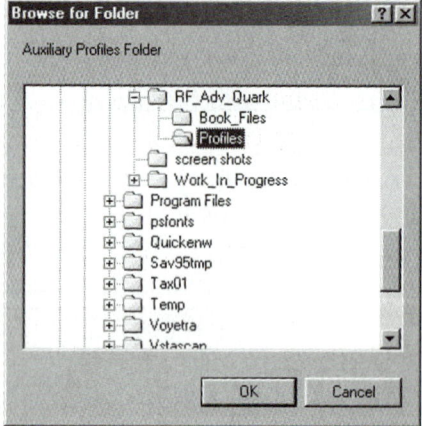

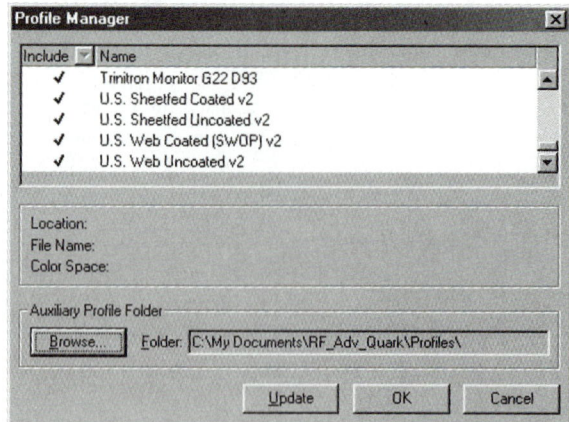

3. Click OK to close the Profile Manager dialog box.

4. Save the file and leave it open.

Assigning Image Profiles

When you import a color TIFF file into a Quark layout, you can attach a source profile to the image so that the color-management module correctly translates the color space to the appropriate monitor. The bottom half of the Get Picture dialog box allows you to choose the Profile and Rendering Intent for the imported image.

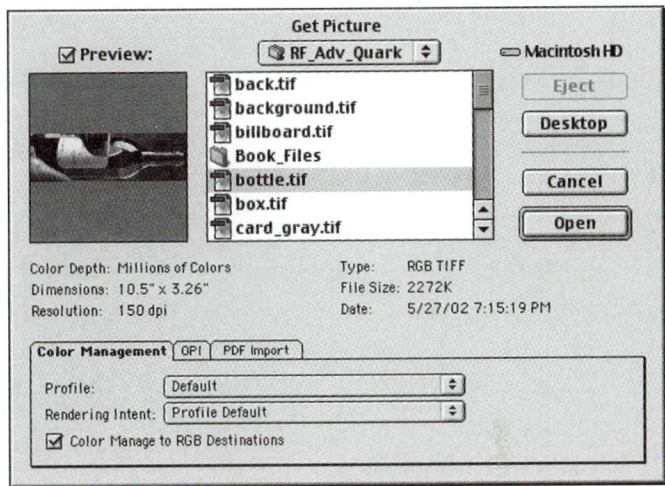

When an image is scanned, photographed, or otherwise created, the profile of the capturing device is saved with the image (in a color-managed environment). Although you can change the profile of a specific image, it is not recommended.

When an image is captured by a profiled device or saved from an image-editing application such as Adobe Photoshop, a profile is attached to the image file. When that image is imported into QuarkXPress, the Profile menu defaults to Embedded. There is, however, no way to determine exactly to what profile "Embedded" refers. You can replace the embedded profile by choosing another profile from the Profile menu.

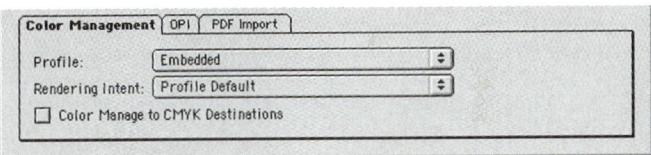

You can also change the profile of an image that is already placed. The Profile Information dialog box (View>Show Profile Information) shows the Picture Type, File Type, and Color Space of the image selected in the document window. The Profile and Rendering Intent menus can be changed to any other existing profile.

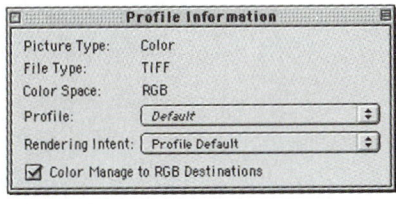

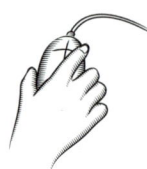

Assign Image Profiles

1. In the open document, create a picture box on the page.

2. Choose File>Get Picture, and locate the file **troller.tif** in the **RF_Adv_Quark** folder. Notice that the Profile menu shows an Embedded profile. Click Open.

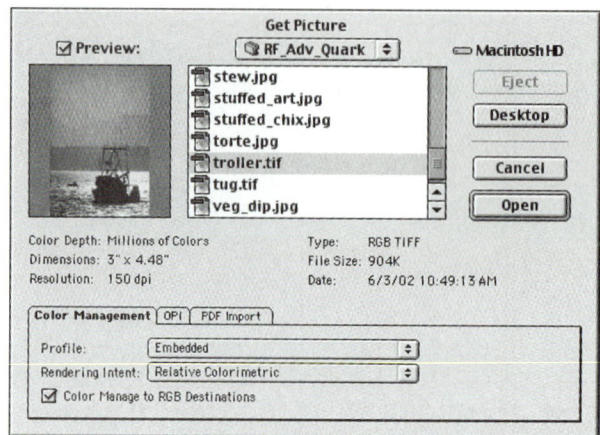

3. Choose Style>Fit Box to Picture.

4. Draw another picture box on the page. Choose File>Get Picture, and locate **tug.tif** in the **RF_Adv_Quark** folder. Notice that the Profile menu shows Default — this image was not saved with an embedded profile. Click Open.

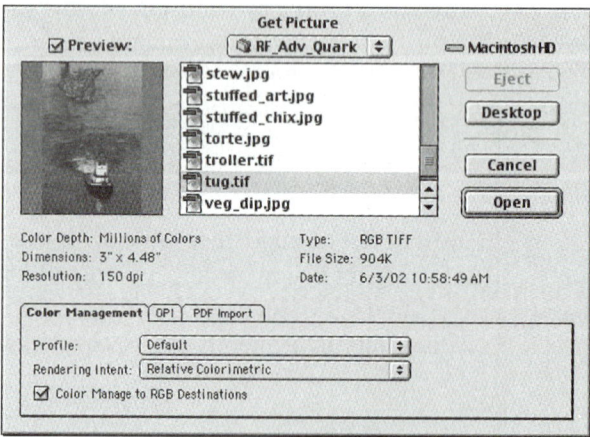

5. With the tugboat image selected in the document, select View>Show Profile Information.

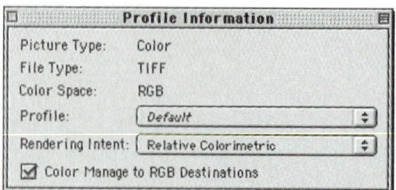

6. Select Microtek 600ZS in the Profile menu. Notice the difference in the image appearance on the document page.

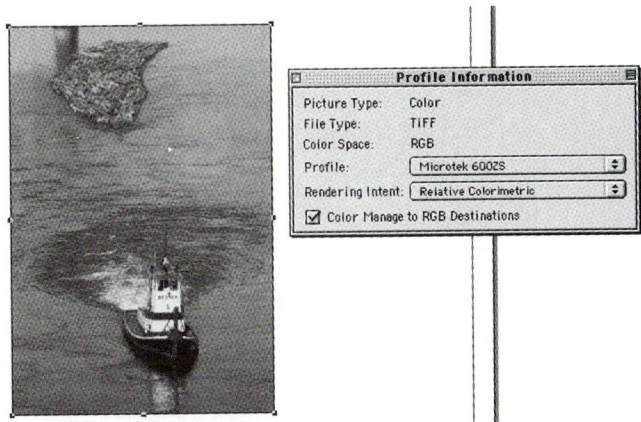

7. Save the document and leave it open.

Managing Profiles

A color profile is a data file. Just as the font files used in a document have to be present for successful output, the color-profile files must also be available when the document is printed. You can manage the color profiles used in a document in the Profiles tab of the Usage dialog box (Utilities>Usage). Every profile used in a document is listed in the Profile menu. The lower half of the Usage dialog box displays a list of the Objects (the specific images) that use the profile shown in the Profile menu.

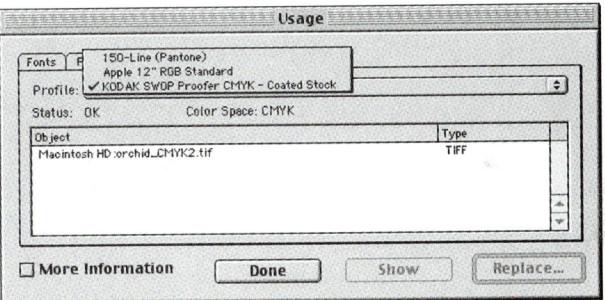

You can change the profile for a particular object by highlighting that object in the dialog box and clicking Replace. The Replace Profile dialog box shows the Current Profile; the Replace With menu lists the other available profiles. Clicking OK changes the profile of the selected object.

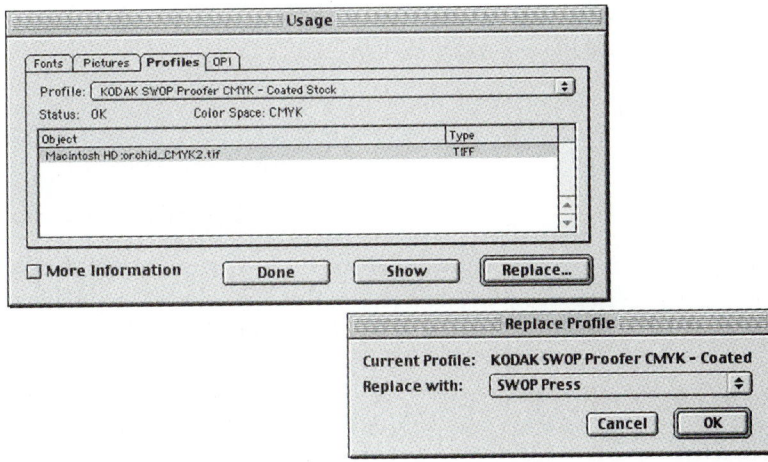

Exporting Profiles

If you have built color-management profiles into your document, you have to include the necessary color profiles with the job package that you send to the service provider. Checking the Color Profiles option in the Collect for Output dialog box will export the necessary files.

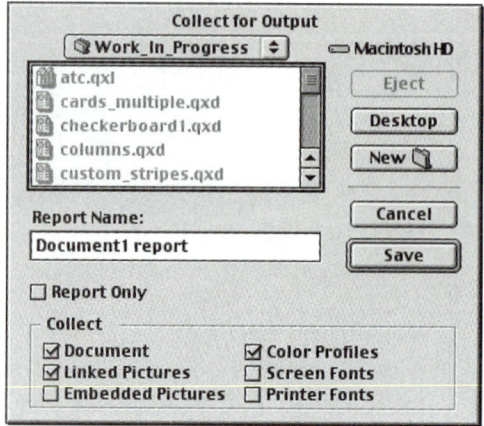

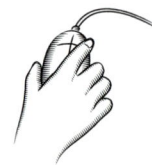

Manage Profiles

1. Select Utilities>Usage and click the Profiles tab.

2. Select Kodak Generic DCS Camera Input from the Profile menu.

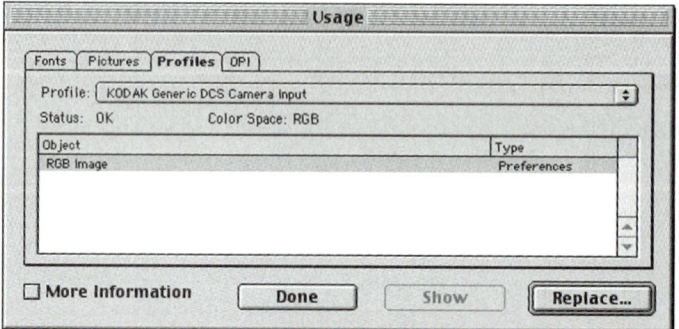

3. Highlight RGB Image in the Object list and click Replace.

4. Choose Microtek 600ZS from the Replace With menu, and click OK.

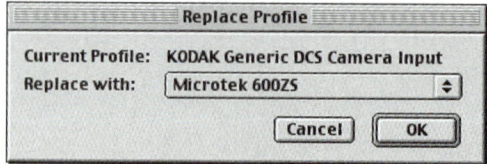

5. Notice that the Profile menu automatically changes to Microtek 600ZS. The Object list now shows that the selected profile is used in the Preferences, and for one image in the document.

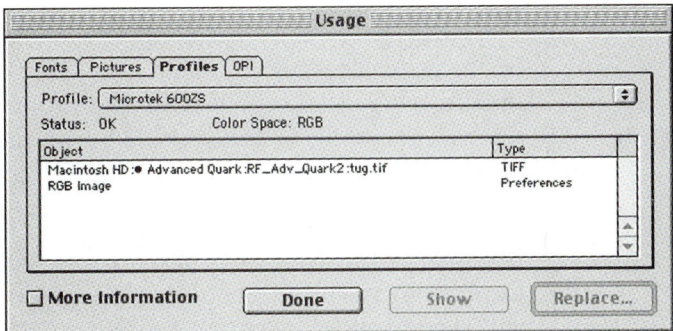

6. Click Done/Close to close the Profiles Usage dialog box.

7. Select the troller image in the document window, and look at the Profile Information dialog box. The Profile is Embedded.

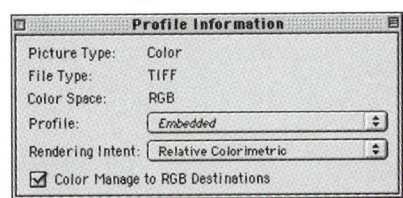

8. Choose Microtek 600ZS from the Profile menu.

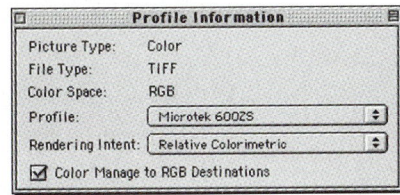

9. Save the document.

10. Choose File>Collect for Output.

11. Create a new folder called "Color" in your **Work_In_Progress** folder. Activate the Color Profiles check box and click Save.

12. You will see the warning about font license agreements. Because we are discussing color profiles, and because this document does not include type, click Don't Collect Fonts.

13. When the collect process is complete, close the Quark file and open the **Color** folder (**Work_In_Progress>Color**) on your desktop. You will see a separate Profiles folder, which should be sent to the service provider as part of the job package.

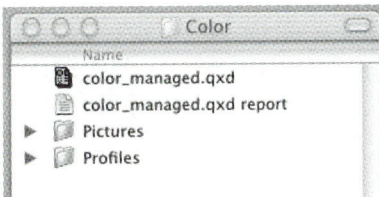

Trapping

In process-color printing, the four process colors (cyan, magenta, yellow, and black) are imaged or *separated* onto individual printing plates. Each color separation is printed on a separate unit of a printing press. The semitransparent inks, when printed on top of each other in varying percentages, produce the range of colors in the CMYK gamut. Spot colors are printed using specially formulated inks as additional color separations.

Because printing is a mechanical process, some variation between the different units of the press is possible (if not likely). Paper moves through the units of a press at considerable speed, and some movement from side to side is inevitable. Each printing plate has one or more registration marks (crosshairs) that are used to monitor the registration of each color. If the units are in register, the cross hairs from each color plate will print exactly on top of each other.

When a press is out of register, the individual colors are discernible.

Misregistration can cause a noticeable gap of uninked paper between adjacent elements, particularly when these elements are comprised of different ink colors.

C:50

K:100

Misregister results in a thin but visible gap between the two objects.

If any misregister occurs on press, type can become blurry or, worse, virtually unreadable. Any time multiple ink colors are placed on top of each other, you run the risk of misregister.

As a general rule, small type and type with thin serifs should not be printed with more than one color ink.

Misregister

Misregister

Even slight misregister will blur the sharp edges of type, especially thin serifs like this Minion font.

Trapping is the compensation for misregister of the color plates on a printing press. Trapping minimizes or eliminates these errors by artificially expanding adjacent colors so that small areas of color on the edge of each element overlap and print on top of one another. If sufficiently large, this expansion of color, or *trap*, fills in the undesirable inkless gap between elements. Trapping procedures differ based upon your workflow; most service providers will perform trapping before generating film or plates. The specific amount of trapping to be applied varies, depending on the ink/paper/press combination.

Caveat

If you are a designer, you may never have to touch the trapping controls in QuarkXPress. Remember this rule: ask your service provider whether or not they want you to apply trapping, and, if so, what settings you should use.

Many service providers and printers have high-end solutions that apply trapping to your documents. If they do, any trap settings that you make in Quark will be overwritten. Smaller firms without dedicated trapping solutions may use the Quark trapping options to prepare the document in the prepress department.

Knockouts and Overprints

A *knockout* is an area of background color that is removed so that a lighter foreground color is visible. To achieve white (paper-colored) type on a black background, for example, the black background is removed wherever the type overlaps the black. Any time a lighter color appears on top of a darker color, the area of the lighter color is knocked out of the background.

Overprint is essentially the converse of knockout. A darker-color foreground object is printed directly on top of a lighter-color background, which means that slight variation in the units of the press will not be as noticeable, especially if the darker color is entirely contained within the lighter color. Black is commonly set to overprint other colors, as are some special colors that are printed using opaque inks. Black is particularly effective when overprinted since it becomes visually richer when other process colors — especially cyan — are mixed with it.

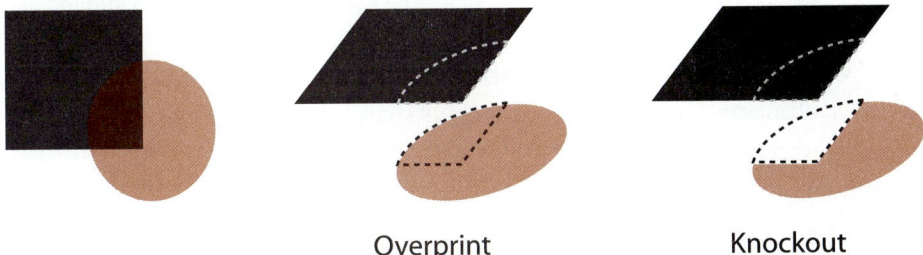

Overprint   Knockout

When a color is set to knock out, anything beneath that color will not be printed. If the black knocks out the cyan, any misregistration may result in a paper-colored gap where the two objects meet. Setting black to overprint eliminates the possibility of a gap caused by misregistration. (The dashed lines in the graphic are for illustration only and will not print.)

Chokes and Spreads

A *choke* means that the edge of the background color is expanded into the space in which the foreground color will be printed. A *spread* means that the edge of the *foreground* color is expanded to overprint the edge of the background color. As a general rule, the lighter object should be trapped into the darker area. This rule helps determine whether you should choke or spread.

- If the background is darker than the foreground object, the lighter color of the foreground object should be spread to overprint the darker background.

- If the foreground color is darker than the background color, the lighter background color is choked so it overprints the darker foreground color.

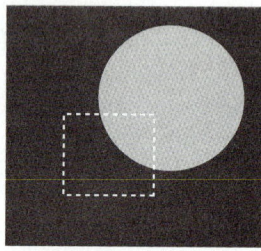 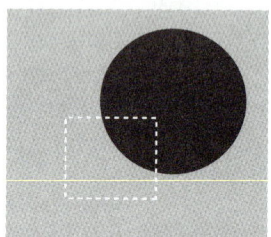

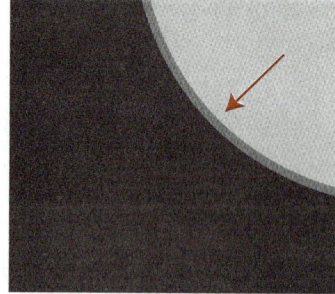 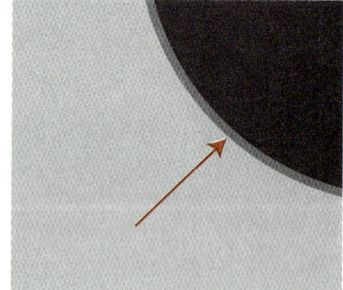

In the left image, the foreground circle is spread into the darker background. In the right image, the background color is choked into the darker foreground.

Using Common Colors

If adjacent elements share a large percentage of one or more common colors, trapping between those elements is not necessary. If both elements contain a lot of magenta, for example, the continuity of the magenta between the two objects will mask any gaps that occur between the other process colors in the two images; this makes trapping unnecessary. The general rule is that if two adjacent elements share one process color that varies by less than 50%, or if the two elements share two or more process colors that vary by less than 80%, don't bother with trapping — the continuous layer of the inks common to both elements will effectively mask any gaps.

If two adjacent elements share one process color that varies by less than 50%, or if the two elements share two or more process colors that vary by less than 80%, trapping is generally not necessary.

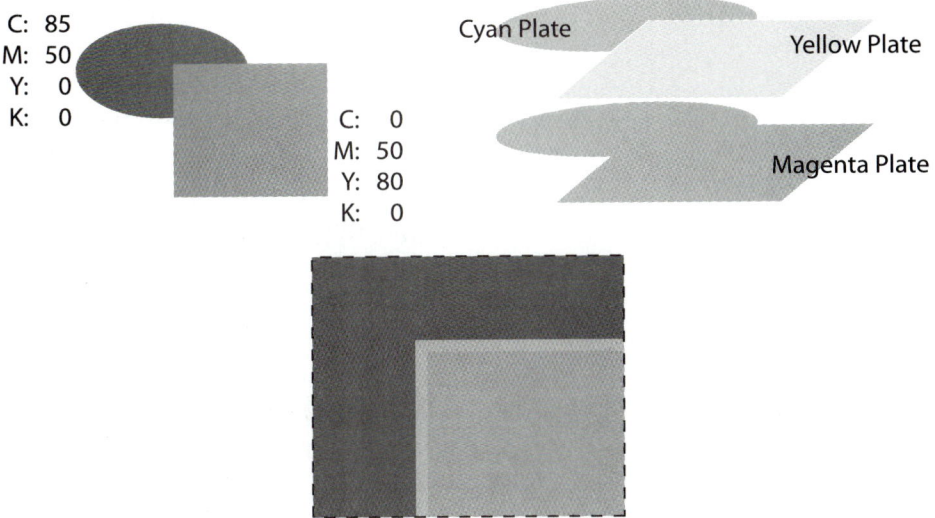

C: 85
M: 50
Y: 0
K: 0

Cyan Plate

Yellow Plate

C: 0
M: 50
Y: 80
K: 0

Magenta Plate

The enlargement (bottom) shows where the two objects overlap.
Even if the cyan or yellow press unit is out of register, the paper will not show through
since the magenta is printed as a common element.

Trapping Preferences

QuarkXPress incorporates three different types of trapping:

- **Default Trapping**. This option automatically applies to the entire document and is modified in the Trapping Preferences dialog box (Edit>Preferences> Preferences>Document>Trapping).

- **Color-Specific Trapping**. You can change the trap settings for specific colors in a document. These settings are accessed in the Edit Colors dialog box (Edit>Colors) by clicking Edit Trap.

- **Item-Specific Trapping**. You can change the trap settings for specific objects in the Trap Information dialog box (View>Trap Information).

QuarkXPress trapping preferences control the settings that are used to trap the elements of your document automatically.

You can change the default trapping preferences by opening the Trapping Preferences dialog box with no document open.

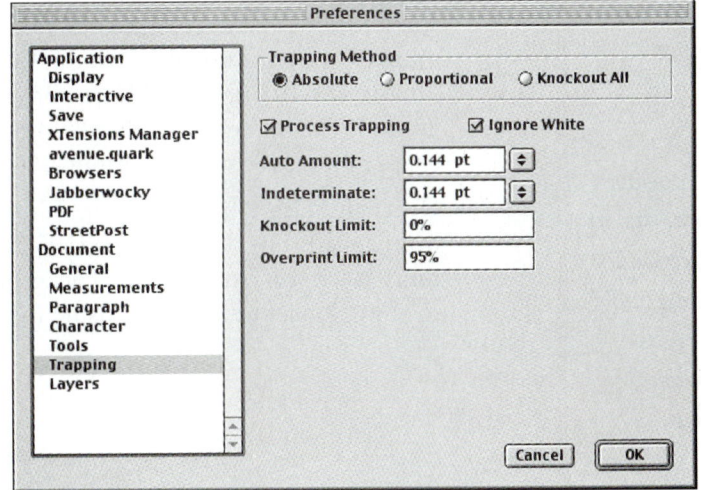

Though called White in the QuarkXPress Colors palette, this color would be more appropriately named "Paper." Any object colored White in the document will show the color of the paper for the job. To print the color White, you would have to designate specially formulated opaque inks.

Many printers consider the default Auto Amount of 0.144 pt. to be far too small for quality trapping.

Ask your service provider whether or not you should apply trapping in a Quark document. If you do apply your own trapping, ask your service provider for the correct settings.

- **Trapping Method**. The trapping method option determines how traps are applied. Absolute applies trapping based on the Auto Amount and Indeterminate values. Proportional applies trapping based on a comparison of the color *luminance* (relative lightness or brightness) values of the foreground and background object. Knockout All effectively turns trapping off.

- **Process Trapping**. Activating the Process Trapping check box means that the individual separations of a document are trapped separately. In other words, the cyan component of a foreground object is compared to the cyan component of the background object, the magenta component of a foreground object is compared to the magenta component of the background object, and so on.

- **Ignore White**. If the Ignore White check box is active, any object in front of a white background will overprint. If a foreground object overlays a colored background and a white background, the white is ignored in the trapping consideration.

  The Ignore White option is important when an object overlaps two background objects — one white and one colored. Technically, no trap is necessary when an object overlaps White.

  If a foreground object overlaps a colored object and a white object, the Ignore White check box means that the white background object is not considered when trapping is calculated; the foreground is trapped to the colored background using the Auto Amount value.

  If the Ignore White check box is deselected, the foreground will trap to the colored background using the Indeterminate amount.

- **Auto Amount**. The Auto Amount field determines the amount of trapping that is applied for any object set to trap automatically. The amount of required trapping varies according to the paper, ink, and press used to produce the job. Always ask your service provider before setting a trap value.

- **Indeterminate**. The Indeterminate trap value applies whenever an object overlays a background of indeterminate color value (such as a continuous-tone image with many different colors), or when a foreground object overlays two background objects with different color values.

- **Knockout Limit**. The Knockout Limit field defines the percentage of color that will knock out a background color. The default value, 0%, means that any object set to 0% of a color will knock out the background. If you change the knockout limit to 5%, any object set to 5% or less of a color will knock out the background. The higher this field, the more knockouts are created, which means more chance for visible misregistration.

- **Overprint Limit**. The Overprint Limit field defines the percentage of black that is overprinted. The default value is 95%, which means that any object set to 95% or more black will overprint the background. The Overprint Limit field also applies to any color set to overprint using the color-specific trapping options.

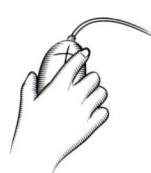

Set Trapping Preferences

1. Open the document **yearbook.qxd** from the **RF_Adv_Quark** folder. If the Colors palette is not visible, choose View>Show Colors. This is a process-color job with a fifth color plate for metallic silver (Pantone 877 C).

2. The printer needs 0.2 pt. traps to ensure quality output. Select Edit>Preferences>Preferences, and click Trapping under Document.

3. Change the Auto Amount field to 0.2 and click OK.

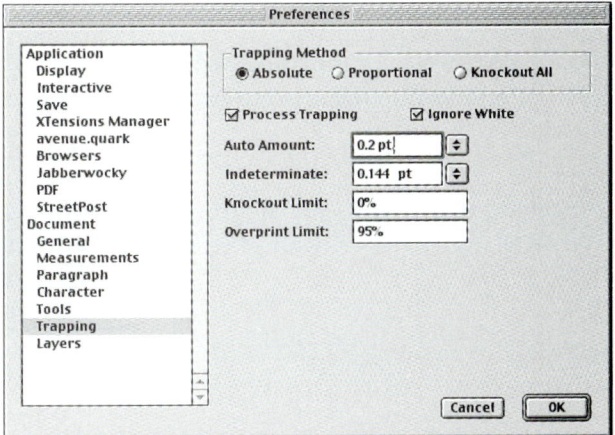

4. Save the file to your **Work_In_Progress** folder, and leave the file open.

Color-Specific Trapping

You can define the trapping behavior of any color in a document by highlighting the color in the Colors dialog box and clicking Edit Trap.

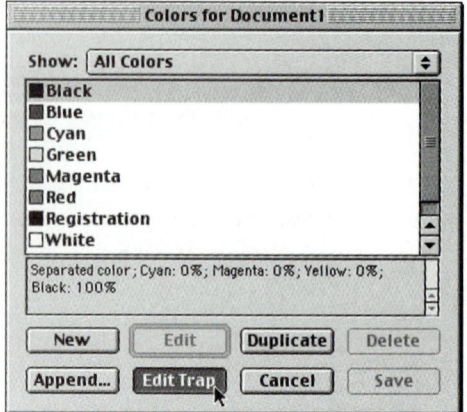

The Trap Specifications dialog box allows you to define how the selected color is trapped to any other color in the document. Changes you make in this dialog box apply any time the color shown in the Menu bar (Trap Specifications For [Color]) is placed in front of the color selected in the Background Color list. For example, you can change the way Black is trapped when placed over a Cyan background by highlighting Cyan in the Background Color list.

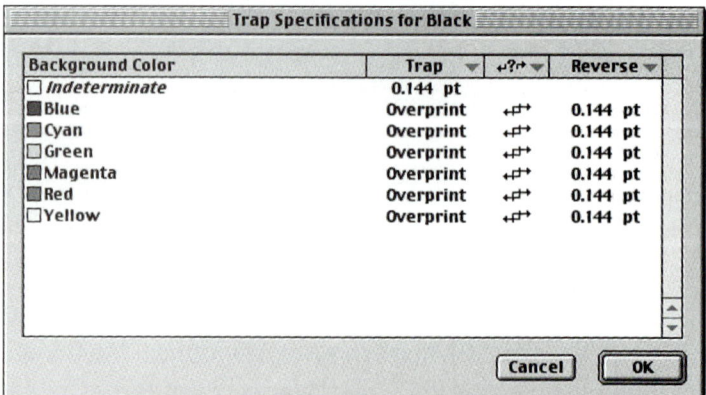

When a color is highlighted in the list, you can change the trapping method by clicking on the Trap menu. Auto Amount (+) applies a spread; Auto Amount (–) applies a choke.

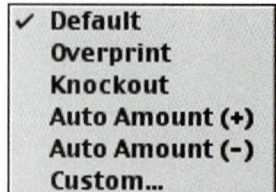

You can also create an amount other than the Auto Amount by choosing Custom.

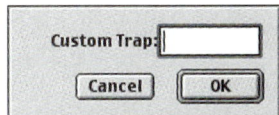

The Custom dialog box allows you to create a trapping relationship other than the value defined in the Auto Amount field.

The Dependent/Independent menu enables you to apply the inverse relationship automatically when the foreground color and background color relationship is reversed. In other words, if you define the trap relationship for any instance of a Cyan object in front of a Black background, the Dependent Traps option automatically calculates the inverse trap value for any time a Black object is in front of a Cyan background. If you do not want the color trap relationship to be inverted, choose Independent Traps from the menu.

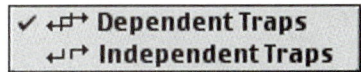

The Reverse column shows the inverse values for the specific trapping relationship. If you change the trap value for Cyan on a Magenta background, for example, the Reverse column will show the trap value that will apply any time a Magenta object is placed over a Cyan background. If Dependent Traps is selected, any change you make to the Reverse column will automatically affect the Trap column.

Create Color-Specific Traps

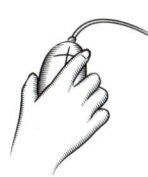

1. In the open document, choose Edit>Colors.

2. Highlight Pantone 877 C in the dialog box, and click Edit Trap.

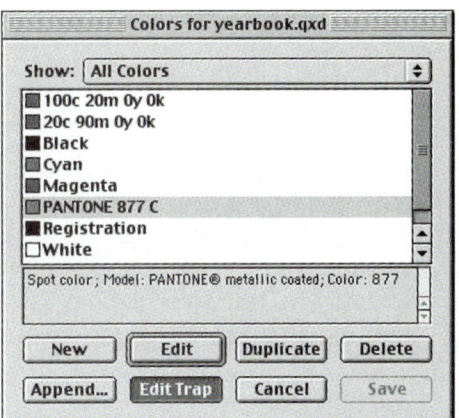

3. Pantone 877 C is an opaque metallic ink. Because it is opaque, it should overprint all other inks instead of knocking out. Highlight Indeterminate in the Trap Specifications dialog box. Click the Trap column heading (Macintosh) or the arrow next to the Trap column heading (Windows), and choose Overprint from the menu.

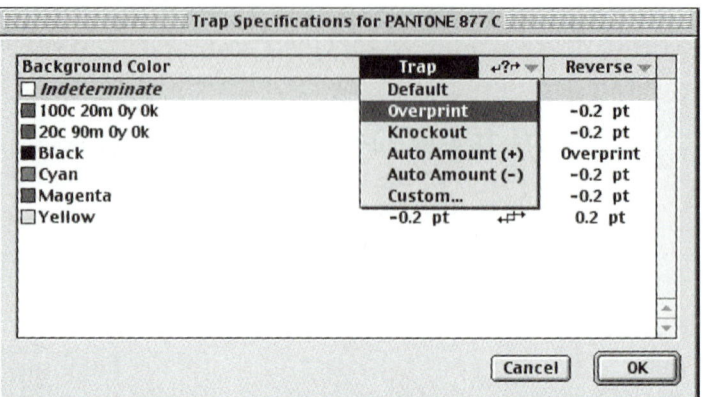

4. Repeat this process for all colors in the list so that Pantone 877 C will overprint all colors in the document. Click OK when you have finished, and click Save in the Edit Colors dialog box.

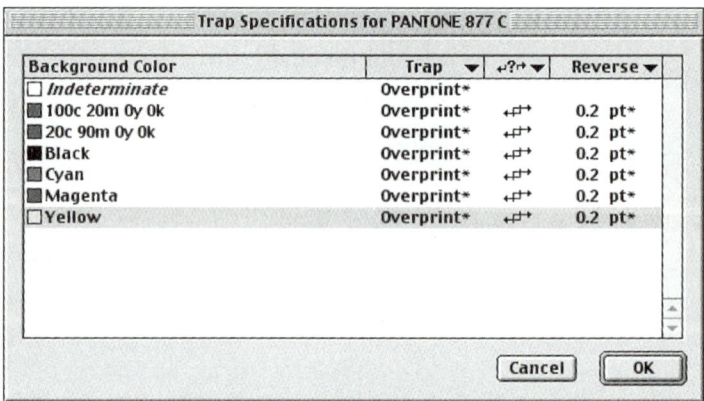

5. Save the file and leave it open.

Item-Specific Trapping

You can apply specific trapping settings to any object in the document except imported pictures. The Trap Information dialog box (View>Show Trap Information) shows the trapping values that are applied for any selected object on the page.

Trapping for imported pictures must be implemented in the picture's native application, or using a stand-alone trapping application.

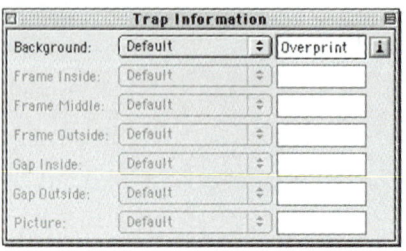

You can modify the trap setting for any available option by choosing a Trap setting from the drop-down menu. These options are the same that are available in the Trap Specifications dialog box.

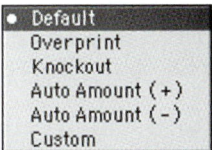

If you click the Information icon (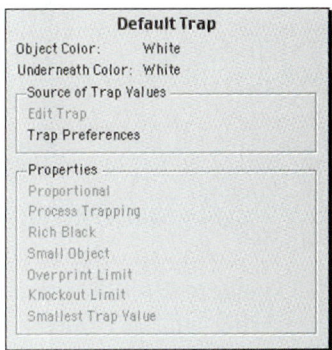) next to any option, you can get the specifics of the trap that will be applied to the selected object.

Different areas of the Trap Information dialog box become available, depending on what is selected in the document window.

- **Background**. This option is available if a box contains a background color (including White).

- **Frame Inside**. This option is available if the selected box has a border greater than 0 pt. It defines how the inside edge of the frame is trapped to the contents of the box, or to the background if the box if filled with None. If the frame style has more than one line, the innermost line of the frame is trapped according to the Frame Inside option.

- **Frame Middle**. This option is available if the frame style has color between the lines of the frame (more than one line) or between the segments of the frame (dashed or dotted). This setting defines the trap for the different pieces of the line.

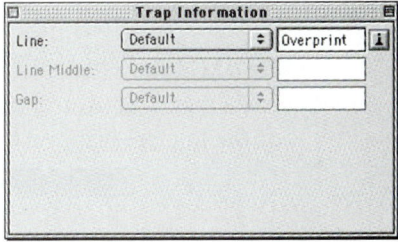

Any line style that defines a gap color other than None activates the Frame Inside, Frame Middle, and Frame Outside options in the Trap Information dialog box.

- **Frame Outside**. This option is available if the selected object has a border greater than 0 pt. It defines how the outside edge of the frame is trapped to any background object. If the frame style has more than one line, the outermost line of the frame is trapped according to the Frame Outside option.

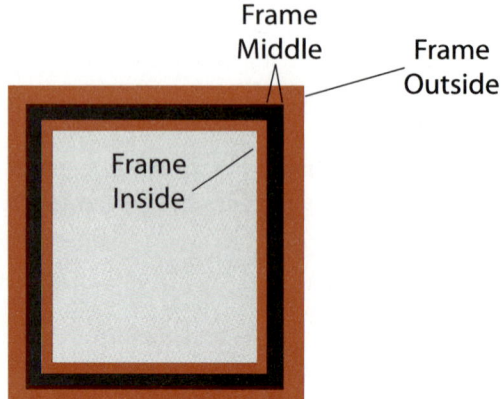

- **Gap Inside**. This option is available if the frame style is dashed or dotted and uses a gap color other than None. It defines how the gap color is trapped to the contents of the box (on the inside edge), or to any background object if the box has a fill of None.

- **Gap Outside**. This option is available if the frame style is dashed or dotted and uses a gap color other than None. It defines how the gap color is trapped (on the outside edge) to any background object.

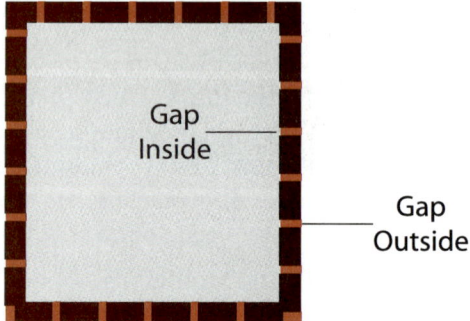

- **Line**. This option is available if the selection is a line with a width greater than 0 pt. It defines how the line color is trapped to any background object.

- **Line Middle**. This option is available if a line style has more than one stroke or is dashed or dotted, and uses a gap color other than None. It defines how the pieces of the line are trapped to each other.

- **Gap**. This option is available for a multistroke line without end treatments (arrowheads), and dashed or dotted line styles with a gap color other than None. It defines how the gap color is trapped to any background object.

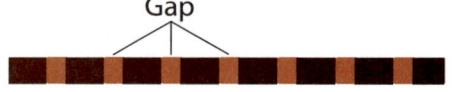

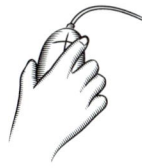

- **Text.** This option is available (replacing Picture) if text is highlighted in a text box. You can trap text to the background color of its box, or to any background color if the box is filled with None.

- **Picture.** This option is available (replacing Text) if the selection is a picture box that contains an EPS picture. Trapping an EPS illustration depends largely on how the file was created. Unless you are sure trapping strokes were applied correctly in the illustration application, do not try to trap pictures in QuarkXPress.

Apply Item-Specific Trapping

1. Highlight the text 2002 in the open document.

2. Choose View>Show Trap Information. The Text field is the only one available.

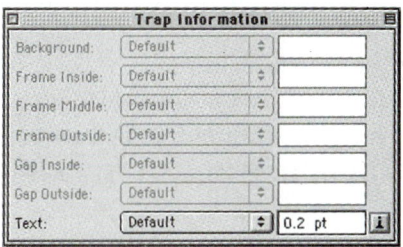

3. Click the Information icon (the small "i") to the right of the Text trap field.

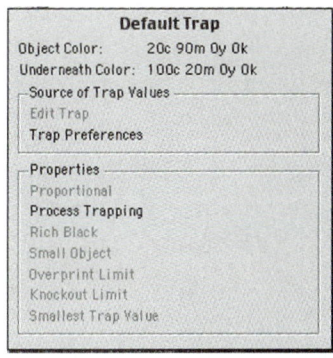

4. Observe that there is some common color between the selection and the background, but not enough to eliminate the need for trapping.

5. Select Custom from the Text menu.

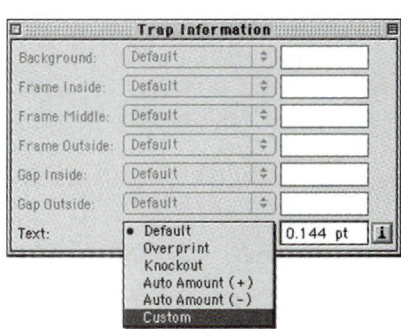

Be aware that large trap values can distort the shape of small type or of small serifs in larger type.

Check with your service provider before changing trap values away from their specifications.

6. Type 0.1 in the field to apply a smaller trap value for the thin text.

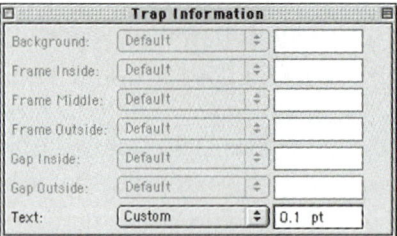

7. Save and close the file.

Summary

You have discovered that quality color reproduction is far more difficult than simply picking colors on your monitor and applying them to objects on the page. You understand that color management and trapping are tools that help you to create predictable output. You have learned the basic concepts of color management, and seen how QuarkXPress can be integrated into a color-managed workflow. You have also learned the basics of trapping, and worked with the different Quark trapping options. Finally, you have discovered the importance of discussing trapping with your service provider or printer.

Managing Output

Chapter Objectives:

Most documents designed in QuarkXPress will eventually be output in some form of PostScript. Even PDF files, which may never be printed on anything more than a desktop laser or inkjet printer, are created from PostScript files. QuarkXPress includes many tools and options that can help you to manage your documents, effectively and efficiently, through the final stages of the workflow. In this chapter, you will:

- Explore the options in the Save Page as EPS dialog box.
- Learn how to manage PPD files from within the Quark environment.
- Discover how to automate the output process using print styles.
- Become familiar with the export options for a QuarkXPress document.
- Learn to create PostScript files from your page-layout documents.
- Review the PDF Export capabilities built into QuarkXPress.

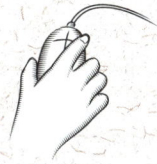

Projects to be Completed:

- Stonington Letterfold Brochure (A)
- Body Solution Booklet (B)
- **Cosciel Poster (C)**

Managing Output

In *QuarkXPress: Introduction to Electronic Documents*, we explored the multitude of options available in the Print dialog boxes. You know that print settings differ from one printer to the next, and from one file to the next. Despite the promises that "what you see is what you get," outputting files is never as easy as just clicking Print. Workflow issues affect the settings that you choose in the Print dialog boxes. Every printer has different color, size, resolution, and layout capabilities; the specific hardware used for output dictates the setup of your final output.

QuarkXPress includes tools that enable you to control the final output, automate certain output tasks, improve the production workflow, and even export a document to a PostScript-based file. In this chapter, we examine the workflow issues that help your jobs to output smoothly, and that give you control over the final quality of your printed page.

Because every user has a different PPD and printer configuration on his or her computer or network, several of the topics in this chapter do not include exercises. Instead, we show you the concepts of managing output options. We suggest that you follow along through the menu options and dialog boxes, but recognize that the PPDs and printers on your computer may be very different than what is shown here.

Exporting EPS

EPS files exported from QuarkXPress do not embed the fonts used in the document.

It is sometimes necessary to export a document as an EPS file, especially when submitting advertisement layouts to a magazine or other publisher. An *EPS file* saved from a Quark document is a single file that contains all of the page elements (except fonts) needed to output your document.

When you choose Save Page as EPS from the File menu, the dialog box defaults to the page active in the document window. The file name (the Save Page As text field) defaults to "Page x.eps" where "x" is the page number of the active page.

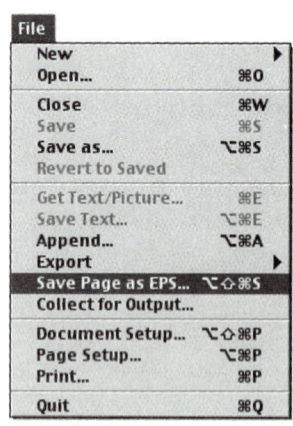
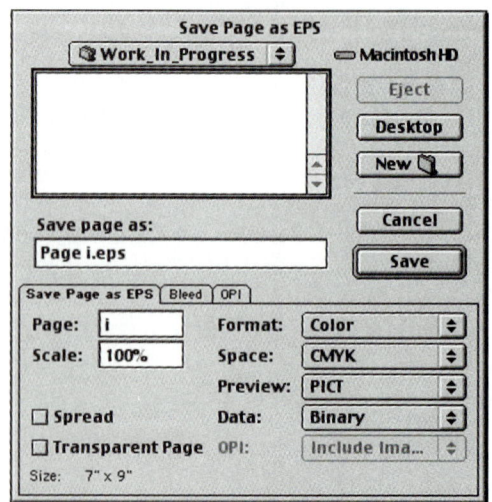

Three tabs in the Save Page as EPS dialog box allow you to define what is saved and how it is saved. In the Save Page as EPS tab, you define the parameters of the file that is created.

- **Page.** This field automatically defaults to the active page in the document window. You can change the Page field to a different page than the active one, and rename the file using some meaningful file name.

- **Scale.** This option defaults to 100% and defines the size at which the page is exported. There are very few cases when you should export a page at any size other than 100%.

- **Format.** This menu allows you to export the page as Color, B&W, DCS, or DCS 2.0.

- **Space.** This menu defines the color space (either CMYK or RGB) of the resulting EPS file. If you choose RGB, you will see a warning that the file cannot be separated for process printing.

- **Preview.** This menu defines the format (TIFF, PICT, or None) used for the low-resolution screen preview of the file. If you are sending the file to a Windows-based computer, you should choose TIFF from this menu. If you choose None, the resulting EPS file will not have a preview image for placement into another document.

When you export an EPS file with a preview of None, the file shows only a gray box with the file name when placed into another document.

- **Data.** This menu defines the format of bitmap data in the page being saved. You can choose Binary, ASCII, or Clean 8-Bit.

- **Spread.** This check box allows you to export both pages of a spread as a single EPS file.

- **Transparent Page.** This check box allows you to save the page with no background. If the option is unchecked, a white background box will exist within the page boundaries in the EPS file. If the exported EPS is placed into a layout over another object, the white box (background) will obscure anything behind it.

The Bleed tab of the Save Page as EPS dialog box allows you to define how bleed objects are treated on the exported page. These options are the same as the Bleed tab in the Print dialog box.

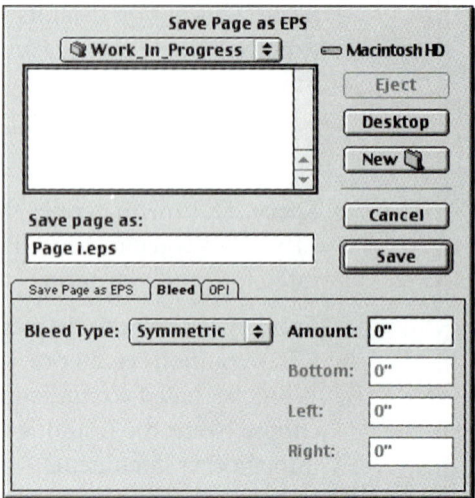

The OPI tab of the Save Page as EPS dialog box enables you to embed TIFF and EPS pictures into the resultant EPS file. If the TIFF Low Resolution check box is active, only a low-resolution preview of the image is stored in the EPS file.

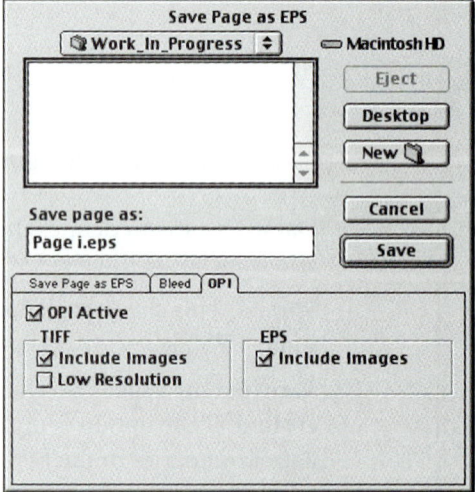

Once a page is exported as an EPS file, you can open it in a vector-illustration program, place it into another page-layout document, parse it into a bitmap-image application, or distill it to a PDF file. The entire page is saved as one file, which means that you don't have to send out all the individual components (with the exception of the necessary fonts).

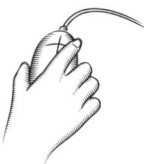

Export a Document as EPS

1. Open the document **beans.qxd** from the **RF_Adv_Quark** folder.

2. Choose File>Save Page as EPS.

3. Navigate to your **Work_In_Progress** folder.

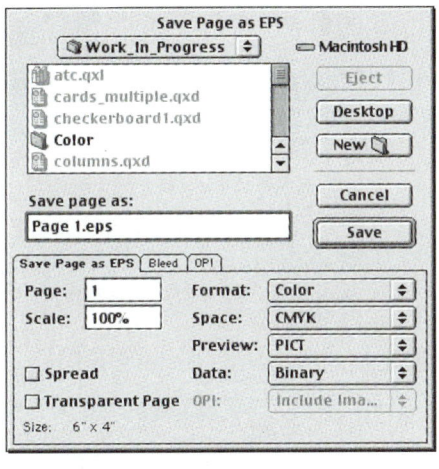 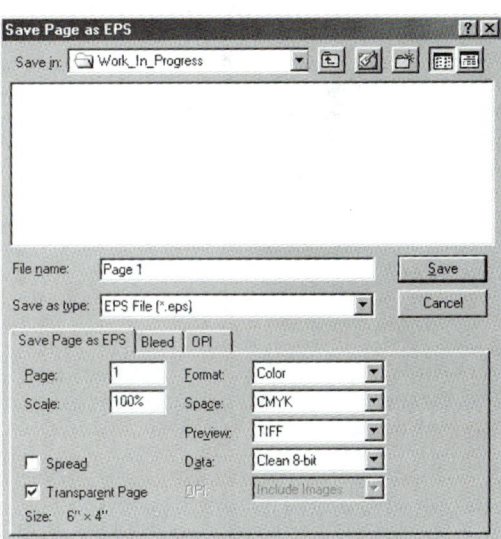

Macintosh (left) and Windows (right) Save Page as EPS dialog boxes.

4. Change the Save Page As/File Name field to "beans_cmyk.eps". Windows users, leave the Save as Type menu at the default EPS File.

5. Choose TIFF from the Preview menu, and activate the Transparent Page check box. Make sure the Format menu is set to Color and the Space menu is set to CMYK. Leave the Data menu at the default setting.

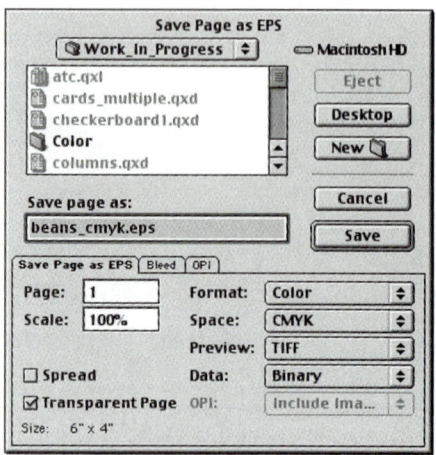

6. Click the Bleed tab. This document contains no bleed objects. Review the settings and leave them at the default.

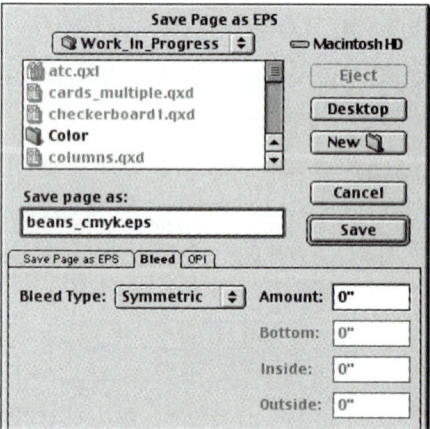

7. Click the OPI tab. Make sure the Include Images check boxes are both active.

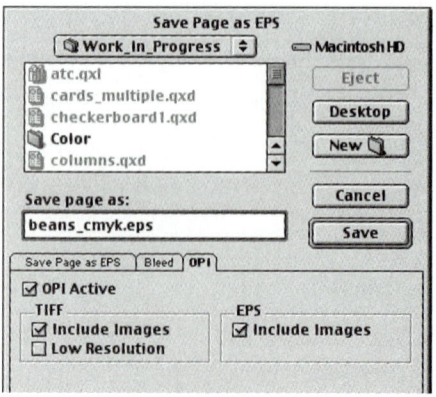

8. Click Save.

9. Create a new letter-sized document using the default margins.

10. Draw a rectangular picture box on the page with the dimensions W: 6 in., H: 4 in.

11. Choose File>Get Picture.

12. Locate the file **beans_cmyk.eps** in your **Work_In_Progress** folder and click Open.

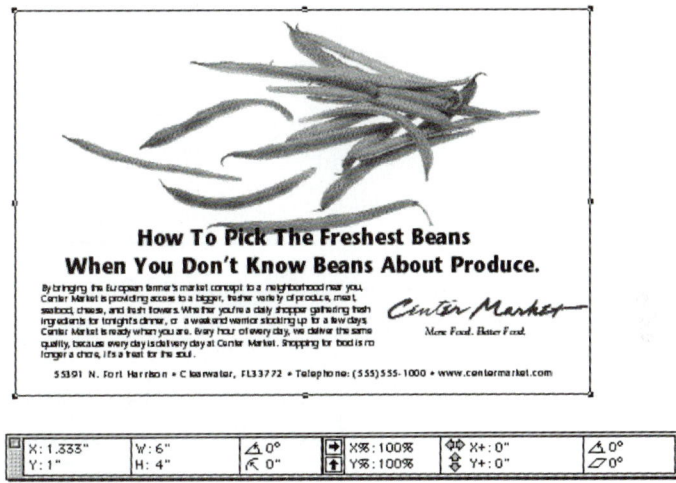

13. Close both files without saving.

Managing PPDs

To access the features and capabilities of a PostScript output device, you have to install a PostScript Printer Description (PPD) file for that device. PPDs are usually installed with the device-driver software or with other software applications. Additional PPDs may exist as a part of the default system software.

The Setup tab of the Print dialog box lists every available PPD. The specific file you choose in this menu defines the options that are available. Because PPD files are installed from various sources, you may have several (or many) PPD files for devices that do not exist in your workflow.

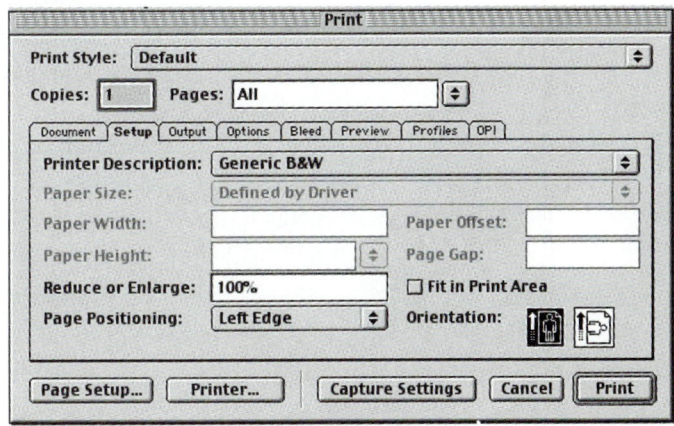

Printer Description files are accessed in the Setup tab of the Print dialog box.

QuarkXPress always looks at the PPDs available on your computer, even if they are turned off in the PPD manager. If many generic or default PPDs are installed on your computer, it is better to remove them at the system level of your computer.

QuarkXPress allows you to control the specific PPDs that are available in the application environment using the PPD Manager (Utilities>PPD Manager). The PPD manager lists every PPD available on your computer. The entire list appears in the QuarkXPress Print dialog box by default, as indicated by the check marks in the Include column.

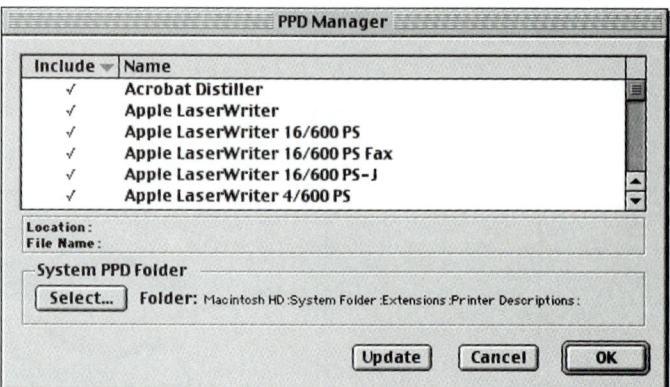

You can deselect one or more PPD files by clicking in the Include column to turn off the check mark. To reactivate a PPD file, you can click in the Include column to replace the check mark.

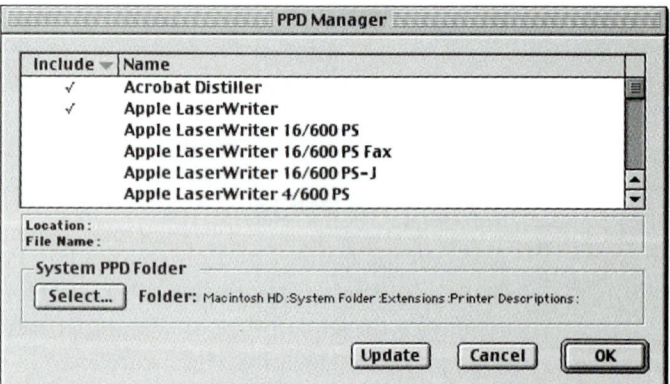

After the unwanted PPDs are deactivated, the list in the Printer Description menu of the Print dialog box is far more manageable.

Working with Nonsystem PPDs

You can also use the PPD manager to locate PPD files that are not stored in your System folder. The Select/Browse button in the PPD Manager dialog box effectively redirects the application to a folder other than the System to determine the available PPDs.

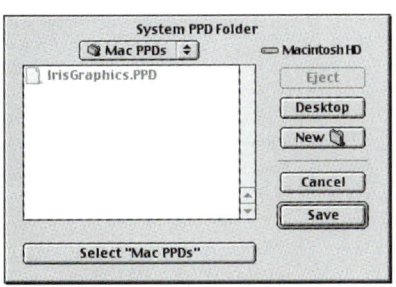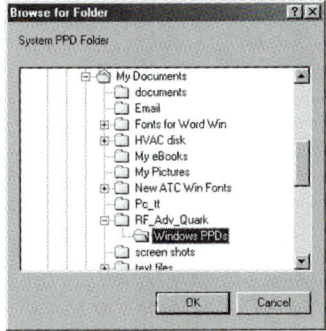

Macintosh (left) and Windows (right) System PPD Folder navigation dialog box.

You can use this option if, for example, a service provider gives you a PPD for their imagesetter. Because you don't have the imagesetter connected to your computer, you should not install the PPD in your System folder.

If you point the PPD Manager to a different folder, you can temporarily access the PPD of the service provider's output device, make your print choices, save the document to PostScript or PDF, then change the PPD Manager back to the System PPD folder. This allows you to choose the right settings for a specific device, even if that device is not connected to your printer.

The PPD Manager list shows the available PPDs that are in the folder you choose in the Select/Browse navigation dialog boxes. Clicking OK applies the changes. The PPDs in the new list will appear in the Printer Description menu of the Print dialog boxes.

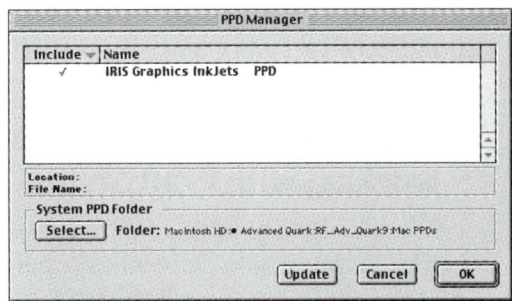

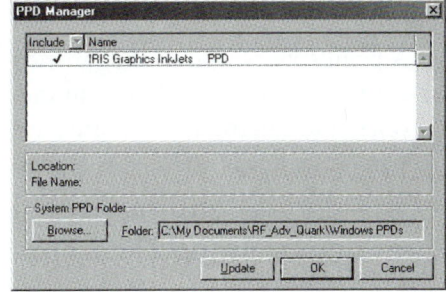

Macintosh (top) and Windows (bottom) PPD Manager. The Select/Browse button allows you to redirect the application to a folder other than the system PPD folder.

To access PPDs, you must have a PostScript printer selected in the Chooser (Macintosh) or in the Printer menu (Windows). If you don't have a PostScript printer, use the LaserWriter (Macintosh) or Generic PostScript Printer (Windows) option. You can then choose the correct PPD from the Printer Description menu of the Setup tab.

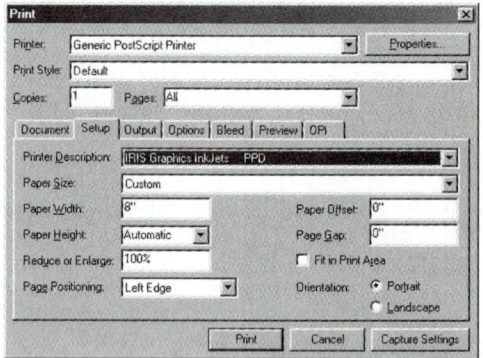

Macintosh (top) and Windows (bottom) Print dialog boxes.

When you have finished with the service provider's PPD, make sure that you reopen the PPD manager and change the System PPD Folder back to the System folder. If you forget this step, you will not be able to output correctly to the printers that are installed on your computer or network.

Working with Print Styles

Because of the number of different settings available in the Print dialog boxes, it can be time-consuming to define the output for a specific document. It is also fairly easy to miss one or more options, which means that the document may not output correctly. QuarkXPress allows you to define Print Styles to help avoid these problems.

A print style works on the same concept as text-formatting style sheets. Print styles contain most of the choices in the Print dialog boxes; you make the appropriate choices once, and call the style as often as necessary. Print styles are not document-specific; when you create a print style, it is stored in the application settings.

Print styles are created by choosing Edit>Print Styles. The Print Styles dialog box presents the same familiar options from other Quark dialog boxes.

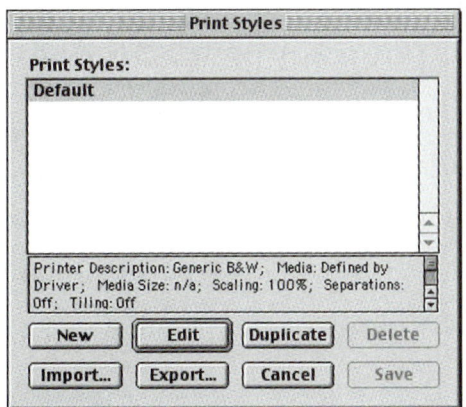

The Edit Print Style dialog box presents most of the print options available in the QuarkXPress Print dialog box.

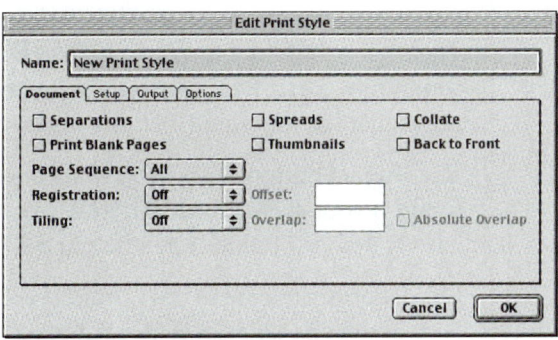

As with all elements you define in QuarkXPress, use a meaningful name for Print Styles.

Four tabs — Document, Setup, Output, and Options — are available to define the choices for a particular print style. The Name field allows you to identify the print style. The name you choose will be listed in the Print dialog box.

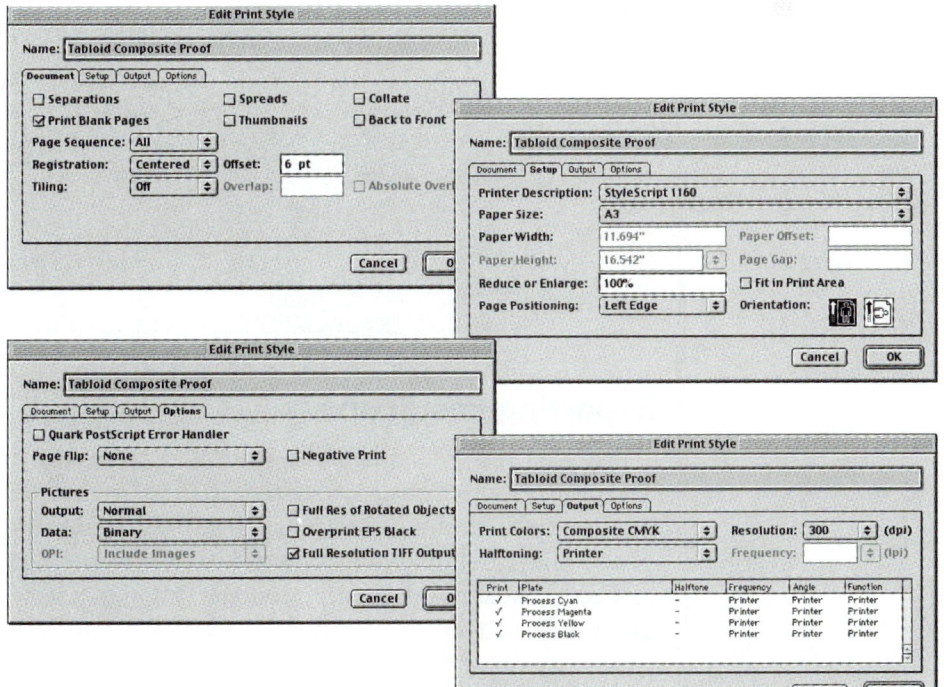

Clicking OK in the Edit Print Style dialog box returns you to the Print Styles dialog box. The styles you create will be listed in the window. To finalize your choices and add the new style to the application preferences, you must click Save in the Print Styles dialog box.

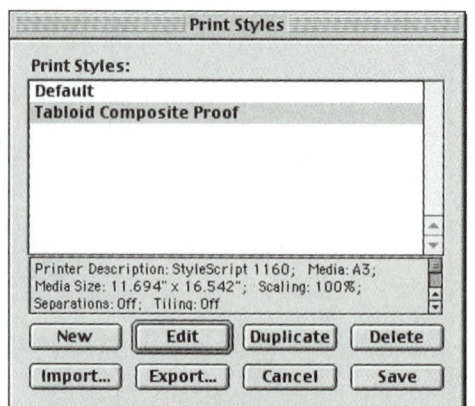

The Export button allows you to export print styles for other users. Service providers sometimes create and distribute print styles for their specific output devices. Keep in mind that the required PPD must be available on any computer that calls a print style.

The extension for a QuarkXPress Print Style is .qpj.

The Import button allows you to import print styles created by other users; this may be useful if your service provider gives you a print-style file, or if another user on a network has created print styles for different output devices on the network.

Once a print style is created, you can access it in the Print Style menu of the Print dialog box. If you choose a defined print style from the menu, the Print dialog box automatically changes to reflect the settings in the style.

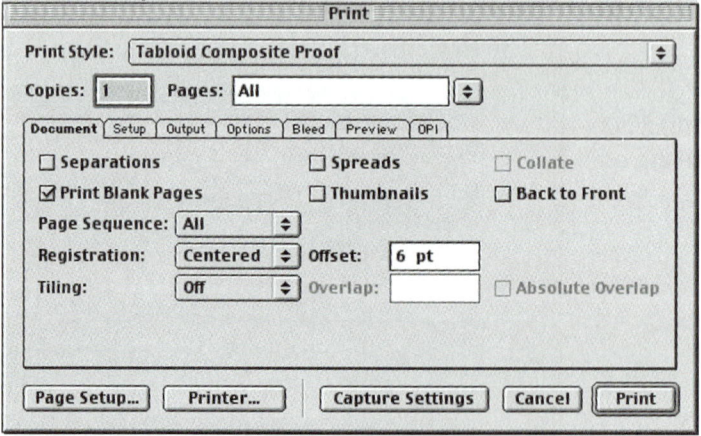

Exporting PostScript

When you print a document, the page is sent as a string of PostScript code to the printer. The printer's raster image processor (RIP) interprets the code and prints the document on the chosen output device. You can also print a Quark document to a PostScript file. This is called "printing to disk," and was once a common way to transport files to a service provider or other output bureau. Though largely replaced by PDF files, printing to disk is still used and is an important concept to understand.

Instead of sending the document's PostScript code directly to a printer, you can choose to print the document to a PostScript file, which contains all of the necessary elements and components — including fonts — required to output the document. The resulting PostScript file can be sent to a service provider for output, distilled into a PDF file, or opened in a bitmap-graphics application.

There are potential problems with printing to a PostScript file. First, the file is uneditable. It cannot be opened and modified at the service provider. Any last-minute changes must be made to the original Quark file, and then the PostScript file must be regenerated and resent.

Another problem with a PostScript file is that the settings in the Print dialog boxes must be correct for the chosen output device. If you print to PostScript with settings for your local desktop printer, the file may not work properly on the service provider's platesetter.

Exporting PostScript on a Macintosh Computer

On a Macintosh, saving a document to PostScript is very similar to printing a document. In the Print dialog box, clicking Printer opens a new dialog box that contains options for the selected printer.

You must have a PostScript printer selected in the Chooser.

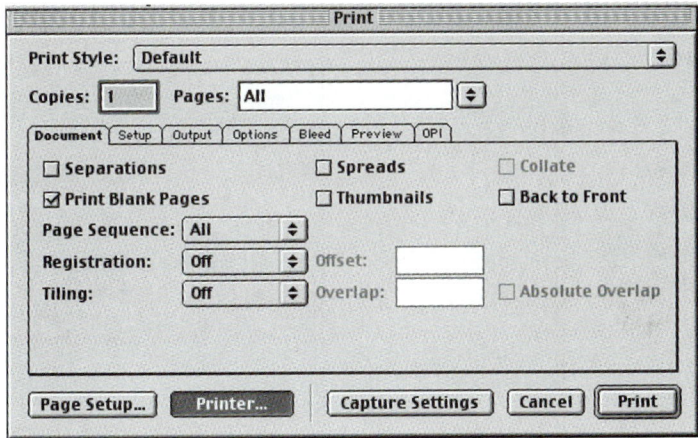

You may see a warning message telling you that clicking Print in the following dialog box does not actually print the document. If you see this warning, simply click OK.

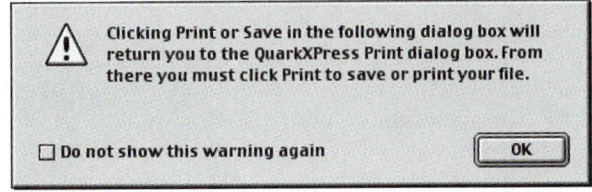

Choosing File in the destination menu means that, when you click Print in the Print dialog box, you will generate a PostScript file. The menu below the Printer option lists different printer-specific choices.

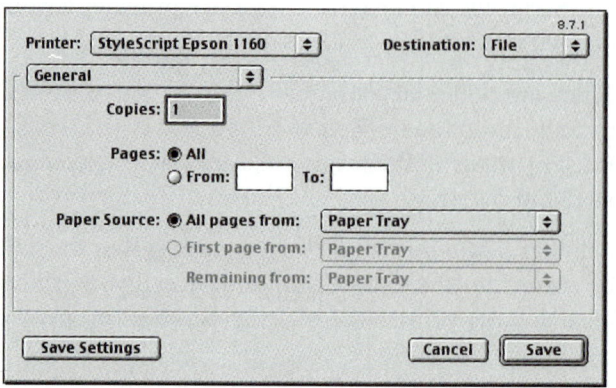

The Save as File options enable you to define the format of the output (PostScript Job is the default and should remain selected to create a PostScript file); the PostScript Level of the code; the Data Format; and the Font Inclusion. To be safe, you should make sure All is selected in the Font Inclusion menu so that the document will output properly.

Most service providers have PostScript Level 2- or 3-compatible devices, but ask to be sure.

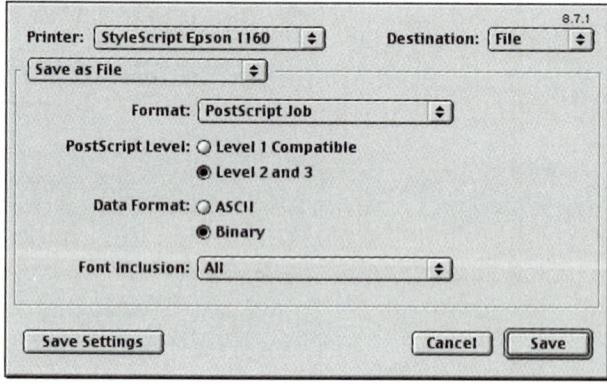

When you have finished setting the printer-specific options, clicking Save presents a navigation dialog box. You can define the name and location for the PostScript file. Clicking Save in this dialog box returns you to the Print dialog box.

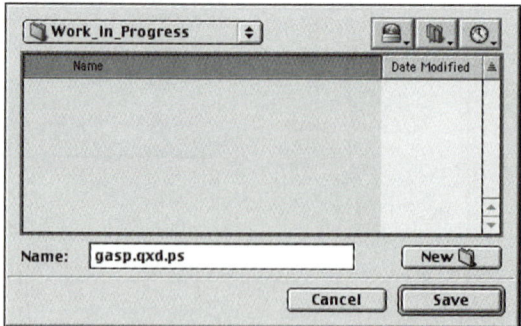

You can define the printing options for the PostScript file, and then click Print to create the file.

Exporting PostScript on a Windows Computer

To save a document as PostScript on a Windows computer, you have to create a printer that is mapped to a file. You can add a printer by choosing Start>Settings>Printers.

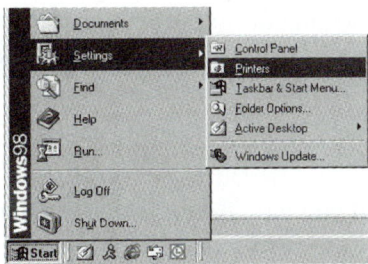

The Add Printer option opens the Add Printer wizard, which walks you through creating a new printer.

When you reach the port dialog box, you can choose FILE from the list to map the printer to a file. The next step allows you to name the printer.

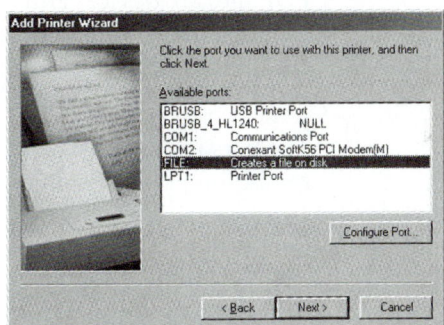

When you finish all of the dialog boxes of the Add Printer wizard, a new printer icon appears in the Printers dialog box. To save a document as PostScript, you can simply choose the file-mapped printer in the Printer menu of the Print dialog box, and then make the appropriate choices before clicking Print.

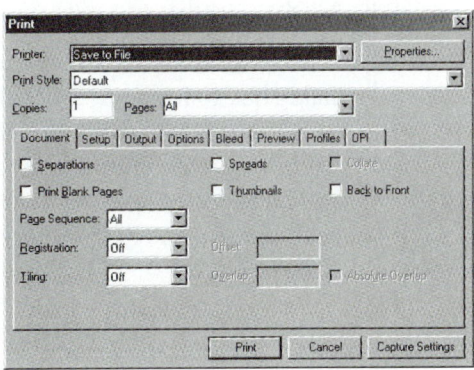

This information is also presented in **QuarkXPress 5: Introduction to Electronic Documents.** *Because more and more service providers are switching to a PDF workflow, we explain it again here.*

PDF files created with PDFWriter rather than by distilling a PostScript file with Acrobat Distiller may not be accurate representations of the job information. PDFWriter does not process PostScript information accurately, including any EPS (encapsulated PostScript) graphics files that are placed in the document.

Exporting PDF Files

PDF (Portable Document Format) files are gaining popularity in the graphic-arts community, for sending proofs to a client (called "soft proofing") and for sending final documents to the service provider for output. PDF files can contain all the elements — page layout, fonts, and image files — that are necessary to output a file, which eliminates the possibility of submitting an incomplete job package. The advantages of PDF files, however, are countered by the fact that if the PDF file is not created properly, the production workflow stops.

If you have Adobe Acrobat, QuarkXPress 5 enables you to interact with Acrobat Distiller from within the Quark environment. Distiller is, in essence, a software-based RIP that interprets the PostScript information to create a PDF file. Successful creation of a PDF file indicates that the document will print correctly on a PostScript output device such as an imagesetter.

One of the defining trends of recent years is the evolution of a PDF workflow. Many printers now accept PDF files from customers instead of requiring original-application files. This workflow offers certain advantages to the service provider:

- Fonts can be embedded in the PDF file, eliminating the problem of missing font files.
- Images and graphics are embedded in the PDF, eliminating the need to send separate files in the job package.
- PDF files are device- and platform-independent, theoretically eliminating problems when crossing from Windows to Macintosh (or vice versa).

PDF workflow also introduces several new potential problems to the production process.

- The person creating the PDF may inadvertently downsample images to low-resolution (Web) graphics.
- The person creating the file may inadvertently change all colors to RGB mode.
- The PDF files may have been created with a PDF Writer instead of distilled with Acrobat Distiller, which may not provide an accurate rendering of the job information.

Software and Hardware Requirements

Exporting a PDF file from a QuarkXPress document requires a PostScript-based printer. In order to use the Export as PDF feature of QuarkXPress 5.0, you must also have Adobe Acrobat Distiller installed on your computer.

You can use the PDF Preferences (Edit>Preferences>Preferences>Application>PDF) dialog box to locate Acrobat Distiller on your computer. The Select button allows you to navigate to the location of Distiller on your hard drive. The Workflow section offers the option to Distill Immediately (create the PDF file at the time you choose to Export PDF) or Create PostScript File for Later Distilling. The Options button in the Default Settings section opens the PDF Export Options dialog box.

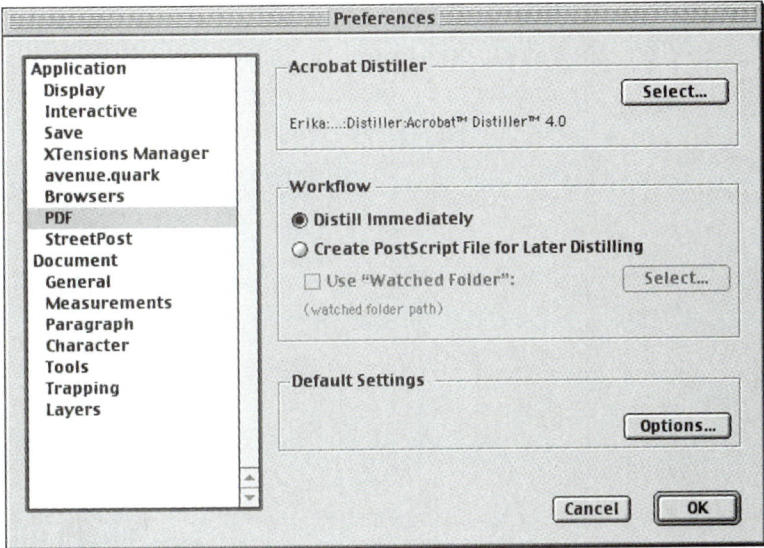

Quark's Export as PDF capabilities require a PostScript printer driver. If you are using a nonPostScript printer, you will not be able to use this feature.

If you have not defined the location of Acrobat Distiller, QuarkXPress will prompt you the first time you choose File>Export as PDF. You can navigate through the folders of your computer and find the Acrobat Distiller application, and then click Open.

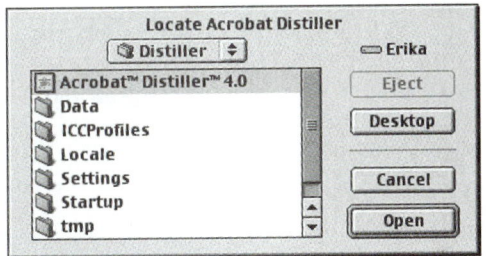

Adobe Acrobat is not the same as the free Acrobat Reader utility. You need to make sure that you install the full version of Acrobat Distiller if you plan to use the Export as PDF features.

Exporting PDF Files

After you have located Acrobat Distiller, the Export as PDF (File>Export>Document as PDF) dialog box enables you to define the location, file name, and which pages to export.

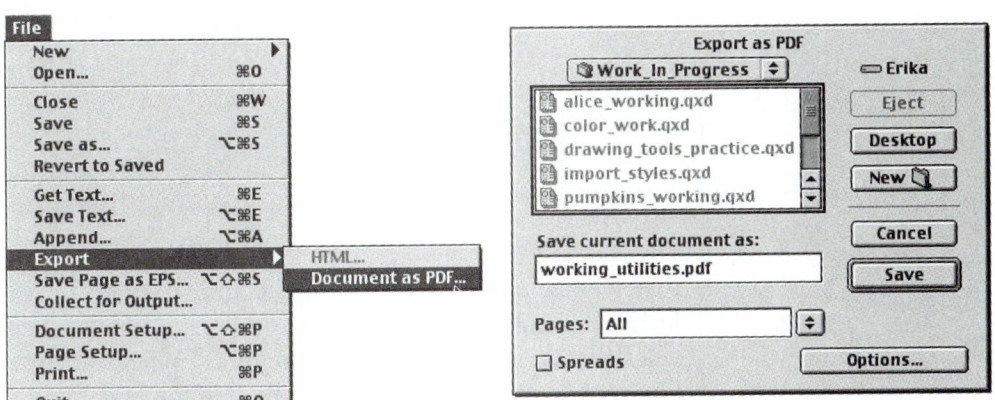

Clicking Options in the Export as PDF dialog box presents the PDF options for the document you are creating. (These are the same dialog boxes you would access by clicking Default Settings Options in the PDF Preferences dialog box.) Any choices you make here override the current settings in the Distiller application.

Job Options

The Document Info and Hyperlinks tabs are not important if you are creating a PDF file for a service provider. These relate to searchability and electronic distribution, and are not relevant for commercial print output.

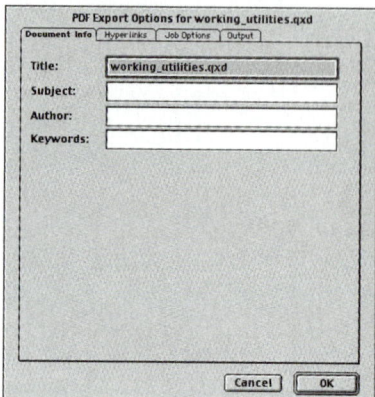
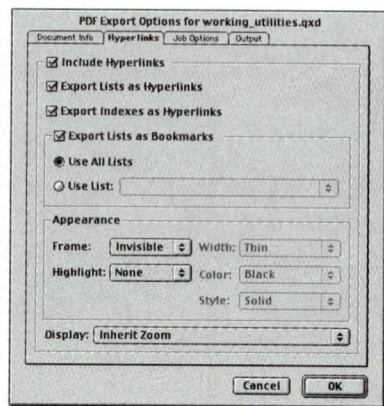

The Job Options tab includes the choices for font embedding and image compression. If you are sending a job to the service provider, the best choice is to Embed All Fonts, set all Compression options to None, and set each Resolution option to Keep Resolution.

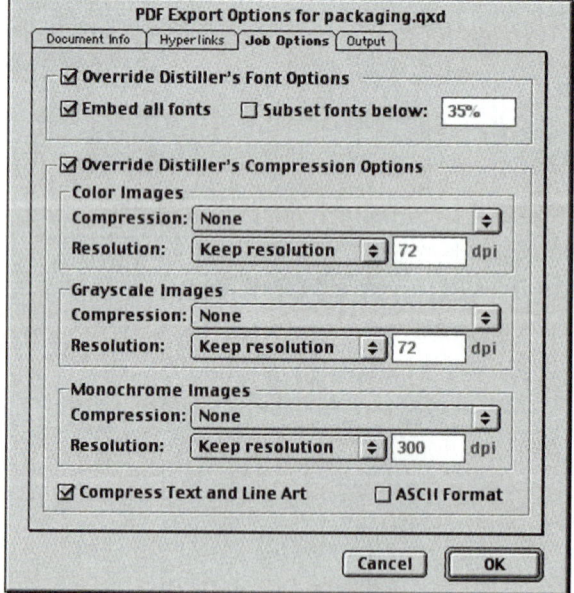

Font Embedding

PDF files are useful for commercial output, partially because they eliminate the need to include font files in the job package; there is a smaller chance that fonts will be missing when the service provider opens the files. Embedding fonts in a document means that the font metrics are incorporated directly into the PDF file.

The option to Subset Fonts Below means that if less than the specified percentage of the font is used, only the necessary (used) characters of that font will be included in the PDF. This helps to keep file size small, but also limits your text-editing capabilities once the PDF is sent to the service provider. If you think there will be any text changes later in the process, it's best to set the subset percentage to 100%.

Image Compression and Downsampling

The compression options can cause the workflow to break down if images are downsampled. Of course, one of the benefits of creating PDF files is portability. If you don't compress the images in a document, your PDF file may be extremely large. For a commercial printing workflow, large file size is preferable to poor image quality.

If you don't have to submit the PDF file via modem transmission, large file size is not an issue. If you do have to compress the files, ask your service provider what settings they prefer you to use. They may have a defined set of job options, which you can load into Distiller to create PDF files.

Output Options

The Printer Description menu defines the PPD that is used to generate the PDF file. Most service providers who accept PDF files for output will provide you with the correct PPD to install and use.

The Color Output section of the Output tab determines whether your PDF file is a composite or separated job. Most of the options in this dialog box are the same as the options in the Print dialog boxes.

You should always consult with your service provider before creating PDF files for output. They are the best source of information about what settings you should use when generating a PDF file for printing.

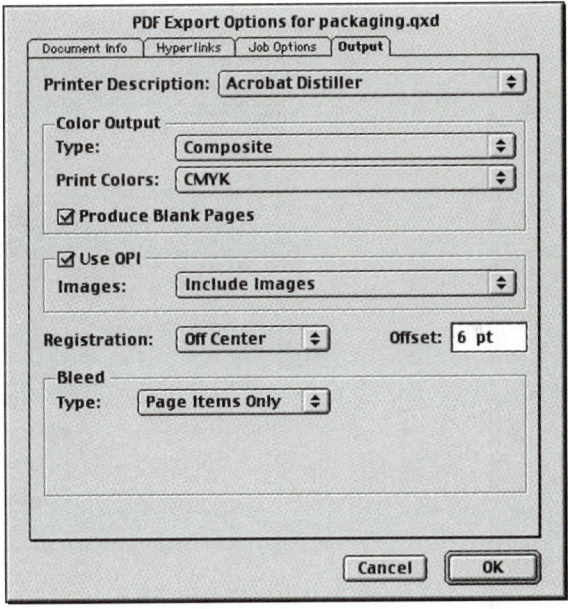

The important point to remember when creating documents for the printing process is that PDF files should not be converted to RGB. When you create a file that will be printed commercially, always ask your service provider how they want you to handle color. If the Type menu is set to Composite, the job will be output to a single PDF page for all colors. If you select Separations in the Type menu, you can choose to separate Used Process & Spot, Convert to Process, or output All Process & Spot, just as you did in the Print Output tab.

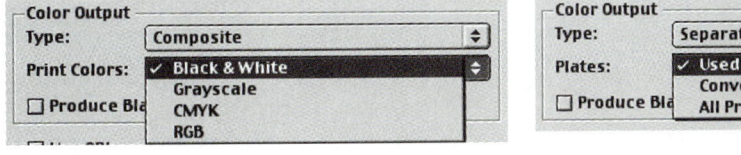

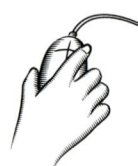

You must have Adobe Acrobat Distiller installed on your computer to complete this exercise.

Acrobat may have a different path on your computer.

Create a PDF File

1. Open **beans.qxd** from the **RF_Adv_Quark** folder.

2. Select Edit>Preferences>Preferences>Application>PDF. Click Select/Browse in the Acrobat Distiller area of the dialog box.

3. Locate the Acrobat Distiller application, probably in the Distiller folder (Applications>Adobe Acrobat>Distiller on the Macintosh or Program Files>Adobe>Acrobat>Distiller on a Windows-based system), and click Open.

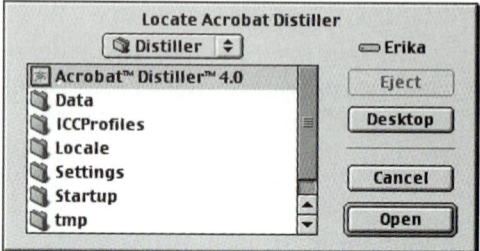

4. In the Workflow area, make sure that Distill Immediately is selected, and click OK.

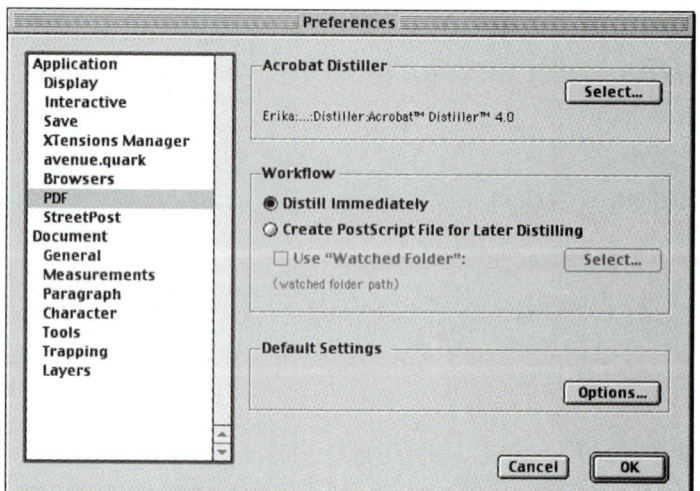

5. Choose File>Export>Document as PDF. Navigate to your **Work_In_Progress** folder, and leave the file name at the default value.

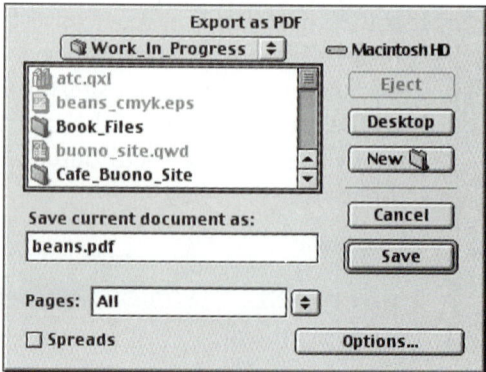

6. Click Options, and choose the Job Options tab. Activate the Override Distiller's Font Options check box, and select Embed All Fonts.

   Activate the Override Distiller's Compression Options. Change all three Compression menus to None, and change all three Resolution menus to Keep Resolution.

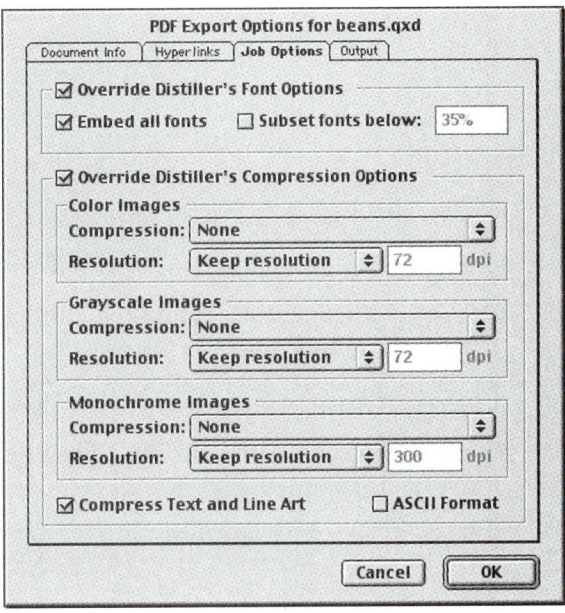

7. Click the Output tab. Choose Acrobat Distiller from the Printer Description menu, if it is not selected by default. Make sure the Type menu is set to Composite and the Print Colors menu is set to CMYK. Activate the Produce Blank Pages check box. Select Off Center from the Registration menu, and leave the Offset value at the default 6 pt. Change the Bleed Type menu to Symmetric, and enter 0.125 in the Amount field.

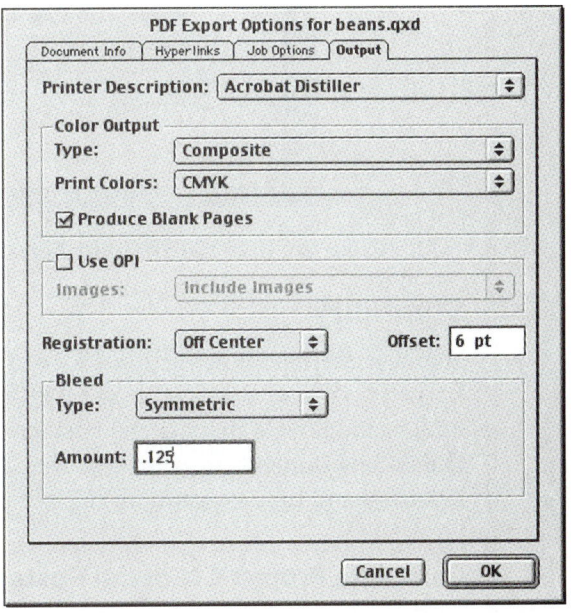

The default compression settings for exporting a PDF downsample image resolution to 72 ppi. This is far too low for high-quality printing.

8. Click OK to close the PDF Export Options dialog box, and click Save to create the PDF. QuarkXPress shows a spool dialog box as if the job were being printed. When the spooling is complete, Acrobat Distiller launches and processes the file automatically.

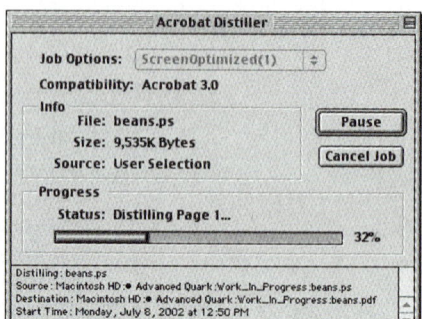

When Distiller is finished, the application quits automatically and returns you to your document in QuarkXPress.

9. Close the Quark document. When asked if you want to save the file, click Yes.

10. You can open your PDF file in Adobe Acrobat or Acrobat Reader. You should have a document that includes registration marks and document information.

11. Close the PDF file and quit Acrobat.

Summary

You have examined the methods for outputting a page-layout document. You have learned how to save a page as an EPS file, and how to print to PostScript. You should understand how to manage the PostScript Printer Description files from within the Quark environment. You also discovered how to use print styles to automate some of the repetitive and time-consuming steps of printing, and how to create a PDF file for output.

Complete Project C: Cosciel Poster

Chapter Objectives:

In response to users' demand for a single application to meet all of their design needs, Quark added Web-design capability to the page-layout application in QuarkXPress 5.0. The Web-design tools in QuarkXPress 5.0 function on a different level of the application. When you create a Web document, you have additional tools and utilities that are not available when working on a page-layout document. This chapter introduces the preferences, tools, and utilities that you can use to build a Web site in QuarkXPress. In this chapter, you will:

- Explore the document environment for designing a Web page in QuarkXPress.

- Create a Web document and define the settings for a Web page.

- Add content to a Web document and understand the limitations imposed by HTML on your design.

- Discover how to repurpose a print document for the Web.

- Create destinations, hyperlinks, and anchors in a QuarkXPress Web document.

- Learn about meta tags, and discover how to create and apply meta tag sets.

- Discover how to preview and export a Web document as HTML.

Projects to be Completed:

- Stonington Letterfold Brochure (A)

- Body Solution Booklet (B)

- Cosciel Poster (C)

Creating a Web Document

The newest and most widely advertised feature of QuarkXPress 5.0 is the ability to design Web pages, using the same environment, tools, utilities, and features with which we are already familiar for designing print documents. Other attempts at a one-size-fits-all layout application have always been lacking, typically attempting to generate HTML code directly from the page-layout file. The fact is, print design and Web design are very different. Features that work well on paper may not work as well on the Web, and vice versa.

The new Web-design capabilities built into QuarkXPress 5.0 are a tremendous improvement over the old model. Rather than exporting HTML directly from a print document, you now have a slightly different interface into which you can copy elements from print jobs. Any feature that is not supported by HTML is not available in the Web-design environment. When you finish creating your site, the application creates HTML code for you. Familiar design features are translated into the appropriate HTML equivalent. The code generated by a QuarkXPress export is not perfect, but it is currently the easiest transition from print to Web design.

The purpose of this book is to help you learn to use the features of QuarkXPress. While we discuss Quark's Web-design features in this chapter, we do not focus on HTML or the Internet. For more background on these and other related topics, we suggest that you consult an HTML resource such as *HTML & XHTML: Creating Web Pages* in the Against the Clock series. Some terms are also defined in the glossary of this book.

Web Document Preferences

When you create a Web document in QuarkXPress, most of the options in the preferences dialog boxes are the same as those for print documents. When a Web document is open, choosing Edit>Preferences>Preferences presents a list of Web Document Preferences (instead of Document Preferences for print page layouts). Several additional choices are available, which are important for successfully viewing and exporting Web documents.

The Browsers Preferences dialog box (Edit>Preferences>Preferences>Application> Browsers) lists the browsers available on your computer, which are used to preview a Web document as you are building it.

The Add button allows you to locate any browser installed on your system. Once you locate the browser application in the Select Browser dialog box, clicking Open adds the browser to the Preferences list. The Default column indicates which browser is used to preview a Web page. You can change the default browser by clicking in this column to the left of the browser you prefer.

To complete the exercises in this chapter, you need to have at least one Web browser application, such as Microsoft Internet Explorer or Netscape Navigator, installed on your computer.

You should define browser preferences with no document open, so that the change will be applied as the default application preferences.

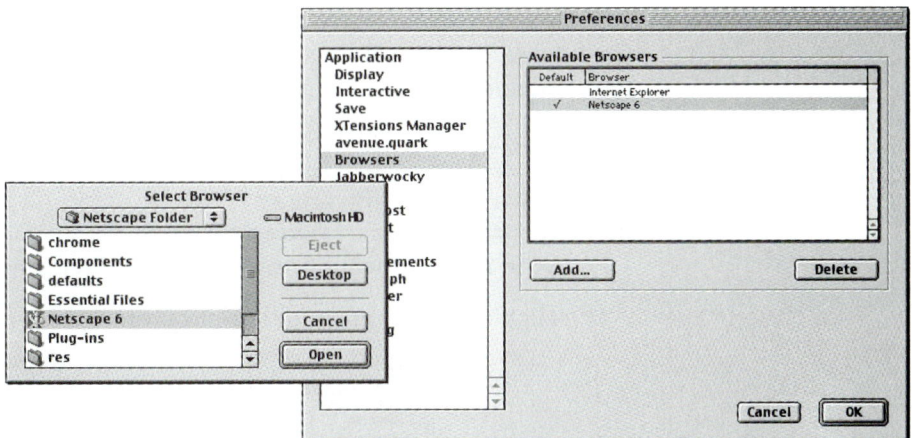

In the General Preferences, you can define the color of anchor icons in the document. (Anchors are discussed in more detail later in this chapter.) General preferences also allow you to define folders to which the components of your Web site are exported using the Image Export Directory and Site Root Directory fields.

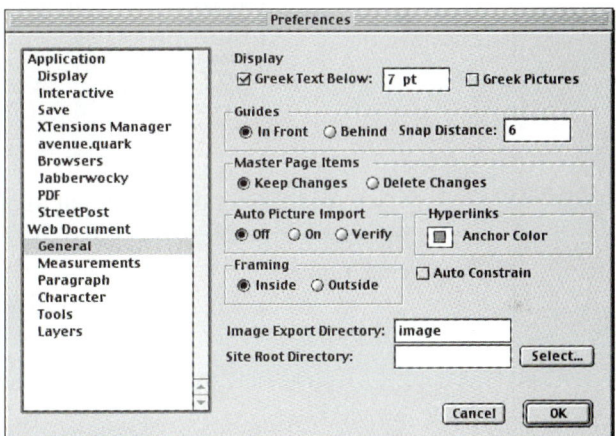

The site root directory is the folder where your Web pages will be saved when you export the Quark documents to HTML. You can navigate to a specific folder on your computer by clicking Select/Browse. When you find the folder you want to be the root directory, the button at the bottom of the navigation dialog box allows you to choose that folder.

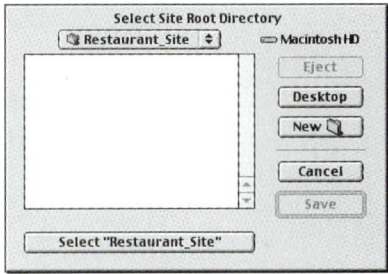

The Image Export Directory is set to Image by default. This means that, when you export a Web page to HTML, a folder called "Image" is created in the root directory folder to contain all of the images in the Web document. If you delete the folder name from the Image Export Directory field, all images will be saved in the root directory folder.

Exercise Setup

The following exercise asks you to add different browsers to the QuarkXPress preferences. You should follow the directions to add whichever browsers you have available on your computer.

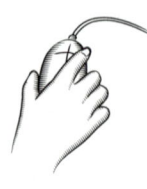

Define Browser Preferences

1. With no document open, choose Edit>Preferences>Preferences.

2. Highlight Browsers under Application.

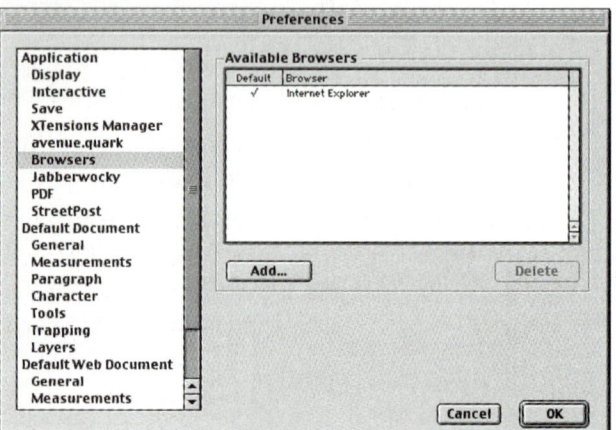

3. Click Add. Depending on what appears in your list and what browsers are installed on your computer, navigate to the Netscape or Internet Explorer application and click Open.

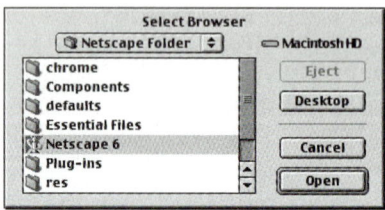

4. When you have finished adding browsers to your list, choose the one you prefer as your default by clicking in the column to the left of the browser name.

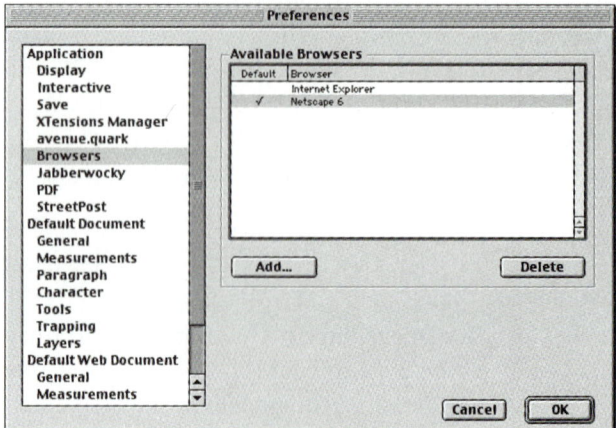

5. Click OK.

Creating a New Web Document

When you choose New from the File menu, you have the option to create a new Web Document. The New Web Document dialog box allows you to define the default behavior for the Web page you are creating, including the colors, layout, and background.

The key command for creating a new document (Command/Control-N) generates a new page-layout document. To create a new Web Document, you must use the File menu.

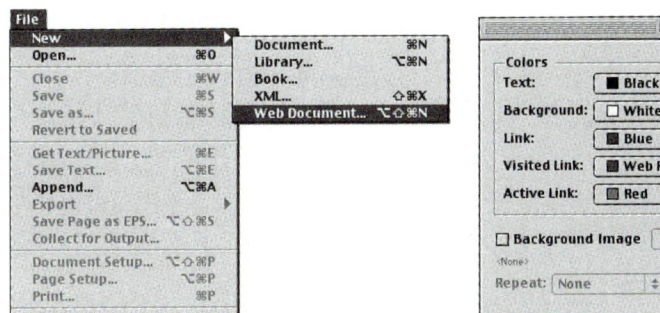

The Colors section of the dialog box defines the default color of the text, background, links, visited links, and active links in the document. Each option has a pop-up menu that lists the available colors including Other, where you can choose a color that is not listed in the default menu.

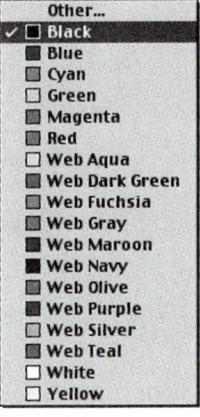

The default colors for a Web document include several Web-specific colors, which are not available in the default Color palette for a print document.

Web-design convention states that, to be visible on a 14-in. monitor, a Web page should be no more than 600 × 400 pixels.

The Layout section of the New Web Document dialog box defines the size of the Web page. You can define a specific number of pixels in the Page Width field, or choose the Variable Page Width check box to create a dynamic Web-page size that changes according to the viewer's browser window. If you chose Variable Page Width, the Width field displays the percent of the browser window that will be filled by the Web page that you create. You can also define the smallest possible page size in the Minimum field.

In general, people dislike scrolling, especially scrolling left-to-right.

Defining a Background Image

If you want your Web page to use an image as the page background, you can activate the Background Image check box. The Select/Browse button opens a navigation dialog box, where you can choose the image that will be used as the background.

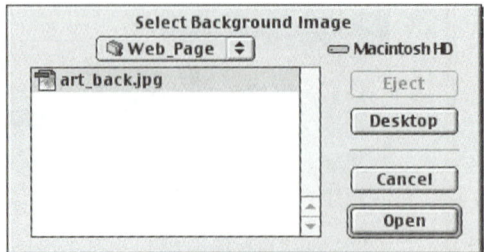

Once a background image has been defined, you can choose a *repeat pattern*, or the way the image is placed to fill the background of the entire page, in the Repeat menu.

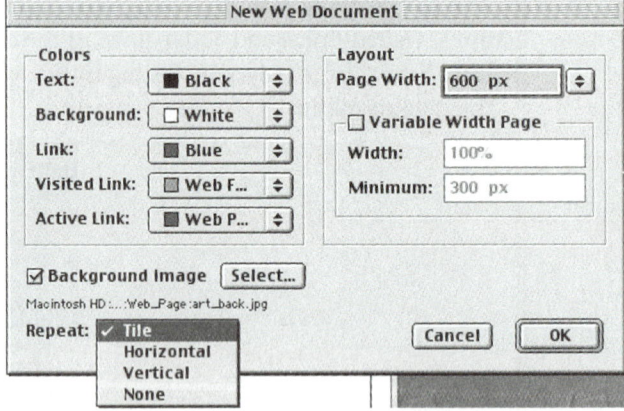

- **Tile.** This option repeats the image horizontally and vertically over the entire Web page.

- **Horizontal.** This option repeats the image horizontally over the width of the entire Web page.

- **Vertical.** This option repeats the image vertically over the height of the entire Web page.

- **None.** This option does not repeat the image.

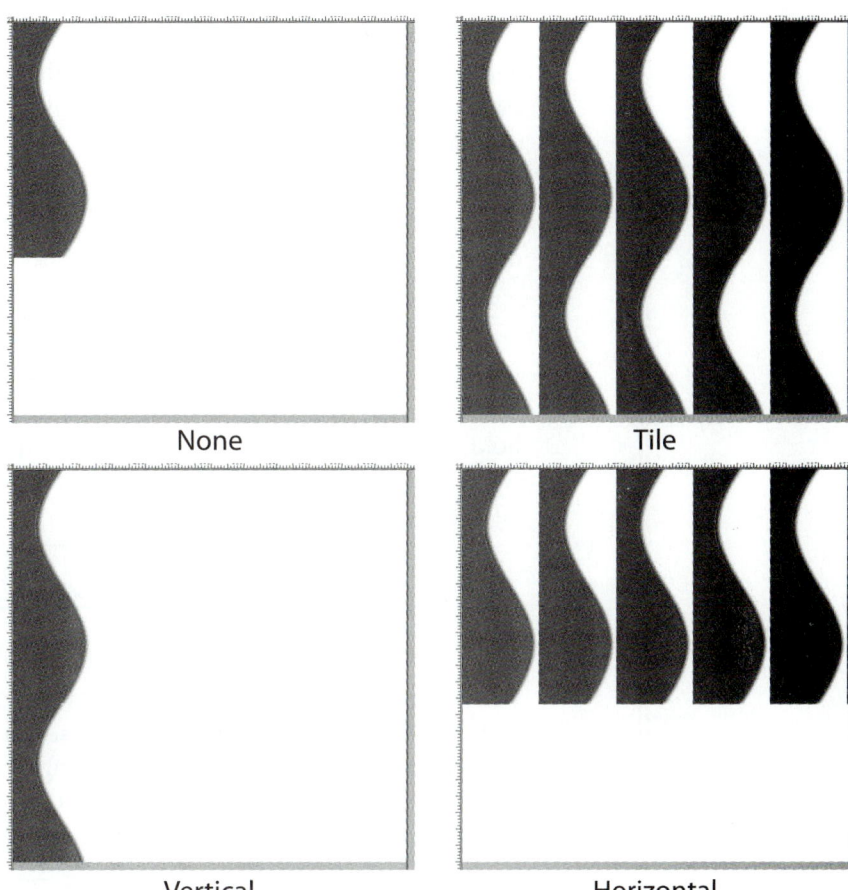

None

Tile

Vertical

Horizontal

The Web Document Environment

When you have finished in the New Web Document dialog box, clicking OK creates the document. The environment is very similar to that of a print document, with a few notable exceptions.

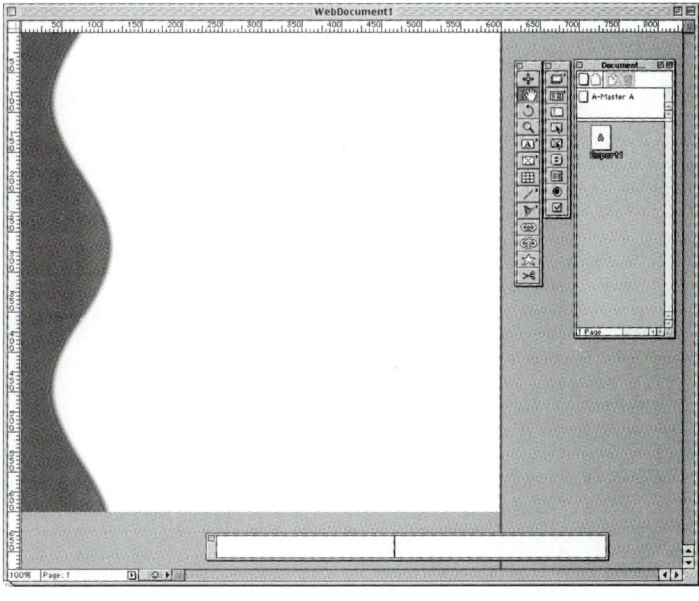

- All measurements are in pixels.

- The document page is square, based on the number of pixels you defined in the Page Width field of the New Web Document dialog box. There is no pasteboard around the document page.

- An HTML Preview button appears to the right of the Page field in the lower-left corner of the window. Clicking this button opens the default browser and displays a sample of the page on which you are working.

If more than one browser is listed in the Browser Preferences dialog box, you can hold down the mouse button until a pop-up menu shows all browsers available. A checkmark indicates the default browser; you can preview your work in nondefault browsers by choosing from the pop-up menu.

- The Facing Page icon is not available in the Document Layout palette.

- Each page icon in the Document Layout palette is labeled according to the Export File Name in the Page Properties. You can change the page name by highlighting the label in the palette and typing a new name. (Export File Names and Page Properties are discussed in the next section.)

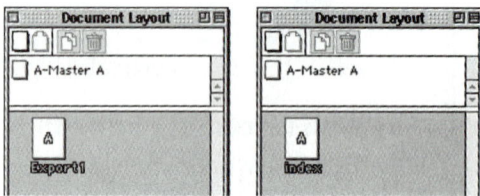

- The default Colors palette includes several Web-specific colors that are not available in the print Colors palette.

Saving Web Documents

The HTML files generated by the export process (with the extension .htm) can be opened and modified in any HTML editor. They cannot, however, be opened in QuarkXPress. Once Web document files are exported, you should also save the Web document using File>Save As. You can then reopen the document, make changes, and re-export the HTML files.

The extension for a Quark Web document is .qwd.

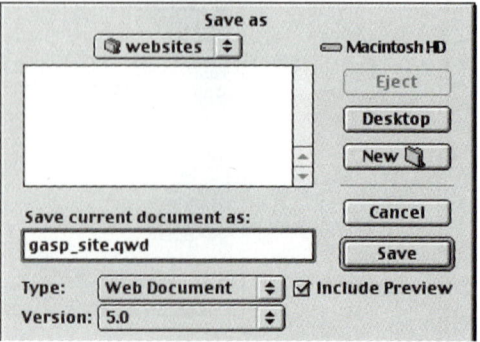

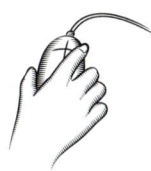

Create a Web Document

1. Choose File>New>Web Document.

2. Activate the Background Image check box and click Select/Browse.

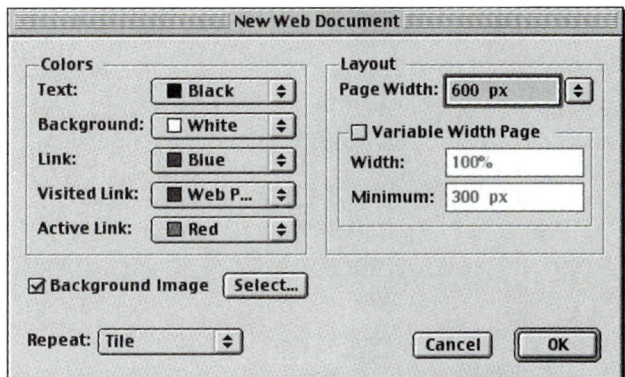

3. Locate the file **art_back.jpg** in the **RF_Adv_Quark** folder and click Open.

4. Choose Vertical from the Repeat menu.

5. Make sure the Page Width field is set to 600 px, and the Variable Width Page check box is deselected.

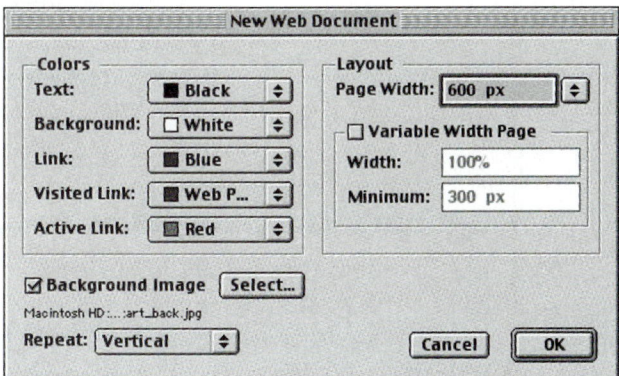

6. Click OK to create the new document.

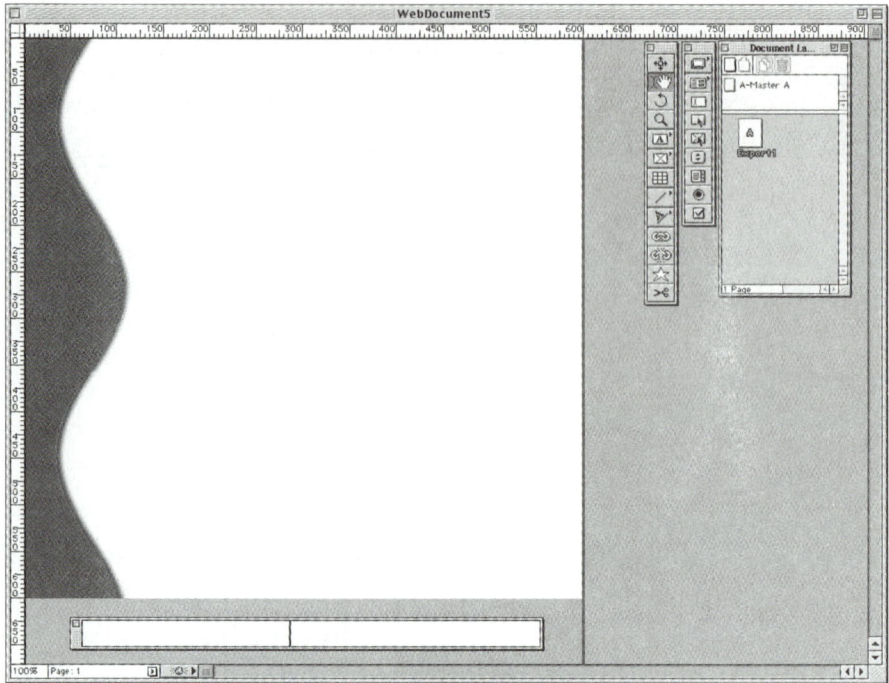

7. Choose File>Save As. Save the file as "buono_site.qwd" in your **Work_In_Progress** folder, and leave the file open.

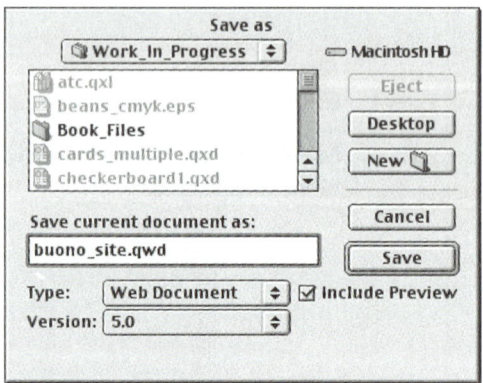

Defining Page Properties

It is not a good idea to use drastically different settings from one page to the next within a single Web site. Continuity is just as important in a Web site as it is in the pages of a printed document.

You can change the settings for any page in a Web document by choosing Page>Page Properties. If a Web document has more than one page, you can define different settings for each page, such as defining a different background image for different pages in your Web site.

The Page Properties dialog box presents the same options as the New Web Document dialog box; when you make changes in the Page Properties dialog box, however, you are only modifying the currently active page.

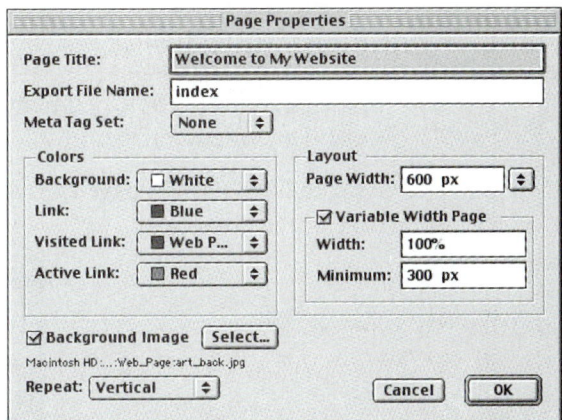

The Page Properties dialog box includes several additional options that are specific to the page you are modifying. In the Page Title field, you define what is displayed in the Title bar of the user's browser when he or she views that specific page.

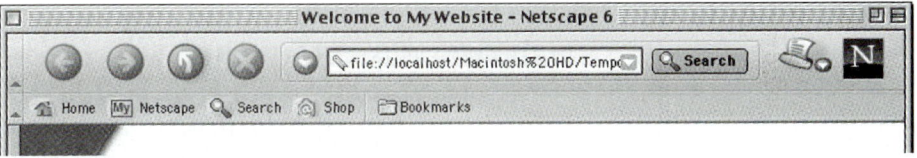

The Export File Name field determines the file name of the page when you export the document to HTML. When you export the Web document, the extension .htm is automatically appended to the file name. The text in this field is used to label the page icon in the Document Layout palette. If you change the page name in the Document Layout palette, this field is changed automatically.

The Meta Tag Set menu allows you to append a defined set of meta tags to the Web page. *Meta tags* are words and phrases that define the content of your Web page, and are used by search engines to index the pages of your Web site. (Meta tag sets are explained later in this chapter.)

Defining Master-Page Properties

If the currently active page is a master page when you choose Page>Page Properties, you can only change settings that can apply to all pages in the Web document. This means that you cannot define a page name or export file name, which are page-specific attributes. You can, however, attach a meta tag set to the master page of your document, which means that you do not have to apply a set to each page individually.

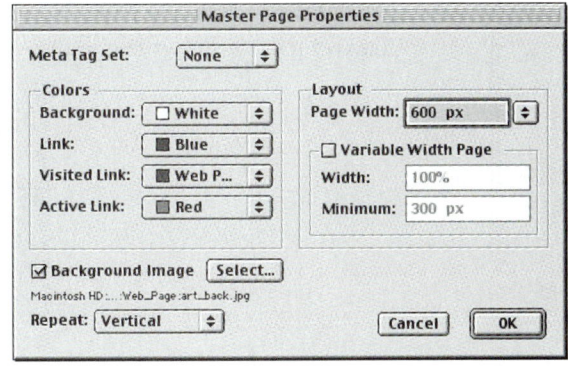

The file name should not contain any spaces or slashes (/), since they are not recognized by Unix- and Windows-based servers.

Master pages in Web documents function just as they do in print documents.

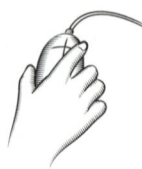

Define Page Properties

1. In the open file, if the Document Layout palette is not already visible, choose View>Document Layout.

2. Drag the A-Master A page icon into the Document Layout palette to add a second page to the document.

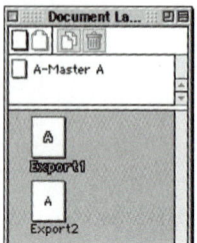

3. Double-click the Export1 page icon to make it the active page, and choose Page>Page Properties.

4. In the Page Title field, type "Welcome to Cafe Buono".

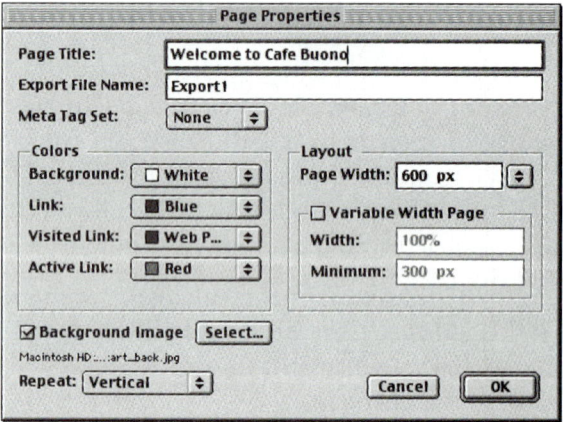

5. Highlight the Export File Name field and type "buono_home".

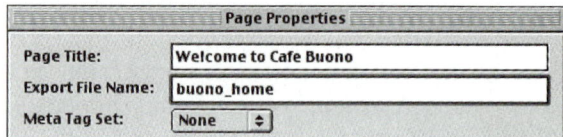

6. Click OK to close the Page Properties dialog box. Notice that the Document Layout palette shows the buono_home label under the first page.

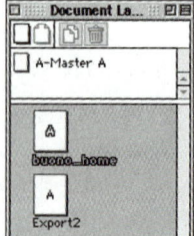

7. In the Document Layout palette, highlight the label (Export2) under the second page icon. Type "menu".

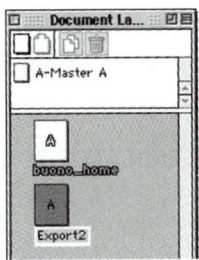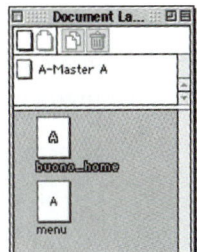

8. Double-click the menu-page icon in the Document Layout palette to make that the active page, and choose Page>Page Properties. Notice that the Export File Name field reflects the change you made in the Document Layout palette in Step 7.

9. Type "Cafe Buono Menu" in the Page Title field and click OK.

10. Add another page to the document by dragging the A-Master A icon into the lower half of the Document Layout palette.

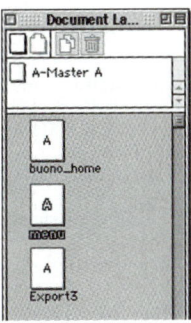

11. Make the new page the active page in the document and open the Page Properties dialog box. Enter "Cafe Buono Reservations" in the Page Title field and "reservations" in the Export Page Name field. Click OK.

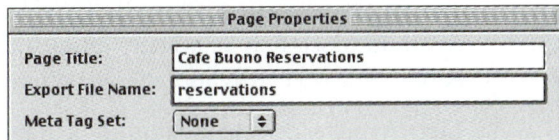

12. Save the document and leave it open.

Adding Content to Your Web Document

Creating a Web document in QuarkXPress is very similar to creating a page-layout document. The tools you use to place text and graphics into a document are the same — text is contained in text boxes and pictures are contained in picture boxes. The primary difference between the two types of layouts is the available options for specific types of content.

Working with Text Boxes

To place text into a Web document, you first must create a text box. Text is imported by choosing File>Get Text, just as it is for a print document.

Typographic options that are not supported by HTML are unavailable in the Measurements palette, Style menus, and Character dialog box.

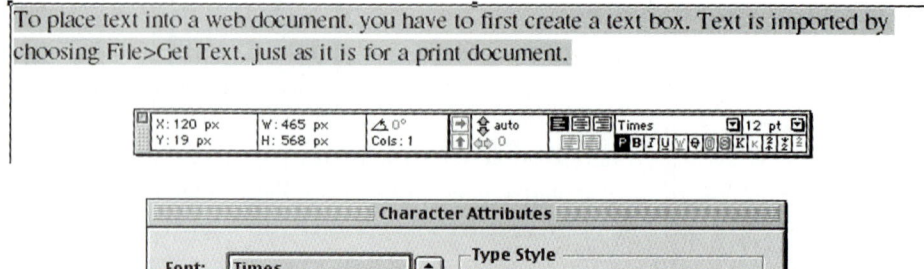

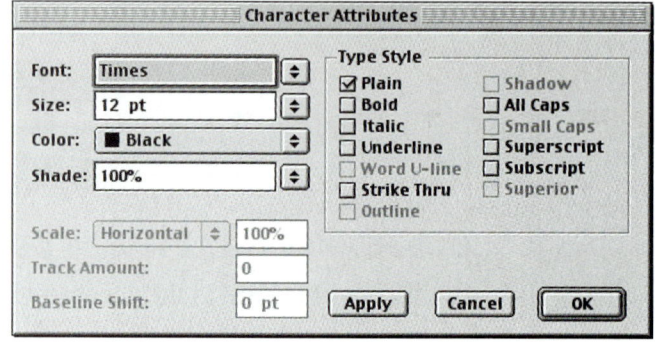

The text styling options that cannot be used for a Web document are:

- Alignment — Forced and Justified
- Character styles — Word Underline, Outline, Shadow, Small Caps, Superior
- Horizontal and Vertical Scale
- Tracking and Kerning
- Paragraph Leading
- Baseline Shift
- H&J Specifications
- Lock to Baseline Grid
- Text Angle and Text Skew

In addition, certain characters (em, en, flex, and nonbreaking spaces, and tabs) are not supported by HTML and will be converted to regular spaces when you export the page.

Like character styling, box options that are not supported by HTML are unavailable in the Modify dialog boxes. The box options that cannot be used for a Web document are:

- Box Angle and Box Skew
- Box Rotation
- First Baseline
- Inter ¶ Max
- Flip Horizontal and Flip Vertical
- Text-box linking

Nonrectangular text boxes and any text on a path are automatically exported as graphic elements. If a text box uses more than one column, the columns will be converted to an HTML table upon exporting.

An HTML table functions very much like a table created with the Quark Table tool. It is the only way to create columns in a Web page.

The header information in an HTML file is transparent to the user, but contains the information that is read by search engines to index your pages.

In addition to these limitations, nonrectangular text boxes and any text on a path are automatically exported as graphic elements. If a text box uses more than one column, the columns will be converted to an HTML table upon exporting.

Using Style Sheets

You can use style sheets to format text in a Web document, just as you would for a print document. The advantages are the same — you can change the appearance of all instances of an entire style at one time. When you export a document to HTML, the style information is embedded into the header information of the HTML code as Cascading Style Sheets (CSS), which define the formatting of different styles used throughout the document.

You can also choose to export an external CSS file when you export the document to HTML. Instead of embedding the styles into every HTML page, each page is linked to a separate .css file that contains the style definitions.

One problem with Cascading Style Sheets generated by the Quark Export to HTML utility is that the style sheets call for a specific font, which users may or may not have. The following shows the code for defining a cascading style sheet.

```
.text {
        font-family:'Times','Times New Roman','serif';
        font-size:10px;
        text-decoration:none;
        color:black;
}
```

The font-family line defines the font called by the style ('Times'). If the user doesn't have Times installed, the browser moves to the next style in the list ('Times New Roman'). You can list as many possible fonts as you like, but lengthy lists of potential fonts aren't particularly valuable or efficient. The third item in the list ('serif') defines the class of font that will be substituted if the user's computer has none of the specific fonts you list.

When you export a Quark Web document to HTML, the application generates the Cascading Style Sheets for you, automatically appending the class of the fonts you used to the appropriate style sheets. The problem, however, is that HTML only recognizes five classes — serif, sans serif, monospace, cursive, or fantasy. If you use a font that has a different class (humanist, modern, and so on) or does not have a defined class, the style sheet generated by Quark only calls for the exact fonts that you used. Inevitably, there will be some substitution.

The only way you can fix this problem is by manually opening the .css file (if you export an external CSS file) or each page created by the HTML export process. For every style sheet listed, you should add a class to the end of the font-family list.

Using Variable-Width Text Boxes

In the Text tab of the Modify dialog box, you can choose the Make Variable Width check box to make the text box resize dynamically according to the size of the browser window. This option is useful if your page is set to Variable Width in the Page Properties dialog box. If the page resizes to fit the browser window, a text box set to Make Variable Width will also be resized according to the relative position on the page. Text will reflow automatically according to the variable width of the text box.

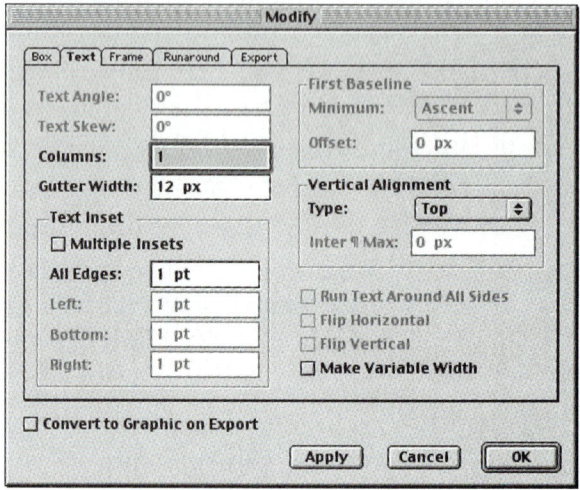

Converting Text Boxes to Graphics

The Convert to Graphic on Export check box at the bottom of the Modify dialog box presents an important choice for handling text boxes in a Web document.

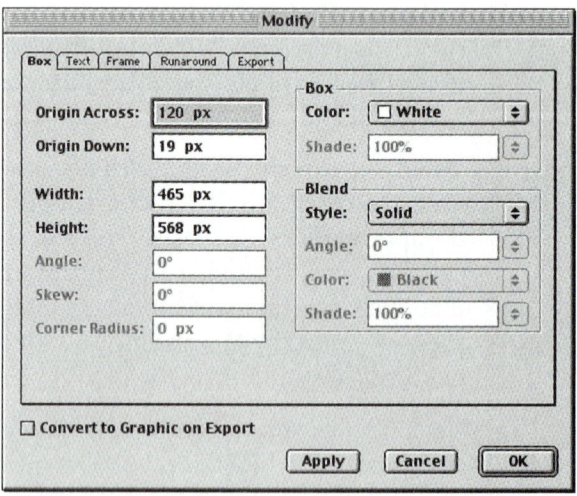

Many Internet users still use dial-up modems. Don't automatically convert all text boxes to graphics without considering your users. If your target is largely corporate, you may be safe to assume that most users have a high-speed connection. If you are creating a Web site for the general consumer or home-computer user, however, you should assume that many people are still dialing in with a 56K (or slower) modem.

Like print design, the fonts used in your document must be present for the user to see the page exactly as you designed it. If the user does not have the same fonts you used, the browser substitutes a user-defined font based on the category of font — serif, sans-serif, monospaced, and so on — that is being replaced.

The only way to prevent this substitution is to export text boxes as graphics. By checking the Convert to Graphic on Export option, the text box will be rasterized into a graphic element when you export your Web page.

The alt text of an image is also used by browsers for the physically impaired, employing voice technology to read the text of a Web page to the user.

The adaptive color palette reproduces the image according to the best-possible color palette on the given display device.

GIF is the default selection for exporting a text box to a graphic.

As a general rule, the Web-safe color palette is the best option because it is limited to the set of colors that are available on most monitors.

Converting a text box to a graphic is an excellent way to control the appearance of text-based buttons and other small text items. When the Convert to Graphic on Export check box is selected, the HTML restrictions on type formatting are lifted because the text will be presented as a graphic. The disadvantage of converting larger blocks of text to graphics is that this can dramatically increase download time for anyone on a slow Internet connection.

Defining Image Settings

When you choose to export a text box as a graphic, you have to define the settings for the exported image in the Export tab of the Modify dialog box. The Alternate Text field allows you to define text, commonly referred to as "alt text," that will be displayed in place of the image if the user's browser is set to text-only (for a slow connection or for using voice technology to read the content of the Web page) or if the image is missing. The Export As menu defines the format for the exported graphic.

- **JPEG.** This format is primarily used for photographic images. JPEG files are compressed, which reduces download time but can also cause data loss. JPEG does not support transparency in an image. When JPEG is selected, you must also choose a compression level from the Image Quality menu. Highest means the least amount of compression will be applied. If the Progressive check box is active, the image will be displayed in progressively greater detail as it is downloaded.

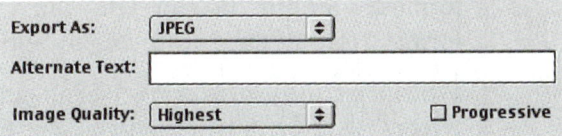

- **GIF.** This format is generally used for images with areas of solid color, and objects with sharp edges (such as type). GIF files are relatively small, and take less time to download than JPEG files. In the Palette menu, you can choose the color model (Web-safe, Adaptive, Windows, or Mac OS) to use for the image.

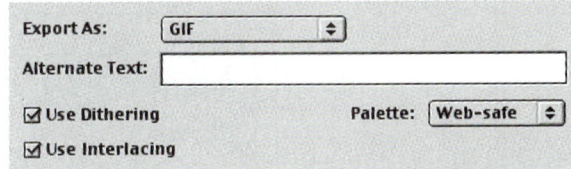

The Use Dithering check box means that the image may be dithered to produce a closer variation of the original color. Dithering is similar to halftoning in print design. The image is converted to small dots of two different colors within the selected palette. When viewed on the monitor, the different-colored dots produce the illusion of a third color. This can artificially increase the colors in the palette, but can also destroy the integrity of fine lines and sharp edges in type.

The Use Interlacing check box has the same function as the Progressive check box for JPEG files.

- **PNG.** This file format is used for photographic images, but does not cause data loss from compression. PNG, unlike JPEG, supports transparent areas in an image. The disadvantage of the PNG format is that some browsers cannot display PNG graphics. The True Color and Indexed Color radio buttons determine how the colors in the image are reproduced. True Color means that the image is reproduced with the most colors possible in the user's browser. Indexed Color compresses the image gamut into the color model you choose in the Palette menu (Web-safe, Adaptive, Windows, or Mac OS). If Indexed Color is selected, you can also choose Use Dithering to artificially increase the range of color. The Use Interlacing option is the same as for GIF files.

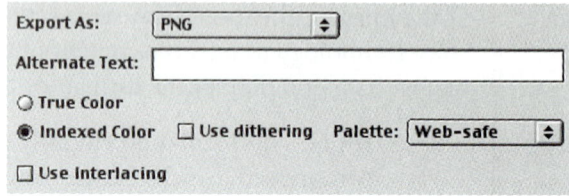

Working with Images

Placing a graphic into a Web document is exactly the same as placing one into a print document — you create a picture box and choose File>Get Picture. In many cases, and especially when repurposing a print document for the Web, the pictures you use are formatted for print documents — high resolution, CMYK color model, TIFF or EPS file format. None of these attributes are appropriate for a Web document.

When a picture is placed in a Web document, the Modify dialog box includes the same Export tab as when you choose to convert text to a graphic. The default values in this tab depend on the type of image that is selected when you open the dialog box. Placed TIFF files are automatically set to export as JPEG; placed EPS files are automatically set to export as GIF. When a Web document is exported to HTML, the export process automatically converts CMYK images to RGB, and decreases high-resolution images to 72 dpi.

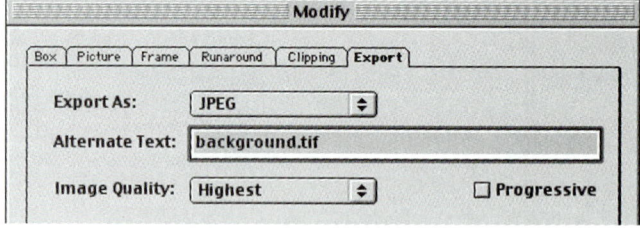

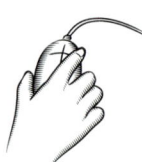

Add Content to Your Document

1. Navigate to the master-page layout of the open document.

2. Create a rectangular text box with the following dimensions:

    X: 10 px   W: 100 px
    Y: 10 px   H: 30 px

3. Type the word "Home" in the text box.

4. Format the text to 14-pt. ATC Maple Medium, All Caps.

5. Open the Colors palette. Change the text color to White, and then change the background color to None.

6. Choose the Item tool. Copy the text box and then paste a copy into the document. Change the position of the copy to X: 10 px, Y: 210 px.

7. With the box still selected, choose Item>Step and Repeat. Make 2 copies of the box with Horizontal Offset: 0 px, Vertical Offset: 50 px.

8. Change the text in the three text boxes (beginning with the box at Y: 210 px) to: "Menu", "Reservations", "Contact Us".

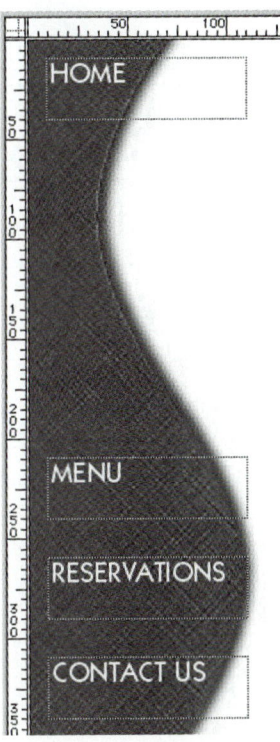

9. Because users are not likely to have ATC Maple Medium installed on their computers, we will set these text boxes (which will be links to different pages) to export as graphics.

   Select the Home text box and choose Item>Modify. Click the Export tab, and activate the Convert to Graphic on Export check box.

10. Type "Cafe Buono Home" in the Alternate Text field. Deselect the Use Dithering check box and leave the remaining options at the default values. Click OK. Notice the camera icon in the top-right corner of the text box. This indicates that the box is set to export as a graphic.

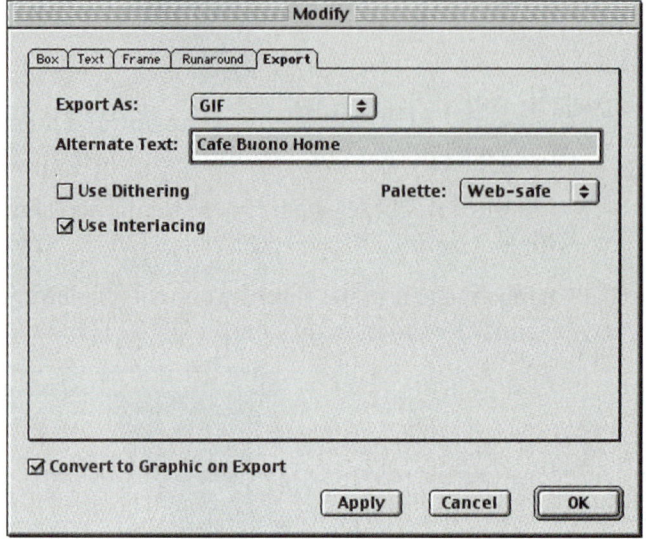

11. Repeat Steps 9–10 to set the other text boxes to export as graphics. Enter appropriate alt text for each box.

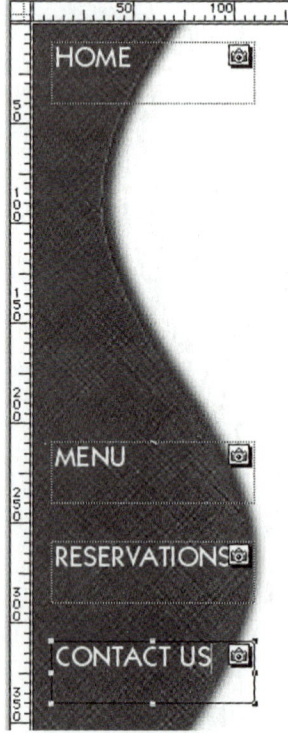

12. Double-click on each page icon in the Document Layout palette. Notice that the text boxes appear on the pages automatically.

13. Save the file and leave it open.

Repurposing Print Documents

Many Web documents created in QuarkXPress are repurposed versions of existing print documents. This process, using the Web-design features introduced in QuarkXPress 5.0, is now much easier than it has been in the past. You can drag elements from an existing print document directly into the Web document, maintaining all of the formatting defined in the original print document.

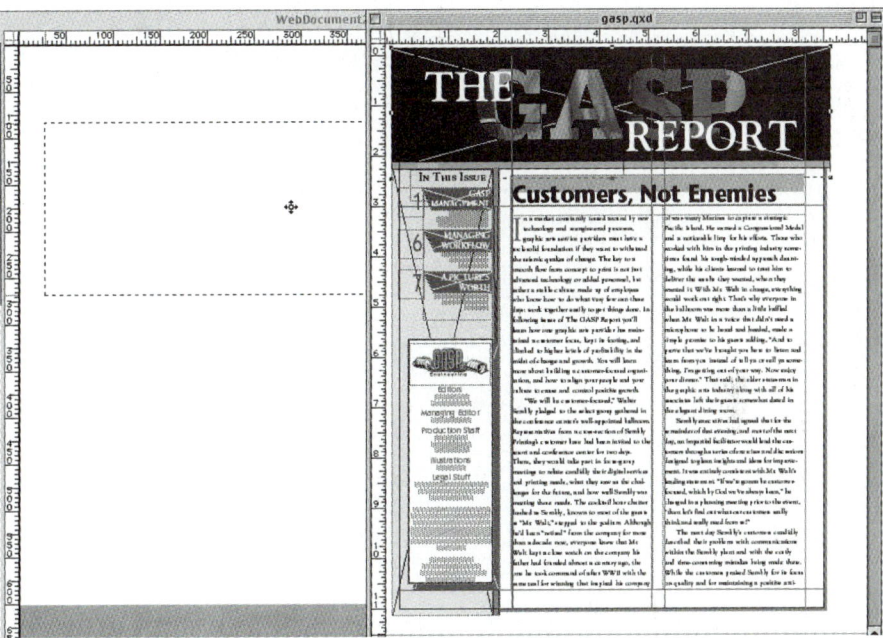

Once the elements are placed, you can make the necessary modifications to prepare the document for the Web. As we already discussed, however, many of the formatting options available for print documents are not supported in HTML.

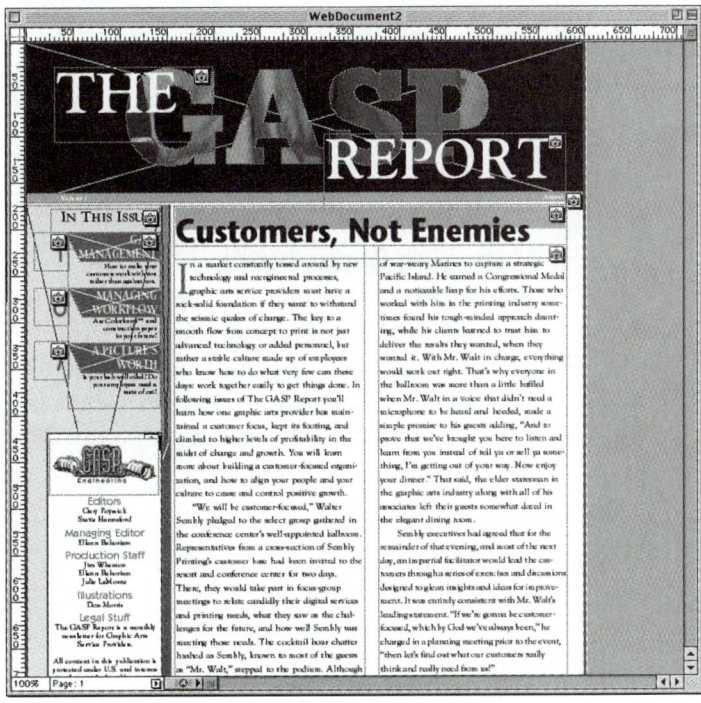

Any text element placed from a print document that uses an unsupported formatting command will be automatically set to export as a graphic. In some cases, this is fine; for long blocks of text, however, you should remove any unsupported formatting. The problem of such formatting is simple to fix. By selecting a text box marked to export as a graphic, you can open the Modify dialog box and deactivate the Export to Graphic on Export check box. Clicking OK in the Modify dialog box effectively removes the unsupported formatting.

Notice the subtle differences between the text set to export as a graphic (left) and the text set to export as text (right). Features such as custom H&Js, tracking, and Lock to Baseline Grid are not supported.

Another problem when moving text from a print document to a Web document is that linked text boxes are not supported. The text box in the Web document contains the story from the entire text chain of the print document. Even if an overset icon indicates that there is more text in the story, the final HTML document will be expanded to contain the entire story.

Managing Runarounds

Box runarounds in Web documents are a touchy subject. You can apply a runaround to elements in a Web document, but runaround is not handled in the same way as it is for a print document. When a page is exported to HTML, overlapping elements (such as picture boxes) within a story are exported as inline graphics. In order for an image runaround to affect the text in a Web document text box, the picture box must exist entirely within the text box.

*The image runaround does not affect the underlying text box (left) until
the image box boundaries are entirely contained within the text box (right).*

Previewing Your Page

The ability to preview your work is invaluable, especially when converting an existing print document. Because so many of the print design features are not supported in a Web document, you should preview your work frequently and make adjustments as necessary.

You can preview your page by clicking the HTML preview button in the bottom of the document window. Your page will be processed and displayed in the default browser. When you preview your page, you will get an idea of what the page will look like in a browser. This is an excellent way to see what works and what *doesn't work* for viewing in a Web browser.

In the following image, a preview of a Web page with columns shows the potential problem of using text boxes with columns in a Web document. The left column ends in the middle of the paragraph at the defined height of the text box. The right column begins the rest of the paragraph as a new paragraph, and extends down the page to contain the entire remaining portion of the story. HTML tables do not function in the same manner as text columns in a Quark print document.

If you are repurposing from a print document, it is a good idea to deactivate the fonts used in the print document so that you can preview what other people will see in their browser window if they don't have the specific fonts you are using.

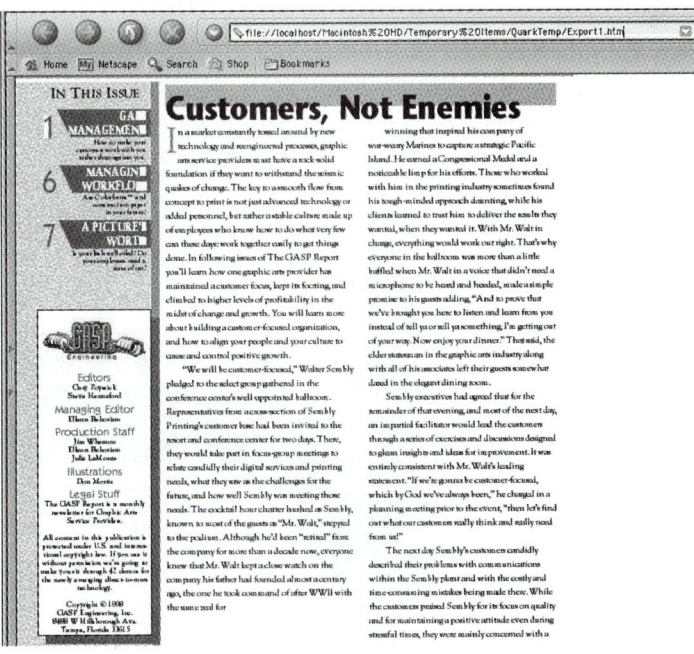

By previewing your document frequently, you can make the changes necessary to create the page you want before the final export process.

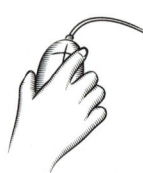

Repurpose a Print Layout

1. With the Web document buono_site.qwd still open, open the document **buono_menu.qxd** from the **RF_Adv_Quark** folder.

2. Change the page view of the print document so that you can see both documents on your monitor.

3. In the Web document, make sure that buono_home is the active page.

4. Using the Item tool, select the logo picture box on the first page of the print document.

5. Drag the selected item from the print document into the Web document. Click on the Web document window to make it the active window.

6. Change the size of the logo to 100% horizontally and vertically, and then choose Style>Fit Box to Picture. Position the image box at X: 175 px, Y: 10 px.

7. Using the Item tool, drag the coffee-cup image from the print document into the Web document.

8. In the Web document, change the picture to 35% horizontally and vertically, then choose Style>Fit Box to Picture. Position the image box at X: 250 px, Y: 180 px. Close up the bottom of the picture box so that the height is 215 px.

9. Save the file and continue.

10. Navigate to the menu page in the Web document, and to page 2 of the print document. In the print document, select the Bagels, Pastries, & Sweet Breads text box with the Item tool and drag this text box into the Web document.

11. In the Web document, change the dimensions of the text box to:

X: 125 px	W: 465 px
Y: 10 px	H: 101 px

12. Notice that the text box is set to export as a graphic, as indicated by the camera icon in the top-right corner. With the box selected, open the Modify dialog box and deselect the Convert to Graphic on Export check box.

13. Expand the bottom of the text box to the bottom of the white area on the page. Choose View>Show Invisibles.

14. Place the insertion point immediately before the next-box character (↓) at the end of the text, and press Return. Delete the next-box character. More text in the story should become visible.

15. Repeat Step 14 to remove the next-box character at the end of the page and display more of the story.

16. Expand the bottom of the text box into the gray area below the page edge. When you release the mouse button, the page is automatically resized to fit the new height of the text box.

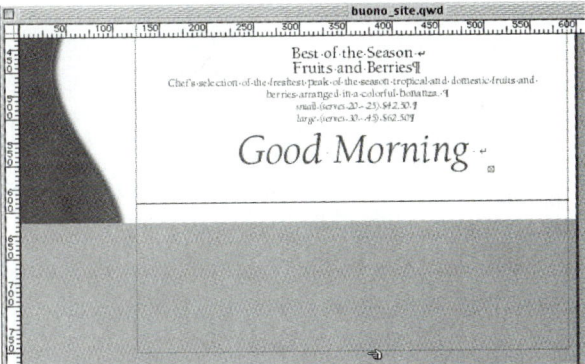

17. Continue removing all of the next-text-box characters and expanding the text box until the overset icon disappears.

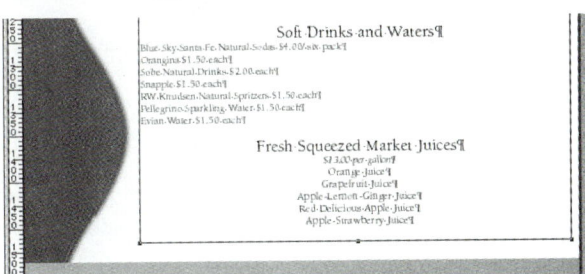

18. Before going any farther, remove any soft-return characters (↵) from the document. Place the text insertion point at the beginning of the text box and press Command/Control-F. Type "\n" in the Find What field and leave the Change To field blank.

19. Click Find Next, and then click Change All. Click OK to the message about the number of changes, and then close the Find/Change dialog box. Scroll back to the top of the text box.

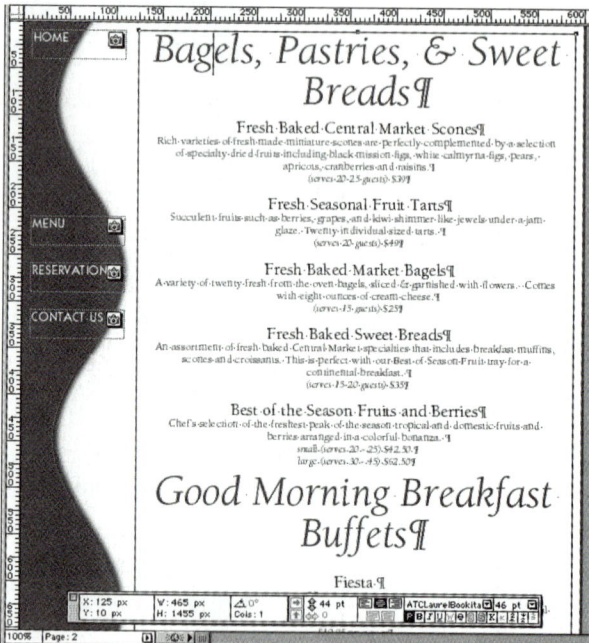

20. If the Style Sheets palette is not already visible, choose View>Show Style Sheets.

21. Control/Right-click on Page Head in the Style Sheets palette, and choose Edit Page Head from the contextual menu.

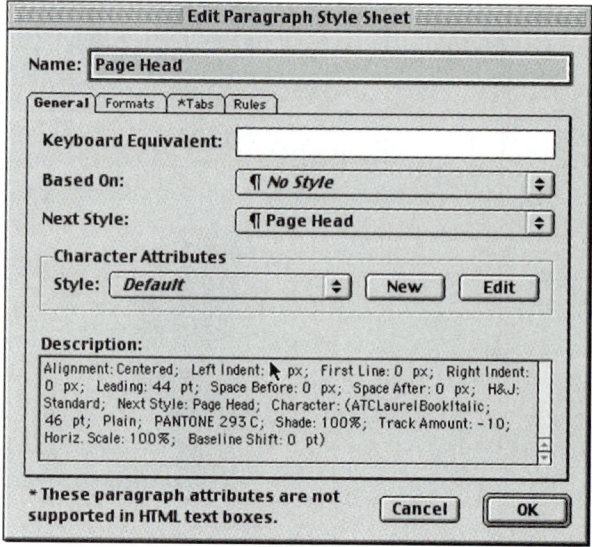

22. Click Edit in the Character Attributes area of the Edit Paragraph Style Sheet dialog box. Change the font size to 30 pt. Click OK, and then click OK again to close the dialog box.

23. Open the Edit dialog box for the Item Name style sheet. Change the font to ATC Maple Medium, click OK, and then OK again to return to the document window.

24. Change the Description Text style sheet to use ATC Pine Normal, and change the left and right indents of the style sheet to 0 px.

25. Change the Item Price style sheet to use ATC Pine Italic.

26. Delete the style Menu List and replace it with Description Text. Click Save.

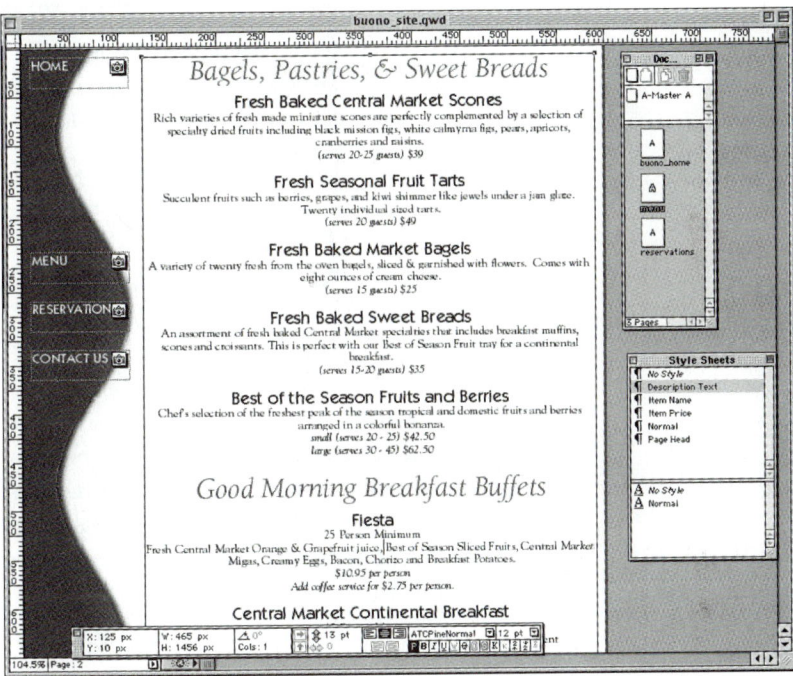

27. Close the print document.

28. Save the Web document and leave it open.

Adding Hyperlinks and Anchors

The most important goal of a Web page is to present content in a clear, intuitive manner. A single Web page can provide volumes of information, but if users have to scroll in six different directions to read everything, they will lose interest and your efforts at presentation are wasted. One advantage of Web publishing is the ability to link from one document to another, breaking up information into small chunks that are clearly and attractively presented. Hyperlinks, which enable this kind of presentation, are the foundation of Web design.

QuarkXPress includes a Hyperlinks palette that is used to create and maintain links from one page to another, from one area of a page to another area on the same page, or from your page to an external source.

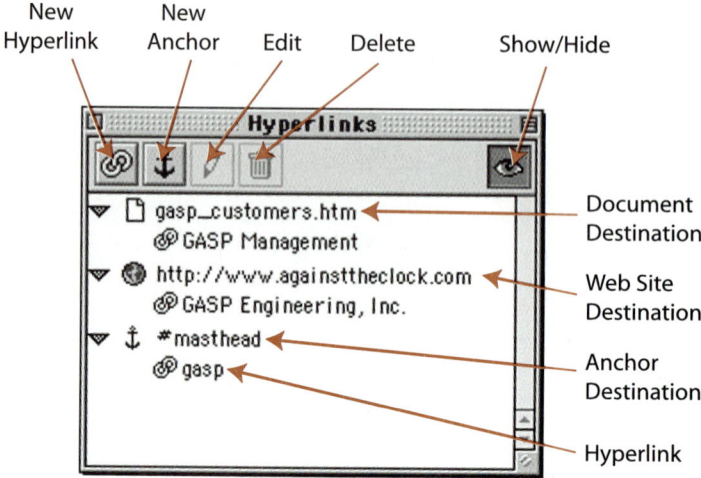

New Hyperlink   New Anchor   Edit   Delete   Show/Hide

Document Destination

Web Site Destination

Anchor Destination

Hyperlink

Creating Destinations

Every hyperlink has two parts — the hyperlink text or object and the destination. The *destination* is the document, location, or other place that is called by clicking on the hyperlink. To create hyperlinks in a Web document, you should begin by creating a list of destinations in the Hyperlinks palette. You can always add more destinations later, but you should at least have a starting point.

There are several ways to create a destination:

- You can simply click the New Hyperlink button in the Hyperlinks palette.
- If a box is currently selected with the Content tool, you can choose Style>Hyperlink>New.
- Control/Right-clicking a box presents a contextual menu, where you can choose Hyperlink>New.

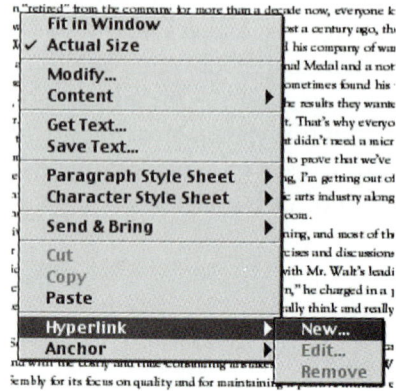

- Control/Right-clicking in the Hyperlinks palette opens a contextual menu, through which you can choose New Hyperlink.

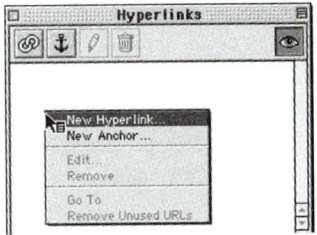

Any of these actions opens the New Hyperlink dialog box, where you can define the destination.

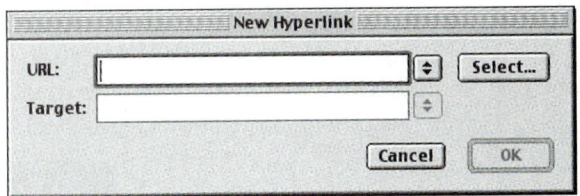

In the URL field, you can enter:

- An anchor name (preceded by the # character). If the anchor is on another page, the destination must also show the file name in the path. (Anchors are explained in the next section.)

      #anchor   jul_page1.htm#anchor

- The name of a file that exists in the same folder level as the file that contains the hyperlink.

                        file2.htm

- The relative path to a file in another level of the directory.
                    ../august/aug_page1.htm

The characters ../ in a URL indicate a *relative hyperlink*, which means that the destination shares a common parent folder with the page containing the hyperlink. As an example, you have two files with the following absolute paths:

    http://www.againsttheclock.com/back_issues/august/aug_page1.htm
    http://www.againsttheclock.com/back_issues/july/jul_page1.htm

If a hyperlink on aug_page1.htm links to jul_page1.htm, the relative link from aug_page1.htm would be:

                    ../july/jul_page1.htm

- The absolute URL of another Web site (preceded by http://, https://, or ftp://)

            http://www.againsttheclock.com

- A URL command that implements an action, such as sending an email (the email address is preceded by "mailto:").

            mailto:someone@address.com

*An **absolute path** lists every folder in the path to the file, beginning with the http address of the page. A **relative path** abbreviates the path by omitting the http address and any common folders.*

In the Target menu of the New Hyperlink dialog box, you can define where the destination will be viewed when the hyperlink is clicked.

- **_blank.** This option opens a new browser window to display the destination page.
- **_self.** This option places the destination in the same window as the hyperlink. If the Web page has frames, the destination is placed into the same frame as the hyperlink.
- **_top.** This option removes any frames and displays the destination in the entire browser window.
- **_parent.** This option is only relevant if you are working with nested frame sets. Otherwise, it functions the same as _top.

Clicking OK places the new destination in the Hyperlinks palette. As a general rule, you should begin creating hyperlink destinations by creating destinations for each page in your document, a site contact (mailto:), and a home page.

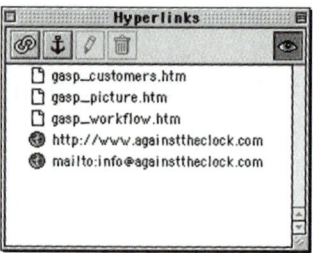

Creating Hyperlinks

Once destinations are created in the Hyperlinks palette, creating a hyperlink is a fairly simple process. You first select the text or object that will be the hyperlink, and then click the intended destination in the Hyperlinks palette.

After defining the destination for a selection, you can expand the destination in the Hyperlinks palette to show the name of the hyperlink. Hyperlink text appears underlined in the document, in the color specified in Page Properties. You can change the format of link text, but remember that users need to be able to easily identify links to information.

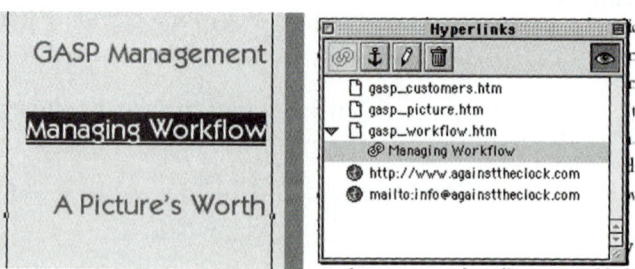

Creating Anchors

Anchors are useful when you have a long block of text that requires the user to scroll through a page to read all of the information. *Anchors* are similar to hyperlinks, but link to a specific spot on a page instead of a page. They are useful, for example, for presenting a list of subheads in a long story. The list of subheads can appear at the beginning of a story, linking to the correct spot in the story. Users can easily jump to the subhead they want without scrolling.

In the following examples, the story "Customers, not Enemies" requires the users to scroll through at least four screens to read all of the text.

Customers, Not Enemies

In a market constantly tossed around by new technology and reengineered processes, graphic arts service providers must have a rock-solid foundation if they want to withstand the seismic quakes of change. The key to a smooth flow from concept to print is not just advanced technology or added personnel, but rather a stable culture made up of employees who know how to do what very few can these days: work together easily to get things done. In following issues of The GASP Report you'll learn how one graphic arts provider has maintained a customer focus, kept its footing, and climbed to higher levels of profitability in the midst of change and growth. You will learn more about building a

The story contains five subheadings. We can create anchors to each of the subheads, and create a list at the top of the story that allows users to quickly jump to a specific subhead. The first step is to create anchors at each subhead. This is accomplished by scrolling through the story, highlighting the subheading with the Content tool, and clicking the New Anchor button in the Hyperlinks palette. The New Anchor dialog box shows the name of the highlighted text (with no spaces). You can change it or click OK to accept the default name of the anchor.

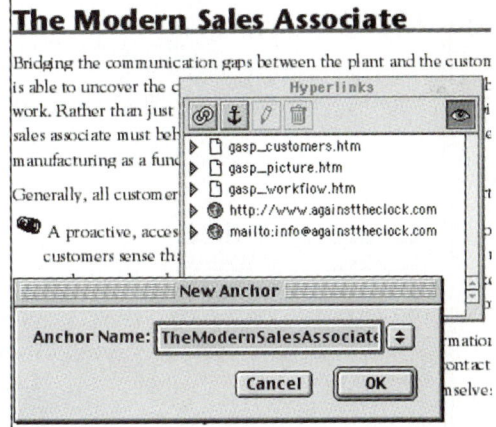

If you look closely at the document, a colored-arrow icon indicates an anchor's location in the document. You can hide these indicators by clicking the Show/Hide button in the Hyperlinks palette.

After creating anchors at each subhead, the next step is to create and format a text box that lists the subheads. The text in this box will provide the links to the anchors. In the following image, notice that the text box we created is entirely within the original text box, so that the runaround applies to the story.

You could also create the links inline with the rest of the story. This is a purely stylistic choice.

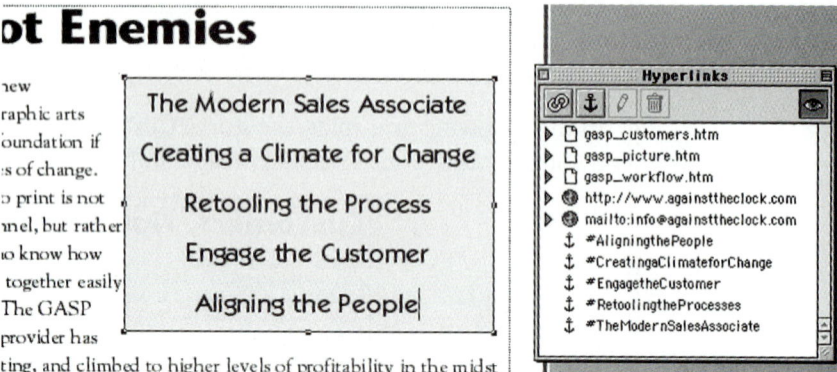

After the anchors and text box are created, linking from the text to the appropriate anchor is the same as creating a hyperlink. You can highlight the text and click on the appropriate anchor in the palette to create the link.

Create Hyperlinks

1. With the document buono_site.qwd open, choose View>Show Hyperlinks.

2. Click the New Hyperlink button in the Hyperlinks palette.

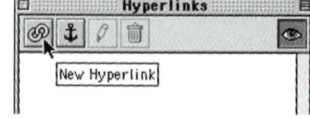

3. In the New Hyperlink dialog box, type "buono_home.htm" (the name of the page in the document, plus the extension .htm that is added when the document is exported).

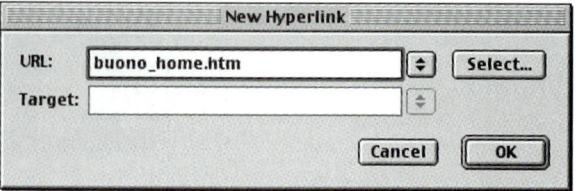

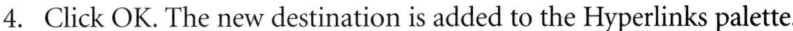

4. Click OK. The new destination is added to the Hyperlinks palette.

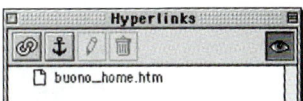

5. Repeat this process to add destinations for the remaining two pages in the document (menu.htm and reservations.htm).

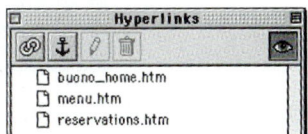

6. Click the New Hyperlink button in the Hyperlinks palette. In the URL field of the Edit Hyperlink dialog box, type "http://www.againsttheclock.com" and click OK to return to the Hyperlinks palette.

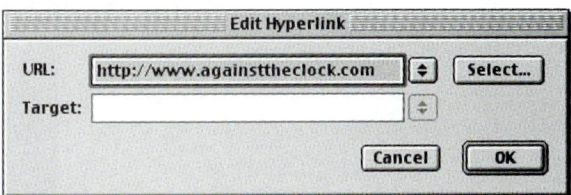

Cafe Buono is fictional, and therefore doesn't have a real Web site.

7. Click the New Hyperlink button. In the URL field, type "mailto:" and then type your email address.

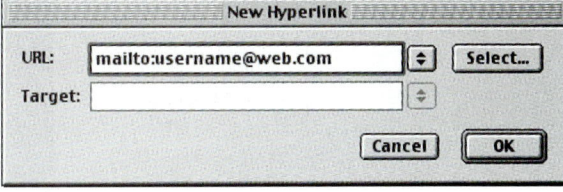

By creating the links on the master page, you are adding the hyperlinks to each page in the document.

8. Navigate to the master-page layout of the document.

9. Select View>Hide Visual Indicators to hide the camera icons in the text boxes.

10. Highlight the word HOME with the Content tool and click buono_home.htm in the Hyperlinks palette.

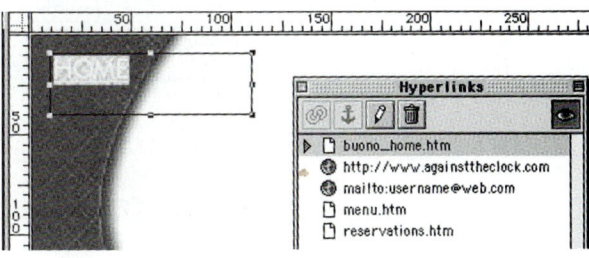

11. Highlight the word MENU and click menu.htm in the Hyperlinks palette.

12. Highlight the word RESERVATIONS and click reservations.htm in the Hyperlinks palette.

13. Highlight the words CONTACT US and click the mailto: destination in the Hyperlinks palette.

14. Notice that the link text is difficult to read over the background.

15. Choose Page>Master Page Properties. Change the Link text color to White. Change the Visited Link and Active Link colors to Web Silver and click OK.

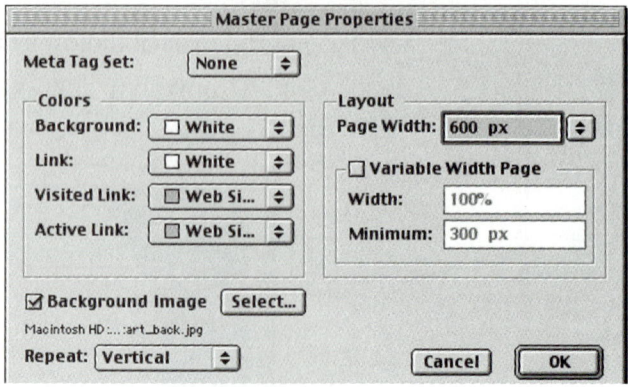

16. Notice that the text color does not change on the master page. Navigate to the first page of the document. The text color is correctly changed to match the settings in the Master Page Properties dialog box.

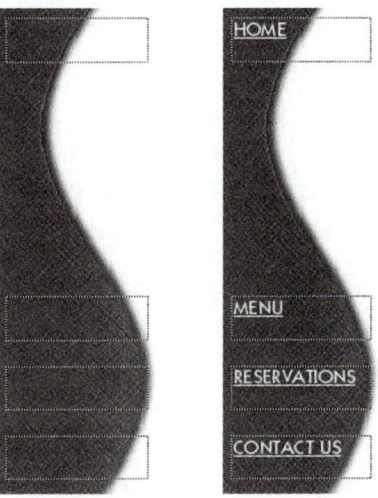

17. Save the document.

Always save your work before clicking the HTML Preview button. This button can cause Quark to crash, especially if the browser is not already open.

18. Click the Preview button. If you click the Contact Us link, you should be able to send an email to yourself. The remaining links will not work properly since the Quark preview feature only exports the active page for preview. If you click on the Menu or Reservations link, you will see a blank page.

19. Close the browser window and return to the Quark document. Leave it open.

Using Meta Tags

A *meta tag* is a hidden element of a Web page and contains some piece of information about the page. The content of a meta tag is contained in < > characters. Meta tags are built into the heading of the HTML code of your Web page, but are transparent to the end user.

QuarkXPress manages meta tags in *sets,* or logical groupings that you define and apply to specific pages. You can create and edit meta tag sets by choosing Edit>Meta Tags. The Meta Tags dialog box includes the same familiar buttons as other Quark dialog boxes. You can create a new set by clicking New.

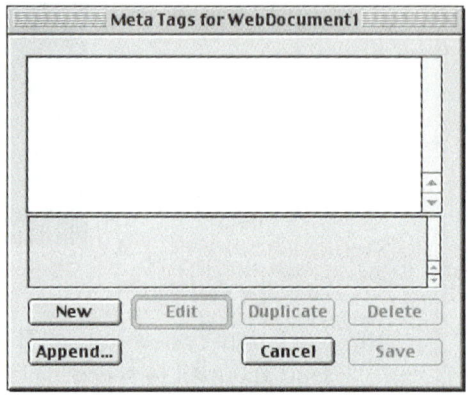

In the Edit Meta Tag Set dialog box, you can define an appropriate name for the set in the Name field. Individual meta tags in the set will be listed in the window.

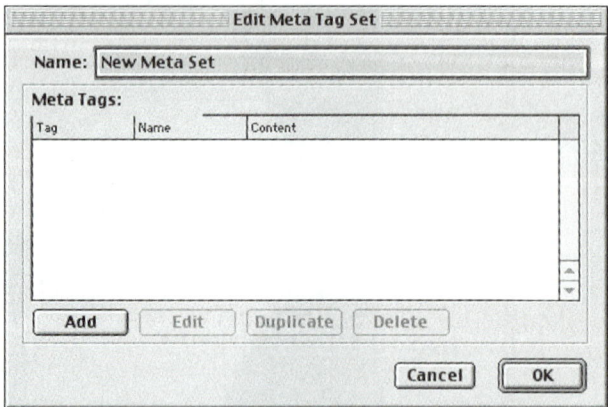

Scripting languages are the codes used to create interactive features in a Web site. JavaScript, which is used to create rollovers (discussed in the next chapter), is an example of a scripting language.

Clicking Add opens the New Meta Tag dialog box. You can choose the type — name or http-equiv — of meta tag from the Meta Tag pop-up menu. Name meta tags simply contain information about the page, such as the page title, author, and keywords. Meta tags of the type http-equiv contain directions that interact with the user's browser, defining items such as the character set used to display the page in the browser and the scripting language used in the page.

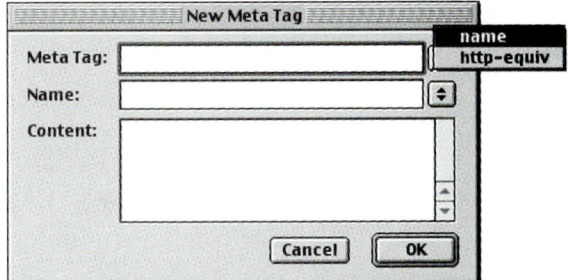

A meta tag appears in the header information of the HTML code for the page, using the following format:

<meta name="generator" content="QuarkXPress 5.0">

In this example, name is the type of tag; generator is the name of the tag; QuarkXPress 5.0 is the value or content of the tag.

When name is selected as the tag type, you can choose from the available list of meta names in the Name pop-up menu, or type other text into the Name field. After choosing the name of the tag, you can type the content of the tag into the Content field.

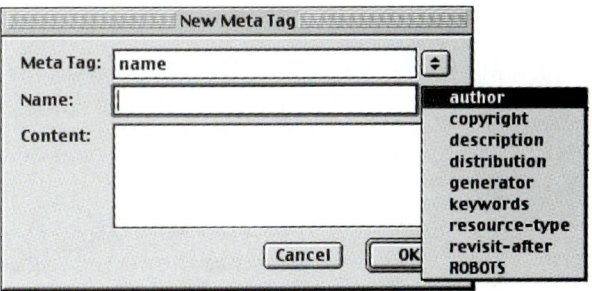

- **Author.** This option identifies the creator of the site.

- **Copyright.** This option lists copyright information.

- **Description.** This option provides a brief textual description of the page contents.

- **Distribution.** This option defines the availability of the site:

  – **Global** for distribution on the Web.

  – **Local** for distribution on a local intranet.

  – **IU** for internal use.

- **Generator.** This option lists the application and version used to create the page.

- **Keywords.** This option lists words or phrases that indicate the content of the page.

- **Resource-Type.** This option determines that the page is a document.

- **Revisit-After.** This option defines how often a search engine should reindex the page.

- **Robots.** This option defines how search engines are allowed to search a page and any pages linked to it:
    - **index** and **noindex** determine whether or not a page is indexed.
    - **follow** or **nofollow** determine whether or not the robot can follow links to other pages.
    - **all** combines **index** and **follow**.
    - **none** combines **noindex** and **nofollow**.

When http-equiv is selected as the meta tag type, the Name pop-up menu presents options that interact with the user's browser to define how it displays the information on the page.

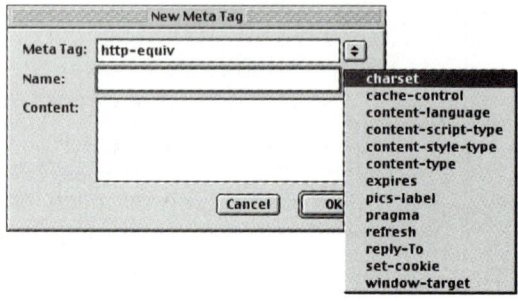

- **Charset.** This option defines the character set used to display information in the user's browser. The most common Western-language character set is ISO 8859-I.

- **Cache-Control.** This option defines how a page can be *cached* (stored) by a browser:
    - **no-cache** means the page cannot be cached.
    - **no-store** means the page can be cached, but not stored in an archive.
    - **public** means the page can be cached and stored in any manner.
    - **private** means the page can only be cached in a private cache.

- **Content-Language.** This option defines the specific language of the page.

- **Content-Script-Type.** This option defines the default scripting language.

- **Content-Style-Type.** This option defines the default style sheet language.

- **Expires.** This option defines the date and time at which a page expires in a browser's cache, after which it must be reloaded.

- **Pics-Label.** This option specifies a rating (similar to the ratings on movies) of the pictures in your page. This is used to identify adult content in a Web site.

- **Pragma.** This option restricts Netscape from caching the page.

- **Refresh.** This option defines how long a page will last in the browser window before it is automatically refreshed. You can also define another page that loads after the defined number of seconds has passed (called a "redirect").

- **Reply-to.** This option defines an email address that is used as the contact information for the page.

- **Set-Cookie.** This option defines the value and expiration date of a cookie.

- **Window-Target.** This option defines the window that will be used to display the page. This option can prevent a page from loading in a frame.

*A **cookie** is a text file that is saved on the user's computer so that the site recognizes return visitors.*

*For more information about meta tags, consult an HTML resource such as **HTML & XHTML: Creating Web Pages** in the Against the Clock series.*

When you have finished defining a meta tag, clicking OK in the Edit Meta Tag dialog box adds the meta tag to the Edit Meta Tag Set list.

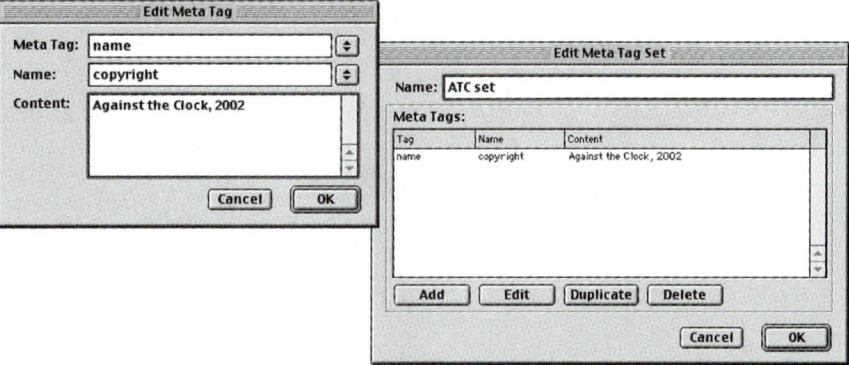

Once a meta tag appears in the Edit Meta Tag Set list, you can Edit, Duplicate, or Delete it using the appropriate button. You can also add more tags to the list by clicking Add.

When you have finished defining the tags in a set, clicking OK returns you to the Meta Tags dialog box. The named set you created will appear in the list. If a set is highlighted in the window, the tags defined in that set appear in the lower window of the dialog box. To use the sets you create, you have to click Save in the Meta Tags dialog box.

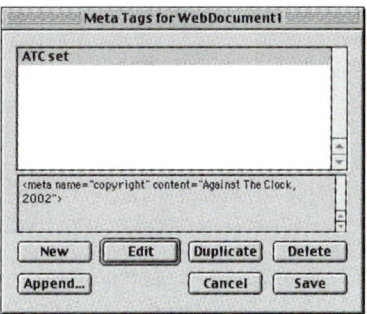

Applying Meta Tag Sets

Once a meta tag set is defined, you can apply it to a page by choosing from the Meta Tag Set menu in the Page Properties dialog box. To apply the same set to all pages in a Web document, navigate to the master page of the document before choosing Page>Page Properties.

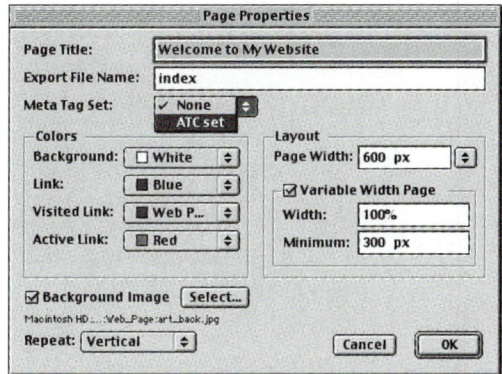

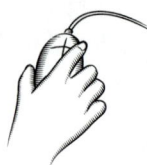

Create Meta Tags

1. In the open file, choose Edit>Meta Tags.

2. Highlight Set 1 and click Edit.

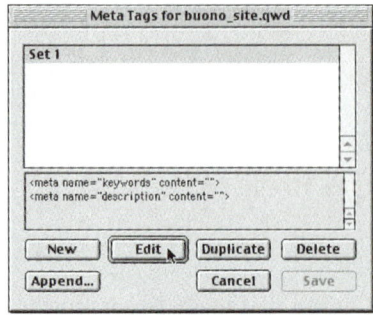

3. Change the Name field to "Cafe Buono".

4. Highlight the keywords item in the list and click Edit.

5. In the Contents field, type "restaurants, catering, dining, food, cafe, bakery, french cuisine, french food, french restaurants".

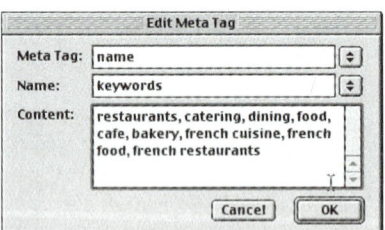

6. Click OK. Notice that the keywords item in the list shows the contents that you just entered.

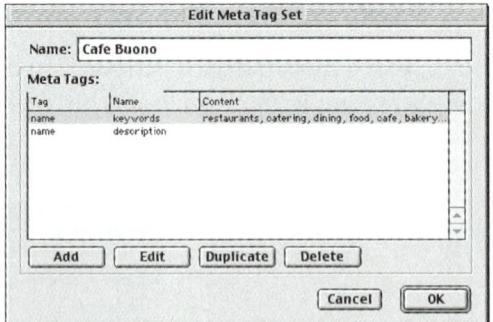

7. Highlight the description item in the list and click Edit.

8. In the Content field, type: "The finest French cafe available in a quaint beach-side setting. Award-winning bakery offerings round out our delicious menu. Catering is also available." Click OK.

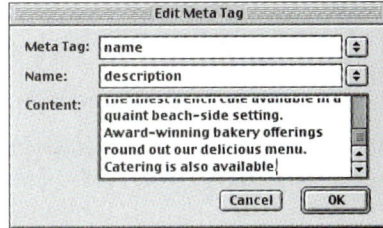

9. Click Add in the Edit Meta Tag Set dialog box.

10. Choose Name in the Meta Tag drop-down menu and choose Generator in the Name drop-down menu. In the Content field, type "QuarkXPress 5.0". Click OK.

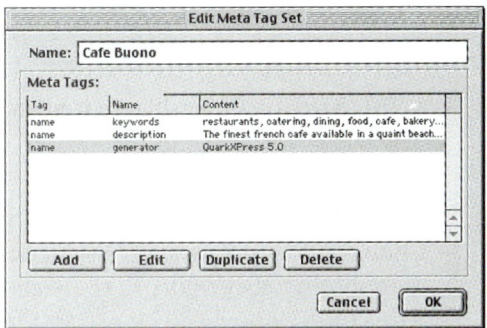

11. Click Add in the Edit Meta Tag Set dialog box.

12. Choose Name in the Meta Tag menu and choose Author in the Name menu. In the Content field, type your name. Click OK.

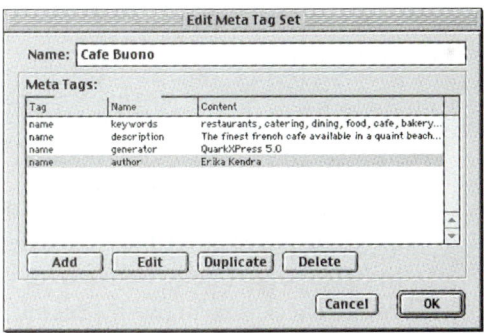

13. Click OK to close the Edit Meta Tag Set dialog box. Click Save in the Meta Tags dialog box to save the set.

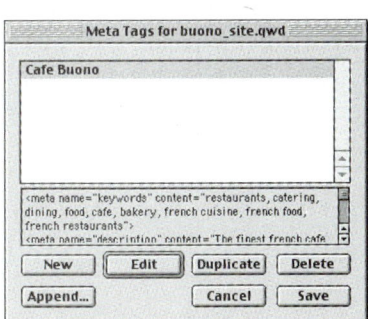

14. Navigate to the master-page layout in the document window, and choose Page>Master Page Properties.

15. Choose Cafe Buono from the Meta Tag Set menu and Click OK.

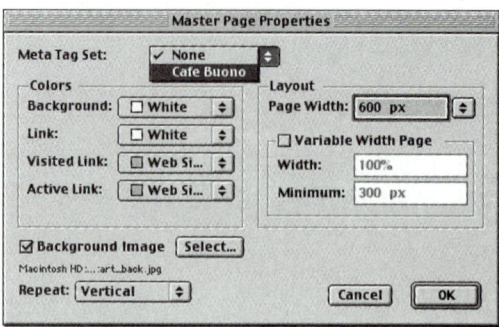

16. Save the file and leave it open.

Exporting HTML

When you have finished designing your Web pages, the export process is fairly simple. Choosing File>Export>HTML opens the Export HTML dialog box. If you have defined a site root directory folder in the Web Document General Preferences, that folder is the default location when you export the document.

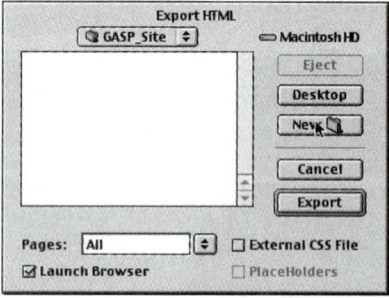

You can choose to export a specific page by changing the Pages field. Even if you have named the pages other than the default Export1, Export2, etc., the pages are still numbered sequentially from top to bottom in the Document Layout palette. The Launch Browser check box, active by default, opens the (first) exported page in the browser window when the export is complete. If your site uses Cascading Style Sheets (CSS), the External CSS File check box places the CSS file into the folder to which you are exporting.

The folder you chose for the export process will contain all of the elements of your exported Web page(s). If you opted to include an image folder in the Web Document General Preferences, any graphic element — including text that is exported as a graphic — is placed in the image folder.

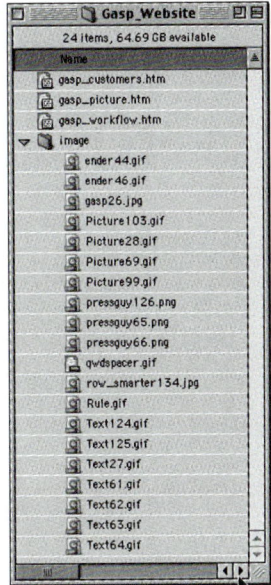

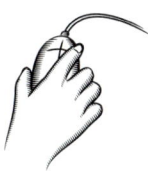

Export Web Pages

1. In the open file, chose Edit>Preferences>Preferences and highlight General under Web Document.

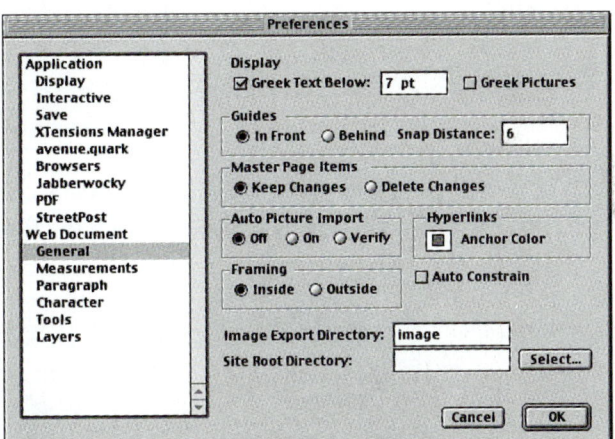

2. Macintosh users: click Select next to the Site Root Directory field. Navigate to your **Work_In_Progress** folder. Create a new folder called "Cafe_Buono_Site" and open the folder. Click Select "Cafe_Buono_Site".

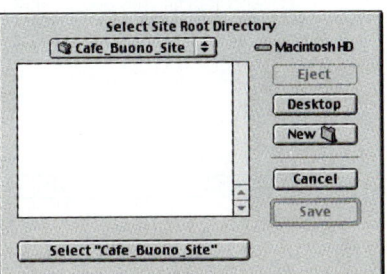

Windows users: on your desktop, create a folder called "Cafe_Buono_Site" in your **Work_In_Progress** folder. Click Browse next to the Site Root Directory field. Navigate to the Cafe_Buono_Site folder and click OK.

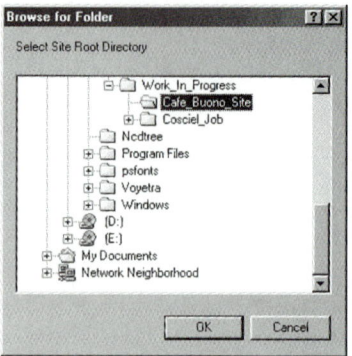

Be sure you have a document page — not a master page — active when you choose Export from the File menu.

3. Click OK to close the Preferences dialog box.

4. Choose File>Export>HTML. Activate the External CSS File check box and click Export.

5. When the exporting is complete, your Cafe_Buono_Site folder should have all of the necessary files. You can open the files in a browser, and the links should all work.

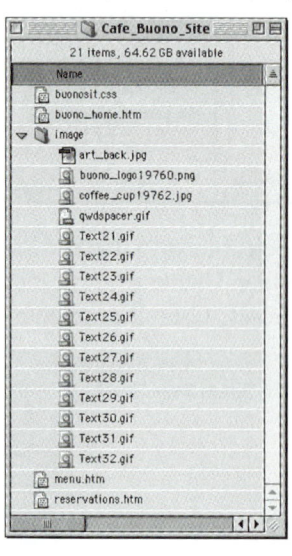

6. Close the browser window. Save the Quark Web document and close it.

7. Using any available text editor (SimpleText, NotePad, and so on), open the file **buonosit.css** from the **Cafe_Buono_Site** folder (**Work_In_Progress>Cafe_Buono_Site**).

```
.text4 {
    font-family:'ATCLaurelBookItalic';
    font-size:30px;
    text-decoration:none;
    color:#003CA9;
}
.text1 {
    font-family:'ATCMapleMedium';
    font-size:18px;
    text-decoration:none;
    color:black;
}
.text2 {
    font-family:'ATCPineNormal';
    font-size:12px;
    text-decoration:none;
    color:black;
}
.text3 {
    font-family:'ATCPineItalic';
    font-size:11px;
    text-decoration:none;
    color:black;
}
```

8. The first four items, the ATC fonts, do not have font classes. At the end of the font-family line in the first style (before the semicolon), type

,'serif'

9. At the end of the font-family line in the second style (before the semicolon), type

,'sans-serif'

10. At the end of the font-family line in the third style (before the semicolon), type

,'serif'

11. At the end of the font-family line in the fourth style (before the semicolon), type

,'serif'

12. Save the .css file (to avoid saving in the wrong file format, don't use Save As) and close it. Deactivate the ATC fonts on your computer. In your browser, open the file **menu.htm** from the **Cafe_Buono_Site** folder. Previewing the file in this way gives you a good idea of what users will see on their browsers. Close the file.

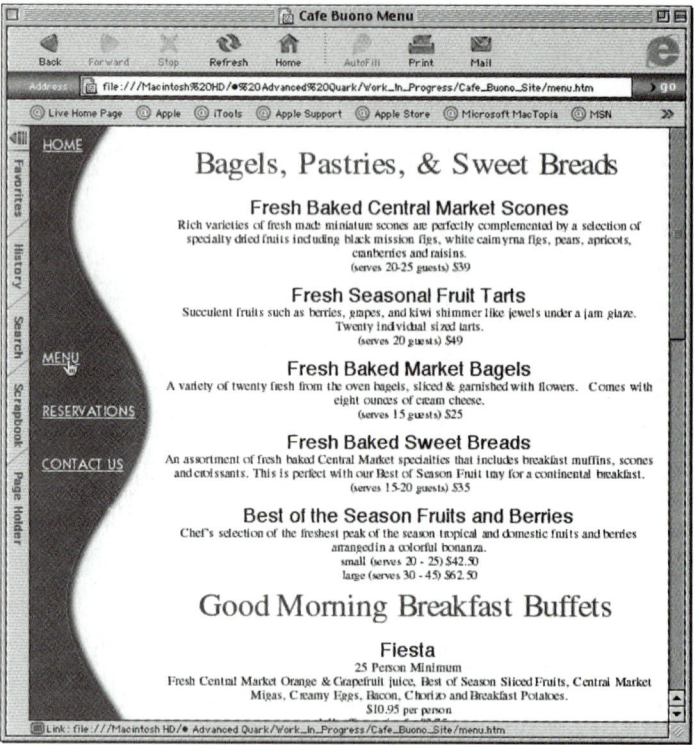

162_QXA_10.tif

Summary

You have learned how to create a QuarkXPress Web document, and should know about the preferences associated with a Web document. You learned how to add content to a Web page by importing files, manually entering text or dragging elements from an existing print document. You have learned some of the stylistic limitations imposed by the HTML language, and you know how to work around those limitations using the Convert to Graphic on Export feature. You should understand hyperlinks, destinations, and anchors, and have a basic knowledge of meta tags. Finally, you should know how to preview and export your Quark Web document to HTML.

11 *Interactive Web Elements*

Chapter Objectives:

The Web-design tools in QuarkXPress 5.0 move beyond basic HTML creation. Like any application that is dedicated to creating Web pages, you can add interactive elements — forms, image maps, and rollovers — to a Web page that you design in QuarkXPress. Rather than simply repurposing existing print documents for Web publishing, these new tools make QuarkXPress a fully functional Web-design application. In this chapter, you will:

- Discover the new tools that are available when you are working on a QuarkXPress Web document.

- Build hyperlinks with an image map.

- Learn how to create rollovers in a QuarkXPress document.

- Create HTML forms that gather information from users.

Projects to be Completed:

- Stonington Letterfold Brochure (A)

- Body Solution Booklet (B)

- Cosciel Poster (C)

Interactive Web Elements

The traditional QuarkXPress tools are used to create a Web document that you can export to HTML, without having to understand the complexities of the HTML language. You can create Web pages from scratch or repurpose existing print documents for the Web. In addition, QuarkXPress 5.0 includes Web-design tools that move beyond the basic display of information.

When you are building a Quark Web document, a new set of Web tools is available that enables you to add interactive elements to your Web pages. Rollovers, image maps, and HTML forms each add interest and variation to a Web page. Creating these elements traditionally required at least some detailed knowledge of the code languages that drive the interactive features. Using QuarkXPress 5.0, you can add interactivity to your Web pages with little (if any) knowledge of HTML, JavaScript, and other languages. This chapter teaches you how to create interactive elements using QuarkXPress.

This chapter does not focus on the code that underlies interactive elements unless a particular setting or dialog box requires a basic understanding of the code to make a good choice.

Web Tools

When you create a QuarkXPress Web document, a palette of Web tools is available in addition to the standard toolbox. The Web-document tools appear in a separate palette, and are used in combination with the basic tool set. These tools are used to create the interactive elements of a Web document such as image maps and forms. We will discuss the specific applications of each tool throughout this chapter. First we'll introduce the tools and briefly define each.

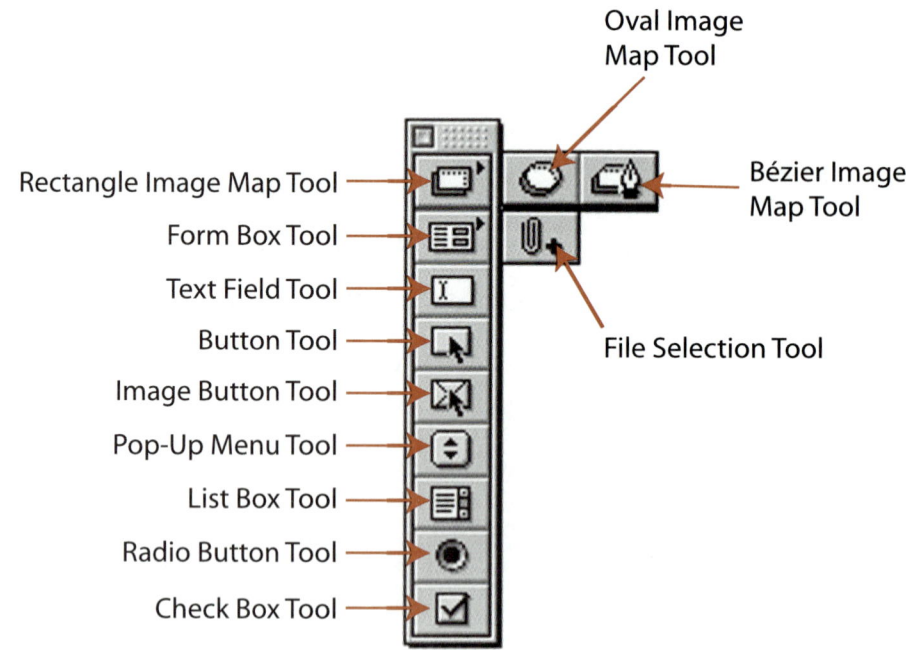

- **Image Map tools.** Three tools — Rectangle, Oval, and Bézier — are available to create image maps.
- **Form Box tool.** This tool is used to create a form box, which contains the elements of a Web document form. All form fields must be contained within a form box.

- **File Selection tool.** This tool is used as an element of the form so that users of the final Web page can submit a file.
- **Text Field tool.** This tool is used to create a text field in a form. Text fields allow the user to enter information, such as a name, address, or email address.
- **Button tool.** This tool is used to create a button that, when clicked, initiates some action.
- **Image Button tool.** This tool is used to create a button from a placed image.
- **Pop-Up Menu tool.** This tool is used to add a pop-up menu in a form. Pop-up menus allow the user to choose from a specific set of options defined by the Web-site administrator.
- **List Box tool.** This tool creates a window where users can choose from a specific set of options. Users can scroll through the list of options rather than choose from a pop-up menu.
- **Radio Button tool.** This tool creates a radio-button form field, where users can choose one of several defined options.
- **Check Box tool.** This tool creates a check-box form field, where users can choose one or more of a specific set of options.

Creating Rollovers

Rollovers are graphic-based hyperlinks that change appearance when the mouse moves over the object, providing a visual indicator that the object is a hyperlink. Rollovers are commonly used to alter the appearance of hyperlink buttons depending on the *state*, or position of the user's cursor. Rollovers are typically created using the JavaScript programming language. The Web-design tools in QuarkXPress include the ability to generate a rollover without knowing the correct JavaScript code.

To create a rollover in a Quark Web document, you have to create different image files for each state of the image. In other words, you create one image that is the default image and a separate image that will appear when the user's cursor rolls over the button. You first place the original image into a picture box in the Web document, just as you would any other image.

To define the rollover, you then select the box containing the original image and choose Item>Rollover>Create Rollover. The Rollover dialog box shows the path to the default image in the Default Image field.

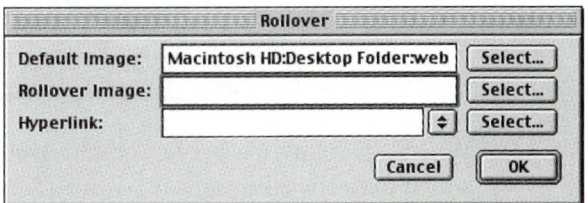

To define the rollover image, you click Select/Browse next to the Rollover Image field, and then navigate to the correct image for the button's rollover state.

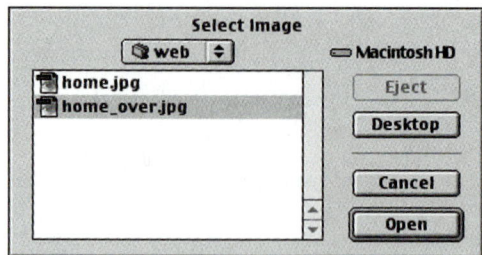

In the Hyperlink field, you can enter either the absolute or the relative path to the URL for the link. When you have defined the three elements of the rollover, clicking OK in the Rollover dialog box returns you to the document window. If Visual Indicators are active (View>Show Visual Indicators), two icons will appear in the top-right corner of the picture box.

Two icons appear in the top-right corner of a picture box that contains a rollover — the rollover icon (left) and the hyperlink icon (right).

Placing and Scaling Rollover Images

When a rollover is created during the export process, the entire rollover image is scaled to fit within the defined size of the picture box. In the following illustration, the default image (left) and rollover image (right) have a lot of extra white space around the actual image.

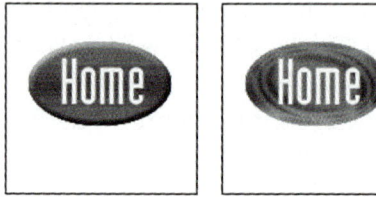

The two images used in a rollover. The bounds of the images are shown as black borders.

The default image is placed and positioned in a picture box, the picture box closed up to contain only the image, and then the rollover is defined.

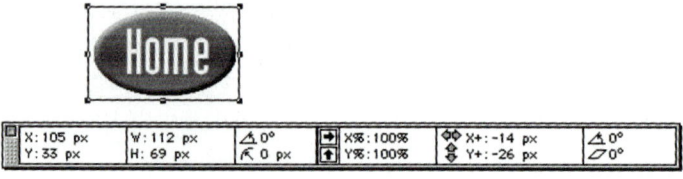

When this rollover is previewed in a Web browser, you can see that the rollover image is scaled to fit the entire image — including the surrounding white space — into the picture box.

To avoid this problem, you should crop images as closely as possible in an image-editing application, or create them with no extra surrounding white space. If the images are the same size and are placed in the picture box at 100% using the Fit Box to Picture utility, the rollover image will not be scaled in the browser window.

The two images used in a rollover, correctly cropped to avoid rescaling of the rollover image in the browser window. The bounds of the images are shown as black borders.

Add Rollovers

1. Open the file **vegan_website.qwd** from the **RF_Adv_Quark** folder.

2. Double-click A-Master A in the Document Layout palette to open the master-page layout.

3. Draw a rectangular image box in the top-right corner of the page with the following dimensions:

      X: 455 px   W: 135 px
      Y: 45 px   H: 32 px

4. Place the file **home.jpg** (from the **RF_Adv_Quark** folder) into the box.

5. With the box selected, choose Item>Rollover>Create Rollover.

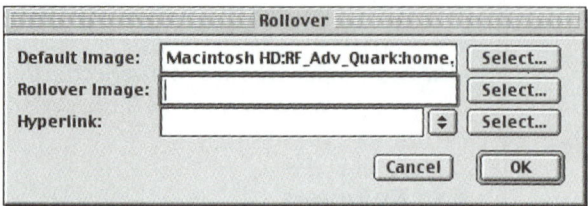

6. In the Rollover dialog box, click Select/Browse next to the Rollover Image field. Locate the file **home_over.jpg** in the **RF_Adv_Quark** folder and click Open.

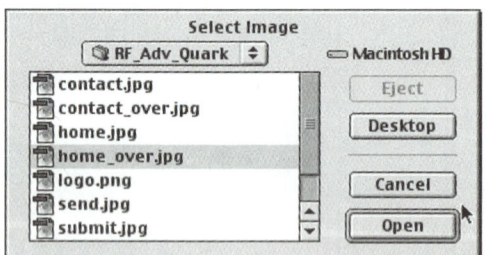

7. In the Hyperlink field, type "index.htm" (the name of the home page).

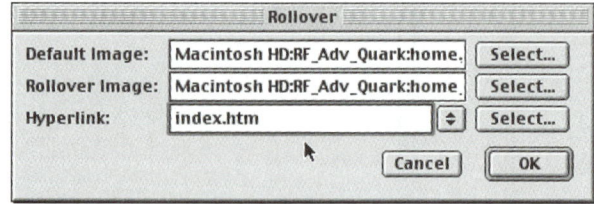

8. Click OK to create the rollover.

9. With the rollover image selected, choose Item>Step and Repeat. Make 2 copies of the image with 0 Horizontal Offset and 45-px. Vertical Offset.

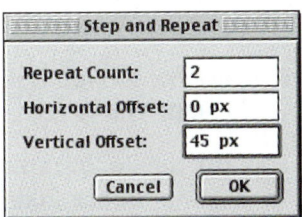

10. Control/Right-click the middle image and choose Edit Rollover from the contextual menu.

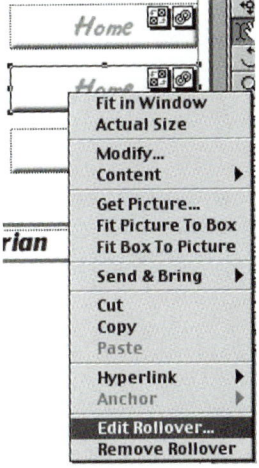

11. Click the Default Image Select/Browse button. Locate **contact.jpg** in the **RF_Adv_Quark** folder and click Open.

12. Click the Rollover Image Select/Browse button. Locate **contact_over.jpg** in the **RF_Adv_Quark** folder and click Open.

13. In the Hyperlink field, type "mailto:", and then type your email address (with no spaces).

14. Click OK in the Rollover dialog box to create the second rollover.

15. Control/Right-click the bottom image and choose Edit Rollover from the contextual menu.

16. Click the Default Image Select/Browse button. Locate **submit.jpg** in the **RF_Adv_Quark** folder and click Open.

17. Click the Rollover Image Select/Browse button. Locate **submit_over.jpg** in the **RF_Adv_Quark** folder and click Open.

18. In the Hyperlink field, type "submit.htm".

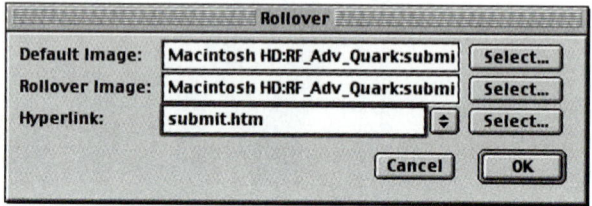

19. Click OK to create the third rollover. Notice that you can also change the Default Image using the Edit Rollover command.

20. Navigate to index.htm in the Document Layout palette. Click the Preview HTML button to view the rollover buttons in your default Web browser.

21. In Quark, save the file as "vegan_site.qwd" in your **Work_In_Progress** folder and leave the file open.

Creating Image Maps

An image map is another way to create graphic-based hyperlinks in a Web document. Using image maps, different areas of a single picture file can initiate actions or link to other pages. Image maps are created by defining *hot areas* of an image, or the specific shapes that contain the hyperlinks. QuarkXPress includes three tools for creating hot areas — the Rectangle Image Map tool, Oval Image Map tool, and Bézier Image Map tool.

The Rectangle Image Map tool, Oval Image Map tool, and Bézier Image Map tool are available in the Web Tools palette.

You cannot preview from a master-page layout.

When you create an image map, it is a good idea to tell the user that the image map exists.

Adding Hot Areas

The Image Map tools work in the same way as the regular box tools. You create a rectangular or oval image map by dragging with the tool; holding down the Shift key while dragging constrains the shapes to a square or circle. The Bézier Image Map tool is used to create nonstandard map shapes, just as you would create a uniquely shaped picture box.

After you create a hot area, you can define the associated hyperlink by clicking on the appropriate item in the Hyperlinks palette while the hot area is selected in the document. You can also Control/right-click the hot area and choose a hyperlink from the contextual menu, or choose New to define a new hyperlink.

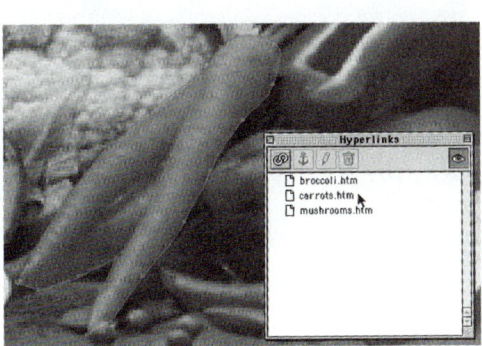
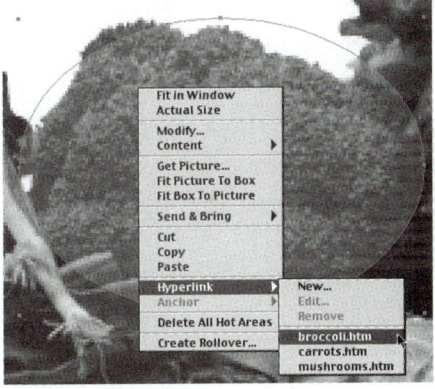

If Visual Indicators are turned on (View>Show Visual Indicators), an Image Map icon will appear in the top-right corner of an image that contains an image map.

When a document containing an image map is exported to HTML, the hot areas should work as hyperlinks when you view the HTML page in a browser.

Managing Hot Areas and Image Maps

To view the hot areas of an image map, you have to choose Show Guides from the View menu, and then select the image with the Content or Item tool.

When a hot area is selected, you can see its anchor points. Make sure that you select the actual area — not the image — before pressing Delete.

Hot areas of an image are only visible (top) when guides are showing and the image is selected. If you choose View>Hide Guides, the hot areas will not be visible in the Web document (bottom).

If you select a hot area with the Item tool and then press Delete, you delete the entire image and all associated hot areas.

You can move a hot area within the bounds of an image by dragging with the Item tool. A hot area can be reshaped by dragging its anchor points. If you move an image that contains hot areas, the hot areas move with the image.

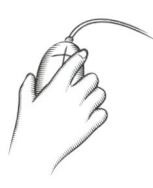

You can delete a hot area by selecting the hot area (not the image) with the Content tool and pressing Delete. If you delete an image that contains an image map, all hot areas associated with that image are also deleted.

Create an Image Map

1. In the open file vegan_site.qwd, make the index.htm page active in the document window.

2. Double-check that guides are visible (View>Show Guides).

3. Draw a rectangular picture box on the page with the following dimensions:

   X: 10 px   W: 580 px
   Y: 262 px   H: 333 px

4. Place the file **veggies.jpg** (from the **RF_Adv_Quark** folder) into the picture box.

5. Draw a rectangular text box with the following dimensions:

   X: 10 px   W: 580 px
   Y: 236 px   H: 17 px

6. In the text box, type:

    (Click your favorite veggie to find the recipes)

7. Change the text to 12-pt. ATC Pine Normal. Choose Centered alignment.

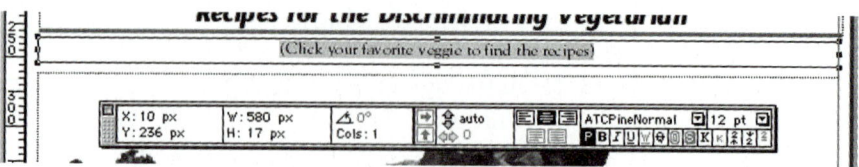

8. Using the Magnification tool, drag a marquee around the carrots in the veggies image to zoom in on that area of the image.

9. Choose the Bézier Image Map tool from the Web Tools palette.

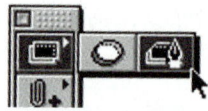

In this context, the hot area doesn't have to be exact. It should, however, be close.

10. Draw a hot area, matching the shape of the carrots as closely as possible.

11. Select View>Show Hyperlinks to display the Hyperlinks palette.

12. With the carrot hot area still active, click carrots.htm in the Hyperlinks palette to define the hot area.

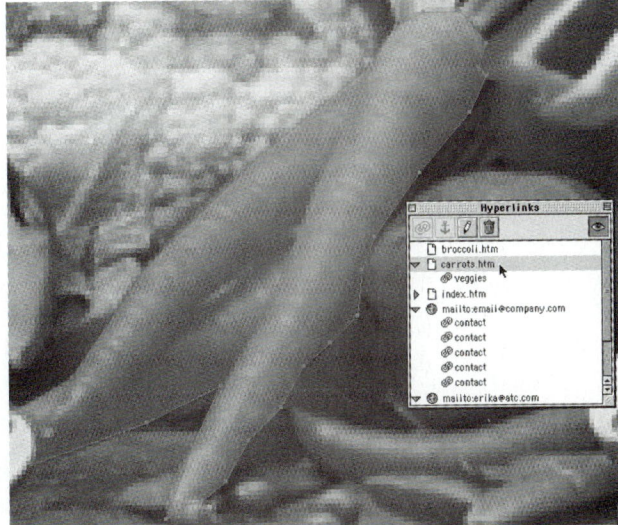

13. Change the view percentage back to 100% by pressing Command/Control-1.

14. Choose View>Hide Guides. Notice that the hot area is not visible while guides are turned off.

15. Choose View>Show Guides. The hot area should be visible as long as the image is selected.

16. Using the Magnification tool, zoom in on the broccoli in the veggies image.

17. Using the Bézier Image Map tool, create another hot area that closely matches the shape of the broccoli.

18. Click broccoli.htm in the Hyperlinks palette to define the hot area.

19. Zoom in on the mushrooms in the bottom-right corner of the image. Draw another hot area, and link it to mushrooms.htm.

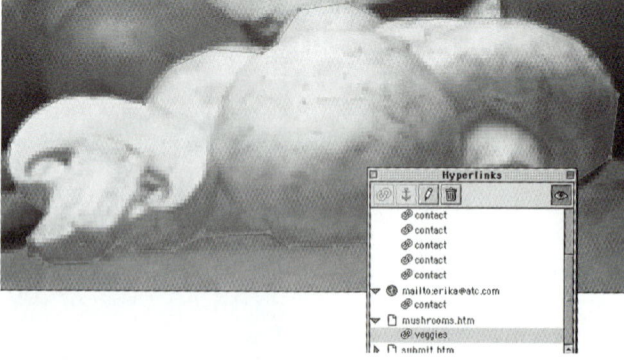

20. Click the Preview HTML button to view your page in the default browser. When you move the cursor over any of the hot spots that you created, you should see the pointing-hand icon.

Recipes for the Discriminating Vegetarian

(Click your favorite veggie to find the recipes)

Link: file://localhost/Macintosh HD/Temporary Items/QuarkTemp/broccoli.htm

21. Close the browser window. Save the Quark file and leave it open.

Building an HTML Form

HTML forms are used to gather information from people who visit your Web site. Forms can include text fields, menus of specific options, radio buttons, check boxes, and buttons that initiate some activity. Forms can be simple, collecting information from the user and sending the information to the site administrator. Forms can also be complex, interacting with the user by presenting different options, depending on the user's choices.

To add a form to a QuarkXPress Web page, you begin by creating a form box with the Form Box tool. This tool is essentially a Rectangle Box tool, used in exactly the same way as it would be for drawing a rectangular text box.

If Visual Indicators (View>Show Visual Indicators) are active, a form box is identified by a Form icon in the top-right corner.

The Form Box tool is used to create a form box in the document; this box will contain all of the elements of a form.

Defining Form Properties

When you create a form box, you define the form's properties in the Form tab of the Modify dialog box. The options in this dialog box are used when Quark generates the HTML code for the form.

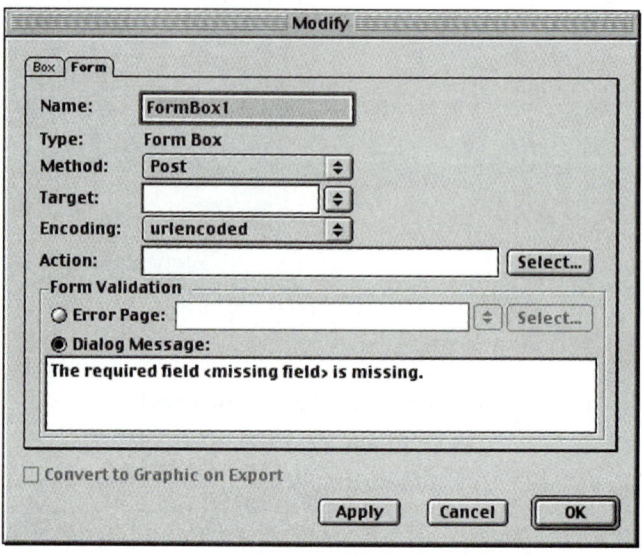

- **Name.** This field defines the name of the form. Each form in your Web site should have a unique, meaningful name.

- **Method.** This menu defines what happens (Post or Get) when the user submits the form.
  - **Post** sends the entered data to the Web server as a separate file. This option is the most common for a form that asks the users to submit data.
  - **Get** attaches the entered data to the end of a URL in the Address line of the browser window, as you might see when you use a search engine.

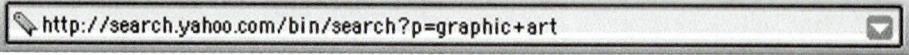

- **Target.** This menu defines where information is displayed after the user submits the form. The options (_self, _blank, _parent, or _top) are the same as for any hyperlink.

- **Encoding.** If you choose Post in the Method menu, the encoding menu defines the MIME (Multi-purpose Internet Mail Extension) type encoding option for submitted data.
  - **Urlencoded** forces data to conform to URL specifications. This option allows data to be translated on most operating systems and applications.
  - **Form-data** tells the server to encode the submitted file as multipart form data. The server is able to read each part of the form data, which is useful if you include required fields.
  - **Plain** means that the data will not be encoded.

- **Action.** This field defines what occurs when the user submits the form. You can enter a URL, or click Select/Browse to locate a CGI script on your computer. (We discuss this in greater detail in the next section.)

If you choose the Get method, submitted data is limited to 100 characters.

MIMEs *are the helper applications used by the browser or Web server to translate data.*

In the Form Validation area, you can define what happens when the user submits a form without filling a required field.

- **Error Page.** If you choose this option, you can define the URL of a specific page that presents an error message. This is most useful if you want to create a stylized error-message page.

- **Dialog Message.** This option presents a simple error dialog box if the user submits a form without some piece of required information. You can define the specific text of the dialog box in the field, as long as the text <missing field> (including the chevrons) appears somewhere in the message.

Defining Post-Form Actions

We have said that you don't need to know much about HTML to design a Web site in QuarkXPress. While this is true, you do need to understand a little about HTML actions to create a form that works.

When you click the Submit button (regardless of the text that appears on that button) on a Web-page form, you are initiating an action that calls some URL. The Action field in the Modify dialog box defines the URL that is called when a user clicks the Submit button.

If you use the Post-form method, the Action URL must contain the name of a CGI script or Active Server Page (with the extension .asp), which are applications run by the server to process the form data.

Many Internet service providers (ISPs) provide CGI scripts for their Web-host clients; some require that you only use the provided CGI scripts. Check with your ISP about their policies and what scripts they provide (if any). Other ISPs allow you to add your own scripts, which you can create or download from resources such as:

http://www.cgiforme.com

http://www.scriptarchive.com

Create an HTML Form Box

1. In the open document vegan_site.qwd, double-click submit.htm in the Document Layout palette to make it the active page.

2. Choose the Form Box tool from the Web Tools palette. Draw a form box with the following dimensions:

X: 10 px   W: 580 px
Y: 240 px   H: 376 px

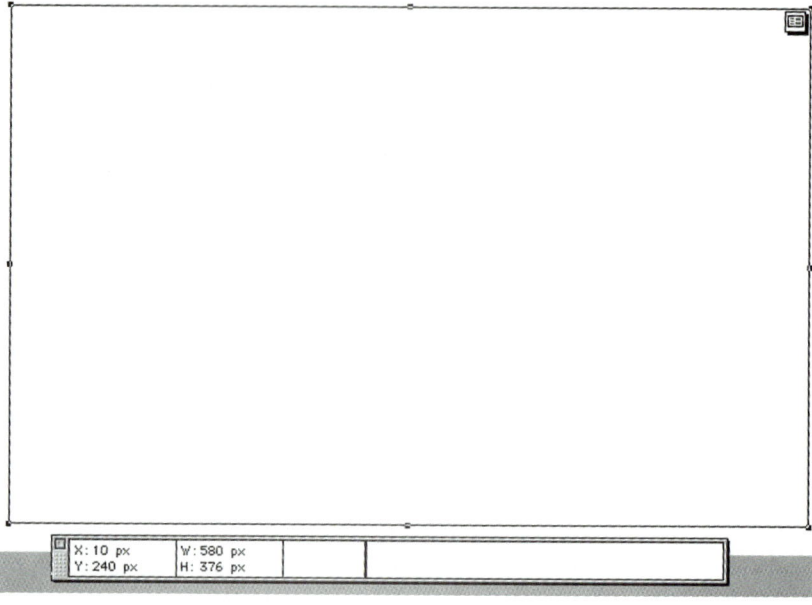

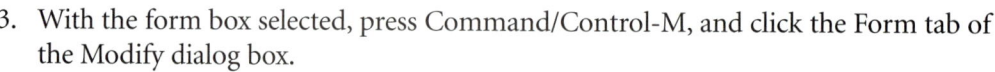

3. With the form box selected, press Command/Control-M, and click the Form tab of the Modify dialog box.

4. In the Name field, type "SubmitRecipe".

5. Choose Get from the Method menu.

6. Choose _self from the Target pop-up menu.

7. In the Action field, type "thanks.htm". Click OK to apply the settings to the Form box.

Ideally, the form you are creating would be a Post form that interacts with a CGI script on your Web server. Since we don't have a server, however, we are using the Get method as an example.

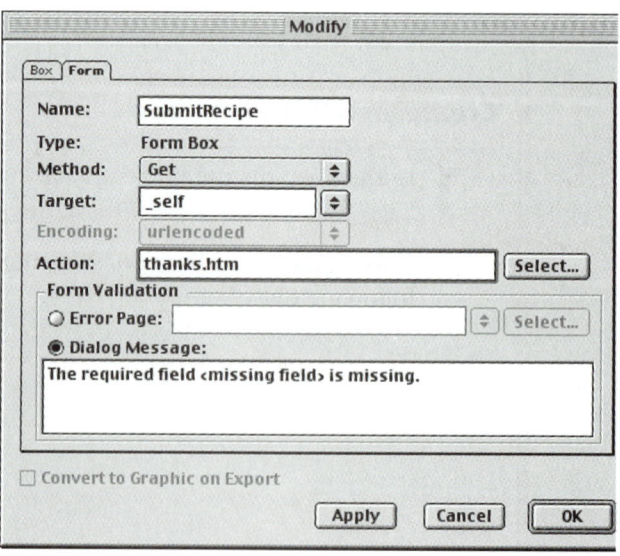

8. Save the file and leave it open.

Adding Form Fields

Form fields are the means used to gather the specific pieces of information that you want to collect. The Web document tools allow you to create eight different kinds of form fields. All form fields must be entirely contained within the form box. If you add a form field outside of a form box, a new form box is created automatically.

Once a field is created, you can define its parameters in the Form tab of the Modify dialog box. In this tab, you should identify each field with a unique name.

Adding Text Fields

The Text Field tool allows you to create a text field in which a user can type information. By default, new text fields are created as single-line fields. You can change the width of the field by dragging the left- or right-center handles of the field, but you cannot change the field height.

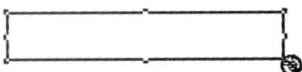

You cannot change the height of a text field. You can only drag the left- or right-center handles of the text field.

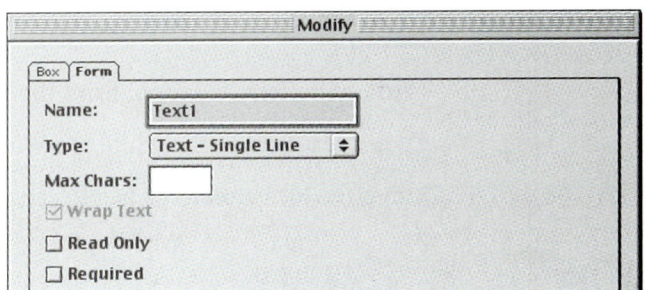

- **Type.** You can use this menu to change the appearance of the text field.

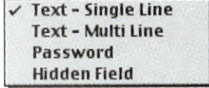

If you choose Text - Multi Line, the text field will display a scroll bar on the right side of the field. You can change the height and width of a multi-line text field by dragging any handle of the field. If you choose this option, you can also determine if entered text automatically wraps to fit the width of the box. Deselecting the Wrap Text check box adds a horizontal scroll bar to the bottom of the text field.

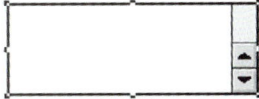

If you choose Password from the Type menu, the text field automatically changes back to a single-line text field.

You can choose Hidden Field from the type menu to add a field that does not appear in the browser window, but which contains some predefined text that is submitted along with the user's form data. If you choose Hidden Field, the other options in the Modify dialog box are unavailable.

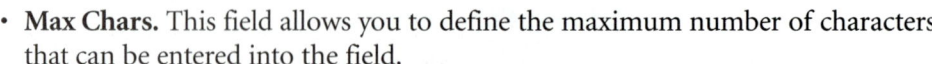

- **Max Chars.** This field allows you to define the maximum number of characters that can be entered into the field.

- **Read Only.** This check box prevents users from changing the text in the field. This is commonly used to present text that the user can read but not alter, such as a Terms-and-Conditions statement.

- **Required.** If you select this check box, the field must be filled in by the user. If the user does not enter information in a required field, an error message (defined for the Form Box) is returned after the user clicks Submit.

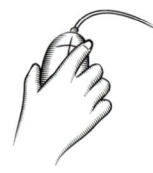

Add Text Fields

1. Drag vertical ruler guides to X: 20, X: 300, X: 350, and X: 575.

2. Drag horizontal ruler guides to Y: 265 and Y: 600.

3. Draw a rectangular text box with the following dimensions:

X: 20 px	W: 270 px
Y: 248 px	H: 17 px

4. In the new text box, type the words "Your Name:". Change the font to ATC Pine Normal.

5. Choose the Text Field tool from the Web Tools palette.

6. Drag a text field in the white space of the page.

7. Using the Measurements palette, change the dimensions of the text field to:

X: 20 px	W: 270 px
Y: 270 px	

8. Notice that you can't modify the height of the text field.

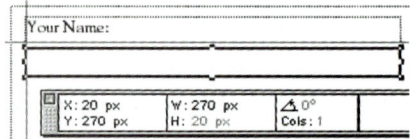

9. With the text field selected, press Command/Control-M and choose the Form tab of the Modify dialog box.

10. Type "UserName" in the Name field and activate the Required check box. Click OK.

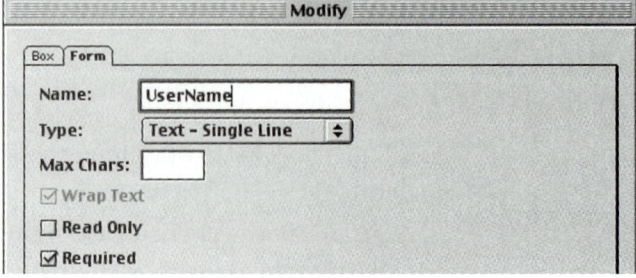

11. Using the Item tool, hold down the Shift key and click on the text box above the field to select both objects. Press Command/Control-D to duplicate both. Using the Measurements palette, change the position of the duplicate to X: 300, Y: 248.

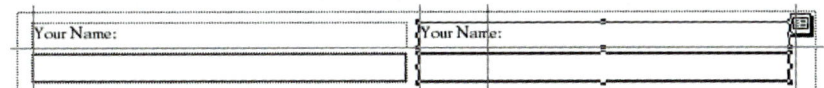

12. Change the text in the duplicate text box to "Email Address:".

13. Select the duplicate text field and open the Form tab of the Modify dialog box (Command/Control-M).

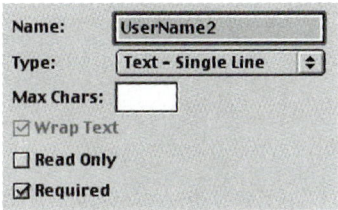

By default, a duplicate field has the same name as the original, with a sequential number added to the name of the field.

14. Change the Name field to "UserEmail" and click OK.

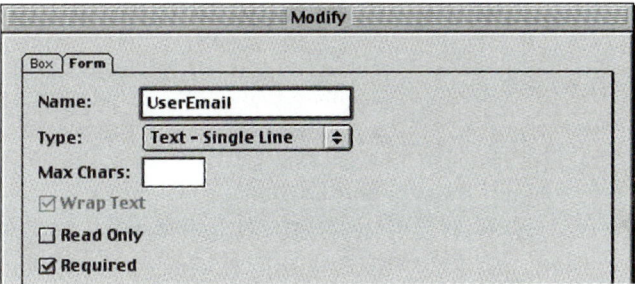

15. Select the original text box and field with the Item tool, and make another duplicate. Position this set of boxes at X: 20, Y: 300. Change the text in the text box to "Enter your recipe here:".

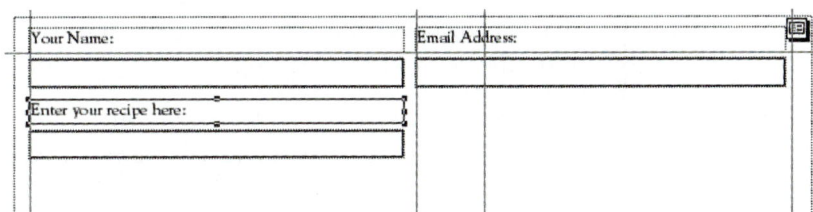

16. Select the new text field and open the Form tab of the Modify dialog box.

17. Change the Name field to "RecipeText". Choose Text - Multi Line in the Type menu and make sure that the Wrap Text option is selected. Click OK.

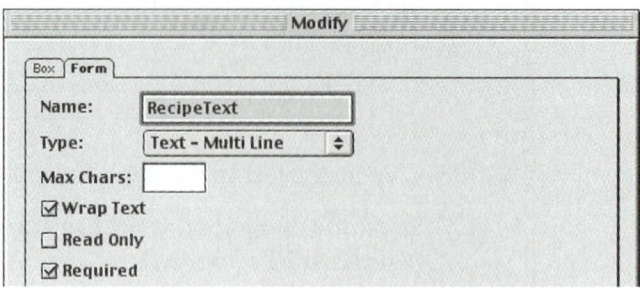

18. In the document window, change the height of the multi-line text field to 190 px.

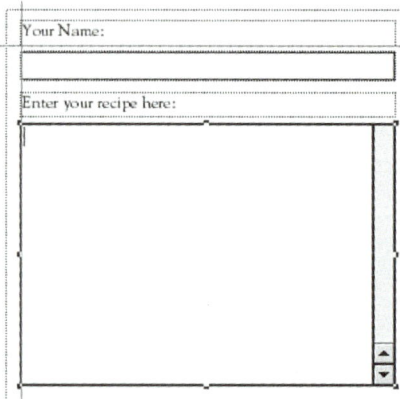

19. Save the file and leave it open.

Defining Menu Sets

An HTML form can include a list of predefined choices, from which the user selects one or more options. Pop-up menus allow the user to select a single option from a defined list, such as the month or year; list boxes can be useful if you want the user to be able to select more than one option from the list.

The advantage of using a pop-up menu or list box is that you can force the user to select from the options that you present. QuarkXPress manages those options in sets, which you can create by choosing Edit>Menus. The Menus dialog box contains the familiar options from other QuarkXPress dialog boxes (e.g., Colors, Style Sheets, etc.). Clicking New opens the Edit Menu dialog box.

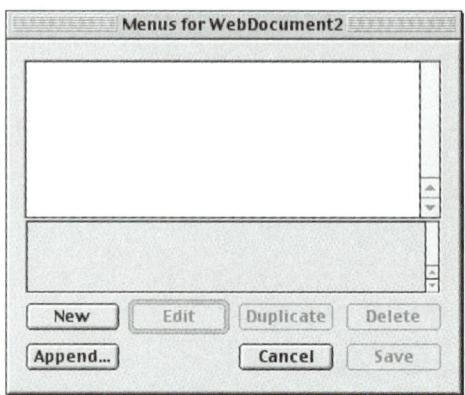

In the Edit Menu dialog box, you should enter a meaningful name for the set of options that you are creating. Think of a menu set as the group of options that will appear in the pop-up menu or list box from which the user will select. If you are asking the user to select a month, the name of the menu set should be Month.

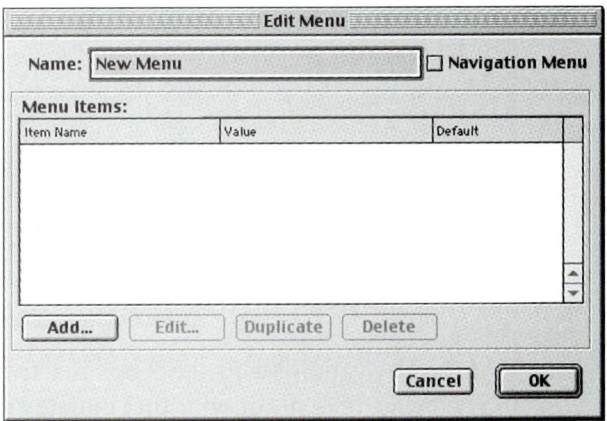

You can define the specific items in a menu by clicking Add in the Edit Menu dialog box. In the Menu Item dialog box, you can enter the Name (the text that will appear in the menu) and the Value (the text that is sent to the server when the form is submitted).

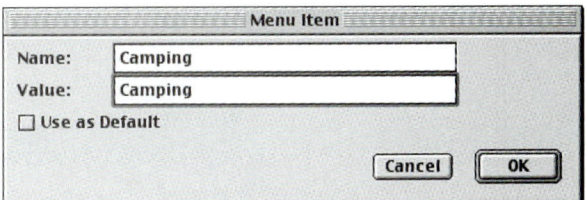

The Use as Default check box allows you to specify the default value of a particular menu set. The default value is the default text in a pop-up menu, and is the automatically high-lighted option in a list box. If you do not specify a default option, the first item you enter will be considered the default.

After adding a menu item to the menu set, the item is listed in the Edit Menu dialog box. You can add as many options as you want before clicking OK to finalize the menu set. Items appear in the final list in the order in which you see them in the Edit Menu dialog box; you can reorder them by dragging an item up or down in the list.

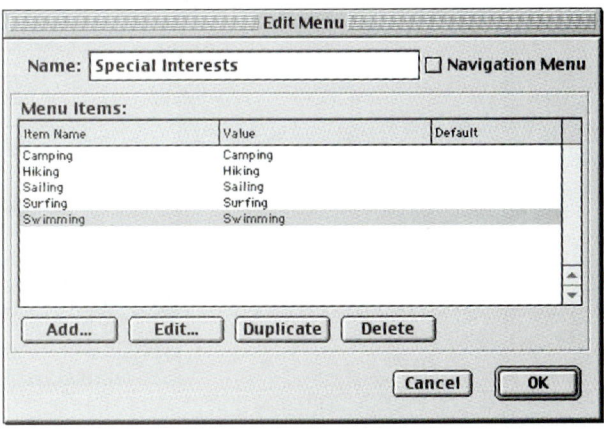

Clicking OK in the Edit Menu dialog box returns you to the Menus dialog box; the new menu set is added to the list.

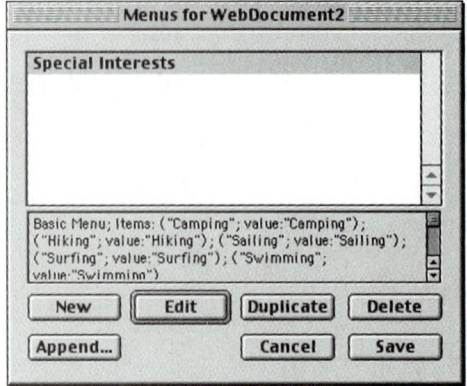

If the Navigation Menu check box is active in the Edit Menu dialog box, the menu set that you create presents options that initiate an action, which is defined in the Value field of the Menu Item dialog box. For a navigation menu, the value of each menu item should be a URL. This is particularly useful for presenting a pop-up menu of people to contact; by choosing a name from the menu, the user automatically opens a new email window addressed to the selected individual's email address.

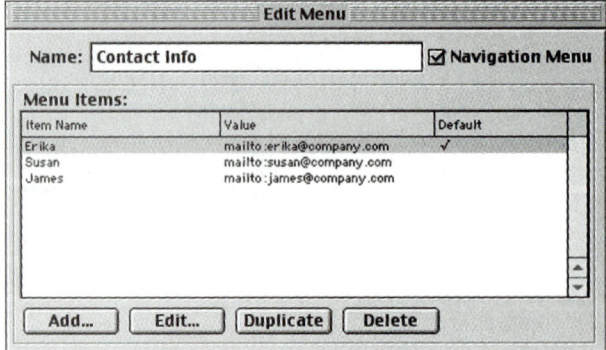

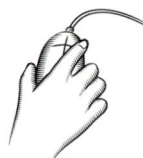

Add Menu Sets

1. In the open file, choose Edit>Menus and click New in the Menus dialog box.

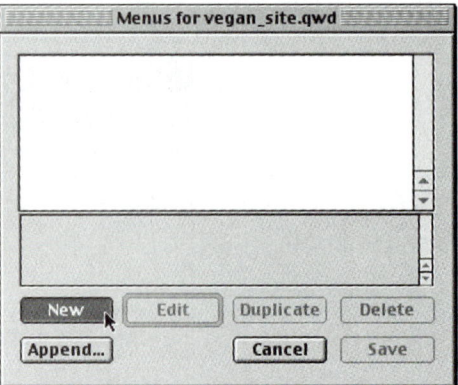

2. In the Edit Menu dialog box, type "Categories" in the Name field.

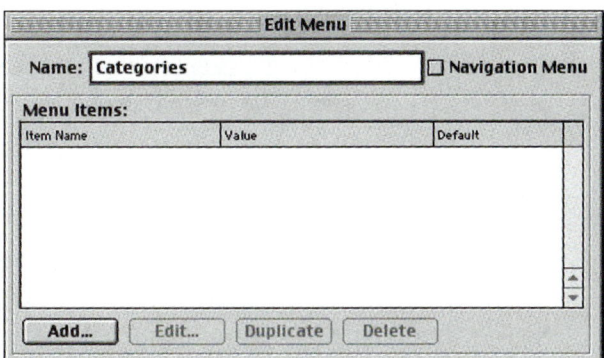

3. Click Add in the Edit Menu dialog box. Type "Beets" in both the Name field and the Value field, and click OK.

4. Notice that Beets is added to the list in the Edit Menu dialog box.

Because we are creating a simple list of options, the name and the value are the same.

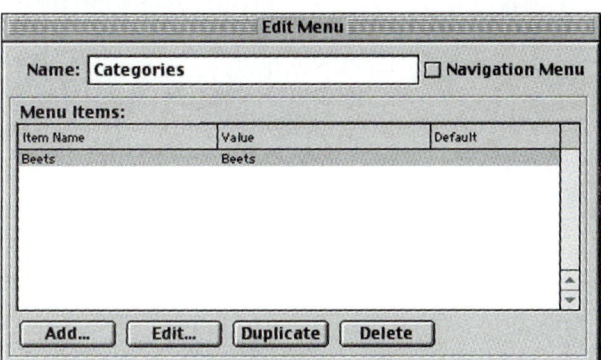

5. Add more list items, using the same Name and Value for each:

Beans, Broccoli, Cabbage, Carrots, Cauliflower, Mushrooms, Peppers, Spinach, Squash

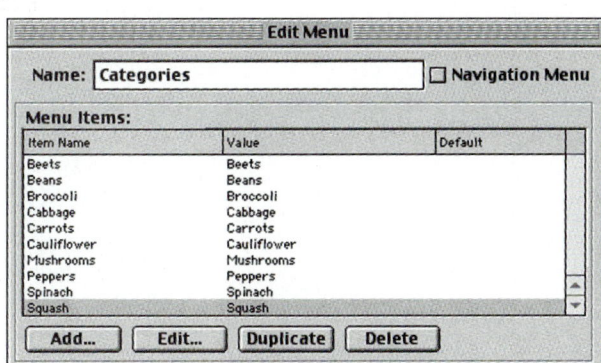

6. Highlight Beets in the list and drag it below Beans, so that the list is in proper alphabetical order.

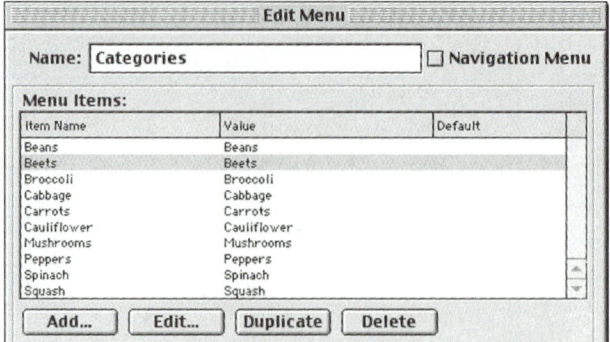

7. Click OK to return to the Menus dialog box.

8. Click New. Create a new menu called "Cost", using the following Names and Values:

Name	Value
Less than $10	<10
$10 to $20	10-20
$21 to $35	21-35
More than $35	35+

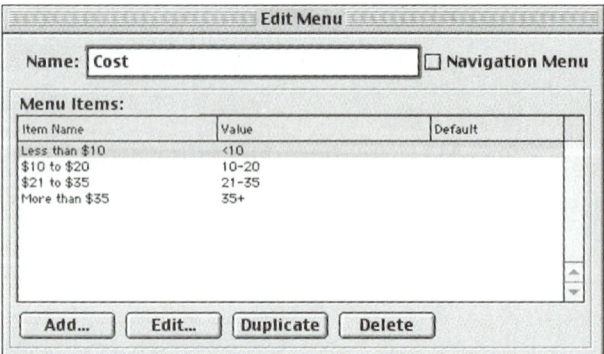

9. Click OK to return to the Menus dialog box, and then click Save to save the menus in the document.

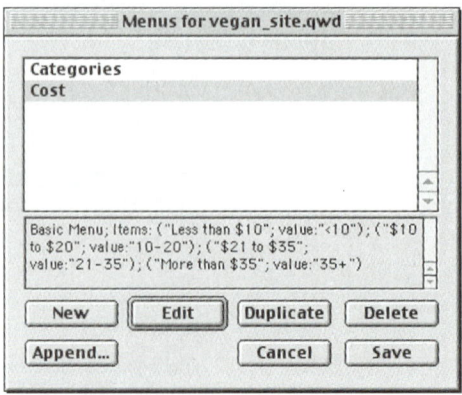

10. Save the file and leave it open.

Adding Pop-Up Menus and List Boxes

Once menus are defined, the Pop-Up Menu tool and List Box tool are used to create form fields that hold the list of options.

A pop-up menu (left) and list box (right) as they appear when first created.

The Form tab of the Modify dialog box defines the content of a pop-up menu or list box. The Type menu allows you to change the selected field from a pop-up menu to a list box, or from a list box to a pop-up menu. The Menu menu lists all sets that appear in the Menus dialog box. You can also click New to create and apply a different menu set.

If you are modifying a list box, you can also select the option to Allow Multiple Selections, and activate the Required check box to force users to choose at least one item from the list.

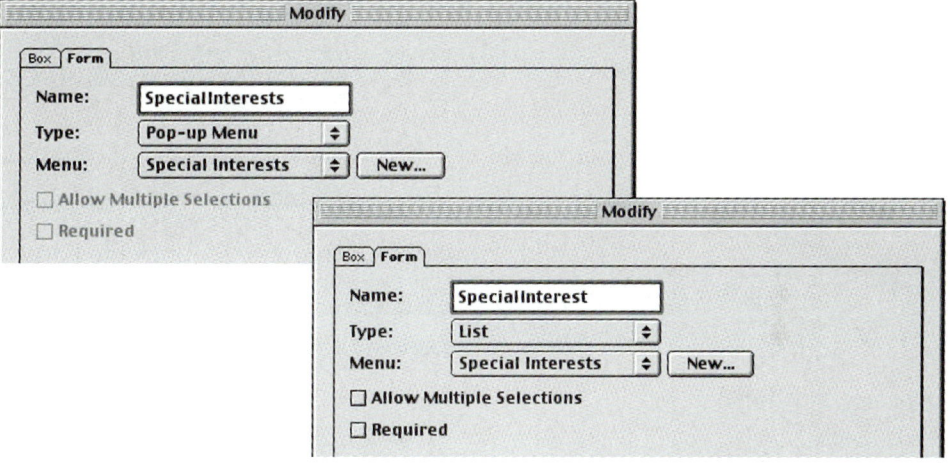

After defining the menu to use for a pop-up menu or list box, the pop-up menu or list box automatically expands to fit the menu items. By default, a list box shows the first three items in the list. You can modify the height of the list box by dragging the top- or bottom-center handle; you cannot modify the box width.

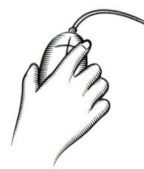

Add a Pop-Up Menu

1. In the open document, draw a rectangular text box with the following dimensions:

   X: 300 px   W: 270 px
   Y: 300 px   H: 17 px

2. In the text box, type: "How much does it cost to make this recipe?". Change the font to ATC Pine Normal.

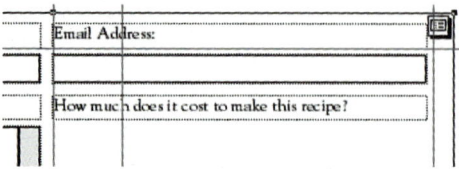

3. Using the Pop-Up Menu tool, draw a pop-up menu on the page. Change the position of the pop-up menu to X: 350, Y: 322. Notice that you cannot change the width or height of the field.

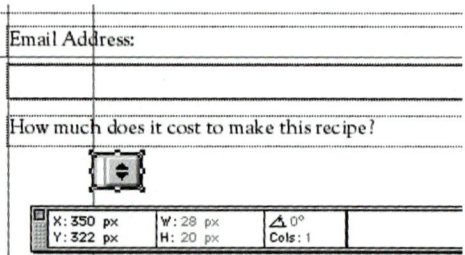

4. With the pop-up menu selected, open the Form tab of the Modify dialog box.

5. Change the Name field to "RecipeCost", and choose Cost from the Menu menu.

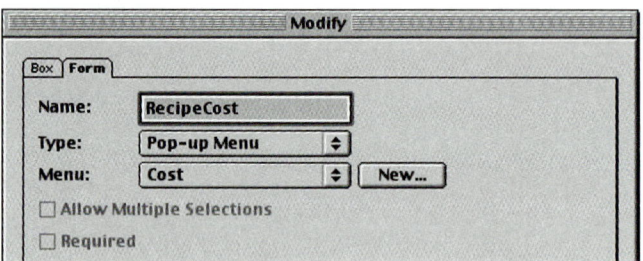

6. Click OK. Notice that the text from the list is automatically entered in the menu field, and the width of the field is adjusted as necessary.

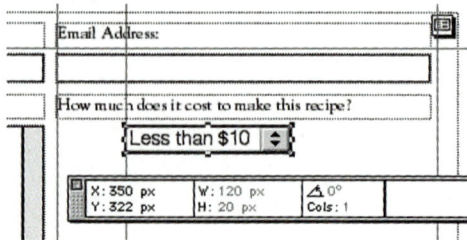

7. Save the file and leave it open.

You have no control over the appearance of text in a pop-up menu.

Create a List Menu

1. In the open file, select the pop-up menu and the text box directly above it. Make a duplicate of both objects, and position the duplicate at X: 300, Y: 350.

2. Change the text in the duplicate box to: "What category does this recipe belong in?"

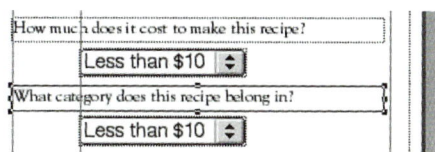

3. Select the duplicate pop-up menu and open the Form tab of the Modify dialog box.

4. Change the Name field to "RecipeCategory", choose List from the Type menu, and choose Categories from the Menu menu. Activate the Allow Multiple Selections check box and deactivate the Required check box.

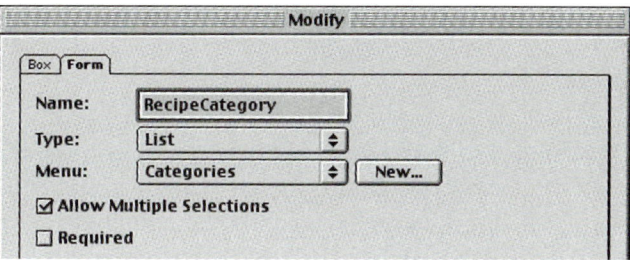

5. Click OK to apply the changes to the field. Notice that the list-box field changes horizontally to match the longest item in the menu, and expands vertically to display the first three items in the menu.

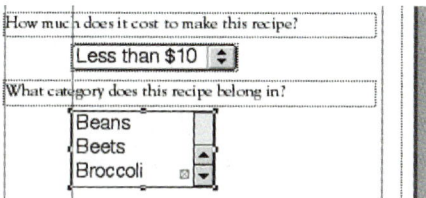

6. Save the file and leave it open.

Adding Radio Buttons

Radio buttons are frequently used to present a list of options from which the user can select only one choice. QuarkXPress allows you to change a radio button into a check box, and a check box into a radio button using the Type menu in the Form tab. The Value field defines the data that is sent to the server if the user selects that option. You can use the Required check box to force a user to select a radio button.

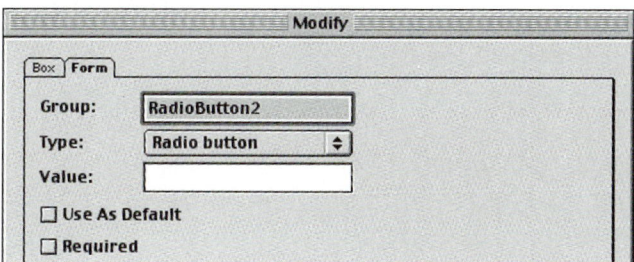

When one radio button in a group is marked as Required, all buttons in the group are Required. This means that the user must choose one radio button in the group.

When modifying a radio button, the Group field replaces the Name field. Radio buttons require the user to select only one of two or more choices. You have to create each radio button option separately, but you can identify them as a group by entering the same name in the Group field. You can assign a default selection by activating the Use As Default check box for the radio button you want to be selected automatically.

You can also group radio buttons by choosing the related radio buttons with the Item tool and opening the Modify dialog box. Only the Group field appears; the text you enter here will automatically be applied to each separate radio button in the group.

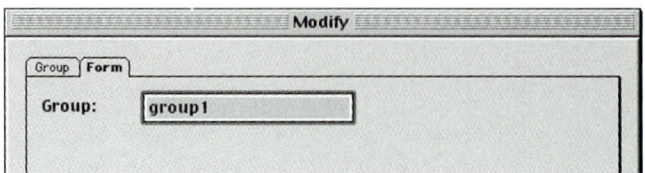

When you create a radio button with the Radio Button tool, a box containing the button is placed automatically.

The box containing the radio button is a kind of text box, which you can resize by dragging any handle. You can label a radio button or add text that defines the radio buttons for the user by selecting the radio button box with the Content tool. The insertion point is placed after the radio button, where you can enter a label. The text in a radio button box can be formatted in any way you like, just as you would format any other text in a Web document.

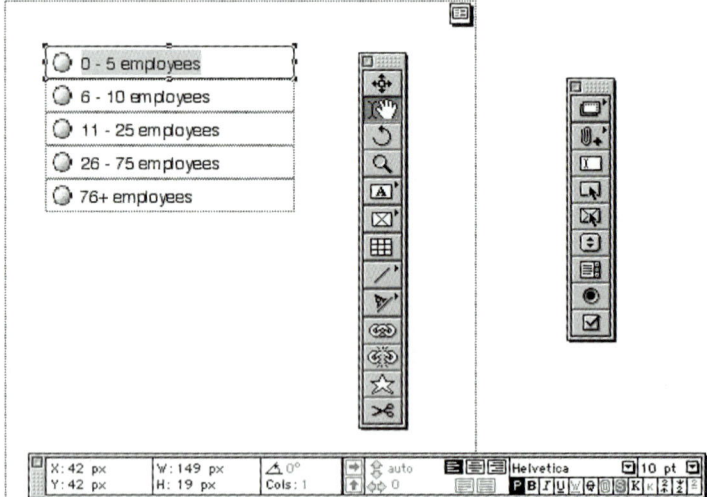

Remember the restrictions on text formatting in HTML. These restrictions also apply to radio-button labels.

To designate a radio button as the default choice in a group, click the radio button with the Content tool.

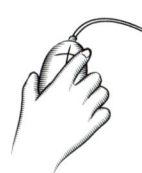

*Notice that when you
create a radio button, the
box automatically
expands to fit the height
and width of the radio
button.*

Add a Radio-Button Group

1. In the open file, duplicate one of the text boxes in the form and position it at X: 300, Y:432. Change the text to "How easy is it to make this recipe?"

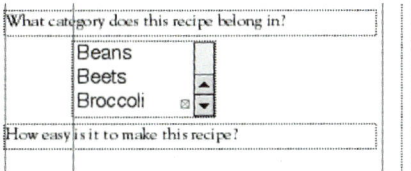

2. Choose the Radio Button tool from the Web Tools palette. Draw a radio button on the page below the text box from Step 1. Position the radio button at X: 350, Y: 453.

3. Change the width of the radio-button box to 150 px, and drag the bottom-center handle of the box to the smallest possible height (19 px).

4. With the radio-button box selected, choose the Content tool. Notice that the insertion point flashes after the radio button.

5. Press the Spacebar, and then type "Easy". Select all of the text in the box and change it to 12 pt.

6. Open the Form tab of the Modify dialog box.

7. In the Name field, type "RecipeSkill". In the Value field, type "Easy". Activate the Required check box. Click OK.

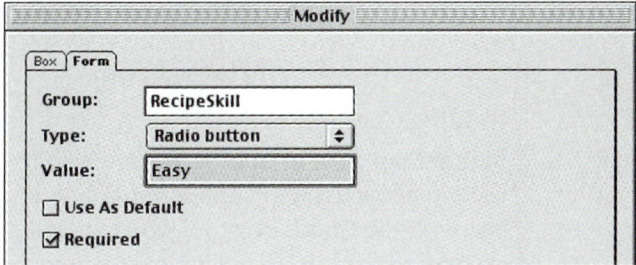

8. Choose Item>Step and Repeat. Make 2 copies of the radio button box with Horizontal Offset: 0, Vertical Offset: 20 px.

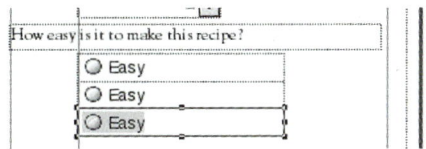

9. Change the text after the second radio button to "Intermediate".

10. Change the text after the third radio button to "Difficult".

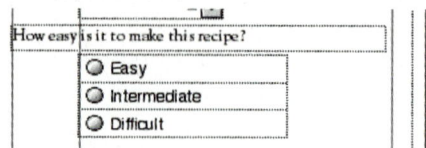

11. Choose the second radio button box and open the Form tab of the Modify dialog box.

12. Delete the 2 at the end of the Name field so that it now reads "RecipeSkill". Change the Value field to "Intermediate". Click OK.

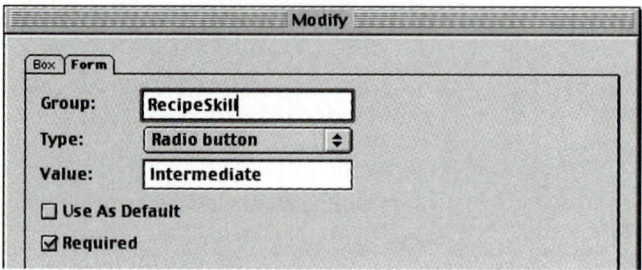

13. Choose the third radio button box and open the Form tab of the Modify dialog box.

14. Delete the 3 at the end of the Name field so that it now reads "RecipeSkill". Change the Value field to "Difficult". Click OK.

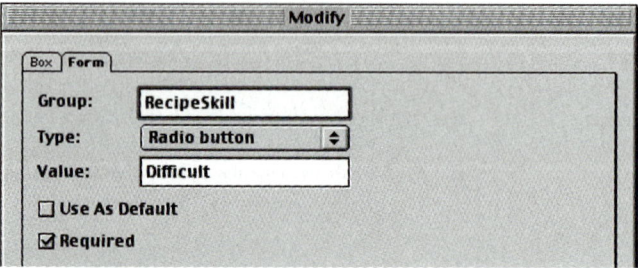

15. Save the file and leave it open.

Adding Check Boxes

Rather than a list of options from which to choose only one, check boxes are frequently used to allow users to choose more than one available option. When you create a check box with the Check Box tool, you can add a label just as you would for a radio button, by expanding the box and using the Content tool.

In the Form tab of the Modify dialog box, each check box must have a unique name; unlike radio buttons, check boxes cannot be grouped. The Value field defines the data that is sent to the server if the user selects that check box. If the Initially Checked option is selected, the check box will be selected when the user first views the form. If the Required check box is selected, the user must check the box to submit the form. This is useful for creating an "electronic signature" check box, acknowledging that the user understands conditions, terms, and so on.

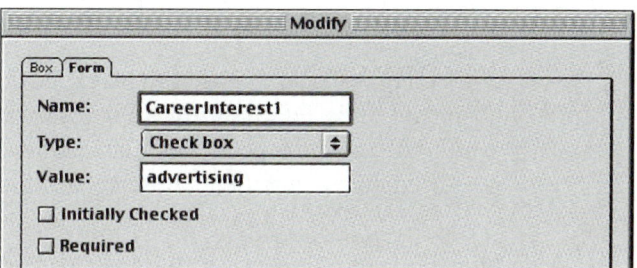

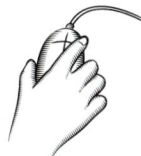

Add a Check Box

1. In the open file, choose the Check Box tool from the Web Tools palette.

2. Draw a check box at X: 20, Y: 520. Notice that the box containing the check box automatically expands to fit the check box.

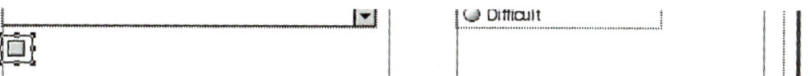

3. Change the width of the check box field to 550 px.

4. With the check-box box still selected, select the Content tool. The insertion point will flash immediately after the check box.

5. Press the Spacebar, and then type "Check this box to authorize publication of your recipe on the Vegan Delight Web site." Select all of the text and change the font to 12-pt. ATC Pine Normal.

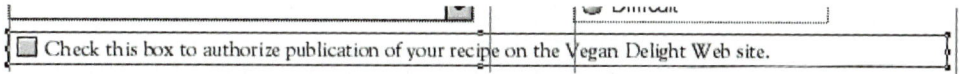

6. Open the Form tab of the Modify dialog box. Type "Authorized" in the Name field, type "yes" in the Value field, and activate the Required check box.

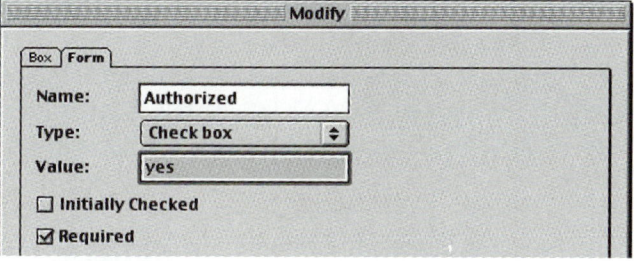

7. Click OK. Save the file and leave it open.

*Consult an HTML resource such as ATC's **HTML & XHTML: Creating Web Pages** for more information about MIMEs.*

Adding File-Selection Buttons

The File Selection tool creates a Browse button in the form; the user can click this button to locate a file that will be uploaded when the form is submitted. A text field appears to the left of the button, which will display the path to the user-selected file. You can drag the left- or right-center handle to enlarge the text field next to the button, but you cannot change the size of the button.

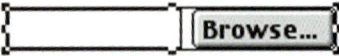

In the Form tab of the Modify dialog box, you can define a name for the file field. The Type option is automatically set to File and cannot be changed. The Accept field allows you to define the type of files that can be uploaded with this button. You can make this a required field using the Required check box.

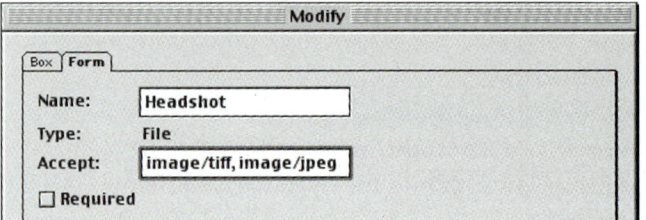

Add a File-Selection Button

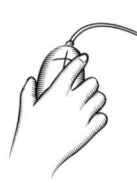

1. In the open file, create a new text box with the following dimensions:

   X: 20 px   W: 270 px
   Y: 544 px   H: 32 px

2. In the text box, type: "Use the Browse button to send us a picture of your finished dish. It will be posted with your recipe." Change the font to 12-pt. ATC Pine Normal.

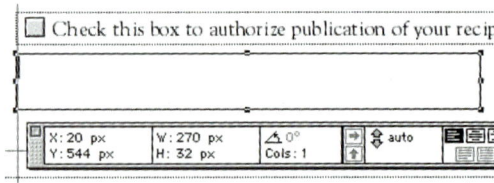

3. Choose the File Selection tool from the Web Tools palette.

4. Drag with the tool to create a file-selection field and button. Position the new field at X: 20, Y: 580. Notice that the created field automatically expands to fit the button and the smallest allowable text field.

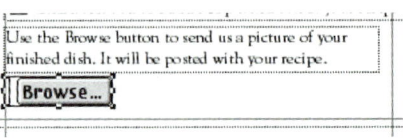

5. Change the width of the field to 270 px. Notice that the button does not change, but the text field next to the button expands to fill the width of the box.

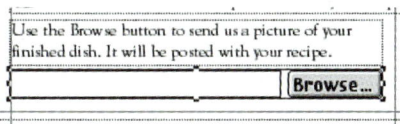

6. With the file-selection field active, open the Form tab of the Modify dialog box.

7. In the Name field, type "RecipePicture".

8. In the Accept field, type "image/jpeg, image/tiff, image/bmp, image/pict" to define the types of files people can send.

9. Make sure the Required check box is not selected. Click OK.

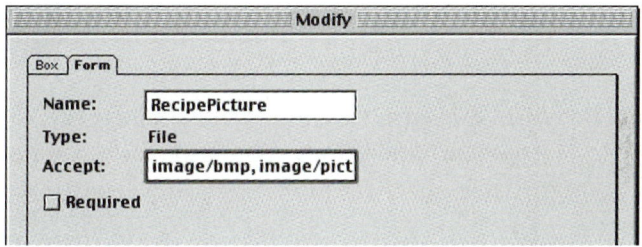

10. Save the file and leave it open.

Adding Text Buttons

The Button tool allows you to create buttons that, when clicked, either submit or reset the form. When you create a button in a Web document, it defaults to 13 pixels wide by 20 pixels high. You cannot drag any handles to resize the button on the page.

You can add text to a button by selecting the button with the Content tool, and then typing as you would in any text box. When you add text to a button, the button automatically resizes horizontally to accommodate the text you enter. You do not, however, have any control over the appearance of the text.

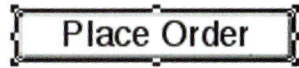

In the Form tab of the Modify dialog box, you can assign a meaningful name to the button. The Type menu presents two options: Submit and Reset. If you choose Submit, clicking the button submits the user's information. If you choose Reset, clicking the button clears any information entered by the user.

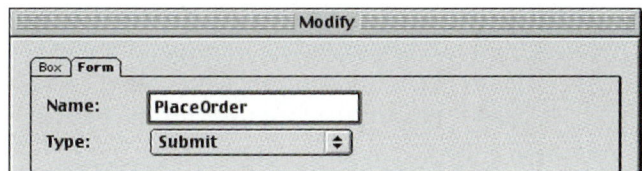

Adding Image Buttons

Because you have very limited control over the appearance of a text-based button, you can use the Image Button Tool to create a stylized submit button using an image created in another application. The Image Button tool creates a picture box that is very similar to a regular picture box.

Once the Image button box is created, you can import an image by choosing File>Get Picture. An image placed into an Image Button tool can be scaled and manipulated as you would modify any other placed image.

In the Form tab of the Modify dialog box, you only have the option to name the button. Image buttons only submit the form and cannot be used to reset the form.

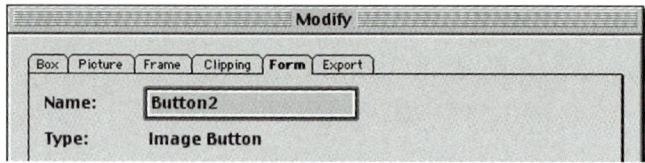

When you are using an image button, the Export tab of the Modify dialog box presents that same options as for any other image used in the Web page. Remember to add alt text that defines the button's function.

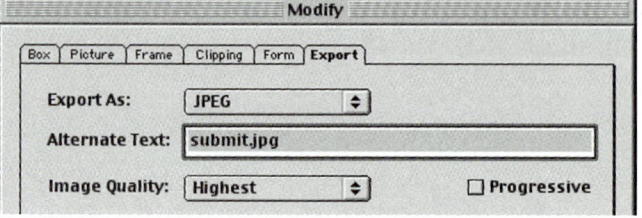

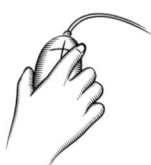

Add Buttons

1. In the open file, choose the Button tool () from the Web Tools palette.

2. Draw a text button on the page, positioned at X: 350, Y: 580. Notice that you cannot change the height or width of the button.

3. With the button selected, chose the Content tool. The insertion point should flash inside the button. Type "Reset". Notice that you have no control over the size of the type or the font used for the button.

4. Open the Form tab of the Modify dialog box. Type "Reset" in the Name field and choose Reset from the Type menu. Click OK.

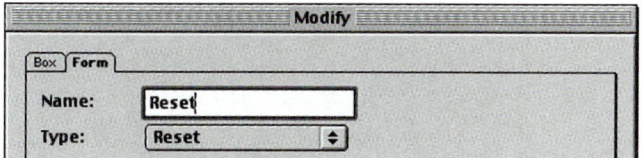

5. Choose the Image Button tool (⊠) from the Web Tools palette.

6. Draw a box with the following dimensions:

   X: 440 px W: 135 px
   Y: 568 px H: 32 px

7. Press Command/Control-E and locate the file **send.jpg** in the **RF_Adv_Quark** folder. Click Open to place the image in the button box.

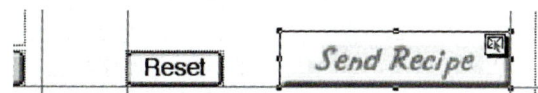

8. With the Image button selected, open the Form tab of the Modify dialog box. Change the Name field to "Submit". Notice that you have no other options. Image buttons are automatically defined as Type: Submit. Click OK.

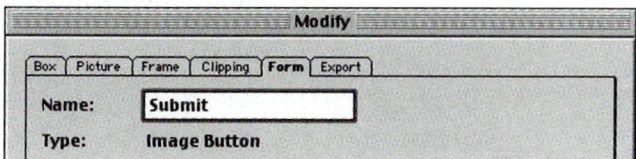

9. Save the file.

10. Choose File>Export>HTML.

11. Create a folder called "Vegan_Site" in your **Work_In_Progress** folder, and choose that folder as the target. Activate the Launch Browser and External CSS File check boxes, and click Export.

12. If you get a missing picture message, click Update and locate the necessary files in the **RF_Adv_Quark** folder. Click Continue when all the images have been located.

13. When the export process is complete, your browser should open and correctly display the rollovers, image maps, and form.

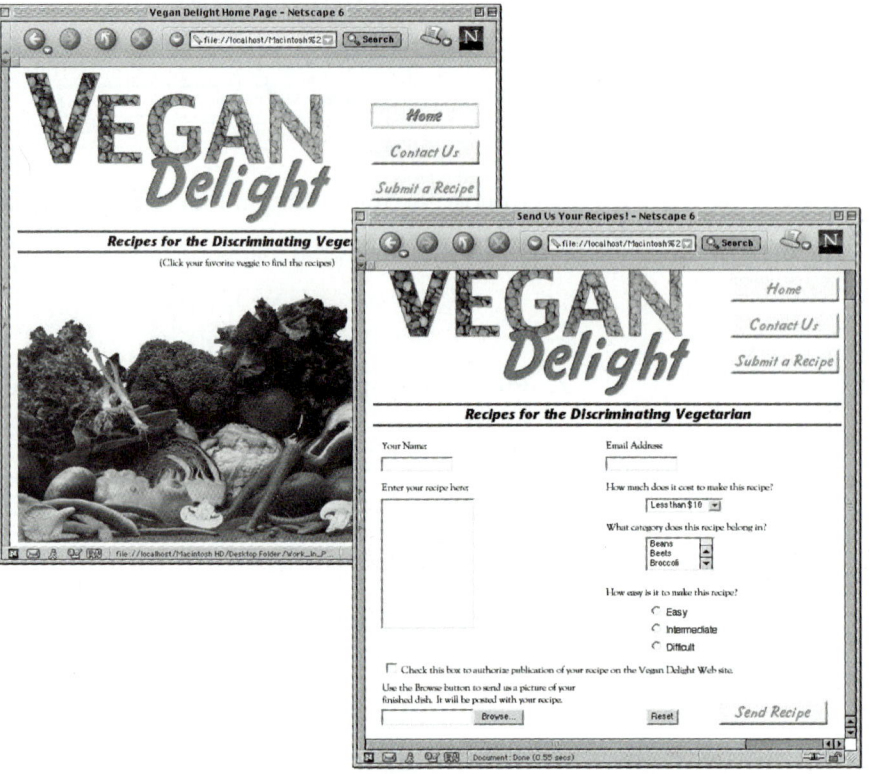

Summary

Using the new Web-design tools in QuarkXPress 5.0, you can now create a fully functional, interactive Web site in the environment with which you are already acquainted. You have learned how to create image maps to add visual interest to your Web pages. You have also discovered how to define rollover buttons without knowing a single line of JavaScript code. Finally, you have learned how to create and define an HTML form, including all of the different fields that you can add to a form. By combining the basic Web-design capabilities that you learned in Chapter 10 with these interactive elements, you can use QuarkXPress to create attractive and effective Web pages.

Free-Form Project #2

Assignment

You are opening a new restaurant with a menu of different pita and roll sandwiches, as well as a monthly "Star," or a special creation that changes monthly. Your assignment is to design the menu for the new restaurant; the menu will then be printed and converted to a Web site. The print menu should be a four-page document, printed two-sided on one sheet and folded in half. Design a cover that includes the restaurant's logo, name, and address. Design the balance of the menu creatively to match the theme of your restaurant. Use an additional layer for the monthly Star specials so that it can be easily changed without affecting the rest of the menu layout. Your online menu should allow customers to place advance orders for large purchases.

Apply Your Skills

To develop your menu, you will use the following methods and features. You will:

- Create a grid that incorporates the correct folding allowances for the final document.

- Use separate layers to create the main layout of the menu, and to create the special Star section that will change monthly.

- Develop a color scheme and text-formatting plan that will communicate the theme of your restaurant. Create and use style sheets to format the document text.

- Plan the layout of the different elements before placing items into the page. Balance type, graphics, and white space to achieve a visually pleasing and easily readable menu.

- Print composite proofs of the menu, including printer's marks, using a PostScript printer.

- Perform a Collect for Output to package the job for the service provider who will print your menus.

- Repurpose the menu into a Web document that includes at least three pages — home page, menu list, and online ordering form. Be sure to include a contact link to your email address, as well.

- Make sure that your Web document is readable on both Internet Explorer and Netscape. Convert text to graphics where appropriate, and use meta tags that indicate the content of the pages.

Print Specifications

Finished Trim Size (flat): 14 × 10 in.

Finished Folded Size: 7 × 10 in.

Color: Process

Included Files

You can develop your own text and graphics, or use the files for the Hollywood Sandwich Shoppe that are provided on the Resource CD in the RF_Free-form folder. You can also modify any of the provided files to suit your needs.

Publisher's Comments

A menu is the single most important tool that a restaurateur can develop to promote the business. Mistakes in a menu — incorrect prices, unavailable items, and poorly organized selections — can adversely affect the revenue of the eatery. It's well known that large chains spend millions of dollars refining, measuring, and redesigning their menus each year. Make your menu an extension of the restaurant's theme. Be creative, but also be sure that the menu is readable.

Review #2

Chapters 6 through 11

In Chapters 6 through 11, you have learned how to use the advanced utilities and tools that control type, pictures, color, and output. You should understand how to customize the application environment using such features as Tracking Tables, Custom Dashes & Stripes, and Print Styles, and create unique effects with text on a path, complex shapes, and clipping paths. You have learned the different output options, and how to create different versions of the same file for different service providers' requirements. You also discovered the Web-design capabilities built into the QuarkXPress environment, and should know how to create a Web page that incorporates interactive tools. After completing this series of discussions, exercises and projects, you should:

- Know how to create and control text on a path to create special effects with type. You should be able to use the Table tool to create and format tables of information, convert text to tables, and convert tables to text. You know how to control the automatic flow of text, and how to define automatic text boxes on master pages. You can also customize the appearance of text by modifying tracking and kerning tables for specific documents or projects.

- Be able to create custom dash and stripe patterns for lines and box frames. You also know how to create, manipulate, and manage complex graphics using the different merging options and by converting text to boxes. You understand clipping paths and runarounds, and know how to create unique visual effects with unusual text runarounds. You know about the different effects that can be used to modify graphics, and know the limitations associated with those effects.

- Understand the basic concepts of color management, and know how to import and apply color profiles to objects in QuarkXPress. You also understand the concept of trapping, how it applies to color printing, and how to specify trapping in QuarkXPress. You can define the trapping preferences for a document or for the application, and apply object-specific and color-specific trapping.

- Know about the different options for outputting files from QuarkXPress, including printing, saving as EPS, exporting PostScript, and exporting PDF. You know how to speed up the output process by creating Print Styles, automating the multiple settings and choices available in the Print dialog boxes.

- Be familiar with the new tools available for creating a Web document in the QuarkXPress environment, including how to create and define pages. You know how to add content to a Web document, and how to repurpose a print document for the Web. You can create and apply hyperlinks and meta tags within a Web document, and export a Web document to HTML.

- Be able to add interactive elements to a Web site, including image maps, rollovers, and forms. You know the different types of form fields, and can create a form that will transmit user-supplied information to a server.

Project A: Stonington Letterfold Brochure

The Stonington Beach Hotel in Bermuda has hired you to create a letterfold brochure that will be placed in racks at travel agencies, tourism boards, and other tourist locations. They want to promote the resort-like atmosphere, and hope to attract individual guests as well as corporate event planners.

The trim size of this job is 8.5 × 11 in., folded twice into a standard rack-card brochure size. The brochure will be printed with four-color process inks on glossy paper. The focus of the brochure is the photographs, with a small amount of text that highlights some of the hotel's offerings. Your job is to include all of the supplied elements in a brochure that looks good when folded.

Create a Document Grid

1. Create a new one-column document with facing pages, 11 × 8.5 in., (landscape orientation) with 0.25-in. margins on all four sides. Make sure Facing Pages is selected and Automatic Text Box is deselected.

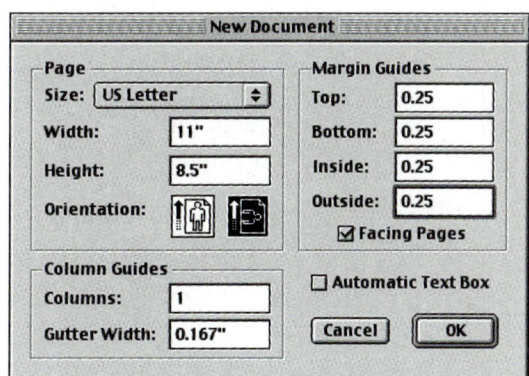

2. If the Document Layout palette is not visible, choose View>Show Document Layout.

3. Double-click A-Master A in the Document Layout palette to display the master-page layout in the document window.

4. Drag vertical guides onto the page for your folds at the following settings:

Left master page	Right master page
3.687 in.	3.625 in.
7.375 in.	7.312 in.

It is much easier to place precise marks with the Measurement palette than by watching the ruler bars. Zooming in can help to place guides at exact positions.

5. Click the Zero-Point Crosshairs, and drag the zero point to the first vertical guide on the left master page.

6. To delineate the live copy area, drag vertical page guides (onto the document page, not the pasteboard) 0.25 in. on both sides of the fold guide.

7. Repeat Steps 5–6 to place page guides 0.25 in. on both sides of all four fold guides.

8. Click the Zero-Point Crosshairs to return the zero point to its original position.

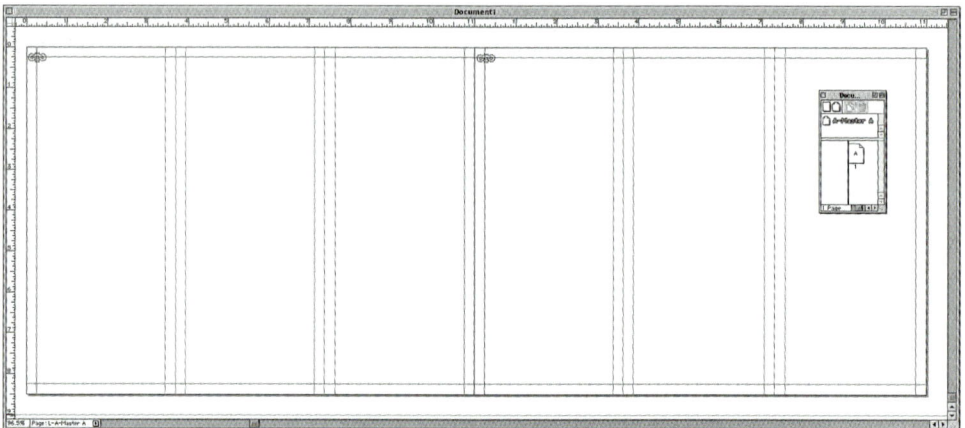

9. Your document grid is finished. Save the file as "stonington_letterfold.qxd" in your **Work_In_Progress** folder and leave the file open.

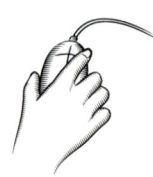

Create Folding Marks

1. Drag a second page into the document using the A-Master A master page.

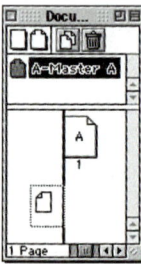

2. Double-click the Page 2 icon in the Document Layout palette to make page 2 active in the document window.

3. Draw a vertical rule of L: 0.5 in. (choose Left Point from the Endpoint menu in the Measurements palette); assign it a 0.25-pt. dotted stroke.

4. Position the rule you just drew at X: 3.687 in., Y: –0.375 in.

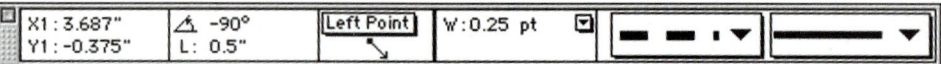

5. Use the Step and Repeat command to duplicate the rule you just created with a Horizontal Offset: 3.687 in., Vertical Offset: 0.

6. Select both of these rules with the Item tool; use the Step and Repeat command to duplicate both rules with a Vertical Offset of 8.75 in. and a Horizontal Offset of 0.

7. Use electronic whiteout. Draw a white box with the following dimensions:

    X: 3.5 in.   W: 4 in.
    Y: –0.125 in.   H: 0.375 in.

8. Duplicate the rectangle, and position it at X: 3.5 in., Y: 8.25 in.

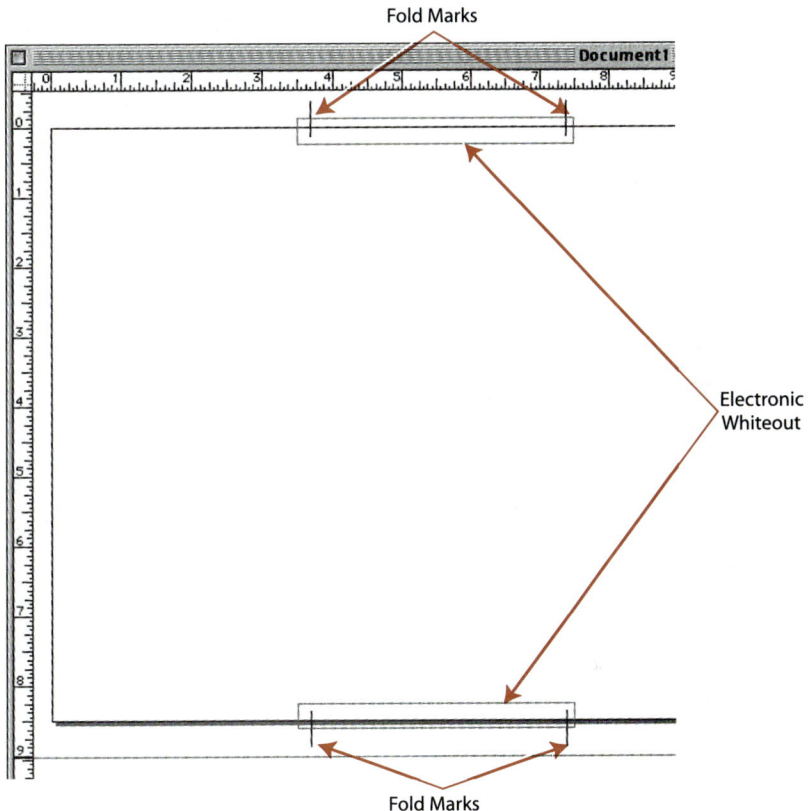

9. With the Item tool selected, press Command/Control-A to select the cut marks and boxes. Press Command/Control-G to group the elements.

10. Paste a copy of the group on page 1 of the document. Position the copy at X: 3.439 in., Y: –0.375 in.

11. Your folding guides are now complete. Save the document and continue.

Define Layers

1. Choose View>Show Layers to open the Layers palette. You placed the folding guides on the default layer — the only layer in the document. You will add the document content to a second layer.

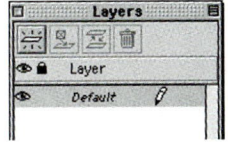

2. In the Layers palette, click the New Layer button to add a layer to the document.

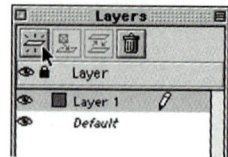

3. Double-click Layer 1 in the Layers palette to open the Attributes dialog box for that layer. Type "Brochure Elements" in the Name field and click OK.

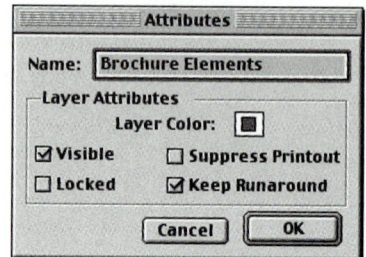

4. In the Layers palette, click to the right of the Visible icon in the Default layer item. You will see a Locked icon.

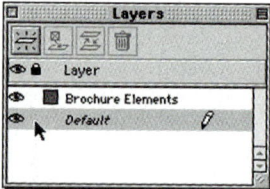

5. Click the Brochure Elements layer in the palette to make that the active layer. You should see the Locked icon in the Default layer. All elements you add to the document will now be placed on the Brochure Elements Layer.

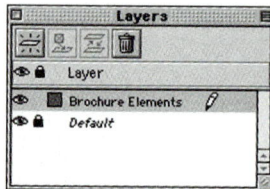

6. Click the Visible icon in the Default layer to hide the layer.

7. Save the document and continue.

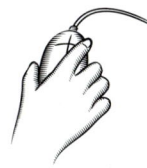

Add Style Sheets

1. Choose Edit>Style Sheets.

2. Highlight the Normal character style sheet and click Edit.

3. Click Edit in the Character Attributes area. Change the Font to ATC Laurel Book and the Size to 11 pt.

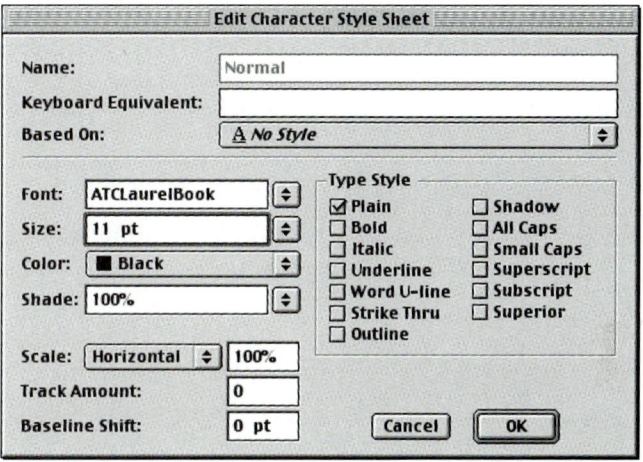

4. Click OK, and then OK again to return to the Style Sheets dialog box.

5. Create the following paragraph style sheets. The items listed here are the ones you need to change for each style sheet. If something is not listed, leave that item at the default value.

Name:	Body Text Justified
Formats Tab:	Space Before: 0.111 in.
	Keep Lines Together: Selected (Start: 2, End: 2)
	Alignment: Justified
Name:	Body Text Left
Based On:	Body Text Justified
Formats Tab:	Space Before: 0.208 in.
	Alignment: Left
Name:	Body Text Right
Based On:	Body Text Justified
Formats Tab:	Space Before: 0.208 in.
	Alignment: Right
Name:	Contact Info
Character:	Size: 8 pt.
	Track Amount: −1
Formats Tab:	Leading: 8 pt.
	Space Before: 0 in.
	Alignment: Centered

Name:	Credit Line
Character:	Font: ATC Oak Normal
	Size: 6 pt.
	Color: White
Name:	Heading
Character:	Font: ATC Laurel Book Italic
	Size: 60 pt.
	Color: White
	Horizontal Scale: 90%
	Track Amount: –6
Formats Tab:	Leading: 55 pt.
	Alignment: Centered
Name:	Subhead
Character:	Size: 26 pt.
	Horizontal Scale: 90%
	Track Amount: –5
Formats Tab:	Leading: 25 pt.
	Alignment: Centered
	Space After: 0.111 in. (for Windows only)

6. Create the following character style sheet:

   Name: Bold Body Text
   Font: ATC Laurel Bold
   Size: 12 pt.

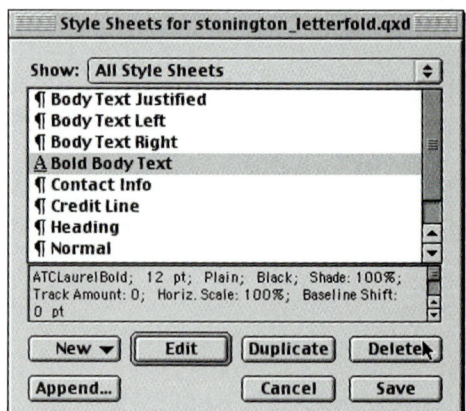

7. Click Save to close the Style Sheets dialog box. Save the file and continue.

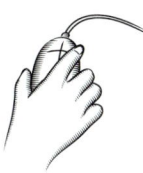

Create the Document Grid

1. On page 1 of the document (the outside of the brochure), drag horizontal page guides to Y: 5.35 in. and Y: 6.75 in.

2. Draw a rectangular text box in the first column of the brochure, snapping to the live-area guides.

If visual indicators are turned on (View>Show Visual Indicators), an icon in the top-right corner of the box indicates that the box is on the Brochure Elements layer.

3. Draw another text box in the second column of the brochure, again snapping to the live-area guides. Change the height of the second text box to 5 in.

4. Using the Linking tool, link the first text box to the second.

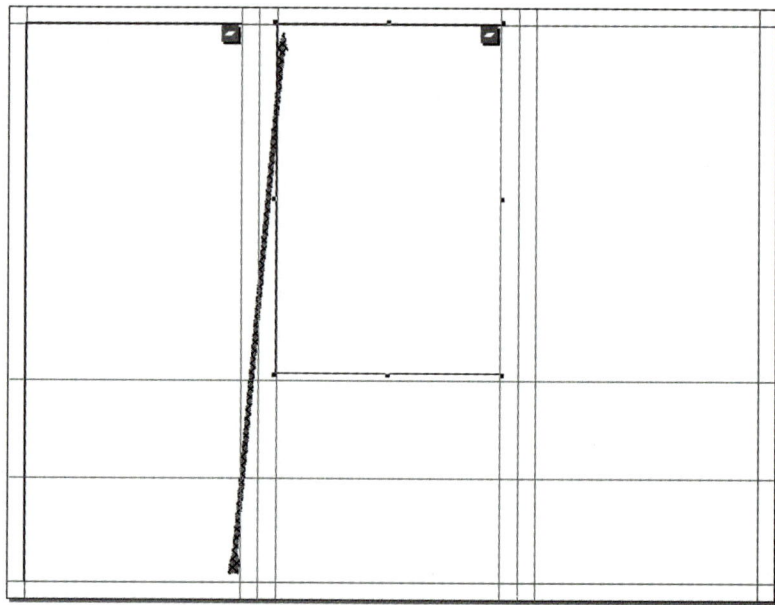

5. Draw another text box in the third column, again snapping to the live-area guides. Do not link this box to the first two.

6. Navigate to page 2 (the inside of the brochure) of the document.

7. Draw rectangular text boxes in all three columns of the brochure, snapping to the live-area guide for each column.

8. Using the Linking tool, link the first-column text box to the second-column text box.

9. Drag horizontal page guides to Y: 2.6 in., Y: 4.5 in., and Y: 6.375 in.

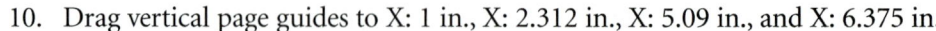

10. Drag vertical page guides to X: 1 in., X: 2.312 in., X: 5.09 in., and X: 6.375 in.

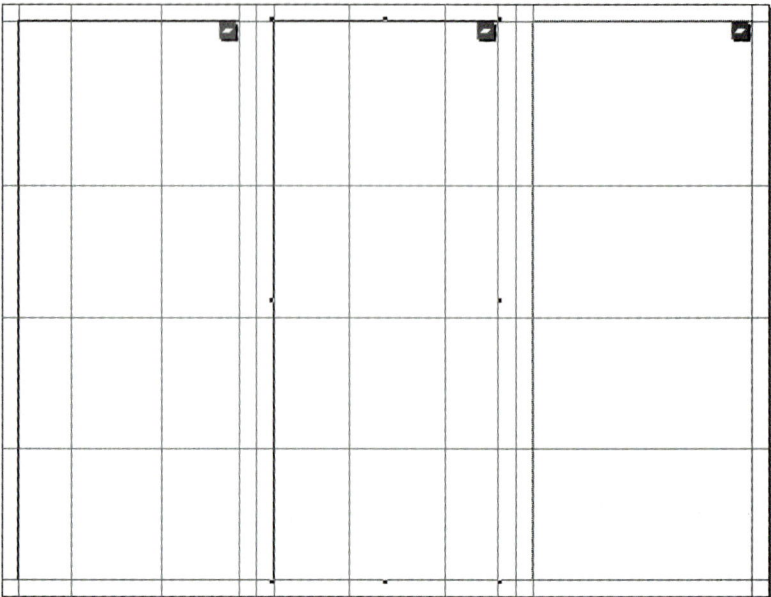

11. If the visual indicators are showing, choose View>Hide Visual Indicators.

12. Save the file and continue.

Add the Outside Brochure Content

1. Navigate to page 1 of the document. Choose the left-most text box with the Content tool and press Command/Control-E. Locate the file **sb_outside.xtg** in the **RF_Adv_Quark** folder. Make sure that the Include Style Sheets check box is selected and click Open.

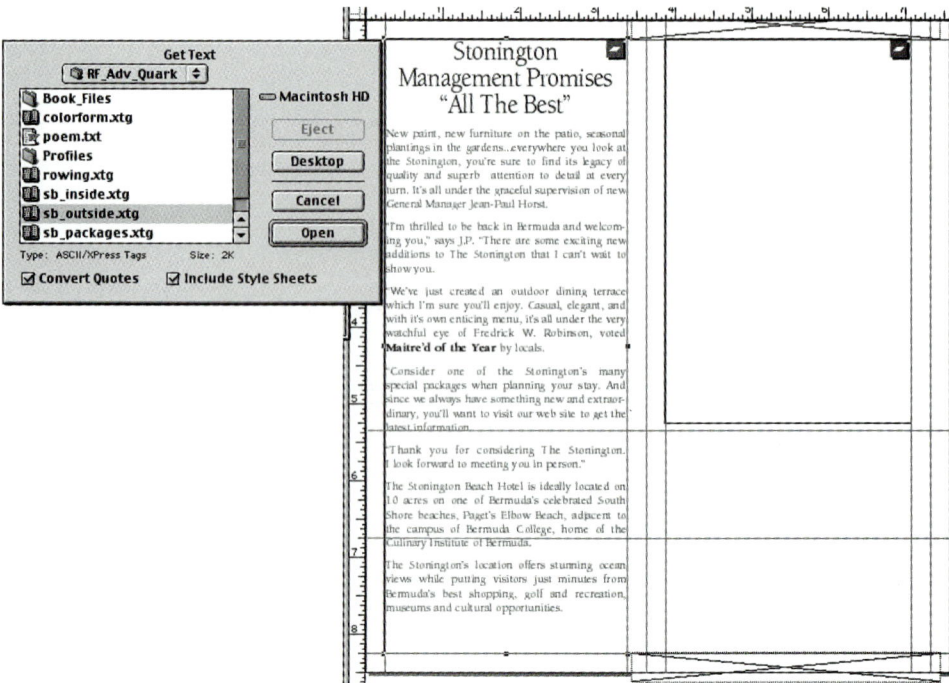

2. Draw a rectangular picture box on page 1 with the following dimensions:

X: 7.312 in.   W: 3.812 in.
Y: –0.125 in   H: 8.75 in.

3. With the box selected, open the Get Picture dialog box. Locate **beach.tif** in the **RF_Adv_Quark** folder and click Open.

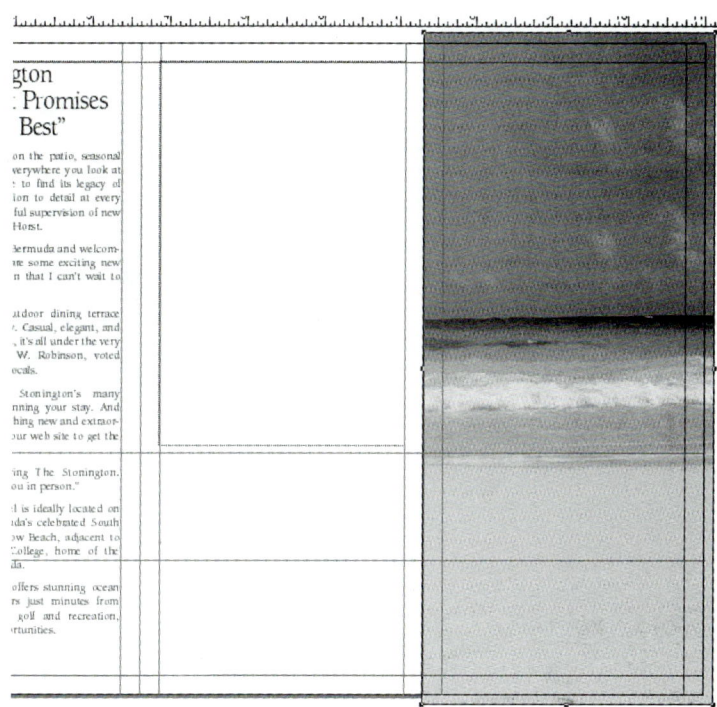

4. Draw a rectangular picture box with the following dimensions:

X: 2.136 in.   W: 1.238 in.
Y: 1.437 in   H: 1.762 in.

5. Place the file **horst.tif** into the box that you created in Step 4.

6. With the box selected, choose Item>Runaround. Change the Left and Right runaround field to 10 pt. and click OK.

You will find all of the resource files in the **RF_Adv_Quark** *folder.*

7. Zoom in to the bottom of the picture box. Create a rectangular text box with the following dimensions:

     X: 2.136 in.   W: 1.239 in.
     Y: 3.228 in   H: 0.16 in.

8. Apply a 10-pt. runaround to the left and right of the text box.

9. In the text box, type "John-Paul Horst" and apply the style Contact Info to the caption.

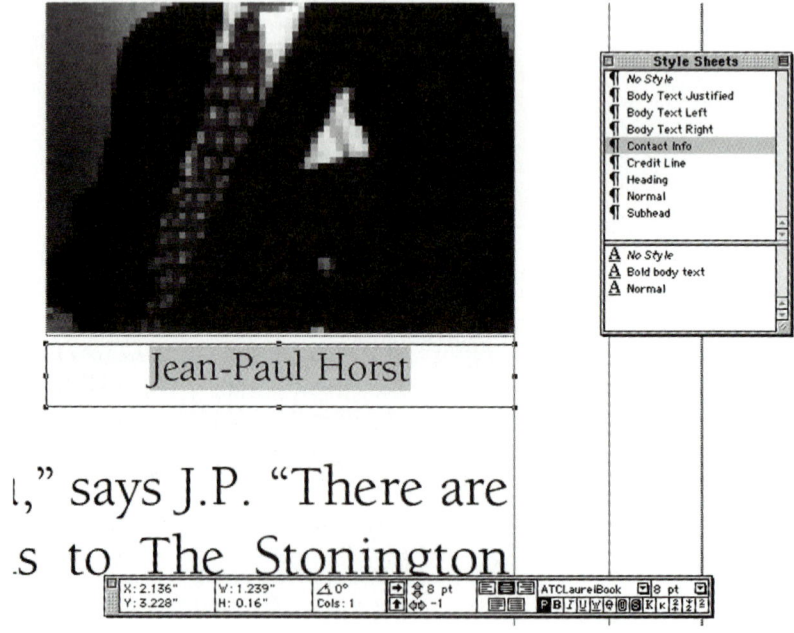

10. Zoom out to view the entire page.

11. Draw a new rectangular picture box with the following dimensions:

     X: 0.25 in.   W: 1.549 in.
     Y: 4.261 in.   H: 1.762 in.

Windows users: change the Y position of the box to 4.261 in.

12. Apply an 8-pt. runaround to the left and right of the box.

13. Place the file **dinner.tif** into the duplicate picture box. Drag the picture within the box so that the food on the plate is centered.

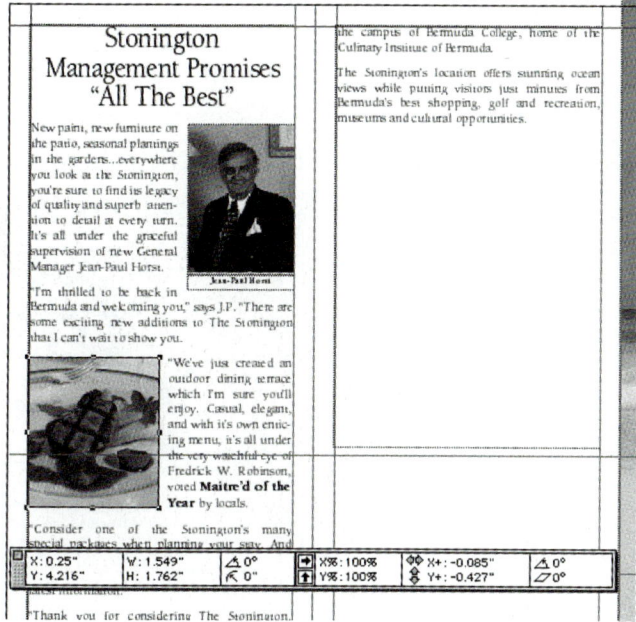

14. Change the height of the left-most text box to 7.375 in.

15. Draw a rectangular picture box in the top of the second column, snapping to the live-area guides on either side. Set the box height to 3.2 in.

16. Place the file **bermuda_map.eps** into the picture box. Scale the picture to 40% horizontally and vertically, and then drag the picture within the box so that the map is centered.

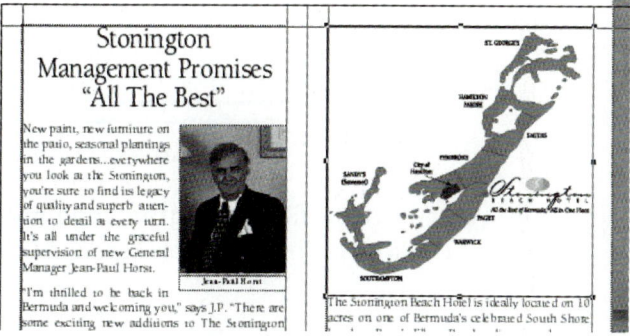

17. Select the beach image in the right column and choose Item>Send to Back.

18. Select the empty text box in the right column. Open the Colors palette and change the background color to None.

19. In the text box, type:

    All the [soft return]
    Best of [soft return]
    Bermuda, [soft return]
    All in [soft return]
    One Place.

20. Apply the Heading style sheet to the text.

21. Draw a rectangular picture box at the bottom of the right column (over the beach picture), snapping to the live-area guides on the top, left, and bottom, and snapping to the page guide at Y: 6.75 in.

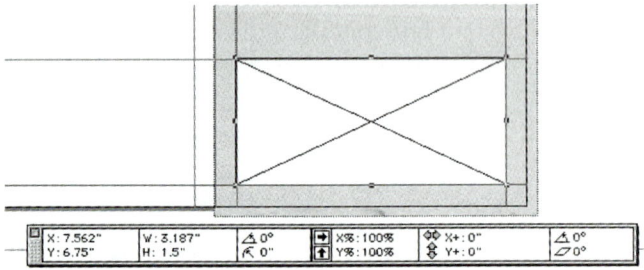

22. Place the file **stonington_logo.eps** into the box, and choose Style>Center Picture. Change the background color of the box to None.

23. Duplicate the logo picture box. Drag the duplicate box into the second column so that it snaps to the page guide at Y: 6.75 in and to the live-area guides on the left and right of the column.

24. Change the horizontal and vertical scale of the logo to 80% and change the height of the box to 0.855 in. Choose Style>Center Picture.

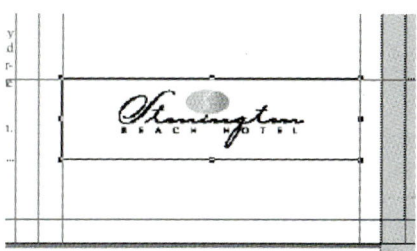

25. Beginning at Y: 7.625 in., draw a rectangular text box in the bottom of the second column, snapping to the live-area guides on the left, right, and bottom.

26. Import the file **contact.txt** into the box. Select all of the text and apply the Contact Info style sheet.

27. Draw a rectangular picture box with the following dimensions:

    X: 3.875 in.   W: 1.5 in.
    Y: 5.35 in.   H: 1.227 in.

28. Make a duplicate of the box and drag it to the right so that it snaps to the live-area guide for the column.

29. Place the file **harbor.tif** into the left box, and place the file **bermuda2.tif** into the right box.

30. Draw a rectangular text box with the following dimensions:

    X: 3.875 in.   W: 1.5 in.
    Y: 6.457 in.   H: 0.121 in.

31. Change the background of the box to None, and type "Photo: Bermuda Dept. of Tourism". Apply the Credit Line style sheet.

32. The outside of the brochure is finished. Save the file and continue.

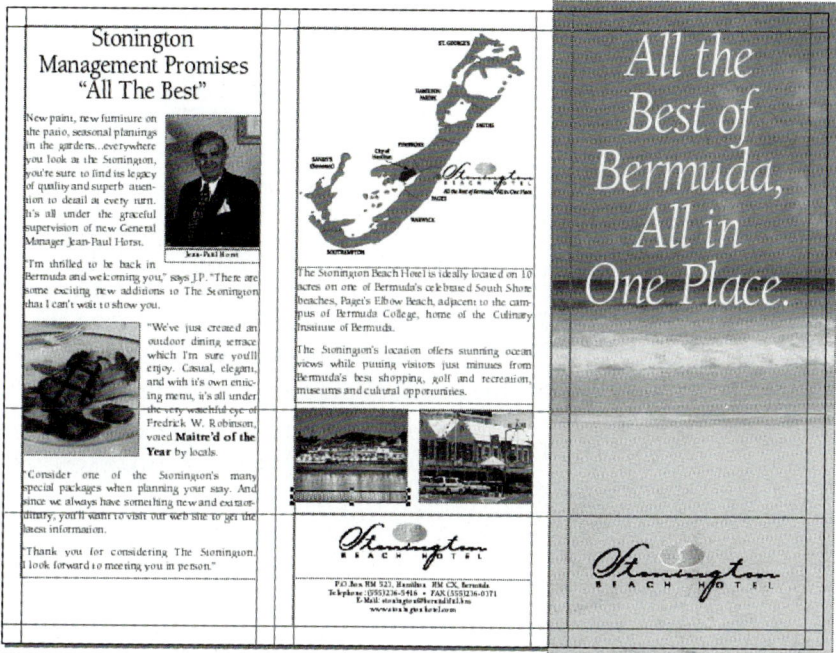

Add the Inside Brochure Content

1. Navigate to page 2 of the document.

2. Select the left-most text box. Drag the top-center handle of the box down until it snaps to the guide at Y: 4.5 in.

3. Repeat Step 2 for the text box in the second column.

4. With the left text box selected, choose File>Get text. Locate the file **sb_inside.xtg** in the **RF_Adv_Quark** folder. Make sure the Include Style Sheets option is selected and click Open.

You've found it. The perfect place to fulfill all your island dreams. The Stonington Beach Hotel has everything you'd hoped for in Bermuda all in one fantastic location.

Located on Bermuda's famed South Shore at Paget's Elbow Beach, Stonington Beach Hotel enjoys one of Bermuda's best beachfront locations. Whether for business or pleasure, the Stonington has everything covered in exquisite detail.

Surrounded by natural seaside flora and rock formations, your room at the Stonington brings the best of Bermuda indoors with touches such as beautiful tiled floors, cooling ceiling fans, and your choice of ocean front or ocean view.

Your room is just a few steps from the beach bar, championship tennis courts, heated pool and, of course... Bermuda's famed pink sand beach and turquoise water.

Inside, you'll find gracious service amid a relaxing island atmosphere. Meet new friends in the lounge. Curl up with a book in the library. Or enjoy something for which the Stonington is famous — unparalleled culinary experiences available in the Norwood dining room.

5. Draw a rectangular picture box at the top of the first two columns, on the left snapping to the guide at X: 1 in., on the right snapping to the guide at X: 6.375 in., and on the top to the margin guide. Set the height of the box to 2.25 in.

6. Place the file **exterior.tif** into the box.

7. Draw a rectangular picture box in the left column, snapping to the live-area guide of the column on either side, and on the top snapping to the guide at Y: 2.6 in. Set the height of the box to 1.806 in.

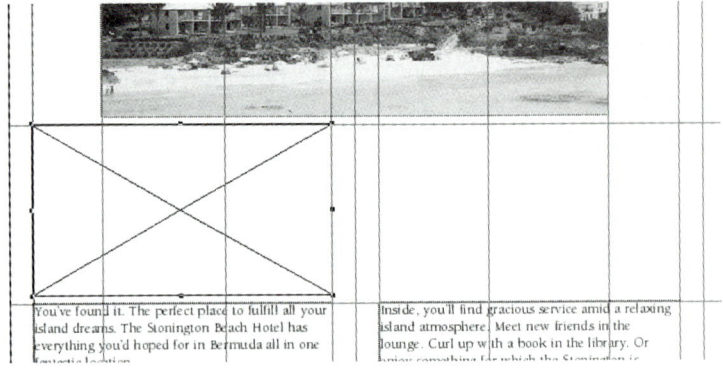

8. Duplicate the box, and drag it to the right so that it snaps to the live-area guides of the second column (on the left and right) and on the top to the page guide at Y: 2.6 in.

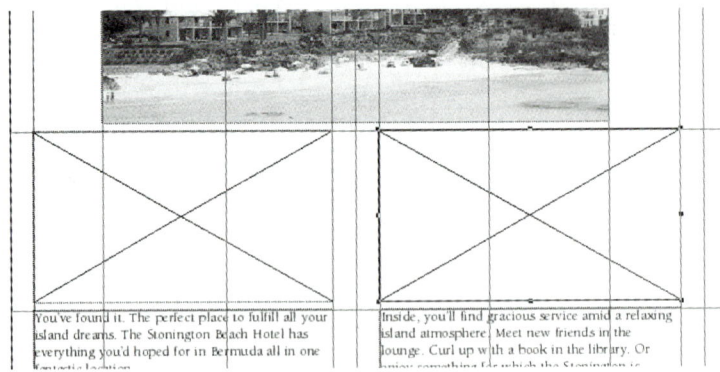

9. Place the file **room.tif** into the left box and place the file **people.tif** into the right box.

10. Draw a rectangular picture box that extends across the first two columns, on the left snapping to the guide at X: 2.312 in., on the right snapping to the guide at X: 5.09 in., and on the top snapping to the guide at Y: 4.5 in. Set the height of the box to 1.8 in.

11. Apply a 6-pt. runaround to the left and right of the box.

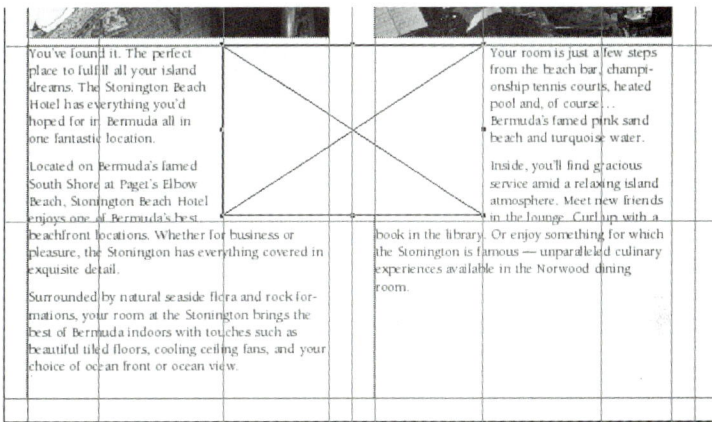

12. Duplicate the box, and drag it down so that it snaps to the guide at Y: 6.375 in.

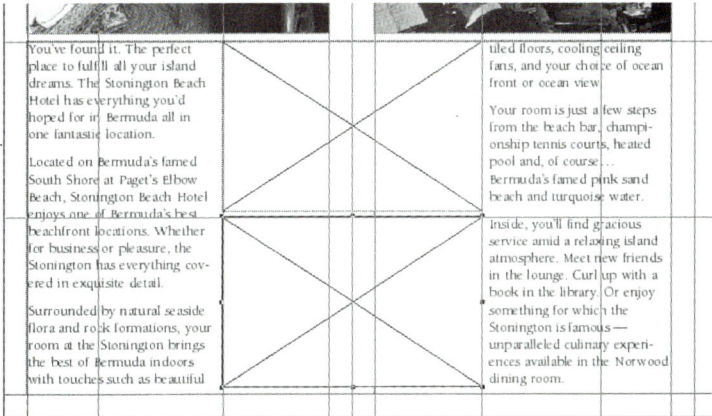

13. Place the file **meeting_room.tif** into the top box and place the file **pool.tif** into the bottom box.

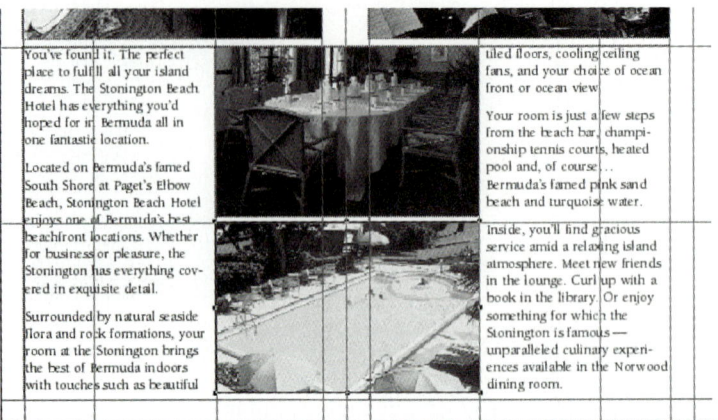

14. Select the text box in the right column. Place the file **sb_packages.xtg** — including the style sheets — into the text box.

15. Draw a rectangular picture box with the following dimensions:

    X: 9.345 in.   W: 1.93 in.
    Y: 1.408 in.   H: 2.258 in.

16. Place the image **tools.tif** into the box.

17. Draw a rectangular picture box with the following dimensions:

> X: 7.625 in.   W: 1.336 in.
> Y: 3.778 in.   H: 1.456 in.

18. Apply a 6-pt. runaround to all four sides, and place the image **golfcourse.tif** into the box.

19. Draw a rectangular picture box with the following dimensions:

> X: 9.313 in.   W: 1.437 in.
> Y: 5.5 in.   H: 2.562 in.

20. Apply a 6-pt. runaround to all sides, and place the image **beach_dining.tif** into the box.

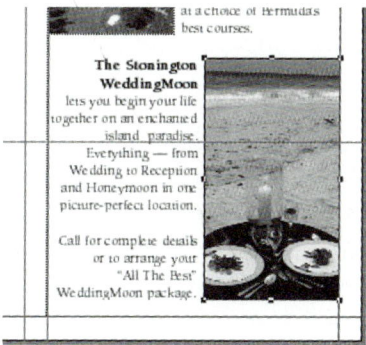

21. Using the Layers palette, make the Default layer visible by clicking to the left of the Locked icon in the Default line.

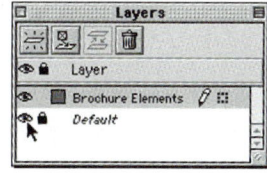

22. The inside of the brochure is finished. Save the file and close it.

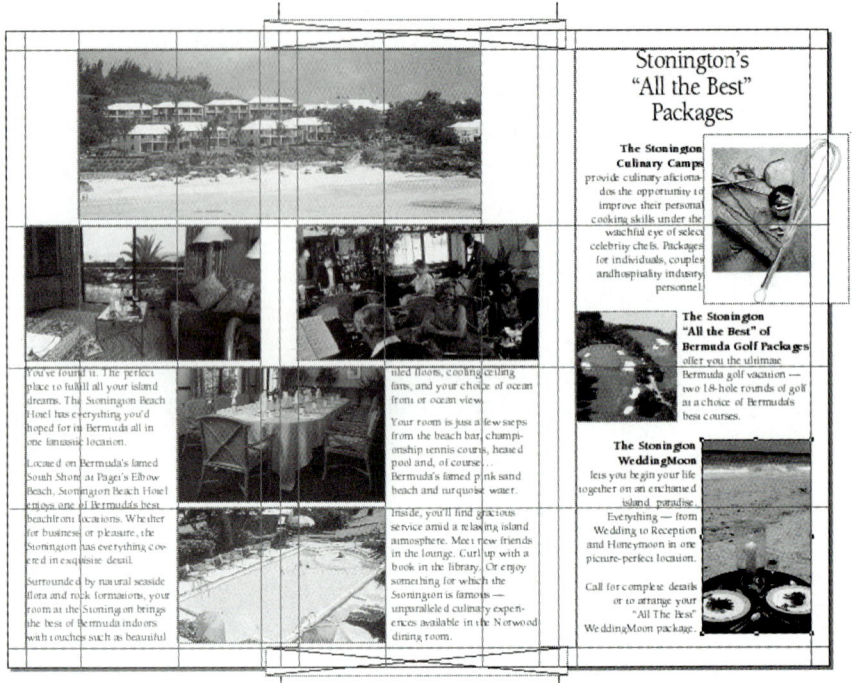

This project required you to create a folding grid for a letterfold brochure. You took advantage of the Layers feature to place folding marks, and then hide them while creating the brochure content. You also created a layout grid to facilitate object placement. By combining style sheets, image placement, and formatting tools with well-planned layout and folding grids, you improved the time required to create the client's brochure. When this job is printed, the margins of each panel will appear even and the brochure will fit into standard rack-card holders.

Project B: Body Solution Booklet

As the lead designer for the Body Solution account, you are coordinating the efforts of three other designers. Each of your designers has created one chapter of a booklet that will be sent to health-care providers around the country as a free handout for patients. As the project coordinator, it is your job to make sure that each chapter of the document is consistent with the others, and to create the front and back matter.

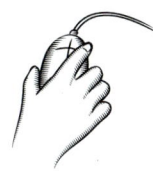

Create the Book File

1. Copy the **Fitness_Files** folder from the **RF_Adv_Quark** folder into your **Work_In_Progress** folder.

2. Windows users: open the Properties dialog box for each file in the **Fitness_Files** folder and deactivate the Read-Only check box.

3. Choose File>New>Book.

4. Navigate to your **Work_In_Progress** folder. Type "fitness_book.qxb" in the Book Name/File Name field and click Create.

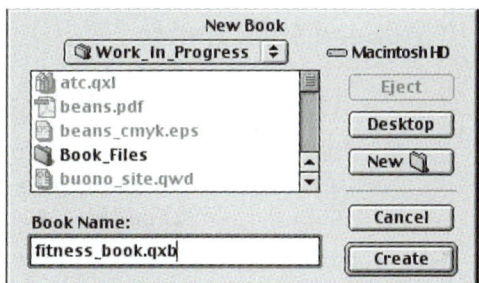

5. Click the Add Chapter button in the book palette.

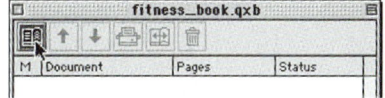

6. Locate the file **fitness_01.qxd** in the **Fitness_Files** folder (**Work_In_Progress>Fitness_Files**) and click Add.

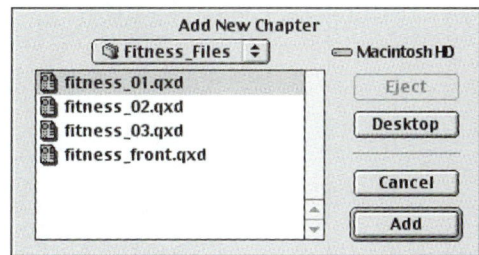

7. Notice that the file is added as the master document, indicated by an "M" in the "M" column.

8. Click the Add Chapter button. Add the file **fitness_02.qxd** to the book.

9. Click the Add Chapter button. Add the file **fitness_03.qxd** to the book.

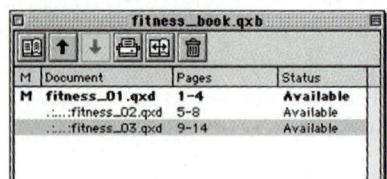

10. Click the Add Chapter button. Add the file **fitness_front.qxd** to the book.

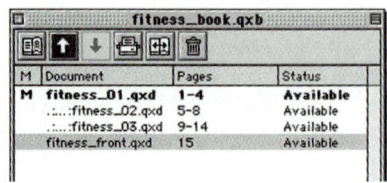

11. Click the Move Chapter Up button three times to place the fitness_front document at the beginning of the list.

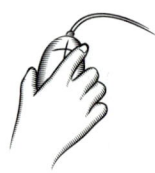

Append Style Sheets

1. Double-click fitness_01.qxd in the book palette to open the file.

2. If the Style Sheets palette is not visible, choose View>Style Sheets. This document was built with different style sheets for the Chapter Header, Chapter Title, Chapter Subtitle, and Subheads.

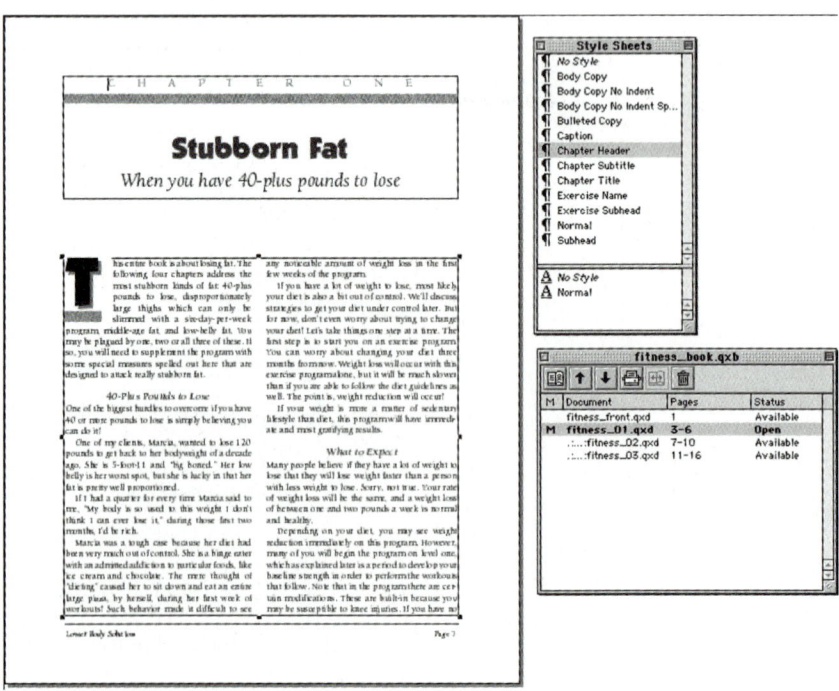

3. Choose File>Append. Locate the file **fitness.qxt** in the **Work_In_Progress>Fitness_Files** folder and click Open.

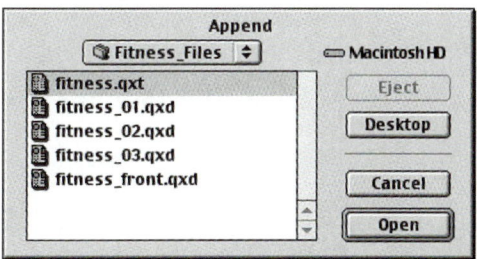

4. In the Style Sheets tab, click Include All, and then click OK.

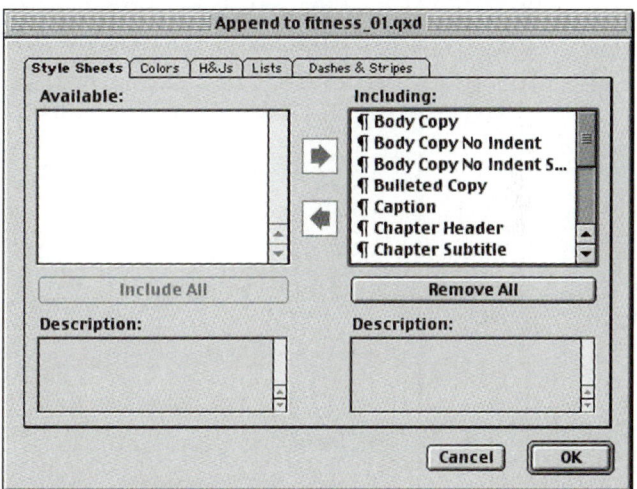

5. You will see a dialog box telling you that embedded elements will also be appended. Click OK.

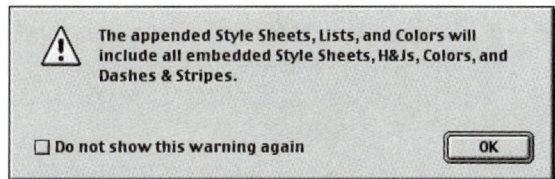

6. In the Conflict warning dialog box, activate the Repeat For All Conflicts check box and click Use New.

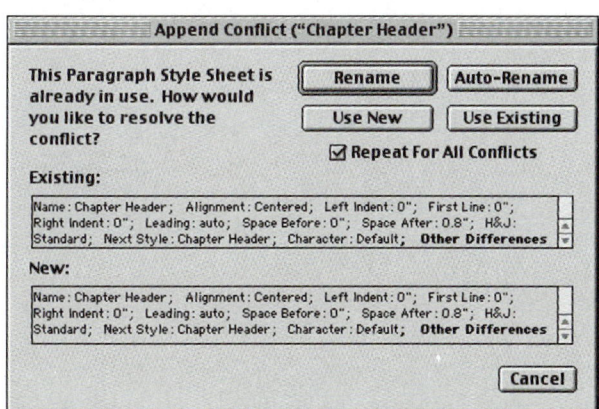

7. Notice that the chapter header in the open file is now set in blue type, and that three style sheets — TOC1, TOC2, and TOC3 — have been added.

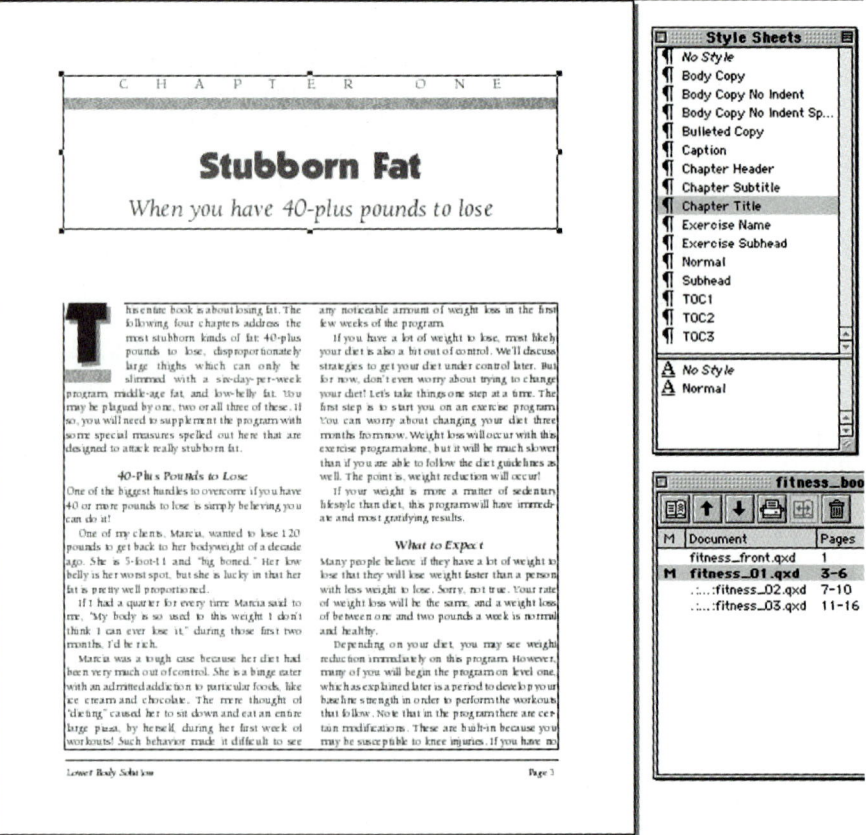

8. Save the open file and continue.

Define the Table of Contents List

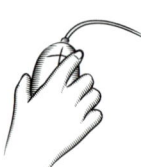

1. With the file fitness_01.qxd still open, choose Edit>Lists. In the Lists dialog box, click New.

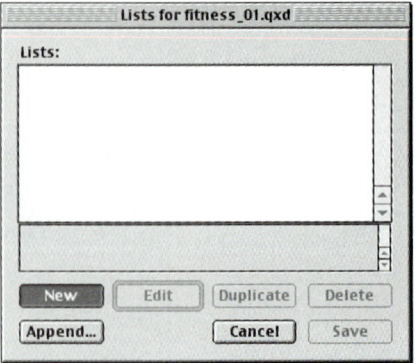

2. In the Edit List dialog box, type "Table of Contents" in the Name field.

3. Highlight Chapter Header in the Available Styles area and click the Add (right-facing arrow) button.

4. Choose TOC1 in the Format As menu.

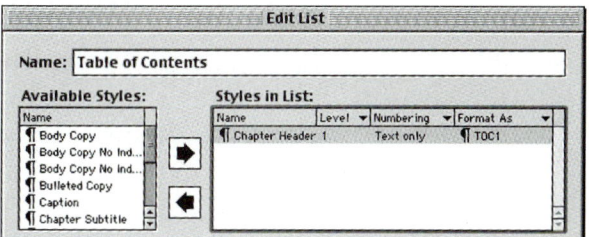

5. Highlight Chapter Title in the Available Styles area and click the Add (right-facing arrow) button.

6. Choose 2 from the Level menu, choose Text… Page # from the Numbering menu, and choose TOC2 from the Format As menu.

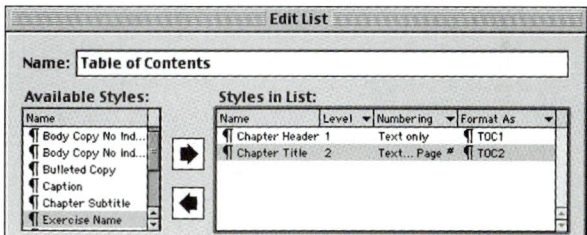

7. Highlight Subhead in the Available Styles area and click the Add (right-facing arrow) button.

8. Choose 3 from the Level menu, choose Text… Page # from the Numbering menu, and choose TOC3 from the Format As menu.

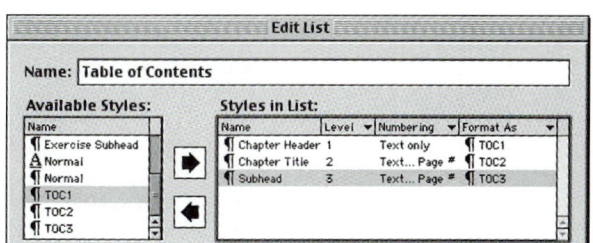

9. Click OK to return to the Lists dialog box, and click Save to add the list to the document.

10. Choose View>Show Lists. Examine the list for the chapter.

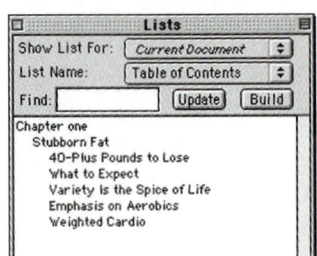

11. Choose fitness_book.qxb from the Show List For menu. Notice that the rest of the palette is now unavailable because the list only exists in this chapter.

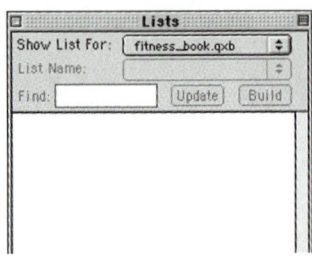

12. Save the file and close it, but leave the book file open.

Synchronize the Book

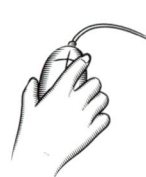

1. Click in the empty space at the bottom of the book palette to deselect all files.

2. Click the Synchronize button in the book palette.

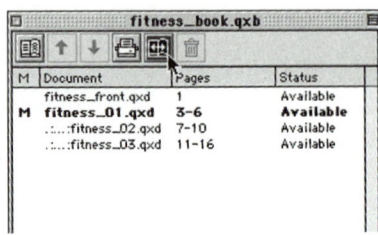

3. In the Style Sheets tab, click Include All to synchronize all style sheets in all documents of the book.

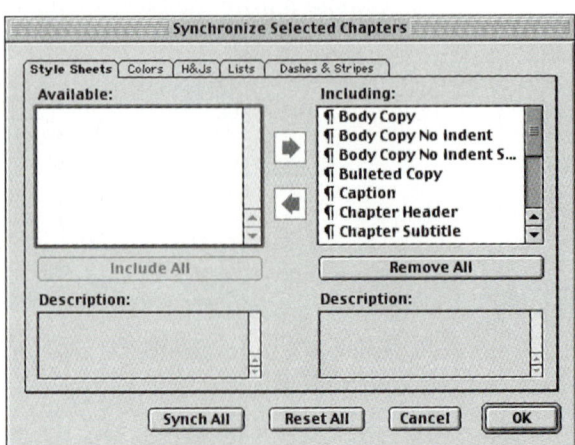

4. Click the Lists tab, and click Include All to add the Table of Contents list to all documents of the book.

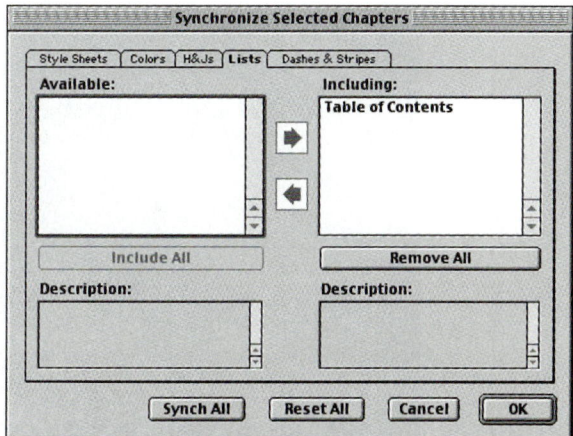

5. Click OK. Click OK to the warning that embedded elements will also be synchronized. When the synchronization process is complete, look at the Lists palette.

6. Notice that the List Name menu defaults to Table of Contents. This is the only list in the book.

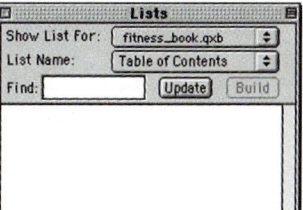

Build the Table of Contents

1. Click Update in the Lists palette. You should see the list for the entire book.

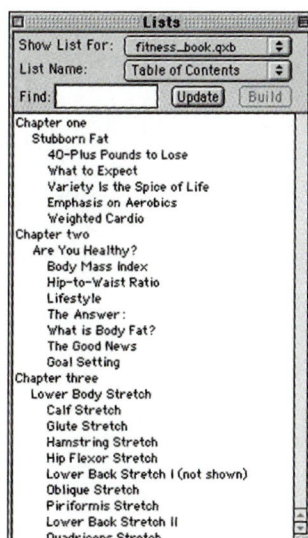

2. Double-click fitness_front.qxd in the book palette to open the document. If the Document Layout palette is not visible, choose View>Show Document Layout.

3. Drag a second page into the open document using the E-Table of Contents master page.

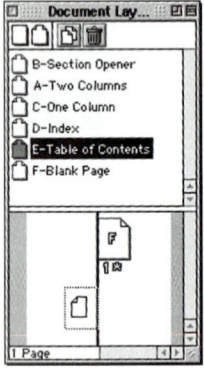

4. Make page 2 of the document active in the document window.

5. Using the Content tool, select the empty text box on the page. Click Build in the Lists palette.

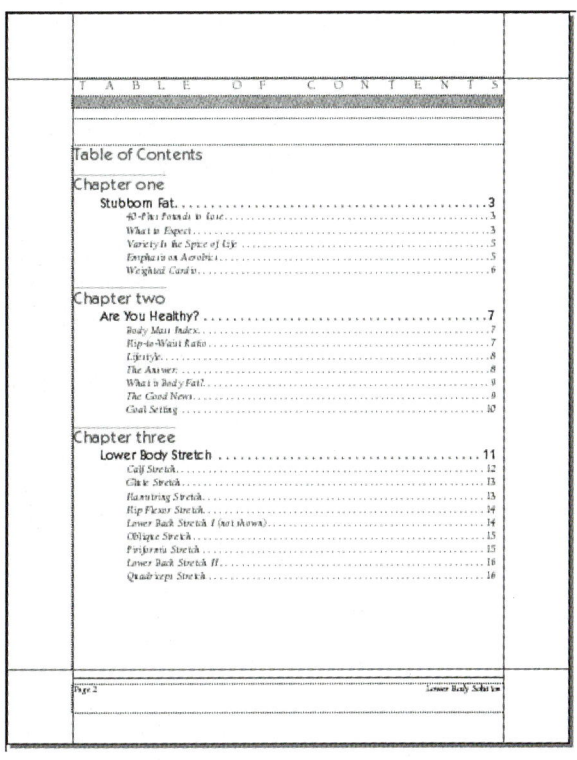

6. Close the Lists palette. Save the open file and close it, but leave the book file open.

Tag Index Terms in the First File

1. Double-click fitness_01.qxd in the book palette to open the file.

2. Choose View>Show Index to open the Index palette.

3. Highlight the word "diet" in the last paragraph of the first column.

4. Click the Add All button in the Index palette to add the term to the index. Notice that nine references to the term are added.

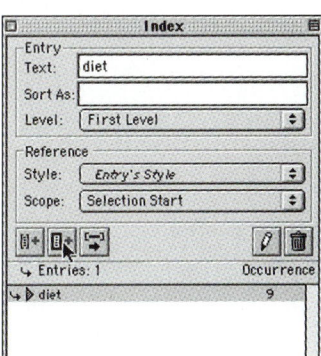

5. Highlight the words "binge eater" in the second line of the same paragraph. In the Index palette, change the Text field to "binge eating" and click the Add button.

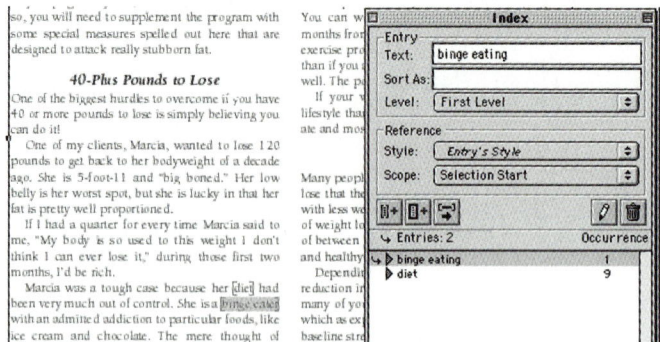

6. In the middle of the first full paragraph in the right column, highlight "exercise program" and click the Add All button.

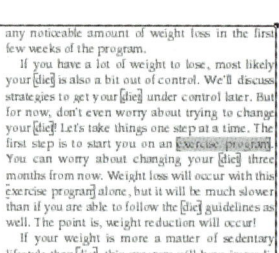
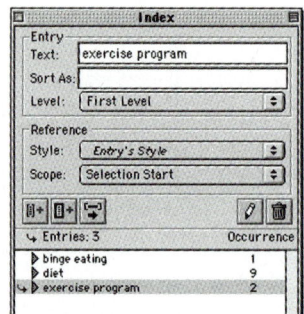

7. In the first paragraph after the What to Expect subhead, highlight "weight loss" and click the Add All button.

8. In the next paragraph, add "weight reduction", "baseline strength", and "injuries" to the list of index terms. Use the Add All button.

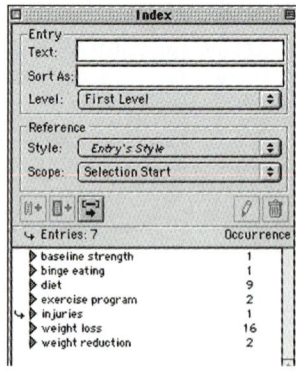

9. Navigate to page 4 of the open document. Highlight "back" in the first line. In the Index palette, change the Level menu to Second Level. Make sure that the target indicator is pointing to the term Injuries and click Add.

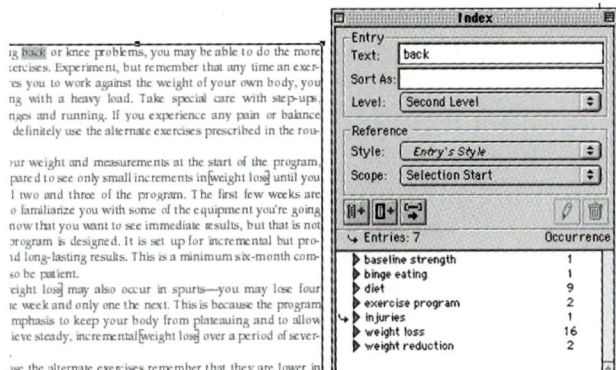

10. Repeat this process to add "knee" as a second-level term under injuries.

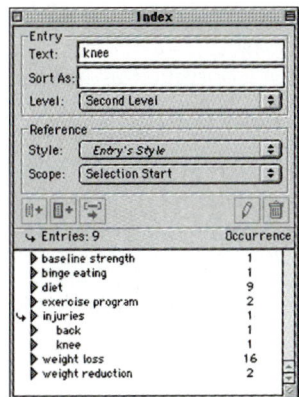

11. Single-click anywhere in the text box to make sure that nothing is highlighted.

12. In the Index palette Text field, type "pain". Change the Level menu to First Level.

13. Windows users: after typing in the Text field, click once in the document text box again. This will allow you to access the Add All button.

14. Click the Add All button. Notice that one reference to the term "pain" is added.

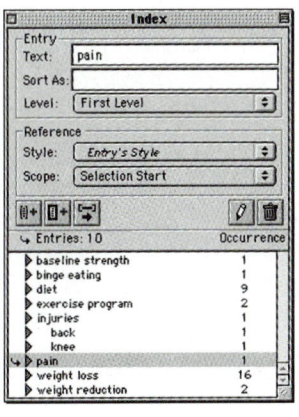

The first time that you try to add an index term with nothing highlighted, you have to click a text box in the document once using the Content tool. This will make the Add All button available. You only have to do this for the first word in a series of words that you add.

15. In the Text field, type "alternate exercises" and click the Add All button. Notice that two references are added for the term "alternate exercises".

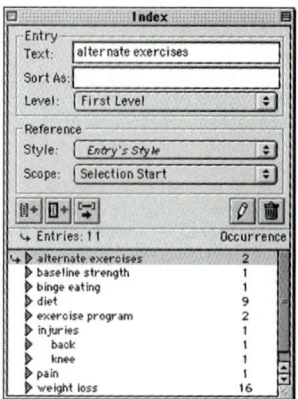

16. Continue this process adding the following terms:

measurements	results	weight training
metabolism	eating habits	strength
routines	aerobics	body fat
interval training	treadmill	stationary bike
stairclimber	calories	weighted cardio
maximum aerobic power training		

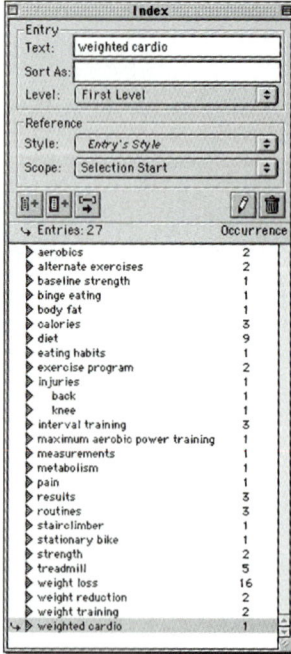

Notice that the terms you add are automatically alphabetized in the bottom half of the Index palette.

17. Navigate to page 4 of the open document. In the second-to-last paragraph, highlight the word "benefits" halfway through the paragraph. Change the Level menu of the Index palette to Second Level. Click in the empty space to the left of the term "exercise program" (in the bottom of the Index palette) to make exercise program the target term, and click the Add button.

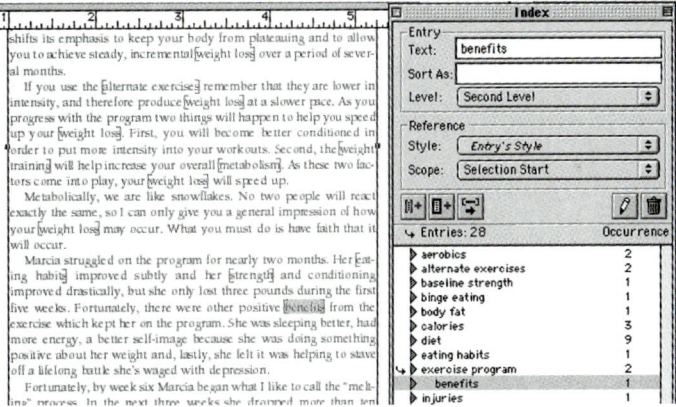

18. Navigate to page 5 of the document. In the third paragraph under the Emphasis on Aerobics subhead, highlight "Daniel Mercer". Change the Level menu to First Level. Hold down the Option/Alt key and click the Add Reversed button.

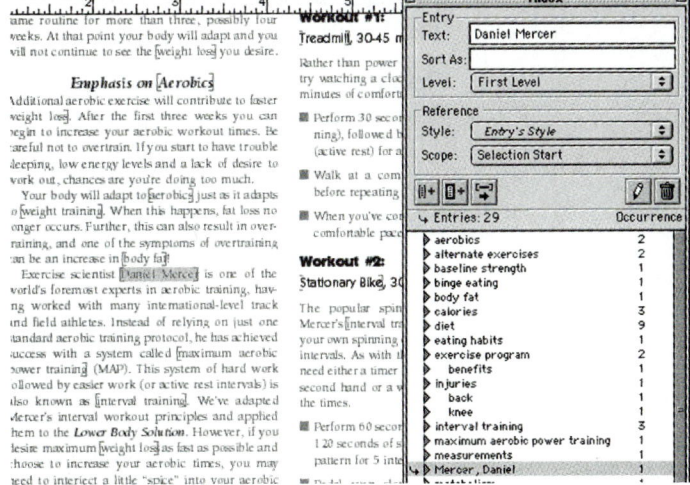

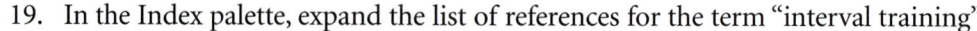

19. In the Index palette, expand the list of references for the term "interval training".

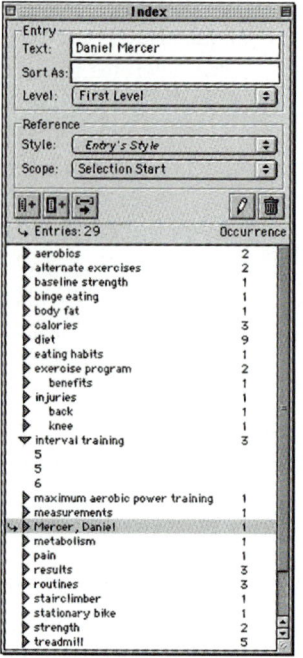

20. Highlight the second page 5 reference to the term and click the Edit button (the Pencil).

21. Change the Scope menu to Cross-Reference, and choose See Also from the Scope submenu.

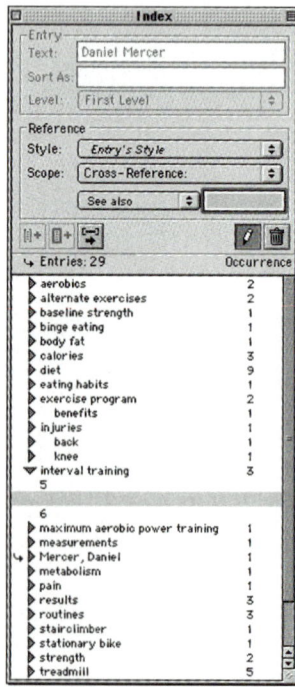

22. While the text field next to the See Also menu is highlighted, click the term "maximum aerobic power training" in the list of index terms. The text field next to the See Also menu should now show the term "maximum aerobic power training".

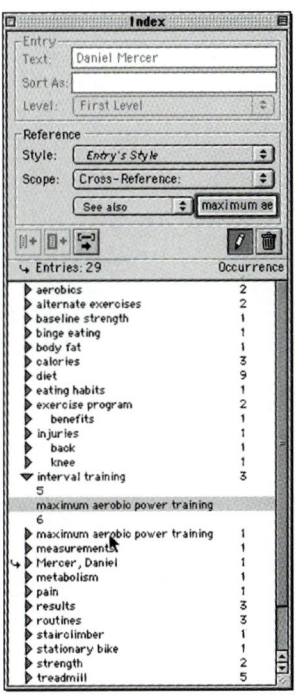

23. Click the Edit button to leave the edit mode.

24. Save the file and close it, but leave the book file open.

Tag Index Terms in the Second File

1. Double-click fitness_02.qxd in the book palette to open the file.

2. Highlight the subhead "Body Mass Index" in the first column. In the Index palette, choose To Style from the Scope menu and choose Subhead from the secondary menu. Click the Add button.

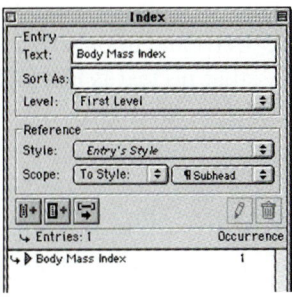

3. Highlight the "Hip-to-Waist Ratio" subhead in the second column. Leave the Scope menu at To Style and click the Add button in the Index palette.

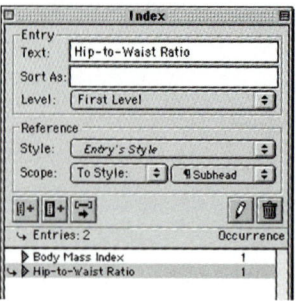

4. Navigate to page 8 of the document. Highlight the "Lifestyle" subhead in the first column. Leave the Scope menu at To Style and click the Add button.

5. Navigate to page 10 of the document. Highlight the "Goal Setting" subhead. Leave the Scope menu at To Style and click the Add button in the Index palette.

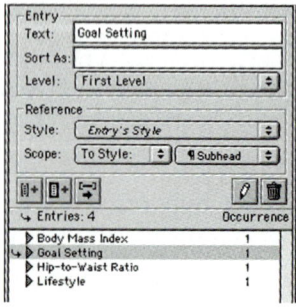

6. Navigate to page 7 of the document. Click in the text box on the page to make sure that no text is highlighted.

7. Change the Scope menu to Selection Start and type "body fat" in the Text field.

8. Windows users: after typing in the Text field, click once in the document text box again. This will allow you to access the Add All button.

9. Click the Add All button.

Remember: When typing in the Text field of the Index palette with nothing highlighted, you have to click a text box in the document once using the Content tool before you can use the Add All button. You only have to do this for the first word in a series of words you add.

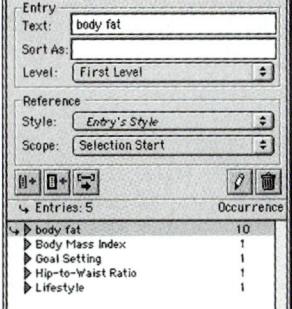

10. Change the Text field to "muscle mass" and click the Add All button.

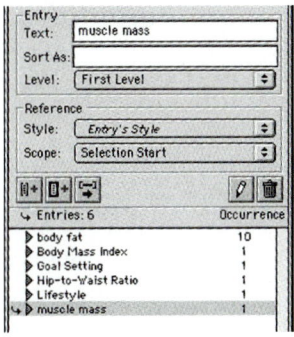

11. Repeat this process to add the following terms to the index.

measurements	diabetes	hypertension
obesity	pregnancy	childbirth
high blood pressure	osteoarthritis	cholesterol
heart disease	cigarettes	stress
weight	Mayo Clinic	National Institutes of Health
Harvard	menopause	weight training
weight loss		

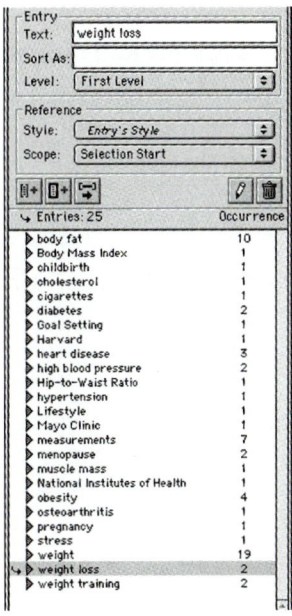

12. Save the open file and close it, but leave the book file open.

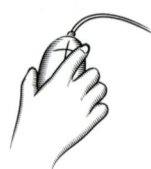

Tag Index Terms in the Third File

1. Double-click fitness_03.qxd in the book palette to open the file.

2. Highlight the word "Stretch" in the chapter heading.

3. In the Index palette, change the Text field to "stretching". Choose To End Of from the Scope menu and choose Document from the secondary menu. Click the Add button.

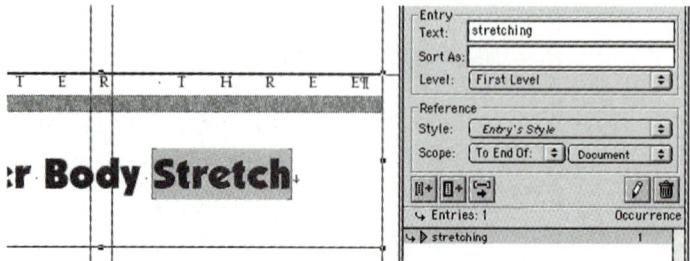

4. Navigate to page 12 of the document and highlight "Calf" in the first subhead. In the Index palette, change the Level menu to Second Level. Choose To Style from the Scope menu, and choose Subhead from the secondary menu. Click the Add button.

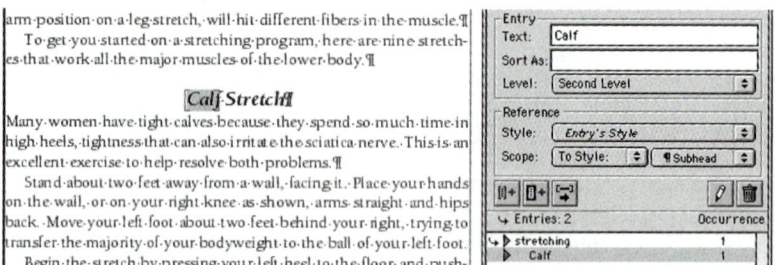

5. Navigate to page 13 of the document and highlight "Glute" in the first subhead. Click the Add button.

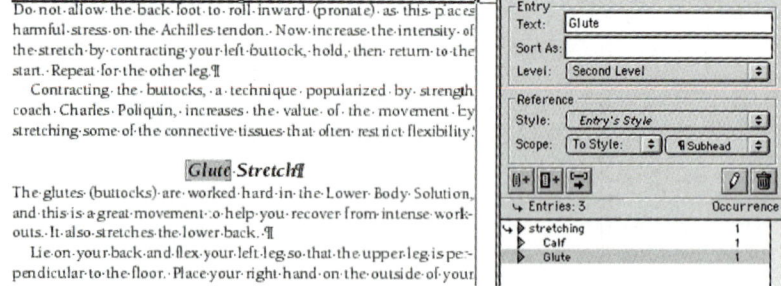

6. Repeat this process to add the topic of each subhead to the index as second-level terms under the first-level term "stretching".

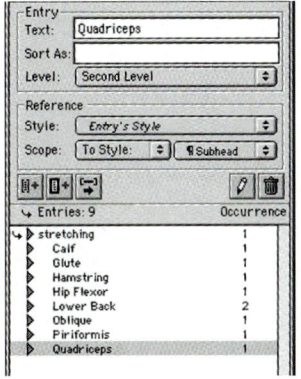

7. Navigate to page 11 of the document and single-click in the text box to deselect any text.

8. In the Index palette, change the Level menu to First Level and change the Scope menu to Selection Start.

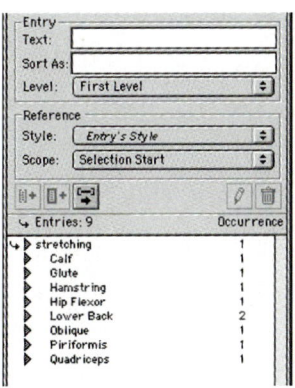

9. Type "workout" in the Text field of the Index palette.

10. Windows users: after typing in the Text field, click once in the document text box again. This will allow you to access the Add All button.

11. Click the Add All button.

Reminder: don't forget that you have to click a text box in the document once using the Content tool the first time you try to add an index term with nothing highlighted. This will make the Add All button available. You only have to do this for the first word in a series of words you add.

12. Repeat this process to add the following index terms:

fitness	weight training	aerobics
flexibility	muscle tension	muscle strains
circulation	heart rate	body temperature
clothing	pain	muscle
posture	spine	ligaments

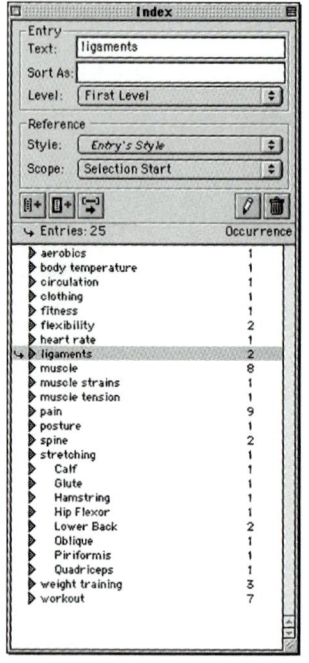

13. Save the file and close it, but leave the book file open.

Build the Index

1. Open the template file **fitness.qxt** from the **Fitness_Files** folder (**Work_In_Progress>Fitness_Files**).

2. Choose Edit>Style Sheets. Define new paragraph style sheets as follows:

Name:	Index Head
Based On:	TOC1

Name:	Index Level 1
Character:	Font Size: 10 pt.
Formats Tab:	Space Before: 0.028 in.

Name:	Index Level 2
Based On:	Index Level 1
Formats Tab:	Left Indent: 0.2 in.

3. Define a new character style sheet:

Name:	Cross Reference
Font:	ATC Laurel Book Italic
Size:	10 pt.

4. Save the file as "fitness_back.qxd" in your **Fitness_Files** folder (**Work_In_Progress>Fitness_Files**) and close the file, but leave the book file open.

5. Click the Add Chapter button in the book palette. Locate the fitness_back.qxd file that you just created and click Add.

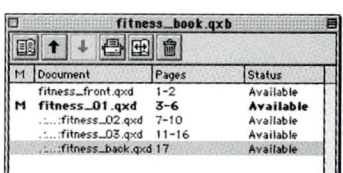

6. Double-click fitness_back.qxd in the book palette to open the file.

7. Choose Edit>Preferences>Index.

8. Type "\n" in the Before Cross-Reference field and choose <u>A</u> Cross Reference from the Cross-Ref Style menu. Click OK.

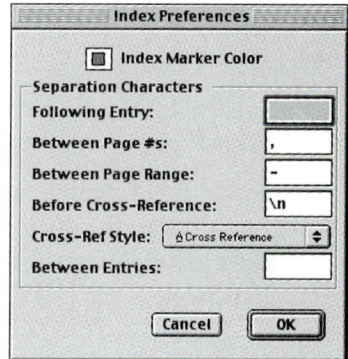

9. Choose Utilities>Build Index.

10. Activate the Entire Book check box.

11. Activate the Add Letter Headings check box and choose Index Head from the submenu.

12. Choose D-Index from the Master Page menu.

13. Choose Index Level 1 from the First Level Level Styles menu, and choose Index Level 2 from the Second Level Level Styles menu.

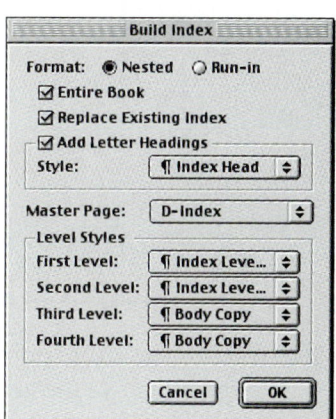

14. Click OK to build the index.

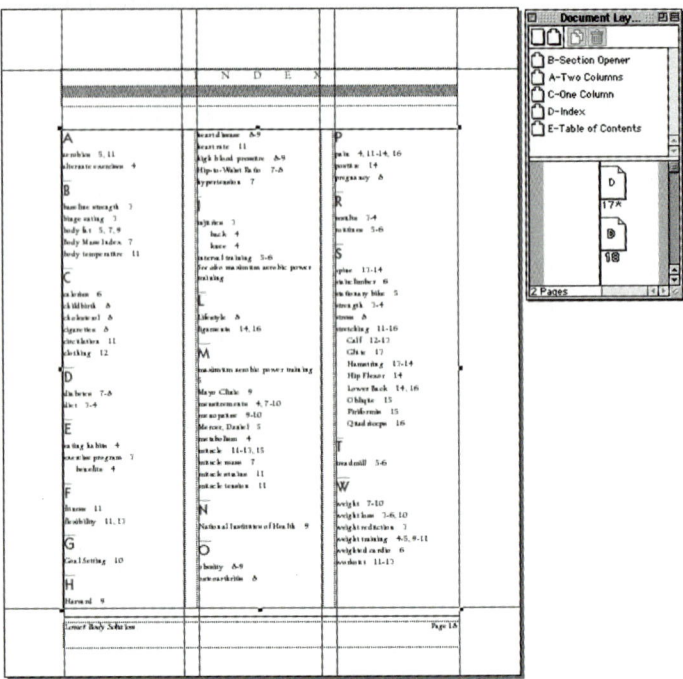

15. Notice that a second page was added to the document to contain the index. Delete page 17 from the document, and then add a blank page to the end of the document to keep the page numbers even. The blank page will be the back cover of the document.

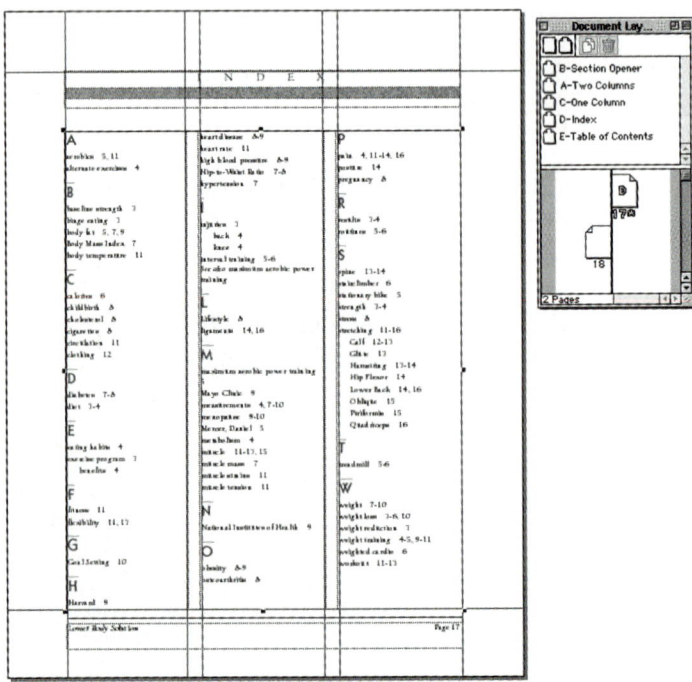

16. Place the insertion point before the "H" heading and press Enter on the numeric keypad to move the heading to the next column.

17. Choose Edit>Style Sheets. Highlight Index Level 1 and click Edit. In the Formats tab, change the Space Before field to 0.014 in. Click OK, and then click Save.

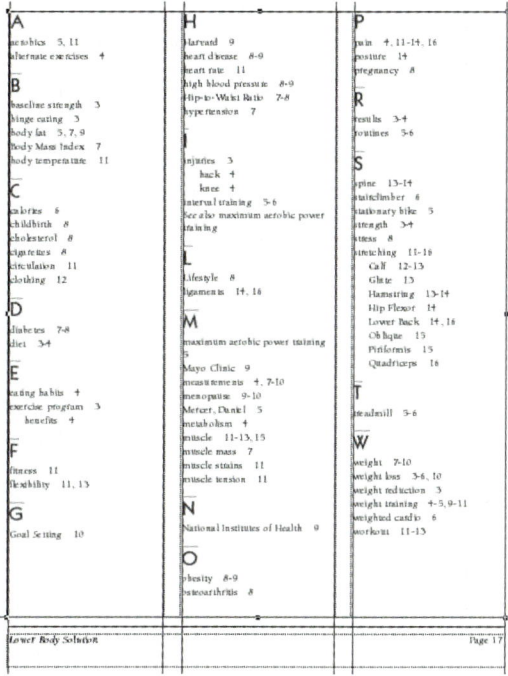

18. Close the Index palette.

19. Save the file and close it, but leave the book file open.

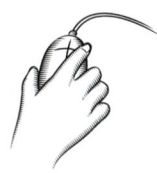

Update the Table of Contents

1. Click in the empty space at the bottom of the book palette to deselect all files. Click the Synchronize button.

2. Click the Lists tab. Move Table of Contents into the Including/Include column and click OK. Click OK to the warning that embedded elements will also be synchronized.

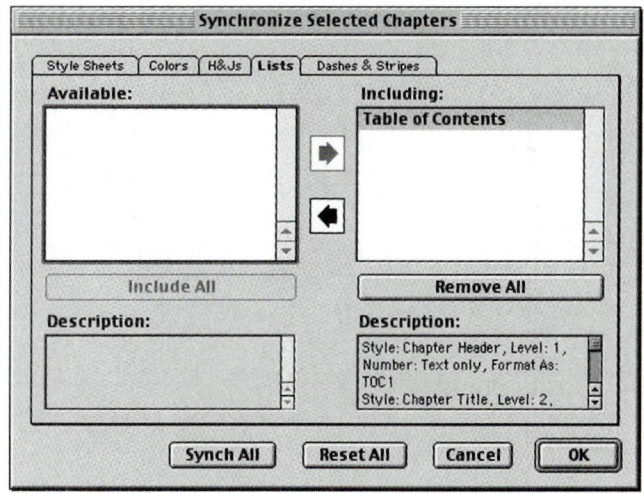

3. Double-click fitness_front.qxd in the book palette to open the file.

4. Navigate to page 2 of the document.

5. Choose View>Show Lists to open the Lists palette.

6. Select fitness_book.qxb from the Show List For menu and click Update.

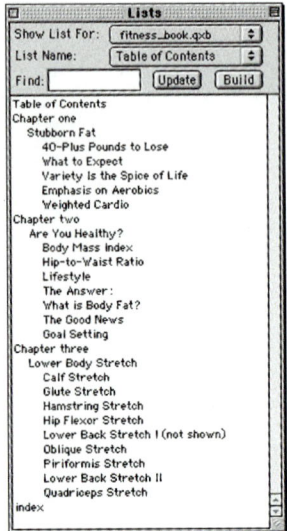

7. In the Lists palette, double-click "index" to open the appropriate file and highlight the appropriate text.

8. Because this header is set to All Caps, you can't tell that the word "index" was typed with a lowercase "i". Highlight the "I" in the Index header and type an uppercase "I".

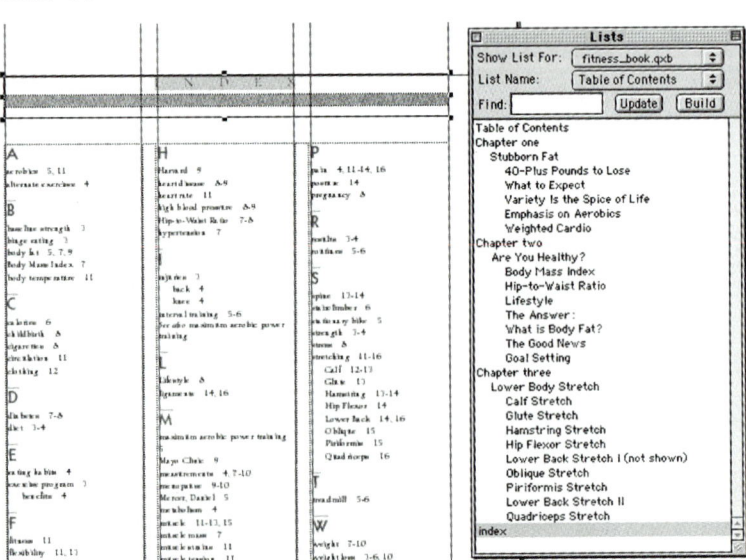

9. Save the fitness_back.qxd file and close it.

10. Click Update in the Lists palette.

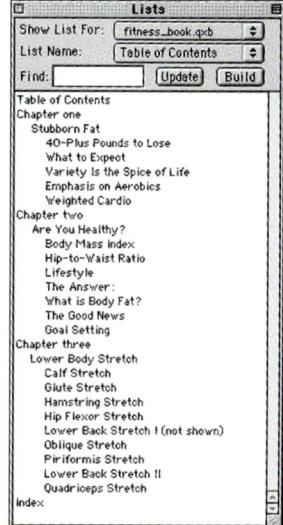

11. Double-click Table of Contents in the Lists palette to highlight the appropriate text.

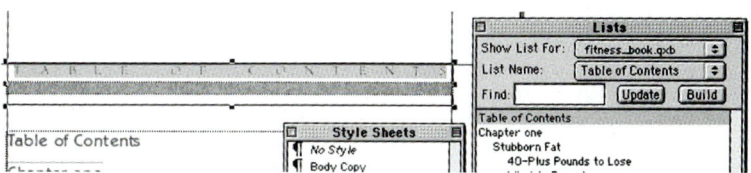

12. Click No Style in the Style Sheets palette to change the style sheet without changing the appearance of the text on the page.

13. Click Update in the Lists palette.

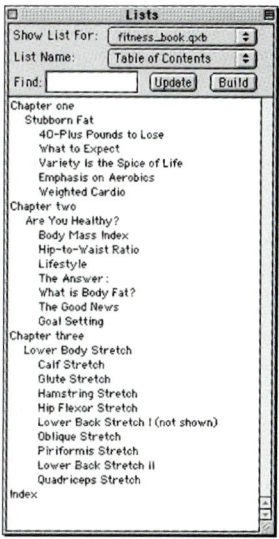

14. Click Build in the Lists palette. In the warning dialog box, click Replace to rewrite the Table of Contents.

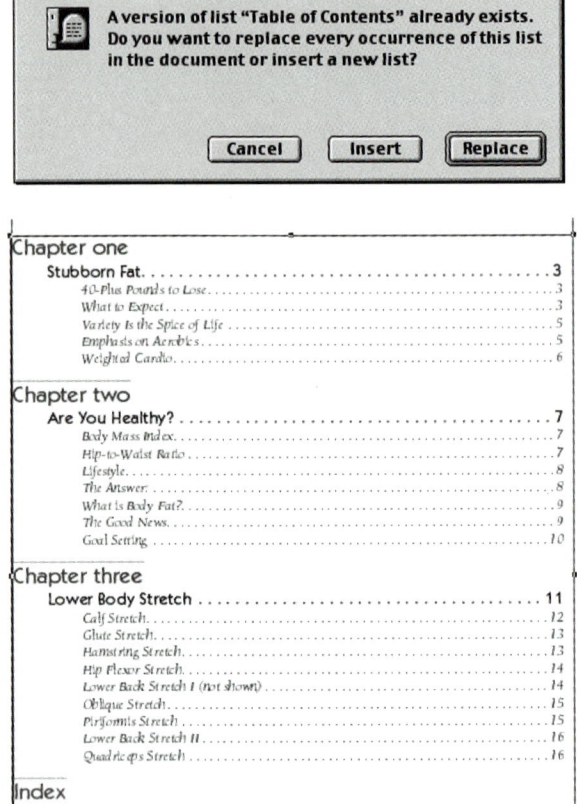

15. The table of contents is now updated. Save the file and close it, and close the book file.

To complete this project, you have used the long-document utilities built into QuarkXPress 5.0. You have combined multiple documents into a book, and synchronized the different files to ensure consistency from one document to the next. You used the Lists feature to build a table of contents, and used the Index utility to create an index for the client's publication. You also used style sheets and master pages to control the appearance of long-document features.

Project C: Cosciel Poster

Your new client, Cosciel Company, has hired you to replace their old design agency. They submit a poster to gourmet grocers and food festivals every year. The company's ad manager wants to redesign the company's poster using the same elements but a different layout. Cosciel wants to be able to send the file to different printers, each of whom has different file-submission requirements.

Your job is to create and prepare the ad using the master document from the former design agency. You will place the same pictures that are in the master, and use the same style sheets and colors. When the ad layout is complete, you will export the layout as an EPS for one printer, and create a job package with the Quark and supporting files for another printer.

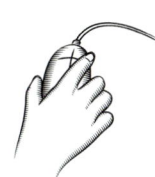

Create the Document Grid

1. Create a new one-column document, 17 in. wide by 11 in. high, with 0.5-in. margins on all four sides. Deactivate the Facing Pages and Automatic Text Box options and click OK.

2. Navigate to the A-Master A layout.

3. Drag horizontal page guides to Y: 2.875 in., Y: 5.5 in., and Y: 8.5 in.

4. Drag vertical page guides to X: 8.5 in. and X: 8.75 in.

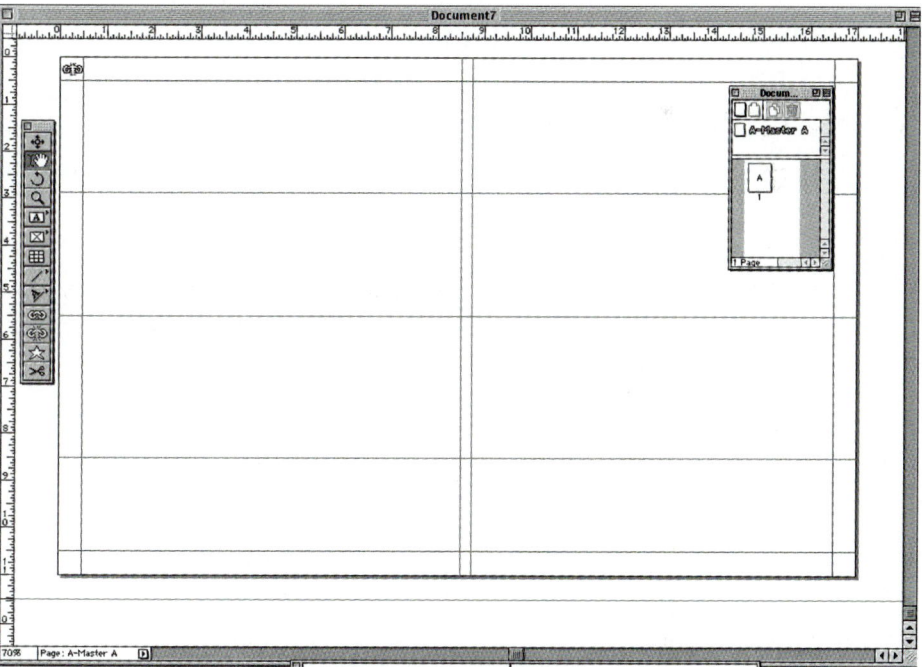

5. Navigate to page 1 of the document.

6. Snapping to the page guides you created, draw a rectangular text box with the following dimensions:

X: 0.5 in.   W: 8 in.
Y: 2.875 in.   H: 7.625 in.

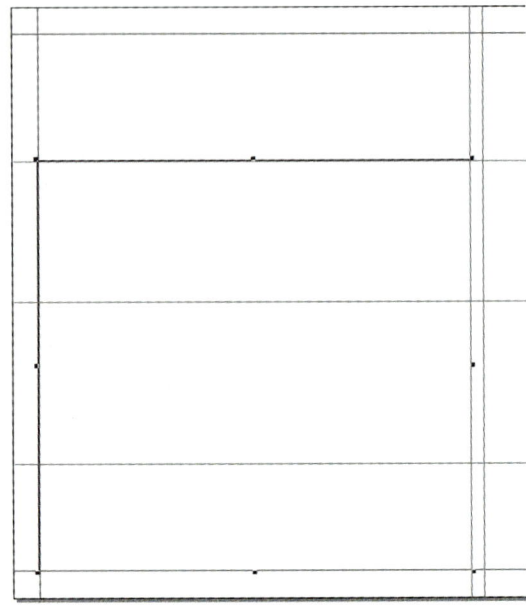

7. Open the Text tab of the Modify dialog box. Change the box to 2 Columns with a 0.25-in. Gutter Width. Click OK.

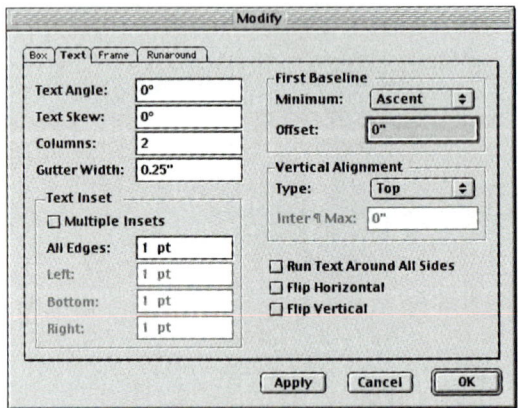

8. Draw another rectangular text box with the following dimensions:

X: 8.75 in.   W: 7.75 in.
Y: 2.875 in.   H: 2.375 in.

9. Draw another rectangular text box with the following dimensions:

X: 8.75 in.   W: 7.75 in.
Y: 8 in.   H: 0.407 in.

10. Open the Text tab of the Modify dialog box. Change the Vertical Alignment Type menu to Bottom. Click OK.

11. Draw another rectangular text box with the following dimensions:

    X: 8.75 in.   W: 7.75 in.
    Y: 8.5 in.   H: 2 in.

12. Open the Text tab of the Modify dialog box. Change the box to 3 Columns with a 0.167-in. Gutter Width. Click OK.

13. Choose the Linking tool. Link the four text boxes together in the order that you created them.

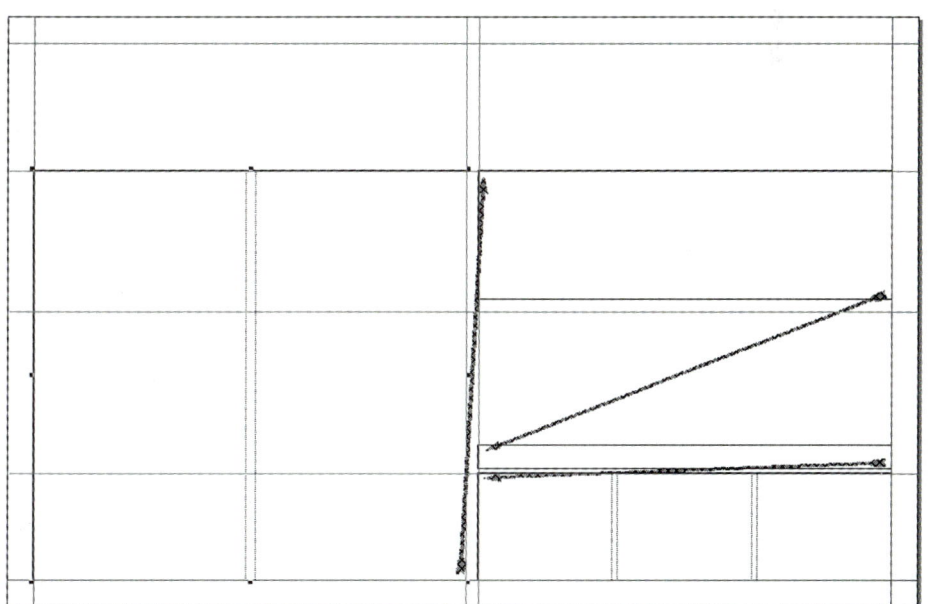

14. Save the file as "cosciel.qxd" in your **Work_In_Progress** folder and continue.

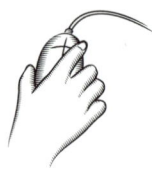

Append Style Sheets and Colors

1. Choose File>Append. Locate the file **cosciel_master.qxd** in the **RF_Adv_Quark** folder and click Open.

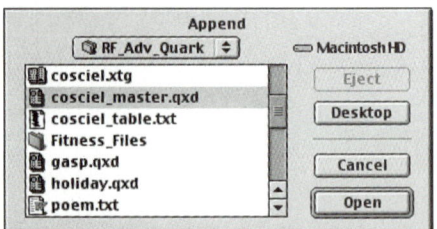

2. In the Style Sheets tab of the Append dialog box, click Include All, then click OK.

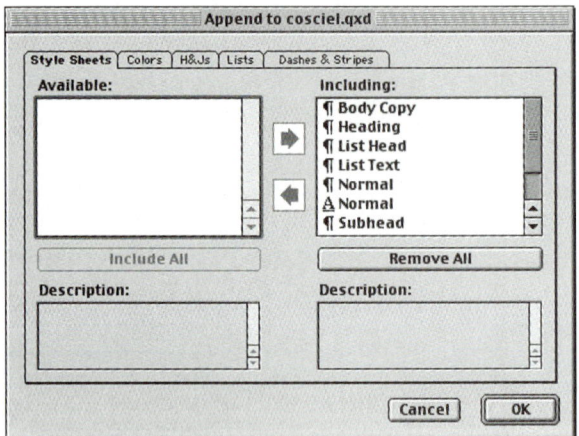

3. Click OK to the warning that embedded elements will also be appended.

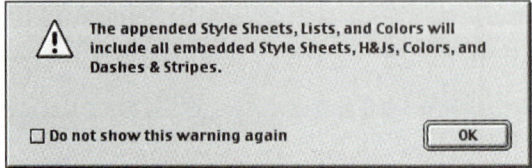

4. In the Append Conflict dialog box, activate the Repeat For All Conflicts check box and click Use New.

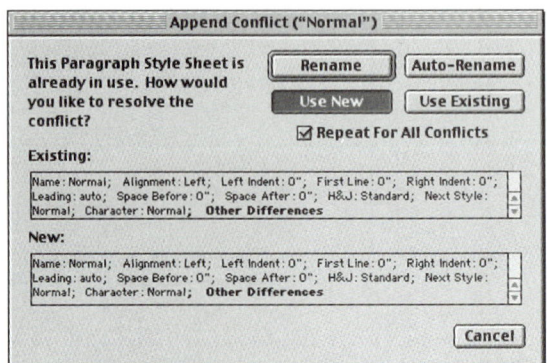

5. Open the Style Sheets palette and the Colors palette if they are not already visible. Notice that the defined style sheets from the client's master have been added to the open document. Also notice that a new color has been added to the Colors palette.

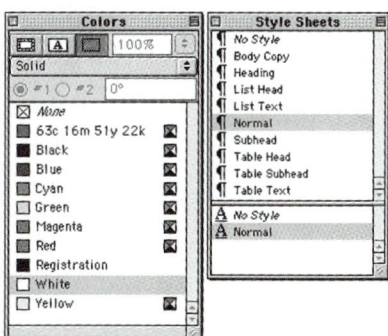

6. Save the file and continue.

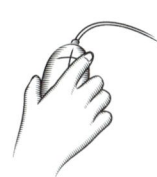

Create a Client Library

1. Choose File>New>Library. Navigate to your **Work_In_Progress** folder. Type "cosciel.qxl" in the Library/File Name field and click Create.

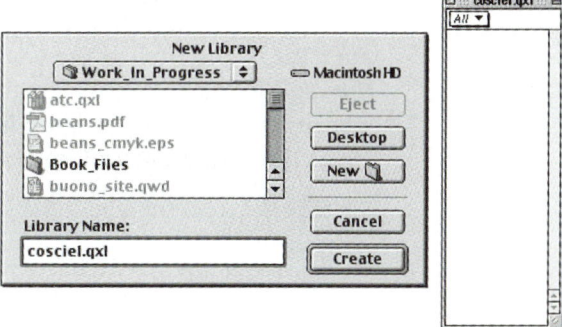

2. Copy the file **cosciel_master.qxd** from the **RF_Adv_Quark** folder to your **Work_In_Progress** folder.

3. Windows users: open the properties dialog box for the cosciel_master.qxd file and deactivate the Read-Only check box.

4. Open the file **cosciel_master.qxd** from your **Work_In_Progress** folder.

5. Open the Pictures tab of the Usage dialog box (Utilities>Usage). Update the Missing/Modified images by highlighting each, clicking Update, and locating the appropriate file in the **RF_Adv_Quark** folder. Click Done/Close when all pictures show OK in the Status column.

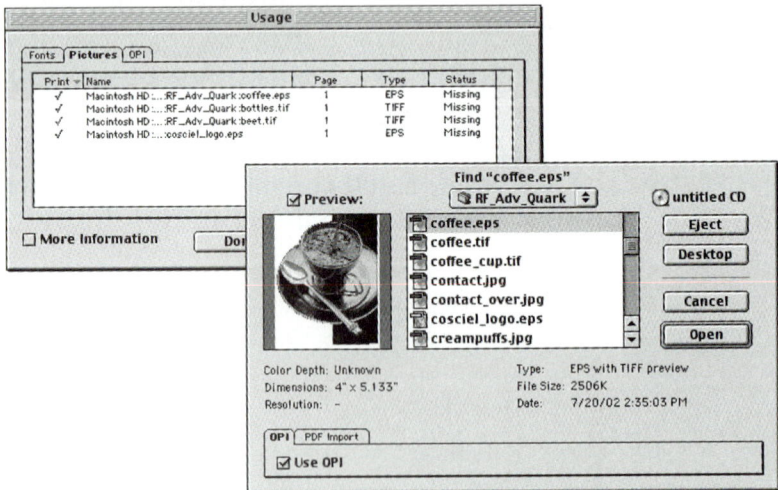

6. Using the Item tool, drag the logo picture box (on the top left of the page) into the Library palette.

7. Repeat Step 6 to place all of the images from the master document into the library.

8. Save and close the cosciel_master.qxd document.

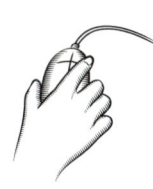

Place the Document Content

1. In the open file cosciel.qxd, select the first text box with the Content tool and choose File>Get Text. Locate the file **cosciel.xtg** in the **RF_Adv_Quark** folder. Make sure that the Include Style Sheets check box is selected and click Open.

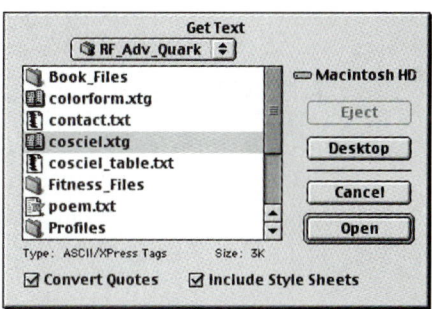

2. Draw a rectangular text box on the right side of the page with the following dimensions:

    X: 8.75 in.   W: 4.397 in.
    Y: 5.5 in.   H: 2.26 in.

3. Place the file **cosciel_table.txt** from the **RF_Adv_Quark** folder into the text box.

4. Drag the logo image from the open library until the box snaps to the top-left margin guides.

5. Drag the bottles picture from the library onto the document page. Using the Measurements palette, place the picture box at X: 2.229 in., Y: 7.31 in.

6. Drag the beet picture from the library onto the document page. Using the Measurements palette, place the picture box at X: 1.681 in., Y: 1.079 in.

7. Drag the coffee cup picture from the library onto the document page. Using the Measurements palette, place the picture box at X: 12.858 in., Y: 2.875 in.

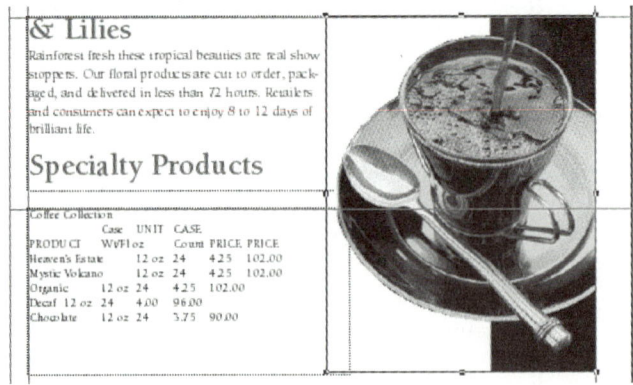

8. Save the file and continue.

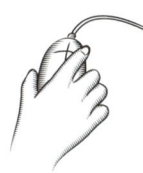

The file path.tif is a template for drawing the text path.

Create Text on a Path

1. Draw a rectangular picture box with the following dimensions:

   X: 3.73 in. W: 12.722 in.
   Y: 0.991 in. H: 1.467 in.

2. Place the file **path.tif** from the **RF_Adv_Quark** folder into the box.

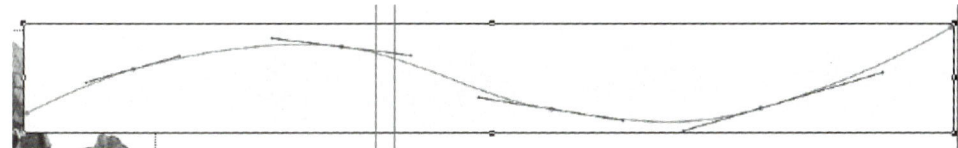

3. Select the Bézier Text-Path tool ( ).

4. Beginning with the left red dot in the path image, draw a Bézier text path. Add points at each red point in the path image, and drag handles to match the blue lines in the path image.

5. Delete the picture box containing the path image.

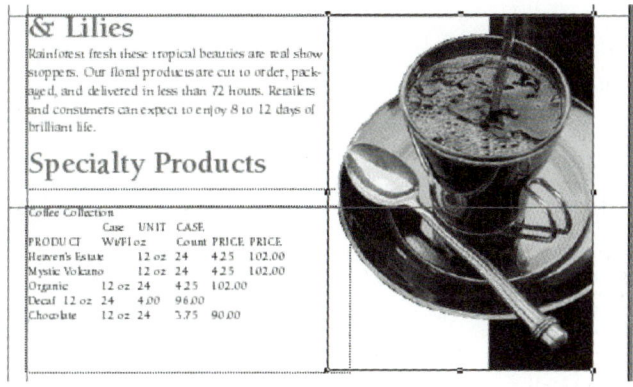

6. Select the text path with the Content tool and type: "All the Best of Costa Rica, Shipped to Your Door".

7. Press Command/Control-A to select all of the text. Style the text as 48-pt. ATC Laurel Book Italic, 90% Horizontal Scale. Change the text color to "63c 16m 51y 22k", and change the paragraph alignment to Centered.

8. Save the file and continue.

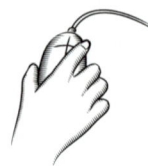

Create a Table

1. Using the Content tool, select the text box that contains the table text.

2. Press Command/Control-I to show invisible characters.

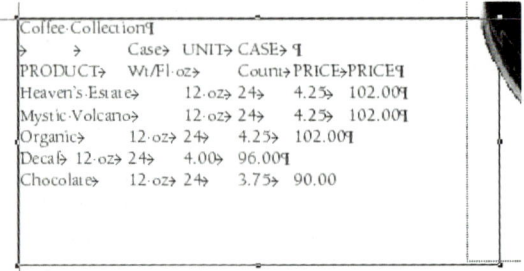

3. Remove the tab character at the end of the second line.

4. Press Command/Control-A to select all of the text.

5. Choose Item>Convert Text to Table. Review the default options in the dialog box and click OK.

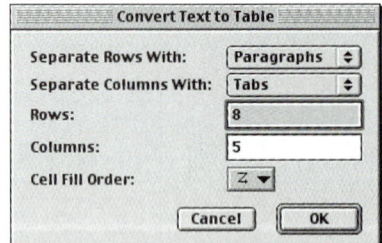

6. Delete the original text box, and drag the table until it snaps to the guides in the original box's position.

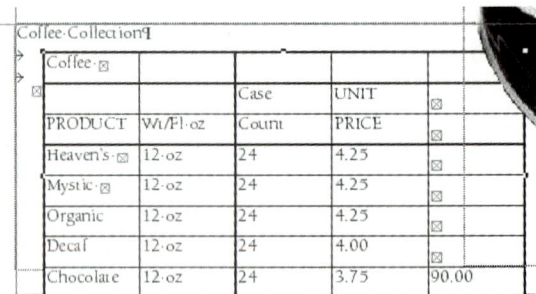

7. Open the Table tab of the Modify dialog box and activate the Maintain Geometry check box. Click OK.

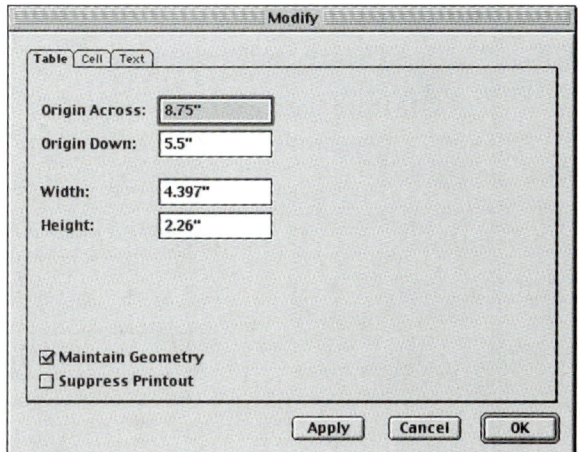

8. Save the file and continue.

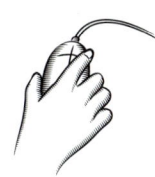

Format Table Content

1. Place the cursor to the left of the first row until the cursor appears as a right-facing arrow.

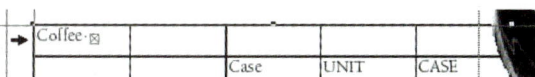

2. While the cursor is a right-facing arrow, click to select the entire row.

3. Choose Item>Table>Combine Cells.

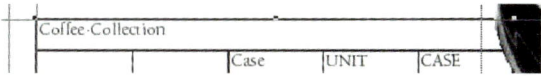

4. Place the cursor before the word Count in the third cell of the third row. Type "Case", and then press the Spacebar.

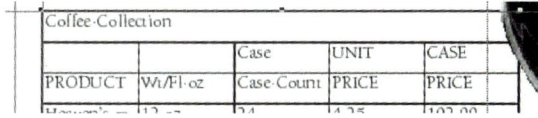

5. Add the word "UNIT" before PRICE in the fourth column of the same row.

6. Add the word "CASE" before PRICE in the fifth column of the same row.

7. Select the entire second row and choose Item>Table>Delete Row.

8. Select all of the rows in the table and open the Text tab of the Modify dialog box.

9. Change the Text Inset for All Edges to 3 pt., and choose Centered from the Vertical Alignment Type menu.

10. Select the entire first row and click the Table Head style in the Style Sheets palette. The type will be overset.

11. Place the cursor over the bottom gridline of the first row (the cursor becomes a two-headed arrow). Drag the gridline down until the text in the first row is visible.

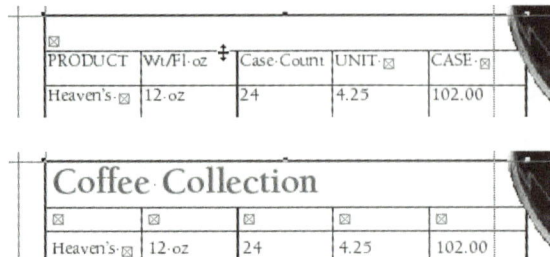

12. Select the second row of the table and apply the Table Subhead style sheet. Drag the bottom gridline of the second row down until all of the text in the row is visible.

13. Select the third through seventh rows and apply the Table Text style sheet.

14. With the five rows selected, open the Table tab of the Modify dialog box and deactivate the Maintain Geometry check box.

15. Click the Cells tab, and click the Height Distribute Evenly button. Click Apply.

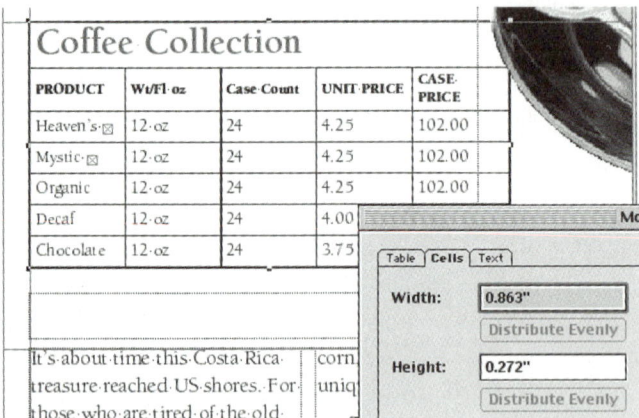

16. Click the Table tab and reactivate the Maintain Geometry check box. Click OK.

17. Place the cursor over the right gridline of the first column until it becomes a two-headed arrow. Drag the gridline to the right until all of the text in the first column is visible.

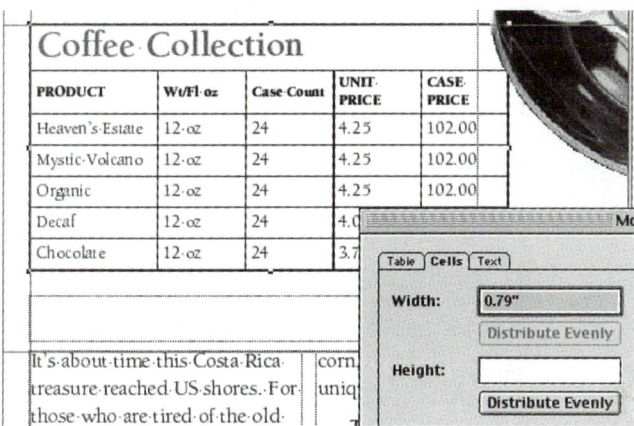

18. Select the second through fifth columns and open the Modify dialog box.

19. In the Table tab, deactivate the Maintain Geometry check box.

20. In the Cells tab, click the Width Distribute Evenly button and click Apply.

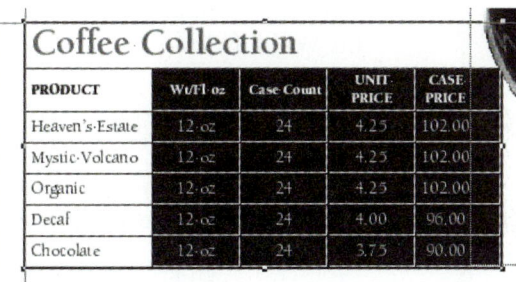

21. Click the Table tab and reactivate the Maintain Geometry check box. Click OK.

22. With the same cells selected, Press Command/Control-Shift-C to center the text within the cells.

23. Select the second row of the table and open the Text tab of the Modify dialog box. Choose Bottom from the Vertical Alignment Type menu and click OK.

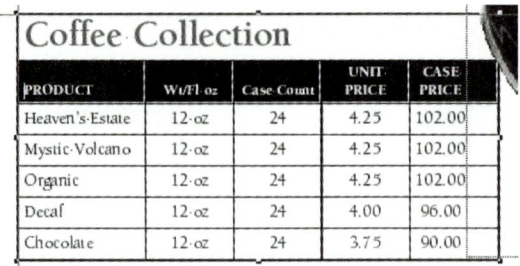

Coffee·Collection				
PRODUCT	Wt/Fl·oz	Case·Count	UNIT·PRICE	CASE·PRICE
Heaven's·Estate	12·oz	24	4.25	102.00
Mystic·Volcano	12·oz	24	4.25	102.00
Organic	12·oz	24	4.25	102.00
Decaf	12·oz	24	4.00	96.00
Chocolate	12·oz	24	3.75	90.00

24. Save the file and continue.

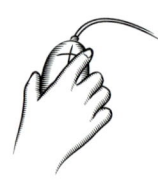

Format Table Gridlines

1. Select the table with the Item tool and open the Grid tab of the Modify dialog box.

2. Click the Vertical Gridlines button to the right of the Preview window and change the Color to White. Click Apply.

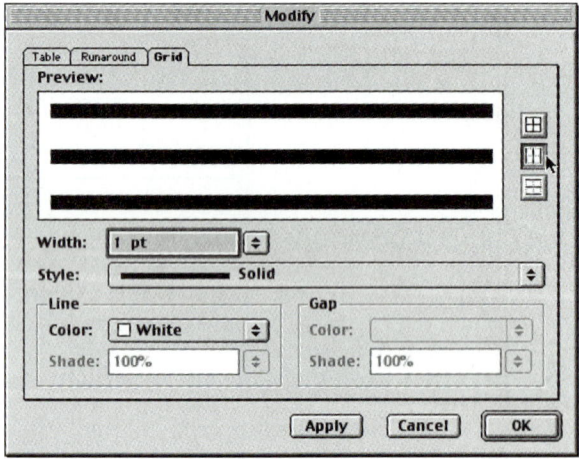

3. Click the Horizontal Gridlines button to the right of the Preview window. Change the Width field to 0.5 pt and choose "63c 16m 51y 22k" from the Color menu. Click OK.

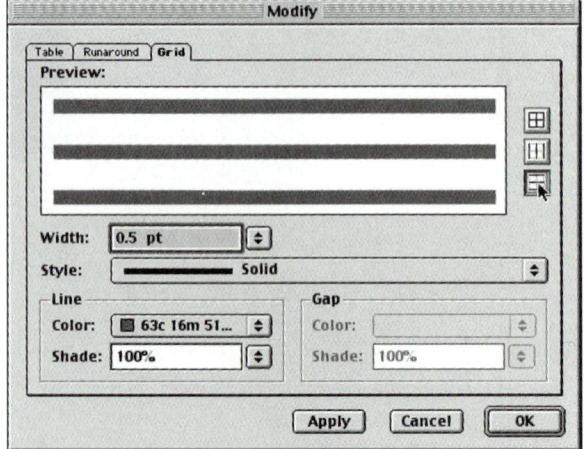

4. With the table still selected, choose the Content tool. Choose Item>Gridlines>Select Borders.

5. Open the Grid tab of the Modify dialog box. Type "1 pt." in the Width field and choose Black from the Color menu. Click OK.

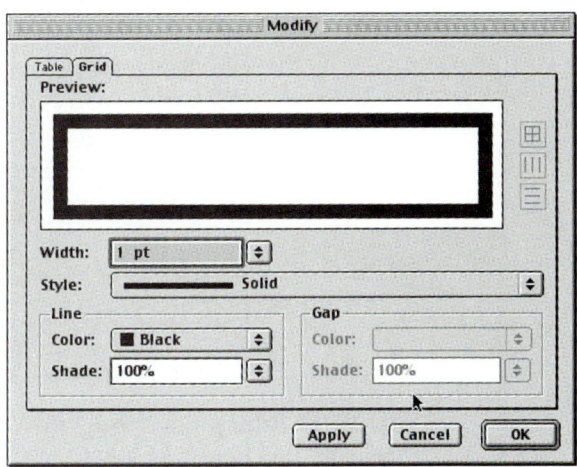

6. The table is finished. Save the file and continue.

Coffee·Collection				
PRODUCT	**Wt/Fl·oz**	**Case·Count**	**UNIT· PRICE**	**CASE PRICE**
Heaven's·Estate	12·oz	24	4.25	102.00
Mystic·Volcano	12·oz	24	4.25	102.00
Organic	12·oz	24	4.25	102.00
Decaf	12·oz	24	4.00	96.00
Chocolate	12·oz	24	3.75	90.00

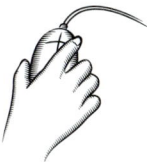

Modify Image Runarounds

1. Select the beet image on the page and open the Clipping tab of the Modify dialog box.

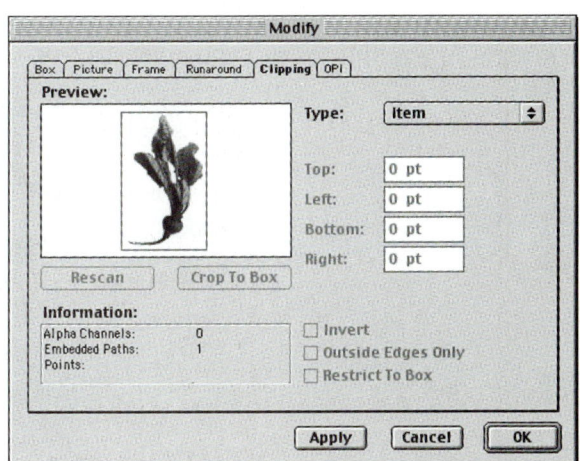

2. Choose Embedded Path from the Type menu. The Path menu should default to Clip (the name of the file's embedded path). Click Apply.

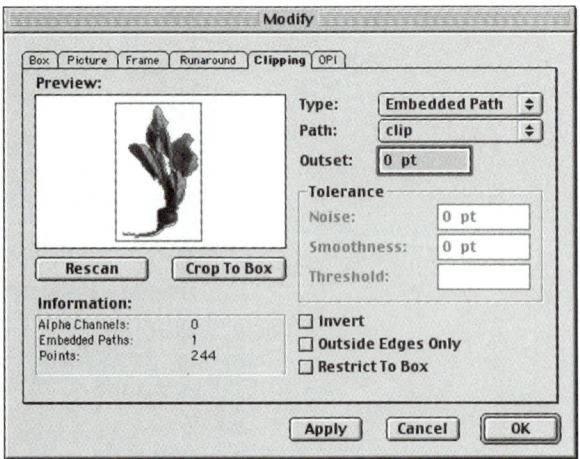

3. Click the Runaround tab. Choose Same as Clipping from the Type menu and change the Outset field to 12 pt. Click OK.

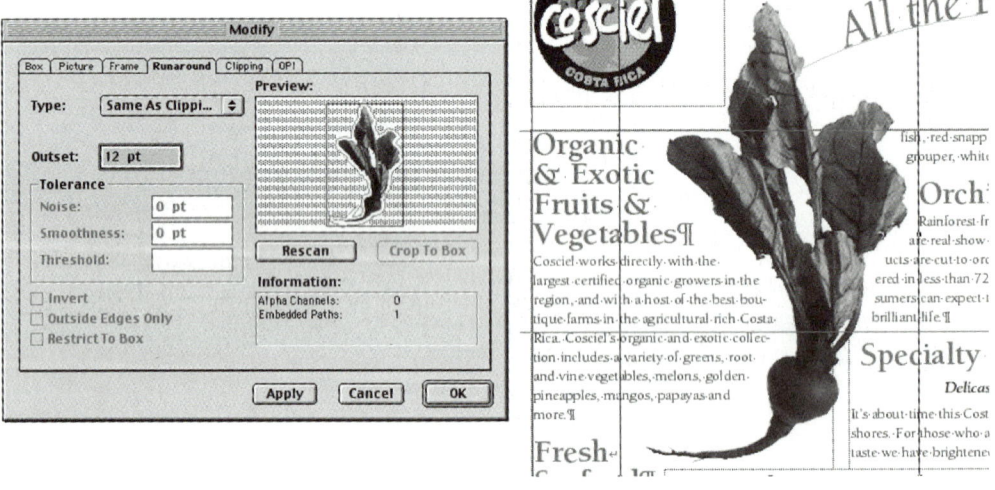

4. Repeat Steps 1–3 for the bottle image, using the image's embedded path as the clipping path and apply a 12-pt. runaround.

5. Select the coffee cup image on the document page and open the Clipping tab of the Modify dialog box. Notice that the Type menu is unavailable because this is an EPS image saved with a clipping path.

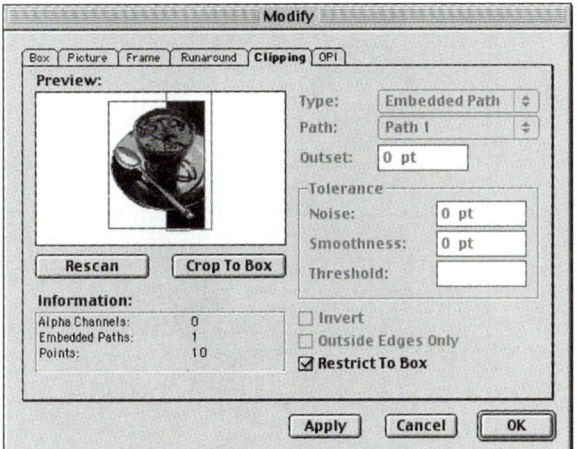

6. Click the Runaround tab. Choose Same as Clipping from the Type menu and change the Outset field to 12 pt. Click OK.

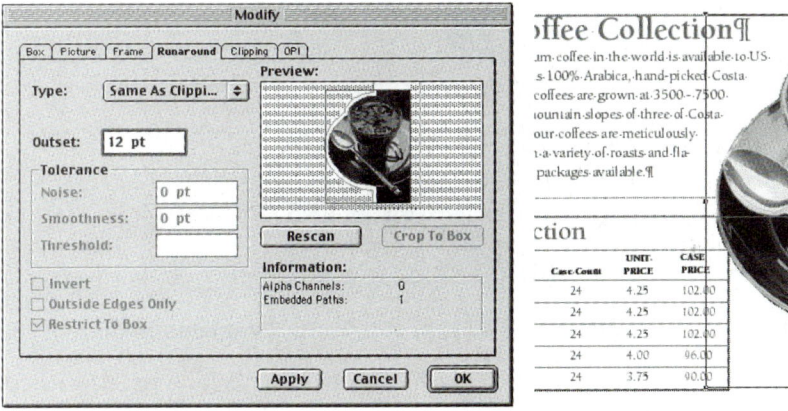

7. Windows users: press Enter on the numeric keypad to place a next-box character (↓) before the words "Available soon…" to move that text below the table.

8. Using the Orthogonal Line tool, draw an 8-pt. horizontal line on the page at Y: 2.687 in., snapping to the left and right margin guides. Apply the color "63c 16m 51y 22k" to the line and choose Item>Send to Back.

9. The layout is now complete. Save the file and continue.

Export the Document as EPS

1. Choose File>Save Page as EPS.

2. Navigate to your **Work_In_Progress** folder.

3. In the Save Page As/File Name field, type "cosciel.eps".

4. Activate the Transparent Page check Box, and change the Preview menu to TIFF.

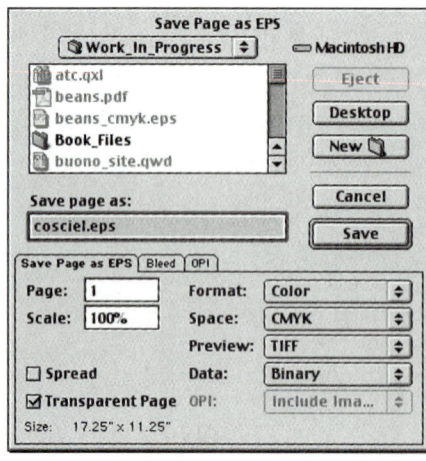

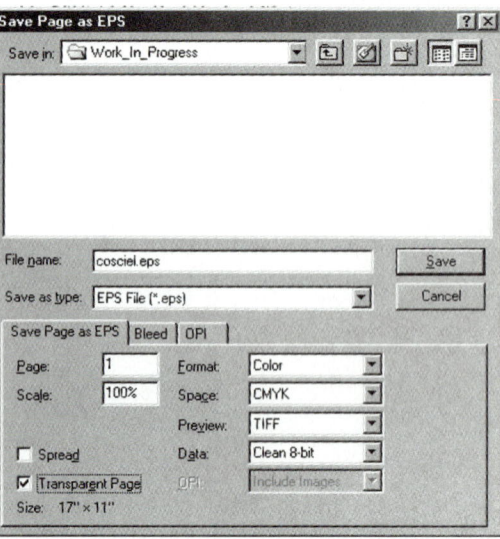

5. Click the Bleed tab. Since this document does not include bleed elements, leave these options at the default values.

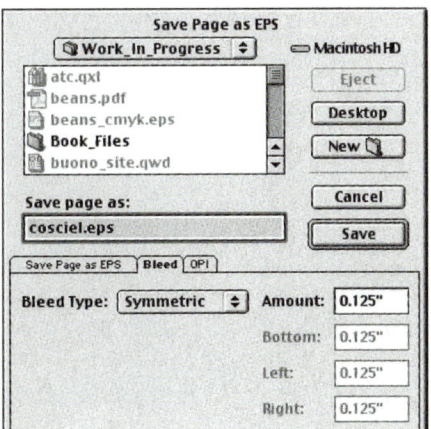

6. Click the OPI tab. Make sure that the OPI Active and both Include Images check boxes are selected. Make sure that the TIFF Low Resolution option is not selected.

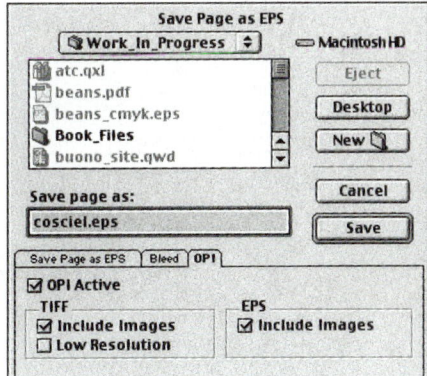

7. Click Save. Your document will be exported as an EPS file that you can send to the service provider.

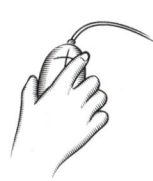

Print Composite Proofs

1. Macintosh users: make sure a PostScript printer is selected in the Chooser.

   Windows users: make sure a PostScript printer is selected in the Print menu.

2. With the cosciel.qxd file still open, choose File>Print.

3. In the Document tab, choose Centered from the Registration menu. Choose Automatic from the Tiling menu and change the Overlap field to 0.5 in.

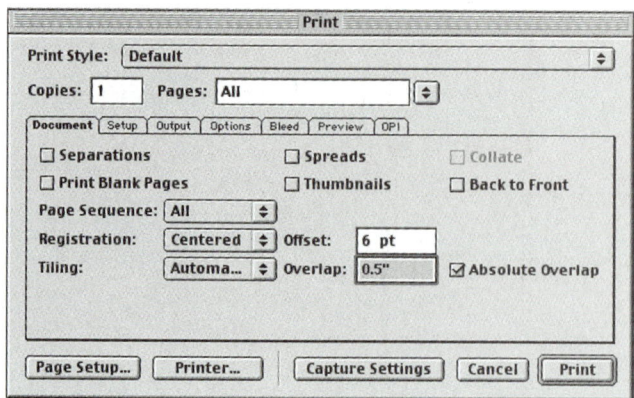

Many service providers require an offset of 12 pt. or higher. Ask your service provider before changing the Offset field in the Print Document dialog box.

4. In the Setup tab, make sure that the correct PPD file for your PostScript printer is selected in the Printer Description menu.

5. If your printer can print tabloid-size paper, choose Tabloid (or A3) from the Paper Size menu and choose the Portrait paper orientation icon.

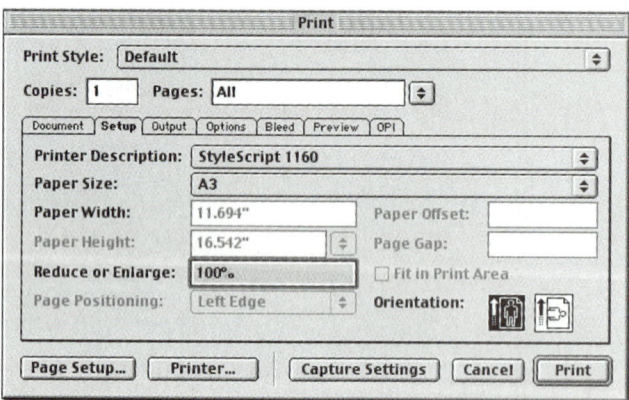

If your printer can only print letter-size paper, choose Letter from the Paper Size menu and choose the Landscape paper orientation icon.

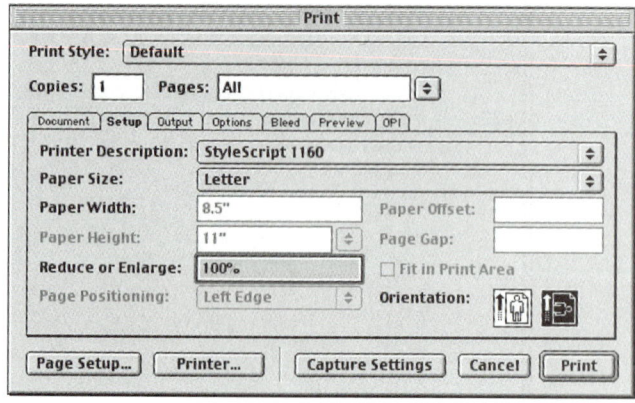

6. In the Output tab, choose Printer from the Halftoning menu to take advantage of the built-in information in the printer's PPD file.

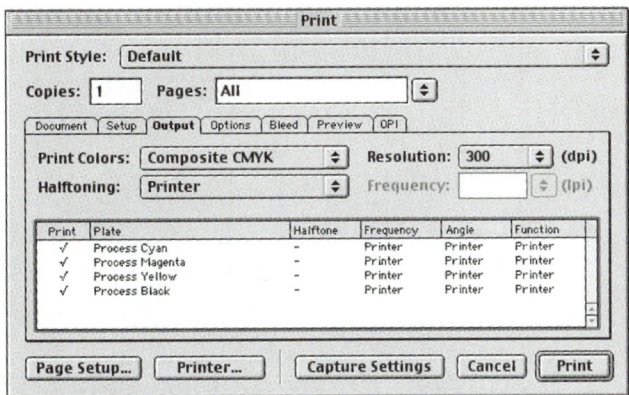

7. Click the Preview tab. If you are printing to Tabloid (A3) size paper, your document will tile to two pieces of paper. If you are printing to letter-size paper, your document will tile to four pieces of paper.

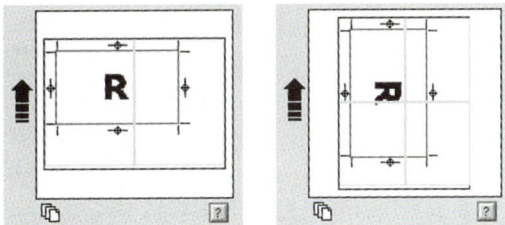

The Preview for tabloid (left) and letter-size (right) paper.

8. Click Print.

Collect the Job for Output

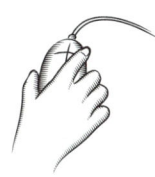

1. With the file cosciel.qxd still open, choose File>Collect for Output. If you see a warning asking to save the file before proceeding, click Save.

2. Create a new folder called "cosciel_job" in your **Work_In_Progress** folder and make that the target folder.

3. Make sure that the Document, Linked Pictures, Screen Fonts and Printer Fonts (Macintosh) or Fonts (Windows) check boxes are active and click Save.

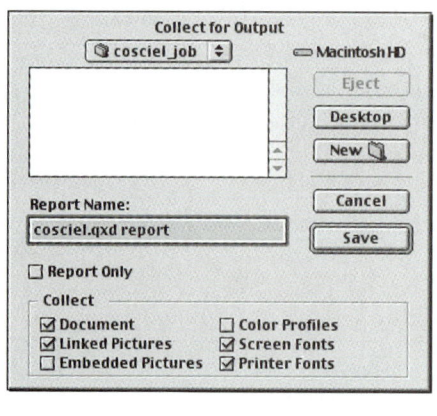 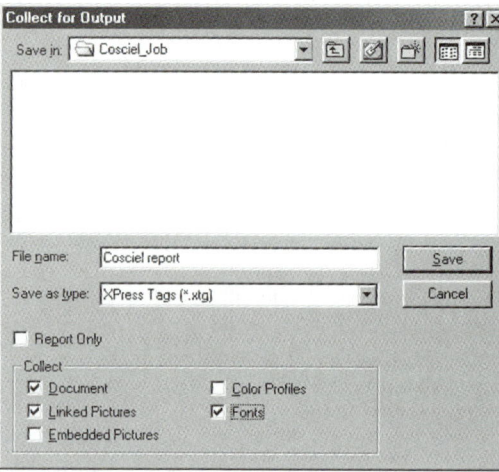

4. Click OK in the warning about illegal distribution of fonts.

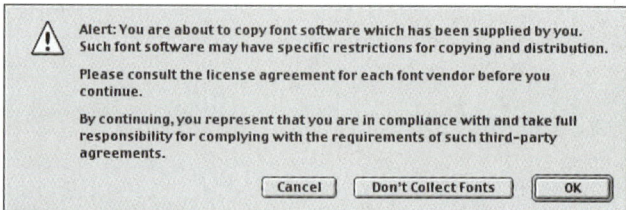

5. When the collect process is complete, close the open file.

6. On your desktop, open the **cosciel_job** folder from your **Work_In_Progress** folder. You should have a complete job package.

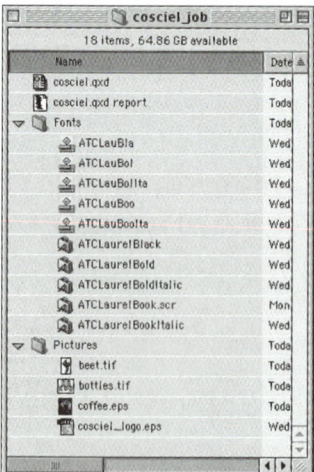

Your poster layout successfully meets the client's requirements, using the same fonts, colors, and images from the old poster. You have created a custom page-layout grid using linked text boxes with different properties, and added a cleanly formatted table with the pricing information. The headline is placed on a path, which adds visual interest and fills the large white space at the top of the poster. You have also prepared the job to output both as a single EPS file, and as a complete job package.

GLOSSARY

Absolute Path

A URL that includes all information needed to find the resource. The location of the current page is irrelevant.

Additive Color Process

The additive color process is the process of mixing red, green, and blue light to achieve a wide range of colors, as on a color television screen. See *Subtractive Color*.

Algorithm

A specific sequence of mathematical steps to process data. A portion of a computer program that calculates a specific result.

Alt Text

Text that can be displayed in lieu of the image, if necessary.

Anchor

In a Web page, a type of hyperlink destination in which the destination is a specific location on a page.

ANSI

American National Standards Institute, the recognized standards-making body for the United States. ANSI code is used by some Windows computers for addressing text.

Ascender

Parts of a lowercase letter that exceed the height of the letter "x". The letters b, d, f, h, k, l, and t have ascenders.

ASCII

The American Standard Code for Information Interchange, which defines each character, symbol, or special code as a number from 0 to 255 (8 bits in binary). An ASCII text file can be read by any computer, and is the basic mode of data transmission on the Internet.

Baseline

The implied reference line on which the bases of capital letters sit.

Bézier Curves

Curves that are defined mathematically (vectors), in contrast to those drawn as a collection of dots or pixels (raster). The advantage of these curves is that they can be scaled without the "jaggies" inherent in enlarging bitmapped fonts or graphics.

Binding

In general, the various methods used to secure signatures or leaves in a book. Examples include saddle-stitching (the use of staples in a folded spine), and perfect-bound (multiple sets of folded pages sewn or glued into a flat spine).

Bleed

Page data that extends beyond the trim marks on a page. Illustrations that spread to the edge of the paper without margins are referred to as "bled off."

Border

A continuous line that extends around an object.

Bounding Box

The imaginary rectangle that encloses all sides of a graphic.

Browser

A software program used to view content over the World Wide Web.

Bullet

A marker preceding text, usually a solid dot, used to add emphasis; generally indicates that the text is part of a list.

Cache

A copy of files the browser has already seen and can reference without downloading a second time.

Calibration

Making adjustments to a color monitor and other hardware and software to make the monitor represent as closely as possible the colors of the final printed piece.

Callout

A descriptive label referenced to a visual element, such as several words connected to the element by an arrow.

Cap Line

The theoretical line to which the tops of capital letters are aligned.

Caption

The line or lines of text that identify a picture or illustration, usually placed beneath it or otherwise in close proximity.

Cascading Style Sheet (CSS)

A file or section of a file listing properties that affect the appearance of content, the content to which those properties apply, and their values.

Center Marks

Press marks that appear on the center of all sides of a press sheet to aid in positioning the print area on the paper.

CGI Script

A CGI (Common Gateway Interface) program used to process a Web form or provide other dynamic content.

Check Box

A square that can be clicked to cause the form to send a name-value pair to the action; a form element that allows a user to choose zero or more choices.

Choke

See *Trapping*.

Cicero/Didot Point

The cicero is a unit of horizontal distance slightly larger than the pica, used widely in continental Europe. A cicero equals 0.178 inches, or 12 Didot points.

Clipboard

The portion of computer memory that holds data that has been cut or copied. The next item cut or copied replaces the data already in the Clipboard.

CMYK

Acronym for cyan, magenta, yellow, and black, the four process-color inks which, when properly overprinted, can simulate a subset of the visible spectrum. These colors form the subtractive primaries. See *Color Separation*.

Code

Code consists of HTML or programming text that provides instructions to the browser, such as to display a header or an alert box.

Color Balance

The combination of yellow, magenta, and cyan needed to produce a neutral gray. Determined through a Gray Balance analysis.

Color Chart

A printed chart of various combinations of CMYK colors used as an aid for the selection of "legal" colors during the design phase of a project.

Color Conversion

Changing the color "mode" of an image. Converting an image from RGB to CMYK for purposes of preparing the image for conventional printing.

Color Gamut

The range of colors that can be formed by all possible combinations of the colorants of a given reproduction system (printing press) on a given type of paper.

Color Management System

A process or utility that attempts to manage color of input and output devices in such a way that the monitor will match the output of any CMS-managed printer.

Color Model

A system for describing color, such as RGB, HSL, CIE L*a*b*, or CMYK.

Color Proof

A printed or simulated printed image of the color separations, intended to produce a close representation of the final reproduction for approval and as a guide to the press operator.

Color Separation

The process of transforming color artwork into four components corresponding to the four process colors. If spot colors are used, additional components may be created containing only those items that will appear in the corresponding spot color layer. Each component is imaged to film or paper in preparation for making printing plates, or directly to printing plates that correspond to each ink.

Color Space

A three-dimensional coordinate system in which any color can be represented as a point. It is three-dimensional because a color must be represented by three basic characteristics depending on the color model.

Column

A vertical area for type, used to constrain line length to enhance design and readability.

Commercial Printing

Typically, printing on high-capacity, high-resolution presses. High-resolution commercial printing processes include offset lithography, flexography, gravure, and screen printing. Offset printing is the most widely used commercial printing process.

Comp

Also known as comprehensive artwork, a rendering used to present the general color and layout of a page.

Compose

To set copy into type or lay out a page.

Composite Proof

A version of an illustration or page in which the process colors appear together to represent full color. When produced on a monochrome output device, colors are represented as shades of gray.

Condensed Type

A typeface in which the width of the letters is narrower than that of the standard letters of the font. Condensed type can be a designed font, or the effect may be approximated using a horizontal scaling feature.

Continuous Tone

An image (such as a photograph) in which the subject has a range of shades of color or gray tones through the use of an emulsion process. Continuous-tone images must be screened to create halftone images to be printed.

Contrast

The relationship between the dark and light areas of an image.

Cookie

A text file that is saved on the user's computer so that the Web site recognizes return visitors.

Copyright

Ownership of a work by the originator, such as an author, publisher, artist, or photographer. The right of copyright permits the originator of material to prevent its use without express permission of the originator. Copyright may be sold, transferred, or given up contractually.

Creep

The progressive extension of interior pages of the folded signature beyond the image area of the outside pages.

Crop Marks

Printed short, fine lines used as guides for final trimming of the pages within a press sheet.

Cropping

The elimination of parts of a photograph or other original that are not required to be printed.

Crossover

An element in a book (text, line art, or other graphic) that appears on both pages of a reader's spread, crossing over the gutter.

Default

A specification for a mode of computer operation that operates if no other is selected. The default font size might be 12 point, or a default color for an object might be white with a black border.

Desktop

The area on a monitor screen on which the icons appear before an application is launched.

Destination

The page or part of a page to which a link points.

Dictionary

A collection of words, used to determine appropriate spelling and hyphenation.

Dithering

A technique used in digital images wherein a color is represented using dots of two different colors displayed very close together. Dithering is often used to artificially extend the gamut of reproduceable colors in graphics that will be displayed on the Internet.

Document

The general term for a computer file containing text and/or graphics.

Double-Page Spread

A design that spans the two pages visible to the reader at any open spot in a magazine, periodical, or book.

DPI (Dots Per Inch)

The measurement of resolution for page printers, phototypesetting machines, and graphics screens. Currently graphics screens use resolutions of 60–100 dpi, standard desktop laser printers work at 600 dpi, and imagesetters operate at more than 1500 dpi.

Duotone

The separation of a black-and-white photograph into black and a second color having different tonal values and screen angles. Duotones are used to enhance photographic reproduction in two-, three-, and sometimes four-color work. Often the second, third, and fourth colors are not CMYK inks.

Element

The smallest unit of a graphic, or a component of a page layout or design. Any object, text block, or graphic might be referred to as an "element of the design."

Embedding

Including a complete copy of a text file or image within a document, with or without a link. See *Linking*.

EPS (Encapsulated PostScript)

Acronym for file format used to transfer PostScript data within compatible applications. EPS files can contain text, vector artwork, and images.

Export

To save a file generated in one application in a format that is readable in another application.

Film

Non-paper output of an imagesetter or phototypesetter.

Flop

To make a mirror image of visuals such as photographs or clip art.

Folder

A mechanical device that folds preprinted pages into various formats, such as a tri-fold brochure.

Folding Dummy

A template used for determining the page arrangement on a form to meet folding and binding requirements.

Font Subsetting

Embedding only part of a font. If you use only a small number of characters from a font, say for drop caps or for headlines, you can embed only the characters you used from the font. The advantage of font subsetting is that it decreases the overall size of your file. The disadvantage is that it limits the ability to makes corrections at the printing service.

Font Substitution

A process in which your computer uses a font similar to the one you used in your publication to display or print your publication. Although the substitute font may be similar to the original font, your publication will not look exactly as you intended; line breaks, column breaks, or page breaks may fall differently, which can affect the entire look and feel of the publication.

Form

A page that enables a user to type information and send it to a Web site via form elements such as text boxes and pull-down menus. Form information is normally processed by an application on the server.

Four-Color Process

See *Process Colors*.

FPO

Acronym for For Position Only, a term applied to low-quality art reproductions or simple shapes used to indicate placement and scaling of an art element on mechanicals or camera-ready artwork. In digital publishing, an FPO can be a low-resolution TIFF file that is later replaced with a high-resolution version. An FPO is not intended for reproduction, but only as a guide and placeholder for the prepress service provider.

Frame

A section of the browser window displaying a content document that is independent of all other areas within the browser window. This window-within-a-window can be referenced by links in other frames.

Frame Set

The document defining the layout on a framed page and breaking it into one or more frames.

Gamut

See *Color Gamut*.

GASP

Acronym for Graphic Arts Service Provider, a firm that provides a range of services somewhere on the continuum from design to delivery.

Get

A method for sending form data by appending it to the URL of the action. See also *Post*.

GIF

An acronym for Graphics Interchange Format. A popular graphics format for online clip art and drawn graphics. Graphics in this format look good at low resolution. See *JPG*.

Global Preferences

Preference settings that affect all newly created files within an application.

Gray Balance

The values for the yellow, magenta, and cyan inks that are needed to produce a neutral gray when printed at a normal density.

Grayscale

1. An image composed in grays ranging from black to white, usually using 256 different tones of gray.
2. A tint ramp used to measure and control the accuracy of screen percentages on press.
3. An accessory used to define neutral density in a photographic image.

Greeking

1. A software technique by which areas of gray are used to simulate lines of text below a certain point size.
2. Nonsense text used to define a layout before copy is available.

Grid

A set of horizontal and vertical guides that define the areas into which text or graphics may be placed accurately.

Gripper Edge

The leading edge of a sheet of paper, which the grippers on the press grab to carry the paper through a press.

Gutter

Extra space between pages in a layout. Sometimes used interchangeably with "alley" to describe the space between columns on a page. Gutters can appear either between the top and bottom of or between the sides of adjacent pages. Gutters are often used because of the binding or layout requirements of a job — for example, to add space at the top or bottom of each page or to allow for the grind-off taken when a book is perfect bound.

H & J

Hyphenation and justification. Parameters used by a page-layout program to determine how a line of text should be hyphenated, or how its inter-word and inter-character space should be adjusted.

Hairline Rule

The thinnest rule that can be printed on a device. A hairline rule on a 1200-dpi imagesetter is 1/1200 of an inch; on a 300-dpi laser printer, the same rule would print at 1/300 of an inch.

Hot Area

The portion of an image that will, when clicked, initiate some action, such as linking to another Web page.

HSL

A color model that defines color based on its hue, saturation, and luminosity (value), as it is displayed on a video or computer screen.

HTML

An acronym for HyperText Markup Language. The language written in plain (ASCII) text using simple tags that is used to create Web pages, and which Web browsers are designed to read and display. HTML is used to mark, or code, the content of your design (text, graphics, sounds, and animation).

Hue

The wavelength of light of a color in its purest state (without adding white or black).

Hyperlink

An HTML tag directs the computer to a different anchor or URL (Uniform Resource Locator). The linked data may be on the same page, or on a computer anywhere in the world. A hyperlink can be a word, phrase, sentence, graphic, or icon. A hyperlink can also cause an action, such as opening or downloading a file.

Hyphenation Zone

The space at the end of a line of text in which the hyphenation function examines the word to determine whether it should be hyphenated and wrapped to the next line.

Image Map

An image containing one or more defined regions, called "hot areas", which are assigned hyperlinks. As the pointing device passes into these defined areas, an associated hyperlink is available and can be accessed by selection.

Imagesetter

A raster-based device used to output a digital file at high resolution (usually 1000–3000 dpi) onto photographic paper or film, from which printing plates are made, or directly to printing plates (called a "platesetter").

Imposition

The arrangement of pages on a printed sheet, which, when the sheet is printed, folded, and trimmed, will place the pages in their correct order.

Indexed Color

Color model containing only 256 possible colors. Indexed color is used for graphics that will be displayed on a monitor, such as Web graphics, to better predict what different users will see on different monitors.

Interlacing

Method of saving GIF and PNG graphics so that, when a Web page is downloaded by a user, the image appears in progressive steps as the data is downloaded.

International Paper Sizes

The International Standards Organization (ISO) system of paper sizes is based on a series of three sizes — A, B, and C. Series A is used for general printing and stationery, Series B for posters, and Series C for envelopes. Each size has the same proportion of length to width as the others. The nearest ISO paper size to conventional 8.5 × 11-in. paper is A4.

Internet Service Provider (ISP)

An organization or company that provides access to the Internet for home or corporate users through phone lines, cable lines or special Internet connections such as T1 lines. In addition to Internet access, many ISPs provide other services such as Web hosting, Web-page design, domain name service, and other proprietary services.

Intranet

A play on the word Internet, an intranet is a small network that works like the Web, but is dedicated to information and resources about and for the corporation or organization that maintains it. Typically, access to an intranet is restricted to computers or employees within the organization.

JavaScript

A Java-based language created for scripting.

JPG or JPEG

A compression algorithm that reduces the file size of bitmapped images. Named for the Joint Photographic Experts Group, an industry organization that created the standard. JPEG is a "lossy" compression method, and image quality will be reduced in direct proportion to the amount of compression. JPEG graphics produce better resolution for color photographs than a GIF format. See *GIF*.

Kerning

Moving a pair of letters closer together or farther apart to achieve a better fit or appearance.

Knockout

A printing technique that prints overlapping objects without mixing inks. The ink for the underlying element does not print (knocks out) in the area where the objects overlap. Opposite of overprinting.

L*a*b*

The lightness, red-green attribute, and yellow-blue attribute in the CIE L*a*b* color space, a three-dimensional color mapping system.

Landscape

Printing from the left to right across the wider side of the page. A landscape orientation treats a page as 11 inches wide and 8.5 inches long.

Layer

A function of graphics or page-layout applications in which elements may be hidden from view, locked, reordered, or otherwise manipulated as a unit, without affecting other elements on the page.

Leading (pronounced "ledding")

Space added between lines of type. Usually measured in points or fractions of points. Named after the strips of lead that used to be inserted between lines of metal type. In specifying type, lines of 12-pt. type separated by a 14-pt. space is abbreviated "12/14," or "twelve over fourteen."

Letter Spacing

The insertion or addition of white space between the letters of words.

Ligature

Letters that are joined together as a single unit of type such as œ and fi.

Line Screen

The number of lines per inch used when converting a photograph to a halftone. Typical values range from 85 for newspaper work to 150 or higher for high-quality reproduction on smooth or coated paper.

Linking

An association through software of a graphic or text file on disk with its location in a document. That location may be represented by a "placeholder" rectangle, or a low-resolution copy of the graphic.

Lithography

A mechanical printing process used for centuries based on the principle of the natural aversion of water (in this case, ink) to grease. In offset lithography, the image on a photosensitive plate is first transferred to the blanket of a rotating drum, and then to the paper.

LPI

Lines per inch. See *Line Screen*.

Margins

The nonprinting areas of a page, or the line at which text starts or stops.

Masking

A technique that blocks an area of an image from reproduction by superimposing an opaque object of any shape.

Master Pages

Page layouts that contain elements common to all pages to which the master is applied. Master pages can be equated to templates for a page layout.

Mechanical

A pasted-up page of camera-ready art that is to be photographed to produce a plate for the press.

Menu

A list of choices of functions.

Meta Tag

A tag that contains information about a Web page. These tags are typically used by search engines and other applications, and not seen by the user.

Microsoft Internet Explorer

A common Web browser.

MIME Type

An indication of the kind of data being sent to the browser. Tells the browser what to do with the data.

Misregistration

The unwanted result of incorrectly aligned process inks and spot colors on a finished printed piece. Misregistration can be caused by many factors, including paper stretch and improper plate alignment. Trapping can compensate for misregistration.

Monochrome

An image in which all information is represented with a range of gray shades.

Nesting

Placing graphic files within other graphic files. This unacceptable practice often results in errors in printing.

Netscape Navigator

A common Web browser.

Nonreproducible Colors

Colors in an original scene or photograph that are impossible to reproduce using process inks. Also called out-of-gamut colors.

Offset Lithography

A printing method whereby the image is transferred from a plate onto a rubber-covered cylinder, from which the printing takes place. See *Lithography*.

Opacity

1. The degree to which paper will show print through it.
2. Settings in certain graphics applications that allow images or text below the object whose opacity has been adjusted, to show through.

Orphan

A single or partial word, or a partial line of a paragraph appearing at the bottom of a page. See *Widow*.

Overprint

A printing technique that lays down one ink on top of another ink. The overprinted inks can combine to make a new color. The opposite of knockout.

Page-Description Language (PDL)

A special form of programming language that describes both text and graphics (object or bit-image) in mathematical form. The main benefit of a PDL is that it makes the application software independent of the physical printing device. PostScript is a PDL, for example.

Pasteboard

The desktop area outside of the page area, on which elements can be placed for later positioning on any page.

PDF (Portable Document Format)

Developed by Adobe Systems, Inc. (and read by Adobe Acrobat Reader), this format has become a de facto standard for document transfer across platforms.

Pica

A traditional typographic measurement of 12 points, or approximately 1/6 of an inch. Most applications specify a pica as exactly 1/6 of an inch.

PICT/PICT2

A common format for defining bitmapped images on the Macintosh. The more recent PICT2 format supports 24-bit color.

PNG

An acronym for Portable Network Graphic, a common image format intended to replace GIF images. See also *GIF* and *JPEG*.

Point

A unit of measurement used to specify type size and rule weight, equal to (approximately, in traditional typesetting) 1/72 inch.

Portrait

Printing from left to right across the narrow side of the page. Portrait orientation on a letter-size page uses a standard 8.5-inch width and 11-inch length.

Post

A method for sending form data using headers. See also *Get*.

PostScript

1. A page-description language developed by Adobe Systems, Inc. that describes type and/or images and their positional relationships upon the page.
2. An interpreter or RIP (see *Raster Image Processor*) that can process the PostScript page description into a format for output.
3. A computer programming language.

PostScript Printer Description (PPD) File

A file format developed by Adobe Systems, Inc. that contains device-specific information enabling software to produce the best results possible for each type of designated printer.

PPI

Pixels per inch; used to denote the resolution of an image.

Preferences

A set of defaults that may be modified.

Prepress

All work done between writing and printing, such as typesetting, scanning, layout, and imposition.

Primary Colors

Colors that can be used to generate secondary colors. For the additive system (i.e., a computer monitor), these colors are red, green, and blue. For the subtractive system (i.e., the printing process), these colors are cyan, magenta, and yellow.

Printer Driver

The device that communicates between your software program and your printer.

Printer Fonts

The image outlines for type in PostScript that are sent to the printer.

Process Colors

The four inks (cyan, magenta, yellow, and black) used in four-color process printing. A printing method in which a full range of colors is reproduced by combining four semitransparent inks. Process-color printing is typically used when your publication includes full-color photographs or multicolor graphics, and when you want the high resolution and quality that printing on an offset press provides. See *Color Separation, CMYK*.

Profile

A file containing data representing the color-reproduction characteristics of a device determined by a calibration of some sort.

Proof

A representation of the printed job that is made from plates (press proof), film, or electronic data (prepress proofs). It is generally used for customer inspection and approval before mass production begins.

Proportional Spacing

A method of spacing whereby each character is spaced to accommodate the varying widths of letters or figures, thus increasing readability. Books and magazines are set proportionally spaced, and most fonts in desktop publishing are proportional. With proportionally spaced fonts, each character is given a horizontal space proportional to its size. For example, a proportionally spaced "m" is wider than an "i."

Pt.

Abbreviation for point.

Radio Button

A single round button that can be clicked to cause the form to send a name-value pair to the action. See also *Radio Group*.

Radio Group

A group of radio buttons with the same name. Only one radio button may be selected within a radio group at one time. See also *Radio Button*.

Raster Image Processor (RIP)

That part of a PostScript printer or imagesetting device that converts the page information from the PostScript page-description language into the bitmap pattern that is applied to the film or paper output.

Rasterize

The process of converting digital information into pixels at the resolution of the output device. For example, the process used by an imagesetter to translate PostScript files before they are imaged to film or paper. See *Raster Image Processor*.

Registration

Aligning plates on a multicolor printing press so the images will superimpose properly to produce the required composite output.

Registration Color

A default color selection that can be applied to design elements so they will print on every separation from a PostScript printer. Registration is often used to print identification text that will appear outside the page area on a set of separations.

Registration Marks

Figures (often crossed lines and a circle) placed outside the trim page boundaries on all color-separation overlays to provide a common element for proper alignment.

Relative Path

A URL that uses the current page as its starting point. See also *Absolute Path*.

Resample

To alter the resolution of an image. Downsampling averages the pixels in an area and replaces the entire area with the average pixel color at the specified resolution. Subsampling chooses a single pixel and replaces the entire area with that pixel at the specified resolution; it is not recommended for high-resolution printing.

Resolution

The density of graphic information expressed in dots per inch (dpi) or pixels per inch (ppi).

Reverse Out

To reproduce an object as white, or paper, within a solid background, such as white letters in a black rectangle.

RGB

Acronym for red, green, blue — the colors of projected light from a computer monitor that, when combined, simulate a subset of the visual spectrum. When a color image is scanned, RGB data is collected by the scanner and then converted to CMYK data at some later step in the process. Also refers to the color model of most digital artwork. See *CMYK*.

Rich Black

A process color consisting of solid black with one or more layers of cyan, magenta, or yellow.

Right-Reading

A positive or negative image that is readable from top to bottom and from left to right.

Robot

A program that indexes Web pages and the pages to which they are linked.

Rollover

The changing of appearance of an item, such as an image, when the user rolls the mouse over that item or another item.

Root Directory

The main directory for a Web site.

Rules

Straight lines, often stretching horizontally across the top of a page to separate text from running heads.

Running Head (Header)

Text at the top of the page that provides information about the publication. Chapter names and book titles are often included in a running head.

Saddle-Stitching

A binding method in which each signature is folded and stapled at the spine.

Screen

To create a halftone of a continuous-tone image.

Screen Angle

The angle at which the rulings of a halftone screen are set when making screened images for halftone process-color printing. The equivalent effect can be obtained electronically through selection of the desired angle from a menu.

Screen Frequency

The number of lines per inch in a halftone screen, which may vary from 85 to 300.

Search Engine

A program that enables a user to locate content by means of a keyword or keywords supplied by the user.

Selection

The act of placing the cursor on an object and clicking the mouse button to make the object active.

Server

A computer used as a central repository for information. A Web server, in particular, may house HTML pages, scripts, applications and databases, all of which may be combined to produce the HTML code that reaches the user's browser.

Service Bureau

A business that specializes in producing film for printing on a high-resolution imagesetter. An organization that provides services, such as scanning and prepress checks, that prepare your publication to be printed on a commercial printing press. Service bureaus do not, however, print your publication. To find out if you need to use a service bureau, talk to your printing professional.

Smart Quotes

The curly quotation marks used by typographers, as opposed to the straight marks on the typewriter. Use of smart quotes is usually a setup option in a word-processing or page-layout application.

Snap-to (Guides or Rulers)

An optional feature in page-layout programs that drives objects to line up with guides or margins if they are within a preset pixel range. This eliminates the need for very precise, manual placement of an object with the mouse.

Soft Return

A return command that ends a line but does not apply a paragraph mark that would end the continuity of the style for that paragraph.

Spine

The binding edge at the back of a book that contains title information and joins the front and back covers.

Spot Color

Any premixed ink that is not one of or a combination of the four process color inks, often specified by a Pantone swatch number.

Spot-Color Printing

The printing method in which one or two colors (or tints of colors) are produced using premixed inks, typically chosen from standard color-matching guides. Unlike process colors that reproduce color photographs and art, spot colors are typically used to emphasize headings, borders, and graphics, to match colors in graphics such as logos, and to specify special inks such as metallic or varnish.

Spread

1. Two abutting pages. Reader's spread: the two (or more) pages a reader will view when the document is open. Printer's spread: the two pages that abut on press in a multi-page document.
2. A trapping process that makes the lighter color larger.

Stacking Order

The order of the elements on a PostScript page, wherein the topmost item may obscure the items beneath it if they overlap.

Step-and-Repeat

1. A command which makes multiple copies of selected objects using defined offset values.
2. A layout in which two or more copies of the same piece are placed on a single plate. This is useful for printing several copies of a small layout, such as a business card, on a single sheet. Also called "multiple-up."

Subset

When exporting documents as EPS or PDF files, the ability to include only the portion of a font that actually appears in the document. This is particularly useful when decorative drop caps are used, or when a specific symbol is used from a pi font.

Substitution

Using an existing font to simulate one that is not available to the printer.

Subtractive Color

Color that is observed when light strikes pigments or dyes, which absorb certain wavelengths of light; the light that is reflected back is perceived as a color. See *CMYK, Process Color*.

Tabloid

Paper 11 inches wide × 17 inches long.

Tagged Image File Format (TIFF)

A common format used for scanned or computer-generated bitmapped images.

Tags

The various formats in a style sheet that indicate paragraph settings, page layouts, hyphenation and justification, widow and orphan control, and other parameters.

Target

The physical location in which a hyperlink document will be displayed.

Template

A document file containing layout and styles by which a series of documents can maintain the same look and feel. A model document that you can use as the basis for creating a new publication. A template contains the basic layout and formatting, and perhaps even some text and graphics that can be reused in future publications.

TIFF (.tif)

An acronym for Tagged Image File Format. A popular graphics format. See *Tagged Image File Format*.

Tile

1. Reproducing a number of pages of a document on one sheet.
2. Printing a large document overlapping on several smaller sheets of paper.

Tint

1. A halftone area that contains dots of uniform size; that is, no modeling or texture.
2. The mixture of a color with white: a 10% tint is one part of the original color and nine parts white. See *Shade*.

Tracking

Adjusting the spacing of letters in a line of text to achieve proper justification or general appearance. You may want to squeeze letters closer together to fit into a frame, or spread them apart for a special effect.

Trapping

The process of creating an overlap between abutting inks to compensate for imprecise registration in the printing process. Extending the lighter colors of one object into the darker colors of an adjoining object. This color overlaps just enough to fill areas where gaps could appear due to misregistration.

Trim

After printing, mechanically cutting the publication to the correct final dimensions. The trim size is normally indicated by marks on the printing plate outside the page area.

Trim Page Size

Area of the finished page after the job is printed, folded, bound, and cut.

UNIX

An operating system designed to support multiple users in a multi-tasking environment. Many Internet servers are UNIX-based.

URL

An acronym for Uniform Resource Locator, an addressing scheme for information.

Vector Graphics

Graphics defined using coordinate points, and mathematically drawn lines and curves, which may be freely scaled and rotated without image degradation in the final output. Fonts (such as PostScript and TrueType) and illustrations from drawing applications are common examples of vector objects. Two commonly used vector drawing programs are Adobe Illustrator and Macromedia FreeHand. A class of graphics that overcomes the resolution limitation of bitmapped graphics.

Vertical Justification

The ability to automatically adjust the interline spacing (leading) to make columns and pages end at the same point on a page.

Web-Safe Color Palette

A color palette used for pictures that will be displayed on the Internet. The Web-safe color palette is a specific set that can be displayed by most computer-operating systems and monitors.

Zero Point

The mathematical "origin" of the coordinates of the two-dimensional page. The zero point may be moved to any location on the page, and the ruler dimensions change accordingly.

INDEX

Resource CD-ROM
QuarkXPress® 5
Advanced Electronic Documents
AGAINST THE CLOCK

System Requirements

Windows:

- Intel® Pentium® II, III, or 4 Processor.

- Microsoft® Windows® 98, Windows 98 Special Edition, Windows Millennium Edition, Windows 2000 with Service Pack 2, Windows XP (recommended upgrade procedure)

- 128 MB of RAM

- 180 MB of available hard-disk space

- Color monitor capable of 800 X 600 pixel resolution

- CD-ROM drive

Macintosh:

- PowerPC® processor (G3, G4, or G4 Dual)

- Mac OS software version 9.1, 9.2, or Mac OS X version 10.1

- 128 MB of RAM

- 180 MB of available hard-disk space

- Color monitor capable of 800 X 600 pixel resolution

- CD-ROM drive

To use the additional resources available on this CD-ROM, you will need to have the appropriate applications installed on your system and enough free space available if you copy the files to your hard drive. This product does not come with the application software required to use the data files on this CD-ROM.

classroom use. use of these programs. If media is defective, you may return it for replacement